Preliminary Edition Notice

You have been selected to receive a copy of this book in the fo... ...A preliminary edition is used in a classroom setting to test the overall ... ...s effectiveness in a practical course prior to its formal publication on th...

As you use this text in your course, please share any and all feedback regarding the volume with your professor. Your comments on this text will allow the author to further develop the content of the book, so we can ensure it will be a useful and informative classroom tool for students in universities across the nation and around the globe. If you find the material is challenging to understand, or could be expanded to improve the usefulness of the text, it is important for us to know. If you have any suggestions for improving the material contained in the book or the way it is presented, we encourage you to share your thoughts.

Please note, preliminary editions are similar to review copies, which publishers distribute to select readers prior to publication in order to test a book's audience and elicit early feedback; therefore, you may find inconsistencies in formatting or design, or small textual errors within this volume. Design elements and the written text will undergo changes before this book goes to print and is distributed on the national market.

This text is not available in wide release on the market, as it is actively being prepared for formal publication. This may mean that new content is still being added to the author's manuscript, or that the content appears in a draft format.

If you would like to provide notes directly to the publisher, you may contact us by e-mailing studentreviews@cognella.com. Please include the book's title, author, and 7-digit SKU reference number (found below the barcode on the back cover of the book) in the body of your message.

Race and Ethnicity

The Sociological Mindful Approach

Preliminary Edition

Jacqueline Brooks, Heidy Sarabia, and Aya Kimura Ida

California State University - Sacramento

cognella®
SAN DIEGO

Bassim Hamadeh, CEO and Publisher
Seidy Cruz, Acquisitions Editor
Gem Rabanera, Project Editor
Christian Berk, Production Editor
Emely Villavicencio, Graphic Designer
Trey Soto, Licensing
Celeste Paed, Production Assistant
Natalie Piccotti, Director of Marketing
Kassie Graves, Vice President of Editorial
Jamie Giganti, Director of Academic Publishing

Copyright © 2020 by Cognella, Inc. All rights reserved. No part of this publication may be reprinted, reproduced, transmitted, or utilized in any form or by any electronic, mechanical, or other means, now known or hereafter invented, including photocopying, microfilming, and recording, or in any information retrieval system without the written permission of Cognella, Inc. For inquiries regarding permissions, translations, foreign rights, audio rights, and any other forms of reproduction, please contact the Cognella Licensing Department at rights@cognella.com.

Trademark Notice: Product or corporate names may be trademarks or registered trademarks, and are used only for identification and explanation without intent to infringe.

Cover image copyright © 2016 iStockphoto LP/PeopleImages.

Printed in the United States of America.

3970 Sorrento Valley Blvd., Ste. 500, San Diego, CA 92121

Table of Contents

Section III: Intersectionality: Race, Class, Gender, and Beyond... 99

Section IV: Education 135

Introduction

Purpose of the Book

On March 18, 2008, then presidential candidate Barack Obama delivered a speech on race and politics at the National Constitutional Center. Eight months before his historic presidential win, Obama addressed one of the most salient and complex issues that continually agitates American debate. During his eight-year term, Obama would comment on a range of racially motivated incidents that affected communities of color and faith throughout the United States. Today, these incidents continue. Yet, the leading political response to these acts has changed in tone. Defenders of white supremacy and nationalism have gained a significant foothold on influencing racial discourse and discourse of faith. In the following photo, members of the Alt-right clash with counter-protestors at Emancipation Park in Charlottesville, Virginia, during the August 2017 Unite the Right Rally. Tensions flared over the planned removal of the statue of Confederate general Robert E. Lee. During the conflict, Heather Heyer, a thirty-two-year old civil rights activist, was killed by an Alt-right motorist, who drove into a group of counter-protestors. In a tepid response to the violent rally, President Donald Trump blamed both sides of the confrontation, inflaming an already volatile situation. Public backlash to Trump's comments were swift and abundant. So, which America are we? The one that uses racist rhetoric to defend "American values?" Or the one that engages in anti-racist praxis? Regardless of how you respond to this question, it is hard to deny that the American collective consciousness seems battered and bruised from mixed messages that espouse racial hatred or demonstrate racial unity. It is in the midst of this confusion and uncertainty that we chose to assemble this book. Undergraduate students walk into courses on race and ethnic inequalities with the same confusion, often using their own personal experiences to decide which version of the United States makes most sense to them.

The works reflected in this text elucidate the complexity of racial and ethnic inequalities, referring back to America's long, troubled history with race, emphasizing the role of social institutions in perpetuating race inequalities, and exposing the intersection of race, class, gender, and other social inequalities. We encourage students to take an active role in the educational process, using each work as a source of individual and collective reflection.

The Sociological Mindfulness Approach

Students bring various experiences and assumptions into the classroom that can foster anxieties about offending someone or being offended themselves. As a result, students become passive learners, making it difficult to comprehend complex issues and subsequently detaching from the course material. In order to grasp the breadth of racial discourse and ease tensions that arise when engaging in such discussions, we frame our approach using *sociological mindfulness*. As articulated by Schwalbe, sociological mindfulness encourages us to see the world for what it is, reinforcing "how our lives are intertwined and how our words and deeds help or harm others in nonobvious ways" (2005:4). Employing sociological mindfulness allows students and instructors to remain actively conscious of the ideas, events, and interactions that shape our lives, even when these factors seem separate from our own experiences. The *sociological mindfulness* framework allows the reader to remain engaged and holds each student accountable for the development of their own sociological consciousness. We encourage students to become problem solvers in the arena of race discourse, rather than passive observers or casual critics of social events.

Organization of the Book

We invite students to reflect on their own observations and experiences by providing a range of scholarly works from theoretical macro-level works to micro-level narratives. Overall, we highlight four main goals: introduce students to fresh narratives about current issues of race and ethnic inequality; connect larger macro-level explanations of race and ethnic inequalities with personalized experiences; reveal how theory connects to the gathering of empirical evidence; and fuel critical discussion by confronting the concerns students hold about present-day race discourse.

We organize the book into nine sections. Each section begins with an engaging student narrative, followed by an editor's introduction. The subsequent chapters presented in each chapter offer discussion questions and resources to support knowledge building.

Section I: Theorizing Race, Racism, and Race Inequalities: Sociological theory offers explanations as to how race and ethnic inequalities become perpetuated within our social institutions and throughout our social interactions. This section addresses a range of sociological explanations, such as intersectionality, color-blind racism, race formation theory, critical race theory, and race group positioning.

Section II: Identity, Wellness, and Society: This section addresses the complex relationship between the social construction of race and one's identity development. We focus on the present-day challenges that individuals face in negotiating their identities in a society that maintains racial stereotypes yet desires to be "race neutral." The chapters in this section address the experiences of South Asian Americans, implicit bias, and the relationship between race and ethnic inequalities and health outcomes.

Section III: Intersectionality: Race, Class, Gender, and Beyond: This section addresses the intersections of race, class, gender, and religious identity. In addition, this section introduces students to how race and ethnic inequalities are perpetuated within the social institutions of work, the economy, religion, and the criminal justice system. The chapters in this section discuss Sandra Bland, the experiences of American Muslims, and how race informs the experiences of individuals employed as care workers.

Section IV: Education: In this section we challenge students to reflect on their educational careers before college, their present-day experiences, and their lives after graduation. The chapters in this section address how university campuses negotiate racial discourse, the lack of inclusivity in education, and the experiences of students of color in high school and college.

Section V: Popular Culture and the Media: This section is tailored to meet the concerns of students who find it difficult to navigate the terrain of popular culture, which is saturated with racialized and sexualized images. The sociological mindfulness approach will allow students the opportunity to reflect on their own actions as consumers and creators of popular culture. The chapters in this section address racialized images, the commodification of race, especially in entertainment, how technology informs racial discourse and collective activism, and how documentary film can help to address America's sordid, racialized past.

Section VI: Family and Partnerships: As a social institution, the family represents one of the most powerful mechanisms through which we develop our social identities and learn about other social groups. In this section, students will engage in narratives that reveal how broader race and ethnic inequalities shape family dynamics. The chapters in this section address parenting after Ferguson, raising a child in a foreign country, and interracial relationships.

Section VII: Racialized Immigration Policies: In this section we seek to engage students in classroom dialogue that provokes them to think about who they are as public individuals. What does it mean to have a "voice" in American politics? What does it mean to be marginalized in American politics? Current political rhetoric has made us confront how we interpret and connect with varying perspectives, especially views related to immigration. Students will use the sociological mindfulness approach to evaluate where they stand in the milieu of political discourse, especially given that race shapes much of the dialogue. The chapters in this section address violence at the US-Mexico border, the criminalization of immigrant status, and the influence of public policy on educational attainment for immigrant populations.

Section VIII: Coloniality in the Twenty-first Century: Moving students beyond a discussion of domestic ethnic and race relations allows them to see the universality of racial prejudice and discrimination. It is important for students to understand that race inequality is not solely a "US problem," but exists as a destructive force in many areas around the globe. The sociological mindfulness approach will allow students to see commonalities with groups they may think of as "the other." The chapters in this section address colonialism, race and ethnic discourse in Guatemala, the politics of borders, and racial dynamics in Colombia.

Section IX: Mobilizing for Social Change: In this section, we will round out each student's journey by addressing the active ways that we can reimagine race and ethnic relations and support anti-racist praxis. The chapters in this section address the activism of immigrant groups, community activism, and the struggles of African Americans, Asian Americans, and indigenous groups to gain ground against systemic racism.

—Jacqueline Brooks, Heidy Sarabia, and Aya Kimura Ida

References

Schwalbe, Michael. 2005. *The Sociologically Examined Life: Pieces of the Conversation*. 3rd ed. New York, NY: McGraw-Hill.

Section I: Theorizing Race, Racism, and Race Inequalities

Student Narrative

My first day of undergrad at Sacramento State was one of the prime highlights of my life. I was set to accomplish my dream of obtaining my degree—so I could go out into the world and be my "best self." I was thrilled at the thought of being a student at a real university. Yet, my happiness was short lived. Immediately, I noticed that out of thousands of students on campus, I was a part of the minority. In most of my classes I was the only African American. In my Urban Education course, I was one of three African American students in the class. The racial demographic of this class along with the dynamics of the subject matter, revealed the powerful intersections of race and class and the prevalence of structural racism. I began to struggle with these revelations, feeling increasingly uncomfortable and conflicted—feeling that I could not be myself. W.E.B. Du Bois argued that a double-consciousness includes the sense of "twoness," stating that "one ever feels his two-ness, an American, a Negro; two souls, two thoughts, two unreconciled strivings; two warring ideals in one dark body, whose dogged strength keeps it from going asunder" (Du Bois 2007:15). This is how I felt as an African American who grew up poor, studying alongside White students from more privileged backgrounds. I struggled to fit in. My standpoint was definitely different from the other students in the class based on my everyday life experiences and having grown up in an urban neighborhood. I was forced to police my thoughts before I responded to questions presented about the subject material. This was so disheartening to me. I had to police my tone, so as not to evoke emotion when talking about or responding to my classmates and the professor, so as not to come across as the stereotypical "angry Black woman." Eventually, I realized that I was censoring more than my thoughts. I was responding based on how I thought White people view me through the "veil." How sad that I thought about how others felt about me first, before speaking my own truth. It has not been easy, but I have learned to lift the "veil" and see myself as the intelligent African American woman that I am—in and out of the classroom.

Kendra Jackson is pursuing a master's degree in sociology at California State University–Sacramento. She is a McNair Scholar, and her research interests include inequities in education and the school-to-prison pipeline.

Learning Objectives

After you read this section on "Theorizing Race, Racism, and Race Inequalities," you should be able to:

1. Define sociological theory.

2. Compare and contrast race formation theory, critical race theory, color-blind racism, and intersectionality.

3. Define a racial project.

Editor's Introduction

Jacqueline Brooks, PhD

Throughout this text, we will encourage you to be "mindful" of your social location. As Schwalbe explains in the introduction, mindfulness challenges us to consider where we exist in the race hierarchy, the patterns that contribute to our social location, how we benefit from our social location, how we are disadvantaged, and how we disadvantage others. This is a weighty, yet necessary, task if we hope to make strides in dismantling structural and interpersonal racism. For Kendra, everyday activities, practices, and interactions consistently remind me of her social location. How frustrating to sit in a college classroom, where the free expression of ideas is encouraged, and feel trapped by stereotypes. In the education section, we will discuss the stereotype threat and its harmful effect on student achievement. For Kendra, identifying the intersections of race, class, and gender was filtered through multiple experiences that challenged her to contemplate her "black-ness," "woman-ness," and class standing.

We tend to think of race as a character flaw rather than a destructive force that is embedded within the fabric of social life. Several years ago, I attended a conference where I was asked to complete an exercise from an "able-centered" perspective. The facilitator of the exercise sought to "snap us out" of our perceived notions of what ability means and recognize our "able-bodied privilege." I found this difficult, as I felt compelled to contextualize the exercise based on my social location as an African American and a woman. I struggled to be mindful of my "able-ness," as I sought to understand the experiences of those with physical and mental challenges. I consider myself well versed in theories of intersectionality, yet I floundered when asked to imagine how ableism exists as an intersecting form of oppression. Like ableism, racism transcends personal likes and preferences; it is a social phenomenon so embedded within the norms of our everyday lives and social structures that we fail to recognize its existence. I am guessing that you, too, will struggle to be mindful of your individual dislikes and preferences, as we ask you to review the works in this text from a "race-centered" or "ethnic-centered" perspective. As you move through the text, remind yourself that mindfulness is a process, not a solitary, one-time act. This means that although you may have experienced racism or ethnocentrism yourself, it is still necessary to be mindful of your own assumptions, beliefs, values, and behaviors. What better place to start than with sociological theory—the process of explaining how and why we do what we do?

In sociology, pondering why our social behavior takes certain forms is just as important as gathering the empirical evidence that reveals the existence of social patterns. This reader highlights the many ways in which marginalized groups experience race and ethnic inequalities. Most of the readings rely on quantitative and qualitative data to illustrate the effect of structural racism, the daily struggle of negotiating race and ethnic identities, or the economic, health, or financial effect of racism. In addition, you will find that many of these readings steep their arguments in **sociological theory**, which unlike theories in the natural sciences tends to be more evaluative and critical (Appelrouth and Edles 2015). We utilize theory to organize the observations and facts that make up social life. Appelrouth and Edles (2015) state that, in essence, theory helps us make sense of the world around us "because it holds assorted observations and facts together." As we struggle to organize our social world, we rely on "implicit assumptions and unacknowledged presuppositions that mean interpretations of social reality rely more on *what we think we observe and know*, rather than what is factual." Yet, as Sears and

Cairns (2016) argue, it is difficult to make the argument for theory in a data-driven world, preoccupied wit h collecting empirical evidence. "Formal theories guide and inform the process of study and observation, helping to define what the problems are in the first place and how they might be addressed" (Sears and Cairns 2016:45). Theory is a tool of investigation, not a hindrance to it.

So, how do we make sense of race and ethnic inequalities, especially when the idea of "race" is socially constructed, rendering it fluid and vulnerable to change? The story of race in the United States is complex and tenuous—its discourse has been shaped by religion, politics, law, economics, and geography. The social constructions of race and ethnicity have become so embedded in the American psyche that we have lost much of our creative power to rethink how they exist within our lives and social institutions, through a process of **reification**. Thus, the race and ethnic categories that we socially construct become interpreted as fixed, discrete social-psychological spaces that do not offer much room for change. The theories discussed in this reading attempt to break race and ethnicity out of this constraint.

We will discuss two camps of sociological theory: **structural theories of inequality** and **theories of interaction**. Structural theories emphasize the historical shaping of racial hierarchies through the power of social institutions. Most significant among these theories are **critical race theory, race formation theory, and color-blind racism**. Theories of interaction emphasize relational spaces, how our interpretations of race and ethnicity influence our identities (i.e., relationship to oneself based on collective meaning) and how these interpretations influence our interactions with others (i.e., interpersonal relationships). We will focus specifically on **intersectionality** and its use as an analytical framework within the study of race and ethnic inequalities.

Critical Race Theory

Critical Race Theory (CRT) stems from the theorizing of Karl Marx, which placed great emphasis on the role of the economic order in structuring (mostly) class inequalities (e.g., as corporate profit increases, the value of the worker decreases). It reinvigorates Marxist ideas by addressing inherent inequalities in many of our social institutions, such as law, politics, education, and religion, that affect the lives of marginalized groups, especially race and ethnic minorities. Thus, the power and privileges of social institutions maintain an inverse relationship to the quality of life of marginalized groups (e.g., the militarization of the police force and its effect on predominantly black and brown low-income communities). CRT's emphasis on social institutions challenges us to consider how we legitimize and perpetuate racial hierarchies and their subsequent harmful effects on individuals and groups.

Collectively, works that utilize critical race theory claim the following: 1) racism is *not* abnormal; 2) racism benefits the privileged, thereby solidifying its existence; 3) racism is a fluid, changing feature of social life that works in tandem with other social inequalities; and 4) racism influences our personal and interpersonal experiences (Delgado and Stefancic 2001, and Matsuda, Lawrence, Delgado, and Crenshaw 1993). Further, CRT critiques the production of race and race identities within social institutions, exposing how racial categories and definitions are used to subjugate communities of color. For example, within the criminal justice system, consciously or unconsciously, labeling communities of color as "thugs" or "aggressive" influences their interactions with law enforcement and the court system. Similarly, constructing negative perceptions of students of color, such as "emotionally disturbed" or "unteachable," influencing their interactions with faculty, administrators, and their peers.

It is important to note that within the disability literature, researchers apply DISCRIT, which explains the structural disadvantages related to the marginalization of individuals with disabilities. For example, how we conceive of "ability" and "disability" frames the experiences of people with disabilities.

Race Formation Theory

As mentioned above, Marxist theorizing touted class as the paramount force creating social inequalities. Simultaneously, it marginalized the power and influence of other forms of social inequalities, such as race and gender. Omi and Winant responded to this problem in *Racial Formation in the United States*, walking us through the historical changes that have shaped shifting racial ideologies (1994). Arguing that race is not reducible to class, Omi and Winant illustrated how race functions separately from class, deserving of its own sociological inquiries. Further, they describe the *racialization process*—revealing how race becomes contextualized within social arenas, such as politics, education, and the criminal justice system. More specifically, they describe how racial projects contribute to the birth and perpetuation of racial ideologies. They state:

> A racial project is simultaneously an interpretation, representation, or explanation of racial dynamics, and an effort to reorganize and redistribute resources along particular racial lines. Racial projects connect what race means in a particular discursive practice and the ways in which both social structures and everyday experiences are racially organized, based upon that meaning.

Specifically, what is a *racial project*? For Omi and Winant, anything from a racial stereotype presented in a reality TV show to a conscious social movement exemplify racial projects. They control racial discourse, coaching us to interpret, respond, and identify in specific ways. Let us use the Black Lives Matter movement as an example. In response to ongoing police brutality, especially against black men, BLM challenges us to consider how racial stereotypes, racial prejudice, and racial hatred shape interactions between African Americans and the police. Regardless if you actively participate in BLM or not, you have an opinion about its objectives and actions. Thus, you become drawn into the discourse, debating the relevance of the movement, its connection to your personal life, and its overall objectives. Similarly, we can classify the white nationalist rally in Charlottesville, Virginia, which protested the removal of Confederate statues as a racial project as well. Shielding their protest under the banner of "Unite the Right," white nationalist protestors referenced President Donald Trump's 2016 campaign promises, stating their goals were in line with Trump's efforts to "take back the country." This coded language, used widely in American politics, masks underlining racial prejudice and bigotry. Again, whether one was present at the rally or not, we interpret, respond, and identify with its actions in ways that draw us into the larger, national, race discourse. You will learn more about Omi and Winant's theorizing in this section.

Color-Blind Racism

You may have heard someone state the following: "I'm not a racist! I have a black friend," or "I get along with everyone. I don't see color!" For Bonilla-Silva (2013), these retorts exemplify color-blind racism, a perspective that ignores the existence of a racial hierarchy, overlooking the multiple inequities served upon people of color. The stories that we tell about racism, our experiences or others', illustrates the structure of racial grammar—the rules, semantics, and logics that justify, legitimize, and present the racial order as normal. We communicate the existence and power of the racial order through storytelling (racial grammar) that "normalizes" white privilege and demonizes the powerless. For example, rather than cite historical, structural racism as a contributor to residential segregation, a color-blind perspective argues that people self-segregate, so we can live next to people "just like us." Bonilla-Silva (2013) identifies four central frames used by whites that mask racist views and perceptions: abstract liberalism, naturalization, cultural racism, and the minimization of racism. Each frame reduces or erases the existence of a racial hierarchy and its harmful effects on communities of color. Abstract liberalism refers to the use of "equal opportunity" and "meritocracy" arguments to eschew racism (e.g., "There are plenty of jobs out there, why can't you find one?"). Naturalization anecdotes identify personal motives or reference the status quo as factors in social phenomena such as residential segregation (e.g. "People choose to be like people just like themselves," or "This is how it's always been."). A descendant of biological racism, cultural racism shoves blame onto communities of color (e.g., "They're lazy," or "It's just part of their culture to have so many kids."). Minimization tactics draw attention away from historical, structural inequities (e.g., "Slavery happened a long time ago," or "People are just people. No one is trying to be racist."). Each central frame flies in the face of real experiences of racism, historical injustices, and ongoing racial inequities, which makes it harder to eradicate racism.

Intersectionality

Many trace the origins of intersectionality to Crenshaw's 1991 article in the *Stanford Law Review*, in which she skillfully explains how race and gender social inequalities particularly disadvantage women of color. More specifically, Crenshaw details how intersecting race and gender inequalities creates different experiences of sexual assault and domestic violence for women of color than white women. However, decades earlier, black women scholars such as Anna Julia Cooper and Ida B. Wells-Barnett addressed the harmful consequences of gendered and raced social hierarchies. Collins offers a definition of intersectionality that attempts to encapsulate its interdisciplinary use. Intersectionality "references the critical insight that race, class, and gender, sexuality, ethnicity, nation, ability, and age operate not as unitary, mutually exclusive entities, but as reciprocally constructing phenomena that in turn shape complex social inequalities" (2015:3). Intersectionality views social inequalities as multiplicative, often simultaneous experiences, which do not outrank one another. Thus, race, class, and gender nest within one another, as multiplicative social inequalities. See Collins's reading in this section for a full discussion.

Drawing from racial formation theory, intersectionality emphasizes the influence of racial hierarchies on the lived experiences of marginalized groups. For example, how people are situated within racial hierarchies denotes whether their lives are protected through privilege or vulnerable to disadvantage. In addition, racial formation theory and critical race theory inform how race meaning and race identity influence social interaction and behavior. For example, after 9/11, Arab and/or Muslim groups in the United States were targeted as "terrorists" and portrayed as such in the media, on television, and in films. Although the racial hierarchy did not shift, the perception of Arab and Muslim Americans as untrustworthy influenced their experiences in the workplace, in school, and traveling in and outside the United States. The contentious travel restrictions, ordered by the Trump administration and referred to as the "Muslim Ban," indefinitely denies immigrant and nonimmigrant visas to seven countries—five Muslim-majority (i.e., Libya, Iran, Somalia, Syria, and Yemen) and Venezuela and North Korea. In this case, the intersections of race and religious social inequalities influence the creation of oppressive social policy. For a full discussion, please see the Introduction to the Intersectionality section.

Mindfulness

Theory encourages us to remain flexible. Theoretical perspectives do not offer definitive, concrete conclusions to racial discourse. Rather it is important for theory to remain flexible, open to change and reinterpretation. This means that theory, like individuals, must be self-reflective. None of the theoretical approaches we have discussed could survive academic scrutiny without, at times, analyzing their own arguments, suppositions, and assumptions. Often, when teaching, I communicate to students that beliefs—what we hold to be true—are difficult for humans to change. Think about your journey through higher education. Have you ever encountered an idea or a fact that you found difficult to *believe*? One of the hardest things to do as an undergraduate is confront the many ideas, values, and norms that we learned from our families and peers. In fact, this may be the first time that you have been asked to reconsider what you learned in the past. In order to engage the educational process, you will need to develop the ability to be self-reflective. This does not mean you should tear down everything that went into your upbringing. It means asking, is there another way to look at this? I grew up in a charismatic, fundamentalist church. My family members were preachers, evangelists, deacons, and Sunday school teachers. When I was older, I joined an even stricter church. I was not allowed to wear pants, cosmetics, or jewelry or date. In many ways the church was an extension of what I learned as a youth. In other ways it challenged me to question what I truly believed. For a long time, I thought my belief was revealed in my actions. However, as I grew more disgruntled with the behavior of the church, I realized what I believe is separate from what I was being asked to do. Aha! A moment of self-reflection. I am not sure if you will experience such a dramatic shift in your educational journey; however, I encourage you to remain open to it. Just like the theoretical perspectives we discussed, a moment of self-reflection can help strengthen your worldview.

Section Readings

This section presents three readings that discuss the application of sociological theory to race and ethnic inequalities. Each reading focuses on a specific sociological theory(ies).

In "Intersectionality's Definitional Dilemmas," Patricia Hill Collins reflects on how researchers and theorists define intersectionality across multiple disciplines. Often, diffusing terms and concepts across academic fields leads to diluted and fragmented meanings. Given its importance in elucidating how social inequalities converge, generating different experiences for social groups, how we define and apply intersectionality requires a common approach. Collins attempts to provide some clarity and direction regarding the assumptions of intersectionality. Rather than produce definitive, fixed assumptions, Collins establishes a guiding framework that when wielded, is amenable to diverse perspectives, approaches, and applications.

In "Racial Formation Rules: Continuity, Instability, and Change," Omi and Winant revisit their seminal work on the construction and persistence of racial hierarchies within American society. The authors address the shifting definition and constructions of racial hierarchies within a range of social institutions such as criminal justice and education.

In "Obstacles to White Anti-racist Praxis: Notes on Sociological Theory," Brooks addresses the relationship between social protests and the development of a white race consciousness. Using Blumer's Race Group Position theory, Du Bois's notion of the "veil," Brooks argues that how whites identify as members of "race groups" and how they perceive of the "other" can hinder or encourage anti-racist sentiments and behaviors.

Intersectionality's Definitional Dilemmas

Patricia Hill Collins

RACIAL FORMATION THEORY, KNOWLEDGE PROJECTS, AND INTERSECTIONALITY

Intersectionality faces a particular definitional dilemma—it participates in the very power relations that it examines and, as a result, must pay special attention to the conditions that make its knowledge claims comprehensible. Because analyzing the relations between knowledge and power is the traditional bailiwick of the sociology of knowledge, this field provides important theoretical vocabulary for conceptualizing intersectionality as both reflecting and shaping the power relations that house it. A sociology of knowledge framework suggests that knowledge—including knowledge aimed at better understanding intersectionality—is socially constructed and transmitted, legitimated, and reproduced. Yet within this core tenet, scholars have placed various emphases on the types of knowledge deemed worthy of study, the conceptions of social structure that house and/or are shaped by knowledge, and the influence of knowledge itself in shaping power relations (Balibar 2007, Berger & Luckmann 1966, Foucault 1980, Mannheim 1954, Swidler & Arditi 1994).

Within a broader critical race theory landscape (Delgado & Stefancic 2013), racial formation theory shows special promise for addressing intersectionality's definitional dilemma [Omi & Winant 2014 (1994)]. Because it conceptualizes race as situated within the recursive relationship between social structures and cultural representations, racial formation theory conflates neither discourses about race (e.g., racial meanings, representations, and social identities) nor the power relations in which racial meanings are situated. Both are held separate yet interconnected. Historically constructed, ever-changing racial formations organize racialized groups, the specific patterns of racial inequality that link racialized populations, and social problems that ensue. For example, in the United States, the racial formation of color-conscious racism has relied on a deep-seated logic of segregation that was applied to all aspects of social structures and cultural representations. In contrast, contemporary color-blind racism constitutes a differently organized yet equally powerful racial formation that manages to replicate racial hierarchies, often without overt attention to race itself (Bonilla-Silva 2003, Brown et al. 2003). Despite being more visible in different historical periods or across cross-national settings—both South Africa's racial apartheid and Brazil's racial democracy established racial hierarchies that persist—color-conscious and color-blind racial formations do not displace one another. As structural forms of power, one or the other racial formation may predominate, yet typically they coexist.

Racial formations have distinctive configurations of racial projects for which interest groups advance various interpretations of racial inequality. Within racial formation theory, ideas matter, not simply as hegemonic ideologies produced by elites but also as tangible, multiple knowledge projects that are advanced by specific interpretive communities. Because groups aim to have their interpretations of racial inequality prevail, knowledge lies at the heart of racial projects.

The question is less whether race is real or whether racial projects exist, but rather what kinds of racial projects appear and disappear across specific racial formations and why. For example, African American intellectual production has a storied history of protesting both the social structural dimensions of racism and the cultural representations of people of African descent (Kelley 2002). Yet despite these efforts, the richness of these knowledge projects rarely make it into the legitimated canon of established fields. Similarly, the eugenics projects that advanced widely accepted scientific knowledge about race had significant impact on the public policies of the United States, Germany, and many nation-states. Eugenics arguments fell out of favor in the post–World War II era, suggesting that counterarguments claiming that race was socially constructed with no connections to biology had prevailed. Yet in a postgenomic age, the resurgence of race in science, law, and medicine points to the resiliency of biological understandings of race within contemporary racial projects of science itself, typically without racially discriminatory intent (Duster 2015). The word "eugenics" fell out of favor, but ideas about the centrality of biology, newly defined in determining various aspects of human social behavior, have been more difficult to uproot. Just as racial formations change in response to racial projects, racial projects change in relation to changing racial formations.

Racial formation theory offers one additional benefit for intersectionality. Through its analysis of racial projects, racial formation theory can account for change in ways that retain the agency of individual human actors and group-based action. In contrast to the sociology of knowledge's traditional emphasis on individual intellectuals as superior if not the sole producers of knowledge—whether Mannheim's intelligentsia or Gramsci's organic intellectuals—this theory makes room for multiple interpretive communities. Because understanding racial inequality remains central to racial formation theory, it provides intellectual and political space for subordinated social groups such as African Americans, Latinos, Asians, and indigenous peoples. Such groups find intellectual and political space within racial formation theory for the group-based knowledge of racial projects that oppose racial hierarchy and racial inequality (Collins 1998a, pp. 201–28). Racial formation theory offers social actors guidance as to how their individual and collective actions matter in shaping racial inequality.

The strength of racial formation theory lies in how it links specific knowledge projects (racial projects) with historically constructed power relations (racial formations). Intersectionality can build on this foundation by moving beyond a mono-categorical focus on racial inequality to encompass multiple forms of inequality that are organized via a similar logic. As an initial step, this framework can be applied to other social formations and knowledge projects that reproduce inequality, for example, social formations of patriarchy, capitalism, heterosexism, and their characteristic knowledge projects. Yet intersectionality goes farther than this mono-system analysis, introducing a greater level of complexity into conceptualizing inequality. Whereas racial formation theory (ironically, itself a knowledge project) focuses on racism as a mono-categorical system of power, intersectionality examines social formations of multiple, complex social inequalities. In order to build on racial formation theory's promise, however, intersectionality would need to flesh out a more nuanced sociological understanding of how social structures and cultural representations interconnect. Knowledge projects are not free-floating phenomena; they are grounded in specific sociological processes experienced by actual people. Here a robust analysis of the new politics of community provides a way of grounding the more theoretical arguments in both racial formation theory and intersectionality (Collins 2010). Linking power with knowledge, the construct of community provides an important framework for understanding the interpretive communities that advance intersectionality's many knowledge projects.

Intersectionality can be conceptualized as an overarching knowledge project whose changing contours grow from and respond to social formations of complex social inequalities; within this overarching umbrella, intersectionality can also be profitably conceptualized as a constellation of knowledge projects that change in relation to one another in tandem with changes in the interpretive communities that advance them. The broader knowledge project provides a set of ideas that provide moments of definitional consensus. Overarching intersectional frameworks have been so successful because they remain broad and unspecified. They provide the illusion that the constellation of smaller knowledge projects can be uncritically categorized under intersectionality's big tent umbrella. Yet the sets of practitioners that lay claim to intersectionality via multiple cross-cutting and competitive intersectional knowledge projects reveal a lack of consensus about intersectionality's history, current organization, and future directions. Intersectionality's definitional dilemma occurs in this intellectual and political space.

In consideration of this framework, intersectional knowledge projects typically focus on three interdependent concerns. The first focal point makes intersectionality as a field of study the object of investigation. Examining the content and themes that characterize the field constitutes the main task. Why does this field exist? How is this field of study situated within prevailing power relations? How does this social location shape the kinds of themes and approaches that characterize intersectionality as a field of study?

The second focal point of intersectional knowledge projects examines intersectionality as an analytical strategy. These projects rely upon intersectional frameworks to produce new knowledge about the social world. Garnering the lion's share of attention within intersectionality as a field of study, this approach uses intersectional frameworks to investigate social phenomena, e.g., social institutions, practices, social problems, and the epistemological concerns of the field itself.

The third focal point emphasizes intersectionality as a form of critical praxis, especially its connections with social justice. This praxis perspective does not separate scholarship from practice, with scholarship providing theoretical frameworks that people are encouraged to apply to practice. Instead, both scholarship and practice are recursively linked, with practice being foundational to intersectional analysis.

PRODUCING NEW KNOWLEDGE: INTERSECTIONALITY AS AN ANALYTICAL STRATEGY

Despite intersectionality's ongoing definitional ambiguities, intersectionality as a field of study has catalyzed a copious outpouring of new knowledge, much of it produced by researchers, faculty members, and students who use intersectionality as an analytical strategy. Cho et al. (2013) view intersectionality as an analytical sensibility, arguing "what makes an analysis intersectional is not its use of the term 'intersectionality,' nor its being situated in a familiar genealogy, nor its drawing on lists of standard citations. Rather, what makes an analysis intersectional...is its adoption of an intersectional way of thinking about the problem of sameness and difference and its relation to power" (p. 795). Although the claim of an "analytic sensibility" is an improvement over merely "mentioning" intersectionality, both understandings resemble the "we know it when we see it" definitional approach.

Here I propose a way of proceeding that pushes beyond mere sensibility. Just as using Crenshaw to set intersectionality's canonical boundaries may be premature, designating selected theories and methods, especially one's own, as intersectional using an amorphous and perhaps idiosyncratic sensibility may be similarly shortsighted. Instead, examining patterns in the new knowledge that has been produced under the rubric of intersectionality as an analytical strategy may be more productive. The books, articles, conference papers, pamphlets, syllabi, and other products that claim intersectionality constitute data points that lend themselves to discourse analysis. Surveying the corpus of scholarship that draws upon intersectionality as an analytical strategy is daunting because intersectional publications are vast and growing exponentially (Collins & Chepp 2013). Because the field itself is dynamic, here I draw from my long-standing involvement within Black feminism, race/class/gender studies, and intersectionality to identify six selected focal points within intersectional literature that stand out for me. I present two questions: What themes characterize intersectional scholarship, and what assumptions might this disparate work share?

One important area of intersectional scholarship rethinks work, family, identity, the media, and similar core constructs. Work constitutes one important concept that contains highly nuanced scholarship on how labor market organization, occupational segregation, work-family balance, and other aspects of paid and unpaid reproductive labor underpin complex social inequalities. These topics have provided an especially rich terrain for intersectional scholarship from the race/class/gender period through contemporary analyses of global capitalism. Reflecting the social movement origins of race/class/gender studies, early intersectional scholarship on work examined segmented labor markets and the ways in which women and people of color were shunted to bad jobs and dirty work (Amott & Matthaei 1991). Building on analyses of capitalism that examined how the good jobs and bad jobs of labor markets were organized using social inequalities of gender, race, and economic class, studies of domestic work in particular showed how work was central to the exploitation of women and men of color (Glenn 2002, Hondagneu-Sotelo 2001). This foundational scholarship on work foreshadowed important directions within contemporary social science research, such as Browne & Misra's (2003) intersection of race and gender in the labor market, Tomaskovic-Devey's (2014) analysis of the relational nature of workplace inequalities, Wingfield & Alston's (2012) intersectional work on African American professional men, and Duffy's (2007) work on paid reproductive labor.

A second area expands the focus on race, class, and gender to incorporate sexuality, nation, ethnicity, age, and ability as similar categories of analysis (Kim-Puri 2005). Specifically, a sustained attention to the themes of nation, nationalism, nation-state, and national identity has aimed to align the power relations of nation with structural analyses of racism, capitalism, and patriarchy (Yuval-Davis 1997). Literature on the nation-state and its citizenship policies has benefited from intersectional frameworks, e.g., the case of Goldberg's (2002) analysis of the racial state or Glenn's (2002) study of work, American citizenship, and nation-state power. Intersectional frameworks have also deepened our understanding of nationalist ideologies, as evidenced in Nagel's (1998) analysis of masculinity and nationalism or Mosse's (1985) classic work on nationalism and sexuality. The political behavior of subordinated groups as they aim to empower themselves has also garnered intersectional analysis; for example, Ramos-Zayas's (2003) ethnographic study of Puerto Rican identity within a Chicago neighborhood illustrates the benefits of incorporating nationalism into studies of local politics. Intersectional analyses of nation-state power have expanded to consider transnational processes, for example, placing analyses of tourism in the Bahamas within intersectional processes of erotic autonomy, decolonization, and nationalism (Alexander 1997, 2005).

A third area uses intersectional frameworks to rethink violence and similar social problems. Recasting violence as a social problem for many groups has catalyzed a broader conception of complex social inequalities and how heterogeneous forms of violence are essential in maintaining them (Collins 1998b). Because violence against women has been such a powerful catalyst for intersectionality itself, intersectional analyses of this topic not only are widespread but have informed political activism and public policy. Solutions to violence against women remain unlikely if violence against women is imagined through mono-categorical lenses such as gender lenses of male perpetrators and female victims or racial lenses that elevate police violence against Black men over domestic violence against Black women. Intersectional frameworks that analyze violence reappear across a wide array of topics such as violence against women in Iraqi Kurdistan (Alinia 2013), nation-state violence of militarism and war (Peterson 2007), the treatment of sexual violence and ethnicity in international criminal law (Buss 2009), and hate speech itself as part of relations of violence (Matsuda et al. 1993).

A fourth area emphasizes identity. Identity has garnered considerable scholarly attention, ranging from a strong interest in the theme of studying how intersecting identities produce distinctive social experiences for specific individuals and social groups, to claims that intersectionality constitutes a feminist theory that deals with issues of identity (Goldberg 2009). In contrast, scholarship that examines identity in relation to social inequality, such as the possibilities of identity categories as potential coalitions (Carastathis 2013) or case studies on how attending to intersecting identities creates solidarity and cohesion for cross-movement mobilization (Roberts & Jesudason 2013), remains in the minority.

The fifth area critiques the epistemological workings of intersectionality itself. Here conceptualizations of intersectionality seem to be as varied as the individual scholars themselves. Intersectionality has been conceptualized as a perspective (Browne & Misra 2003, Steinbugler et al. 2006), a concept (Knapp 2005), a type of analysis (Nash 2008, Yuval-Davis 2006), or as a "nodal point" for feminist theorizing (Lykke 2011). Other scholars emphasize intersectionality's placement in the research process, with some approaching intersectionality as a methodological approach (Steinbugler et al. 2006, Yuval-Davis 2006), a research paradigm (Hancock 2007b), or a measurable variable and a type of data (Bowleg 2008). Still, others draw upon existing social theories, aiming to deepen intersectionality's analysis of inequality by bringing the field in alignment with complexity theory (Walby 2007).

Last, researchers remain preoccupied with questions of methodology. Because of the vacuum in scholarship that explicitly examines how intersectionality's emphasis on relational thinking affects research methodology, McCall's (2005) taxonomy of intersectional categorization has been widely taken up within the field. Similarly, extant literature on intersectionality, methodology, and empirical validity (see, e.g., Bowleg 2008; Hancock 2007a,b) is likely a response to the critique that intersectionality scholarship lacks a precise and diverse methodological approach (Nash 2008). When it comes to intersectionality and methodology, the core question concerns how intersectionality can be conceptualized within a particular research design that is attentive to the contradictions that characterize intersectional knowledge projects and that makes a good faith effort to deploy appropriate theories and methods in the face of such uncertainty. Looking beyond intersectionality's mainstream, however, yields other epistemological insights. Feminist scholar Chela Sandoval (2000) contends that methodology is not politically impartial, proposing instead a "methodology of the oppressed." Fonow & Cook's (2005) analysis of feminist methodology remains especially useful in parsing out the distinctions among epistemology, methodology, and methods that might inform intersectionality as an analytical strategy.

Collectively, the patterns of emphasis (and the patterns of absence) within intersectional scholarship provide a template for seeing the benefits and costs of legitimation for intersectionality as a field of study. The benefits may be visible, but the costs are more difficult to identify without assessing how these particular focal points advance not only the interests and careers of particular scholars, but also intersectionality as a broader knowledge project. Seeing patterns of emphasis and absence can be difficult for a field with a constellation of knowledge projects that reflect the power relations that they study. For example, in the US context, intersectional scholarship on work and labor markets has the potential to influence public policy, yet doing so requires claiming particular perspectives on stratification and class. Class is routinely mentioned across intersectional scholarship, yet it remains underutilized as an analytical category to explain complex social inequalities. Writing in 1999, Acker (1999, p. 44) suggested that, with the development of postmodern/poststructuralist feminism, several leading feminist theorists turned to issues of culture, representation, and identity, in effect abandoning class as a central theoretical construct. By overemphasizing class as a descriptive category of economic stratification and underemphasizing class as an analytical category of economic relations, empirical scholarship that relies on descriptive analyses of class inadvertently elevates race and gender as explanatory categories while appearing to treat class in a similar fashion.

The European context reads race, class, and gender quite differently. In the European context of engagement with Marxist social thought, class analyses have long explained social inequality, leaving race and gender as descriptive interlopers. Yet reducing race to a descriptive identity category that is important to racial/ethnic minorities but not to mainstream scholarship leaves intersectional scholarship that privileges class incomplete. Elevating intersectionality sans race as a more theoretical and therefore preferred discourse on inequality erases racism, displacing its effects onto the United States, South Africa, and similar color-conscious racial formations (Lewis 2013).

Epistemological Challenges

Neither the new knowledge created within these areas of intersectional scholarship nor the research methodologies used to produce it stand outside power relations; both are deeply embedded in what they aim to study. Philosopher Kristie Dotson's (2013) analysis of epistemic oppression claims that knowledge is not politically neutral. Intersectionality would do well to consider how epistemic oppression might play out against and within its own parameters. When empirical work that claims to be using intersectionality fails to consider the epistemological assumptions of its own practice, such work can unwittingly uphold the same complex social inequalities that it aims to understand. Proceeding as though intersectionality, as much as any other theoretical framework, is already a social theory that can be used and critiqued within prevailing academic norms misreads this field.

In the same way that my earlier discussion of Black feminism and its shift to race/class/gender studies provided a context for the themes that characterized these projects, my selective rendition of how scholars use intersectionality as an analytical strategy constitutes a comparable preliminary entry point into similar epistemological terrain. The thematic emphases described above—(a) attending to social institutions such as work, (b) expanding systems of power beyond race, class, and gender, (c) applying an intersectional lens to social problems, (d) giving considerable attention to identity, and (e) casting a self-reflexive eye on intersectionality's epistemological and methodological issues—produce a loose set of guiding assumptions or guiding themes. Stated differently, based on a cursory survey of publications as data for analysis, these guiding assumptions may flesh out intersectionality's analytical sensibility discussed above. These guiding themes need not be present simultaneously, nor is each theme unique to intersectionality.

My reading of intersectional knowledge projects is that they embrace one, some combination, or all of the following provisional list of guiding assumptions:

- Race, class, gender, sexuality, age, ability, nation, ethnicity, and similar categories of analysis are best understood in relational terms rather than in isolation from one another.
- These mutually constructing categories underlie and shape intersecting systems of power; the power relations of racism and sexism, for example, are interrelated.
- Intersecting systems of power catalyze social formations of complex social inequalities that are organized via unequal material realities and distinctive social experiences for people who live within them.
- Because social formations of complex social inequalities are historically contingent and cross-culturally specific, unequal material realities and social experiences vary across time and space.
- Individuals and groups differentially placed within intersecting systems of power have different points of view on their own and others' experiences with complex social inequalities, typically advancing knowledge projects that reflect their social locations within power relations.
- The complex social inequalities fostered by intersecting systems of power are fundamentally unjust, shaping knowledge projects and/or political engagements that uphold or contest the status quo.

The current unevenness across how scholars use intersectionality as an analytical strategy reflects differing degrees of emphasis on specific guiding assumptions. Some themes are definitely more popular than others. For example, work and identity constitute popular topics, whereas sustained attention to the connections between complex social inequalities and social justice is less prominent. Overall, this provisional list of guiding assumptions is far from a working definition, but it does elucidate how intersectionality as an analytical strategy is unfolding.

But this all begs the underlying epistemological question of how these emerging patterns contribute to clarifying intersectionality's definitional dilemmas. One way to understand intersectionality as an analytical strategy is to place the earlier themes of community organizing, identity politics, coalitional politics, interlocking oppressions, and social justice in dialogue with the guiding assumptions of contemporary intersectional scholarship. Stuart Hall's construct of articulation may prove highly useful in examining the dynamic patterns of how scholars use intersectionality as an analytical strategy. Hall posits that a theory of articulation is "both a way of understanding how ideological elements come, under certain conditions, to cohere together within a discourse, and a way of asking how they do or do not become articulated, at specific conjunctures, to certain political struggles" (Grossberg 1996, pp. 141–42). Stated differently, how do and how might these two sets of ideas articulate to shape intersectionality's emerging canonical knowledge?

With hindsight, I see how this unanswered (and, some would say, unanswerable) question of how to articulate multiple points of view on intersectionality frames its definitional dilemmas. Yet the epistemological issues that affect any use of intersectionality as an analytical strategy may take a different form outside the scholarly requirements of the academy. When it comes to intersectionality as critical praxis, practitioners might use both sets of ideas differently.

WHAT'S AT STAKE? INTERSECTIONALITY AS A FORM OF CRITICAL PRAXIS

In 2013, I delivered a keynote address on US Black feminism and intersectionality at the Afro-Latin and Afro-Caribbean Women's Festival in Brasilia, Brazil. A small group of Afro-Brazilian women scholar-activists approached me after my talk (Collins 2012). They were surprised by my argument that US Black feminism and intersectionality were interconnected knowledge projects, stating bluntly, "We thought intersectionality was for white feminists and that it had nothing to do with us." In our discussion, I learned how their experiences resonated not just with the guiding assumptions that shape contemporary intersectional scholarship on work, social issues such as violence, and the significance of identity politics, but also with the broader themes from US Black feminism as a social justice project. They seemed to be working within one particular space of articulation between, on the one hand, the core ideas that I have attributed to US Black feminism and race/class/gender studies and, on the other hand, the guiding assumptions that I identified via a preliminary content analysis of intersectional scholarship. Ironically, their interpretive community advanced an intersectional knowledge project that did not claim the term intersectionality.

For these scholar-activists, intersectionality as a form of critical praxis made sense for their social justice projects aimed at remedying complex social inequalities. Despite their suspicions of intersectionality, they understood how using a more expansive understanding of intersectionality potentially constituted an important tool for political engagement. This connection between social justice and remedying complex social inequalities seems more prominent outside academic settings than within them. Once I became more mindful of how practitioners were using intersectionality, even when, as in this case, it was not called intersectionality, I encountered different patterns of articulation between understandings of intersectionality.

Practitioners are often frontline actors for solving social problems that are clearly linked to complex social inequalities, a social location that predisposes them to respond to intersectionality as critical praxis. Teachers, social workers, parents, policy advocates, university support staff, community organizers, clergy, lawyers, graduate students, and nurses often have an up close and personal relationship to violence, homelessness, hunger, illiteracy, poverty, sexual assault, and similar phenomena. Intersectionality is not simply a field of study to be mastered or an analytical strategy for understanding; rather, intersectionality as critical praxis sheds light on the doing of social justice work. As was the case for intersectional scholarship, the types of actions that characterize intersectionality as critical praxis are vast. Again, I offer suggestive avenues of investigation.

Local, grassroots, small-scale, and/or temporary groups that draw upon intersectionality to guide their critical praxis can often escape public notice. Typically, these groups are composed of society's overlooked populations, specifically the young, women, people of color, and poor people. Yet groups such as these have a vested interest in drawing upon intersectional frameworks to address social inequalities. For example, Clay's (2012) study of youth activism in Oakland, California, shows how young people of color draw upon intersectional frameworks to confront the persisting inequalities in schooling that face them. Similarly, Harrison's (2009) research on the hip-hop underground in San Francisco reveals how a multiethnic group of youth renegotiate racial identifications within a performative place of poetry and politics. Both studies show how young people engage intersectionality as critical praxis in venues that often escape scholarly scrutiny.

In some cases, social institutions do aim to make intersectionality as critical praxis central to their organizational mission and practice. For example, Simon Fraser University's Intersectionality-Based Policy Analysis (IBPA) initiative, housed at the Institute for Intersectionality Research and Policy, aims to generate research with direct applicability to Canadian health policy. Because public health remains connected to the practices of health care professionals, the challenge for this field lies in integrating intersectional frameworks into both health care delivery practices and public policies. Aiming to make their materials user friendly to stakeholders in health policy arenas, the IBPA organizers developed an iterative, participatory process that involves researchers, practitioners, and consumers. The mission statements from the IBPA illustrate the aspirations of social actors who wish to bring intersectionality into public policy areas: "IBPA provides a new and effective method for understanding the varied equity-relevant implications of policy and for promoting equity-based improvements and social justice within an increasingly diverse and complex population base" (Hankivsky 2012, p. 33).

Human rights is another vitally important area for intersectionality as critical praxis. The ideas expressed in the 1948 Universal Declaration of Human Rights bear a strong family resemblance to strands of intersectionality that are aligned with social justice initiatives. Article 1 affirms that all human beings "are born free and equal in dignity and rights"; Article 2 states everyone "is entitled to all the rights and freedoms set forth in this Declaration without distinction of any kind, such as race, colour, sex, language, religion, political or other opinion, national or social origin, property, birth or other status" (Freeman 2011, p. 5). Yet because the protected categories gain meaning only in relation to one another, actualizing human rights means transcending the limitations of a strictly legal statement of human rights. Intersectionality potentially helps address three main concerns. First, human rights requires more effective tools for identifying the kinds of distinctions that constitute discrimination. In a world where petitions for human rights violations could be brought under various categories, conceptualizing discrimination becomes important. When discrimination is legally framed either by sex or gender or race, how does one best serve people who bring claims that touch on more than one area? Second, there is the need for better assessments of pain, suffering, and injury. What types of pain and suffering are appropriate for bringing forth a human rights claim? In what ways do questions of human dignity matter? The third concern is the search for appropriate reparations and remedies to victims of human rights abuses. What are state responsibilities if harm has been documented and suffering has occurred?

Despite its ubiquity, intersectionality as critical praxis remains underemphasized within intersectionality as a field of study and within scholarship that draws on intersectionality as an analytical strategy. This underemphasis may be due in part because these areas valorize studying or writing about intersectionality over practicing it. In addition, the underemphasis on intersectionality as critical praxis within academia most likely reflects efforts to avoid the implicit political implications of intersectionality itself. The qualifier *critical* is important. Practitioners who would be drawn to intersectionality as critical praxis seek knowledge projects that take a stand; such projects would critique social injustices that characterize complex social inequalities, imagine alternatives, and/or propose viable action strategies for change.

The value of critical praxis reflects the norms of any given interpretive community. For example, from her pathbreaking work on women, race, and class to her sustained attention to prison abolition, the storied career of Angela Davis (1981, 2012) speaks to a sustained engagement with intersectionality as critical praxis. Yet on the basis of their respective agendas, activist and scholarly circles can interpret Davis's intellectual production differently. In scholarly settings, the critical dimensions of Davis's work open her up to accusations of bias—her analyses of capitalism, neoliberalism, racism, and prisons can read as too polemical and therefore unscholarly. In contrast, in activist venues searching for a critical analysis of social inequality, these same ideas remain well-received, precisely because her work remains critical. Davis's stature as a public intellectual has provided a platform for her ideas, making it difficult if not impossible to exclude them from academic venues. Increasingly, intersectionality's ideas can travel across diverse interpretive communities, a shift that has important implications for intersectionality as critical praxis. The changing political economy of publishing and social media provides new venues for circulating intersectional analyses both outside and inside academia. For example, Canadian activist Harsha Walia's (2013) analysis of border imperialism is written for, not about, activists. Her book is unlikely to be selected for ASA sessions on "Intersectionality" or to appear as assigned reading on course syllabi. Yet critical scholarship linked to critical practice such as this is also part of a broader intersectional knowledge project that increasingly transcends the traditional boundaries of academic projects. Scholars may know less about intersectionality as critical praxis simply because they fail to look for it.

When it comes to intersectionality's definitional dilemmas, much is at stake. As Carbado (2013) points out, "Scholars across the globe regularly invoke and draw upon intersectionality, as do human rights activists, community organizers, political figures and lawyers. Any theory that traverses such transdemographic terrains is bound to generate controversy and contestation" (p. 811). Despite the visibility of scholars as the public face of intersectionality, practitioners such as hip-hop poets, Afro-Brazilian feminists, IBPA scholar-activists, and intellectual activists such as Angela Davis and Harsha Walia may be equally if not more likely to put forth the innovative, cutting-edge intersectional analyses that will advance the field. In this context, intersectionality as a knowledge project faces the fundamental challenge of sustaining its critical edge. Holding fast to the creativity of this dynamic area of inquiry and practice yet finding a common language that will be useful to its practitioners *is* the cutting-edge definitional dilemma for intersectionality.

DISCLOSURE STATEMENT

The author is not aware of any affiliations, memberships, funding, or financial holdings that might be perceived as affecting the objectivity of this review.

LITERATURE CITED

Acker J. 1999. Rewriting class, race, and gender: problems in feminist rethinking. In *Revisioning Gender*, ed. MM Ferree, J Lorber, BB Hess, pp. 44–69. Thousand Oaks, CA: Sage

Alexander MJ. 1997. Erotic autonomy as a politics of decolonization: an anatomy of feminist and state practice in the Bahamas tourist industry. In *Feminist Genealogies, Colonial Legacies, Democratic Futures*, ed. MJ Alexander, CT Mohanty, pp. 63–100. New York: Routledge

Alexander MJ. 2005. Imperial desire/sexual utopias: white gay capital and transnational tourism. In *Pedagogies of Crossing: Meditations on Feminism, Sexual Politics, Memory, and the Sacred*, ed. MJ Alexander, pp. 66–88. Durham, NC: Duke University Press

Alexander-Floyd NG. 2012. Disappearing acts: reclaiming intersectionality in the social sciences in a post-black feminist era. *Fem. Formations* 24:1–25

Alinia M. 2013. *Honor and Violence Against Women in Iraqi Kurdistan*. New York: Palgrave Macmillan

Amott TL, Matthaei J. 1991. *Race, Gender, and Work: A Multicultural Economic History of Women in the United States*. Boston: South End

Andersen ML, Collins PH, eds. 2012. *Race, Class and Gender: An Anthology*. Belmont, CA: Wadsworth

Anderson CD. 1996. Understanding the inequality problematic: from scholarly rhetoric to theoretical reconstruction. *Gender Soc.* 10:729–46

Anzaldúa G. 1987. *Borderlands/La Frontera*. San Francisco: Spinsters/Aunt Lute Press

Anzaldúa G, Moraga C, eds. 1983. *This Bridge Called My Back: Writings by Radical Women of Color*. Watertown, MA: Kitchen Table

Balibar E. 2007. *The Philosophy of Marx*. New York: Verso

Berger M, Guidroz K, eds. 2009. *The Intersectional Approach: Transforming the Academy Through Race, Class, and Gender*. Chapel Hill, NC: Univ. North Carolina Press

Berger PL, Luckmann T. 1966. *The Social Construction of Reality: A Treatise in the Sociology of Knowledge*. New York: Anchor

Bilge S. 2013. Intersectionality undone: saving intersectionality from feminist intersectionality studies. *Du Bois Rev.* 10:405–24

Bonilla-Silva E. 2003. *Racism Without Racists: Color-Blind Racism and the Persistence of Racial Inequality in the United States*. Lantham, MD: Rowman & Littlefield

Bowleg L. 2008. When black + lesbian + woman ≠ black lesbian woman: the methodological challenges of qualitative and quantitative intersectionality research. *Sex Roles* 59:312–25

Brown MI, Carnoy M, Currie E, Duster T, Oppenheimer DB, et al. 2003. *Whitewashing Race: The Myth of a Color-Blind Society*. Berkeley: Univ. Calif. Press

Browne I, Misra J. 2003. The intersection of gender and race in the labor market. *Annu. Rev. Sociol.* 29:487–513

Buss D. 2009. Sexual violence, ethnicity, and intersectionality in international criminal law. In *Intersectionality and Beyond: Law, Power and the Politics of Location*, ed. D Cooper, pp. 105–23. New York: Routledge

Carastathis A. 2013. Identity categories as potential coalitions. *Signs* 38:941–65

Carbado DW. 2013. Colorblind intersectionality. *Signs* 38:811–45

Carbado DW, Crenshaw K, Mays VM, Tomlinson B. 2013. Intersectionality: mapping the movements of a theory. *Du Bois Rev.* 10:302–12

Cho S, Crenshaw K, McCall L. 2013. Toward a field of intersectionality studies: theory, applications, and praxis. *Signs* 38:785–810

Choo HY, Ferree MM. 2010. Practicing intersectionality in sociological research: a critical analysis of inclusions, interactions, and institutions in the study of inequalities. *Sociol. Theory* 28:129–49

Clay A. 2012. *The Hip-Hop Generation Fights Back: Youth, Activism, and Post-Civil Rights Politics*. New York: New York Univ. Press

Collins PH. 1998a. *Fighting Words: Black Women and the Search for Justice*. Minneapolis: Univ. Minn. Press

Collins PH. 1998b. The tie that binds: race, gender and U.S. violence. *Ethn. Racial Stud.* 21:918–38

Collins PH. 2000. *Black Feminist Thought: Knowledge, Consciousness, and the Politics of Empowerment*. New York: Routledge

Collins PH. 2007. Pushing the boundaries or business as usual? Race, class, and gender studies and sociological inquiry. In *Sociology in America: A History*, ed. C Calhoun, pp. 572–604. Chicago: Univ. Chicago Press

Collins PH. 2010. The new politics of community. *Am. Sociol. Rev.* 75:7–30

Collins PH. 2012. *On Intellectual Activism*. Philadelphia: Temple Univ. Press

Collins PH, Chepp V. 2013. Intersectionality. In *Oxford Handbook of Gender and Politics*, ed. L Weldon, pp. 31–61. New York: Oxford

Combahee River Collective. 1995. A black feminist statement. In *Words of Fire: An Anthology of African-American Feminist Thought*, ed. B Guy-Sheftall, pp. 232–40. New York: The New Press

Cooper AJ. 1892. *A Voice from the South; By a Black Woman of the South*. Xenia, OH: Aldine

Crenshaw KW. 1991. Mapping the margins: intersectionality, identity politics, and violence against women of color. *Stanford Law Rev.* 43:1241–99

Davis AY. 1981. *Women, Race, and Class*. New York: Random House

Davis AY. 2012. *The Meaning of Freedom and Other Difficult Dialogues*. San Francisco: City Lights Books

Delgado R, Stefancic J, eds. 2013. *Critical Race Theory: The Cutting Edge*. Philadelphia: Temple Univ. Press

Dill BT. 2009. Intersections, identities, and inequalities in higher education. See Dill & Zambrana 2009, pp. 229–52

Dill BT, Zambrana R, eds. 2009. *Emerging Intersections: Race, Class, and Gender in Theory, Policy, and Practice*. New Brunswick, NJ: Rutgers Univ. Press

Dotson K. 2013. Conceptualizing epistemic oppression. *Soc. Epistemol.* 14:1–23

Duffy M. 2007. Doing the dirty work: gender, race and reproductive labor in historical perspective. *Gender Soc.* 21:313–36

Duster T. 2015. A post-genomic surprise: the molecular reinscription of race in science, law and medicine. *Br. J. Sociol.* 66:1–27

Fonow MM, Cook JA. 2005. Feminist methodology: new applications in the academy and public policy. *Signs* 30:2211–30

Foucault M. 1980. *Power/Knowledge: Selected Interviews and Other Writings, 1972–1977*. New York: Pantheon

Freeman M. 2011. *Human Rights*. London: Polity

Glenn EN. 2002. *Unequal Freedom: How Race and Gender Shaped American Citizenship and Labor*. Cambridge, MA: Harvard Univ. Press

Goldberg DT. 2002. *The Racial State*. Malden, MA: Blackwell

Goldberg SB. 2009. Intersectionality in theory and practice. In *Intersectionality and Beyond: Law, Power and the Politics of Location*, ed. D Cooper, pp. 124–58. New York: Routledge

Grossberg L. 1996. On postmodernism and articulation: an interview with Stuart Hall. In *Critical Dialogues in Cultural Studies*, ed. D Morley, K-H Chen, pp. 131–50. New York: Routledge

Grzanka PR, ed. 2014. *Intersectionality: A Foundations and Frontiers Reader*. Boulder, CO: Westview

Guidroz K, Berger MT. 2009. A conversation with founding scholars of intersectionality: Kimberlé Crenshaw, Nira Yuval-Davis, and Michelle Fine. In *The Intersectional Approach: Transforming the Academy Through Race, Class and Gender*, ed. K Guidroz, M Berger, pp. 61–78. Chapel Hill, NC: Univ. North Carolina Press

Hancock A-M. 2007a. Intersectionality as a normative and empirical paradigm. *Polit. Gender* 3:248–55

Hancock A-M. 2007b. When multiplication doesn't equal quick addition: examining intersectionality as a research paradigm. *Perspect. Polit.* 5:63–79

Hankivsky O, ed. 2012. *An Intersectionality-Based Policy Analysis Framework*. Vancouver, BC: Inst. Intersect. Res. Policy, Simon Fraser Univ.

Harrison AK. 2009. *Hip Hop Underground: The Integrity and Ethics of Racial Identification*. Philadelphia: Temple Univ. Press

Hondagneu-Sotelo P. 2001. *Domestica: Immigrant Workers Cleaning and Caring in the Shadow of Affluence*. Berkeley: Univ. Calif. Press

Kelley RDG. 2002. *Freedom Dreams: The Black Radical Imagination*. Boston: Beacon

Kim-Puri HJ. 2005. Conceptualizing gender-sexuality-state-nation: an introduction. *Gender Soc.* 19:137–59

Knapp G-A. 2005. Race, class, gender: reclaiming baggage in fast travelling theories. *Eur. J. Women's Stud.* 12:249–65

Lamont M, Molnár V. 2002. The study of boundaries in the social sciences. *Annu. Rev. Sociol.* 28:167–95

Lewis G. 2013. Unsafe travel: experiencing intersectionality and feminist displacements. *Signs* 38:869–92

Lorde A. 1984. *Sister Outsider: Essays and Speeches*. Freedom, CA: Crossing Press

Lutz H, Vivar MTH, Supik L, eds. 2011. *Framing Intersectionality: Debates on a Multi-Faceted Concept in Gender Studies*. Surrey, UK: Ashgate

Lykke N. 2011. Intersectional analysis: black box or useful critical feminist thinking technology? See Lutz et al. 2011, pp. 207–20

Mannheim K. 1954. *Ideology and Utopia: An Introduction to the Sociology of Knowledge*. New York: Harcourt, Brace & World

Matsuda MJ, Lawrence C III, Delgado R, Crenshaw K. 1993. *Words that Wound: Critical Race Theory, Assaultive Speech, and the First Amendment*. Boulder, CO: Westview

McCall L. 2005. The complexity of intersectionality. *Signs* 30:1771–800

Mohanty CT. 2013. Transnational feminist crossings: on neoliberalism and radical critique. *Signs* 38:967–91

Morley D, Chen K-H, eds. 1996. *Stuart Hall: Critical Dialogues in Cultural Studies*. New York: Routledge

Morrison T. 1970. *The Bluest Eye*. New York: Vintage Books

Morrison T. 1987. *Beloved*. New York: Knopf

Morrison T. 1992. *Playing in the Dark: Whiteness and the Literary Imagination*. Cambridge, MA: Harvard Univ. Press

Mosse GL. 1985. *Nationalism and Sexuality: Middle-Class Morality and Sexual Norms in Modern Europe*. New York: H. Fertig

Nagel J. 1998. Masculinity and nationalism: gender and sexuality in the making of nations. *Ethn. Racial Stud.* 21:242–69

Nash JC. 2008. Rethinking intersectionality. *Fem. Rev.* 89:1–15

Omi M, Winant H. 2014 (1994). *Racial Formation in the United States*. New York: Routledge

Parker J, Samantrai R. 2010. Interdisciplinarity and social justice: an introduction. See Parker et al. 2010, pp. 1–33

Parker J, Samantrai R, Romero M, eds. 2010. *Interdisciplinarity and Social Justice: Revisioning Academic Accountability*. Albany: SUNY Press

Peterson VS. 2007. Thinking through intersectionality and war. *Race Gender Class* 14:10–27

Ramos-Zayas 2003. *National Performances: The Politics of Class, Race, and Space in Puerto Rican Chicago*. Chicago: Univ. Chicago Press

Roberts D, Jesudason S. 2013. Movement intersectionality: the case of race, gender, disability, and genetic technologies. *Du Bois Rev.* 10:313–28

Roth B. 2004. *Separate Roads to Feminism: Black, Chicana, and White Feminist Movements in America's Second Wave*. New York: Cambridge Univ. Press

Said EW. 1983. *The World, the Text, and the Critic*. Cambridge, MA: Harvard Univ. Press

Sandoval C. 2000. *Methodology of the Oppressed*. Minneapolis: Univ. Minn. Press

Schutz A, Sandy MG. 2011. *Collective Action for Social Change: An Introduction to Community Organizing*. New York: Palgrave Macmillan

Steinbugler AC, Press JE, Dias JJ. 2006. Gender, race and affirmative action: operationalizing intersectionality in survey research. *Gender Soc.* 20:805–25

Swidler A, Arditi J. 1994. The new sociology of knowledge. *Annu. Rev. Sociol.* 20:305–29

Taylor V. 1989. Social movement continuity: the women's movements in abeyance. *Am. Sociol. Rev.* 54:761–75

Tomaskovic-Devey D. 2014. The relational generation of workplace inequalities. *Soc. Curr.* 1:51–73

Tomlinson B. 2013. To tell the truth and not get trapped: desire, distance, and intersectionality at the scene of argument. *Signs* 38:993–1017

Valk AM. 2008. *Radical Sisters: Second-Wave Feminism and Black Liberation in Washington, D.C.* Urbana: Univ. Illinois Press

Walby S. 2007. Complexity theory, systems theory, and multiple intersecting social inequalities. *Philos. Soc. Sci.* 37:449–70

Walia H. 2013. *Undoing Border Imperialism*. Oakland, CA: AK Press

Weber L. 1998. A conceptual framework for understanding race, class, gender, and sexuality. *Psychol. Women Q.* 22:13–32

Wells-Barnett IB. 2002. *On Lynchings*. Amherst, NY: Humanity Books

Wingfield AH, Alston RS. 2012. The understudied case of black professional men: advocating an intersectional approach. *Sociol. Compass* 6:728–39

Yuval-Davis N. 1997. *Gender and Nation*. Thousand Oaks, CA: Sage

Yuval-Davis N. 2006. Intersectionality and feminist politics. *Eur. J. Women's Stud.* 13:193–210

Yuval-Davis N. 2011. *The Politics of Belonging: Intersectional Contestations*. London: Sage

Racial Formation Rules

CONTINUITY, INSTABILITY, AND CHANGE

Michael Omi and Howard Winant

A LONG, STRANGE TRIP

When we initially advanced our concept of racial formation in the mid-1980s, we did not have the slightest inkling that it would prove both durable and flexible as a framework for understanding the changing meaning of race. The credit for its vitality goes not to us alone but also to scholars and activists from a wide range of fields who have creatively engaged racial formation theory and given it much of its ongoing significance, coherence, and utility. The contributors to this collection are among those leading the way in deepening our understanding of ongoing processes of racialization and interpreting the broader political meaning of "racial projects" both historically and in the present.

With this essay we seek both to situate racial formation theory in the historical period from which it first emerged and to apply it to racial politics today in the age of Obama. In the first subsection, "The Origins of Racial Formation Theory," we consider the problems that the theory was initially designed to address, and the thinkers and movements who influenced us. In a short transition, "Breaking with the Past: Trajectories of Racial Politics," we move to the present, drawing attention to the breadth and depth of the shifts in the meaning and social structure of race that the United States and the world as a whole have experienced over just the past few decades. In the following subsection, "Post-racial Scenarios?" we survey some contemporary analyses of changing U.S. racial dynamics and their implications.

After that, we present our own take on new patterns of race and racism. In "Racial Classification and Its Discontents," we examine the ongoing instability and changing meaning of the race concept and discuss such matters as census politics, the "new racial science," and concepts of race in popular culture. In "The Racial Regime and Its Discontents," we consider such issues as "colorblind" racial ideology, the U.S. demographic shift toward a "majority-minority" population, the role of race in electoral politics, race and empire, immigrant rights and resurgent nativism, and the racial dimensions of neoliberalism.

As this long list of topics indicates, we continue to see race and racism as fundamental dimensions of U.S. politics and society—deeply structuring social life at both macro and micro levels and profoundly shaping political discourse and ideology. Our concluding subsection, "Reconstructing Race," looks at U.S. racial prospects: a combination of chronic racial crisis and glimmers of hope for an expanding and deeper democracy.

THE ORIGINS OF RACIAL FORMATION THEORY

Our concept of racial formation emerged in the 1980s as a reaction to the then-dominant modes of theorizing about race in mainstream social science. We were trained in the social sciences; we were experienced anti-racist activists. We had come to reject the way race was conceptualized and operationalized, both in social science research and in left anti-racist thought and political practice. In mainstream social science, scholars failed to address the changing meaning of race over historical time and in distinct social settings. Race was ubiquitous, but the changing meaning of race and the "content" of racial identity went largely unnoticed. Conceiving race in a fixed and static way meant that researchers did not have to engage the very category of race itself and its social determinants. Treating race in a binary manner, for example as present/absent, 0/1, allowed researchers to correlate it simply and nonreflexively with the other variables in assessing patterns of residential segregation, income inequalities, health disparities, and so on. Of course, understanding racial inequality is important. But what is the meaning of race itself? How did race assume a given reality, a given significance, at a specific historical moment and in a specific social site? Such questions were rarely, if ever, asked.

Trying to address these problems ourselves led us to think of race as a social concept, something that needed to be critically engaged in its own right. One could not effectively analyze patterns of residential segregation, for example, without considering the racial categories that were utilized and encoded in research, in public documents, and in legal decisions at a given place and time. One had to ask not only how race shaped segregation but also how segregation reciprocally shaped race, how it invested racial categories with content and meaning. To assert that race is a social concept marks the beginning, not the conclusion, of "doing" racial theory.

Our initial take was to emphasize the "political determination" of race. This emphasis came from our simultaneous engagement and disenchantment with theories of race and racism on the political left. While firmly committed to the democratic, egalitarian, and social justice goals espoused by the left, we were critical of several assumptions that guided Marxist analyses of race. Race was seen as epiphenomenal to class, while racism was regarded as a specific form of "false consciousness" that muted class-based opposition to capitalist exploitation. From this perspective, race was strategically utilized by the capitalist class to sow discontent and create divisions within the working class, thus preventing the emergence of unified class consciousness and organization.[1] The task for the left was to challenge false racial consciousness and promote the primacy of class-based politics.

Skeptical of this position, we began to consider race as a legitimate and salient social category in its own right, on par with class. Adopting this approach allowed us to think about race as a fundamental principle of social organization in the United States. From there, we could discover how race could shape class categories as well as be shaped by them, and also how race was inextricably bound up with other axes of stratification and difference such as gender and sexuality.

Of course the concept of racial formation did not emerge out of thin air. We were inspired by some of the magnificent scholars who had gone before us, and we pillaged and borrowed from a variety of sources. The pioneering work of W. E. B. DuBois, E. Franklin Frazier, and Oliver C. Cox, among others, helped us understand the multiple ways in which race was a foundational and organizing principle of U.S. society, and how profoundly it had shaped social stratification historically. In particular, DuBois's notion of "double consciousness" (1969) was fundamental to how we thought about individual identity and collective consciousness. Bob Blauner's concept of "internal colonialism" (1972) was also instrumental in our rethinking of race. Although we criticized that paradigm in *Racial*

Formation, Blauner's treatment of the distinctions between "colonized and immigrant minorities" and the attention he directed toward the problem of cultural domination influenced us greatly. His efforts to link the "Third World abroad" to the "Third World within" continue to hold relevance for contemporary racial theory. Herbert Blumer (1958) and Troy Duster's symbolic interactionist account of race and racism (Blumer and Duster 1980) allowed us to think about "group position" and the consolidation of racial hierarchy. They showed how racial stratification profoundly shapes relations between racially defined groups. A crucial insight we took from symbolic interactionism was its emphasis on individual and collective agency and the ways identities and relationships were continually forged in social interaction.

The writings of Antonio Gramsci (1971) spurred us to rethink Marxism and supplied the key conceptual frames for understanding the transition from racial dictatorship to racial democracy. Gramsci's notion of *hegemony,* constituted by a combination of coercion and consent, allowed us to explore the consolidation, depth, and persistence of racial power. Through Gramsci we were able to conceptualize historical changes in the U.S. racial system and the ways in which a "war of maneuver"—a pitched battle between clearly located antagonists, between dominant and subordinate racialized groups—had given way to a "war of position," a pervasive conflict being fought out everywhere at once. Adam Przeworski's concept of "class formation" (1977) not only helped us rethink class but also provided a reference point for theorizing about race. Przeworski critiqued the notion that class was a distinct location within a mode of production and instead emphasized the highly relational and contingent political dimensions of class conflict. Ernesto Laclau's work (1977) demonstrated that ideological positions did not necessarily reflect discrete class positions but that themes such as populism and nationalism could be taken up and refashioned to express the interests and aspirations of different and antagonistic political blocs. Populism or nationalism could have authoritarian or emancipatory political framings. From such work we grasped the importance of political struggles over racial meaning and adopted the concept of *rearticulation* to illustrate how racial ideology could be refashioned to suit a variety of different and sometimes competing political positions.[2] To us, these were "better" Marxian analyses.

The theoretical insights of feminist scholars such as Sheila Rowbotham, Shulamith Firestone, and bell hooks, among others, also shaped our ideas in several important ways. Second-wave feminism was flowering as we wrote, and questions of race-gender "intersectionality" were first being raised. Thinking about gender as a distinct axis of stratification and difference prodded us to conceptualize the category of race in a parallel fashion. The feminist movement advanced an understanding of gender, both analytically and politically, as a social category—arguing convincingly that gender was not reducible to class. Feminism facilitated and deepened our critique of Marxist and left analyses of race and racism. Feminist theory also insisted on comprehensively linking both the micro and macro levels of social analysis. It dramatically revealed how concepts of gender were deeply embedded at all levels of human interaction and organization—from intimate relations within the family to the overall structure of pre- and postindustrial societies. Such an analysis was succinctly expressed by radical feminist Carol Hanisch's notion that "the personal is political."[3] We took such formulations to heart in our analysis of race. We paid attention to the ways race was conceived, constructed, and practiced at both the micro level of everyday social relationships and at the macro level of institutional arrangements and social structure.

Our concept of racial formation was forged in struggle. We were inspired by and engaged in the new social movements of the 1960s and 1970s: the black power movement, the feminist movement, the antiwar movement, the student movement, the insurgent labor movement, and the struggles for ethnic studies on university campuses. The insights, issues, and contradictions generated by these social justice struggles became foundational to our work. Racial formation also reflected debates between the two of us. We worked out our positions through intense discussion, endless rewriting, and compromise. Our collaboration, now more than thirty years old, is a model for collective political and intellectual labor. It sometimes seems like a miracle, a marvelous gift that we have been able to give each other. Our work has truly been sustained by a great friendship.

The concept of racial formation was first advanced in a two-part article, "By the Rivers of Babylon: Race in the United States," published in the journal *Socialist Review,* with which we were associated (Omi and Winant 1983). The first edition of the book *Racial Formation in the United States* appeared in 1986.

Then came disappointment. We were dismayed that our work was ignored for several years by the very social scientists we sought to influence. Anti-racist activists took no notice. Much to our surprise, our initial fans were from other academic disciplines, notably history, literary studies, and law. Historians used our ideas to examine and periodize shifts in the racial order, literary theorists and critics analyzed racial representations and discourse in their canonical texts, and legal scholars interrogated the fluidity and ambiguity of race in doctrinal law, jurisprudence, and legal practice. The fact that contemporary introductory sociology textbooks on race and ethnicity now have a section on "racial formation" is quite gratifying for us. We can at last find validation in our own discipline—one that had initially ignored our call to critically examine the social construction of race.

Over the years, numerous criticisms have been made of the concept of racial formation. The political determinism we embraced early in our collaboration has often been challenged, but we continue to uphold our commitment to *the primacy of the political*. Such an emphasis, we think, allows us to discern the contours of the current racial order, to understand what racial hegemony looks like, to specify its contradictions, and to envision alternative scenarios.

We continue to emphasize the *instability* of the race concept. This condition derives from the multiply determined "social space"—both very broad and very deep—that race occupies. Race operates at the crossroads between social structure and experience.[4] It is both historically determined and continuingly being made and remade in everyday life.[5] In this sense, race is simultaneously synchronic and diachronic, as Lévi-Strauss (1966) might say.

The instability of race accounts for both the ongoing volatility and the continuity of the concept. Why, for example, are racial attributions so prone to violence, so "hot," so fiercely upheld and contested, so necessary in the modern world as components of both self and social structure? Why is race so available as a "scavenger concept": a default variable on the basis of which so many disparate phenomena are supposedly explained (Fredrickson 2002; Gilroy 1999)? How can a social distinction be both so determining—of life chances and status, of freedom, of social structure, of identity itself—and at the same time so undetermined, inchoate, and indeed unreal on so many levels? These are but a few of the many questions we were asking about race and racism more than three decades ago.

We are asking them still. And while racial conditions have changed dramatically since our book was first published, the legacy of the past, the vast *waste* of structural racism,[6] accumulated over the centuries, continues to weigh us down as well. We do indeed live in history.

BREAKING WITH THE PAST: THE TRAJECTORIES OF RACIAL POLITICS

There have been "cycles" or "trajectories" of racial reform and reaction since the rise of the race concept in tandem with the development of the "modern world-system." But the post–World War II racial "break" was the most profound transformation in world racial history. Never before had there been a racial upsurge so *wide*: so comprehensively driven by extensive global conflicts—such as World War II and the Cold War—and so propelled by mass action, by vast demographic transformations, massive migrations, urbanization, and above all, by popular mobilization. Never has any racial upheaval cut so *deep*: indeed, under intense pressure that was often radical and sometimes revolutionary, many racial states officially "switched sides" in the postwar years, shifting from upholding apartheid, racial exclusion, and colonial rule to opposing—at least officially—these policies and practices (Winant 2001).

Enormous changes have occurred over the past few decades as parts of a shift, a rupture, a break that we called (*pace* Polanyi) the "great trans-formation" (Polyani 2011 [1944]). De jure segregation and state-enforced Jim Crow were effectively challenged in the 1960s, and the South African apartheid system finally fell in 1994. Some explicitly "racist regimes" (Fredrickson 2002) have been overthrown, and the ideologies that undergirded them have been largely discredited.[7]

The U.S. encounter with race and racism in the second half of the twentieth century and beyond constitutes a case study of a global racial transition. The great transformation, the worldwide racial "break," was the cumulative result of states, empires, and elites on a world scale being challenged by their own people—by "natives," and by the descendants of former slaves and colonial subjects—to "pay up" for the practices of superexploitation, exclusion, domination, and nonrecognition to which they had been so long subjected. The former "wretched of the earth" demanded greater social equality, a fundamental expansion of democracy, and a dramatic extension of *popular sovereignty*. The great wave of postwar political movements—anti-imperialist movements, civil rights movements, and the "identity politics" of the 1960s—all contributed to the radical transformation of the global racial order.

Not only was the vast upsurge of demands for racial justice more than merely a U.S.-based phenomenon, but the resistance to those demands, what we called the "racial reaction," was correspondingly global in scope. Neoconservatism, nonracialism, neoliberalism, backlash, multiculturalism, rollback, colorblindness,[8] and racial differentialism—to pick some of the key terms of that reaction—were responses, sometimes right-wing and sometimes centrist or even liberal,[9] to the hugely disruptive, redistributive, democratic, and egalitarian demands of the worldwide racial upsurge. Here too the United States was but a "case," however important, of a global process in which displaced elites, empires, and ideologies struggled to reconstruct and indeed reimagine their racial regimes after the war.

POST-RACIAL SCENARIOS?

This brings us to the present moment. Have racist regimes been dismantled as a result of the "great transformation," or has racism simply mutated into new and perhaps more flexible and less discernible forms? Some political observers have interpreted the election of Barack Obama as the dawning of a new, "post-racial" era. Obama's ascent to the highest post in the land is popularly regarded as stunning testimony of how far the nation has come in moving beyond the racial barriers and exclusions of the past. This post-racial optimism reflects contemporary "colorblind" racial ideology: the belief that the goals of the civil rights movement have been substantially achieved, that overt forms of racial discrimination are a thing of the past, and that the United States has successfully transitioned to a "post-" or even "nonracist" society. As an ideological frame, colorblindness denies that race should inform perceptions, shape attitudes, or influence individual or collective action. Indeed from a colorblind standpoint any hints of race consciousness are tainted by racism; hence, the most effective anti-racist gesture, policy, or practice is simply to ignore race. The hope is that by ignoring race, we can transcend racism and embrace a post-racial future.[10]

Such an optimistic scenario, of course, misses the enduring persistence and significance of race, and the ways that structural racism continues to shape present conditions.[11] The "colorblind" framework has been the target of scathing criticism across the social sciences, humanities, and professions that has demonstrated the persistence of racial inequalities and argued for "race conscious" policies and practices to address them (Carbado and Harris 2008; Brown et al. 2003; Feagin 2006; Bonilla-Silva 2006).

But while race still matters, changes are always afoot. The color line itself has been rendered more complex in the twenty-first century transition to a majority-minority society. How will racial transformations reshape issues of racial hierarchy and broader patterns of racial domination and subordination?

Many have speculated about these questions, peering through a glass darkly in their attempts to predict the racial future. Jennifer L. Hochschild (2005) assesses future racial trends and poses several possible scenarios contingent on different racial constructions and practices. In her "black exceptionalism" scenario, a black/nonblack racial divide is the crucial axis of racial division: Asians and Latinos are slowly drawn to the white side of the color line. An alternative is the "white exceptionalism" scenario, which posits a white/nonwhite racial divide in which groups of color would share a common subordinate status. Her third possibility is the "South African" scenario, in which the nation is re-sorted into three groups: whites and "honorary whites" (most Asians, some Latinos, and some biracials), coloreds (some Asians, most Latinos, some biracials and a few blacks), and blacks and almost-blacks. This last "triracial" system is similar to Eduardo Bonilla-Silva's notion (2004) of the "Latin Americanization" of race relations. A fourth scenario Hochschild considers is the dramatic growth of a "mixed-race" or multiracial population with the requisite blurring of distinct racial and ethnic groups. "A crucial divide in this scenario," writes Hochschild, "would be between those who identify as monoracials and seek to protect cultural purity and those who identify as multiracials and celebrate cultural mixing" (2005, 81).

Certainly persistent white supremacy has historically required that groups of color be politically and economically marginalized and subject to cultural forms of domination. Such a position of subordination found expression, for example, in the internal colonialism account: there, groups of color shared a common situation of oppression that offered a potential basis for political unity. But just as previous "outsiders" such as the Irish and Jews have been incorporated into prevailing notions of who is white,[12] some scholars speculate that groups such as Asian Americans and Latinos are increasingly being included in an expanded definition of whiteness. For example, George Yancey (2003) argues that Latinos and Asian Americans are undergoing significant structural, marital, and identity-based assimilation and that a black/nonblack divide is emerging as these groups become "white," while blacks continue to experience what Yancey calls "racial alienation." The emergence of a triracial order in which some groups are positioned as intermediate buffers between black and white might at first glance appear more pluralistic and fluid than a biracial order shaped by the rule of hypodescent, the so-called one-drop rule. But, as Bonilla-Silva warns, a triracial system of stratification would also be an effective means of maintaining white supremacy. The "Latin Americanization of race" thesis anticipates a U.S. transition to a society with "more rather than less racial inequality but with a reduced forum for racial contestation" (Bonilla-Silva 2006, 198).

We question aspects of the "Latin Americanization of race" thesis. Because the United States now relates to the global South and global East through a master policy of "accumulation by dispossession,"[13] it fosters immigration. Displaced and impoverished workers and peasants from Latin America and the Caribbean, as well as from the Pacific Rim, continue to immigrate, their human flow modulated but hardly contained by boom and bust, "bubble," and recession.[14] And because the United States has also become more predatory domestically, practicing a similar policy of "accumulation by dispossession" in post-Katrina New Orleans or the subprime housing crisis—to pick just two prominent examples—it is less able to integrate immigrants than it was in previous historical periods. Where will the United States find an "engine of mobility" to parallel that of the late nineteenth and early twentieth centuries, the epochs of mass labor recruitment to the industrial economy? In short, the country's economic capacity to absorb enormous numbers of immigrants, low-wage workers and their families, and a new, globally based (and largely female) servant class (see Glenn 2002), without generating the sort of established subaltern groups we associate with the terms *race* and *racism,* seems to us more limited than was the "whitening" of Europeans a century earlier, this argument's key precedent.[15]

And then there is the question of "mixed-race" or multiracial individuals, another key aspect of the "Latin Americanization" thesis. The issue of multiraciality problematizes deeply held notions of race, racial classification, and racial identity itself. Indeed, the very concept of being of "mixed race" presupposes the existence of clearly defined, discernible, and discrete races.[16] Our view is that any discussion of multiraciality must resist "racial lumping": the tendency to locate multiracial individuals in a collective category that fails to consider not only the enormous diversity within multiracial populations but also the varied political and cultural meanings of multiraciality itself. For example, the *mestizaje* framework conflicts with the white/nonwhite North American system. And in many social or institutional settings the experience and consciousness of being mixed-race white-Asian is significantly different from that of being black-Asian. Whether multiracial identity, consciousness, and organization will seriously subvert or merely reinforce racial hierarchy in the United States remains very much an open question.

An opposite and equally pernicious tendency is to reject group identity *tout court* by elevating social constructionist approaches to ethnicity, race, and nationality to an all-encompassing framework, a sort of universal solvent of all identity, all particularity. Perhaps driven by frustration that not only racial but also ethnic and national identities remain flexible and unstable and resist social scientific specification, Rogers Brubaker, Mara Loveman, and Peter Stamatov (1994; see also Brubaker 2004) repudiate "groupism" across the board. They argue that ethnic, racial, and national social categories can be more effectively conceived as matters of social psychology. Ethnic, racial, or national identities are thereby reduced to quite subjective processes: how one (or many) interpret their social location, their differences or similarities with others, and so forth. This has the consequence of diminishing the political dimensions of these themes, as well as relegating lived experience, not to mention world-historical events and widely distributed beliefs, to little more than commonly held illusions.

All these issues—the possibility or desirability of a post-racial society, the realities of demographic transformation and racial stratification, the varieties of multiracial consciousness, and the parameters of collectivity as well—continually and inexorably point to the continuing instability of the concept of race itself. This instability is a fundamental preoccupation of the racial formation approach. It is reflected, for example, in the endemic mismatches between state-based racial classifications and individual/collective social identities. Such inconsistencies are political in nature and embody profound differences over racial meaning—differences that reveal who wields power in establishing definitions and categories and how such boundaries are contested and negotiated.

Consider the U.S. census. As this is written the 2010 census is under way. We cannot yet evaluate its findings. But according to the Census Bureau, 40 percent of Latinos in the 1980, 1990, and 2000 censuses filled out the race and ethnicity questions "wrong." The bureau's preference was to have Latinos respond both to the question "Is this person Spanish/Hispanic/Latino?" *and* the question "What is this person's race?" A dark-skinned Puerto Rican, for example, might check off that she or he was "Hispanic/Puerto Rican" *and* "Black," while a light-skinned Mexican might describe himself or herself as "Hispanic/Mexican" *and* "White." But many Latino respondents did not understand, or perhaps did not accept, the racial and ethnic categories presented. They did not know how—or perhaps refused—to situate themselves within the choices the census offered. It is estimated that about 95 percent of respondents who simply checked "some other race" were in fact Latino (Omi 1997; Rodríguez 2000).

The shifting context of race has a profound impact on claims for recognition that are validated (or ignored) in state-sanctioned racial categories. In the mid-1990s, during the planning for Census 2000, key Arab American civil rights organizations unsuccessfully lobbied the Office of Management and Budget for a "Middle Eastern" category on the census. They were critical of the classification of Arab Americans as "white" and argued that with respect to hate crime reporting (among other social indicators and issues), Arab Americans should be a distinct racial category. We are not surprised that in the wake of 9/11 *no* Arab American organization is now lobbying for such a separate "Middle Eastern" category. The line between group recognition and racial profiling is a thin one.[17]

The issue of racial profiling reveals an intriguing contradiction in the meaning of race and its relationship to the racial ideology of colorblindness. Profiling raises questions of when and under what circumstances we want to "notice" race. When do we want to be race-conscious, and when do we want to be "colorblind"? After decades of touting colorblindness as the only appropriate guide to policymaking regarding race, some conservative political figures and commentators are now finding it expedient to make exceptions. In the context of the continuing "war on terror," it is argued that our national security may rest on the state's adoption of explicitly *race-conscious* policies. Since the 9/11 attacks, the 2004 Atocha railroad bombings in Spain, the July 2005 attacks in London, and various other similar events, renewed calls have gone out for authorities to use racial and ethnic profiling to identify potential terrorists at airports and elsewhere. The "scavenger concept" of race resurfaces.

After the attempt to blow up a passenger jet in December 2009, New York assemblyman Dov Hikind (D-Brooklyn) introduced legislation to "authorize law enforcement personnel to consider race and ethnicity as one of many factors that could be used in identifying persons who can be initially stopped, questioned, frisked and/or searched." In 2005 Hikind had sponsored a bill to allow New York state police to zero in on "Middle Easterners" when conducting terrorism prevention searches. "They all look a certain way," he said. "It's all very nice to be politically correct here, but we're talking about terrorism."[18] This is a call for policies and practices that *notice* race and attempt to rationalize and justify such moves as serving a broader public interest. Law professor John Banzhaf states, "A very compelling argument can be made that the government's interest in protecting the lives, safety and health of thousands of its citizens from another major terrorist attack similar to those carried out in New York, London and other cities . . . is at least as 'compelling' as a racially diverse student body."[19]

The pervasive instability of the concept of race is revealed not only in ongoing policy debates but also in the biological sciences. The dominant mantra in the social sciences and humanities is that "race is a social construction, not a biological one." This view reflects scientific critiques of race as a biological concept that emerged at the close of World War II as a direct response to the eugenic ideologies and practices of Nazi Germany. An editorial in the *New England Journal of Medicine* in 2001 sought to provide the definitive word on the subject by flatly stating that "race is biologically meaningless." But in the wake of the Human Genome Project, geneticists are once again debating whether race is a meaningful and useful genetic concept.

Geneticist Neil Risch contends that genetic differences have arisen among people from different continents and employs the term "race" to aggregate the human population into five major groups. This recognition of race, he contends, is important for understanding genetic susceptibility to certain diseases and receptivity to medical interventions such as drug treatments.[20] This biological turn has repercussions in fields such as pharmacogenomics. The ultimate goal of pharmacogenomics is to deliver the precise type of medication—and the precise dose—to a patient based on her or his individual genome. Drugs would be specifically tailored for the treatment of an individual's specific condition. Given that an individual's genome has yet to be sequenced in a quick and cost-effective manner, the question has been raised as to whether one's race can serve as a suitable proxy for determining how one might fare with a specific drug.

The question is not an abstract one. Consider the introduction of BiDil as the first "ethnic designer drug." Produced by the biotech firm NitroMed, BiDil is marketed to African Americans who suffer from congestive heart failure. Some medical researchers fear that BiDil sets a dangerous precedent by linking race and genetics in ways that could distract from alternative ways of understanding the causes of a disease and the means to treat it (Kahn 2004). Legal scholar and bioethicist Jonathan Kahn suggests that by approving BiDil, the federal government was "giving its imprimatur, its stamp of approval, to using race as a biological category. To my mind, it's the road to hell being paved with good intentions."[21]

The issue of race and genetics finds expression in popular culture as well. In 2010, PBS aired *Faces of America, with Henry Louis Gates, Jr.,* a four-episode documentary series that traced the ancestral roots of prominent celebrities through "genealogy and genetics." Gates's series inspired a growing popular quest by individuals to find their "roots" through purportedly scientific means. There are currently at least two dozen companies that market "genetic ancestry tests"; more than 460,000 people have purchased these tests over the past six years (Bonick et al. 2007). In 2007 Gates stated: "We are living through an era of the ascendance of biology, and we have to be very careful. We will all be walking a fine line between using biology and allowing it to be abused."[22] There is indeed a fine line. The rebiologization of race will significantly contribute to and trouble debates about the very concept of race.

Somewhat ironically, new patterns and developments in racialization, such as the rebiologization question, destabilize the prevailing racial ideology of colorblindness. It is hard to maintain a colorblind posture if there is indeed a "scientific" basis to race and racial categories. Given the inherent instability of the race concept, it becomes increasingly important to make clear distinctions between colorblind and race-conscious policies and practices, and to discern their larger purpose and intent.

In August 2006 Mark Burnett, the creator of CBS's *Survivor,* caused a furor when he revealed that in the upcoming fall season, the twenty *Survivor* contestants would be divided into four "tribes"—Asian American, black, Hispanic, and white. Local and national protests ensued. Several

New York City Council members demanded that CBS cancel the show. Their demand prompted *New York Times* columnist Clyde Haberman to observe sarcastically that the very city officials incensed by the show were members of the black, Latino, and Asian caucuses that operate in New York City's political system. "In other words," wrote Haberman, "leading the condemnation of CBS for creating teams defined by race and ethnicity was a team that created itself using race and ethnicity as the definition."[23]

Haberman's comment is indicative of the dilemmas of racial classification. Those engaged in challenging racial inequality need to specify with greater clarity (and consistency) when, where, and under what circumstances we want to be "colorblind" and when we want to be race-conscious in the broader pursuit of social justice.

THE RACIAL REGIME AND ITS DISCONTENTS

The instability of the race concept and the controversies it generates are emblematic of the *racially contradictory* society in which we live. In the United States a system of racial rule has always been in place, operating not merely through macro-level, large-scale activities but also through micro-level, small-scale practices. The racial regime is enforced and challenged in the schoolyard, on the dance floor, on talk radio, and in the classroom as much as it is in the Supreme Court, electoral politics, or the battlefield of Helmand province. Because racial formation processes are dynamic, the racial regime remains unstable and contested. We live in racial history.

While the "great transformation" contributed to the demise of explicitly racist state policies, discredited essentialist racial ideologies, and ushered in a set of (ostensibly) egalitarian reforms, it obviously did not complete those tasks. Given the persistence of structural racism and racial inequality in the "post–civil rights era," is the racial regime's supposed "switching of sides," the supposed transition "from domination to hegemony" we described in *Racial Formation,* anything more than a thinly veiled cosmetic makeover? In the United States, after all, segregation proceeds quite effectively without explicit state sponsorship, and indeed still receives quite a bit of tacit state support. Anti-discrimination laws are barely enforced, and when an occasional plaintiff of color wins a rare victory in court, the costs to discriminators don't even begin to offset the benefits derived from discrimination in the first place. The old forms of systematic voter disenfranchisement—by terror—have largely ended, but new forms of election rigging (for example, "vote caging" and the permanent denial of voting rights to ex-felons) achieve many of the same effects. Since the enactment of civil rights laws, incarceration rates in the United States have increased so dramatically (nearly a tenfold increase since 1980; see Mauer 2006; Alexander 2010; Gilmore 2007), and with such extreme racial disproportionality, that carceral policy has now to be viewed as a prime example of "backlash" racial politics.

And come to think of it, how relegated to the past is the question of empire? In the modern world, empires are always distinctively racist; race and empire walk hand in hand. Occupying and subduing other nations is justified today by reference to the putative backwardness of the "natives" (Afghanistan) as well as by claims that they are suffering under horrific regimes that fail to provide elementary democratic or human rights (Iraq). How different is this from the French *"mission civilisatrice"* or the British "white man's burden"—or for that matter, the U.S. "manifest destiny"—of past epochs?[24] One notes that the effort to tutor these "backward" peoples in the "higher values" of advanced civilization also involves dispossessing them of resources and/or labor, not to mention mass slaughter (Mbembe 2001). As for popular sovereignty, forget it. In 2008 the United States maintained military bases in 132 countries. While publically fighting wars of occupation in Iraq and Afghanistan, it was covertly involved in military operations in at least a dozen other supposedly sovereign nations. The meaning and structure of race, both in the United States and worldwide, remain fundamentally unstable and troubled and are the source of unresolved contradictions and dilemmas.

The "great transformation" after World War II overturned the old racial logics, enabled anti-racist movements to enter mainstream politics and initiate racial "wars of position," and resulted in the rearticulation and reorganization of racial regimes in more incorporative and less coercive forms. This shift transformed but hardly precluded the recurrence of "old school" racial repression and violence. In many respects it allowed the perpetuation of discrimination, profiling, nativism, empire, and other forms of racial injustice as it "regrooved" these practices, making use of the very racial reforms for which earlier civil rights and anti-imperialist activists had successfully struggled.[25] Condoleeza Rice compared the U.S. occupation of Iraq to the 1963 movement led by Dr. Martin Luther King Jr. in her native Birmingham, Alabama.

The crisis of race is now a chronic condition. "Crisis," Gramsci wrote, "consists precisely in the fact that the old is dying and the new cannot be born: in this interregnum, morbid phenomena of the most varied kind come to pass" (1971, 276). On the one hand, the old verities of established racism and white supremacy have been officially discredited, not only in the United States but fairly comprehensively around the world; on the other hand, racially informed action and social organization, racial identity and race consciousness, continue unchecked in nearly every aspect of social life.

Given this, why doesn't the manifest contradiction between the *repudiation* of race—both official and personal—and the continuing, constant, and near-ubiquitous *recognition* of race in virtually every aspect of social and political life provoke enormous uncertainty and confusion in public life, political activity, and personal identity? Why don't our heads *explode* under the pressures of such cognitive dissonance?

The answer once again lies in the instability of the race concept, the processual characteristics of racial formation. Because racial categories remain unstable and subject to contention, and because the trajectory of racial reform and racial reaction remains volatile, the U.S. racial regime is permanently unstable as well. Here we note, necessarily very briefly, some of the major contradictions of the present U.S. racial system.

Electoral Politics

The election of Barack Obama transformed the U.S. presidency in ways we cannot yet fully appreciate. Obama is not simply the first nonwhite (that we know of) to occupy the office. He is the first to have lived in the global South, the first to be a direct descendent of colonized people, the first to have a genuine movement background. Without question Obama is by far the most progressive, the most "left" person ever to have occupied the White House. But he is no more powerful than any of his predecessors; he is constrained, as they were, by the U.S. system of rule, by the U.S. racial regime, by structural racism.

Not just the Obama victory but also a host of recent developments have demonstrated the isolation and marginalization of the Republican Party. It has become the white people's party, driven in large measure by racial, religious, and gender/sexuality-based *ressentiment*. In U.S. history, there has generally been one political party that took charge of racial rule. This has been especially true vis-à-vis black-white demarcations; for example, the organization by the Democratic Party of white supremacist rule in the Jim Crow era. But rapid swings are possible. After the critical election of 1932 U.S. blacks (those who could vote) shifted their loyalties away from the "party of Lincoln" en masse (Weiss 1983; Katznelson 2005). This occurred even though Roosevelt's New Deal coalition effectively delegated control of the South to the plantocratic/agrarian/racist/Dixiecrat wing of his party. After the civil rights reforms of the mid-1960s, large numbers of white voters, particularly those based in the South, similarly embraced the Republicans.

The appearance of the "Tea Party" movement since the 2008 election signals a clearly reactionary racial agenda. This "movement"—white, predominantly male, and very much in the Republican Party orbit—is both an "Astroturf" phenomenon, a loose network of fake grass-roots organizations cobbled together by corporate lobbyists, and a genuine right-wing populist phenomenon rooted in resentment of Obama and the resurgence—still quite feeble—of the welfare state. Its whining politics— "I want my country back!"—incarnates a certain incredulity directed at present political conditions, both class-based and race-based. The "movement" has greater disruptive potential than it has adherents: just whose country is the United States, anyway?[26]

Resurgent Nativism and Immigrants' Rights

Reforms in 1965 and 1986 removed many of the overtly racist components of the immigration laws that had shaped U.S. policy since the 1920s, and thereby set off enormous shifts in U.S. racial demography. These changes in turn have dramatically heightened nativist ideologies and mobilizations, reiterating racially framed political conflicts that stretch back to the founding of the U.S. nation-state (Ngai 2005; Chavez 2008).

The ineluctable demographic transition to a majority-minority population may impose some limits on the intensity and depth of contemporary nativist mobilization, however. Although nativism continues to flourish, it confronts other obstacles that did not exist in past cycles of alternating clampdowns and relaxations of immigration laws. In contrast to the sweeping anti-immigrant upsurges of the past (Higham 2002), a significant immigrants' rights movement exists today in the United States; nothing like it has ever developed before. The civil rights connection to immigrants' rights remains strong—most notably embodied in the legacy of the Immigration Reform Act of 1965, a civil rights bill in its own right and a priority of the Kennedys. And immigration reform has huge consequences for voting patterns, especially over the medium and long term; this has been clear with respect to Latino voting patterns since 1994, when what had been seen as a swing constituency was pushed over to the Democrats as a result of California governor Pete Wilson's promotion of Proposition 187 (R. Jacobson 2008; Ono and Sloop 2002; Wroe 2008).

In contrast, before the "great transformation" and the rise of the modern civil rights movement, exhortations on behalf of "Anglo-conformity" (M. Gordon 1964) were taken quite seriously. Virulent nativist assaults such as the anti-Irish movements of the 1840s (the American Native party or "Know-Nothings"), the 1870s and 1890s assaults on West Coast Asian communities (Saxton 1971; Pfaelzer 2007), and the 1930s mass deportations of Mexicans from Southern California (Balderrama and Rodríguez 1995) would prove considerably harder to stage today. The outcome of present-day immigration struggles depends on much political contention at the local, national, and global levels. Catastrophic events on the order of the 9/11 tragedy are always possible—and such tragedies remain susceptible to racialization. In the past the United States often recurred to "domestic foreign policy" in response to political threats. The country has tended to address major social conflicts (and sometimes international ones) by recourse to racist domestic practices. This is exemplified by the internment of Japanese Americans during World War II, the Palmer raids on Eastern and Southern Europeans in the 1920s, and the enormous waves of Islamophobia that followed the 9/11 attack.

In April 2010 the state of Arizona enacted SB 1070, an act "relating to unlawfully present aliens" that authorized police to stop suspected "illegal immigrants" and to demand proof of citizenship. National polls conducted in the wake of the law's passage revealed significant popular support for the law[27]—an ominous sign that immigration reform and the racialization of undocumented workers continue to be vexing issues. Does Arizona SB 1070 represent a new instance of "domestic foreign policy" in addition to being an obvious reiteration of U.S. nativism? Or is it a "gift to the Democrats," as some political commentators have suggested, cementing the loyalties of Latino voters to the Democratic Party, much as Proposition 187 did in California in 1994?[28]

As the Republican Party locks in its identity as the U.S. white people's party, and as the rise in the U.S. Latino population continues, it is hard to avoid the impression that Arizona's institutionalization of racial profiling via SB 1070 represents a last-ditch and probably doomed effort to deny brown people access to the ballot. But that's in the medium to long term, when demographic trends favor another cycle of legalization, as happened in 1965 and 1986. The sheer impracticality of deporting large numbers of undocumented denizens from the United States, and the ferocious state repression that would be required to carry out such a policy, seem to rule out the strategy of *la mano dura* that SB 1070 implies. Numerous other negative consequences would also derive from such measures, notably massive disruptions in the labor market and untold amounts of personal suffering. In the short term, though, there are undoubtedly some political gains to be made through immigrant-bashing.

The Crisis of Neoliberalism and the Assault on the Welfare State

The shifting demographics of race also affect other key political and policy arenas, such as education, labor policy, and social security. The rise of neoliberalism, which began under Reagan, meant the vitiation of an already beleaguered welfare state: notably in the 1996 Clinton welfare "reforms" that abandoned AFDC in favor of the more draconian policies of TANF.[29] By shredding the "safety net" that had been established in the 1930s and was only belatedly and grudgingly extended to racial minorities in the 1960s, the U.S. racial regime greatly widened the gap between the formal ("visible"), largely white economy and the informal ("invisible"), largely nonwhite economy. This trend also increased the distance between city and suburb, hardened policing and criminal "justice" patterns (often relying on a "national security" rationale),[30] and reinforced segregation in schooling and residential patterns—vis-à-vis both blacks and Latinos (Boger and Orfield 2005).

Education is a key battleground in the racial restructuring of U.S. society. The student body in the U.S. public education system is moving toward majority-minority status, though it is still some decades away from that. Census Bureau estimates of that transition locate it around the year 2025.[31] Who will teach these students? What career prospects will they have? As the U.S. economy becomes increasingly centered in the "knowledge industries," it will require major investments in public education and far more effective integration between curricular content and shifting patterns of employment. Neoliberal educational policy ("No Child Left Behind," "Race to the Top," the privatization of higher education) is headed in precisely the opposite direction: disinvesting; relying on mechanistic and formulaic testing of basic skills rather than teaching adaptive and creative thought processes ("intelligence" in the Deweyan use of the term); and abandoning large numbers of low-income children (disproportionately black and brown) to permanent subemployment.

A closely related question is the *racial composition of the U.S. workforce.* As informal labor markets grow (Vogel 2006) in size and importance, it becomes more difficult to assess employment patterns with specificity (Toossi 2002). Consider the Social Security system, perhaps the most durable element of the New Deal–based welfare state. Already there are fewer and fewer white workers paying the FICA taxes to support social security payments to largely white baby boomers. The Social Security system—forced savings through regressive payroll taxation, pay-as-you-go financing—has long been seen both as a powerful guarantor of political legitimacy and as a "third rail" of the welfare state: a New Deal achievement that worked to curtail and regulate excessive and highly ideological "free market" pressures from the political right. George W. Bush's blundering campaign for Social Security "privatization" was but the most recent assault on that system from the HQ of reaction.[32] But by the mid-twenty-first century a majority of U.S. workers will be nonwhite. To the extent that they are employed in the formal economy, they will be paying their FICA/payroll taxes (as of now still organized regressively, exempting annual incomes above $106,800 in 2009) to support those largely white retirees born in the mid-twentieth century and later. Well before 2050, in short, the calculus of cost and benefit in the Social Security system will shift: it will no longer afford political legitimacy or constitute an unshakeable pillar of support to many working people. We may very well see revolts against this remaining bastion of the welfare state (or against its inadequacy) on the part of people of color. Might we see future opposition to Social Security from the "left"? Now that would be something new![33]

Racial rule is increasingly difficult to maintain. The *costs of racial repression*—imprisonment and arming the U.S.-Mexican border, for example—directly compete with the costs of social investment. *Postcolonial warfare*—a distinctly racial policy—is perhaps the most egregious example of this: the cost of U.S. wars since 2001 is now in the trillions.[34] *Cultural transformations* generally tend to delegitimize racial rule, especially in the context of demographic transition toward a majority-minority society: in the arts, popular media, language use, "styles," the dynamics of personal life and intimate relationships, and indeed in working concepts of identity, racial rearticulation is commonplace.

Racial rule *requires* repression, not because of some functionalist law, but because it inspires resistance. Exclusion, superexploitation, violence, and despotism inevitably generate opposition. In the past the opposition of those who were not white, who lacked citizenship rights and therefore could not access the political system, necessarily took subversive and largely spontaneous forms: sabotage, slacking, subaltern forms of action (Scott 1990). After "the great transformation," after the movement "from protest to politics" (Kelley 1992; Tate 1993; see also Waskow 1966), however, the racially subordinate could both act within mainstream political parameters and continue to subvert those boundaries in search of greater democratic and human rights. Yet racial repression remains very much a part of everyday life and social structure in the United States.

RECONSTRUCTING RACE

The prevailing ideology of colorblindness is a failed attempt to construct a new racial hegemony, based on the limited reforms of the civil rights era. Center-right in political orientation, informed by an uneasy admixture of new right and neoconservative racial ideology,[35] colorblind racial ideology cannot overcome the gap between the promises of reform and the realities of ongoing inequality and racial despotism.

While advocates of "colorblind" racial ideology vehemently argue against state policy "taking race into account," the state also *needs* race to rule. This is true in virtually every area of state activity. Structural racism persists; democratic reforms have not undone the legacy of systematic exclusion, violence, exploitation, and marginalization that race embodies. Thus social control via race continues: in criminal "justice," in corporate welfare as well as the evisceration of the welfare state, in the organization of labor, credit, and housing markets, and of course in the U.S. militarization of the world. Racial repression continues to furnish brutal reminders of the incompleteness of democracy and the shallowness of post-racial celebrations. Consider the victims: who are the prisoners, the families dropped from the welfare rolls, the permanent residents deported, and those disproportionately dispossessed by the home mortgage crisis (Rivera 2008)?

But while the state needs race to rule, it is also confronted by anti-racist opposition and constrained by its own commitment to the achievement of racial hegemony through the colorblindness construct. In general, it is forced to exercise racial rule covertly. The effects of the "great transformation" still resonate. The contradictions of this situation, in which the racial regime must simultaneously disavow its raciality and deploy it as broadly and deeply as ever, is arguably the greatest single factor in the continuing instability of race in the state's unavoidable ratification of neoliberal policies of superexploitation and "accumulation by dispossession." Here we see the limits of President Obama's post-racial appeals, the enormous difficulties involved in stemming, much less cleaning up, the ongoing accumulation of racial "waste."

So what does the crisis of colorblindness suggest for the racial future? What does it mean for the United States that a new racial hegemony cannot be consolidated, that achieving some new post–civil rights era racial commonsense seems very unlikely, at least for now? Does it mean persistent structural racism, unremitting racial despotism, the impossibility of democratization? Or does our present racial condition contain hints and suggestions about *alternative routes*—not toward racial "progress" (a much too incrementalist, too meliorist term), but at least toward a greater and deeper democracy? Can we see new ways of situating the racial self, of inhabiting our racial identities—both individually and collectively—in greater freedom?

The desire remains strong—not only in our hearts but in those of millions—for a more emancipatory concept of race and a more fulfilling, less conflicted race consciousness. What would that look like? To be very specific, what do you want *your* race consciousness to be?

If the "colorblind" perspective has failed to achieve hegemony, failed to consolidate a new racial "common sense," what comes next? From a "colorblind" perspective, one is exhorted not to "notice" race, not to see it, for if one did, one wouldn't be "blind" to it, right? But what happens to *race consciousness* under conditions of "colorblind" hegemony? Quite clearly, awareness of raciality does not dry up like a raisin in the sun. Just as "colorblind" racial ideology serves as a means to occlude recognition of race beneath the veneer of a supposedly already accomplished universality, race consciousness works to highlight racial differences and particularities. It can be linked to despotic or democratic ends, articulated in defense of coercion, privilege, and undeserved advantage; alternatively it can be deployed in support of inclusion, human rights, and social justice.

Yet despite our strong criticism of racism and of the "colorblind" racial project, race consciousness exhibits certain contradictions as well. We can make errors in conceptualizing race or in attributing racial identity. Just when does race matter, anyway? Always? Sometimes? If the answer is "sometimes," what about those situations when race "doesn't matter"? Are there situations in which we should *not* notice race? Isn't racial identity often ambiguous and contradictory? What is its significance for transracial solidarity and alliance? What is its significance for transracial friendship, or indeed love? These old themes no doubt retain something of their transgressive and unsettling character, but they are also increasingly normal, regular, and unremarkable. Can trust and solidarity exist across racial lines? Is it possible either in individual or collective social practice to "get beyond" race, and what exactly would that mean? How definitive is racial identity, and what are the implications for democracy, humanism, and antiracism (Gilroy 2002)?

Parallel to the question, What do you want *your* race consciousness to be? is another: What would a racial justice–oriented *social policy* look like *to you*? What types of policies and practices—at the level of the state, civil society, and major institutions—would help us achieve a more comprehensive, deeper, and longer-lasting racial democracy in the United States?

Some General Answers to These Questions

Since racism is so large, combating it must also be a large-scale practice. The historically recurrent theme of racial reparations provides a valuable guidepost here (Henry 2007). *Reparation* means repairing, making whole, making good what was evil. As a sociopolitical project, reparations can be seen to extend from the large to the small, from the institutional to the personal (Yamamoto 1999). Clearly, abolishing the debt (not "forgiving," for who is to forgive and who is to be forgiven?) fits within the reparations logic, as does affirmative action.

Redistribution fits as well, but here we must be careful: the politics of income and wealth distribution are "double-entry" bookkeeping items. Not only the allocation of resources but also the derivation of revenues are involved. If reparations were to be paid for the crime against humanity that was African slavery, it would be important to look at both the inflow and the outflow sides of the process. On the outflow side, reparations should take the form of social investment (think of a "Marshall Plan for the Cities" or something similar). On the inflow side, there is a danger that reparations would be paid out of general revenues, unduly assessing present-day working people for the crimes of past colonialists and elites, perpetuating rather than attenuating racial conflicts, and allowing new variants of the "colorblind" argument to loom up in the future. An alternative revenue-oriented strategy would raise the money by means of a wealth tax, thus recognizing how many present-day capital hoards had their origins in slavery.[36]

Beyond reparations, anti-racist practice can be understood macropolitically in terms of *social citizenship* and micropolitically in terms of *acculturation and socialization*. The concept of social citizenship was proposed by T. H. Marshall (1950) as an obligation of the postwar welfare state, the proximate stage in the achievement of popular sovereignty. Rights, Marshall argued, had been acquired by the populace in stages: first economic, then political. The time had now come for the achievement of social rights. Of course, this formulation was offered when the British flag still flew over Lagos and Singapore and Jim Crow still flourished in the United States; it was proposed when postmodern criticism of the limits of "rights talk" (in critical race theory, for example) had not yet been made; and it certainly did not encompass the diasporic and globalized issues anti-racists face today. Yet we can make use of it to think anew about political inclusion, social provision, even world citizenship.

By *acculturation and socialization* we mean the reawakening of the 1960s concept that "the personal is political" as a key principle of anti-racist personal practice. No one—no matter what their racial identity is—can be free of racism in their heads or hearts; it is too deeply ingrained a social structure. Yet a great deal of thought and action has been devoted to the problem of fostering anti-racist practice at the individual and experiential level. Developing these skills, fostering the interruption and interrogation of racism, and extending the reach of anti-racism in family, school, and cultural life constitute an important dimension of the practice we want to support.

While we have offered here some tentative and sketchy answers to these questions, on a deeper level such serious issues can be adequately addressed only through the creative thought and political action of many people—the masses, the multitudes, whose "freedom dreams" (Kelley 2003) can transfigure and rearticulate the unstable and conflicted racial system yet again. We began this essay by noting that racial formation theory emerged from an earlier set of challenges to the system of racial oppression. Surely those movement-based challenges were not the last we shall ever know. If our approach has any value, it lies in the suggestion that racial politics is an ongoing creative practice, both individual and collective. Our actions and ideas—both individual and collective—should be seen as political projects that have the potential to undo racial injustice and generate broader racial equality, and indeed greater freedom in every way. Racial formation theory should help us think about race and racism as *continuing encounters between despotic and democratic practices*, in which individuals and groups, confronted by state power and entrenched privilege but not entirely limited by those obstacles, make choices and locate themselves over and over in the constant racial "reconstruction" of everyday life.

NOTES

1. A neo-Marxist critique of this approach that influenced us in important ways was Bonacich 1972.

2. In retrospect we can see that we were developing arguments that paralleled emerging perspectives in post-structural and in radical pragmatist theoretical approaches. This was not our primary purpose, though; we sought better explanations for race/racism dynamics, and reinvented the wheel only in pursuit of that specific aim.

3. There is some debate as to the origins of the phrase. "The Personal Is Political" was the title of an essay by Carol Hanisch, an early second-wave feminist activist and veteran of the civil rights movement. The essay was published in 1969 by the Redstockings organization. See Carol Hanisch, "The Personal Is Political," http://www.carolhanisch.org/CHwritings/PIP.html (accessed January 19, 2012).

4. The crossroad is deeply significant in the black vernacular. Cf. Robert Johnson, "Cross Roads Blues," originally Vocalion Records, catalog no. 3519 (1937); reissued on idem, *King of the Delta Blues Singers,* Columbia catalog, no. CL 1654 (1966); see also Litwack 1998, 410–411.

5. In a well-known article (1997), Eduardo Bonilla-Silva argued for a "structural interpretation" of racism. Focusing on rac*ism,* he did not deeply explore the race concept, instead invoking the notion of "racialized social systems" to link race to racism. Lévi-Strauss's approach effectively grasps the interplay between the everyday (synchronic) and historically imbedded (diachronic)

dimensions of "social structure"; that's why we cite him here. Although we have some disagreements with the Bonilla-Silva piece, we still consider it a major contribution.

6. On racism as "waste," see Feagin, Vera, and Batur 2000. The concept is drawn from Georges Bataille.

7. Of course, others remain: Israel-Palestine, Kurdistan, the conditions of many indigenous peoples . . . It's a long list.

8. This term requires some clarification. *Colorblindness* is a problematic term, a neologism twice over. First and most obviously, it is rooted in an ophthalmic condition that has no relevance to race, unless we understand race as being "about" skin color, which involves a deep reductionism in the race concept's meaning. Second, the term's application to the race concept derives from its appearance in the dissent of Justice John Marshall Harlan in the 1896 *Plessy v. Ferguson* case, where the justice's insistence that "our Constitution is colorblind," coexists blissfully with a range of support claims for eternal white superiority and supremacy (see Gotanda 1995).

9. We use the term *liberal* here in the U.S. sense, signifying "center-left."

10. We discuss colorblindness more extensively later in this essay.

11. The structural racism perspective allows us to see racism in terms of its consequences, not as a matter of intentions or beliefs. In *Racial Formation* we describe it this way as well: "a structural feature of US society, the product of centuries of systematic exclusion, exploitation, and disregard of racially defined minorities" (Omi and Winant 1994, 69). Grant-Thomas and powell offer a similar interpretation: "We can describe a social system as structurally racist to the degree that it is configured to promote racially unequal outcomes. For example, a society marked by highly interdependent opportunity structures and large interinstitutional resource disparities will likely be very unequal with respect to the outcomes governed by those institutions and opportunity structures" (Grant-Thomas and powell 2006, 5).

12. Of the vast literature on this topic, see Jacobson 1998; Roediger 2005; and Guglielmo 2003.

13. "Accumulation by dispossession" is an idea taken from David Harvey (2004). Among its many theoretical and analytical applications, the concept effectively describes such exploitative and predatory practices as "payday lending" (spatially concentrated in ghetto and barrio locations) and "steering" of subprime mortgages to working-class black and brown borrowers.

14. Elsewhere in the global system, parallel patterns prevail, overlapping to a large extent with U.S. processes: Maghrebines and Caribbeans migrate to France, Spain, and Italy; sub-Saharan Africans and South Asians are on the move; in the Philippines the state exports labor (particularly female labor) systematically; the global economy of remittances constitutes the most reliable and "progressive" (so to speak) foreign aid. For a good overview, see Massey et al. (2005).

15. See also Perlmann and Waters 2005; Perlmann 2005; Foner and Fredrickson 2004.

16. "Mixed-race" identity is also a race-gender/sexuality issue of "intersectionality" par excellence. See Stoler 2006b.

17. In 2003 the Census Bureau shared data on Middle Eastern, Arab, and South Asian Americans with the Department of Justice and the newly created Department of Homeland Security. The details of this cooperation—which seems to have violated pledges on the confidentiality of census data and on the bureau's abstention from politics—remain themselves confidential.

18. Quoted in Edward Epstein, "Calls for Racial, Ethnic Profiling Renewed after Transit Attacks" *San Francisco Chronicle,* August 10, 2005.

19. Ibid.

20. Nicholas Wade, "Race Is Seen as Real Guide to Track Roots of Disease," *New York Times,* July 30, 2002.

21. Quoted in Carolyn Johnson, "Should Medicine Be Colorblind?" *Boston Globe,* August 24, 2004.

22. Quoted in Amy Harmon, "In DNA Era, New Worries about Prejudice," *New York Times,* November 11, 2007.

23. Clyde Haberman, "NYC: Separating Common Sense from Reality," *New York Times,* September 1, 2006.

24. Indeed contemporary U.S. imperial misadventures generally take place on the very same terrains on which Americans' European predecessors sought in vain to impose their will in the past. "Globalization" is hardly a new phenomenon.

25. Contemporary civil rights jurisprudence exemplifies these trends. The Supreme Court has proved unwilling, in case after case, to tackle the ongoing dynamics of racial discrimination, unless that discrimination is construed to harm the interests of white people (Kairys 1996). The Court now thinks that whites are the main victims of racial discrimination in the United States. In a 2007 decision on two school desegregation cases, the Court outlawed school desegregation plans that were voluntary and had substantial community support, on the grounds that they invoked racial categories. See *Parents Involved in Community Schools Inc. v. Seattle School District No. 1,* and *Meredith v. Jefferson County (Ky.) Board of Education,* 551 U.S. 701 (2007).

26. For recent survey research on the Tea Party and its members' racial attitudes, conducted by a team of University of Washington political scientists, see Christopher S. Parker, "2010 Multi-State Survey of Race & Politics," WISER (University of Washington Institute for the Study of Ethnicity, Race, and Sexuality), http://depts.washington.edu/uwiser/racepolitics.html (accessed January 23, 2012).

27. According to a Pew Research Center poll conducted May 6–9, 2010, 73 percent approved of requiring people to produce documents verifying legal status, while 67 percent approved of allowing police to detain anyone unable to verify legal status. See "Broad Approval for New Arizona Immigration Law," Pew Research Center for the People & the Press, http://people-press.org/report/613/arizona-immigration-law (accessed January 23, 2012).

28. Conservative columnist Michael Gerson, writing in the *Washington Post,* noted opposition to the law from many Republican elected officials, and argued: "Unlike, say, a conservative magazine or blog, it is the purpose of a political party to win majorities within the broad bounds of its convictions. And each time a portion of the conservative movement demonstrates this particular form of ideological purity—in California's Proposition 187, the 2006 House immigration debate and now Arizona—they create resentments toward the Republican Party among Latinos that will last for generations. In all these cases, Republicans have gained little, sacrificed much, and apparently learned nothing." See Michael Gerson, "The Authors of Arizona's Immigration Law Retreat," *Washington Post,* May 3, 2010.

29. Clinton's welfare program (Temporary Assistance to Needy Families, or TANF), which replaced the previous, Aid to Families with Dependent Children (AFDC) program in 1996, forced welfare recipients (particularly women of color) into "workfare" jobs and substantially eroded the well-being of low-income children across a wide range of health, housing, education, and indeed survival issues. See Edelman 2004.

30. For a good overview of these connections, see Hayden 2004.

31. Calculated from Table M, U.S. Census Bureau, Current Population Reports, *Population Projections of the United States by Age, Sex, Race, and Hispanic Origin: 1995 to 2050* (issued February 1996; updated April 13, 1999), 16–17.

32. Social Security privatization was also presented as benefiting blacks, a claim doubtful at best. See Peter Wallsten and Tom Hamburger, "Blacks Courted on Social Security," *Los Angeles Times,* February 28, 2005; Paul Krugman, "Little Black Lies," *New York Times,* January 28, 2005.

33. We are indebted to Joe Feagin for first drawing our attention to this point.

34. See National Priorities Project, http://costofwar.com/ (accessed January 23, 2012); see also Stiglitz and Bilmes 2008.

35. New right and neoconservative racial ideologies are quite distinct; their political alliance remains shaky. The new right diverges from neoconservatism in its willingness to practice racial politics subtextually, through coding, manipulation of racial fears, and so on. De facto, it recognizes the persistence of racial difference in United States society. The new right understands perfectly well that its mass base is white and that its political success depends on its ability to interpret white identity in positive political terms. The resurgent nativism discussed above, the hostility and indeed blatant attacks on President Obama (and threats of violence against him), the return to talk of "states' rights" and even secession in the "Tea Party" and Republican far right, all show that the strategy of authoritarian populism addressed to the mass base of the white people's party (the Republicans) is far from exhausted. Neoconservatism at least professes postraciality and "colorblindness." It has not, and could not, deliver such tangible political benefits, and in fact lacks an equivalent mass political base. Thus the uneasy alliance between the two tendencies.

Reading 1.3 Obstacles to White Anti-racist Praxis: Notes on Sociological Theory

Jacqueline Brooks, California State University–Sacramento

Keywords: White anti-racist praxis, group-conflict theory, race consciousness, and double-consciousness.

Chapter Objective

This chapter will introduce students to two important ideas within sociological theorizing: group conflict theory and race consciousness. Each idea has a long history within sociological thinking, yet each has become overshadowed by explanations that focus more on interaction and structural processes (e.g., intersectionality and critical race theory). By the end of the chapter, students should be able to define group-conflict theory and race consciousness. In addition, students should be able to define and apply tangential concepts, such as white anti-racist praxis, double-consciousness, the "veil," affective knowledge, tacit knowledge, and propositional knowledge. Finally, students should be able to connect how each theoretical concept relates to the perception of present-day actions of civil unrest focusing on race-based social injustices.

> *By every civilized and peaceful method we must strive for the rights which the world*
> *accords to men, clinging unwaveringly to those great words which the sons of the Fathers*
> *would fain forget: "We hold these truths ..." (Du Bois 1903:25)*

Introduction

In the early 1990s, the acquittal of police officers who used excessive force against Rodney King sparked massive social protests. Since then, this scenario has been repeated multiple times—an unarmed person of color has a fatal or near fatal encounter with law enforcement; the offending police officers escape conviction; the public responds to the egregious use of force and lack of justice. More so today than in 1991, these events play out in front of news cameras and cell phones, transmitting 24 hours a day into our homes, schools, and places of work. Sociological research warns that a barrage of images watched repeatedly creates a desensitizing effect: reality becomes just another source of entertainment. According to Herbert Blumer (1958), highly publicized events such as Black Lives Matter marches constitute "big events," which have the ability to influence the thinking of race groups. In this chapter, I question whether prominent news stories about police shootings of unarmed people of color and subsequent collective social activism can penetrate the white gaze. Despite shifting race demographics, white, hegemonic structures remain entrenched throughout US social institutions. The perpetuation of racial hierarchies, which create real, lived disadvantages for people of color, relies on the promotion of white supremacy. Further, racial meaning and the development of race identities are bound to cultural imagery that communicates where people exist within the racial hierarchy. The mass media reflects just one social institution that reproduces social chasms among race groups. Thus, it is not prudent to expect the mass media to have such an overwhelming effect on people, that it alone can alter an individual or groups' consciousness. Yet, given the pervasiveness of technology within society and the diffusion of news across multiple platforms, it is important to access our immersion into twenty-four-hour news. In this chapter, I ask whether coverage of social protests in response to police brutality can influence the development of a race consciousness among white observers.

Thompson (2001) contends developing a white anti-racist praxis rarely involves a neat, smooth, linear trajectory. Rather, it tends to take seekers down a winding road, often filled with self-doubt and fear as they confront their own biases, and for some their upbringing. A journey that may begin with "naïveté and obliviousness about the politics of race" can lead people to "new places, often more secure and whole than the places they left" (Thompson 2001:38). An anti-racist praxis constitutes "conscious thought and action to dismantle racism and end racial inequalities in U.S. society," which ranges from explicit behaviors to challenge racism to daily activities, which comprise regular work and home routines (Perry and Shotwell 2009:34). Perry and Shotwell's (2009) work on the connection between knowledge attainment and white anti-racist praxis argues that the production and internalization of **affective**, **tacit**, and **propositional knowledge** serve as critical mechanisms that can lead to the emergence of a white anti-racist praxis. Their argument rests in the supposition that a lack of knowledge about one another creates social distancing marked by a chasm of distrust and ignorance; thereby stifling the maturation of the relational understanding (i.e., the dynamic process of identity formation in the context of societal structures) needed to connect with the "other."

Affective knowledge refers to "feelings or structures of feelings" that we use to make sense of the world around us (Perry and Shotwell 2009:34). For example, "empathy" serves as a necessary step in moving one toward race consciousness (Feagin 1991). During the Occupy movement, whites chanted "We're all N****!" During the Ferguson protests, people of varying races chanted, "I Am Michael Brown!" even donning T-shirts expressing the mantra. These acts seem to illustrate a feeling of connectedness to the other, allowing one to champion social justice despite one's own race or ethnicity.

Tacit knowledge refers to the library of "common sense" that we use to build assumptions about our social world. For example, historically, the educational system has taught whiteness as tacit knowledge, presenting it as a normalized feature of the larger cultural structure (Perry 2002, Blau 2003, Lewis 2003). As Du Bois (1920) asserts:

> *How easy, then, by emphasis and omission to make children believe that every great soul the world ever saw was a white man's soul; that every great thought the world ever knew was a white man's thought; that every great deed the world ever did was a white man's deed; that every great dream the world every sang was a white man's dream. (Du Bois 1920)*

Propositional knowledge refers to how we use language—the basis of the construction of our social realities—to shape our view of the social world. For example, the word *thug* has negative and racist connotations. The mere use of the term invokes stereotypical images that conjure up derogatory images of African American men and Latinx men.

Finally, the development of a white anti-racist praxis depends on how people construct an understanding of themselves in relationship to their own identities, the construction of the "other," and society itself (Perry and Shotwell 2009:34). Thus, how one is situated within each context affects our ability to shift, change, or alter our point of view. This goes beyond asking the perennial question, "Who am I?" It requires one to confront their own belief system, to know and understand how they have become situated in the world based on race, class, gender, and other markers of social inequality. Further, it relies on one's ability to examine their group identity and how group membership has exacerbated social injustices. Thus, although the experiences whites have as members of privileged groups is important, a substantive shift in white racism requires a multiplicative dose of alternative experiences, which results in relational understanding (Perry and Shotwell, 2009). In a study of white faculty, staff, and administrators at a "majority-minority" university, Brooks-Immel and Murray (2019) found that whites who engaged in and practiced anti-racism achieved this through a process of dialogue. Thus, for some, as the racial climate changed, the need to engage students more in racial discourse cultivated the emergence of white anti-racist praxis.

Perry and Shotwell (2009) offer a convincing argument that highlights the need to connect one's identity formation to the racial projects that perpetuate, or challenge racial hierarchies. Their work recognizes and advances the theory of social positioning, color-blind racism, and intersectionality; yet maintains the acquisition of affective, tacit, and propositional knowledge as central to developing a white anti-racist praxis. In this chapter, we discuss Blumer's social-group positioning and Du Bois's notion of the veil to highlight the difficulties in altering belief systems, values, and norms. White anti-racist praxis, though aided by knowledge building, relies on a thorough examination of group positioning, forcing whites to question their position in the social hierarchy, and how this position may propagate human social suffering. Further, I discuss the difficulty in lifting the "veil," the invisible barrier that keeps race groups from identifying with each other's experiences and interests.

Theoretical Arguments

Challenging Social-Group Identity

Challenging racial prejudice requires connecting the experiences and interests of the dominant group with the experiences and interests of the minority group. Dominant group positioning is structured in many ways—access to and wielding of societal resources, reinforcement of favorable ideologies, and the normalization of the dominant group's values, belief systems, and cultural practices. Often unseen, and unrecognized as "privileges," the dominant group carries an "invisible knapsack of special provisions, assurances, tools, maps, guides, codebooks, passports, visas, clothes, compass, emergency gear, and blank checks" (McIntosh 1997:291). Whites exchange these privileges for societal rewards (e.g., better interest rates on home loans, higher pay, or reserved employment positions) and social protection (e.g., perceptions of being trustworthy, reliable, and credible). Despite the pervasiveness of these transactions, they generally go unnoticed, unrecognized, or confronted. On the other hand, minority race group membership comes with unequal access to societal rewards, and while the dominant group's knapsack is filled to the brim, minority group members are denied equal access to the bag itself.

Blumer (1958) reinforces the idea that the dominant group conceptualizes minority groups as "the other," thus creating an "abstract image" that is solidified in the public arena. Blumer (1958) discounts everyday, minute social interaction as pivotal in the construction of one's racial consciousness and gives greater credence to the goings-on within the public arena. Racial prejudice is not based in one's sentiments or emotions, but an attachment to the status, privileges, and interests of the larger social group. Blumer argues that the dominant group views the "other" in four distinct ways that exemplify racial prejudice (1958):

- Dominant group feels superior to the minority group.
- Dominant group feels that the minority group is different and alien.
- Dominant group feels that they are entitled to privileges and advantages.
- Dominant group feels that the minority group is a threat to its resources, possessions.

Further, Blumer makes note of four implications (1958):

- The construction of the abstract group is formed by *remoteness,* not nearness.
- The public arena is crucial in establishing the grammar and manner in which the minority group is depicted and perceived.
- Representatives with considerable amounts of "standing, prestige, authority, and power" frame the discussions in the public arena.
- "Strong interest groups" influence the "direction" and "interpretation" of public discussions.

The collective sentiment of the group as a whole is constructed and reinforced within the public sphere, where dominant group members not only shape but also *own* the discourse. Media discourse, including its imagery, decides the winners and losers, the offenders and the victims, the deserving and the undeserving. Yet, the growth of social media threatens this power, offering marginalized groups real-time platforms to create their own narratives. In what Blumer (1958) would classify as "big events," twenty-four-hour news channels and social media feeds streamed anti-racist demonstrations as they spewed onto American streets and highways, lending support to well-established movements such as #BlackLivesMatter (BLM), which was birthed via

Twitter. Reportedly, the BLM hashtag has been used 30 million times, nearly 17,000 times per day, since its inception in 2013 (Anderson et al. 2018). Highly publicized "big events," especially those related to themes of race, violence, and law enforcement, such as the killings of Alton Sterling, Philando Castile, and the shooting deaths of Dallas and Baton Rouge police officers, tend to increase use of the BLM hashtag (Anderson et al. 2018).

The Problem of the "Veil"

Throughout his prolific writings, but most notably in *The Souls of Black Folk* (2007, 1903), Du Bois calls for the development of race consciousness among black Americans, charging them with the duty of confronting institutional racism. A heavy burden indeed, yet a necessary component in the move toward social justice. In Marxist theorizing, those who view their fellow workers as allies in the struggle against capitalist exploitation and actively work to demolish the capitalist structure—more importantly, its sociopolitical ideology—engage their *class-consciousness*. Thus, consciousness reflects more than an awareness of one's position within a social hierarchy; it reflects an understanding of the structural mechanisms that create one's place within the hierarchy. Following Marx, Du Bois presents collective social action as an inherent and essential feature of race consciousness. Thus, opposition to racial injustice emerges from a race-conscious mind that not only knows where it exists in the racial hierarchy, why it is there, but *what keeps it in its place*.

In *Darkwater: Voices from Within the Veil (1920),* Du Bois shifts his focus from black Americans to white Americans, challenging them to face their *white racial consciousness*. As Du Bois quips, the establishment of a racial hierarchy relied heavily on the advent of whiteness, a fairly new historical construct, which posits whiteness as normal, acceptable, and pleasing.

> *The discovery of personal whiteness among the world's peoples is a very modern thing—a nineteenth and twentieth century matter, indeed. The ancient world would have laughed at such a distinction. The Middle Age regarded skin color with mild curiosity; and even up into the eighteenth century we were hammering our national manikins into one, great, Universal Man, with fine frenzy, which ignored color and race even more than birth. Today we have changed all that, and the world in a sudden, emotional conversion has discovered that it is white and by that token, wonderful!*

Yet, whiteness blends itself into the normative features of American culture. As notable law scholar Flagg (1993) articulates, "Whites' endeavors to understand our own and blacks' ways of thinking about blackness are never unimportant, but a thorough reexamination of race consciousness ought to feature a careful consideration of whites' racial self-conception." Further, she states, "the tendency of whites not to think about whiteness, or about norms, behaviors, experiences, or perspective that are white-specific" is detrimental to the development of race consciousness. How one engages the racial order (i.e., viewing other race groups from a position of privilege or perceiving other race groups through a lens of oppression) influences how one sees the world around them. Du Bois elegantly refers to this as the *veil*: an invisible barrier that exists between race groups used as a lens through which we view one another. Cumulative experiences of subjugation (subordinate group) or privilege (dominant group) alter our perspectives. As those within the veil (subordinate group) strive for a better socioeconomic position, those on the other side of the veil (dominant group) often conflate race with class, arguing that a rise in the latter will lead to an improved perception of the former. Du Bois (1903) stated, "the ignorant Southerner hates the Negro, the workingmen fear his competition, the money-makers wish to use him as a laborer, some of the educated see a menace in his upward development, while others—usually the sons of the masters—wish to help him to rise. National opinion has enabled this last class to maintain the Negro common schools, and to protect the Negro partially in property, life, and limb" (80). Yet, this speaks to those whites who share a similar class grouping as blacks. Their ability to develop race consciousness is impeded by their economic struggles, viewing blacks as unnecessary competition. While lower-class whites resent the economic competitiveness blacks provide, middle- and upper-class whites implore blacks, especially poor blacks, to accept their lot in life: "Be content to be servants, and nothing more; what need of higher culture for half-men?" It is as if blacks must heed the dictate:

My poor, un-white thing! Weep not nor rage. I know too well, that the curse of God lies heavy on you. Why? That is not for me to say, but be brave! Do your work in your lowly sphere, praying the good Lord that into heaven above, where all is love, you may, one day, be born—white!"(DuBois 1920)

In *The Souls of Black Folk* (1903), Du Bois famously asks, *"How does it feel to be a problem?"* This question was asked of the striving black, pushing for a better spot on the social ladder. How does it feel to be perceived of as undeserving? How does it feel to be perceived of as unqualified? How does it feel to be perceived of as a threat? The presence of the veil creates a barrier that allows one group to see and experience disadvantage (e.g., objects of prejudice and discrimination) and the other group to continuously benefit from a position of advantage. Their continued advantage does not rely on seeing or consciously identifying social inequities. Yet, the suffering of those at the bottom of social hierarchies fortifies the position of the dominant group, justifying their privilege. In order to remove the veil, one must believe people on the other side of the veil deserving of it. Thus, this is a crucial, necessary step in the development of race consciousness on the part of the dominant group. Yet, it is important to note that those on the opposite side of the veil steep their attitudes, beliefs, and behaviors in racial hatred. Du Bois (1920) argues that the lowering of the veil requires a shift how the dominant group perceives blacks—one that does not espouse the following sentiments: "Darker peoples are dark in mind as well as in body; of dark, uncertain, and imperfect descent, of frailer, cheaper stuff, ... they have no feelings, aspirations, and loves; they are fools, illogical idiots—half-devil and half-child."

Police Brutality, Social Protests, and the Enduring Race Divide

Whereas past collective social action organized around structural mechanisms that propagate racial injustice, (e.g., segregation, educational inequality, and workplace discrimination), recent civil unrest seems focused on a singular issue, one that presents the victim as culpable in his own undoing. Thus, today's civil unrest may be viewed by onlookers as sparked by random, individual incidences rather than capacious structural forces. Combined with stereotypes about race minority groups and crime, an invisible social boundary materializes, creating an inability to identify with the victim in meaningful ways, ultimately preventing the development of a race consciousness. Additionally, observers of social protests may fail to connect police killings of unarmed black and brown individuals with economic inequality. Intersections among economic inequality, the hyper-criminalization of people of color, and police violence, especially toward men of color, go unseen. The social control of poor areas is a business, even more so when the community is predominantly black or brown. In the wake of Michael Brown's death, the Department of Justice concluded that the Ferguson Police Department (FPD) and the local court system profited from targeting blacks with excessive fines and fees, stating that the "FPD appears to bring certain offenses almost exclusively against African-Americans" (US Department of Justice 2015). Further, DOJ researchers "discovered emails circulated by police supervisors and court staff that stereotype racial minorities as criminals including one email that joked about an abortion by an African American woman being a means of crime control" showing that racial stereotyping serves as an effective means of institutionalizing racism and justifying economic subjugation (US Department of Justice 2015:5).

Second, previous research shows that whites' perception of police action is more favorable than that of black and Latinx communities. Although instances of police brutality negatively influence confidence in law enforcement, race disparities in the perception of overall police action remain (Sigelman et al. 1997). Weitzer and Tuch (2004) found that across multiple types of police misconduct (i.e., verbal abuse, excessive force, unwarranted stops, and corruption), blacks are much more likely to maintain highly negative views of law enforcement; whites are least likely to harbor negative perceptions of law enforcement; and Latinx attitudes fall somewhere in between. As Smith (2010) points out, distrust in the police is tied to historical institutionalized discrimination and contemporary racism—whether perceived or experienced. Further, the representation of the police as "credible sources" rather than as public officials willing to misrepresent events in order to protect their own interests and jobs contributes to the divide. We tend to look beyond the fact that police officers work in bureaucratic structures, replete with formal and informal norms that foster allegiance building among colleagues and sanction police violence. In response to "tough on crime" measures that resulted in harsh law enforcement policies and unfair sentencing, the arrest and incarceration rates of black and Latinx individuals grew disproportionately. Police murders align with extensive fear of *suspected bodies* and growing militarization of the police.

Third, the reinforcement of stereotypical images of the victims (e.g., depiction as "thugs" and "criminals") furthers the divide. Immediately following the killings of Michael Brown and Trayvon Martin, narratives that characterized both young, black men as troubled became fodder for news channels and social media. This is a tried-and-true media ploy that distracts us from the negligent behavior of the perpetrator (e.g., police or "concerned citizen") and reinforces images of black and brown men as "suspicious" and deserving of brute force.

Finally, with each failed conviction of law enforcement, the racial gap widens. In a review of fifteen high-profile police killings of people of color that occurred between 2014 and 2016, the *New York Times* reports that of the eight incidences that resulted in an indictment or charges, only three produced a conviction (2018). The slogan "No Justice, No Peace" belies more than a chant that builds solidarity among protestors. It speaks to the reality that marginalized groups endure relentless social inequities, yet rarely receive amends, reparations, or often even an acknowledgment of wrongdoing. We have become accustomed and desensitized to routine press conferences held by police officials and members of the court, offering condolences to the victims' families, yet refusing to indict or charge offending police officers. Even when police face indictment or charges, these efforts seldom lead to a conviction.

Conclusion

Bonilla-Silva (2012) contends that the power of racial domination generates a racial grammar (e.g. rules, semantics, and logics) that justifies, legitimizes, and presents the racial order as normal. This racial grammar shapes "… in significant ways how we see or do not see, how we frame, and even what we feel about race-related matters" (Bonilla-Silva 2012:2). More specifically, racial grammar provides the semantics by which we interpret racial matters, largely developed through interaction and communication (Bonilla-Silva 2012). Bonilla-Silva (2012) offers many examples of how racial grammar influences the larger cultural narrative. For example, American culture, largely propagated by the media, highlights the stories of "beautiful" white women who go missing while ignoring the fact that women of color, who are rarely referred to in such glowing terms, are victims of similar crimes as well. Or the fact that the movie industry forces people of color to suspend their belief in racism in order to enjoy a bit of entertainment. In order to engage in "normal" everyday activities, people of color must forget that a racial order exists. Or that school shootings are presented as morally reprehensible when they occur in majority white schools, but not in urban, majority black and/or brown schools (Bonilla-Silva, 2012). We communicate the existence and power of the racial order through storytelling (racial grammar) that "normalizes" white privilege and demonizes the powerless.

Can social protests help to redefine this racial grammar in ways that encourage the development of a white anti-racist praxis? If we situate media imagery and the reconstruction of race narratives via social media as knowledge production, then affective, tacit, and propositional knowledge become mechanisms of change. Since white anti-racist praxis stems from the "confluence of experiences and understanding" that knowledge building generates, then social protests offer several distinct opportunities: 1) they reveal the harmful and long-lasting consequences of institutionalized racial discrimination; 2) they highlight the material realities of social injustice as it is experienced by race and ethnic groups; and 3) they reveal the intersection among varying forms of social inequalities (e.g., gender, class, disability, age, and religion). As the seeds of knowledge germinate in the consciousness of white onlookers, the possibility to relate to the victims of police shootings in meaningful ways that humanize the victims (affective knowledge) exposes whitewashing in the narratives that develop about police shootings (tacit knowledge) and questions the language used to criminalize even the most basic activities of race minority groups (propositional knowledge) exists.

Yet, as suggested throughout this chapter, this insight must occur against the powerful influence of race-group positioning and a racial divide articulated by the "veil." This is exacerbated when media imagery and stories focus on individual decision-making rather than structural inequalities because this is how we tend to process racism—as an individual character flaw rather than a product of structural forces. As Blumer (1958) states, we must question public discourse when it "takes the form of a denunciation of the subordinate racial group, signifying that is unfit and a threat, the discussion becomes particularly potent in shaping the sense of social position" (1958:6). Simply, it is easier to identify with people with whom you share a neighborhood, work space, and church pews, than yet another black or brown face killed by the police. As the media imagery of social protests takes over our news channels and social media feeds, we must acknowledge the moment at which the veil descends, coloring our perceptions of one another, reinforcing the staunch, historical racial divide. It is at this moment that a shift in race consciousness can occur.

Discussion Questions

1. In thinking about the civil unrest surrounding the Unite the Right rally in Charlottesville, Virginia (2017 and 2018), do the counter-protests support or refute the author's argument? Why or why not?

2. In thinking about the Black Lives Matter movement, how are race consciousness and group-conflict theory tied to its perception and overall ability to achieve its goals?

3. What does it mean to be an "ally?" How does the experience of an ally differ from those who directly experience race and ethnic inequalities? For example, can a person who benefits from white privilege truly support social justice causes for race and ethnic minorities? What has to occur for people to become allies?

References

Anderson, Monica, Skye Toor, Lee Raine, and Aaron Smith. 2018. "Activism in the Social Media Age." Retrieved Nov. 16, 2018 (http://www.pewinternet.org/2018/07/11/activism-in-the-social-media-age/).

Bjornstrom, Eileen E.S., Robert L. Kaufman, Ruth D. Peterson, and Michael D. Slater. 2010. "Race and Ethnic Representations of Lawbreakers and Victims in Crime News: A National Study of Television Coverage." *Social Problems* 57(2):269–93. doi: 10.1525/sp.2010.57.2.269

Blau, Judith. 2003. *Race in the Schools: Perpetuating White Dominance?* Boulder, CO: Lynne Rienner Publishers.

Blumer, Herbert. 1958. "Race Prejudice as a Sense of Group Position." *The Pacific Sociological Review*, 1(1): 3 – 7.

Bobo, Lawrence, and Vincent L. Hutchings. 1996. "Perceptions of Racial Group Competition: Extending Blumer's Theory of Group Position to a Multiracial Social Context." *American Sociological Review* 61(6):951–72.

Bonilla-Silva, Eduardo. 2012. "The Invisible Weight of Whiteness: The Racial Grammar of Everyday Life in America." *Michigan Sociological Review* 26:1–15.

Du Bois, W.E.B. (1903). 2007. *The Souls of Black Folk.* New York: Oxford University Press.

Du Bois, W.E.B. (1920). 1999. *Darkwater: Voices From Within the Veil.* Mineola, NY: Dover.

Esposito, Luigi, and John W. Murphy. 1999. "Desensitizing Herbert Blumer's Work on Race Relations: Recent Applications of His Group Position Theory to the Study of Contemporary Race Prejudice." *Sociological Quarterly* 40(3):397–410.

Feagin, Joe R. 1991. "The Continuing Significance of Race: Antiblack Discrimination in Public Places." *American Sociological Review* 56(1):101–16.

Flagg, Barbara J. 1993. "'Was Blind, but Now I See': White Race Consciousness and the Requirement of Discriminatory Intent." *Michigan Law Review Association* 91(5):953–1017.

Lewis, Amanda. 2003. *Race in the Schoolyard: Negotiating the Color Line in Classrooms and Communities*. New Brunswick, NJ: Rutgers University Press.

Perry, Pamela. 2002. *Shades of White: White Kids and Racial Identities in High School*. Durham, NC: Duke University Press.

Perry, Pamela, and Alexis Shotwell. 2009. "Relational Understanding and White Antiracist Praxis." *Sociological Theory* 27(1):33–50. doi: 10.1111/j.1467-9558.2009.00337.x

Prendergast, Catherine, and Ira Shor. 2005. "When Whiteness Is Visible: The Stories We Tell About Whiteness." *Rhetoric Review* 24(4):377–85.

Shibutani, Tamotsu. 1988. "Herbert Blumer's Contributions to Twentieth-Century Sociology." *Symbolic Interaction* 11(1):23–31.

Sigelman, Lee, Susan Welch, Timothy Bledsoe, and Michael Combs. 1997. "Police Brutality and Public Perceptions of Racial Discrimination: A Tale of Two Cities." *Political Research Quarterly* 50(4):777–91.

Thompson, Becky. 2001. *A Promise and a Way of Life: White Anti-Racist Activism*. Minneapolis, MN: University of Minnesota Press.

Ulmer, Jeffery T. 2001. "Mythic Facts and Herbert Blumer's Work on Race Relations: A Comment on Esposito and Murphy's Article." *Sociological Quarterly* 42(2):289–96.

US Department of Justice. 2015. *Investigation of the Ferguson Police Department*. US Department of Justice, Civil Rights Division.

Weitzer, Ronald, and Steven A. Tuch. 2004. "Race and Perceptions of Police Misconduct." *Social Problems* 51(3):305–25.

Discussion Questions

1. Discuss instances where you have struggled to understand a social phenomenon from someone else's perspective.

2. Compare and contrast two theoretical perspectives within a specific social institution. For example, would you approach racial profiling from a critical race perspective and an intersectional perspective? How do the theoretical approaches converge? How do they deviate?

References

Appelrouth, Scott, and Laura D. Edles. 2015. *Classical and Contemporary Sociological Theory: Text and Readings*. 3rd ed. Los Angeles: Sage Publication.

Bonilla-Silva, Eduardo. 2013. *Racism Without Racists: Color-Blind Racism and the Persistence of Racial Inequality in America*. Lanham, MD: Rowman & Littlefield.

Collins, Patricia Hill. 2015. "Intersectionality's Definitional Dilemma." *Annual Review of Sociology* 41:1–20.

Crenshaw, Kimberlé. 1991. "Mapping the Margins: Intersectionality, Identity Politics, and Violence Against Women of Color." *Stanford Law Review* 43:1241–99.

Delgado, Richard, and Jean Stefancic. 2001. *Critical Race Theory: An Introduction*. New York: New York University Press.

Matsuda, M., C. Lawrence, R. Delgado, and K. Crenshaw. 1993. *Words That Wound: Critical Race Theory, Assaultive Speech, and the First Amendment*. Boulder, CO: Westview Press.

Omi, Michael, and Thomas Winant. 1994. *Racial Formation in the United States: From the 1960s to the 1990s*. 2nd ed. New York: Routledge.

Sears, Alan, and James Cairns. 2016. *A Good Book in Theory: Making Sense Through Inquiry*. 3rd ed. Ontario, Canada: University of Toronto Press.

Section II: Identity, Wellness, and Society

Student Narratives

In 2016, my father decided to move back to Oakland so he could commute to his work in San Francisco. I helped him pack up his belongings, put it on some rental trucks, and we were off to Oakland. On the way, there was a weigh station where all trucks must go through for inspection. As we were driving slowly through the weighing area, an officer got on a microphone to tell us that they wanted further inspection. My father, who has been driving trucks for the past 30 years, thought it was strange that a rental truck would need further examination. We complied and listened for further instruction. As we drove toward their desired location, I saw many rental trucks driving through the weigh stations without being flagged down. We waited for about 20 minutes, and I was beginning to lose my patience. I got out of the truck and was immediately greeted by a loudspeaker to "Get back in the truck now!" I stood there confused, and my father told me to do as they say. Five minutes later, an officer finally came out. He walked up toward my side of the door and said, "Why did you get out of the car? Were you going to hide something in the back?" I responded, "We were tired of waiting, and I was going to ask why the long wait." They ignored my response and asked for our license, registration, and to open the back for inspection. We did as we were told. When they finished the inspections, they smiled at us and acted more friendly. They said, "We're sorry for the long wait. Sometimes we catch people smuggling illegal things in the back." I asked, "Are they mostly Asians?" and they responded, "Yes. You are free to go." I sat there confused and angry at what just happened. Right then, I now knew what millions of minorities in America felt when they were racially profiled by someone of authority. Helpless.

Jourbert Chiu is a Sociology MA Candidate at California State University–Sacramento.

When I had my first child, I consulted with my doctor and read many websites to prepare myself for labor. None, however, prepared me for what I experienced in the midst of excruciating labor pain. I was admitted to the hospital after my water broke when I was one centimeter dilated. My decision for a natural birth (vaginal and no medication) was a personal decision, and this was communicated to every nurse who cared for me as soon as I was admitted. When I was 5–6 centimeters dilated, I was in agonizing pain. In at least three attempts, the white male doctor on shift suggested I get an epidural to minimize the pain. He further added that my hips were too small to deliver a baby, implying I should prepare myself for a cesarean section. I was 4'11 and just over 140 lbs. at full term. I have known women my size—and some smaller—who have given vaginal births. In his last attempt to try to force me to take the epidural, he said that I looked "Americanized" and asked why I was letting my "culture" dictate my decision, suggesting my culture did not believe in Western medicine and further implying I was culturally backwards. This was no less than a manifestation of color-blind racism. Despite the pain and anger I felt, I refused to get an epidural. After 27 hours of labor, I naturally delivered a beautiful and healthy baby boy.

Chia Xiong is a PhD candidate at University of California–Merced. Prior to her studies in the social sciences, she was a pre-nursing student and has a general understanding of human anatomy and physiology. She came to the United States as a refugee when she was five.

Learning Objectives

After you read this section on "Identity, Wellness, and Society," you should be able to:

1. Recognize social factors influencing one's racial and ethnic identities.

2. Distinguish unconscious bias from racism, prejudice, discrimination, and stereotypes.

3. Understand the consequences of racism for one's well-being.

Editor's Introduction

Aya Kimura Ida, PhD

When you receive a questionnaire asking your racial and/or ethnic identity, do you find the category easily or do you struggle to pick a category that fits how you see yourself? Figure 1 shows the racial and ethnic categories that the US Census 2010 used based on the Office of Management and Budget's (OMB) standards (Humes, Jones, and Ramirez 2011:1), and much of other research has adopted the similar racial and ethnic classifications. Respondents are asked whether they are "Hispanic, Latino, or Spanish origin" and then are asked to identify their racial identification(s): White, Black or African American, American Indian or Alaska Native, Asian, and Native Hawaiian or Other Pacific Islander. These categories are adopted widely beyond the US Census, and you may find similar race and ethnicity questions on other surveys. The US Census 2010 reported 72.4 percent of the US population self-identified as White, 12.6 percent reported Black or African American, 0.9 percent selected American Indian and Alaska Native, 4.8 percent chose Asian, Native Hawaiian and Other Pacific Islander was 0.2 percent, and some other race and two or more races accounted for 6.2 percent and 2.9 percent, respectively. Of all, 16.3 percent reported Hispanic or Latino origin. When asked about their racial identity, over half of the Hispanic or Latino persons identified themselves as White. One-third of the Hispanic or Latino persons reported their race as Latino, Mexican, Puerto Rican, Salvadoran, or other ethnicities, not being able to find a race category that fit their self-identity, and therefore were later classified as "some other race" for statistical purposes. This example shows how the widely used categories may not fit one's own identification. Also, these categories are too vague to understand the race/ethnicity-related experiences of individuals. For example, when these categories are presented, I would pick "Asian" (or "Japanese" if the option was available). At the same time, however, I would feel ambivalent about the choice because this Asian category includes such a wide range of skin colors, cultures, languages, and socioeconomic and historical backgrounds in the United States (see Zhou 2004). In this section, we explore the social factors that shape our self-identification of race and ethnicity, the biases we develop based on the socially constructed categories, and the consequences of such biases.

Figure 1.
Reproduction of the Questions on Hispanic Origin and Race From the 2010 Census

→ **NOTE: Please answer BOTH Question 5 about Hispanic origin and Question 6 about race. For this census, Hispanic origins are not races.**

5. Is this person of Hispanic, Latino, or Spanish origin?

☐ **No,** not of Hispanic, Latino, or Spanish origin
☐ Yes, Mexican, Mexican Am., Chicano
☐ Yes, Puerto Rican
☐ Yes, Cuban
☐ Yes, another Hispanic, Latino, or Spanish origin — *Print origin, for example, Argentinean, Colombian, Dominican, Nicaraguan, Salvadoran, Spaniard, and so on.* ↗

[ ][ ][ ][ ][ ][ ][ ][ ][ ][ ][ ][ ][ ][ ][ ][ ]

6. What is this person's race? *Mark* ☒ *one or more boxes.*

☐ White
☐ Black, African Am., or Negro
☐ American Indian or Alaska Native — *Print name of enrolled or principal tribe.* ↗

[ ][ ][ ][ ][ ][ ][ ][ ][ ][ ][ ][ ][ ][ ][ ][ ]

☐ Asian Indian   ☐ Japanese   ☐ Native Hawaiian
☐ Chinese   ☐ Korean   ☐ Guamanian or Chamorro
☐ Filipino   ☐ Vietnamese   ☐ Samoan
☐ Other Asian — *Print race, for example, Hmong, Laotian, Thai, Pakistani, Cambodian, and so on.* ↗   ☐ Other Pacific Islander — *Print race, for example, Fijian, Tongan, and so on.* ↗

[ ][ ][ ][ ][ ][ ][ ][ ][ ][ ][ ][ ][ ][ ][ ][ ]

☐ Some other race — *Print race.* ↗

[ ][ ][ ][ ][ ][ ][ ][ ][ ][ ][ ][ ][ ][ ][ ][ ]

Source: U.S. Census Bureau, 2010 Census questionnaire.

Figure SII.1

Race, Ethnicity, and Self

Self is a process of defining who we are from our own perspective while also considering other persons' views toward us (Gecas 1982). Social psychologists argue that humans are reflexive in that we define ourselves not only subjectively (how we see ourselves), but also objectively (how we believe others see us). An **identity** is a description of the self. Throughout our lives, we develop a collection of many identities that are unique to us based on various social statuses, roles, characteristics, and personalities that we have and social groups to which we belong. *Racial* and *ethnic* identities are **social identities** in that they are based on perceived membership(s) in certain groups. We define our racial and ethnic identities subjectively, but also objectively through interactions with others in the society. For example, being raised as part of the majority race and ethnicity in Japan, I did not feel so strongly about my Japanese-ness growing up. However, my Japanese identity has suddenly become more salient since I moved to the United States over twenty years ago, because I have become part of the minority group. Here, my race and ethnic identity became something to be scrutinized, intrigued, questioned, and challenged by society, and it became something that I consciously needed to protect, assert, and sometimes let go. There were many instances where people asked me, "What [ethnicity] are you?," commented on (or joke about) my "Japanese-ness" and accent, and made assumptions about my personality through stereotypes of an Asian woman. It is those mundane social experiences that have made me feel more Japanese in the United States than when I lived in Japan. And it is important to realize that such individual everyday interactions are shaped by the social, political, and historical climate in the society. Thus, we may feel our racial and ethnic identities are stable and innate within us, but they are in fact changeable, depending on the social, political, and historical environment that surrounds us. The first chapter in this section, written by Radha Modi, analyzes how second-generation South Asians understand their ethnic and racial identities. This work by Modi is a wonderful example demonstrating the importance of sociopolitical contexts, such as the continued support for multiculturalism, the backlash after 9/11, and the growth of the Latinx community in the United States, to fully understand how South Asians identify themselves based on race and ethnicity.

Racial and ethnic identities are more salient among racial and ethnic minorities than among whites in the United States, simply because whites, or persons of European descent, do not have to think about their race as the majority group (see Wise 2008). Not having to think about race and ethnic identity in everyday life is part of the **white privilege**. Taking a survey question on race and ethnicity (as in Figure 1) may cause everyone to become more conscious of their racial and ethnic identity, but minority individuals tend to encounter experiences that make them think about their social positions in everyday life more often than the majority group. In the first vignette, MA student Jourbert Chiu shared his experience of receiving unfair treatment on the road. At the beginning, he and his father were not sure why their truck was singled out for further investigation, but when they realized their racial appearance triggered the suspicion for "smuggling illegal things," his racial identity became salient. Minorities tend to encounter these experiences more often than whites; therefore, minorities are socialized to view the society and their experiences through two different standpoints—also called **double consciousness** (Du Bois 1903). An influential early sociologist, W.E.B. Du Bois coined the term and described the idea of double consciousness as "this sense of always looking at one's self through the eyes of others, of measuring one's soul by the tape of a world that looks on in amused contempt and pity" (Du Bois 1903:3). Although he focused on African Americans in his work, this idea can be applied to many other racial and ethnic minorities in a society (e.g., Spickard 1997). Joubert may have felt "helpless" in the end, realizing that he and his father have to always be more vigilant, knowing that they are viewed through their racial appearances and the generalizations based on stereotypes.

Us Versus Them

We not only categorize ourselves but also other people around us using the existing social groups (Tajfel 1981). As the earlier section showed, race and ethnicity are socially constructed. There is no meaningful biological or genetic distinction between races, but those categories were developed and have been used for political, economic, and social reasons to justify a superiority of European race and inferiority of other groups. When we do categorize others consciously or unconsciously, a likely consequence is the association of stereotypes. **Stereotypes** refer to biased images and assumptions about a group. Throughout the socialization, we learn those distorted images of a group from our family, friends, school, and media. Holding such biased images and assumptions can lead us to develop **prejudice**, or unfair attitudes toward a given group. The second chapter in this section, by Lisa Harrison, warns us that we may not realize at the conscious level that we hold prejudice toward other groups, which is called **unconscious bias**. It is important to carefully examine our unconscious bias because it can result in **discrimination**, which is an action that treats others unfairly on the basis of their group membership. In other words, one may not think they are racist, but the bias they hold at an unconscious level can lead them to treat individuals of certain races unfairly. Stereotypes, prejudice, unconscious bias, and discrimination all have real and serious consequences in society.

Consequences of Race and Ethnicity

While it is difficult to develop valid and reliable measures of racial and ethnic identities, it is crucial to keep collecting information about those identities because the consequences of the racial/ethnic hierarchy are undeniably real. The second vignette, shared by PhD student Chia Xiong, shows how a highly educated person like a medical doctor could hold an unconscious bias and act based on color-blind racism. **Color-blind ideology** is the belief that race no longer matters and therefore does not have any impact on our lives and that race-conscious policies and practices would only make racism worse (Bonilla-Silva 2003). In Chia's example, the doctor assumed her body was too small to give birth naturally and she looked too "Americanized" to follow her "backward" cultural belief. These assumptions held by medical professionals have real consequences, even though such biases are held at the unconscious level. Not only that the bias held by medical professionals could lead to uncomfortable interactions, accumulations of these experiences in the US health care system could also discourage one to trust the professionals and seek care when needed. The last chapter in this section is an excerpt from an article written by David R. Williams and Michelle Sternthal that provides a great overview of ways in which race and migration impact health disparities in the United States. Their work demonstrates that the stress of having to deal with discrimination adversely impacts one's health, although this serves as just the tip of the iceberg in explaining the racial disparities in health. They offer the complex ways in which race impacts one's health through structural and social psychological pathways.

Researchers who study racial and ethnic identities recognize that these identities are actually multidimensional, arguing that the identities are more than just simple categories or labels (see, e.g., Cross 1985; Hughes and Demo 1990; Broman, Neighbors, and Jackson 1988; Gurin, Miller, and Gurin 1980; Shelton 2008; Phinney 1992). For example, researchers have measured ethnic and racial group identity based on the sense of closeness and/or commitment to, evaluation/pride associated with, curiosity about, and behavioral tendencies reflecting one's own ethnic/racial group. Thus, it is more than the single word a person uses to describe their group membership(s). Furthermore, these studies on ethnic identities and racial identities tend to recognize that the degree to which one identifies with the ethnic and racial group varies from one person to another. In other words, two persons from the same ethnic and racial group could identify themselves in different strengths, one feeling the ethnic identity more strongly than the other. Strong and positive ethnic and racial identities are generally shown to be beneficial for minority individuals' mental health (Carter 1991; Munford 1994) and provide resiliency to cope with discrimination in daily lives (Mossakowski 2003). While maintaining positive and strong ethnic and racial identities may not be easy in a society where assimilative adaptation is still required for minorities to climb up the socioeconomic ladder and mitigate discriminatory treatment, these findings suggest that we should not overlook the importance of ethnic and racial identities as coping resources for minority individuals. These findings also suggest that it is important to recognize that racial and ethnic identities are more than a mere category or label.

Mindfulness

Biased images and attitudes that we sometimes hold even at the unconscious level could lead to discriminatory behaviors and institutional practices, which can result in internalized racism as well as poorer health consequences. As the concept of sociological mindfulness suggests, it is important that we first reflect on the stereotypes and prejudice that we may hold about others. Like any bad habit, the first step is to recognize the problem in order to work toward correcting it.

Not only being sensitive and reflective on our own unconscious biases, we should also work toward holding institutions accountable for their mindfulness and actions. For example, the United States Census Bureau has collected information on racial and ethnic identities of US residents since its first data collection in 1790 and continues to revise the racial categories as society changes politically, culturally, and economically (Humes et al. 2011). In the past decades, there has been an effort to further divide the White category to recognize the persons of Arab or Middle Eastern origins separately from other persons of European descent. Also, it was not until the US Census 2000 that people were allowed to report more than one race. It is important to note that the measurement of race and ethnicity in US censuses has always been based on self-identification. Without the voices from the mindful citizens, such continued efforts (and funding to support such efforts) to develop and revise more accurate and reliable measures of race and ethnicity that reflects the social climate would not be possible.

Reading 2.1 "Brown Like Us": Reflections from South Asian Americans on Race, Ethnicity, and Skin Color

Radha Modi, Florida State University

Keywords: Racialization, Racial Identity, Ethnic Identity, Pan-ethnic Identities, Multiculturalism, Phenotype

The day after 9/11, I felt like there was a neon sign above my head that read "terrorist!" Everywhere I went, I just got stares. Suddenly, my brownness was the only thing people saw.

—Nabin (Bangladeshi American)

Introduction

The use of "brown" as an identity label among South Asians has vague beginnings. Vijay Prashad, the author of *The Karma of Brown Folk*, is one of the earlier scholars to use "brown" to refer to the South Asian diaspora (Indians, Pakistanis, Bangladeshis, Sri Lankan, Nepalese, as well as others from the subcontinent). *The Karma of Brown Folk* is a modern-day response to W.E.B. Dubois's analysis on the spiritual crisis of black Americans stereotyped as a "problem" race incapable of assimilating in the United States. Prashad, a century later, identifies a spiritual crisis for South Asians, who are being politically used by the United States as the stereotypical "model minority" against blacks. Prashad could not have foretold that a year after publishing his book, the September 11, 2001, attacks would occur, and soon after South Asians would experience a racialization under the US War on Terror. The South Asian diaspora has now largely begun to self-identify as "brown." Using reflections from interviews with second-generation South Asians, the next few pages explore the potential micro and macro underpinnings behind this shift in identity.

Background

A Look at South Asian Identity

South Asians are a critical group to study because they are characterized as the model group for contemporary assimilation due to their high levels of attainment, similar levels of attainment by their immigrant parents, and proximity to whiteness (Portes and Rumbaut 2006). However, under this glossy image of upward mobility and integration, there is a great deal of heterogeneity.

Previous literature has found that second-generation South Asians express and understand their identity primarily through a cultural lens (such as language, tradition, and food) consistent with other ethnic groups in the United States (Purkayastha 2005; Dhingra 2007), with religion playing an important role in that formation (Joshi 2006; Kurien 2007). Unlike their first-generation parents, second-generation South Asians strongly identify with being American as well.

Further, despite being categorized under the larger Asian racial category on the census, second-generation South Asians do not readily embrace the pan-ethnic label of Asian (Koshy 1998). One reason for the ambivalence toward the Asian identity is that the Asian American identity has historically been linked with East Asians, with "Asian Indian" only being added to the classification within the last thirty years.[1] Additionally, other South Asian groups, such as Pakistani, Bangladeshi, or Sri Lankans, are not explicitly listed on the census and must select "Other" (Kibria 2007). Kurien (2003) also suggests that differing South Asian religious affiliations[2] may also contribute to the ambivalence South Asians have for pan-ethnic connections. While it is clear that place of birth, culture, and religion do play a role, missing in this Asian American literature is a systematic investigation of the role of skin color in ethno-racial identification.

Does Skin Color Matter?

Developments in research on phenotype do find connections between skin color and racial identification but focus heavily on black and Latinx communities (Golash-Boza and Darity 2008; Quiros and Dawson 2013; Roth 2014; Dowling 2014; Joseph 2015). This literature reveals that darker skin color increases the likelihood of identifying as black for Latinxs (Golash-Boza and Darity 2008), but lighter skin color does not consistently align with identifying as white (Dowling 2014). Other factors, such as discrimination, language background, and immigration status (Golash-Boza and Darity 2008; Roth 2014; Dowling 2014), as well as socioeconomic status (Schwartzman 2007; Roth 2014), and gender (Garcia and Abascal 2015) complicate the relationship between skin color and identity. With evidence showing skin color informing the identities of blacks and Latinxs, what role does it play for the Asian racial identity? Ocampo (2016) demonstrates second-generation Filipinos also feel proximity to Latinos partly due to their phenotype. South Asians also exhibit skin tones from very light to very dark.

Investigating the role of skin color may provide a final piece to the puzzle over the current status of the racial and ethnic identities of second-generation South Asians as well as provide insights into the larger racialization processes of Asians in the United States.

Larger Sociopolitical Context

Further, we cannot make sense of racial and ethnic identities without taking into consideration the sociopolitical context in the United States (Omi and Winant 2014). As participant reflections will illustrate, the meanings attached to identity do not exist in a vacuum but are grounded in a larger context. Three contemporary sociopolitical events are relevant for second-generation South Asian identity: the 9/11 attacks, the rise of multicultural ideology, and the growth of the Latinx community.

September 11, 2001

The September 11, 2001, attacks may have transformed the South Asian identity, and this transformation is likely linked to the rise of Islamophobia. The Council on American Islamic Relations (CAIR) reported an increase in anti-Muslim hate crimes between 2004 and 2005, as well as processed nearly 2,000 civil rights complaints, up 30 percent from the previous year (Esposito and Kalin 2011). The growing Islamophobia post-9/11 contributed to the racialization of differing groups by bringing them under a larger umbrella of Muslim (Garner and Selod 2015). South Asians have been absorbed into that racialization due to their phenotype

---

[1] The Association of Indians in America (AIA) successfully negotiated for reclassification of Indians from the "Other" racial category to Asian Indians under the Asian category starting with the 1980 US Census (Espiritu 1993).
[2] South Asians not only identify with a nationality but also have strong ethno-religious identities of Sikh, Muslim, Christian, Hindu, or Buddhist (Kurien 2007).

signaling a perceived "Muslimness." In what ways does the post-9/11 racialization of "darkness" and "brownness" relate to second-generation South Asian racial and ethnic identification?

Multiculturalism

The rise of multiculturalism post–civil rights movement has also become a central framework in incorporating newer minority groups into the United States. The focus has largely been on the celebration of cultural diversity and the importance of diverse representation (Modood 2013). Modood (2013) suggests that multiculturalism can assist in integrating immigrants as they can keep their cultural traditions and still be, for instance, American. There does not need to be total assimilation into white America. While the multicultural framework celebrates the ethnic diversity of immigrants, it conversely ignores the lived reality of systemic discrimination that blocks mobility for blacks.

Under the multicultural framework, Asians position themselves in the US racial system as a cultural ethno-racial group. South Asians, for instance, utilize the multicultural framework by strategically altering their ethnic identities across contexts of home and work to manage xenophobia and racial discrimination (Dhingra 2007) and form ethno-religious identities as well (Kurien 2007). Due to its significance, in what ways does the multicultural framework influence second-generation South Asian identity construction and understanding of their skin color?

Growth of the Latinx Community

The growth of the Latinx community in the United States may also fuel the changing identity of South Asians. Latinxs are now the largest minority group in the United States. Their presence may have shifted the traditional black-white divide into a tri-racial system (Bonilla-Silva 2004). With the "Latin Americanization" of the US racial system as described by Bonilla-Silva (2004), there is a growing "racial middle" that acts as a buffer between whites and the collective black. The racial middle will incorporate multiple groups, including South Asians and light-skinned Latinxs. This positionality may result in some shared racial experiences between Latinxs and South Asians. Thus, the growth of the Latinx community and the Latin Americanization of US racial classification may impact second-generation South Asian identity formation.

Methods

This study employs in-depth interviews to address identity formation among second-generation South Asians. The total sample of 120 participants from the New York metro area from 2013 to 2015 varies by gender, religion, and class. I define *working class* as having parents who work blue-collar jobs and rent their current place of residence. Those who did not meet these criteria fell into the middle-/upper-class category. The religion category is representative of religious identities common in the South Asian community: Hindu, Muslim, Christian, and Sikh. All the participants have second-generation immigrant status (meaning that they are born in the United States or migrated to the United States before school age and are the children of foreign-born parents).

Results

A Repertoire of Identities

The results from the interviews reveal identity patterns consistent with previous literature as well as new diverging patterns. First, I find that second-generation South Asians utilize a mix of ethnic/national, religious, pan-ethnic, and phenotypical identifications as part of their repertoire. A nationality identity in combination with American is the most commonly employed, such as *Indian American, Pakistani American*, or *Bangladeshi American*. In addition to the nationality identity, Sikh and Muslim South Asians also regularly use an ethnic-religious identity, such as *Sikh American* or *Muslim American*. Hindus, Jains, Christians, Buddhists, in contrast, did not use religious identity as part of their racial and ethnic identity toolbox.

Pan-ethnic identities of *South Asian* and *Asian* only become relevant for South Asians in institutional and political contexts, such as college applications, the census, and in some cases, for political organizing. In fact, my participants only came to know they are Asian through participation in schools. In a similar regard, older participants recalled that the term "South Asian" is newer to the scene. For instance, South Asian organizations began to use the umbrella term to build coalitions across diverse South Asian groups post-9/11.

Two additional pan identity terms that are prevalent in everyday conversations are *Desi* and *Brown*. "Desi," a colloquial pan-cultural term made popular by Bollywood, is used by South Asians around the world to identify each other. However, a few participants conveyed their reluctance in using "desi," as it centers a specific cultural image from India over other South Asian cultures. In contrast, the use of "brown" is widespread among all South Asians and has its origins among the later-generation diasporas outside of South Asia. I discuss the identity of "brown" in more detail in a later section of this chapter.

Skin Color as Secondary to Culture

The hyphenated nationality (i.e., Indian American) and religious categories (i.e., Sikh American) as noted are the most popular among South Asians. Throughout conversations with participants, I came to realize that participants understand their identity primarily in cultural and geographical terms. To demonstrate, Mandeep (Sikh American, mid-thirties) voices:

> "I'm not Indian. I'm Sikh American. Even though I may not be perceived that way … I can't be anything but American. I was born here. I only speak English. This is my home."

Mandeep emphasizes his US birthplace as relevant for his ethno-racial identity. Similarly, Laila (Pakistani American, early thirties, Muslim) reflects:

> "American … Pakistani American … American Pakistani … all of them are very important. For a long time, culturally I felt all I did was American. I mean that's all I knew. If more Pakistanis were around then maybe I would have known but yeah American definitely."

Laila highlights her cultural habits as American habits and not Pakistani habits, which makes the American part of her identity important. Regarding geography, participants discuss how their place of birth in the United States signifies their level of American identity. Participants also indicate that they are Pakistani, Indian, or Bangladeshi because their parents or grandparents were born there. The tracking of ancestry to the Indian subcontinent is important for South Asian identity. Even South Asians with parents who came from England, South Africa, or the Middle East identify more strongly with being Indian, Pakistani, or Bangladeshi.

Further, as South Asians view their racial and ethnic identity as cultural and geographical, the negotiating of identity and making sense of how different identities fit together is central to their experiences as children of immigrants. Participants believe that identity can be molded by picking and choosing parts that they value and discarding the parts they find undesirable. Surya (Indian American, mid-thirties, Hindu background) explains:

> "I am both Indian and American. I'm American because I don't show off with money and material goods like the way Indians do. Who has the biggest house … the most expensive car (shaking head). I don't do that. The ways that I am Indian are I take care of my parents. I know how to save money. Americans don't do that."

In the above quote Surya demonstrates that his ability to save money and take care of his parents are cultural behaviors that make him Indian, and the fact that he does not show off his wealth like other South Asians makes him American.

While culture and geography are primary in how South Asians make sense of their racialized ethnic identity, phenotype—in particular, skin color—plays a secondary role. For second-generation South Asians, the relationship between racial and ethnic identity formation and skin color may be implicit until larger sociopolitical events push the issue of skin color to the forefront in their lives.

During interviews, participants demonstrated difficulty in indicating how their skin color impacts their racial and ethnic identification. They were more likely to view their identity directly related to culture, ancestry, and geography. From light-skinned to very-dark-skinned South Asians, skin color was not an obvious lens through which to understand their most common racial and ethnic identity of racialized nationality such as Bangladeshi American. For example, Rena (Indian American, early thirties, Hindu) explains:

> "Uhhh. I mean I'm Indian because my parents are Indian. But I'm not Indian Indian like them. They are really religious and conservative. I'm more progressive. All their friends are Indian. They eat mostly Indian food. I mean I love Indian food but you know I eat other stuff too. I don't know. [pause] Also of course if I look in the mirror, I look Indian."

As can be seen, Rena only mentions phenotype after discussing cultural and geographical aspects of her racial and ethnic identity. This excerpt highlights how second-generation South Asians place skin color as a secondary source of their racial and ethnic identity.

However, skin color becomes central to their racial experience when they reflect on sociopolitical events such as 9/11. In their reflections, second-generation South Asians describe a shift in the visibility of their embodiment after the 9/11 attacks as well as more recent terrorist attacks such as the Boston Marathon bombing in 2013. Common themes in these reflections highlight feelings of phenotypical hypervisibility: "standing out" or "feeling exposed." Nabin, a Bangladeshi American in his late thirties, exclaims:

> "The day after 9/11, I felt like there was a neon sign above my head that read "terrorist!" Everywhere I went, I just got stares. Suddenly, my brownness was the only thing people saw."

These reflections signal a clear shift in racialization from invisibility to hypervisibility of phenotype, resulting in being treated as a suspect. Hypervisibility and the accompanying racialization may add to the constellation of South Asian identity. Whether this hyper-racialization of the South Asian community will continue is dependent on the larger sociopolitical context related to 9/11 and national policies on terrorism, the demographic shift with increased Latinx communities, and the durability of multicultural ideology in the United States.

Use of "Brown"

Even though skin color seems to play a secondary role in identity formation, it nonetheless has an impact on how second-generation South Asians deploy the identity term "brown" and also may point to future trends. "Brown" is one of the most frequently used pan identity terms by South Asians, with 118 participants out of 120 utilizing it for self-identification. Participants across the skin color spectrum use the term "brown." The age of the participant also matters for the frequency and ease of use. Participants between the ages of eighteen and thirty-five deploy the term "brown" regularly, while those older than thirty-five express it rarely as they do not always feel comfortable with the term. The differences across age may be a cohort effect since the term seems to have become ubiquitous as the number of South Asian students increased at colleges and universities. Participants of the study explain that their first exposure to the term "brown" occurred on college campuses as they came in contact with other South Asians. Second-generation South Asians deploy the term "brown" in many interesting and revealing ways. Three of the most common ways are: phenotypically, culturally, and politically.

Phenotypically

One of the most striking ways South Asians indicate their use of "brown" is in association with their skin color, unlike with other ethno-racial identifiers. For example, Ritu, a Bengali American, explains why she uses "brown:"

> "I don't know. Everyone uses it. But I think it makes sense. We are brown (pointing to her arm). You can't deny that. We're not white and we're not black."

Similarly, other participants also indicate the obvious color of their skin as the reasoning behind the use of "brown." The interview with Ritu demonstrates that color matters in US racial hierarchy. Participants seem to indicate that to find their place in the United States, they had to identify along the color line. "Brown" seems like an appropriate identifier that accurately represented their nonwhite and nonblack complexions. They do not want to identify with white or black. The lack of identification with black may have to do with a long history of immigrant communities distancing themselves from blackness and espousing anti-black attitudes (Prashad 2000). The distancing from whiteness is also revealing, as it may indicate a movement toward a third racial position by second-generation South Asians. This third racial position is theorized as the racial middle as part of a tri-racial system that Bonilla-Silva (2004) calls the "Latin Americanization" of the United States due to the growth of the Latinx community.

Culturally

Cultural use of "brown" is another common use among South Asians. For instance, Tahir, a Pakistani American male, uses the term "brown" interchangeably with South Asian, Pakistani, and Desi throughout the interview. When I ask him to elaborate on this use, he confirms my conclusions:

> "Brown is all of us from the subcontinent whether you are Indian or Pakistani. You know like Desi. We have similar food and cultures. I also use it because I hate it when everyone always just uses Indian as the main group. I'm not Indian. I'm Pakistani but we all look the same."

Tahir is deploying "brown" to indicate shared culture with other South Asians. At the same time, he also wants to use a more inclusive identifying term of "brown" and not the dominating identity of Indian. Finally, Tahir points out that "brown" for him is like the term Desi (a cultural term representing all South Asians).

Similar to Tahir, participants found the term "brown" to be an extension of their ethnic identity that was situated in cultural expression. Further, the sentiment is also an indicator of the influence of "multiculturalism" ideology that often shapes how groups in the United States discuss identity. Racial and ethnic identity is viewed as a contribution to the diversity but is stripped of its connection to discrimination and larger systemic inequality. For example, during the interview, when I brought up the option to make "Brown" an official census category, participants became uncomfortable and thought that such a change would be too racial and would minimize their unique heritage. The fear is not only of losing cultural heritage but also with coming to terms with the reality of racial injustice in the United States.

Politically

A smaller portion of my participants understands the utilization of "brown" as a consequence of the current political climate. Particularly, they bring up common experiences of South Asians, Middle Easterners, and Muslims post-9/11. Moreover, these participants also indicate that brown-colored groups were often confused for each other after 9/11, and thus the term "brown" can be unifying. Soniya, a young Indian American female who currently works in New York City, explains her use of "brown" after she uses it to describe her South Asian friends:

Soniya: "You know brown people. They always gossip about each other. It's so annoying!"

Modi: Who do you mean by Brown?

Soniya: "You know … Indians … Desis."

Modi: Do you include anyone else when you say Brown?

Soniya: "Just Desis … Indian, Paki, Bangla … you know."

Modi: How about blacks, Latinos, Asians, or Middle Easterners?

Soniya: (Shakes head no) "Well … maybe Middle Easterners … but that's it."

Modi: Why Middle Easterners?

Soniya: People basically think we're Middle Eastern. Look what happened after 9/11!

It is clear from Soniya's interview that the term "brown" enables boundary making with some groups being included in the "Brown" category and others being excluded. While Soniya is willing to include Middle Easterners due to how others perceive South Asians, she does not make the same allowance for Latinxs, blacks, and Asians. Other participants did expand the term to include Latinxs and sometimes blacks, but this, as one Bangladeshi college student explained, is based on "who else was around." He clarifies:

"You can't say brown for only South Asian when you are with a diverse group of people. It's just easier to say us all brown folks."

Participants agree that "brown" could at times be synonymous with the term "people of color." The use of "brown" then may signal a changing understanding of South Asian positionality in the United States and changing relations with other communities of color. The term seems to be a response to the traditional black/white dichotomy. The dichotomy does not capture the experiences of brown-skinned people. Participants also contend "brown" is an applicable identifier, since brown-skinned people are routinely confused for each other.

Conclusion

Overall, second-generation South Asians understand their racial and ethnic identity through a mix of cultural, geographical, and phenotypical frameworks. Skin color has a growing relevance in South Asian identity with the use of the identifying term "brown." This pattern of identification diverges from previous research as it shows a move away from the black/white binary and toward a racial middle identity. It also shows that nonblack and nonwhite children of immigrants are identifying in ways different from their first-generation parents.

Second-generation South Asians often utilize "brown" as an all-inclusive concept to represent the cultural similarities across groups and link the groups under a common umbrella term. The cultural use of "brown" allows participants to engage in a multicultural framework of identity and distance themselves from the issues of race in the United States.

Phenotypic use of "brown" is also common among second-generation South Asians. Participants link their brown skin color with their use of "brown" as something logical, obvious, and relevant. They point out that their brown skin color does play a role in how they identify themselves and others. While some shy away from making "brown" a racial category, others find the term to be useful in locating themselves in the US racial hierarchy.

A smaller portion of my participants understands "brown" as a political identity that allows them to be in solidarity with other people of color. The responses range from including only some non–South Asian groups to all people of color. Participants also see "brown" as a political outcome of anti-Muslim racialized backlash against many immigrant communities post-9/11.

The use of "brown" by South Asians signals both a shift in understanding racial identity as well as a replication of cultural identity that often creates distance from racialization. The role of the multicultural framework, the growth of the Latinx community, and the racialization post-9/11 all are relevant for understanding the deployment of "brown" by second-generation South Asians.

Discussion Questions

1. Based on the reflections presented in this chapter, what are the differences and similarities between ethnic identity and racial identity?

2. Reflect on the ways larger sociopolitical events, processes, or ideologies connect with your racial and ethnic identity.

3. What are the pros and cons of including "Brown" as a racial category in the US Census?

Resources

Chou, Rosalind, and Joe R. Feagin. 2008. *The Myth of the Model Minority: Asian Americans Facing Racism.* New York: Routledge.

Dowling, Julie. 2014. *Mexican Americans and the Question of Race.* Austin: University of Texas Press.

Glenn, Evelyn. 2009. *Shades of Difference: Why Skin Color Matters.* Palo Alto, CA: Stanford University Press.

Ocampo, Anthony. 2016. *The Latinos of Asia: How Filipino Americans Break the Rules of Race.* Palo Alto, CA: Stanford University Press.

References

Bonilla-Silva, Eduardo. 2004. "From Bi-racial to Tri-racial: Towards a New System of Racial Stratification in the USA." *Ethnic and Racial Studies* 27(6):931–50.

Dhingra, Pawan. 2007. *Managing Multicultural Lives: Asian American Professionals and the Challenge of Multiple Identities.* Palo Alto, CA: Stanford University Press.

Dowling, Julie. 2014. *Mexican Americans and the Question of Race.* Austin: University of Texas Press.

Du Bois, William Edward Burghardt. 1994 (1903). *The Souls of Black Folk.* Unabridged edition. New York: Dover Publications.

Esposito, J., and I. Kalin (eds.). 2011. *Islamophobia: The Challenges of Pluralism in the 21st Century.* New York: Oxford University Press.

Garcia, Denia, and Maria Abascal. 2015. "Colored Perceptions: Racially Distinctive Names and Assessments of Skin Color." *American Behavioral Scientist* 60(4):420–41.

Garner, Steve, and Saher Selod. 2015. "The Racialization of Muslims: Empirical Studies of Islamophobia." *Critical Sociology* 41(1):9–19.

Golash-Boza, Tanya, and William Darity Jr. 2008. "Latino Racial Choices: The Effects of Skin Colour and Discrimination on Latinos' and Latinas' Racial Self-identifications." *Ethnic and Racial Studies* 31(5):899–934.

Joseph, Tiffany. 2015. *Race on the Move: Brazilian Migrants and the Global Reconstruction of Race*. Palo Alto, CA: Stanford University Press.

Joshi, Khyati Y. 2006. *New Roots in America's Sacred Ground: Religion, Race, and Ethnicity in Indian America*. New Brunswick, NJ: Rutgers University Press.

Koshy, Susan. 1998. "Category Crisis: South Asian Americans and Questions of Race and Ethnicity." *Diaspora: A Journal of Transnational Studies* 7(3):285–320.

Kurien, Prema A. 2003. "To Be or Not to Be South Asian: Contemporary Indian American Politics." *Journal of Asian American Studies* 6(3):261–88.

Kurien, Prema. 2007. *A Place at the Multicultural Table: The Development of an American Hinduism*. New Brunswick, NJ: Rutgers University Press.

Modood, Tariq. 2013. *Multiculturalism*. London, UK: John Wiley & Sons.

Ocampo, Anthony. 2016. *The Latinos of Asia: How Filipino Americans Break the Rules of Race*. Palo Alto, CA: Stanford University Press.

Omi, Michael, and Howard Winant. 2014. *Racial Formation in the United States*. New York: Routledge.

Portes, Alejandro, and Rubén G. Rumbaut. 2006. *Immigrant America: A Portrait*. Berkeley: University of California Press.

Prashad, Vijay. 2000. *The Karma of Brown Folk*. Minneapolis: University of Minnesota Press.

Purkayastha, Bandana. 2005. *Negotiating Ethnicity: Second-Generation South Asian Americans Traverse a Transnational World*. New Brunswick, NJ: Rutgers University Press.

Quiros, Laura, and Beverly Araujo Dawson. 2013. "The Color Paradigm: The Impact of Colorism on the Racial Identity and Identification of Latinas." *Journal of Human Behavior in the Social Environment* 23(3):287–97.

Roth, Wendy. 2012. *Race Migrations: Latinos and the Cultural Transformation of Race*. Palo Alto, CA: Stanford University Press.

Schwartzman, Luisa Farah. 2007. "Does Money Whiten? Intergenerational Changes in Racial Classification in Brazil." *American Sociological Review* 72(6):940–63.

Reading 2.2 Implicit Bias

Lisa A. Harrison, California State University

Keywords: implicit bias, explicit bias, prejudice, stereotype, discrimination, shooter bias

Introduction

Imagine you are driving home one evening. You are exhausted after taking your last exam. You are hungry and tired. While waiting at a stoplight, you see two black teenage boys walking on the sidewalk by your car. Without thinking, you check the locks and roll up the windows. When the light turns green, you watch the boys' faces in the rearview mirror as you drive away.

What just happened? What caused you to behave as you did? Racism? No, of course not! You're enlightened. You're an egalitarian. You are not a racist! Besides, you didn't do anything wrong. You didn't hurt anyone. You decide to put it out of your mind. It just didn't mean anything. Nothing at all.

This chapter briefly reviews what scientists have learned about implicit bias. The chapter begins by explaining how explicit and implicit bias differ. Three major characteristics of implicit bias are identified, and there is a discussion of how implicit biases influence health care decisions. Examples of strategies to reduce implicit bias are provided. These include an empirically tested intervention that has been used successfully by organizations and techniques individuals can practice to reduce their implicit biases.

How Are Explicit and Implicit Bias Different?

Negative attitudes toward social groups contain three components. *Prejudice* is the evaluation (usually negative) and emotional responses toward a social group and its members. *Stereotypes* are beliefs about the traits, attributes, and behaviors of a social group and its members. *Discrimination* is the unfair treatment of individuals and groups based upon their group membership. *Explicit bias* refers to overt prejudicial evaluations, stereotypes, and discriminatory behaviors that are consciously expressed and experienced. Because explicit bias is consciously experienced, it can also be deliberately hidden when social cues or motivational goals prohibit their expression. For example, even if Justine is explicitly biased toward older people, she can hide her explicit biases when visiting her grandparents (at least for short periods of time) because she hopes to inherit their money.

Implicit biases are prejudicial evaluations, stereotypes, and discriminatory behaviors that people may not be aware of and may not be able to control. They differ from explicit biases in three ways (Dovidio and Gaertner 2010). First, implicit biases tend to be automatically activated upon perception of a social group or its members. Second, implicit biases are unintentionally activated and used. Third, we are often unaware of how implicit biases influence us. These processes are exemplified when Justine meets her sister's new boyfriend. Her implicit race bias is automatically activated when she realizes he is Latino. Throughout the evening, Justine's body language and facial expressions are unintentionally negative toward him, but she is not consciously aware of this. She thinks she was friendly to him. Her implicit race bias was automatically activated, it unintentionally influenced her behavior, and she was unaware of how it influenced her behavior.

It is tempting to think of explicit and implicit bias as two different forms of a singular negative attitude, but research does not support this notion. The relationship between implicit and explicit biases is small to moderate (Cameron, Brown-Iannuzzi, and Payne 2012; Cunningham, Nezlek, and Banaji 2004). Also, it seems that different brain structures are associated with implicit and explicit bias. Implicit bias is associated with the activation of the amygdala, an area of the brain linked to emotions. In contrast, explicit bias is associated with the activation of the prefrontal cortex, an area of the brain linked to higher cognitive processes such as decision-making and planning (Cunningham et al. 2004). Because implicit and explicit bias appear to be two separate constructs, it is possible for a person to be explicitly non-biased and have strong implicit biases.

Development of Implicit Bias

One basic way that implicit biases develop is through *mere exposure* (Zajonc 1968). Research suggests that repeated exposure to members of a social category via school, TV, movies, and so forth tends to increase liking for that group. Thus, if whites are overwhelmingly represented in a culture, it is likely that individuals' repeated exposure to whites will lead to the development of an implicit pro-White bias relative to attitudes toward other ethnic/racial groups. Thus, representation—or the lack thereof—matters in regard to the development of implicit biases.

Implicit biases also form through associative learning, which is the process of linking positive or negative associations to previously neutral stimuli (Banaji and Heiphetz 2010). Children are not born with implicit group biases, but if they are repeatedly exposed to media representations of a group as violent and lazy, they begin to associate these negative characteristics to all members of that group. Associative learning is an important process in the development of implicit biases, especially among people who have limited interactions with diverse groups of people.

Implicit biases also develop in very young children via three social learning processes, which are direct teaching, observational learning, and vicarious learning (Kite and Whitley 2016). Direct teaching of bias occurs in different ways, such as when children learn to gain parents' approval by playing with children from certain groups and avoiding children from other groups. Children indirectly acquire implicit bias via observational learning when they watch and imitate how different social groups are treated by parents, peers, and the media. Lastly, children indirectly acquire implicit biases when they see others receive approval for expressing their explicit biases. For example, hearing a father tell sexist jokes that make others laugh might serve as the foundation for implicit sexism.

Effects of Implicit Bias

Implicit biases can profoundly influence our judgments and behaviors. For example, an experimental study demonstrated that white participants were quicker to identify guns paired with photos of five-year black boys and adult black men than guns paired with similar white boys and men. This suggests that implicit racial biases link violence to black men and young boys (Todd, Thiem, and Neel 2016). Likewise, simulation studies demonstrating the "shooter bias" indicate that people are quicker to shoot black criminal suspects (Plant, Goplen, and Kunstman 2011) and Arab Muslim suspects than they are to shoot white suspects (Essien et al. 2017). The shooter bias has been found among college students and police officers (Plant and Peruche 2005), appears to be unrelated to explicit racial prejudice, and is likely to occur even when people consciously try to avoid it (Payne 2006).

Implicit biases also influence whom to vote for (Payne et al. 2010), whom to hire (Ziegert and Hanges 2005), and what products to buy (Dempsey and Mitchell 2010). Implicit biases also influence eye contact (Dovidio et al. 1997), posture (Meadors and Murray 2014), and other forms of nonverbal behaviors that suggest unconscious hostility and dislike (Dovidio, Kawakami, and Gaertner 2002). Implicit biases are also related to the reported use of slurs, exclusion, physical harm to others, and the willingness to defund programs that help ethnic minorities (Rudman and Ashmore 2007).

Effects of Implicit Bias on Health Care Judgments

Substantial research has been conducted examining whether implicit biases influence health care providers' decisions and behaviors. Findings suggest that medical clinicians are just as likely to be implicitly biased as the general population and that patient race/ethnicity are likely to bias clinicians' judgments (FitzGerald and Hurst

2017). A study of primarily white physicians found that at least 70 percent of them showed some level of implicit bias against Latinos and blacks, even though they reported explicitly nonbiased racial attitudes (Blair et al. 2013a). Consistent findings emerged in a large-scale study of almost half a million Americans, including 2,535 medical doctors, which had participants complete an implicit racial bias test (Sabin et al. 2009). As shown in Figure 2.1, all test takers showed implicit bias for whites relative to blacks. In addition, white, Asian American, and Latino medical doctors showed strong implicit bias toward whites relative to blacks. This implicit race bias was greater among men doctors than women doctors, and they often contribute to impaired physician-patient relations (Penner et al. 2010). Physicians and nurse practitioners with stronger implicit race bias are rated by black patients as being patient centered and caring (Cooper et al. 2012) and as providing lower quality of care (Blair et al. 2013b). This is important because patients are less likely to have positive health outcomes when they believe their physicians are not patient centered (Kim et al. 2007).

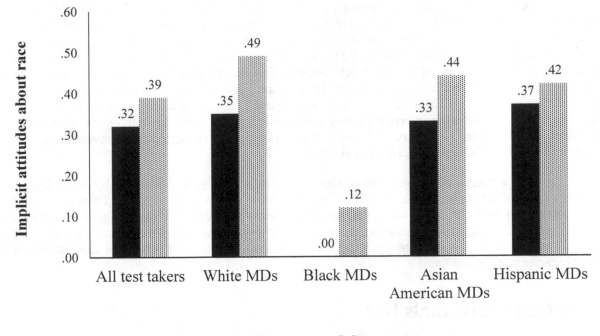

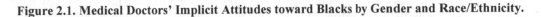

Figure 2.1. Medical Doctors' Implicit Attitudes toward Blacks by Gender and Race/Ethnicity.

The implicit measure ranged from -2 to +2, with zero indicating no bias. A positive mean indicates a preference for whites relative to blacks.

Sabin, Janice A., Brian A. Nosek, Anthony G. Greenwald, and Frederick P. Rivara. 2009. "Physicians' Implicit and Explicit Attitudes About Race by MD Race, Ethnicity, and Gender." *Journal of Health Care for the Poor and Underserved* 20(3):896–913.

Although implicit biases tend to operate automatically, without intent and awareness, it is not inevitable that clinicians' implicit biases will lead to neglectful or even harmful health care. A study that found implicit race bias among the majority of physicians in the research sample also found no evidence of significant differences in physicians' treatment of white, black, and Latino patients with hypertension (Blair et al. 2014). It was theorized that physicians' implicit race biases did not affect patient care because 1) over a three-year period, strong relationships had developed between physicians and their patients; 2) there was significant diversity among primary team members, which served as checks and balances against biased treatment; and 3) there were organizational guidelines that mandated the systematic care of patients, regardless of their race/ethnicity. Thus, although the majority of physicians showed evidence of implicit race bias, they were unlikely to explicitly harm their patients as a result of their implicit bias. The implication of this research is that organizations can develop systems to effectively combat negative effects of implicit bias.

Reducing Implicit Bias

Recently, Patricia Devine has developed a promising intervention designed to reduce implicit bias (Devine et al. 2012). The intervention is based upon the theory that implicit bias is a "habit" that can be broken by motivated people who are a) willing to learn how their implicit biases influence them; and b) practice bias-reduction strategies. In Devine's intervention, people complete a measure of implicit bias and receive feedback about their implicit biases. Next, they participate in an interactive narrated slideshow that educates them about implicit bias, how it is measured, and how it affects racial and ethnic minorities. They are taught implicit bias can be reduced or even eliminated, with motivated awareness and the effortful practice of five bias-reduction strategies. These strategies teach them to 1) replace their stereotypes with non-stereotypical thoughts; 2) use counter-stereotypic imaging by replacing stereotypical thoughts with examples of people who prove stereotype to be inaccurate; 3) think about racial/ethnic minorities as individuals rather than as group members; 4) practice taking the perspective of targets of implicit bias; and 5) seek out more social contact with ethnic/racial minorities. Participants in the intervention also generate realistic ways they can integrate bias-reduction strategies into their lives. Evidence suggests that two weeks after the intervention, people 1) were more likely to notice bias when they saw it; 2) were more likely to identify bias as wrong; and 3) interacted more frequently with racial/ethnic minorities. Two years after the intervention, they were more likely to think stereotyping was wrong and were more likely to publicly say so (Devine et al. 2012). Recent research has replicated this intervention with a larger sample and found similar results (Forscher et al. 2017).

Devine theorizes that her intervention reduces the negative effects of implicit bias by increasing people's sensitivity to the effects of implicit and explicit biases (Devine et al. 2012). This increased concern about biases in oneself and others is associated with a heightened sensitivity to discrimination and a greater willingness to speak out against discrimination. Although the habit-breaking intervention may not eliminate the root underlying processes associated with implicit biases, it can change beliefs about implicit biases and subsequently reduce biased judgments and behavior.

What Can Individuals Do?

How can you reduce your implicit biases? Well, if you have access to a training workshop on implicit bias at your school or within your community, you should go to it. Learning about implicit bias can be an effective intervention. If you do not have access to a training program, consider creating one for yourself by learning more about implicit biases and how they can influence you. Use the resources at the end of this chapter to enhance your understanding of your implicit biases, how they developed, and the harm they can do. You can also practice bias-reduction strategies on a daily basis, which can weaken implicit biases over time. Remember, implicit biases are acquired and strengthened through mere exposure, associative learning, and social learning processes. Egalitarian implicit attitudes can also be strengthened by a) increasing your social interactions with diverse groups of people; b) learning about positive aspects and accomplishments of diverse groups of people; c) consciously reflecting on instances in which implicit biases may have influenced you and developing strategies to avoid such responses in the future; d) consciously thinking about people as individuals, rather than as group members; and e) trying to understand the experiences of other social groups (Kite and Whitley 2016). These strategies are very similar to those recommended in Devine's prejudice habit-breaking intervention. Remember, although implicit biases operate automatically, unintentionally, and generally outside our awareness, that does not mean they cannot be altered or inhibited (Monteith, Parker, and Burns 2016). Just like people learn to lower their blood pressure by practicing good health behaviors, they can also learn to inhibit their implicit biases by practicing bias-reduction strategies.

Conclusion

Implicit bias can unintentionally how we interact with others. Learning about implicit biases, reflecting on their potential to influence us, and practicing bias-reduction strategies can go a long way in freeing us from the negative tentacles of implicit bias. In addition, egalitarian policies and procedures can reduce the impact of implicit biases in organizations and institutions.

Let's now return to our example at the beginning of the chapter in which you imagined your response to seeing two black teenage boys walking by your car. Use this experience as an opportunity to reflect on the possible causes of your behavior. Is it possible your spontaneous response of checking the door locks and rolling up the windows was caused by implicit race bias? Would you have behaved differently if the boys had been white? What if they had been girls? Adults? Nuns? Was your behavior consistent with your explicit racial attitudes? Use such experiences as opportunities to practice bias-reduction strategies. For example, you can consciously think about black boys you know who are gentle and kind. Remember the look in the boys' eyes when they saw your responses to them and consider how it must feel to be automatically perceived as a threat. If you are motivated to put in the work required to reduce and/or eliminate your implicit biases, perhaps you will eventually replace them with implicit egalitarian attitudes.

Discussion Questions

1. The **Project Implicit** website lets you assess your implicit biases toward various social groups. Go to the website and take several implicit bias tests. How do your results compare to others who have taken the test? Describe your reaction to your results. The website URL is https://implicit.harvard.edu/implicit/takeatest.html

2. Imagine you are a parent and want your child to be as free as possible from implicit biases. How can you use your understanding of the three major developmental processes involved in implicit bias development to reduce the development of implicit biases?

3. Research on the shooter bias indicates race and gender influence whether a person is likely to shoot a criminal suspect. Develop a plan to reduce the likelihood the shooter bias will influence police officers' reactions to criminal suspects based upon what you have learned about implicit bias.

4. If implicit biases are automatic, unintentional, and generally operate outside of conscious awareness, should a police officer be convicted of murder or manslaughter if the officer shoots a black male suspect after mistakenly perceiving the suspect had a gun in his hand? Explain your answer.

Exploratory Research Questions

1. Describe how individual characteristics (e.g., ethnicity, age, gender, socioeconomic status) might influence different kinds of implicit bias and individuals' motivation to eliminate their implicit biases.

2. Research suggests motivation to inhibit prejudice is essential for the implementation of bias-reduction strategies. How do physical states such as hunger and fatigue influence motivation to engage in these strategies and whether the strategies are successfully implemented?

3. Implicit bias reduction strategies have not been systematically tested on people with strong explicit bias. If explicitly biased people could be convinced to practice bias-reduction strategies, explain how their implicit and explicit biases might change.

References

Banaji, Mahzarin R., and Larisa Heiphetz. 2010. "Attitudes." Pp. 353–93 in *Handbook of Social Psychology*. Vol. 2. 5th ed., edited by Susan T. Fiske, Daniel T. Gilbert, and Gardner Lindzey. Hoboken, NJ: John Wiley & Sons Inc.

Blair, Irene V., Edward P. Havranek, David W. Price, Rebecca Hanratty, Diane L. Fairclough, Tillman Farley, Holen K. Hirsh, and John F. Steiner. 2013a. "Assessment of Biases Against Latinos and African Americans Among Primary Care Providers and Community Members." *American Journal of Public Health* 103(1):92–98.

Blair, Irene V., John F. Steiner, Diane L. Fairclough, Rebecca Hanratty, David W. Price, Holen K. Hirsh, Leslie A. Wright, Michael Bronsert, Elhum Karimkhani, David J. Magid, and Edward P. Havranek. 2013b. "Clinicians' Implicit Ethnic/Racial Bias and Perceptions of Care Among Black and Latino Patients." *Annals of Family Medicine* 11(1):43–52.

Blair, Irene V., John F. Steiner, Rebecca Hanratty, David W. Price, Diane L. Fairclough, Stacie L. Daugherty, Michael Bronsert, David J. Magid, and Edward P. Havranek. 2014. "An Investigation of Associations between Clinicians' Ethnic or Racial Bias and Hypertension Treatment, Medication Adherence and Blood Pressure Control." *Journal of General Internal Medicine* 29(7):987–95.

Cameron, C. Daryl, Jazmin L. Brown-Iannuzzi, and B. Keith Payne. 2012. "Sequential priming measures of implicit social cognition: A meta-analysis of associations with behavior and explicit attitudes." *Personality and Social Psychology Review* 16(4):330–50.

Cooper, Lisa A., Debra L. Roter, Kathryn A. Carson, Mary Catherine Beach, Janice A. Sabin, Anthony G. Greenwald, and Thomas S. Inui. 2012. "The Associations of Clinicians' Implicit Attitudes About Race with Medical Visit Communication and patient Ratings of Interpersonal Care." *American Journal of Public Health* 102(5):979–87.

Cunningham, William A., Marcia K. Johnson, Carol L. Raye, J. Chris Gatenby, John C. Gore, and Mahzarin R. Banaji. 2004. "Separable Neural Components in the Processing of Black and White Faces." *Psychological Science* 15(12):806–13.

Cunningham, William A., John B. Nezlek, and Mahzarin R. Banaji. 2004. "Implicit and Explicit Ethnocentrism: Revisiting the Ideologies of Prejudice." *Personality and Social Psychology Bulletin* 30(10):1332–46.

Dempsey, Melanie A., and Andrew A. Mitchell. 2010. "The Influence of Implicit Attitudes on Choice When Consumers Are Confronted with Conflicting Attribute Information." *Journal of Consumer Research* 37(4):614–25.

Devine, Patricia G., Patrick S. Forscher, Anthony J. Austin, and William T.L. Cox. 2012. "Long-term Reduction in Implicit Race Bias: A Prejudice Habit-breaking Intervention." *Journal of Experimental Social Psychology* 48(6):1267–78.

Dovidio, John F., and Samuel L. Gaertner. 2010. "Intergroup bias." Pp. 1084–121 in *Handbook of Social Psychology*. Vol. 2. 5th ed., edited by Susan T. Fiske, Daniel T. Gilbert, and Gardner Lindzey. Hoboken, NJ: John Wiley & Sons Inc.

Dovidio, John F., Kerry Kawakami, and Samuel L. Gaertner. 2002. "Implicit and Explicit Prejudice and Interracial Interaction." *Journal of Personality and Social Psychology* 82(1):62–68.

Dovidio, John F., Kerry Kawakami, Craig Johnson, Brenda Johnson, and Adaiah Howard. 1997. "On the Nature of Prejudice: Automatic and Controlled Processes." *Journal of Experimental Social Psychology* 33(5):510–40.

Essien, Iniobong, Marleen Stelter, Felix Kalbe, Andreas Koehler, Jana Mangels, and Stefanie Meliß. 2017. "The Shooter Bias: Replicating the Classic Effect and Introducing a Novel Paradigm." *Journal of Experimental Social Psychology* 70:41–47.

FitzGerald, Chloë, and Samia Hurst. 2017. "Implicit Bias in Healthcare Professionals: A Systematic Review." *BMC Medical Ethics* 18.

Forscher, Patrick S., Chelsea Mitamura, Emily L. Dix, William T.L. Cox, and Patricia G. Devine. 2017. "Breaking the Prejudice Habit: Mechanisms, Timecourse, and Longevity." *Journal of Experimental Social Psychology.*

Kim, Theresa W., Jeffrey H. Samet, Debbie M. Cheng, Michael R. Winter, Dana Gelb Safran, and Richard Saitz. 2007. "Primary Care Quality and Addiction Severity: A Prospective Cohort Study." *Health Services Research* 42(2):755–72.

Kite, M.E., and B.E. Whitley. 2016. *Psychology of Prejudice and Discrimination.* 3rd ed. UK: Taylor & Francis.

Meadors, Joshua D., and Carolyn B. Murray. 2014. "Measuring Nonverbal Bias through Body Language Responses to Stereotypes." *Journal of Nonverbal Behavior* 38(2):209–29.

Monteith, Margo J., Laura R. Parker, and Mason D. Burns. 2016. "The Self-regulation of Prejudice." Pp. 409–32 in *Handbook of Prejudice, Stereotyping, and Discrimination.* 2nd ed. Edited by Todd D. Nelson. New York: Psychology Press.

Payne, B. Keith. 2006. "Weapon Bias: Split-Second Decisions and Unintended Stereotyping." *Current Directions in Psychological Science* 15(6):287–91.

Payne, B. Keith, Jon A. Krosnick, Josh Pasek, Yphtach Lelkes, Omair Akhtar, and Trevor Tompson. 2010. "Implicit and Explicit Prejudice in the 2008 American Presidential Election." *Journal of Experimental Social Psychology* 46(2):367–74.

Penner, Louis A., John F. Dovidio, Tessa V. West, Samuel L. Gaertner, Terrance L. Albrecht, Rhonda K. Dailey, and Tsveti Markova. 2010. "Aversive Racism and Medical Interactions with Black Patients: A Field Study." *Journal of Experimental Social Psychology* 46(2):436–40.

Plant, E. Ashby, Joanna Goplen, and Jonathan W. Kunstman. 2011. "Selective Responses to Threat: The Roles of Race and Gender in Decisions to Shoot." *Personality and Social Psychology Bulletin* 37(9):1274–81.

Plant, E. Ashby, and B. Michelle Peruche. 2005. "The Consequences of Race for Police Officers' Responses to Criminal Suspects." *Psychological Science* 16(3):180–83.

Rudman, Laurie A., and Richard D. Ashmore. 2007. "Discrimination and the Implicit Association Test." *Group Processes & Intergroup Relations* 10(3):359–72.

Sabin, Janice A., Brian A. Nosek, Anthony G. Greenwald, and Frederick P. Rivara. 2009. "Physicians' Implicit and Explicit Attitudes About Race by MD Race, Ethnicity, and Gender." *Journal of Health Care for the Poor and Underserved* 20(3):896–913.

Todd, Andrew R., Kelsey C. Thiem, and Rebecca Neel. 2016. "Does Seeing Faces of Young Black Boys Facilitate the Identification of Threatening Stimuli?" *Psychological Science* 27(3):384–93.

Zajonc, Robert B. 1968. "Attitudinal effects of mere exposure." *Journal of Personality and Social Psychology* 9(2, Pt. 2):1–27.

Ziegert, Jonathan C., and Paul J. Hanges. 2005. "Employment Discrimination: The Role of Implicit Attitudes, Motivation, and a Climate for Racial Bias." *Journal of Applied Psychology* 90(3):553–62.

Further Resources

General Information

Banaji, Mahzarin R., and Anthony G. Greenwald. 2013. *Blindspot: Hidden Biases of Good People*. New York: Delacorte Press.

Staats, Cheryl, Kelly Capatosto, Robin A. Wright, and Victoria W. Jackson. 2016. "State of the Science: Implicit Bias Review 2016." Kirwan Institute for the Study of Race and Ethnicity, Ohio State University. Retrieved June 1, 2017 (http://kirwaninstitute.osu.edu/my-product/2016-state-of-the-science-implicit-bias-review/).

The Project Implicit website. https://implicit.harvard.edu/implicit/takeatest.html

Implicit Bias and Health Care

Kang, Jerry. 2015. "Implicit Bias Within Medicine." Retrieved June 5, 2017 (https://vimeo.com/146838436).

Roberts, Dorothy. 2015. "The Problem with Race-based Medicine." Retrieved June 5, 2017 (https://www.ted.com/talks/dorothy_roberts_the_problem_with_race_based_medicine).

Reducing Implicit Bias

Forscher, Patrick S., Chelsea Mitamura, Emily L. Dix, William T.L. Cox, and Patricia G. Devine. 2017. "Breaking the Prejudice Habit: Mechanisms, Timecourse, and Longevity." *Journal of Experimental Social Psychology* 72:133-146.

Nordell, Jessica. 2017. "Is This How Discrimination Ends?" *Atlantic*. Retrieved June 6, 2017 (https://www.theatlantic.com/science/archive/2017/05/unconscious-bias-training/525405/?utm_source=nl-atlantic-daily-050817).

Understanding Racial-ethnic Disparities in Health: Sociological Contributions

David R. Williams[1] and Michelle Sternthal[1]

SOCIAL STRUCTURE AND RACE

Sociological research has long explored the role of social structure and social stratification as a key determinant of health. Social structure refers to enduring patterns of social life that shape an individual's attitudes and beliefs, behaviors and

Table 2. Years of Life Expectancy at Age 25, United States

Group	White	Black	Difference
All (1998)[a]	53.4	48.4	5.0
By Education (1988–1998)[b]			
0–12 Years	50.1	47.0	3.1
12 years	54.1	49.9	4.2
Some College	55.2	50.9	4.3
College Graduate	56.5	52.3	4.2
Difference	6.4	5.3	

[a]Murphy 2000.
[b]Braveman et al. 2010, National Longitudinal Mortality Study 1988–1998.

actions, and material and psychological resources. Among the social structures investigated within sociology, social class, usually operationalized as socioeconomic status (SES), has proven particularly relevant for understanding racial disparities in health. In a seminal study in the 1840s, Engels ([1844] 1984) showed how life expectancy in Liverpool, England varied by the occupation of the residents. Moreover, he showed how specific exposures in both occupational and residential environments were related to the elevated risk of particular diseases. More recent sociological research has found that SES is inversely associated with high quality health care, stress, exposure to social and physical toxins, social support, and healthy behaviors. Accordingly, SES remains one of the strongest known determinants of variations in health status (Williams and Collins 1995).

Sociological work on class informs the study of racial disparities in health, because, as Du Bois ([1899] 1967) noted at the turn of the century, race is strongly intertwined with SES. Recent research continues to find that SES differences among the races account for a substantial component of the racial-ethnic differences in health (Hayward et al. 2000; Williams and Collins 1995; Hummer 1996). However, sociologists have emphasized that race and SES are two related but distinct systems of social ordering that jointly contribute to health risks (Navarro 1990; Williams and Collins 1995). Accordingly, attention needs to be given to both race-based and class-based factors that undergird racial health disparities.

Table 2 illustrates the complex relationship between race and SES by presenting national data on life expectancy at age across categories of race and education. It shows that there is a five-year racial difference in life expectancy at age 25, but an even larger difference within each race by education. It also indicates that the racial differences in health cannot be simply reduced to SES, because there are residual racial differences at every level of education. These data illustrate the notion of the potential "double jeopardy" facing those in nondominant racial groups who experience health risks associated with both their stigmatized racial status and low SES (Ferraro and Farmer 1996). The life expectancy data at age 25 also reveal that the racial gap in life expectancy is greater at the higher levels of education compared to the lowest level. This is generally consistent with the "diminishing returns" hypothesis, which argues that racial minorities receive declining health returns as SES increases (Farmer and Ferraro 2005). This pattern exists for some but not all health outcomes. Sociologists have also shown that race and SES can combine with gender and other social statuses in complex ways to create patterns of interaction and intersectionality (Schulz and Mullings 2006).

Sociological work on social class has also contributed to our understanding of racial disparities by underscoring the multidimensionality of SES indicators (Hauser 1994). Sociologists have shown that it requires assessing the multiple dimensions of SES to fully characterize its contribution to racial disparities in health. Moreover, all of the indicators of SES are nonequivalent across race. For example, compared to whites, blacks and some other racial minorities have lower income at every level of education; less wealth (net assets) at every level of income; higher rates of unemployment at all levels of education; higher exposure to occupational hazards, even after adjusting for job experience and education; and less purchasing power because of higher costs of goods and services in their residential contexts (Williams and Collins 1995). Sociological research has also highlighted the role of SES at the community level, as captured by neighborhood-level markers of economic hardship, social disorder, and concentrated disadvantage (Wilson 1990; Massey and Denton 1993). Other sociological research has called attention to large racial-ethnic inequalities in wealth, and they have documented that these gaps reflect, at least in part, the historical legacy of institutional discrimination (Conley 1999; Oliver and Shapiro 2006). While income captures the flow of economic resources (such as wages) into the household, wealth captures the economic reserves that are reflected in savings, home equity, and other financial assets. National data reveal that, for every dollar of wealth that white individuals have, blacks have 9 cents and Hispanics have 12 cents (Orzechowski and Sepielli 2003). These striking disparities exist at every level of income. For example, for every dollar of wealth that poor whites in the lowest quintile of income have, poor blacks have one penny and poor Latinos have two pennies.

RACISM AND HEALTH

Sociological research has also shed important light on how factors linked to race contribute to racial differences in health. This work has identified multiple ways in which racism initiates and sustains health disparities (Williams and Mohammed 2009). This research explicitly draws on the larger sociology literature on racism and conceptualizes it as a multilevel construct, encompassing institutional and individual discrimination, racial prejudice and stereotypes, and internalized racism (Feagin and McKinney 2003; Bonilla-Silva 1997; Massey and Denton 1993).

At the institutional level, sociological research has underscored the role of residential racial segregation as a primary institutional mechanism of racism and a fundamental cause of racial disparities in health (Massey and Denton 1993; LaVeist 1989; Williams and Collins 2001), and it has helped shape local and federal policies. Sociologists have documented how segregation produces the concentration of poverty, social disorder, and social isolation, and how it creates pathogenic conditions in residential environments (Massey 2004; Schulz et al. 2002; Williams and Collins 2001). For example, an examination of the 171 largest U.S. cities found that the worst urban context in which white individuals lived was better than the average context of black neighborhoods (Sampson and Wilson 1995). These differences in neighborhood quality and community conditions are driven by residential segregation by race, a neglected but enduring legacy of institutional racism in the United States. Considerable evidence suggests that, because of segregation, the residential conditions under which African Americans, American Indians, and an increasing proportion of Latinos live are distinctive from those of the rest of the population.

Sociologists have also identified multiple pathways through which segregation can adversely affect health (Morenoff 2003; Williams and Collins 2001; Schulz et al. 2002). First, segregation restricts SES attainment by limiting access to quality elementary and high school education, preparation for higher education, and job opportunities. Second, the residential conditions of concentrated poverty and social disorder created by segregation make it difficult for residents to eat nutritiously, exercise regularly, and avoid advertising for tobacco and alcohol. For example, concerns about personal safety and the lack of recreation facilities can discourage leisure time physical exercise. Third, the concentration of poverty can lead to exposure to elevated levels of financial stress and hardship, as well as other chronic and acute stressors at the individual, household, and neighborhood levels. Fourth, the weakened community and neighborhood infrastructure in segregated areas can also adversely affect interpersonal relationships and trust among neighbors. Fifth, the institutional neglect and disinvestment in poor, segregated communities contributes to increased exposure to environmental toxins, poor quality housing, and criminal victimization. Finally, segregation adversely affects both access to care and the quality of care. Research has linked residential segregation to an elevated risk of illness and death, and it has shown that segregation contributes to the racial disparities in health (Williams and Collins 2001; Acevedo-Garcia et al. 2003).

Segregation probably has a larger impact on the health of African Americans than other groups because blacks currently live under a level of segregation that is higher than that of any other immigrant group in U.S. history (Massey and Denton 1993). In addition, the association between segregation and SES varies by minority racial group. For Latinos and Asians, segregation is inversely related to household income, but segregation is high at all levels of SES for blacks (Massey 2004). The highest SES blacks (incomes greater than $50,000) in the 2000 Census were more segregated than the poorest Latinos and Asians (incomes less than $15,000) (Massey 2004).

At the individual level, experiences of discrimination have been shown to be a source of stress that adversely affect health (Williams and Mohammed 2009). Research has documented elevated levels of exposure to both chronic and acute measures of discrimination for socially stigmatized racial and immigrant groups in the United States, Europe, Africa, Australia, and New Zealand (Williams and Mohammed 2009). Exposure to discrimination has been shown to be associated with increased risk of a broad range of indicators of physical and mental illness. In addition, discrimination, like other measures of social stress, adversely affects patterns of health care utilization and adherence behaviors, and it is predictive of increased risk of using multiple substances to cope with stress, including tobacco, alcohol, and illicit drugs. Several studies have found that, in multiple national contexts, racial discrimination makes an incremental contribution to SES in accounting for observed racial disparities in health (Williams and Mohammed 2009).

While much research has focused on the pervasive role of racism in perpetuating health disparities, sociologists have also enhanced our understanding of the complex ways communities respond to discrimination. Some research has explored the harmful health effects of internalized racism, in which minority groups accept the dominant society's ideology of their inferiority (Williams and Mohammed 2009). Other research has identified cultural and psychosocial resources that foster resilience. For example, sociological research has found that religious involvement can enhance health in the face of racial discrimination, and that it can also buffer the negative effects of interpersonal discrimination on health (Bierman 2006; Ellison, Musick, and Henderson 2008). Other research indicates that ethnic identity can serve as a resource in the face of discrimination (Mossakowski 2003). Having a sense of ethnic pride and engaging in ethnic practices can enhance mental health directly, and the strength of ethnic identification can reduce the stress of discrimination on mental health.

MIGRATION AND HEALTH

Du Bois's ([1899] 1967) insight that immigrant status affects the health profile of a population is relevant to understanding contemporary patterns of health. Asians and Latinos have lower overall age-adjusted mortality rates than whites. In the 2000 U.S. Census, 67 percent of Asians and 40 percent of Latinos were foreign-born (Malone et al. 2003). Processes linked to migration make an important contribution to the observed mortality rates for these groups. National data reveal that immigrants of all racial groups have lower rates of adult and infant mortality than their native-born counterparts (Hummer et al.1999; Singh and Miller 2004; Singh and Yu 1996). Moreover, across multiple immigrant groups, with increasing exposure to American society, health tends to decline. This pattern is especially surprising for Latinos. Hispanic immigrants, especially those of Mexican background, have high rates of poverty and low levels of access to health insurance in the United States. However, their levels of health are equivalent and sometimes superior to that of the white population. This pattern has been called the Hispanic paradox (Markides and Eschbach 2005).

Sociological research has shed important light on the complex association between migration and health. First, research has shown that when a broad range of health outcomes are considered, a complex pattern emerges. For example, although Hispanics have comparable levels of infant mortality to whites, women of all Hispanic groups have a higher risk of low birth weight and prematurity than whites (Frisbie, Forbes, and Hummer 1998). Similarly, in the California Health Interview Survey (CHIS), virtually all immigrants reported better physical health status than the native-born (Williams and Mohammed 2008). In contrast, for psychological distress, many immigrant groups (most Latino groups, Pacific Islanders, and Koreans) reported worse health than the native-born, while other immigrants groups (blacks, Puerto Ricans, and Filipinos) had better health, and still others (Vietnamese, Japanese, and Chinese) did not differ from their native-born counterparts.

Second, sociological research has shown that migration status combines in complex ways with SES to affect health. Immigrant populations differ markedly in SES upon arrival in the United States (Rumbaut 1996). For example, Asian and African immigrants have markedly higher levels of education than other immigrant groups and U.S.-born whites. In contrast, immigrants from Mexico have low levels of education at the time of migration to the United States, and they face major challenges with socioeconomic mobility in the second generation. Sociological research has shown that these differences in SES affect patterns and trajectories of health in important ways. For immigrant populations largely made up of low SES individuals, traditional indicators of SES tend to be unrelated to health in the first generation, but they exhibit the expected associations in health by the second generation (Angel, Buckley, and Finch 2001). In addition, the socioeconomic status of immigrants upon arrival to the United States appears to be a determinant of the immigrant group's trajectory of health. For example, the gap in mortality between immigrants and the native-born is smaller for Asians than for whites, blacks, and Hispanics (Singh and Miller 2004), and recent national data reveal that declines in mental health for subsequent generations were less marked for Asians (Takeuchi et al. 2007) than for blacks (Williams et al. 2007b) and Hispanics (Alegria et al. 2007). Thus, although black, Latino, and Asian first generation immigrants all have lower disorder rates than the general population of blacks and whites, by the third generation the disorder rates of Latino and black but not Asian immigrants are higher (Alegria et al. 2007; Takeuchi et al. 2007; Williams et al. 2007b; Miranda et al. 2008). One of the factors contributing to the good health profile of immigrants is their selection on the basis of health. Recent sociological research has shown that differences in the SES of immigrant streams is the key determinant of variation in health selection among immigrants, with immigrants to the United States from Mexico having lower levels of positive health selection than immigrants from all other regions of the world (Akresh and Frank 2008). That is, the surprisingly good health of immigrants from Mexico is not primarily due to the better health of Mexican immigrants relative to Mexicans who did not migrate. Future research is needed to clearly identify the relative contribution of various factors to the health status of immigrants and how these may vary across various immigrant populations.

Third, sociological research has begun to characterize how risk factors and resources in immigrant populations can affect the health of immigrants. Specifically, stressors and strains associated with migration and adaptation, inadequate health care in the country of origin, and factors linked to larger social structures and context (e.g., institutional racism and interpersonal discrimination) can affect health among immigrants (Angel and Angel 2006). For example, a study of adult migrant Mexican workers in California found that stressors linked to discrimination, legal status, and problems speaking English were inversely related to self-reported measures of physical and mental health, and that they partially accounted for the declines in these health indicators with increasing years in the United States (Finch, Frank, and Vega 2004).

Finally, sociologists have also shown that a full understanding of the health effects of migration requires an assessment of the ways in which migration impacts the health of sending communities. For example, a study of infant health in two high-migration sending states in Mexico found that infants born to fathers who had migrated to the United States had a lower risk of low birth weight and prematurity compared to infants born to fathers who had never migrated (Frank 2005). This study also found that women with partners in the United States had lower levels of social support and higher levels of stress during pregnancy than women with nonimmigrant partners, but the benefits of the receipt of remittances and the practice of better health behaviors led to improved infant health outcomes. These findings highlight the importance of attending to the bidirectional effects of migration processes.

At the same time, the good health profile of immigrants highlights how much we still need to learn regarding the determinants of health and the policies needed to improve the health of all Americans and to reduce inequities in health across population groups. Especially striking and intriguing are the data for Mexican immigrants. Despite having levels of poverty comparable to those of African Americans, and despite having among the lowest levels of access to health care of any racial-ethnic group in the United States, Mexican immigrants nonetheless have levels of health that are often equivalent and sometimes superior to those of whites (Williams et al. 2010). These data emphasize that health is not primarily driven by medical care but by other social-contextual factors. However, precisely what these social determinants of health are, and how they may operate in the absence of high levels of SES, and why they change over time is less clear. Accordingly, for both research and policy reasons, there is an urgent need to identify the relevant factors that shape the association between migration status and health for Mexicans and other immigrants. Moreover, we need to identify and implement the interventions, if any, that can avert or reverse the downward health trajectory of immigrants with increasing length of stay in the United States.

CONCLUSIONS AND POLICY IMPLICATIONS

Sociological research on racial disparities in health has many important lessons for policies that seek to address social inequities in health. First, there are implications for how data on social inequalities in health are reported. For over 100 years, the U.S. public health system has routinely reported national health data by race. Instructively, although SES differences in health are typically larger than racial ones, health status differences by SES are seldom reported, and only very rarely are data on health status presented by race and SES simultaneously. Moreover, striking differences are also evident by sex. Given the patterns of social inequalities and the need to raise awareness among the public and policy makers of the magnitude of these inequities and their social determinants, we strongly urge that health data should be routinely collected, analyzed, and presented simultaneously by race, SES, and gender. This will highlight the fundamental contribution of SES to the health of the nation and to racial disparities in health. Failure to routinely present racial data by stratifying them by SES within racial groups can obscure the social factors that affect health and reinforce negative racial stereotypes. The inclusion of gender must be accompanied by research that seeks to identify how biological factors linked to sex and social factors linked to gender relate to each other and combine with race and SES to create new identities at the convergence of multiple social statuses that predict differential access to societal resources.

Sociological research indicates that race and SES combine in complex ways to affect health. There has been some debate regarding the advisability of race-specific versus universal initiatives to improve outcomes for vulnerable social groups. Extant research that clearly documents residual effects of race at every level of SES suggests that race-specific strategies are needed to improve outcomes for disadvantaged racial groups. The research reviewed here indicates that both the legacies of racism and its continued manifestations matter for health. For example, unless and until serious attention is given to addressing institutional racism such as residential segregation, reducing racial inequities in health will likely prove elusive. More research and policy attention should be given to identifying and implementing individual and, especially, institutional interventions that would be effective in reducing the levels and consequences of racism in society. For instance, state or federal policies that expand the stock of safe, stable, low-income and mixed-income housing or funding for section 8 vouchers could increase access to high-opportunity neighborhoods, while more robust enforcement of housing and financial regulations could help curb predatory lending and housing discrimination practices in minority or underserved neighborhoods.

There are many good reasons for reducing societal racism and improving the racial climate of the United States. The substantial health benefits of such interventions are an important benefit that is not widely recognized. Similarly, some evidence suggests that many of the most promising efforts to improve health are likely to widen disparities because the most advantaged social groups are likely to extract the greatest benefit from them (Mechanic 2002). Accordingly, policies are needed that improve the health of vulnerable social groups more rapidly than that of the rest of the population so that health gaps can be narrowed.

The evidence documenting that race is primarily a social rather than a biological category provides insight into the types of interventions that are needed to improve the health of disadvantaged racial populations. Effective interventions will be those that are targeted not at internal biological processes, but those that seek to improve the quality of life in the places where Americans spend most of their time: their homes, schools, workplaces, neighborhoods, and places of worship (Williams, McClellan and Rivlin 2010). For example, incentive programs for farmers' markets and full-service grocery stores, along with more stringent regulations on fast food and liquor stores, could increase availability of nutritious, affordable foods in underserved areas. Other potential interventions include (1) restructured land-use and zoning policies that reduce the concentration of environmental risks (e.g., close proximity of bus depots to schools or daycares); (2) public transportation options that encourage physical activity and minimize pollution risks; (3) the creation of public green spaces that promote walking, exercise, and community cohesion; and (4) educational initiatives aimed at equalizing access to K–12 education and higher education, improving teacher quality, raising graduation rates, and reducing the achievement gap.

Historically, sociological research on racial disparities in health has directly contributed to action and debate in the policy arena. For example, informed by Robert Bullard's groundbreaking research on environmental racism (Bullard 2000; Bullard and Johnson 2000), President Clinton signed an executive order which required federal agencies to ensure that their policies and programs did not disproportionally adversely affect minorities or the poor (Clinton 1994). More recently, an influential report co-authored by sociologist Thomas LaVeist (LaVeist, Gaskin, and Richard 2009) is helping to transform the policy debate about racial disparities in health by emphasizing that these differences in health have substantial economic costs for society. This report estimated that the medical care and lost productivity costs for racial disparities in health amount to a $309 billion annual loss to the economy. These economic costs are a compelling additional policy justification for eliminating health inequities. Sociologist David Williams also recently served as the staff director for the Robert Wood Johnson Foundation Commission to Build a Healthier America, a national bipartisan initiative focused on improving Americans' health and reducing socioeconomic and racial disparities in health. The recommendations of this commission have shaped recent federal spending and budget priorities on nutrition and investments in early developmental support for children (Williams, McClellan and Rivlin 2010).

Since health is embedded in policies far removed from traditional health policy, success will depend on integrative and collaborative efforts across multiple sectors of society that seek to leverage resources to enhance health. It was earlier noted that black women experienced a large decline in life expectancy between 1950 and 2006. This success was likely due to improvements in the SES of African American women. A review of studies of the health effects of the civil rights movement found that black women experienced larger economic gains than black men during the 1960s and 1970s. Further, the study showed that during this period of the narrowing of the income gap between blacks and whites, blacks, especially black women, experienced larger improvements in health, relatively and absolutely, than whites (Williams et al. 2008).

The magnitude and persistence of racial inequities in health call on U.S. policy makers to seriously confront what Du Bois ([1899] 1967) referred to as the "peculiar indifference" to the magnitude of human suffering that racial disparities in health reflect. Policy makers need to identify the real and perceived barriers to implementing comprehensive societal initiatives that are necessary to eliminating racial differences in health. More systematic and sustained attention should be given to how to frame such efforts in ways that resonate with dominant American ideals. Widely cherished norms of equal opportunity and the dignity of the individual could be creatively harnessed to build the needed political support to improve the health of all Americans, including those that currently live shorter and sicker lives than the rest of the population.

REFERENCES

Acevedo-Garcia, Dolores, K. A. Lochner, T. L. Osypuk, and S. V. Subramanian. 2003. "Future Directions in Residential Segregation and Health Research: A Multilevel Approach." *American Journal of Public Health* 93:215–21.

Akresh, Ilana R. and Reanne Frank. 2008. "Health Selection among New Immigrants." *American Journal of Public Health* 98:2058–64.

Alegria, Margarita, Norah Mulvaney-Day, Maria Torres, Antonio Polo, Zhun Cao, and Glorisa Canino. 2007. "Prevalence of Psychiatric Disorders across Latino Subgroups in the United States." *American Journal of Public Health* 97:68–75.

American Sociological Association. 2003. "The Importance of Collecting Data and Doing Social Scientific Research on Race." Washington, DC: American Sociological Association.

Angel, Jacqueline L. and Ronald J. Angel. 2006. "Minority Group Status and Healthful Aging: Social Structure Still Matters." *American Journal of Public Health* 96:1152–59.

Angel, Jacqueline L., Cynthia J. Buckley, and Brian Karl Finch. 2001. "Nativity and Self-Assessed Health among Pre-Retirement Age Hispanics and Non-Hispanic Whites." *International Migration Review* 35:784–803.

Bierman, Alex. 2006. "Does Religion Buffer the Effects of Discrimination on Mental Health? Differing Effects by Race." *Journal for the Scientific Study of Religion* 45:551–65.

Blauner, Robert. 1972. *Racial Oppression in America.* New York: Harper and Row.

Bonilla-Silva, Eduardo. 1997. "Rethinking Racism: Toward a Structural Interpretation." *American Sociological Review* 67:465–80.

Braveman, Paula A., Catherine Cubbin, Susan Egerter, David R. Williams, and Elsie Pamuk. 2010. "Socioeconomic Disparities in Health in the United States: What Can We Learn from the Patterns?" *American Journal of Public Health* 100:S186–S196.

Bullard, Robert. 2000. *Dumping in Dixie: Race, Class, and Environmental Quality.* Boulder, CO: Westview Press.

Bullard, Robert D. and Glenn S. Johnson. 2000. "Environmental Justice: Grassroots Activism and Its Impact on Public Policy Decision Making." *Journal of Social Issues* 56:555–78.

Clinton, William J. 1994. "Federal Actions to Address Environmental Justice in Minority Populations and Low-Income Populations." Executive Order 12898. *Federal Register* 59:FR7629.

Conley, Dalton. 1999. *Being Black, Living in the Red: Race, Wealth, and Social Policy in America*. Berkeley: University of California Press.

Cooper, Richard S., Jay S. Kaufman, and Ryk Ward. 2003. "Race and Genomics." *New England Journal of Medicine* 348:1166–70.

Du Bois and William E. B. [1899] 1967. *The Philadelphia Negro: A Social Study*. New York: Schocken Books.

Duster, Troy and Karen Garrett. 1984. "A Social Frame for Biological Knowledge." Pp. 1–40 in *Cultural Perspectives on Biological Knowledge*. Norwood, NJ: Ablex Publishing.

Ellison, Christopher G., Marc A. Musick, and Andrea K. Henderson. 2008. "Balm in Gilead: Racism, Religious Involvement, and Psychological Distress among African-American Adults." *Journal for the Scientific Study of Religion* 47:291–309.

Engels, Frederick. [1844] 1984. *The Condition of the Working Class in England*. Chicago, IL: Academy Chicago.

Farmer, Melissa M. and Kenneth F. Ferraro. 2005. "Are Racial Disparities in Health Conditional on Socioeconomic Status?" *Social Science and Medicine* 60:191–204.

Feagin, Joe R. and K. D. McKinney. 2003. *The Many Costs of Racism*. Lanham, MD: Rowman and Littlefield Publishers.

Ferraro, Kenneth F. and Melissa M. Farmer. 1996. "Double Jeopardy to Health Hypothesis for African Americans: Analysis and Critique." *Journal of Health and Social Behavior* 37:27–43.

Finch, Brain K., Reanne Frank, and William A. Vega. 2004. "Aculturation and Acculturation Stress: A Social-Epidemiological Approach to Mexican Migrant Farmworkers' Health." *International Migration Review* 38:236–62.

Frank, Reanne. 2005. "International Migration and Infant Health in Mexico." *Journal of Immigrant Health* 7:11–22.

Frank, Reanne. 2008. "Functional or Futile?: The (In)utility of Methodological Critiques of Genetic Research on Racial Disparities in Health. A Commentary on Kaufman's 'Epidemiologic Analysis of Racial/Ethnic Disparities: Some Fundamental Issues and a Cautionary Example.'" *Social Science and Medicine* 66:1670–74.

Frazier, E. Franklin. 1947. "Sociological Theory and Race Relations." *American Sociological Review* 12:265–71.

Frisbie, W. Parker, Doulgas Forbes, and Robert A. Hummer. 1998. "Hispanic Pregnancy Outcomes: Additional Evidence." *Social Science Quarterly* 79:149–69.

Guo, Guang and Michael E. Roettger. 2008. "The Integration of Genetic Propensities into Social-Control Models of Delinquency and Violence among Male Youths." *American Sociological Review* 73:543–68.

Hauser, Robert M. 1994. "Measuring Socioeconomic Status in Studies of Child Development." *Child Development* 65:1541–45.

Hayward, Mark D., Toni P. Miles, Eileen M. Crimmins, and Yu Yang. 2000. "The Significance of Socioeconomic Status in Explaining the Racial Gap in Chronic Health Conditions." *American Sociological Review* 65:910–30.

Heron, Melonie, Donna L. Hoyert, Sherry L. Murphy, Jiaquan Xu, Kenneth D. Kochanek, and Betzaida Tejada-Vera. 2009. "Deaths: Final Data for 2006." *National Vital Statistics Reports* 57:1–135.

Hummer, Robert A. 1996. "Black-White Differences in Health and Mortality: A Review and Conceptual Model." *The Sociological Quarterly* 37:105–25.

Hummer, Robert A., Richard G. Rogers, Charles B. Nam, and Felicia B. LeClere. 1999. "Race/Ethnicity, Nativity, and U.S. Adult Mortality." *Social Science Quarterly* 80:136–53.

Jaynes, Gerald David and Robin M. Williams. 1989. *A Common Destiny: Blacks and American Society*. Washington, DC: National Academy Press.

Krieger, Nancy. 1987. "Shades of Difference: Theoretical Underpinnings of the Medical Controversy on Black/White Differences in the United States, 1830–1870." *International Journal of Health Services* 17:259–78.

Kuzawa, Christopher W. and Elizabeth Sweet. 2009. "Epigenetics and the Embodiment of Race: Developmental Origins of U.S. Racial Disparities in Cardiovascular Health." *American Journal of Human Biology* 21:2–15.

LaVeist, Thomas A. 1989. "Linking Residential Segregation and Infant Mortality Race Disparity in U.S. Cities." *Sociology and Social Research* 73:90–94.

LaVeist, Thomas A., Darrell J. Gaskin, and Patrick Richard. 2009. "The Economic Burden of Health Inequalities in the United States." Washington, DC: Joint Center for Political and Economic Studies.

Link, B. G. and J. Phelan. 1995. "Social Conditions as Fundamental Causes of Disease." *Journal of Health and Social Behavior* 35:80–94.

Malone, N., K. F. Baluja, J. M. Costanzo, and C. J. Davis. 2003. *The Foreign-Born Population: 2000*. Washington, DC: U.S. Census Bureau.

Markides, Kyriakos S. and J. Coreil. 1986. "The Health of Hispanics in the Southwestern United States: An Epidemiologic Paradox." *Public Health Reports* 101:253.

Markides, Kyriakos S. and Karl Eschbach. 2005. "Aging, Migration, and Mortality: Current Status of Research on the Hispanic Paradox." *Journals of Gerontology: Series B* 60B:68–75.

Massey, Douglas S. 2004. "Segregation and Stratification: A Biosocial Perspective." *Du Bois Review: Social Science Research on Race* 1:7–25.

Massey, Douglas S. and Nancy A. Denton. 1993. *American Apartheid: Segregation and the Making of the Underclass*. Cambridge, MA: Harvard University Press.

Mechanic, David. 2002. "Disadvantage, Inequality, and Social Policy." *Health Affairs* 21:48–59.

Miranda, Jeanne, Thomas G. McGuire, David R. Williams, and Philip Wang. 2008. "Mental Health in the Context of Health Disparities." *American Journal of Psychiatry* 165:1102–1108.

Morenoff, Jeffrey D. 2003. "Neighborhood Mechanisms and the Spatial Dynamics of Birth Weight." *American Journal of Sociology* 108:976–1017.

Mossakowski, Krysia N. 2003. "Coping with Perceived Discrimination: Does Ethnic Identity Protect Mental Health?" *Journal of Health and Social Behavior* 44:318–31.

Murphy, Sherry L. 2000. "Deaths: Final Data for 1998." *National Vital Statistics Reports* 56:4–26.

Navarro, Vincente. 1990. "Race or Class Versus Race and Class: Mortality Differentials in the United States." *Lancet* 336:1238–40.

Oliver, Melvin L. and Thomas M. Shapiro. 2006. *Black Wealth, White Wealth: A New Perspective on Racial Inequality*. New York: Routledge.

Omi, Michael and Howard Winant. 1994. *Racial Formation in the United States: From the 1960s to the 1990s*. New York City: Routledge.

Orzechowski, Shawna and Peter Sepielli. 2003. *New Worth and Asset Ownership of Households: 1998 and 2000*. Washington, DC: U.S. Census Bureau.

Risch, Niel, Esteban Burchard, Elad Ziv, and Hua Tang. 2002. "Categorization of Humans in Biomedical Research: Genes, Race and Disease." *Genome Biology* 3:1–12.

Rumbaut, Ruben G. 1996. "Origins and Destinies: Immigration, Race, and Ethnicity in Contemporary America." Pp. 21–42 in *Origins and Destinies: Immigration, Race, and Ethnicity in America*, edited by S. Pedraza and R. G. Rumbaut. Belmont, CA: Wadsworth Publishing Co.

Sampson, Robert J. and William J. Wilson. 1995. "Toward a Theory of Race, Crime, and Urban Inequality." Pp. 37–54 in *Crime and Inequality*, edited by J. Hagan and R. D. Peterson. Stanford, CA: Stanford University Press.

Schulz, Amy J. and Leith Mullings. 2006. *Gender, Race, Class and Health*. San Francisco, CA: Jossey-Bass.

Schulz, Amy J., David R. Williams, Barbara A. Israel, and Lora B. Lempert. 2002. "Racial and Spatial Relations as Fundamental Determinants of Health in Detroit." *The Milbank Quarterly* 80:677.

Serre, David and Svante Paabo. 2004. "Evidence for Gradients of Human Genetic Diversity within and among Continents." *Genome Research* 14:1679–85.

Shields, Alexandra E., Stephanie M. Fullerton, and Kenneth Olden. 2009. "Genes, Environment, and Cancer Disparities." Pp. 49–82 in *Toward the Elimination of Cancer Disparities*, edited by H. K. Koh. New York: Springer Publishing.

Singh, Gopal K. and Barry A. Miller. 2004. "Health, Life Expectancy, and Mortality Patterns among Immigrant Populations in the United States." *Canadian Journal of Public Health* 95:I14–I21.

Singh, Gopal K. and Stella M. Yu. 1996. "Adverse Pregnancy Outcomes: Differences between U.S. and Foreign-Born Women in Major U.S. Racial and Ethnic Groups." *American Journal of Public Health* 86:837–43.

Smedley, Brian D., Adrienne Y. Stith, and Alan R. Nelson. 2002. *Unequal Treatment: Confronting Racial and Ethnic Disparities in Health Care*. Washington, DC: National Acadamies Press.

Smelser, Neil J., William J. Wilson, and Faith Mitchell. 2001. *America Becoming: Racial Trends and their Consequences*. Washington, DC: National Academy Press.

Takeuchi, David T., Nolan Zane, Seunghye Hong, David H. Chae, Fang Gong, Gilbert C. Gee, Emily Walton, Stanley Sue, and Margarita Alegria. 2007. "Immigration-Related Factors and Mental Disorders among Asian Americans." *American Journal of Public Health* 97:84–90.

Wilkinson, Doris Y. and Gary King. 1987. "Conceptual and Methodological Issues in the Use of Race as a Variable: Policy Implications." *The Milbank Quarterly* 65:56–71.

Williams, David R. 1997. "Race and Health: Basic Questions, Emerging Directions." *Annals of Epidemiology* 7:322–33.

Williams, David R. and Chiquita Collins. 1995. "U.S. Socioeconomic and Racial Differences in Health: Patterns and Explanations." *Annual Review of Sociology* 21:349–86.

———. 2001. "Racial Residential Segregation: A Fundamental Cause of Racial Disparities in Health." *Public Health Reports* 116:404–16.

Williams, David R., Manuela V. Costa, Adebola O. Odunlami, and Selina A. Mohammed. 2008. "Moving Upstream: How Interventions that Address the Social Determinants of Health Can Improve Health and Reduce Disparities." *Journal of Public Health Management and Practice* 14(Supplement):S8–S17.

Williams, David R., Hector M. Gonzalez, Harold Neighbors, Randolph Nesse, Jamie M. Abelson, Julie Sweetman, and James S. Jackson. 2007a. "Prevalence and Distribution of Major Depressive Disorder in African Americans, Caribbean Blacks, and Non-Hispanic Whites: Results from the National Survey of American Life." *Archives of General Psychiatry* 64:305–15.

Williams, David R., Rahwa Haile, Hector M. Gonzalez, Harold Neighbors, Raymond Baser, and James S. Jackson. 2007b. "The Mental Health of Black Caribbean Immigrants: Results from the National Survey of American Life." *American Journal of Public Health* 97:52–59.

Williams, David R., Mark B. McClellan, and Alice M. Rivlin. 2010. "Beyond the Affordable Care Act: Achieving Real Improvements in Americans' Health." *Health Affairs* 29:1481–88.

Williams, David R. and Selina A. Mohammed. 2008. "Poverty, Migration, and Health." Pp. 135–69 in *The Colors of Poverty*, edited by A. C. Lin and D. R. Harris. New York: Russell Sage Foundation.

———. 2009. "Discrimination and Racial Disparities in Health: Evidence and Needed Research." *Journal of Behavioral Medicine* 32:20–47.

Williams, David R., Selina A. Mohammed, Jacinta Leavell, and Chiquita Collins. 2010. "Race, Socioeconomic Status and Health: Complexities, Ongoing Challenges and Research Opportunities." *Annals of the New York Academy of Sciences* 1186:69–101.

Wilson, William J. 1990. *The Truly Disadvantaged: The Inner City, the Underclass, and Public Policy*. Chicago: University of Chicago Press.

Discussion Questions

1. How often do you think about your race and/or ethnicity? When and where do you find yourself thinking more about your race and/or ethnicity? Why?
2. What are the examples of stereotypes, prejudice, and discrimination? What are the conceptual differences among the concepts?
3. Discuss whether a person can be prejudiced without being discriminant. Can a person discriminate but not be prejudiced? Look up Robert Merton's (1949) four-square typology and discuss the examples for each typology.
4. Find an ethnic identity measure, such as the Multi-Ethnic Identity Measure developed by Jean Phinney (1992), and discuss whether the measure accurately captures your ethnic identity or not.

Resources

Census Blogs "Measuring Race and Ethnicity Across the Decades: 1790–2010." By Beverly M. Pratt, Lindsay Hixson, and Nicholas A. Jones. Blog: https://www.census.gov/newsroom/blogs/random-samplings/2015/11/measuring-race-and-ethnicity-across-the-decades-1790-2010.html Interactive Tool: https://www.census.gov/data-tools/demo/race/MREAD_1790_2010.html

New York Times Videos: "25 Mini-Films for Exploring Race Bias and Identity with Students." Available at: https://www.nytimes.com/2017/03/15/learning/lesson-plans/25-mini-films-for-exploring-race-bias-and-identity-with-students.html

"Overview of Race and Hispanic Origin: 2010" by Karen R. Humes, Nicholas A. Jones, and Roberto R. Ramirez. Available at: https://www.census.gov/prod/cen2010/briefs/c2010br-02.pdf

Video, *A Girl Like Me*: A replication of the doll study by Clark and Clark by a teen filmmaker, Kiri Davis. Available at: http://understandingrace.org/ (Lived Experience → *A Girl Like Me*)

References

Bonilla-Silva, Eduardo. 2003. *Racism without Racists: Color-Blind Racism and the Persistence of Racial Inequality in the United States*. Lanham, MD: Rowman & Littlefield.

Broman, Clifford, Harold Neighbors, and James S. Jackson. 1988. "Racial Group Identification Among Black Adults." *Social Forces* 67:146–58.

Carter, Robert T. 1991. "Racial Identity Attitudes and Psychological Functioning." *Journal of Multicultural Counseling and Development* 19:05–14.

Cross, William. 1985. "Black Identity: Rediscovering the Distinction Between Personal Identity and Reference Group Orientation." Pp. 155–71 in *Beginnings: The Social and Affective Development of Black Children*, edited by Margaret Spencer, G.K. Brookins, and W.R. Allen. Hilldale, NJ: Erlbaum.

Du Bois, W.E.B. 1903. *The Souls of Black Folk*. New York: Dover Publications.

Gecas, Viktor. 1982. "The Self-Concept." *Annual Review of Sociology* 8:1–33.

Gurin, Patricia, Arthur H. Miller, and Gerald Gurin. 1980. "Stratum Identification and Consciousness." *Social Psychology Quarterly* 43:30–47.

Hughes, Michael, and David H. Demo. 1989. "Self-perception of Black Americans: Self-Esteem and Personal Efficacy." *American Journal of Sociology* 95:132–59.

Humes, Karen. R., Nicholas A. Jones, and Roberto R. Ramirez. 2011. "Overview of Race and Hispanic Origin: 2010." Washington, DC: US Census Bureau. Retrieved April 9, 2019 (http://www.census.gov/prod/cen2010/briefs/c2010br-02.pdf).

Merton, Robert. 1949. "Discrimination and the American Creed." Pp. 99–126 in *Discrimination and the National Welfare*, edited by Robert W. MacIver. New York: Harper and Brothers.

Mossakowski, Krysia. 2003. "Coping with Perceived Discrimination: Does Ethnic Identity Protect Mental Health?" *Journal of Health and Social Behavior, 44*, 318–31.

Munford, Maria B. 1994. "Relationship of Gender, Self-Esteem, Social Class, and Racial Identity to Depression in Blacks." *Journal of Black Psychology* 20:157–74.

Phinney, Jean. 1992. "The Multigroup Ethnic Identity Measure: A New Scale for Use with Diverse Groups." *Journal of Adolescent Research* 7:156–76.

Shelton, Jason E. 2008. "The Investment in Blackness Hypothesis: Toward Greater Understanding of Who Teaches What during Racial Socialization." *Du Bois Review: Social Science Research on Race* 5:235–57.

Spickard, Paul R. 1997. "What Must I Be? Asian Americans and the Question of Multiethnic Identity." *Amerasia Journal* 23(1):43–60.

Tajfel, Henri. 1981. *Human Groups and Social Categories*. Cambridge, England: Cambridge University Press.

Wise, Tim. 2008. *White Like Me*. Brooklyn, NY: Soft Skull Press.

Zhou, Min. 2004. "Are Asian Americans Becoming 'White'?" *Contexts* 3(1):29–37.

Section III: Intersectionality: Race, Class, Gender, and Beyond

Student Narratives

The murder of Trayvon Martin was my introduction to understanding race and police brutality. Like many Black people, I mourned the day his murderer was let free. I remember crying and not knowing what to do with myself; just feeling disbelief and the weight of the collective grief of the Black community. I went to a protest that night, because that was the only place I felt that my grief would be understood. Trayvon Martin was more than a black child: he represented Black boys all over the United States. His murder was also what showed me that not only can Black adults be targeted for violence, Black children can be, too. This grief was bigger than Trayvon; it was mourning for the entire Black community, our past, present, and future.

Unfortunately, this wouldn't be the first time I would mourn for a Black person killed. Over the days, weeks, months, and years, countless of other Black men, women, and children would be beaten and/or killed by police officers, security guards, and racist community members. So many people have been murdered that I'm desensitized to it. Week after week, I expect to hear about a Black person being murdered by police and it breaks my heart. These cases of police brutality affect much more than the person being murdered. It affects that person's family; it affects their community, their city, state, race, and culture.

To be Black is to perpetually feel a threat to your safety, to constantly feel a threat of terror, no matter what your class or work background is. When you look at cases of police brutality, you don't just find one "type" of person, such as a stereotypical criminal getting caught committing a crime. You find children, regular adults, professors, professionals, students, activists, even people who work for the police themselves. You find that they became victims by doing normal things like walking, grocery shopping, calling for help, or hanging out with friends. It is difficult to feel safe in a country where you could be beaten or killed just by living your everyday life.

Nyree Hall is a master's student in the Department of Sociology at California State University–Sacramento. She was born in Santa Clara, California, and relocated to Sacramento in 2009, where she completed her bachelor's degree in Ethnic Studies and minor in Deaf Studies. She is also an activist in the Sacramento area and a doula.

I still remember like it was yesterday—my family trying to cross the California border in 1993. My mom, baby sister, twin sister, and me. *Atascados* (stuck) in *lodo* (mud) somewhere close to San Ysidro. Our "coyote" (smuggler) telling me to keep quiet and not panic by handing me a piece of that *yerba buena*–taste gum. My body slowly sinking in the *pantano* (swamp), the radio transmissions from the *migra* (border patrol) talking to my ears. The inability to advance because of the fear of getting caught. We manage to move close to a gas station store, but the "coyote" (smuggler) warned my mom not to purchase anything there. The only currency my mom had was food stamps. Walking onto the freeway, we were stopped by a migra telling us to stay and wait to get picked up. A verbal fight between la migra and the "coyote" (smuggler) over a *maleta* (luggage bag) which the migra (border patrol) had thrown over the bridge. I don't think there was anything in the maleta (luggage bag), but the coyote kept insulting the migra in English—using words not appropriate for me to hear. The *perrera* (border vehicle, aka dog kennel) took us away to a detention center. Then we were deported back to Mexico.

La Casa del Inmigrante in Tijuana was our home for a month. *Ya desperto peto pelon* (he already awoke) a young sibling, told his brothers and sisters at the *casa*. Everyone laughs. The mother with more than five kids who has struggled for years to cross, waits days on end for her husband to come for her. My mother looks for *leche* (milk) for my newborn sister, but no luck. Only milk available is pasteurized and it does not smell or taste good. We see the coyote once again. My mom desperately calls my uncle Juan from New York for money to cross again. *Seis cientos dolares* ($600). The price it will cost to cross three US-born children and a *madre indocumentedad* (undocumented mother). *Corriendo por los cerros* (running through the mountains) my mom holds my sister and her *Biblia* (Bible) in her *maleta blanca* (white luggage bag) that contains our birth certificates and photo album. *El Mosco* (helicopter) looking for us with its bright light. We hide underneath a tree. *La casa en el monte* (the house in the mountain) with a *gabacho* (white man) that owns it. *Hombres, mujeres solas* (males, females alone). I think we were the only children in the house. *Mi cuata* (my twin sister) got her shoe left stuck in mud that night. The coyote (smuggler) goes out to find it in the morning. We're given *Sopas de vaso* (cup noodles), *bolas y ules para los pies en el cruce del lago* (plastic bag for the feet for the creek to cross). *Todos durmiendo, cansados, esperanzados en llegar a sus destinos.* (Everyone sleeping, tired, hopeful to get to their destination). *Los Angeles por fin llegamos al "correcaminos"* (Greyhound bus) *para Salinas.*

William Medrano Rojas is a graduate student in the Department of Sociology at California State Univeristy–Sacramento. He is finalizing his thesis on Latinx Parental Educational Expectations and Aspirations for Their Children. He was born and raised in Salinas, California, by a single mother.

Learning Objectives

1. Define intersectionality.

2. Discuss how sociologists use intersectionality to analyze overlapping social inequalities such as race, class, and gender.

3. Describe extensions of intersectionality beyond race, class, and gender to embrace other social inequalities such as disability, religion, and nation.

4. Identify how intersecting forms of social inequalities influence your own standpoint.

Editor's Introduction

Jacqueline Brooks, PhD

In their narratives, Nyree describes her response to Trayon Martin's murderer escaping justice. William highlights the struggles of crossing the US-Mexico border. First, both elucidate the intersection of multiple social inequalities. Nyree exposes the intersection of race, class, and gender social inequities. William sheds light on the intersection of race, class, and nation social inequities. Second, both present examples that illustrate the real, lived consequences of unequal power relations. For example, the death of Trayvon Martin, a black teenager, at the hands of a white man, reinforced how white privilege benefits those at the top of the race hierarchy, and how anti-blackness disadvantages those at the bottom. For many black Americans participating in everyday tasks, such as walking down the street, driving to work, or mowing their lawn, can be dangerous, or even fatal, when confronted by the police or "concerned citizens." For white Americans—even poor white Americans—it is rare that someone challenges their right to take a nap on school property where they study, sell lemonade in front of their homes, or have an event in a public park. Although these incidences of racial bias play out at the micro level, they reflect structural racism. William offers a vivid example that details how lack of privilege equates to lack of protection. As a child from a low-income, Mexican family, the families described in the narrative endured a barrage of hardships reserved for those who could not "cash in" on the privilege of emigrating from a European country, being white, and/or in the possession of a visa. Research finds that increased military presence along the US-Mexico border has dire consequences for those crossing into the United States (Sarabia and Perales 2019). As crossing undocumented becomes increasingly labeled as "criminal," people simply seeking better opportunities become suspects, vulnerable to physical and psychological harm at the hands of border authorities (Sarabia and Perales 2019).

Third, each focuses their experiences of multiple inequalities within specific **social institutions**—an aggregation of people, ideologies, practices, and relationships with expressed goals (e.g., government, education, religion, or families). Social institutions influence how we structure and organize our lives. For example, technology, as a social institution, functions to advance progress and promote efficiency. It has redesigned how we communicate, work, and learn. Social institutions also serve as arenas in which we re-produce social hierarchies. Nyree suggests that perceived negative representations of black Americans influence their treatment within the criminal justice system and the mass media, thereby re-producing racial hierarchies. William discusses how immigration, replete with racially biased policies, influences each family's experience as they journey into the United States undocumented. William vividly illustrates this experience from the perspective of a child, describing the anxiety that builds in families from one stop on their journey to the next.

Finally, based on their experiences, each forms a distinct **standpoint** that is unique to their individual experiences of social inequality. Each person develops their own standpoint, based on their unique experiences, which they use to filter their understanding of the social world and their position within it. As a young, black woman, Nyree reacted to the acquittal of Trayvon Martin's offender with acrimony and a growing distrust in the criminal justice system. Her standpoint led her to a protest march. William expands his interest in the experiences of those crossing the border, to study immigrant groups and education.

Intersectionality views social inequalities as multiplicative, often simultaneous experiences, which do not outrank one another. Thus, race, class, and gender nest within one another, as multiplicative social inequalities. Nyree and William offer insight into how intersecting social inequalities frame one's worldview and sense of positioning within the social world.

Historical Overview

Defining intersectionality is not an easy task (Collins 2015). Since the coining of the term in the late 1990s, intersectionality as a theory, field of study, and analytical framework has spread across and within multiple academic disciplines (e.g., psychology, anthropology, economics, and history) (Collins 2015). This diffusion renders it vulnerable to change or alternate conceptions that may render it too general or specific (Collins 2015). Collins offers a definition of intersectionality that attempts to encapsulate its interdisciplinary use. Intersectionality "references the critical insight that race, class, and gender, sexuality, ethnicity, nation, ability, and age operate not as unitary, mutually exclusive entities, but as reciprocally constructing phenomena that in turn shape complex social inequalities" (2015:3). Collins makes note of knowledge projects similar to how Omi and Winant (1994) employ the idea of racial projects (see Theory Introduction and Chapter 1.2). Due to its emphasis on power structures and multiple social inequities, Collins discusses intersectionality as a knowledge project (2015). Further, due to its consideration of diverse groups, Collins highlights the voices of multiple interpretive communities as integral to intersectionality.

Many trace the origins of intersectionality to Crenshaw's 1991 article in *the Stanford Law Review* in which she skillfully explains how race and gender social inequalities particularly disadvantage women of color. More specifically, Crenshaw details how intersecting race and gender inequalities create different experiences of sexual assault and domestic violence for women of color than white women. Even when seeking help, women of color experience different treatment. Crenshaw notes, "Where systems of race, gender, and class domination converge, as they do in the experiences of battered women of color, intervention strategies based solely on the experiences of women who do not share the same class or race backgrounds will be of limited help to women who because of race and class face different obstacles" (1246). In describing the experiences of immigrant women, Crenshaw (1991) draws attention to an amendment in the marriage fraud provision of the 1990 Immigration and Nationality Act, requiring any person who married a US citizen or permanent resident to remain espoused for at least two years. This left immigrant women who were victims of domestic violence and sexual assault at the hands of the US citizen or permanent resident spouses, without a means of escape. A further amendment stipulated that marital partners, trapped in abusive relationships, could leave their marriages, but only with an explicit waiver. Immigrant women often lacked the resources to gain access to these waivers, and often feared that deportation would be a consequence of ending their martial unions (Crenshaw 1991).

Although Crenshaw's use of the term *intersectionality* sparked a new direction in racial discourse, analyses that blended race and class existed for quite some time. The scholarship of black women intellectuals, such as Anna Julia Cooper and Ida Wells Barnett, drew linkages between race and class as they discussed the social positioning of black Americans within politics, law, and education (Collins 2015). Although these contributions to sociology drew connections among social inequities, they were initially not accepted into white, male-dominated, mainstream academic discourse. Decades would pass before the voices of marginalized groups—in particular women of color—would break through the vehement resistance of white, male, privileged scholarship.

Mindfulness

As intersectionality studies gain prominence throughout academia, it is also moving beyond traditional analyses of the overlap among race, class, and gender inequalities. For example, feminist approaches to gender and sexuality have incorporated nationalism as a fluid, shifting dynamic into their scholarship, arguing that the social construction of states, nations, and nationalisms intersect with other social inequalities such as race, gender, and sexuality (Kim-Puri 2005). In addition, extensions of intersectionality have embraced ability, religion, and age as intersecting social inequalities which shape social experiences. Since social constructions reflect dynamic, shifting social phenomena, leaving the door open to extensions of theoretical approaches and analyses is prudent. How people are situated within systems of inequalities changes over time and thusly alters their experiences, meaning intersectional scholarship should respond in ways that reflect these new directions. For example, shifting US demographics suggests that the American population has not only aged, but people are living longer. By 2030 all Baby Boomers will be at least 65 years old, meaning 1 in every 5 US residents will be retirement age (US Census Bureau 2019). Further, the old-age dependency ratio will continue to shift. Currently, there are about 3.5 working-age adults for every retirement-age person (US Census Bureau 2019). By 2060 there will be 2.5 working-age adults for every retirement-age person (US Census Bureau 2019). As people age, they experience increased vulnerability to economic inequalities, illness, and physical abuse. The social construction of the elderly as weak and no longer useful colors their experiences with the workplace, health care systems, and housing. When we incorporate social inequalities relative to race and gender inequalities, the picture for some groups worsens.

In 2018, the case of Cyntoia Brown garnered national attention, reinforcing how intersections of race, class, gender, and age inequalities structure the experiences of women of color in the criminal justice system. In 2004, Cyntoia Brown, an African American sixteen-year-old, was tried as an adult for killing a forty-three-year old white man. At the time of her arrest, young Cyntoia was in the grips of an abusive drug dealer who forced her into sex work. The man she killed was her "john." She was sentenced to life in prison at the Tennessee Prison for Women with the stipulation that she serve fifty-one years before being eligible for parole. Cyntoia's story was the focus of a PBS documentary, which generated national interest and led to a massive petition drive requesting her release from prison. As a result of a petition campaign, **Tennessee governor Bill Haslam granted Cyntoia clemency. After serving fifteen years in prison, she will be released in August 2019. Cyntoia's story is about her arrest, the harsh sentencing, and her time in prison. From an intersectional approach, Cyntoia's experiences highlight the intersections of race (black), class (working class), gender (woman), and ability (mental health issues exacerbated by sexual trauma) inequalities.**

Section Readings

In "More than Just Fear of Islam: Muslims in the United States Experience Anti-Muslim Racism," Zopf explains how anti-Muslim sentiment and behavior extend beyond religion and encapsulate race as well. In addition to enduring prejudice and hatred based on stereotypes and misconceptions about Islam, Muslim Americans also face racial prejudice and hatred. These intersecting social oppressions create unique obstacles and issues for Muslim Americans.

In "Race, Ethnicity, and Migration in the Context of Care Work," Wu examines the gendered and race world of domestic work. Sex segregation characterizes most domestic work performed in the United States. In addition, domestic work relies heavily on the manual and emotional labor of women of color. Wu assesses the experiences of immigrant women of color and white women employed as nannies in the northeastern United States. She finds that gendered and race occupational structures make workers of color more susceptible to discrimination and abuse than their white peers.

In "The Sandra Bland Case: Dissecting Intersectionality and Institutional Segregation in Post-racial America," Brooks and Sarabia analyze the case of Sandra Bland, a young black woman who died while incarcerated. We situate our analysis in intersectionality, highlighting the influence of racist and gendered authority structures that rely on those labeled as *suspicious*. In addition, we explain how everyday activities can become fatal for people marginalized within the intersections of race, class, and gender. Finally, we shed light on the need to analyze how social institutions re-produce gender, class, and race hierarchies, clarifying how intersectional systems of oppression function.

Reading 3.1 More than Just Fear of Islam: Muslims in the United States Experience Anti-Muslim Racism

Bradley J. Zopf, Carthage College

Keywords: Orientalism, Islamophobia, Anti-Muslim Racism, War on Terrorism, Hate Crime, and Ideology

Chapter Goals

In this chapter, you will be able to:

1. Identify and define Orientalism and Islamophobia as key ideologies of anti-Muslim racism;

2. Describe and explain how state-based policies and institutions contribute to the targeting and surveillance of Muslims in the United States;

3. Explain why and how Muslims experience racism; and

4. Discuss the consequences of anti-Muslim racism for Muslims and those perceived to be Muslim.

A Portrait of Muslims in the United States

The now-famous photo of Munira Ahmed adorning a *hijab* in the design of the American flag was taken nearly a decade ago by Ridwan Adhami, not far from where the World Trade Center once stood. In an interview with the *Guardian*, Ahmed described the purpose of the photo: "It's about saying, 'I am American just as you are. I am American and I am Muslim, and I am very proud to be both'" (Helmore 2017).

Islam is the second-largest religion worldwide behind only Christianity and is the fastest-growing religion in the United States (Mohamed, Smith, Cooperman, and Schiller 2017).Islam began in Saudi Arabia in the seventh century by the Prophet Muhammed, who Muslims believe is the Messenger of God, or Allah. Muslims are spread across the globe with sizable populations in South Asia and the Middle East. Though Muslims are expected to surpass Jews as the second-largest religious group in the United States by 2050, Muslims remain a small percentage of the overall US population (approximately 1.1 percent) (Lipka 2015). The rise in the US Muslim population has led to a misperception that the United States is in danger of Islam taking over Christianity as evidenced by a viral YouTube "Muslim Demographics" video with more than 16 million views (2019).

The majority of Muslims in the United States are foreign born, most having immigrated since 2010, representing more than 75 different national-origin backgrounds. Muslims in the United States are phenotypically, racially, ethnically, and religiously diverse. Most Muslims in the United States are citizens, are proud to identify as American, and feel they have a lot in common with Americans. Though Muslim Americans feel they have a lot in common with Americans, prefer to assimilate to American culture, and pursue the American dream, many identify racism as the most important problem facing Muslims in the United States (Mohamed, Smith, Cooperman, and Schiller 2017; Kohut, Keeter, and Smith 2011). Muslims in the United States encounter many misconceptions of Islam, including inaccurate stereotypes about them as religious fanatics and/or terrorists. In addition, nearly 75 percent surveyed believe that there is a lot of discrimination against

Muslims in the United States, with nearly half having experienced various forms of discrimination in the past year (Mohamed, Smith,Coooperman, Schiller 2017). In particular, the Council of American-Islamic Relations received reports of nearly 3,000 bias incidents in 2017, ranging from harassment in public spaces to violent hate crimes, as well as FBI and TSA racial profiling (Council on American-Islamic Relations 2018).

Questions for Reflection and Discussion:

1. What do you know about Islam and/or Muslims? Where does this knowledge come from? (i.e., personal experience, books, classes, movies and television, social media, other)

2. Complete the Arab-Muslim Implicit Association test (https://implicit.harvard.edu/implicit/takeatest.html) and reflect on your results.

3. What are your assumptions about Islam and Muslims? How accurate are these assumptions?

Anti-Muslim Racism: Ideologies and Structures

Racism is a system of power relations resting on both ideologies of difference and structures of domination and power (Golash-Boza 2016). Anti-Muslim racism can be defined as a collection of ideas about Islam and Muslims manifesting in a set of prejudicial attitudes and ideas (i.e., ideology) expressed in actions and enacted as a system of policies and practices (i.e., structures) designed to surveil and restrict Muslims' everyday lives in ways that erode Muslims' sense of safety and belonging. Anti-Muslim racism is more than simply Islamophobia, often defined as an irrational fear or prejudice against Muslims, because the notion of "–phobia" emphasizes "individual and psychological" attitudes rather than the "collective and the structural" practices that define Muslims as religious, cultural, and indeed racial others (Garner and Selod 2015). Anti-Muslim racism, therefore, turns our focus away from personal biases and prejudices and highlights the integration of shared attitudes, practices of discrimination, and systematic policies that target Islam and victimize Muslims. The following three sections examine the historical antecedent of modern-day anti-Muslim racism by tracing the ideologies of Orientalism and Islamophobia that gave rise to structures and state-based policies impacting US Muslims today.

Ideologies of Anti-Muslim Racism: Orientalism and Islamophobia

Anti-Muslim racism rests on mutually reinforcing ideologies of Orientalism and Islamophobia. Together, these ideologies contribute to stereotypical images and narratives of Arabs, Muslims, Islam, and the Middle East. Persistently negative, homogenizing, and essentializing tropes about Islam (as a religion), Arabs (as a civilization), and Muslims (as people) can be seen in modern-day movies, newspaper stories, and social media posts.

Said (1978) describes orientalism as a set of ideologies and practices that produce distorted knowledge about the geographies, cultures, religions, and people of the Orient (often referred to as the Middle East). These frameworks depict an imaginary, immoral, and exotic Orient that serves as a juxtaposition to the virtuosity of Christianity and rationality of the West. Scholars, artists, and writers alike produced ideas, images, and narratives about the Middle East and Islam that distinguished it from the West and Christianity (Said 1978). For example, *The Arabian Nights*, a collection of short stories and narratives compiled over decades, fascinated Western audiences during the eighteenth century. Similarly, the nineteenth century gave rise to Orientalist art, such as Eugène Delacroix's *Women of Algiers in Their Apartment* (1834), Vernet's *The Arab Tale Teller (*1833*)*, or Jean-Léon Gérôme's *Snake Charmer* (1870). Orientalist scholars, artists, and writers produced inaccurate and highly stereotypical images and narratives representing Arabs, Muslims, and the Middle East as backward yet exotic, highly sexualized yet oppressed, and as fanatical and dangerous. Modern-day movies, such as *The Dictator*

(2012), *Zero Dark Thirty* (2012), and *American Sniper* (2014) continue to depict the Middle East, Arabs, and Muslims and continue to rely on that hegemonic framework.

Islamophobia is the second ideological pillar of anti-Muslim racism. The term *Islamophobia* was popularized by the *Runnymede Trust* (1997). Though initially defining Islamophobia as an irrational fear, dread, or hatred of Islam, an updated definition is as follows:

> Islamophobia is any distinction, inclusion, or restriction towards, or preference against, Muslims (or those perceived to be Muslim) that has the purpose or effect of nullifying or impairing recognition, enjoyment or exercise, or an equal footing, of human rights and fundamental freedoms in the political, economic, social, cultural, or any other field of public life (Elahi and Khan 2018).

With an emphasis on the consequences of Islamophobia rather than individual prejudices, this definition more clearly fits within an anti-Muslim racism framework. Islamophobia contributes to a homogenized and essentialized view of Islam as a radical and violent religion. As an ideology, Islamophobia perpetuates a distorted fear of Muslims as unwelcome foreigners and dangerous terrorists (Zopf 2018). For example, President Donald Trump's call for a ban on immigration from seven Muslim-majority countries can directly be attributed to this fear of Muslims. Trump signed *Protecting the Nation from Foreign Terrorist Entry into the United States* in January 2017, which banned admission from Iraq, Syria, Iran, Libya, Somalia, Sudan, and Yemen. While a district judge ruled the ban unconstitutional in February 2017, there remains a series of battles between the Trump administration, community activists, and federal courts, culminating in the Supreme Court agreeing to hear oral arguments concerning the immigration ban. While Islamophobia provides the justification for such a ban, the fear is manifestly overstated, as the total number of people killed by immigrations from those seven countries since 1975 is zero (Nowrasteh 2017).

Orientalist and Islamophobic ideologies are collectively held beliefs and assumptions, including stereotypes, that contribute to pervasive and negative stereotypes that essentialize and homogenize Arabs, Muslims, and the Middle East. As a defining feature of anti-Muslim racism, these two ideologies lead to increased fear of Muslims, incite violence directed toward Muslims, and often justify discrimination in social, political, and state-based policies targeting Muslims.

Structures of Anti-Muslim Racism: War on Terror and the US State

On September 11, 2001, terrorists hijacked four planes, two taking down New York City's World Trade Center towers, a third hitting the Pentagon in Washington, DC, and a fourth crashing in a field in Pennsylvania. Nearly 3,000 people died in these attacks perpetrated by known terrorist group al-Qaeda. Soon after the attacks, President George W. Bush announced a US-led war on terrorism. Since 9/11, the United States has been involved in long-standing wars in Iraq and Afghanistan, despite killing Osama bin Laden, lead orchestrator of 9/11, in 2011. These wars, along with domestic surveillance and detention policies, have been justified in the name of national security.

Though the term *war on terrorism* appeared as early as the 1980s in response to a series of terrorist attacks in Lebanon, Europe, and the United States, it was not until 9/11 that a global war on terrorism, led by the United States, became an institutionalized and state-sponsored system of surveillance, detention, and war. Though this current "War on Terrorism" ostensibly targets domestic and foreign terrorist organizations, scholars have noted how domestic policies have indiscriminately targeted US citizens, mostly of Arab descent and/or Muslim faith (Cainkar 2010).

Shortly after 9/11, the PATRIOT Act (2002) was passed, authorizing increased measures to prevent and deter terrorism against the United States. The federal government increased funding for antiterrorist programs, including enhancing the capabilities of FBI surveillance and screening, especially for their ability to secure FISA warrants used for wiretaps and monitoring of electronic mail. Altogether, nearly fifteen new governmental policies and laws targeted Muslims as potential terrorists. Soon after 9/11, thousands of Arabs and Muslims—

even US-born citizens—were brought in for questioning, some detained without official charges having been established (Cainkar 2002). In 2002, the Department of Homeland Security was established, and the NSEERS, or National Security Entry-Exit Registration System, created protocol for monitoring individuals entering and exiting the United States. As part of the system, Homeland Security, along with the Immigration and Naturalization Service (INS), began collecting fingerprints, facial photographs, and personal information recorded (Cainkar 2002). By June 2003, nearly 83,000 Arabs and/or Muslims had been registered through NSEERS (Bayoumi 2006). Though NSEERS has officially ended, President Trump's call for extreme vetting and a travel ban on several Muslim-dominant countries rests on the same state polices, agencies, and language.

While Arab and Muslim organizations and individuals continue to be surveilled and questioned by the FBI and Homeland Security, racial profiling in airports by TSA has risen in the past decade (Council on American-Islamic Relations 2018). Phrases such as "flying while brown," "flying while Arab," and "flying while Muslim" have entered the common lexicon in the same way as "driving while black" (Baker 2002; Blackwood, Hopkins, and Reicher 2015; Chandrasekar 2003; According to Schildkraut (2009), support for "counterterrorism profiling" is higher than traditional forms of racial profiling, and stories like Mohamed Ahmed's have become more commonplace. On July 20, 2016, Ahmed was singled out by an American Airlines flight attendant who announced his seat number and said "I'll be watching you." Ahmed was eventually removed from the plane (Revesz 2016). Heightened surveillance by TSA, flight attendants, and other passengers constitutes a form of "terror profiling" in which Muslims—and those appearing to be Muslim—experience "selectively negative treatment by both government and private entities of individuals and groups thought to be associated with terrorist activity, based on race, ethnicity, national origin, and/or religion" (Chon and Arzt 2005). Combining elements of skin color, religious dress, name, national origin, and/or language, terror profiling challenges Muslims' belonging in public places, especially airports. The US-led war on terrorism has contributed to several state-based policies and structures that surveil Muslims in the United States and contribute to experiences of marginalization, discrimination, and unequal treatment.

Victimized by Anti-Muslim Terrorism: Microaggressions, Hate Crimes, and Discrimination

CAIR has recently reported 2,599 bias incidents against Muslims, including 359 experiences of verbal or physical assaults, 300 hate crimes, 348 encounters with Customs and Border Patrol, 225 workplace discriminations, and 270 harassment complaints lobbed at the FBI (Council on American-Islamic Relations 2018). In this section, you will explore three spheres in which anti-Muslim racism impacts Muslims in the United States. From verbal harassment and physical assaults to institutionalized discrimination, Muslims in the United States experience racism.

Daily Encounters: Microaggressions

Microaggressions are brief, often daily, encounters where Muslims experience verbal and/or behavioral harassment designed to convey an unwelcoming or hostile attitude, challenge their sense of belonging, or erode their sense of safety and security (Noble 2005). Nadal et al. (2010) define religious microaggressions as "subtle behavior and verbal exchanges (both conscious and unconscious) that send denigrating messages to individuals of various religious groups" (Nadal, Issa, Griffin, Hammit, and Lyons 2010). These encounters take place in schools and at work, in restaurants and the airport, and on the street and contribute to heightened levels of stress and anxiety, as well as negative health outcomes (Jasinskaja-Lahi, Liebkind, and Perhoniemi 2006).

Microaggressions range from subtle forms of avoidance to explicit forms of harassment, including physical assault. Muslims, and those perceived to be Muslim, can, and often do, experience all forms of microaggression. In my own work, I found some Egyptians were asked if they owned a camel or lived in a tent. The Orientalist stereotype evident here communicates a romanticized and exotic view of Egypt stuck thousands of years in the past. A more common microaggression involves answering "Where are you from?" This question, which assumes they are immigrants, challenges Muslims' belonging in the United States, especially for those who have been born and raised here. Additionally, Muslims often face negative—and incorrect—assumptions about their religion. Being told to go back home or being called a terrorist reminds Muslims that they are not welcome in the United States (Zopf 2018). Daily encounters where their belonging is challenged, their religious faith is denigrated, and their personal space and safety are violated demonstrate the pervasiveness of anti-Muslim racism.

Hate Crimes

The FBI defines hate crime as a violent or property crime that is "motivated in whole or in part by the offender's bias against race, religion, disability, sexual orientation, ethnicity, gender, or gender identity" (FBI Year). A nineteen-year-old Muslim woman wearing a *hijab* was violently attacked in a Detroit hospital. Victims of hate crimes, like the young Muslim woman in the video, have their sense of safety and security taken away CBS News 2018). While 2001 remains the year with the highest number of reported hate crimes against Muslims, the previous two years have seen a rapid increase. According to FBI statistics, there were 307 hate crimes against Muslims in 2016 and 257 in 2015. This two-year average of 282 per year represents a 122 percent increase over the previous 13-per-year-average of 127 from 2002–20014. This surge, according to the Southern Poverty Law Center, can in part be attributed to President Donald Trump's inflammatory discourse on Muslims during his presidential campaign, especially his call for a Muslim ban on immigration (Splcenter.org 2017). Additionally, the SLPC has reported a rise in anti-Muslim hate groups since 2016, especially the rise in ACT for America chapters across the United States (Splcenter.org 2017). While hate crimes remain relatively rare, the past two-year increase in hate crimes suggests that anti-Muslim racism is not likely to disappear anytime soon.

Discrimination in Employment and Housing

Though Muslims in the United States have comparative educational attainment, income levels, and employment levels, studies show that Muslims experience discrimination in employment and housing (Mohamed, Smith, Cooperman, and Schiller 2017). Using field audits, Widner and Chicoine (2011) randomly assigned both white-sounding and Arab-sounding résumés to 265 jobs over a fifteen-month period. They found that white-sounding names, such as John Mueller, received a callback 5.25 percent of the time, while Arab-sounding names, such as Abd al-Malik Khalil received a callback only 1.89 percent of the time (Widner and Chicoine 2011). Similarly, using an experimental design, Nausheen et al. (2014) found that participants viewed women wearing a *hijab* less employable than women without a veil (Nausheen, Masson, and Pennington 2014). Additionally, Padela et al. (2015) found that 14 percent of Muslims reported religious discrimination in their workplace. These studies suggest Muslims are facing discrimination in employment at various points (Padela, Adam, Ahmad, Hosseinian, and Curlin 2015). From initial application, Arab- and/or Muslim-sounding names are receiving fewer interview offers, Muslim women in a *hijab* are viewed as less employable, and once hired, Muslims may expect some level of religious discrimination.

Similar studies have found that Muslims may find trouble finding housing because of discrimination. Gaddis and Ghosal (2015) responded to 560 "roommate-wanted" advertisements in Los Angeles, New York, Detroit, and Houston with both white- and Muslim-sounding names. They found that in every city, white-sounding names received more replies, with the biggest in New York. Just as residential segregation by race reduces the level of integration and inclusion for many blacks and Hispanics, limited housing choices further isolates many Muslims in the United States (Gaddis and Ghoshal 2015).

Case Study: #PunishaMuslim

A series of anonymous letters sent to six communities in London proclaimed April 3, 2018, "Punish a Muslim day" (Joseph 2018). The vitriolic rhetoric in these letters warned Europe's and North America's "white majority" they were in danger of being "over-run by those who would like nothing more than to do us harm and turn our democracies into Sharia led police states." In the letters, the author assigned a point system that included verbally harassing a Muslim, removing a Muslim woman's *hijab*, physically assaulting a Muslim, burning or bombing a mosque, and other hateful and violent actions. The hateful message illustrates both long-held fears and prevailing stereotypes of Muslims as unwelcome foreigners, religious fundamentalists, and *jihadi* terrorists. These Islamophobic and racist letters were met with immediate rejection and heightened awareness by police departments, community organizations, and mosques. The Council on American-Islamic Relations (CAIR), the largest Muslim American advocacy organization in the United States, released the following statement in a community advisory:

> While the "Punish a Muslim Day" threat seems to target British Muslims exclusively, it would only be prudent to increase security at Islamic institutions and in public spaces, and to remain vigilant to any potential bias-motivated actions (Council on American-Islamic Relations 2018).

Echoing this call for vigilance, the American-Arab Anti-Discrimination Committee similarly released a statement saying:

> Originating in London, where they were left at the steps of several mosques, the fliers have alarmed communities across the U.S. From a school district in Vermont to the Chicago Police Department, authorities are worried that the planned day—Tuesday, April 3—may lead to hate crimes against Arabs and Muslims and anyone suspected of being Arab and/or Muslim (American-Arab Anti-Discrimination Committee 2018).

Additionally, social media responded with the competing message of #LoveAMuslimDay, complete with points for such actions as buying a Muslim a coffee, inviting a Muslim to your home, and buying a *hajj* package for a Muslim family (Khatami 2018). Fortunately, April 3, 2018, did not see any major spike in violence against Muslims, yet the fear and trepidation felt by the Muslim community have not abated as anti-Muslim sentiment in Europe and the United States continues to rise, and Muslims, and those perceived to be Muslim, have faced increased violence and discrimination (Elahi and Khan 2018). Though #PunishAMuslim did not produce a day filled with violence against Muslims, the letters—and especially the message contained within them—serve as a powerful example of anti-Muslim racism.

Conclusion

While #PunishAMuslim was likely penned by a single individual with clearly prejudicial attitudes toward Muslims, the message conveyed in that letter called upon collective feelings of Muslims as racial others, unwelcome foreigners, and dangerous terrorists. The author employed ideologies of Orientalism and Islamophobia to stir people's fear of Muslims into actions targeting individual Muslims, Islamic institutions, and the *umma* (global Islamic community) more generally. Thus, #PunishAMuslim is but one example of how the ideology and structure of anti-Muslim racism operates and can potentially impact Muslims in the United States and beyond. Because anti-Muslim racism cannot be reduced to individual prejudice or solitary acts of harassment or violence, Muslims of all phenotypes, national origins, and ethnic ancestries collectively shoulder these attacks. This chapter, thus, extends our understanding of race and racism beyond merely skin color, illustrating how religion intersects with the beliefs, practices, and structures of racism.

Critical Thinking Questions

1. What experiences do you have with Muslims? How have these contributed to your views and understandings of Islam and/or Muslims?

2. How does viewing the experiences of Muslims in the United States through the lens of racism expand our understanding?

Exploratory Research Questions

1. How are the experiences of Muslims in the United States similar to and different from other racialized groups, such as blacks, Latinx, Native Americans, and/or Asian Americans?

2. Watch the following YouTube videos: *Muslim Demographics* https://www.youtube.com/watch?v=6-3X5hIFXYU; BBC's *Muslim Demographics: The Truth* https://www.youtube.com/watch?v=mINChFxRXQs. What do you notice about the number of views for each video? Considering the information presented, the source, and the number of views, reflect on how social media contributes to the spread of misinformation about Islam and Muslims. What are the potential consequences of such inaccurate information?

References

American-Arab Anti-Discrimination Committee. March 29, 2018. "ADC on Alert: 'Punish a Muslim Day.'" Retrieved June 8, 2018. (http://www.adc.org/2018/03/adc-on-alert-punish-a-muslim-day/)

Bayoumi, Moustafa. 2006. "Racing Religion." *New Centennial Review* 6(2):267–93.

Council on American-Islamic Relations. 2018. *Targeted: 2018 Civil Rights Report.* (*http://www.islamophobia.org/reports/224-2018-civil-rights-report-targeted.html*)

Baker, Ellen. 2002. "Flying while Arab—Racial Profiling and Air Travel Security." *Journal of Air and Law Commerce.* 67:1375.

BBC. 2019. Muslim Demographics the Truth. Retrieved July 2019 (https://www.youtube.com/watch?v=mINChFxRXQs).

Blackwood, Leda, Nick Hopkins, and Stephen Reicher. "'Flying while Muslim': Citizenship and Misrecognition in the Airport." *Journal of Social and Political Psychology* 32(2):148–70.

Cainkar, Louise. 2002. "Special Registration: A Fervor for Muslims." *Journal of Islamic Law and Culture* 7(2): 73–01.

Cainkar, Louise. 2010. *Homeland Insecurity: The Arab American and Muslim American Experience after 9/11.* New York: Russell Sage Foundation.

Cainkar, Louise. 2010. *Homeland Insecurity: The Arab American and Muslim American Experience after 9/11.* New York: Russell Sage Foundation.

Chandrasekhar, Charu. 2003. "Flying while Brown: Federal Civil Rights Remedies to Post 9/11 Airline Profiling of South Asians." *Asian American Law Journal* 10(2):215–52.

Chon, Margaret, and Donna Arzt. 2005. "Walking While Muslim." *Law and Contemporary Problems*, 238.

Council on American-Islamic Relations. 2018. "Targeted: 2018 Civil Rights Report." Retrieved June 8, 2018. (*http://www.islamophobia.org/reports/224-2018-civil-rights-report-targeted.html*)

Elahi, Farah, and Omar Khan. 2018. "Islamophobia: Still a Challenge for Us All." *Runnymede Trust*. London, UK: London School of Economics. P. 2.

FBI. 2019. Retrieved July 2019 (https://www.fbi.gov/investigate/civil-rights/hate-crimes).

Gaddis, S. Michael, and Raj Ghoshal. 2015. "Arab American Housing Discrimination, Ethnic Competition, and Contact Hypothesis." *ANNALS AAPSS* 660(1):282–99.

Garner, Steve, and Saher Selod. 2015. "The Racialization of Muslims: Empirical Studies of Islamophobia." *Critical Sociology* 41(1):13.

Golash, Boza. 2016. "A Critical and Comprehensive Sociological Theory of Race and Racism." *Sociology of Race and Ethnicity* 2(2): 129–41.

Helmore, Edward. January 23, 2017. "Munira Ahmed: The Woman Who Became the Face of the Trump Resistance." *Guardian*. Retrieved June 8, 2018. (https://www.theguardian.com/us-news/2017/jan/23/womens-march-poster-munira-ahmed-shepard-fairey-interview)

Jasinskaja-Lahti, Inga, Karmela Liebkind, and Riku Perhoniemi. 2006. "Perceived Discrimination and Well-Being: A Victim Study of Different Immigrant Groups." *Journal of Community & Applied Social Psychology* 16:267–84.

Joseph, Yonette. 2018. "'Punish a Muslim Day' Letters Rattle U.K. Communities." *New York Times*, March 11, p. A7. (https://www.nytimes.com/2018/03/11/world/europe/uk-muslims-letters.html)

Khatami, Elham. April 3, 2018. "'Punish a Muslim Day' Backfired Spectacularly." *Think Progress*. Retrieved June 8, 2018. (https://thinkprogress.org/xenophobic-punish-a-muslim-day-campaign-backfired-5e1a42ef99ec/)

Kohut, Andrew, Scott Keeter, and Gregory Smith. 2011. "Muslim Americans: No Signs of Growth in Alienation or Support for Extremism." Pew Research Center, August 30, 2011. Retrieved June 8, 2018.

(http://www.people-press.org/2011/08/30/muslim-americans-no-signs-of-growth-in-alienation-or-support-for-extremism/)

Lipka, Michael. 2015. "Muslims Expected to Surpass Jews as Second-Largest U.S. Religious Group." Pew Research Center for the People and the Press. April 14, 2015. Retrieved June 8, 2018. (http://www.pewresearch.org/fact-tank/2015/04/14/muslims-expected-to-surpass-jews-as-second-largest-u-s-religious-group/).

Mohamed, Besheer, Gregory A. Smith, Alan Cooperman, and Anna Schiller. 2017. "U.S. Muslims Concerned About Their Place in Society, but Continue to Believe in the American Dream: Findings from Pew Research Center's 2017 survey of U.S. Muslims." Pew Research Center, July 26, 2017. Retrieved June 8, 2018. (http://www.pewforum.org/2017/07/26/findings-from-pew-research-centers-2017-survey-of-us-muslims/)

Muslim Demographics. 2019. Retrieved July 2019 (https://www.youtube.com/watch?v=6-3X5hIFXYU).

Nadal, Kevin L., Marie-Anne Issa, Katie E. Griffin, Sahran Hamit, and Oliver B. Lyons. "Religious Microaggressions in the United States: Mental Health Implications for Religious Groups." Pp. 287–310 in *Microaggressions and Marginality: Manifestation, Dynamics, and Impacts,* edited by D.W. Sue. Hoboken, NJ: John Wiley & Sons: p. 297.

Nausheen, Pasha-Zaidi, Tiffany Masson, and M. Nan Pennington. 2014. "Can I Get a Job If I Wear Hijab? An Exploratory Study of the Perceptions of South Asian Muslim Women in the US and the UAE." *International Journal of Research Studies in Psychology* 3(1):13–24.

Noble, Greg. 2005. "The Discomfort of Strangers: Racism, Incivility and Ontological Security in a Relaxed and Comfortable Nation." *Journal of Intercultural Studies* 26(1):107–20.

Nowrasteh, Alex. 2017. "Little National Security Benefit to Trump's Executive Order on Immigration." Cato Institute. Retrieved June 8, 2018. (www.cato.org/blog/little-national-security-benefit-trumps-executive-order-immigration)

Padela, Aasim, Huda Adam, Maha Ahmad, Zahra Hosseinian, and Farr Curlin. 2015. "Religious Identity and Workplace Discrimination: A National Survey of American Muslim Physicians." *AJOB Empirical Bioethics* 0(0):1–11.

Revesz, Rachael. 2016. "Muslim Passenger Kicked off American Airlines Flight After Attendant Announces: 'I'll Be Watching You.'" Retrieved August 15, 2016. (http://www.independent.co.uk/news/world/americas/muslim-kicked-off-plane-american-airlines-racial-discrimination-cair-uncomfortable-a7147311.html)

Runnymede Trust. 1997. "Islamophobia: A Challenge for Us All." (*https://www.runnymedetrust.org/companies/17/74/Islamophobia-A-Challenge-for-Us-All.html*)

Said, Edward. 1978. *Orientalism*. London, UK: Vintage Books.

Schildkraut, Deborah. 2009. "The Dynamics of Public Opinion on Ethnic Profiling After 9/11:

Results from a Survey Experiment." *American Behavioral Scientist* 53(1):61–79.

Splcenter.org. 2019. Retrieved July 2019 from (https://www.splcenter.org/hatewatch/2017/11/14/latest-fbi-numbers-show-anti-muslim-hate-crimes-continue-rise-suggest-growing-shift-toward).

Widner, Daniel, and Stephen Chicoine. 2011. "It's All in the Name: Employment Discrimination Against Arab Americans." *Sociological Forum* 26(4): 806–23.

Zopf, Bradley J. 2018. "A Different Kind of Brown: Arabs and Middle Easterners as Brown, Foreign, and Anti-American Muslims." *Sociology of Race and Ethnicity* 4(2): 178–91.

Reading 3.2 Race, Ethnicity, and Migration in the Context of Care Work

Tina Wu

Work and labor inequalities in society are profoundly shaped by race and ethnicity, migration, and gender. One example is domestic work, work that is performed in or for the home. Such work includes activities such as household cleaning and maintenance, food preparation, child care, and care for the elderly or disabled. When domestic work is performed in or for a private household for a wage, it is considered domestic labor, one of the oldest forms of paid work in society (Daniels, 1987; England, 2005).

Domestic work is commonly associated with care work and reproductive work, because they, too, are often performed in private homes. Care work entails providing care to other people, whether paid or unpaid. Examples of unpaid care work include the care parents provide to children or the care family members give to the elderly or disabled. Jobs that entail care work include those performed by teachers, nurses, doctors, and therapists. Reproductive work, a related concept, involves activities that help to sustain people on a daily and intergenerational basis. Such activities may include activities associated with child care, such as preparing children for school, and elder care, such as scheduling doctor appointments. Reproductive work, too, may be unpaid and informal, or paid. These terms, *domestic work*, *care work*, and *reproductive work* are often synonymous and are conceptually linked.

What these work categories have in common is that, with rare exceptions, these kinds of work typically offer low financial rewards and limited, if any, labor protections on the job. In many cases, these kinds of work are also socially devalued or invisible. For example, the unpaid care work performed by mothers is considered devalued in societies with limited paid maternal leave policies in workplaces. The babysitters and nannies who are paid to care for children are paid wages that typically range from just above minimum wage to much under the minimum wage. Their work is "precarious" in that they often cannot anticipate their work hours or count on a steady income (Kalleberg, 2009). Furthermore, today, these workers are either not protected by labor regulations—such as those governing legal minimum wage, sick pay, protection from workplace abuse—or, when they are, cases of violations remain unreported or uninvestigated.

Scholars agree that domestic work and associated forms of work are socially devalued, low paid, and precarious because of long-standing gendered divisions of labor. The work of taking care of a household and family members has traditionally been women's responsibilities. While women and men historically worked side by side to sustain a livelihood (for example, tending to, slaughtering, and cleaning livestock, tanning leathers) (Davis, 1983), by the nineteenth century, American households—particularly white middle- and upper-middle-class ones that could afford it—emphasized a division of labor by gender. Men were considered breadwinners, working outside the home in paid jobs and bringing home paychecks that supported the entire family. Women were considered "angels of the house," working inside the home, doing the unpaid work of cleaning and caregiving that sustains and reproduces family life. This gendered division of labor renders the unpaid work of women invisible to society. It does not bring a wage, making women economically dependent on men, and until the last few decades, was not recognized in divorce proceedings. Even today, much of this work remains informal and unaccounted for or undervalued in public policies, or lack thereof, like paid family leave for new parents or caregivers of the elderly or disabled. In summary, domestic work has a history of being associated with women and being unpaid and undervalued (Daniels, 1987; Duffy, 2011).

While domestic work has been shaped by the context of gender, it has also, simultaneously, been shaped by race and ethnicity and migration. Differences in women's racial and ethnic identities, and personal and group experiences of migration, influence women's specific experiences with both paid and unpaid domestic work. Scholars and theorists observe that domestic work has been further divided in society into two categories: nurturant and non-nurturant work. Nurturant work refers to work that is interpersonal and relational and that relies on complex skills in attending to the emotional needs of others—such as teaching or caregiving. Non-nurturant work, in contrast, refers to work that is menial, repetitive, and/or dirty—such as scrubbing floors or doing laundry. Domestic work and its related categories of care work and reproductive work often entails nurturant and non-nurturant components. Taking care of children, for example, may involve teaching as well as changing dirty diapers and cleaning soiled clothing. Sociologists and historians have found that the distribution of nurturant and non-nurturant components of domestic work has not been even; it has followed local patterns of racial and ethnic inequality, patterns that exist to this day. In the United States, enslaved women, immigrant women, and women from minority racial or ethnic groups were historically disproportionately tasked with the non-nurturant, "dirty" components of domestic work, while native-born white women performed the nurturant work. Today, immigrant women and women of color (including women brought involuntarily to the country for work) continue to perform domestic work, and especially non-nurturant domestic work, at a disproportionate rate (Duffy, 2011; Glenn, 1992, 2002).

In the United States, geography and history have played a large role in shaping the distinct work experiences of African American, Latina American, and Asian American women as well as that of white women of European origin. In the nineteenth century, European immigrant women, particularly those of Irish and German origin, were commonly employed as domestic servants in the Northeast. Meanwhile, in the South, African American women constituted a "servant caste" working for white households. Up until the First World War, 90 percent of African American women employed in nonagricultural work were employed in domestic labor. In the Southwest, Chicanas (US-born and immigrant women of Mexican origin) were disproportionately employed in domestic labor. In the Far West, particularly in California and Hawaii, Chinese and Japanese immigrants, women and men, were commonly employed in this line of work. Asian men became involved in domestic work because of gender imbalances in immigration (in the nineteenth century, most East Asian immigrants to the United States were men seeking work; women remained in the home countries) and the race-based exclusion of these men from other jobs. During this period, the growing professions of medicine and nursing in the United States explicitly excluded women and African Americans from their ranks. Instead, many African American women were relegated to specifically nonmedical caring and domestic service jobs. These patterns in domestic work continued into the twentieth century, as local immigrant populations and racial and ethnic prejudices determined the supply of workers for cheap domestic labor on one hand and the lack of alternative jobs for these workers on the other (Boris and Klein, 2012; Glenn, 2002).

In the late twentieth century and the beginning of the twenty-first century, immigrant women and women of color continue to perform domestic work and care work at disproportionately higher rates than other groups. These patterns are true across jobs in house cleaning, child care, and elder care. Sociologists have documented the working conditions of Latinas working as domestic workers and nannies in California, black Caribbean women employed as nannies in New York, and home care aides for the elderly from across racial and ethnic groups in the Midwest. They have found that in addition to low wages, unpredictable pay, and lack of job security and employer-provided benefits, these workers also sometimes experience isolation, emotional or physical abuse, surveillance, and racial discrimination on the job. Due to precarious immigration status, some workers are especially vulnerable to exploitation (Brown, 2011; Hondagneu-Sotelo, 2001; Stacey, 2011).

However, these women are not simply victims. Researchers have also documented the ways domestic workers and care workers utilize social networks to share information, pool resources, and protect one another from abuse. For example, drawing on racial and ethnic ties, immigrant women use public spaces like parks and playgrounds to buffer against the isolation of caring for children in private homes. These communities become spaces to learn about job opportunities, give or receive financial loans, and organize local social and labor movements. Immigrants and women of color actively find ways to make meaningful connections at work, despite the isolation, precariousness, and prevalence of abuse (Armenta, 2009; Brown, 2011).

These communities build on workers' sense of shared identity, often rooted in racial and ethnic familiarity, shared language, and countries or regions of origin. Movements such as Domestic Workers United, a founding member of the National Domestic Workers' Alliance, have grown out of these local communities to organize toward political action, such as demands for legislative labor protections. These activities have led to local, state-level, and national movements, and are among some of the most prominent social and labor movements in the country today.

One of the tasks these movements must accomplish is building collective identity across racial, ethnic, and immigrant groups. In many parts of the country, US-born and white women participate in the same labor market with immigrant women and women of color, performing caring jobs such as nannies and home care aides. Transcending these identity boundaries can be challenging to organizing, particularly when the workers come from vastly different personal backgrounds and have different priorities. For example, while Domestic Workers United and National Domestic Workers' Alliance have vocally aligned with other movements for racial justice and immigration reform, organizations like Nannypalooza, an international nanny conference with corporate sponsors, professional workshops, conference attendance fees, and podcasts, prioritize professionalization, which especially appeals to US-born white workers. In order for organizations like NDWA to achieve large-scale, broad-based organizing, they must appeal to disparate workers with different priorities, which first requires an understanding of how workers think about their identities in relation to their work (Goldberg, 2014).

In a study conducted between 2012 and 2013, I compared the work experiences of two groups of women working as nannies: one mostly immigrant women of color (black, Latina, and Asian) with high school–level or equivalent education or less, and the other mostly white, US-born women with college-level education or more (Wu, 2016). I relied on in-depth interviews with thirty-two nannies working in the Northeastern United States. I found that they share some precarious aspects of the job, such as low wages and uncertain work hours, but immigrant workers and nonwhite workers are more likely to experience vulnerability to discrimination and abuse. Immigrants and women of color, confronting historical and present-day social contexts of disrespect and discrimination, use stories of resistance to proudly defend their personal dignity and the value of their work. In contrast, US-born women, white women, and/or women from middle-class or upper-middle-class households report embarrassment, stigma, and shame from working as nannies. They feel they have, or ought to have, other employment options, and they are more likely to downplay or hide their jobs from their friends and family or distance themselves from their work, labeling it temporary. I suggest that broad-based mobilization of care workers requires understanding the attitudes and self-concepts of a diverse range of workers.

Self-concept refers to one's overarching image of oneself, and it is achieved as a compromise between one's personal identity, which is self-designated, and one's social identity, which is ascribed or attributed by others. This process has been termed identity work: "the range of activities individuals engage in to create, present, and sustain personal identities that are congruent with and supportive of the self-concept"(Snow and Anderson, 1987; Snow and McAdam, 2000). These concepts are useful for comparing the experiences of two different groups of nannies.

I conducted my study by visiting local parks and playgrounds in upper-middle-class and affluent residential neighborhoods of a city's downtown area. The nannies I interviewed for the study represented a diverse range of backgrounds, falling into two broad categories. In one group were mostly US-born white women in their twenties and thirties. They spoke English as their native language, and many either finished college or were in college at the time of the interview. Many had been working as nannies for a few years. Some had started during college. One respondent had worked as a nanny for the past thirteen years. In another group were mostly immigrant women of color. They were black, Latina, or Asian and in their thirties to fifties. They spoke English as a second language with varying degrees of proficiency. None held a college degree, and one woman identified her immigrant status as undocumented. A couple explained they had been undocumented in the past while working as nannies. In this group, respondents reported having worked as nannies for a few to over twenty years. Some reported having worked in other caretaking settings; for example, as home health aides for the elderly. While a few respondents in each category did not fully conform to these cleavages—for example, there were US-born white women who were not college educated—these two categories are consistent with findings in other comparable cities and are useful for analysis. Finally, all of the respondents were women, and the vast majority worked for white employers and white children at the time of the interview. Their employers were mostly professionals who worked full time. At the time of the interviews, the respondents were typically working full time—about thirty to forty hours a week—for one family. They were not live-in nannies, although some had worked as live-in nannies in the past. A few were not working as nannies at the exact time of the interview, but had recently worked as full-time nannies. The respondents drew from their experiences with their employers at the time of the interview as well as from past experiences with other families.

According to my interview schedule, I asked questions along some key themes, including: how respondents found their jobs, how they came to do this kind of work, how they felt about their work and their current jobs, their view on childrearing, their views on unions and labor and/or political organizing, and details about their pay rates, job benefits, and contracts (if any). The interviews typically lasted sixty to ninety minutes each and were digitally audio recorded and later transcribed for analysis. In subsequent analyses of the data, salient themes that emerged included: stigma of care work, racial and ethnic discrimination, and framing the work as temporary or "just for now." I coded for these themes in the interview data to look for patterns, which are presented here. I use pseudonyms to protect the anonymity of the respondents and their employers. Inconsequential details have been removed or changed.

Comparing the two groups, I found that both groups of nannies experience the precarious nature of the work. In both cases, the respondents were paid about $13 to $16 an hour, or $500 to $600 a week. The majority did not have contracts, did not receive medical benefits from their employers or other benefits, such as overtime pay, sick days, or paid time off. They all reported having uncertain work hours and schedules, which often caused anxiety because of the uncertain income week to week. In addition, some discussed the uncertain terms of the job and job responsibilities and pay cuts, cutbacks, or job termination with sometimes little or no notice. While most of the respondents worked about thirty to forty hours per week, many reported experiencing these uncertainties that are common in this line of work. As a result, several hold or have in the past held other part-time jobs in addition to their primary jobs as nannies. These other jobs include other caretaking jobs, office temp jobs, online sales, and short-term creative work such as in acting and theater. All in all, respondents in both groups reported experiencing uncertainty that is characteristic of precarious work.

For example, Deliah, a twenty-nine-year-old white woman who was born and raised in the United States and holds a bachelor's degree in English and Film Studies, recounts an experience working for a family whose child was about to enter preschool:

> For about three weeks, my hours had been cut in half, so I was only getting paid for half. There was no discussion of—Sometimes she [the employer and mother of the child] would just cut my hours for a week. This was three weeks, and I was like, "Uh, all right, is it going to be like this forever now, or …" And she said, "Oh! I've been meaning to talk to you about that. Now that Jamie's in preschool, we just don't really need you as much."

Deliah describes this experience as frustrating, as it led to unanticipated reduction of her income. This experience is common for nannies. Even permanent reduction of work hours, such as in this case, can happen with little advance notice. These occurrences create both feelings of uncertainty about one's pay and actual fluctuations of income.

Immigrant women, particularly those with uncertain immigration status in the United States, are substantially more vulnerable to precarious working conditions and abuse. Mirabel is a twenty-eight-year-old woman from Guatemala who immigrated to the United States when she was twenty years old. She was brought to this country by a former employer under the pretense of working as a live-in au pair in their home in the suburbs. Mirabel was not employed through an au pair program or agency and came to the country on a tourist visa. When her tourist visa expired, she continued to live and work in her employer's home without a contract and without friends or family in the United Sates. She reported working in isolation and fear:

> I remember just working and being left with the baby. There was no sense of orientation … I was pretty much working 17 hours a day, 7 days a week. I was being paid $150 per week, cooking, cleaning, taking care of the children, laundry, gardening, taking out the trash … I was

put to clean the floors with hot buckets of water pretty much by hand—all five bedrooms, three floors, huge house, cooking for the whole family, washing the dishes … After a while, I started feeling depression. I lost a lot of hair. I developed arthritis in my hands. For a year, I was [completely] isolated … It was horrible. I was scared. I thought I was going to be judged over time, and I always lived in fear.

Mirabel told her story in tears during her interview. She has since left that former employer and at the time of the interview she was working for a different family, with a written contract—one of the few respondents to have a contract at all. She is still undocumented, but she discussed having learned over the years how to advocate for herself and for other immigrants like her with the help of local nonprofit and community-based organizations. While Mirabel's story of exploitation and abuse is the most extreme of the interviews I conducted, it was not the exception. Other immigrant women also reported feeling isolation and fear, particularly as undocumented immigrants or immigrants on uncertain, short-term visas. They reported feeling pressured to accepted low wages or abusive relationships with employers to a far greater extent than US-born women.

The two groups also experience stigma and low social status associated with child care work. However, they experience the stigma and low status in different ways. Immigrant women of color report being discriminated against based on their racial and ethnic identities and immigrant status both by some employers and by the general public in public places such as parks and playgrounds. As nonwhite women taking care of white children in upper-middle-class neighborhoods, they are visibly marked as nannies. Some give explicit examples of slights or confrontations. Others report that it is an ever-present feeling of being watched or judged. For example, Stella, a thirty-nine-year-old black woman who immigrated to the United States from St. Vincent in the Caribbean says, "I used to think that they might say she looks young and she is black and working in the house. She doesn't have any education. She's just [an] uneducated nanny. I used to think like that, but now I'm done. I'm done." When I asked why she felt judged in public, she says, "It's just the negative feeling. It's just a feeling you have. No one ever said anything to me personally, but it's just the thought in your head."

Priya, a thirty-eight-year-old woman of Indian descent who immigrated to the United States from the Caribbean, recounted an interaction with a previous employer. The mother of a child she cared for once gave her a book to read. She says:

> I read the book, and it was a hard book to read, and she said, "Well, my therapist was really impressed that you read that book." So I said, "Because I'm a nanny I'm dumb? Like I don't have any knowledge or anything?" It's like, I went to school, I have an education [Priya holds an associate's degree and some training to be a certified nursing assistant], you know what I mean? A lot of people see you and [when] you say you're a nanny, they kind of look down on you like you don't know much, you don't have much knowledge, and that you're limited in your views, but it's not true.

Like Stella, Priya is conscious of slights and judgment, particularly of the assumption that nannies are uneducated. She vehemently states, "I went to school, I have an education," resisting this assumption and saying that "it's not true." In her response to this interaction with her employer, she echoes Stella's sentiment: "I used to think like that, but now I'm done. I'm done." In each case, the respondents refuse to internalize perceived public opinion and disrespect.

These nannies' resistance of public scrutiny and disrespect occur even when their jobs may be on the line. Hanna is a thirty-nine-year-old woman from Morocco. She has dark hair and a tan complexion, and she clearly looks different from the blond, white baby she brings to public parks and playgrounds. Her physical characteristics and those of the child she takes care of reveal her role as a nanny, and she says that judgment from bystanders in public places is common. She says:

> Something happened to me with one of the moms [a bystander in the park]. The girl that I'm watching, she took something from another child, and she was rough with it. It was time to show her—that's my job—how to share, how to play with other kids. I was like, come over

here, we don't do this. You need to say sorry. This is what the family agreed with me, too. One of the moms [in the park], she came from the middle of nowhere, and she's like, "Oh, excuse me, I think you're too tough with her!" Like, you see, she wants to put something on me. She doesn't know the situation. She doesn't know what I'm saying to the little girl, and she just show [off] to the other moms that I'm doing something wrong … I told her, "Please don't ever tell me what I'm doing. I can give you her mom's number and you can call her. Thank you!"

In this incident, Hana is aware that she was judged and her job performance was scrutinized by one of the mothers in the public park that parents and nannies frequent in the neighborhood. Instead of tacitly accepting this scrutiny and critique or avoiding conflict, Hana actively resists. She believes she is doing a good job, one that the family she works for agrees with, and asserts herself to the stranger in the park. I did not witness any of these interactions recounted by the respondents, so it is unknown what actually occurred in these instances. However, it is notable that in each case, respondents pride themselves in standing up for themselves and resisting perceived judgment or condescension, even when they may be risking their jobs.

In contrast, US-born women with college degrees respond to the stigma of being nannies by tacitly accepting that stigma and distancing their identities from their jobs. They commonly reported feeling judged by family or friends for working as nannies, and that they feel they ought to be doing other, more respected jobs. Lisa, a twenty-six-year-old white woman who holds a bachelor's degree in health care studies, reported that her family was "supportive" of her working as a nanny, but only because she was taking courses to go back to school to become a nurse. She says:

They support that I'm going back to school, so they know why I'm doing it. They know it's a passing thing, and I think if I said, "Yeah, this is what I'm going to do for a while," they'd be like, "Well, what are you going to do next?" They would push me.

Lisa agrees with these expectations that her family has set out for her. She says, "I think they [my family] expect more of me, and they know I expect more of myself." She continues "I sometimes look at it, like, how did I get here? I have a lot of friends that are very successful, and we all went to the same college, and we all started in the same place." Lisa has internalized the judgment of her friends and family. She implicitly agrees that working as a nanny is not "successful" enough, and that she ought to be doing "more." Lisa frames her job as a nanny as temporary work while she pursues going back to school.

Some US-born women with bachelor's degrees emphasize other work that they do to deflect the stigma associated with working as a nanny. Deliah, the twenty-nine-year-old white woman who holds a bachelor's degree in English and film, says, "When I was working at the market research place [a part-time evening job she held while working as a nanny], that was what I would say" when people asked her, "What do you do?" She continues, "I might have also said, 'I also babysit during the day,' or something like that …'" She explains why: "As much as I complain this whole time about them [her employers] not considering it to be my job, my real honest-to-goodness job—sure, I don't have a degree in babysitting, but I may as well, you know, it's my job—I almost don't … It's hard for me to justify it as a 'job.'" She says, "I know it's difficult work. But in my mind, sitting at a desk in front of a computer is a job. Babysitting is like, I don't know. Anybody can do that. Anybody can babysit." Deliah's internal dilemma reflects one that many US-born women, particularly those with college degrees, experience. She acknowledges the social devaluation of child care—"Anybody can babysit"—and while she intellectually disagrees with it—"I know it's difficult work"—she also struggles to "justify it as a 'job,'" especially because it does not look like the image of a typical white-collar job that she has in mind. As a result, she distances her identity from her work as a nanny, in order to maintain her image of herself.

For those US-born white women, particularly those from middle- or upper-middle-class households who cannot easily justify the temporality of their work, working as a nanny elicits shame. Lars, a thirty-two-year-old white woman whose father is a lawyer, grew up in an upper-middle-class household. She does not hold a bachelor's degree, and her work as a nanny is a source of embarrassment. She says, "I think my family would rather I was doing something different … My mom will be like, 'I told your grandmother you own a store. And it's like, 'Ok mom, got it, you're really embarrassed.'" She continues:

My mom is very concerned about what people think and how things look. She's pretty not happy about it. I think she feels a little ashamed, like she can't—like, even when people ask her what I'm doing, she'll be like, "Oh, she owns a house." She's not trying to broadcast it. I think she thinks it's not—which I can understand—I have mixed feelings about it. It's not where I thought I'd be at 32.

Like Lisa, Lars feels social and family pressure to be doing other, more respectable forms of work. She has internalized this pressure, as evidenced by her statement, "I have mixed feelings about it. It's not where I thought I'd be at 32." Many US-born white women who hold college degrees or who come from upper-middle-class households feel the stigma of working as nannies. It is seen as socially acceptable for young people, particularly as temporary work while pursuing more education, but as women age and as it becomes harder to emphasize the work's temporality, respondents report feeling shame or embarrassment.

The experiences that US-born white women report are markedly different from those of the immigrant women of color. While US-born white women report distancing themselves from their work, which they know is socially devalued, immigrant women of color equally recognize the social devaluation of their work but respond with active resistance. Many US-born white women, particularly those with college degrees, feel they have or should have other, more respectable job options; in contrast, many immigrant women of color, especially those without advanced degrees or credentials, recognize they must both actively defend their self-respect in the face of social devaluation as well as advocate for material conditions of their jobs, such as wages and job agreements. By comparing immigrant women of color and US-born whites, I show that these two groups think about their work and themselves differently, despite doing similar work. Although both groups experience child care as precarious and socially devalued work, I suggest that their responses may pit their efforts against each other. US-born white women's internalization of social stigma and shame tacitly reinforces the notion that child care is menial work and, implicitly, work suited for immigrant women of color who are low on the status hierarchy. In order for collective organizing to reach broad-based mobilization, I suggest that it is first important to recognize the identity work that different groups of workers engage in in response to the longstanding, historic social devaluation of care work in society. Students of social inequalities and race, ethnicity, and migration also benefit from these perspectives.

References

Armenta, A. (2009). "Creating Community: Latina Nannies in a West Los Angeles Park." *Qualitative Sociology, 32*(3), 279–92. https://doi.org/10.1007/s11133-009-9129-1

Boris, E., and Klein, J. (2012). *Caring for America: Home Health Workers in the Shadow of the Welfare State.* New York: Oxford University Press.

Brown, T.M. (2011). *Raising Brooklyn: Nannies, Childcare, and Caribbeans Creating Community.* New York: New York University Press.

Daniels, A.K. (1987). "Invisible Work." *Social Problems, 34*(5), 403–15. https://doi.org/10.2307/800538

Davis, A.Y. (1983). *Women, Race, & Class* (1st Vintage Books edition). New York: Vintage.

Duffy, M. (2011). *Making Care Count: A Century of Gender, Race, and Paid Care Work.* New Brunswick, NJ: Rutgers University Press.

England, P. (2005). "Emerging Theories of Care Work." *Annual Review of Sociology, 31*, 381–99.

Glenn, E.N. (1992). "From Servitude to Service Work: Historical Continuities in the Racial Division of Paid Reproductive Labor." *Signs, 18*(1), 1–43.

Glenn, E.N. (2002). *Unequal Freedom: How Race and Gender Shaped American Citizenship and Labor*. Cambridge, MA: Harvard University Press.

Goldberg, H. (2014). "Prepare to Win: Domestic Workers United's Strategic Transition Following Passage of the New York Domestic Workers' Bill of Rights." In *New Labor in New York* (p. 266). Ithaca, NY: Cornell University Press.

Hondagneu-Sotelo, P. (2001). *Doméstica: Immigrant Workers Cleaning and Caring in the Shadows of Affluence*. Berkeley: University of California Press.

Kalleberg, A.L. (2009). "Precarious Work, Insecure Workers: Employment Relations in Transition." *American Sociological Review, 74*(1), 1–22.

Snow, D.A., and Anderson, L. (1987). "Identity Work Among the Homeless: The Verbal Construction and Avowal of Personal Identities." *American Journal of Sociology, 92*(6), 1336–371.

Snow, D.A., and McAdam, D. (2000). "Identity Work Processes in the Context of Social Movements: Clarifying the Identity/Movement Nexus." In *Self, Identity, and Social Movements* (Vol. 13, pp. 41–67). Minneapolis: University of Minnesota.

Stacey, C. (2011). *The Caring Self: The Work Experiences of Home Care Aides*. Ithaca, NY: Cornell University Press.

Wu, T. (2016). More than a paycheck: Nannies, work, and identity. *Citizenship Studies 20*(3–4), 295–310. https://doi.org/10.1080/13621025.2016.1158358

Reading 3.3 The Sandra Bland Case: Dissecting Intersectionality and Institutional Segregation in Post-racial America

Jacqueline Brooks, California State University–Sacramento

Heidy Sarabia, California State University–Sacramento

Keywords: Intersectionality, Criminal Justice, Oppression, and Suspicious Body

Chapter Objectives

In this chapter students will create connections between structural racism and inequitable treatment of marginalized groups with the criminal justice system. While many works that address racial inequities within the criminal justice system, this chapter focuses on the intersection of race, class, and gender. Students will address and evaluate how the intersecting oppressions of race, class, and gender create different material realities and experiences for women of color. Further, students will analyze how the criminal justice system perpetuates social inequities.

Introduction

In July 2016, social media exploded when the video of Breaion King's traffic stop in Austin, Texas, went viral. It showed Officer Bryan Richter, a white police officer, throwing King, a black schoolteacher, to the ground during an arrest. Dismayed by her brutal treatment, King engaged in a conversation with a different arresting officer about race as she sat, handcuffed, in the back of a police cruiser.

> Officer Spradlin asks King, "Let me ask you this. Why are so many people afraid of black people?" King responds, "That's what I want to figure out, because I'm not a bad black person." Then, Officer Spradlin offers his own explanation, "I can give you a really good, a really good idea why it might be that way. Violent tendencies. I want you to think about that. I'm not saying anything, I'm not saying it's true, I'm not saying I agree with it or nothing, but 99 percent of the time, when you hear about stuff like that, it is the black community that is being violent. That's why a lot of white people are afraid. And I don't blame them." (Miller 2016)

In the exchange, Officer Richter suggested that the perceived aggressiveness of black Americans creates public fear, thus justifying King's violent arrest. Later, Austin's police chief, Art Acevedo, issued an apology to King. stating, "Police officers have a sworn duty to try to calm things down, approach incidents, approach people in a manner that enhances the probability that everyone will get to go on with their day, especially over a speeding ticket" (Miller 2016).[i] Yet, this is not an isolated incident. The treatment of people of color, especially women, in the custody of law enforcement officials has garnered much media attention recently due to new technological means to record and disperse interactions between law enforcement and people of color—making it an undeniable issue in need of urgent attention.

In the context of violent encounters between law enforcement officers and people of color, the experiences of women of color have often been largely ignored, in part due to the number of men of color targeted and affected by these violent interactions.[ii] Thus, this chapter focuses on the case of Sandra Bland, emphasizing how women's experiences with law enforcement are uniquely shaped by their intersectional experiences of race, gender, class, and mental health.

Sandra Bland

In the summer of 2015, the dash cam video of an incident between a young black woman and a police officer became fodder for social media. The video shows the violent arrest of Sandra Bland by Brian Encinia, a white police officer—an incident that yielded irreparable consequences. Within three days of her arrest, Bland was found dead in her jail cell. Immediately after, the public questioned how a traffic stop for a minor violation (failure to signal a lane change) led to such a contentious interaction between a black motorist and a white law enforcement officer, which culminated in her reported suicide.

In this chapter, we analyze the case of Sandra Bland, utilizing the reports of law enforcement in communities of color and newspaper accounts to argue two points. First, we root our analysis in intersectionality, arguing that racist and gendered authority structures rely on the construction of *suspicious* bodies to determine the type of treatment people receive. The *suspicious* label emerges from dangerous perceptions (e.g., "angry black woman," "thug," or "*illegal*") marring the experiences of minority groups. As in Bland's case, everyday minor infractions become potentially fatal situations when committed by individuals who lack intersectional social privileges (e.g., race, class, gender, and ability), since these privileges offer certain groups assurances that guard against maltreatment. Second, we argue that we must always take into account the institutions that treat bodies differently to understand how intersectional systems of oppression operate.

Intersectionality: Racist and Gendered Structures

Emerging in the late 1980s, intersectionality theory sought to expose the relational feature of social inequalities, attaching these linkages to power structures. Moving inequality discourse away from singularly themed explanations, intersectionality highlighted the multiplicative power of social inequalities, exposing the simultaneous interaction of different forms of oppression (Crenshaw 1992; Crenshaw 1991). Since its inception, intersectionality has spread throughout academia, inspiring theoretical works, research that assesses structural arrangements, analyses of identity construction, and applied work, especially in the realm of social justice (Collins 2015).

In *Intersectionality's Definitional Dilemmas*, Collins (2015) lays out the guiding assumptions of intersectionality. Here, she argues that relational bonds exist among various forms of social inequality (e.g., race, class, gender, sexual orientation, nation, age, ethnicity, and ability), and these relational bonds are situated within systems of power. In order to understand inequality, then, we must pay close attention to the systems of power meshed within relational bonds that create unequal access to societal rewards. It is important to underscore that inequality is not fixed, as these inequalities vary across time and space. Subsequently, different groups develop perspectives based on their own particular experiences. Ultimately, Collins argues, we must acknowledge that social inequalities emerging from intersecting systems of power "are fundamentally unjust" (Collins 2015:14).

The intersectional approach constructs an interpretive understanding that challenges the positioning of black women who experience mental distress and financial hardship in the larger social structure. This interpretive, or reflexive understanding, is shaped by the application of intersectionality, which can "excavate and expose multilayered structures of power and domination by adopting a grounded praxis approach" (Sumi, Crenshaw, and McCall 2013:804). We connect relational social inequalities to intersecting systems of power, mainly the racialized and gendered authority of the state via the criminal justice system. We argue that overarching patriarchy renders women, especially those in the hands of the state, powerless. We acknowledge that systemic class inequality disenfranchises people of color, making them targets of police harassment. As these systems of power intersect, justification for maltreatment becomes nurtured and emboldened.

Arresting the Suspicious Body

Michelle Alexander (2012) argues that the criminal justice system is not only one more institution where inequality exists or a single institution that exemplifies racialized unequal treatment. She argues that the criminal justice system is the very systematic process by which inequality is not only created and perpetuated, it is also the ideological tool used to justify such inequality. In other words, not only does the criminal justice system create a system of racial injustice, but it also produces the justification that supports and perpetuates racial inequality.

The criminal justice system perpetuates racial inequality by labeling people of color as "criminals." Once labeled a criminal, hegemonic ideology justifies the removal of rights (Wacquant 2005). The criminal is constructed as undeserving, even though this criminality is explicitly racially differentiated, affecting nonwhites in disproportionate ways. Thus, by paying close attention to the way in which bodies are read—explicitly or implicitly—as suspicious, we can better approach the way in which race and racism operate to criminalize nonwhite bodies in the United States. In other words, while race is a socially constructed "template for the subordination and oppression of different social groups" (Omi and Winant 1994:108), it also signifies difference in particular ways; that is, in ways that make certain bodies suspect.

When Sandra Bland was pulled over and arrested after attempting to make way for the police cruiser quickly approaching behind her on July 10, 2015, it was not Bland's first incarceration. In 2010, she served thirty days for marijuana possession in Harris County Jail, a facility cited for numerous civil rights violations (Nathan 2016). At the time, her lawyer claimed that Bland admitted to smoking marijuana daily, thinking that she was possibly self-medicating. He represented her on a previous marijuana charge and worked to have a DUI charge dropped. In the years following her graduation from Prairie View A&M University, Bland racked up a dizzying amount of fines and fees largely related to traffic stops. She eventually spent a night in jail for not appearing in court related to several traffic citations. A subsequent DUI charge indicates that emotional stress was apparent in Bland's life.

Bland's experiences with law enforcement reflect a pattern of racial targeting that occurs widely across the United States. In fact, the practice of generating substantial revenue through tickets, fees, and fines is not specific to Texas; nor is targeting people of color with this practice. For example, in an investigation of the Ferguson Police Department in Ferguson, Missouri, the US Justice Department concluded that the city relies heavily on court fees and fines as a source of revenue, a practice that is in concert with the racist treatment of African Americans (US Department of Justice 2015). In a city where they comprise 67 percent of the population, African Americans make up 85 percent of vehicle stops, 90 percent of citations, and 93 percent of arrests (US Department of Justice 2015). Further, African Americans are "more likely to be cited and arrested following a stop regardless of why the stop was initiated and more likely to receive multiple citations during a single incident (US Department of Justice 2015:4). In fact, the report goes as far as to state that the Ferguson Police Department "appears to bring certain offenses almost exclusively against African-Americans … 95% of Manner of Walking in Roadway charges, and 94% of Failure to Comply charges" (US Department of Justice 2015:4). Invariably, poverty becomes criminalized as municipalities levy heavy fines and fees against individuals, mostly people of color, for minor violations. Each year, the amount of revenue Ferguson collects from the courts increases. In 2011, they generated $1.41 million from fines and fees, and in 2015 they expected the court's revenue share to balloon to $3.09 million (US Department of Justice 2015).

Bland's actions contributed to her criminal record, yet we cannot discount the racist authority structure that squashes people of color under the weight of arrests, fines, and fees. After graduating college, Bland returned to Illinois several times seeking gainful employment (Nathan 2016). Here, she resided in an area where "black drivers … are up to four and a half times more likely than white drivers to be searched" (Nathan 2016:14). Sporadic employment, a reported miscarriage, a ton of debt related to traffic fines and fees, and the death of her grandmother seemed to factor into Bland's reported battle with depression (Nathan 2016). Bland's file of misdemeanors kept permanent employment out of her reach, consistent with research that finds criminal records disadvantage blacks in the labor market far greater than they disadvantage whites (Pager 2003). Thus, even though Bland moved around, she could not escape the system of racial inequality, perpetuated through the criminal justice system. She was continuously caught in the web of *illegality*—that is, the state production of individuals outside of the law (DeGenova 2002).

When Trooper Encinia stopped Bland for a minor traffic infraction in 2015, he might have been engaging in racial profiling—as numerous studies have exposed the racialized perception of law enforcement and its negative consequences on blacks and Latinos (Weitzer and Tuch 2002, 2005; Wilson, Dunham, and Alpert 2004). For example, New York City discarded its notorious Stop and Frisk policy after its own report revealed that the majority of New Yorkers who were stopped and frisked were innocent (NYCLU 2016). Between 2002 and 2015, approximately 4 million New Yorkers, mostly black and Latino, were "subjected to police stops and street interrogations" (NYCLU 2016). In fact, in 2013, a federal judge ruled the practice unconstitutional for violating Fourth Amendment rights (CCR 2013).

Bland had changed lanes to allow the police car to pass her, so she was dismayed by the officer's actions. Bland appeared frustrated and repeatedly challenged the officer's directives (her right to do so), attempted to record her encounter (her right to do so), and consistently proclaimed her astonishment with the officer's behavior (her right to do so). The crucial turning point in the police encounter occurred when the trooper asked Bland to extinguish her cigarette in her private vehicle. When Bland curtly refuses, this becomes one challenge too many. Threatening Bland with a stun gun, stating, *"I will light you up,"* Trooper Encinia forces Bland to exit her vehicle. Later, he handcuffs Bland and throws her to the ground, claiming that she was being combative. In a recorded conversation with his superior, he is heard struggling to find a reason to arrest her.[iii] Both officers settled on using assault of a public servant as the reason for the arrest. After being seen by paramedics, Bland is transferred to Waller County Jail in Hempstead, Texas.

It is in the context of intersectional experiences that "suspected" bodies are treated differently; and gender is a paramount structure that significantly shapes these treatments. The following chart reflects data compiled by the *Washington Post*, in efforts to track the number of fatal police shootings that occur annually in the United States. As reported, men and whites reflect the majority of victims shot by law enforcement. The *Washington Post* database also reveals that in each reported year, blacks make up approximately one fourth of fatal police shootings. Combined, Hispanics and blacks make up nearly 40 percent of fatal police shootings across each year. Although women make up a small percentage of individuals shot and killed by law enforcement, their consistent representation across each year is troubling.

Fatal Police Shootings in the US by Gender, Race, Mental Illness, and Age

	2015	2016	2017
Gender			
Men	953	923	940
Women	42	40	45
Race			
White	497	466	457
Black	259	234	223
Hispanic	179	160	179
Other/Unknown	67	103	128
Mental Illness			
Sign of Mental Illness	257	242	236
No Sign of Mental Illness	738	721	751

Age			
Under 18 years old	18	16	28
18 years old and older*	966	922	926
Total	995	963	987

This table was compiled from data reported by the Washington Post. *Data was collected from news reports, police records, Internet databases, and journalistic accounts. www.washingtonpost.com/graphics/national/police-shootings/*

*Individuals listed as "age unknown" were not included in the table.

Yet, women are victimized by law enforcement in many ways that are gender specific and that do not always result in death, but with grave consequences nonetheless. In an investigation of the Baltimore Police Department, for example, the US Department of Justice found many examples of sexual misconduct by police officers (USDJ 2016). In one case, a woman filed an official complaint after two Baltimore Police Department (BPD) officers "fondled her when conducting a search and called her a 'junkie, whore bitch'" (143). Not only was inquiry into the complaint long and inadequate, by the time they reached out to the victim, she had passed away. In another case, a woman reported to BPD investigators "she met with a certain officer and engaged in sexual activities in the officer's patrol car once every other week 'in exchange for U.S. currency or immunity from arrest'" (149). But the case was administratively closed. Ten months later, an anonymous tip revealed that the same officer was "'having sex in his patrol vehicle' with a different person involved in the sex trade" (150); however, the state attorney's office declined to prosecute. Then, a third tip came from another police department "that the same officer was engaging in sexual activities with the same woman involved in the sex trade" (150). This time, when a "BPD detective attempted to interview the woman; [she] postponed the interview because she was in ill health. Two days later, the woman passed away" (150).

In light of the findings that BPD officers were found to be "deeply dismissive of sexual assault victims and hostile toward prostitutes and transgender people," the *New York Times* accurately published an article titled "Some Women Won't 'Ever Again' Report a Rape in Baltimore" (Stolberg and Bidgood 2016). In the article, Jacqueline Robarge, the director and founder of Power Inside, reported knowing a female sex-industry worker who "said a police officer had ordered her into his car and coerced her to have sex" (Stolberg and Bidgood 2016). These examples reinforce the finding that sexual misconduct is the second most reported form of police misconduct (AAPF 2016:5). Thus, violence against women often takes place in the form of sexual violence.

In light of this evidence of explicit sexual violence, the framing of intersectionality highlights how race and racism operate in the United States simultaneously with gender and patriarchal oppression. Thus, we must pay close attention to the ways in which racialized and gendered bodies are systematically treated—not in an abstract sense—but in concrete everyday experiences within institutions. These treatments, although sometimes explicitly discriminatory, do not have to be explicitly differentiated to be racist or sexist (Van Cleve 2016), as differential treatments ultimately result in outcomes that perpetuate the oppression of people of color in general, and women of color in particular.

Convicting the Suspicious Body

Institutions are the building blocks of social life; they structure our daily routines, provide meaning to our social world, and determine practices that become normalized in society. They reflect the persistent social relationships that endure over time. For example, in addition to the criminal justice system, religion, education, family, and the economy reflect patterned behavior that has become entrenched within the social fabric of our lives. Patricia Fernandez-Kelly (2016) argues that state institutions have two purposes: they can either be mainstream or liminal. Mainstream state institutions deal with citizenship affairs (e.g., issuing marriage certificates, collecting taxes, or providing official identification) and treat individuals as citizens and consumers; while liminal institutions (e.g., welfare offices, correctional facilities, and public schools) treat individuals as "burdens on the society, perennial outsiders, and sources of pollution" (Fernandez-Kelly 2016: xii). These liminal institutions deal with individuals mostly through surveillance and policing, such as mass incarceration, militarized spaces, or criminal courts.

Yet, from our previous discussion of intersectionality, we can see that whether institutions serve their "mainstream" ideal or the "liminal" purpose depends largely on the individual—and their intersectional positionality within the system. For example, Princeton professor Imani Perry was arrested over a three-year-old unpaid ticket. She complained that she was mistreated by not being allowed to make a phone call, being patted down by a male police officer, and being handcuffed to a table (Knapp 2016). She further explained on social media:

> This was my first time in handcuffs. They were very cold on my arthritic wrists. I have been thinking about how vulnerable they make you feel. And how some people, often my people, from childhood on experience that naked vulnerability over and over again because they happen to live in places deemed "bad." (Perry 2016)

Although the police department immediately responded that the officers had followed standard procedure, Janice Fine, a white woman and a professor just like Perry, explained how in a similar circumstance her treatment was significantly different.

> I am a Rutgers prof[essor] who lives in Princeton. A few years ago I did a u turn w[ith] my son in the car on Nassau street. I was pulled over. The police took a very long time to come back w[ith] my license. As it turned out, I too had an old parking ticket that I had forgotten about and it had apparently morphed into a warrant for my arrest. Maybe b[e]c[ause] my 6th grade son was in the car and maybe also b[e]cause] I am a white woman who was driving a minivan the woman cop was very nice to me. She had me park the van, drove my son and I to the middle school, let me walk him in and then took me to the station. She said I know this is ridiculous and i am supposed to cuff you but I won't unless my chief sees me. So they put me in a room, fingerprinted and processed me but were really nice about it. They took away my license and I had to drive to Trenton without one to get a new one! Sounds like disparate treatment for sure. (Fine 2016)

Perry's and Fine's disparate treatment clearly show how the very same institution, the police, operates differently depending on how bodies are read: as legitimate citizens in need of protection and guidance or as suspicious bodies requiring surveillance and policing. These examples suggest the very same institution—the police—acts as mainstream with white bodies and as liminal with black bodies. Thus, even in mainstream institutions (e.g., schools), nonwhite bodies are read as suspicious and therefore experience oppression. These differential practices within institutions, ideologically couched as neutral, reveal the extent to which explicit racism is no longer acceptable, but disparate treatment and outcomes are largely tolerated and are not seen as discriminatory (Bonilla-Silva 2006).

Sandra Bland, much like Imani Perry, was treated not like a citizen who was rightfully upset in her circumstances. She was stopped by a police officer for a minor traffic violation—failure to signal a lane change—and then was ordered to put out a cigarette: an order meant to reinforce who was in control, who had the authority, and who had the power to command. The arrest was not necessary, but unlike Perry—a Princeton professor with a stable job—Bland was in a more tenuous economic situation. Although she had just landed her first permanent position in a long time, she needed to borrow money to post bail. For Bland, a minor traffic stop yielded harsh consequences because her body was read as suspect and treated as *illegal*—that is as outside of the law. The case of Sandra Bland highlights the extent to which intersectionality operates to produce different effects in the same liminal circumstances. Namely, Perry had the resources to avoid the further escalation of her precarious legal situation, while for Bland, a series of minor infractions escalated to the point where she reportedly committed suicide.

The most troubling part of Bland's story is speculating over what happened after she was incarcerated. The numerous civil rights violations levied against the guardians of suspicious bodies (e.g., police departments, jails, and prisons) suggest that the extension of civil and human rights does not reach many prisoners. The violation of an inmate's rights becomes more urgent when they suffer from physical and mental health issues. The question—asked by Bland's family in a civil lawsuit—becomes where was her protection, if she was battling suicidal ideations? Since 2000, suicide has remained the leading cause of unnatural death in county jails (US Department of Justice 2015). In 2013, the rate of inmate suicides in county jails reached 46 per 100,000, outpacing the prison system by far, which reached 15 per 100,000 (US Department of Justice 2015). Distinct differences between the jail and prison experience may contribute to this gap (Konrad et al. 2007; Blaauw, Kerkhof, and Hayes 2005). County jails often work with little information about inmates, maintain looser checks and balances regarding the physical and mental health of inmates, and do not have the institutional structure to provide inmates with quality care. After Bland's death, state authorities cited the Waller County Jail for not adequately supervising inmates with mental health risks and not providing documentation that jailers had received proper training in dealing with inmates with suicidal ideations (*Chicago Sun-Times* 2015). In addition to poor supervision, jails nurture powerlessness and hopelessness as inmates await decisions about their futures, often falling into despair as they experience the *shock of confinement* (Cox and Morchauser 1997; Goss et al. 2002; Konrad et al. 2007; Kaste 2015; Chammah and Meagher 2015). Behind bars, fears of lost job opportunities, financial destruction, and public humiliation and embarrassment can rattle even the strongest of wills. One can speculate that perhaps Bland thought her days of financial upheaval and bouts with the law were in the past, only to find that the fears she expressed about police brutality had become her reality. Without proper care, negotiating these fears can be disastrous.

Conclusion

Ultimately, Sandra Bland was not arrested by a police officer concerned for her safety, working to protect her, or determined to seek out her best interests. Instead, the police officer that arrested her read her citizenship entitlement as dangerous, her defiance as aggressive, and her resistance as threatening. "She found out her bond was $5,000, and no one—she was calling and calling—and no one was answering, and then after that she just broke down. She was crying and crying," her lawyer said (quoted in Sanchez 2015). The system broke Sandra Bland, not because of this one incident, but because this one incident was the culmination of a series of events that are emblematic of inequality in this society. She felt like she did not have the money, the resources, the network, or the means to post bail. She saw her whole life derailed in front of her—her new job was now out of reach, her time in that jail cell now felt eternal, and her voice had been effectively silenced.

Yet, Sandra Bland was not the only black woman is this precarious situation. Her own mother reminded Congress that

> … other six [women] died in jail. We're not talking about that year, we're talking about the month of July. 18–50 [years old]. Kindra Chapman allegedly stole a cell phone; 20 hours later she hung herself. Alexis McGovern downstairs in the infirmary dead, her family upstairs paying the bond. Nobody has spoken these names. And as I go around the country speaking, the fact that no pen is raised in a room, where six other women, aside from my daughter, have died. And nobody knows their names. That's a problem. (Reed-Veal 2016)

The case of Sandra Bland and others reminds us of the fragility of citizenship rights for people of color in the United States. US citizens have certain rights, but when confronted by the police, people of color have mostly despair—there is not much you can do or say to avoid going down the rabbit hole of social injustice. In a second, your whole life can derail into chaos and despair because throughout the whole process, your body will not be read as a citizen body entitled to certain rights and privileges, but as a suspect body that rather than prove its guilt will have to prove its deservedness of rights.

Sandra Bland was never passive, as she drew on a strong and large network, her interpretive community, to voice her perspective and created kinship with victims of police brutality; entangling her own experiences of inequality with the experiences of others. In April of 2015 she had said in a video posted on social media, "Being a black person in America is very, very hard … At the moment black lives matter. They matter" (quoted in Sanchez 2015). By exposing police brutality via social media, Bland and others have created opportunities for strangers within and across communities to build commonality through shared experiences. For example, immediately following the news of Kindra Chapman's suicide in a jail cell, hashtag "If I Die in Police Custody" trended, showcasing the visceral effect of her death on communities of color.[iv] Bland, in response to police killings of unarmed black men (e.g., Michael Brown, Eric Garner, and Walter Scott) posted numerous Facebook videos exhibiting dismay with the criminal justice system and reinforcing camaraderie with her larger community. Her interpretive community was and continues to be broad and specific, racialized and gendered, ostracized by wealth and mental well-being, known and unknown, vocal and silent.

References

AAPF. 2016. "#SayHerName. Resisting Police Brutality against Black Women: A Social Media Guide." New York. http://static1.squarespace.com/static/53f20d90e4b0b80451158d8c/t/555e2412e4b0bd5f4da5d3a4/143223 2978932/SAYHERNAME+Social+Media+Guide.compressed.pdf.

Alexander, Michelle. 2012. *The New Jim Crow: Mass Incarceration in the Age of Colorblindness.* New Press.

Blaauw, E., J.F.M. Kerkhof, and L.M. Hayes. 2005. "Demographic, Criminal, and Psychiatric Factors Related to Inmate Suicide." *Suicide and Life-Threatening Behavior* 35 (1): 63–75.

Bonilla-Silva, Eduardo. 2006. *Racism without Racists: Color-Blind Racism and the Persistence of Racial Inequality in the United States.* Lanham, MD: Rowman & Littlefield.

CCR. 2013. "Floyd, et al. v. City of New York, et al." http://ccrjustice.org/home/what-we-do/our-cases/floyd-et-al-v-city-new-york-et-al.

Chammah, Maurice, and Tom Meagher. 2015. "Why Jails Have More Suicides than Prisons." *The Marshall Project.* https://www.themarshallproject.org/2015/08/04/why-jails-have-more-suicides-than-prisons#.uz9Y6uLwj.

Collins, Patricia Hill. 2015. "Intersectionality's Definitional Dilemmas." *Annual Review of Sociology* 41 (1): 1–20.

Cox, J.F., and P.C. Morchauser. 1997. "A Solution to the Problem of Jail Suicide." *Crisis* 18 (4): 178–84.

Crenshaw, Kimberlé. 1991. "Mapping the Margins: Intersectionality, Identity Politics and Violence Against Women of Color." *Stanford Law Review* 43 (6): 1241–99.

Crenshaw, Kimberlé. 1992. "Whose Story Is It Anyway? Feminist and Antiracist Appropriations of Anita Hill." In *Race-Ing Justice, En-Gendering Power*, edited by Kimberlé Crenshaw and Toni Morrison. New York: Pantheon.

DeGenova, Nicholas P. 2002. "Migrant 'Illegality' and Deportability in Everyday Life." *Annual Review of Anthropology* 31: 419–47.

Fernandez-Kelly, Patricia. 2016. *The Hero's Fight: African Americans in West Baltimore and the Shadow of the State.* NJ: Princeton University Press.

Fine, Janice. 2016. "This from Professor Janice Fine." *Posted by Imani Perry on Facebook.* https://www.facebook.com/imani.perry1/posts/10153908929959919.

Goss, J.R., K. Peterson, L.W. Smith, K. Kalb, and B.B. Brodey. 2002. "Characteristics of Suicide Attempts in a Large Urban Jail System with an Established Suicide Prevention Program." *Psychiatric Services* 53 (5): 574–79.

Kaste, M. 2015. "The 'Shock of Confinement': The Grim Reality of Suicide in Jail." *NPR*, July 27. http://www.npr.org/.

Knapp, Krystal. 2016. "Princeton Professor Imani Perry Releases Statement About Arrest, Police Chief Responds." *Planet Princeton,* February 8. http://planetprinceton.com/2016/02/08/princeton-university-arrest-perry-racism/.

Konrad, N., M.S. Daigle, A.E. Daniel, G.E. Dear, P. Frottier, L.M. Hayes, A. Kerkhof, A. Liebling, and M. Sarchiapone. 2007. "Preventing Suicides in Prisons, Part 1: Recommendations from the International Association for Suicide Prevention Task Force on Suicide in Prisons." *Crisis* 28 (3): 113–21.

Miller, Michael E. 2016. "Video: Austin Police Body-Slam Black Teacher, Tell Her Blacks Have 'Violent Tendencies.'" *Washington Post*, July 22. https://www.washingtonpost.com/news/morning-mix/wp/2016/07/22/video-austin-police-body-slam-black-teacher-tell-her-blacks-have-violent-tendencies/

Nathan, Debbie. 2016. "What Happened to Sandra Bland?: To Answer That Question, You Must Begin Way before She Died in a Texas Jail." *Nation*.

NYCLU. 2016. "Stop and Frisk Practices | New York Civil Liberties Union (NYCLU)—American Civil Liberties Union of New York State." *New York Civil Liberties Union*. http://www.nyclu.org/issues/racial-justice/stop-and-frisk-practices.

Omi, Michael, and Howard Winant. 1994. *Racial Formation in the United States: From the 1960s to the 1990s.* 2nd ed. New York: Routledge.

Pager, Devah. 2003. "The Mark of a Criminal Record 1." *American Journal of Sociology* 108 (5): 937–75.

Perry, Imani. 2016. "My Encounter with Princeton Police & the Aftermath." *Facebook Post.* https://www.facebook.com/notes/imani-perry/my-encounter-with-princeton-police-the-aftermath/10153293546187477.

Reed-Veal, Geneva. 2016. "Read the Short, Devastating Speech Sandra Bland's Mother Just Made to Congressional Leaders." *Fusion2.* http://fusion.net/story/296456/sandra-bland-mother-powerful-speech/.

Sanchez, Ray. 2015. "Who Was Sandra Bland, Who Died in Police Custody?" *CNN.* http://www.cnn.com/2015/07/22/us/sandra-bland/.

Staff, *Sun-Times*. 2015. "What We Know about the Death of Sandra Bland in Texas Jail." *Chicago Sun-Times.* http://chicago.suntimes.com/news/what-we-know-about-the-death-of-sandra-bland-in-texas-jail/.

Stolberg, Sheryl Gay, and Jess Bidgood. 2016. "Some Women Won't 'Ever Again' Report a Rape in Baltimore." *New York Times*, August 11. http://nyti.ms/2bmsmQ8.

Sumi, Cho, Kimberlé Williams Crenshaw, and Leslie McCall. 2013. "Toward a Field of Intersectionality Studies: Theory, Applications, and Praxis." *Signs: Journal of Women in Culture & Society* 38 (4): 785–810. http://proxy.lib.csus.edu/login?url=http://search.ebscohost.com/login.aspx?direct=true&db=a9h&AN=87458019.

United States Department of Justice. Civil Rights Division. 2015. "Investigation of the Ferguson Police Department." Washington, DC.

USDJ. 2016. "Investigation of the Baltimore City Police." https://www.justice.gov/opa/file/883366/download.

Van Cleve, Nicole Gonzalez. 2016. *Crook County: Racism and Injustice in America's Largest Criminal Court.* Stanford Law Books.

Wacquant, L. 2005. "Race as Civic Felony." *International Social Science Journal* 57 (183): 127–42. doi:papers2://publication/uuid/C0814F94-74E1-435B-853B-FC31B56346D7

Washington Post. 2016. "990 People Shot Dead by Police in 2015." *Washington Post,* August 13. https://www.washingtonpost.com/graphics/national/police-shootings/

Weitzer, R., and S. Tuch. 2002. "Perceptions of Racial Profiling: Race, Class, and Personal Experience." *Criminology* 40 (2): 435–56.

Weitzer, R., and S. Tuch. 2005. "Racially Biased Policing: Determinants of Citizen Perceptions." *Social Forces* 83 (3): 1009–30.

Wilson, G., R. Dunham, and G. Alpert. 2004. "Prejudice in Police Profiling: Assessing an Overlooked Aspect in Prior Research." *American Behavioral Scientist* 47 (7): 896–909.

Discussion Questions

1. In thinking about your experiences, what does your standpoint look like? How did you develop this standpoint?

2. Thinking of the various standpoints that exist, to which standpoint would you have difficulty connecting? For example, would you have difficulty relating to some whose standpoint includes ability? Why or why not?

Resources

Food Access Research Atlas: https://www.ers.usda.gov/data-products/food-access-research-atlas/

Racial Dot Map: https://demographics.coopercenter.org/racial-dot-map

References

Collins, Patricia Hill. 2015. "Intersectionality's Definitional Dilemma." *Annual Review of Sociology* 41:1–20.

Crenshaw, Kimberlé. 1991. "Mapping the Margins: Intersectionality, Identity Politics, and Violence Against Women of Color." Stanford Law Review 43:1241–99.

Kim-Puri, H.J. 2005. "Conceptualizing Gender-Sexuality-State-Nation: An Introduction." *Gender & Society* 19:137–59.

Omi, Michael, and Thomas Winant. 1994. *Racial Formation in the United States: From the 1960s to the 1990s.* 2nd ed. New York: Routledge.

Sarabia, Heidy, and Maria Perales. 2019. "Operation Streamline: Producing Legal Violence, Racialized Illegality, and Perpetual Exclusion." In *Race and Ethnicity: The Sociological Mindful Approach*, Jacqueline Brooks, Heidy Sarabia, and Aya Kimura Ida, eds. San Diego, CA: Cognella Academic Publishing.

United States Census Bureau. 2019. Retrieved April 15, 2019 (https://www.census.gov/newsroom/press-releases/2018/cb18-41-population-projections.htmlUS).

Endnotes

[i] Officer Richter received counseling and training, while Officer Spradlin received no punishment. Since the incident occurred more than six months before the video went viral, Police Chief Art Acevedo claimed he could not punish the officers more. However, the Travis County district attorney moved forward with a special investigation into King's arrest (Miller, July 22, 2016).

[ii] In 2015, of the 258 blacks killed by the police, 96.1 percent (248) were black men (WP 2016).

[iii] Video of Sandra Bland's traffic stop was published on YouTube by the Texas Department of Public Safety on July 22, 2015 (https://www.youtube.com/watch?v=CaW09Ymr2BA).

[iv] Kindra Chapman, a black teenager, reportedly committed suicide in the Homewood City Jail. She was arrested for first-degree robbery of a person of a cell phone.

Section IV: Education

Student Narrative

My parents immigrated from the Philippines to the U.S. and taught me that education would be key to my success. They took me out of the public school system in fear that I could go down the "wrong path." I did not know what "wrong path" meant but I was particularly upset that I had to travel on the freeway to get to school instead of going to the high school down the street where I was part of the majority. Why did I have to go to a school where whiteness was the coveted norm and where the girls traveled two hours every morning from Tijuana to get a college-preparatory education? Were not all high schools college-preparatory? It was not until I took my first sociology class in college did I learn to name the systematic disparities that affected my hometown's public school district. I learned how wealth and privilege afforded one the opportunities for social mobility. The sociological imagination gave me a better understanding as to why my parents called their school choice a "sacrifice." Inequality, however, became more apparent as I continued through college and learned about the racial disparities affecting students who were the first in their family to go to college. I spent so much time in college trying to figure out the language of the university that it was not until my junior year did I know what I was doing. This is time lost for some and time gained for others. Yes, we had pre-orientation programs for the "minorities" on campus, but campus race relations seemed to be an unending problem for the university and their students of color—lack of diverse curriculum and faculty, hostile racial climate, poor retention and academic performance. I did not know that being Filipina would precondition me to not only be a subject of diversity but also a diversity worker on a predominantly white campus. I would reveal to my parents later the contradictions of education being a struggle, rather than a key, for success.

Giselle Cunanan is an American Studies PhD candidate minoring in sociology at Indiana University–Bloomington studying US empire through Filipina/o remembrance. Her research interests include women of color feminisms, US empire, and critical ethnic studies. She attributes much of her development to the community organizers in Washington State, San Francisco, and her hometown of Paradise Hills, San Diego, who inform her work and provided her with multiple homes.

Learning Objectives

1. Describe how school cultures produce different experiences for students based on race and class.

2. Compare and contrast school segregation rates before and after the ruling of *Brown v. Board of Education of Topeka, Kansas.*

3. Relate racial disparities in high school graduation rates and dropout rates with life chances.

4. Discuss racial disparities in college enrollment and graduation rates.

Editor's Introduction

Jacqueline Brooks, PhD

Like Giselle, I traveled to schools outside of my neighborhood. I, too, questioned the value of attending classes far from home, just to engage students and teachers who found me different and strange. One day, while in fifth grade, I decided to skip school. Upon hearing of my truancy, my guidance counselor, a black man, called me to his office. He asked why I was absent the previous day. I accepted this meeting as an opportunity to confide in him. I told him that I was feeling isolated, as one of a few black students at the school. Rather than soothe my fears or offer me comfort, he continued to question me, intimated that I was from a "broken home." On the contrary, I lived in a strong, working-class, two-parent household and consistently earned a place on the honor roll. Yet, just questioning the racial makeup of my school and expressing how it made me feel led a school administrator to treat me as a problem that needed to be solved. How prophetic of W.E.B. Du Bois to ask of black Americans—*"how does it feel to be a problem?"* (1903). In a racialized, white-dominated school system, students of color often feel like burdens—never bright enough, wealthy enough, or powerful enough to be anything more.

To further complicate and compound these feelings of marginalization and isolation, **hidden curricula**, nurtured within school cultures that prefer whiteness and middle-class values, weed out "undeserving" students. Thus, informal rules and practices become institutionalized, which communicates to students who and what the school deems worthy. Further, the hidden curriculum becomes embedded in the school culture as teachers and school administrators identify with students similar to them in race and class position. For example, teachers who recognize their own privilege in chosen students (e.g., race, class, sexual orientation, citizenship status, or ability) may interact with students and evaluate student performance in ways that advantage some and disadvantage others. Findings show that white girls who are perceived as "ideal students … considered compliant, pleasant, and reserved" and receive the fewest disciplinary actions, regard education positively; whereas black boys, who are perceived as fearsome, "outspoken and aggressive" and receive the most disciplinary actions, regard education more negatively (Langhout and Mitchell 2008:595, citing Cornbleth and Korth 1980; Morgan, 1991; McFadden 1992; Mikel Brown 1991; Cokley 2002). Further, in comparison to their white peers, black and Hispanic students are retained more often, forcing them to repeat the same grade (National Center for Education Statistics 2017). Hidden curricula create vastly different experiences for students attending the same schools. In a study of low-income students in one elementary school, Langhout and Mitchell (2008) found that disciplinary practices convey a different message to black and Latino students than white students, implicitly stating "their engagement was inappropriate and that learning, and therefore school, was not for them" (603).

Students navigating school cultures that distance and ostracize them may encounter the **stereotype threat**, the pressure to perform *against* prevailing racial stereotypes (Steele 1988, 1992, 1997). According to Steele, the stereotype threat presupposes that:

- Like adults, children seek good self-esteem, and want others to like them;
- As anxiety about performing poorly increases, students' performance worsens, and

- As a result of these anxieties and internalized negative feelings of self, students disengage from the domain in question through a process of disidentification. (Steele 1988, 1992, 1997; Massey and Fischer 2005)

For example, although African American students may value education, some may remove academic achievement as a measure of self-esteem due to stereotype threat (Steele 1988, 1992, 1997). This distancing from the educational system places students of color in jeopardy of performing below their ability levels, potentially leaving school before completing their degrees. Although Steele confirmed the stereotype threat studying black students at the college level, the negative effect of stereotypes affects the work of elementary and secondary students as well. The American school system may have worked to diversify classrooms; however, we have much work to do in decolonizing our approach to education.

Segregation since *Brown v. Board of Education*

Rescinding the law of the land—"separate but equal"—thereby striking a blow against *de jure* school segregation, *Brown v. Board of Education* addressed historical race inequities in elementary and secondary education. Although this historical ecision was confined to the K–12 school system, it sent a provocative message to higher education, which also practiced fervent race segregation. This was not the nation's first challenge to structural racism in the educational system. In 1927, a Chinese American, Gong Lum, sued Mississippi State on behalf of his daughter, Martha, who sought to attend a designated white high school. Similar to many Southern states, Mississippi maintained separate schools for whites and students of color. The Mississippi State Supreme Court denied Martha's entrance to her selected high school, upholding Jim Crow laws, which in this case extended to Chinese Americans. In 1947, the California Supreme Court ruled in favor of the Menendez family, along with other Latinx families, who sued four Orange County school districts to integrate their schools. The state of California used *Menendez v. Westminster* as a precedent to begin desegregation across the state.

However, in the wake of *Brown v. Board of Education*, efforts to integrate schools across the nation presented many problems. Though well intentioned, the plan to desegregate was not clear, and implementation efforts were poorly diffused throughout the country. Today, segregation remains a defining characteristic of the K–12 public school system, with some parts of the United States experiencing levels of school segregation worse than before the landmark US Supreme Court ruling. In comparison to their middle-class, white and Asian counterparts, black and Latinx students experience **double segregation**, an effect of the intersection of race and economic inequalities, which places them in schools segregated by race and class. Since 1988, when desegregation peaked, the nation's share of schools with at least a 90 percent black and Latinx student population more than tripled (UCLA Civil Rights Project 2016). Conversely, the nation's share of schools with at least a 90 percent white population decreased (UCLA Civil Rights Project 2016). "The result of these diverging trends is that whites can perceive an increase in interracial contact even as African American and Latino students are increasingly isolated, often severely so" (UCLA Civil Rights Project 2016).

Further, as shown in Figure 1, the average US school has significantly increased its population of poor students, revealing structural economic inequalities, such as reduced wages and the increasing income gap. While the average white and Asian student receives education alongside a 40 percent low-income student body, the average black and Latino student attends schools with a more than 60 percent low-income student body. This phenomenon highlights the disproportional share of black and Latinx children living in poverty.

Intra-school segregation reflects the segregation of students *within* schools. Thus, although a school may show racial diversity, students may experience racial segregation under the guise of ability grouping (e.g., college preparatory courses, special education courses, and English as a Second Language courses). Asian students make up the largest group of students receiving Advanced Placement Credit (72 percent), followed by white students (40 percent) (McFarland, Cui, Rathbun, and Holmes 2018). In the 2013–2014 academic year, 17 percent of American Indian and Alaska Native students were tracked into special education programs, followed by 15 percent of black students (Musu-Gillette, De Brey, McFarland, et al. 2017). White and Latinx students were tracked at similar percentages (13 percent and 12 percent, respectively). About 6 percent of Asian students were tracked into special education programs. Once placed into special education programming, the chances of being reintegrated into mainstream classrooms remains bleak. One unique characteristic of special education programming that illustrates its relationship to race segregation is the amount of time students enrolled in special education classes spend in a mainstream classroom. This sharply differs by race. Of students tracked into special education classes, white students spend more time in mainstream classrooms, while black students spend the greatest amount of time learning outside mainstream classrooms (U.S. Department of Education 2019).

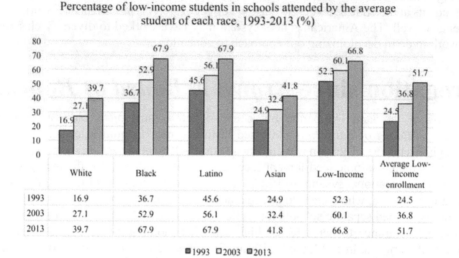

	White	Black	Latino	Asian	Low-Income	Average Low-income enrollment
1993	16.9	36.7	45.6	24.9	52.3	24.5
2003	27.1	52.9	56.1	32.4	60.1	36.8
2013	39.7	67.9	67.9	41.8	66.8	51.7

■1993 □2003 ■2013

Figure SIV.1. Percentage of low-income students in schools attended by the average student of each race, 1993–2013. Source: U.S. Department of Education, National Center for Education Statistics, Common Core of Data (CCD), Public Elementary/Secondary School Universe Survey Data.

Racial Disparities and High School

Research shows that low educational attainment has long-reaching consequences, particularly for communities of color, such as un/underemployment, marital instability, housing instability, arrest, and incarceration. In 2016, the overall US dropout rate was 6.1 percent, reflecting a 55 percent decrease since 2000. The dropout rate for African American students decreased by almost half, closing the statistical gap between blacks and whites. Yet, although the Hispanic dropout rate declined by almost 32 percent, a statistical difference between whites and Hispanics persists (McFarland, Cui, Rathbun, and Holmes 2018). Of those students not completing a high school degree, black and American Indian/Alaska Native adults were most likely to be unemployed (Musu-Gillette, De Brey, McFarland, Hussar, Sonnenberg, and Wilkinson-Flicker 2017). Illustrating the detriment of not finishing high school, white adults who dropped out of high school maintain higher unemployment percentages than their Latinx peers who dropped out of high school (Musu-Gillette, De Brey, McFarland, et al. 2017). In 2016, the US high school graduation percentage reached 84.6, the highest percentage since 2010 (National Center for Education Statistics 2018). Asian/Pacific Islanders and whites outpaced the national average (91 percent and 88 percent, respectively), while Latinx, black, and Native American students fell short of the national average (80 percent, 78 percent, and 72 percent, respectively) (National Center for Education Statistics 2018). Although graduation rates have increased across racial groups, Latinx students complete high school in fewer percentages than white students in 1990. Today, blacks graduate high school in slightly larger percentages than white students in 1990. This lagged effect reveals that the achievements of communities of color often trail the advances of whites by decades.

Racial Disparities in College

Overall, the number of bachelor's degrees awarded in the United States has increased across racial groups since 2003. Within the Latinx community specifically, the number of earned bachelor's degrees has more than doubled. Within all race groups, the percentage of women enrolling in college has steadily increased. In addition, more students graduate college within six years than in the past. Yet, despite these notable gains, racial disparities still exist. For example, almost as many black college students leave their first year of college as enter, resulting in a minimal net gain of enrolled, first-year, black college students. Although more women are enrolling in college, gender gaps exist within race groups. The widest gaps exist for black college students (62 percent to 38 percent) and American Indian/Alaska Native students (60 percent to 40 percent). While 71 percent of Asian students graduate at the six-year mark, 41 percent of black and American Indian/Alaska Native students do the same. Finally, the return on a college education differs by race. Median annual earnings of bachelor and higher degree earners remain highest among Asian workers ($61,000) and lowest among black and Latinx workers (about $46,500) (Musu-Gillette, De Brey, McFarland, et al. 2017).

Mindfulness

In March 2019, the FBI charged fifty individuals with using "fraud, bribes, and lies" to get the children of wealthy parents into elite US universities (Winton and Fay 2019). The enrollment of legacy children into selective universities is traditional practice; at times the rate of "legacies" outpaced the rate of students enrolled under Affirmative Action policies, though it is the latter that has been banned at many colleges and universities. Opponents of Affirmative Action argue that students admitted using race as a deciding factor unfairly stripped "deserving" students of a position. Should we also scrutinize university admissions that use socio-economic status as a deciding factor? Trading in on their class and white privilege, parents were accused of "rigging college entrance exams, bribing test proctors, fabricating athletic credentials, and paying off college coaches and administrators (Winton and Fay 2019). In one of the more popularized tactics, wealthy parents bribed college coaches to place their children on team rosters for sports they never played.

We began this discussion considering the life of Giselle Cunanan, who questioned why she had to travel long distances to gain access to college preparatory classes. Why did her family's tax dollars not provide her with a quality, local education? Although we have focused much of our discussion on race, the intersection of class inequities cannot be ignored. We can easily choose to ignore the racial disparities in education if we think these issues do not affect us. However, when we examine the intersection of race, gender, and class, we begin to understand that inequities in one area influence inequities in other areas. The intersectional approach seeks not to rank order social inequalities, but expose their relational nature. As you move forward with the text, we challenge you to be mindful of your intersecting social characteristics. With a mindful eye, you will be able to see the landscape of intersecting social inequalities while identifying where you exist on the map.

Section Readings

The first two offerings in this section discuss race and socioeconomic issues within the public K–12 public school systems. In "The Hate You Give: A Critical Race Theory Analysis of the U.S. K–12 Education System," Thomas addresses within-school segregation, achieved through racialized tracking and ability grouping. Thomas begins by discussing the short reach of *Brown v. Board of Education*, then develops an argument based in Critical Race Theory that connects increased intra-school segregation and school policies with structural race disparities, such as the school-to-prison pipeline. Thomas calls for counter-storytelling and relying on community as a source of cultural wealth to address race inequities within the K–12 public educational system.

We often ask, what does it take to change the educational system? How do we create a more inclusive educational system? In "Troubleshooting Racial Inequalities Through a Collaborative Network in the Brazilian Educational System: The Case of the 'Color of Culture,'" Rezende and Milagres detail how Brazil, through a dynamic network of organizations, changed their educational system, writing race and ethnic inclusivity into their laws. The authors present a model that incorporates the resources of many stakeholders interested in firmly entrenching the teaching of Afro-Brazilian and African history into the Brazilian educational system.

The final three offerings in this section describe the experiences of faculty, administrators, and students on college campuses. In "'I Know My Place': How Whiteness, White Culture, and White Educators Permeate and Shape Universities," Brooks-Immel and Murray assert that whites rely on color-blind racism, static awareness, or engaged antiracism to navigate racial discourse and interactions with students of color. They base their conclusions on in-depth interviews with thirty white faculty and administrators at a minority-majority university, creating a racialized map of the university. Sampled white faculty and administrators ignore racial hierarchies, claiming "they do not see race," identify racial inequities but neglect to act upon them, or consciously practice antiracism within their classrooms or on the university campus.

In "Racial and Ethnic Macro and Microaggressions, and White Privilege and Supremacy: The Experiences of College Students of Color on Predominantly White Campuses," Chaplin examines acts of micro-aggressions and responses to micro-aggressions, both of which are contextualized by the force of white privilege and white supremacy. Based on interviews and focus groups with students of color, Thomas details multiple experiences with micro-aggressions. Chaplin argues that normative practices of "whiteness" affect not only whites on campus but influence the reactions of students of color to perceived racially charged micro-aggressions.

In "Inequality in the Graduate School Admissions Process: The Chicanx/Latinx Experience," Ramirez argues that the graduate school admissions process marginalizes students of color. Based on interviews with twenty-four Chicanx/Latinx students enrolled in a doctoral program, students report a heavy emphasis is placed on the GRE and the school where you received your undergraduate degree. Further, students discuss the importance of *who* makes decisions about admissions, citing that perhaps too much power is given to one or several people.

As you read Ramirez's work, consider your own path to higher education.

Reading 4.1 The Hate You Give: A Critical Race Theory Analysis of the US K–12 Education System

Richard Thomas, Texas Christian University

Keywords: Critical Race Theory, Counter-Storytelling, School-to-prison Pipeline, Community as Cultural Wealth, Tracking and Ability Grouping, Zero-tolerance Policies, Quarles V. Oxford, Montgomery V. Starkville

Introduction

In 1988, the late Tupac Amaru Shakur gave one of his earliest on-camera interviews at the age of seventeen. During the interview he covered many topics, ranging from what it meant to be an African American youth growing up in the inner city, to issues with police brutality, communal responsibilities, social activism, and even the failures of the public education system. One quote in particular sums up the interconnected challenges that many students of color faced during Tupac's lifetime and beyond. He stated, "We got so caught up in school being tradition that we forgot it was a learning tool" (Winfrey 2018). In other words, the public education system was failing students because educators and administrators were focused more on upholding traditional standards than providing for the welfare of students. Tupac would go on to further advocate for youth education reform through the use of the acronym "THUG LIFE" During several interviews during the early part of the 1990s, he explained that "THUG LIFE" described how the hate given to infants would come back to harm everyone. The harm perpetuated toward children negatively impacts everyone because those children represent future leaders and bear all of the responsibilities of carrying on this world for the next generation. Thus, the damages that children suffer from the K–12 education system not only hurts them in the short term but has a long-term impact on society as a whole.

The life of Tupac Shakur is an appropriate starting point for a sociological analysis of the K–12 education system in the United States because during his lifetime many of the phenomena that have come to be characterized as public education were burgeoning. In the aftermath of the landmark court case *Brown v. Board of Education,* racial barriers to educational opportunities were supposed to be eliminated. In the decades following the decision, racial inequality has continued to persist and in some cases even increased due to a combination of racially biased policies and practices within the public education system. The purpose of this chapter is to provide an overview of a few of the phenomena that perpetuate educational inequalities emphasizing a critical race theory (CRT) lens. CRT will be used to elucidate how tracking/ ability grouping and the school-to-prison pipeline serve as structural impediments that disproportionately impact students of color (particularly African Americans and Latin/x) from educational attainment in public schools. The next part of this chapter will examine educational resources that can enhance the quality of learning for students of color in the classroom. Rather than focusing on structural solutions or policy-making decisions, the critical race theory framework will be used to examine tools that can be used to assess policies that create educational attainment disparities. Two tools that are useful from a critical race theory lens are counter-storytelling and the concept of the community as a source of cultural wealth. At the conclusion of the chapter, the reader should have a better understanding of both some of the causes of educational inequality as well as remedies based on critical race theory.

A Brief Historical Overview of Contemporary Public Education Practices

One of the court cases that has been most influential in determining educational policies from the second half of the twentieth century to the present is the court case *Brown v. Board of Education*. This case has been most prominently described as the court case that integrated the public school system. The court case was actually a combination of four different cases from four different school districts. All of the plaintiffs were African American school children who contended that their Fourteenth Amendment right to equal protection under the law had been violated because of pro-segregation policies that denied them access to public education. At stake during these cases was the precedent that had originally been set over fifty years prior by another Supreme Court Case, *Plessy v. Ferguson*. The ruling in *Plessy v. Ferguson* allowed racial segregation in public spaces as long as there were equal accommodations for each race. The lawyers in the *Brown* case contended that any form of racial segregation in public schools inherently created inequality that could never be remedied (Carter and Roaf 2004). The court agreed with this assessment of racial disparities in the education system.

Two key statements from the court's decision grounds this chapter's analysis of the K–12 public education system. First, the court stated that public education is "the most important function[s] of the state and local government" (Carter and Roaf 2004:493). Second, racially segregating children creates "feelings of inferiority as to their status in the community that may affect their hearts and minds in a way unlikely ever to be undone" (Carter and Roaf 2004:494). The first statement speaks to the importance and ongoing urgency to remedy some of the challenges that exist in the public education system. The next statement speaks to the impact that any form of discriminatory policy can have on children. Contemporary public educational policies either intentionally or unintentionally can cause irreparable harm to children from marginalized racial demographics. They impact the psychological development, socialization process, educational attainment, and overall life chances for many of these children. One of the shortcomings of the *Brown* decision is that although it properly diagnosed the problem in the education system there were no remedies or recommendations on how to fix them. In fact, during the subsequent *Brown v. Board of Education* hearing, the court ruled that state and local school districts should be responsible for remedying the situation. This move began the gradual process of integrating all public schools throughout the United States. As has been well documented, each city moved toward integration at its own pace and with varying degrees of resistance from those opposed to the *Brown* decision.

The integration process created a myriad of multifaceted and complex challenges toward creating an equitable education system. For example, public school districts had to determine how to integrate children from different racial, ethnic, and class backgrounds into the same schools. More often than not, African American or Latin/x students were transferred to predominantly white schools to meet federal regulations. Beyond the often publicized violent resistance to integration from pro-segregation factions, internal conflict also arose on the best policies and practices to educate students once they were in the classroom. Many school districts had to address the historical deprivation of access to educational resources for the families and communities that were integrated into the public school system. Furthermore, state and federal legislatures began to implement more policies for a standardized testing system in every school district to ensure that all students were learning similar material. Finally, educators in the classroom had to adapt to the changing social dynamics of their environment. They had to develop ways to teach normative behavior in multiracial or multiethnic classrooms. The combination of these policies led to two separate yet interconnected phenomena that have profoundly impacted US K–12 education systems, namely, tracking/ ability grouping and the school-to-prison pipeline.

Tracking/Ability Grouping

Both tracking and ability grouping are two separate phenomena that have grown simultaneously in the K–12 education system, although they share similarities that also have their subtle differences as well. The goal of both practices is to optimize the performance of students by adapting class curriculum to the needs of individual students. The practice of tracking typically occurs in middle or high school and involves the placement of students in different classrooms based on their perceived proficiency level on a subject by subject basis

(Brooking 2013). Common levels of placement include Honors or Advanced Placement (AP) courses in topics ranging from English, history, chemistry, algebra, and many more. Honors or AP courses follow a different curriculum, are taught by different professors, and are taught in a different classroom compared to other classes. Students who track with a lower level of proficiency will simply take courses such as general science, chemistry, US history, or algebra. This practice gained popularity in the aftermath of the *Brown* decision, particularly in high school. The primary method for tracking was through exam-based selection in specific subjects. However, today the most common method is through student self-selection or a teacher recommendation into a course (Brown Center Report on American Education 2013).

Alternatively, the practice of ability grouping most frequently occurs in elementary schools. As opposed to tracking, students who are grouped based on perceived proficiency levels are often taught in the same classrooms as the other students. Elementary school teachers typically divide students in the classroom into smaller instructional groups for subjects such as reading or math (Dreeben and Barr 1988). While the teacher provides instruction and guidance for one of the groups in the classroom, the other students are encouraged to work independently or to complete exercises or activities in groups. The teacher also rotates to different groups throughout the duration of the instructional period. Today, the use of computer-aided technology allows students from different tracking groups to work more independently to complete worksheets or assignments to reinforce skills. Research from Johns Hopkins University indicates that ability grouping most often occurs in first grade but features less prominently in subsequent grade school levels (Brown Center Report on American Education 2013). As students move up in grade levels, they are more likely to be tracked in middle and high school.

As both tracking and ability grouping grew in popularity, educational researchers developed studies to analyze patterns within these practices. By the late 1970s and early 1980s, the practices became increasingly controversial because of the way they correlated to the racial and class makeup of school systems. Ray C. Rist's 1970 study indicated that tracking or ability grouping inherently separates students based on academic performance using categories that also correlate with demographic characteristics, such as race, ethnicity, native language, and class. In other words, he argued that tracking and ability grouping intentionally separate students based on categories such as race and socioeconomic status. Rist's research project examined the academic placement of kindergarten students as they aged through the early stages of elementary school. At each grade level, students' socioeconomic status was correlated with the reading or math groups that the students were placed in. His research concluded that teachers consciously or subconsciously developed different academic achievement expectations of their students based on demographic characteristics (Rist 1970).

In 1985, the book *Keeping Track* was published by Jeannie Oakes to describe the impact that tracking had on the public education system in both middle and high school. In her book, she theorized that the practice of tracking both reproduces and facilitates education inequality in the United States. Her research was based on previous ideas postulated by other education scholars on social reproduction theories. According to social reproduction theories, school systems represent one avenue to reproduce inequalities that exist within everyday life. Oakes argued that although tracking is usually a response to addressing the unique educational needs of particular students, it can often have a devastating effect on historically marginalized groups in the classroom. The practice at its core is based on normative assumptions about the race and class of the students (Oakes 1985). Typically, white middle-class to upper-middle-class teachers and parents determine the education standards that are used to evaluate all students in the classroom. This has led to the pattern of middle-class white children densely populated Honors or Advanced Placement courses while African American and Latin/x schoolchildren populate remedial or general studies courses.

The School-to-prison Pipeline

At the same time school systems were adapting curriculum in the aftermath of the *Brown* decision, they were also adapting disciplinary policies as well. In the decades prior to the 1960s, most schools utilized corporal punishment or public punishment as major strategies to discipline schoolchildren (Hanson 2005). However, the influx of integrated school systems where African American and Latin/x students began to attend traditionally white public schools generated a wave of stricter disciplinary procedures that included out-of-school suspensions and zero-tolerance policies. The gradual increase of these policies over the last four decades has had a disproportionate impact on students from African American and Latin/x communities because they suffer the most punitive punishments and are impacted the most by the long-term consequences of the aforementioned policies. The punitive nature of both out-of-school suspension and zero-tolerance policies mirrors statistical data concerning deviance in the criminal justice system. They also criminalize the youth populations and act as a catalyst for the rise in juvenile incarceration rates. The term *school-to-prison pipeline* is used to highlight this connection between educational policies, racial disparities in enforcement of policies, and the subsequent link with the prison-industrial complex.

One of the practical implications of the out-of-school suspensions is that they force schoolchildren away from the classroom and thus serve as an impediment to the student's acquisition of a formal education. Unfortunately, over the last several decades, out-of-school suspensions have become the more prevalent form of disciplinary measures in public schools throughout the United States. The number of students who were penalized with out-of-school suspensions from the 1970s through the 1990s nearly doubled from approximately 1.7 million to over 3 million (Simson 2014). Students who receive this punishment are typically disciplined because of behavioral issues, such as disrespect toward a school educator or another form of classroom disruption. Although no credible research has indicated that suspensions have a deterrent effect on students, they continue to be used as a disciplinary method.

As previously noted, the term school-to-prison pipeline highlights the strong correlation between policies such as suspensions, zero tolerance, and increased youth incarceration rates. Zero-tolerance policies allow strict enforcement of school rules and regulations related to issues of safety. Typically, zero-tolerance policies are enforced against possession of weapons or drugs inside of school facilities. They also allow violations of school policies to be punished through the criminal justice system. Students become subject to what some scholars have referred to as "double jeopardy" (Gonzalez 2012). Double jeopardy entails that students are subject to punishment from both school administrators and law enforcement authorities on issues that have typically been in the jurisdiction of the former. Perhaps one of the best examples of double jeopardy in the public education system is truancy laws. Truancy laws make it a criminal offense for schoolchildren to be absent from school without a valid excuse. Punishments for truancy can vary to a fine or court appearance by both the children and their parents. In some school districts in places such as California, truancy officers are hired to patrol schools and even arrest students who perpetually violate school regulations (Ehrenreich 2009). Thus, school violations become criminal violations, which has led to increased incarceration rates.

Zero-tolerance policies have contributed to the school-to-prison pipeline because of their connection to measures of accountability and scholastic achievement in public schools. Over the past several decades, federal policies such as the No Child Left Behind Act of 2001 (NCLB) have been implemented to bridge the achievement gaps in the classroom. NCLB legislation directly tied academic achievement based on a standardized test scored directly with school funding. In doing so, this created an incentive for public school districts to strictly monitor the classroom. Students who might be considered "problem students" because of classroom behavior were removed from the classroom. Zero-tolerance policies, out-of-school suspensions, or other punitive measures were used to discipline students rather seeking to address potential unmet educational needs that the student might have. Under NCLB legislation, it was much easier to remove students who may be perceived as a problem from the classroom and teach classes in a manner that conforms to the material on standardized exams. In essence, certain students were being forced out of school because many public school districts did not want to risk losing funding by spending resources on perceived "problem students." This practice is known as the push-out phenomenon. The push-out phenomenon has been directly linked with increased youth incarceration rates because suspension rates are a strong predictor of school dropout rates and adolescent encounters with law enforcement authorities (Nussbaum 2018). Subsequently, encounters with law enforcement are correlated with the likelihood of spending time in prison.

A Critical Race Theory Perspective

Critical race theory is a discipline that developed during the 1980s by African American scholars who were exploring the interconnection between race, power, and legal structures. The theory addressed concerns that were absent from similar disciplines, such as critical legal studies or civil rights studies (Crenshaw, Gotanda, Peller, and Thomas 1996). Scholars recognized how the court system did not consider intersectional categories of race, class, and gender on legal policies. Furthermore, they also recognized how racism functioned inherently within legal structures to perpetuate inequalities. Although critical race theory started with legal studies, it has become an important feature in many other disciplines as well, including sociology, literature, education, political science, women's studies, education, and ethnic studies. Critical race theory has also become a movement that encompasses many other sub-disciplines like critical race feminism, Latino critical race studies (LatCrit), Asian American critical race studies (AsianCrit), South Asian American critical race studies (DesiCrit), and American Indian critical race studies (TribalCrit). More recently, a critical race studies framework has been adapted by different racial and ethnic groups across the globe to explore their experiences (Delgado and Stefancic 2017).

One of the key assumptions of critical race theory is that the category of race is primarily a social construction rather than a biological construction. This means that race does not describe a fixed or natural identity but is created through social interactions. The social construction of race carries over the legal construction of race. As such, defining racial categories can never be a neutral phenomenon. In the United States, these racial categories have been defined by those groups who have historically had access to political power, namely Euro-American white people. This group has used the ability to define racial categories as a way to privilege whiteness over subordinate groups that are traditionally described as racial and ethnic minorities (Harris 1993). Another assumption of critical race theory is that race has a performative function. Legal and social constructions of race are solidified through specific notions of racial performance. For example, white Euro-Americans created racial categories such as African American, Asian, Latin/x, etc. Subsequently, performative actions reify the created meaning of those categories.

Critical race scholars have also described how the process of race is socially constructed. The first step is that individuals explore the different ways that race has been defined in the United States. Definitions of race include observations about ancestry, cultural practices, religion, skin color, accents, and behavioral norms (Carbado and Gulati 2003). After individuals determine their own criteria for evaluating race, they use a combination of those criteria to place other individuals they encounter into racial categories. During this step, the performative function of racial identification is important. Both the individuals engaged in the process of creating the racial category and the individuals who are being described observe the performative function of race through assessing language, dress, religion, skin color, cultural practices. The individuals creating the categories evaluate the other group based on perceived assimilation into markers of racial identification. During the next step, social meaning is assigned to individuals based on the racial categories that individuals create. In the United States, the social meaning of race has become inextricably linked with the racial hierarchy that persists in social and legal structures. The structures that are associated with white identity are superiority, dominance, and cultural capital, while on the other hand, African American, Latin/x and other historically marginalized races and ethnicities are associated with subordination or inferiority. Members then act based on whether or not they accept this racial hierarchy, which can create a racial stigma. Racial stigmas are traits or characteristics associated with a particular race used to define a person or group as inferior. Theses stigmas serve as the basis on how to treat specific groups through either everyday interaction or the implementation of laws and policies. For example, if groups such as African Americans and Latin/x are stigmatized as inferior because of their race policies, such as Jim Crow or Juan Crow, are more likely to be viewed as socially acceptable. During the final step, the negative impact of policies and treatment of racial groups confirm and reinforce the perceived inferiority of those groups. The next sections will explain how tracking/ability grouping and the school-to-prison pipeline only reinforce the stigmas concerning historically marginalized races and ethnicities that have been relevant since before *Brown v. Board of Education.*

Critical Race Theory and Tracking/Ability Grouping

The critical race theory perspective on tracking/ability grouping is based on Derrick Bell's critique of the *Brown* decision in his book *Silent Covenant*. The court decision did not specify remedies to the challenges caused by segregation, thus creating the possibility for future policies that could have the exact same effect as the ones prior to *Brown* (Bell 2005). Specifically, the policy of segregation has been replaced with intra-school segregation. Intra-school segregation is the process by which schools systematically separate students based on formal or informal criteria inside the classroom. Bell specifies that the resistance to desegregation at every level impacted court rulings in similar cases after *Brown*. Court systems were filled with cases about integration policies, which severely limited the courts' ability to respond to other cases. Furthermore, the courts also knew that the cases involving integration required more direct supervision and resources that many courts did not have available to spare. As a result, many courts overlooked the practice of intra-school segregation and released public districts from court-ordered obligations to completely desegregate (Bell 2005). The practices of tracking and ability grouping represent the most evident forms of intra-school segregation.

Over the last thirty years, several court cases have demonstrated how tracking or ability grouping have served as forms of intra-school segregation. In the case *Montgomery v. Starkville Municipal Separate School District* (1987), the public school district was equally populated with African American and white students (Cipriano-Walter 2014). Thus, by rule of law, the district was in compliance with court-ordered desegregation policies. However, the racial and ethnic makeup of students inside of each individual classroom was an entirely different story. The district used ability grouping as the primary method to separate students on perceived academic aptitude inside of each classroom. This practice directly led to racial segregation grounded in the perception of student aptitude. Each elementary and middle school placed students in one of three types of classes: low, average, or high ability courses. Approximately 80 percent of the high-achievement classes were composed of the white students, while on the other hand, 80 percent of African American students were placed in low-achievement classes (Cipriano-Walter 2014). The racial and ethnic makeup for the average classes were split evenly between African American and white students. The court ruled in favor of the school district because racial segregation occurred only in the classroom and not throughout the duration of the school day. The court also believed that the school district had made legitimate attempts to desegregate because the average classes were properly integrated. Thus, any form of segregation was incidental and not intentional.

Just a few years later, the court case *Quarles v. Oxford Municipal Separate School District* also had ramifications for public education throughout the United States. The plaintiffs in this case also contested that ability grouping was being used as another way to re-segregate the school district. Specifically, African Americans and other historically marginalized racial groups were being placed primarily into low-achievement classes, while white students were placed into the high-achievement classes. Once again, the focus was on the ability grouping from elementary through middle school. Students were placed in different levels particularly for language arts and mathematics (Cipriano-Walter 2014). Similar to the *Montgomery* case, the racial and ethnic makeup for classes not based on ability grouping meet court-ordered standards for integration. A slightly different method was used to group students once they reached high school. They were tracked by being placed in regular, accelerated, and advanced placement courses. Unsurprisingly, white students were overrepresented in the accelerated or advanced placement classes. The court ruled that because the placement classes were open to everyone, no discrimination had occurred. The court also ruled that the school district had not violated federal regulations at the elementary and middle school levels as well with the practice of ability grouping. Students had the ability to be placed in a different class based on test scores, a teacher recommendation, or a parental request. These circumstances allowed the court to rule that ability grouping did not have the explicit intention of racially segregating classrooms. Both the *Quarles* and *Starkville* cases helped to determine the criteria to evaluate the practices of ability grouping and tracking today.

In both of the previously described cases, the courts failed to realize the role that tracking and ability grouping has on reproducing structural racism through intra-school segregation. Critical race theory can be used to explain how this process occurred. First, public school districts defined racial categories primarily through skin color, ancestry, socioeconomic status, and behavioral norms. These categories are then used to classify students. Historically, formal and informal policies have been used to define race in the United States. For example, individuals from historically marginalized race and ethnic groups have been denied access to specific careers, which has directly impacted the earning potential for those groups. Subsequently, earning potential has been directly related to income and neighborhoods that they can afford to live in. The groups have also been made to believe in their inferior status because of Jim Crow laws and similar legislation. A combination of these factors and many more influences the behavioral norms for the marginalized ethnic groups. During the next phase, both the individuals engaged in racial classification, as well as the individuals who are classified based on the categories, engage with the performative function of race. In the context of the public education system, the previously listed factors that were meant to make students of color inferior carried over into how those students performed in the classroom. They often developed their own sense of normative behavior different from traditional scholastic expectations. Furthermore, students of color (especially African Americans and Latin/x) are also more likely to underperform on standard exams to assess academic achievement for similar reasons. Consequently, these students are then stigmatized based on a perceived inability to meet standard baselines for performance. Racial stigmas influence both the creation and implementation of practices such as tracking and ability grouping. As a result, they simply reinforce the perceived notions about historically marginalized groups—namely, their intellectual inferiority.

From a critical race theory perspective, tracking/ability grouping are both policies that inherently create intra-school segregation. In many instances, the courts have ruled that these policies have a minimal segregation effect on the students in K–12 public education systems. These policies are racist because whether intentional or unintentional, they disproportionately impact students of color. Case after case has indicated how tracking and ability grouping are both intertwined with racial segregation and unequal educational opportunities for students of color. In cases involving tracking or ability grouping, courts should realize that those practices have a disproportionate impact on students of color because they are the result of ongoing values and attitudes that have carried over from previous desegregation cases. In other words, the original failings of the *Brown* decision continue to impact the policies that perpetuate educational inequality in the present.

Critical Race Theory and the School-to-Prison Pipeline

Critical race theory can also be used to posit a similar understanding of how the school-to-prison pipeline is a combination of policies that continues to reproduce racial inequality in the criminal justice system. Teachers and educational administrators who are responsible for school disciplinary policies develop specific criteria to create racial categories. They create these categories using features such as biological ancestry, skin color, dress, and behavioral patterns. They then assign students into white, African American, Latin/x, etc. Racial classification also depends on the specific interpersonal interactions with students. During these interactions, teachers or educational administrators evaluate students partially based on measures of racial performance, such as dress, general demeanor, accent, and other subjective measures. These interactions also create racial stigmas, implicit biases, and stereotypes for the students of color or who come from historically marginalized backgrounds. School officials are then influenced by these racial perceptions as they make disciplinary decisions in the education system.

The preconceived ideas of race help to explain the findings over the last forty years that suggest that students of color, in particular African Americans and Latin/x, are far more prone to face the harshest disciplinary measures in the public school system (Skiba, Homer, Chung, Rausch, May, and Tobin 2011). Research from the Office of Civil Rights during the 1970s indicates that African Americans were more than twice as likely to face suspension or other forms of punishment as a result of classroom misconduct. Sadly, newer data from the same source indicates that the disparity had grown to three times as likely during the early 2000s (Losen 2011). Furthermore, Indiana University professor Russell Skiba's inquiry into public school disciplinary policies discovered that students of color continue to be far more likely to receive out-of-school suspensions at every level from grades K–12. Perhaps more troubling is that the punishments students of color face that place them in the criminal justice system typically stem from more subjective infractions. Stereotyping, implicit bias, and racial stigmas have led school administrators to criminalize youth of color more frequently and thus reproduce racial constructs through the school-to-prison pipeline.

Examples of subjective infractions that students of color are more likely to be punished for include behaviors such as defiance or disrespect. Interpretation of these specific behaviors are usually left to the discretion of the school administrator without outlining rigid guidelines to define them. In fact, conduct such as defiance and disrespect is interpreted through each school's conception of unwritten assumptions known as normative baselines. Normative baselines allow educators to determine appropriate behavior based on criteria that they believe are most important. Factors that determine normative baselines include cultural values, societal/behavioral norms, and racial assumptions. In the United States, white Americans have typically determined normative baselines in most aspects of daily life, including education. Thus, the behavior of white students has traditionally been used to evaluate the behavior of all students in the classroom. The behavioral norms of students of color do not usually fit into the normative assumptions of many public school educators or administrators, which leads to the discrepancy in punishment. Simply stated, African American and Latin/x students are viewed as more dangerous and threatening no matter how they behave in the classroom because of white normative baselines. Ultimately, the refusal or inability to conform to white normative baselines in the classroom exacerbates both the likelihood to be punished as well as the intensity of the punishment for students of color.

A final concept from critical race theory that is helpful in describing how the school-to-prison pipeline reproduces racial inequality is Derrick Bell's concept of racial realism. He described racial realism by stating: "Black people will never gain full equality in this country. Even those herculean efforts we hail as successful will produce no more than temporary 'peaks of progress', short-lived victories that slide into irrelevance as racial patterns adapt in ways that maintain white dominance … We must acknowledge it and move on to adopt policies based on what I call racial realism" (Bell 1992:337). This concept acknowledges that the prevalence of structural racism confers a permanent inferior status on historically marginalized racial and ethnic groups. Until this fact is acknowledged, policies and practices will continue to reproduce racial inequality in virtually every aspect of life. The public education system is a good example of this fact. Policies that were meant to eliminate racial inequality in the education system, such as desegregation, high-stakes testing, and disciplinary reform only served to create new mechanisms by which inequality is reproduced. The roles of both ability grouping/tracking and the school-to-prison pipeline have in this process have already been discussed. Ability grouping/tracking has created intra-school segregation through honor programs, AP courses, and selective school admission practices. The school-to-prison pipeline highlights that both the education system and the criminal justice system do not represent the best interests of historically marginalized groups. Thus, regardless of what policies are enacted, students of color will always suffer the most harm from them (Fasching-Varner, Mitchell, Martin, and Bennett-Haron 2014).

Counter-storytelling and Community Cultural Wealth

The concept of racial realism also serves as a starting point on how critical race theory can be used to address systemic racial inequality in public education settings. Bell's concept of racial realism can be used not only to point out how structural racism permeates the education system in the United States but also to show how working within traditional educational frameworks will not provide an adequate solution. Truly working toward creating a remedy for structural racism does not begin with creating new policies. A much more viable alternative is to critically analyze some of the basic assumptions behind discriminatory policies and practices first. In this vein, critical race theory scholars have developed several tools that can be used to begin this task. The two strategies that will be briefly discussed here are counter-storytelling and using the community as a space of cultural wealth.

The previous sections described how white normative baselines have traditionally been used as the standard to create educational policies that evaluate all students for both educational achievement as well as behavioral expectations in the classroom. White normative baselines create a sense of racial privilege for white students. White students are typically taught in a way that privileges their experiences through the narratives that they hear in class, teaching styles that cater more to their learning styles, and their perspectives are often validated as the default for all students (Solorzano and Yosso 2002). White normative baselines also silence the experiences and perspective of students of color. The students of color who do not meet the normative expectations set by white students are left with two options: they can either assimilate into the prescribed baselines or be dismissed from school.

Therefore, one way to minimize the impact of white normative baselines is for teachers and educational administrators to incorporate counter-storytelling as a tool to evaluate policies and practices in public schools. Counter-storytelling documents the stories and experiences of historically marginalized racial and ethnic groups to counter reliance on norms that are embedded with racial biases. Counter-stories also challenge the dominant and default classroom narratives that reproduce racial privilege for white students, which allows them to believe in their superiority. Counter-storytelling has been a prominent feature of many communities of color for a long time, particularly for African Americans and Latin/x. Counter-stories are CRT only important because they can be used to push back against dominant narratives in the education system that depict students of color as inferior, but they also have their own intrinsic value. Communities of color can use counter-stories as a way to strengthen social and cultural values (Ikemoto 1997).

Three forms of counter-storytelling include: personal stories, other people's stories, and composite stories. Personal stories detail an individual's account of various forms of social inequalities, including racism. Autobiographical stories of events are juxtaposed against policies or practices to offer a strong critique. Personal stories of students of color are helpful in critiquing ability grouping/tracking and the school-to-prison pipeline. Courts ruled in previous cases regarding ability grouping/tracking that in many instances, those policies had a minimum segregative effect. Understanding the personal stories of students who attend these schools would certainly help courts to realize that the segregative effect of those policies is anything but minimum. Personal stories allow the individuals to tell the cognitive, emotional, social, and developmental impact that any form of segregation can have on a student (Solorzano and Yosso 2002). Furthermore, personal narratives can allow students of color to express feelings of implicit inferiority that occurs through both achievement grouping and the discretion used in implementing disciplinary policies. A tool that has a similar effect is the use of other people's narrative. Rather than examining an individual's encounter with systemic racism, a third-person narrative is provided. Teachers and school officials can evaluate effectiveness of certain policies by listening to third-party accounts of those policies. A collection of students of color can have their voices heard in a similar fashion to personal narratives. Finally, composite stories can be used as an evaluative measure. Scholars such as Derrick Bell, Richard Delgado, Tara Yosso, and Daniel Solorzano have written extensively using this method to counter white normative baseline assumptions about students of color. This strategy involves using various forms of data rather than personal experiences to describe the impact that certain policies have on students of color. Often, authors develop fictitious characters based on real or historical events and include accurate data to illuminate the challenges that students of color face in a structurally racist environment. Most frequently, these stories are written about in law reviews, journals, or books as critiques of the inadequate policies that continue to place students of color at a disadvantage.

White normative baselines have been previously established as the traditional standard to create and evaluate public education policies in the United States. They have also been used to describe the forms of social capital necessary to address social inequality. Pierre Bourdieu explains how social capital is typically associated with white normative baselines from the upper or middle class (Bourdieu and Passeron 1997). This framework is used by public school officials and educators to determine the knowledge, skills, and social/cultural capital that all students need to succeed in the classroom. School officials rarely rely on resources that can be found within the communities of color to create tools that enhance the ability of students of color to improve educational attainment. A critical race theory perspective advocates for the use of community cultural wealth as a way to transform the schooling process (Yosso 2005). Wealth from a CRT perspective goes beyond income distribution, salaries, or other monetary description. It includes the total amount of accumulated assets that can be both material and nonmaterial resources. Wealth includes the social capital that exists within communities to help them to navigate through life challenges.

For this analysis, community cultural wealth refers to the unique cultural capital that historically marginalized racial and ethnic groups have developed to empower them to resist both white normative baselines and systemic inequality. Tara Yosso describes six specific forms of social capital that communities of color have relied upon to survive against structural racism. Those forms of capital include: aspirational, linguistic, familial, social, navigational, and resistant capital. Public school education policy makers can consider how to use linguistic, social, and navigational capital as potential resources to help students of color face racial inequality in the classroom.

Linguistic capital describes the intellectual and social skills that someone develops through understanding expressions or interpretations of language through verbal and nonverbal skills by virtue of knowing multiple ways of communication. Often, many students of color enter school systems while having learned multiple ways to communicate with others. In some instances, students of color know multiple languages, such as Spanish, French, or Chinese, that they learn from their communities. Educational curriculum used to assess academic achievement can be more inclusive of the need of bilingual and multilingual students of color. Linguistic capital in the classroom can also refer to how students are able to communicate through visual art, music, and poetry (Yosso 2005). To better utilize linguistic capital, educators can develop policies and practices that take into account the impact that music, poetry, and art forms have on how students of color learn. Students of color can also rely on social capital found within their communities to face educational challenges. One example of social capital that is found in many communities of color is familial bonds. Strong familial bonds can provide students of color with the emotional and social support to survive the education system. This form of social capital can minimize feelings of isolation or inferiority. Strong familial bonds or bonds within the community also create communal knowledge that all members can withdraw from. Students of color are able to learn from the experiences of other communal members to develop their own learning strategies that can be used in the classroom. Educational challenges are able to be transcended through developing a strong social network within the community (Yosso 2005). The previously described forms of capital aid in the development of navigational capital. Navigational capital is the specific set of skills that students of color develop in order to maneuver through social institutions such as schools. Students of color are able find ways to thrive in scholastic environments that were not created to help them be successful. They develop a set of inner resources and cultural strategies that allow them to excel under perilous circumstances. Navigational capital allows these students to rely on other forms of community cultural wealth to help face educational challenges created by structural racism. Finally, students also gain individual agency that can empower them to achieve a greater degree of success in the classroom.

Conclusion

The aim of this chapter has been to elucidate two of the main challenges that students from historically marginalized racial and ethnic groups face in the K–12 public education system, namely, the tracking/ability grouping and the school-to-prison pipeline. A critical race theory perspective has been used to analyze the disparate impact of these practices. The shortcomings of both can be traced to the basic failures of the *Brown* decision, which diagnosed the problem of racial inequality in the education system but did not provide any remedies. Thus, it has continued to be perpetuated over the last half century. Whether it has been education scholars or the late Tupac Shakur, many individuals have pointed out the deficiencies and disparate impacts that policies and practices have on students of color. CRT provides concerned individuals with the opportunity to reimagine how to create a more equitable public education system in the United States. Counter-storytelling and community cultural wealth are just two tools that administrators can use to start conversations about the basic assumptions behind current policies. Until a complete restructuring of both basic assumptions regarding education policies as well as the policies themselves occurs, there can be no remedy to structural racism in K–12 schooling.

References

"Board of Educ. v. Dowell, 498 U.S. 237 (1991)." 2018. Justia. Retrieved July 23, 2018. (https://supreme.justia.com/cases/federal/us/498/237/).

"Brown v. Board of Education of Topeka, 347 U.S. 483 (1954)." 2018. Justia. Retrieved July 23, 2018. (https://supreme.justia.com/cases/federal/us/347/483/).

"Montgomery v. Starkville Mun. Separate School Dist., 665 F. Supp. 487 (N.D. Miss. 1987)." 2018. Justia. Retrieved July23, 2018. (https://law.justia.com/cases/federal/district-courts/FSupp/665/487/1668786/).

"Quarles v. Oxford Municipal Separate School District, 366 F. Supp. 247 (N.D. Miss. 1972)." 2018. Justia. Retrieved July23, 2018. (https://law.justia.com/cases/federal/district-courts/FSupp/366/247/1502717/).

Bell, Derrick. 1992. "Racial Realism." *Connecticut Law Review* 24:363–79.

Bell, Derrick. 2005. *Silent Covenants*. Oxford, England: Oxford University Press.

Bourdieu, Pierre, and Jean-Claude Passeron. 1977. *Reproduction in Education, Society and Culture*. London, England: Sage Publications.

Boyd, Tona. 2009. "Confronting Racial Disparity: Legislative Responses to the School-to-Prison Pipeline." *Harvard Law Review* 44(2):571–80.

Carbado, Devon, and Mitu Gulati. 2003. "The Law and Economics of Critical Race Theory." *Yale Law Journal* 112(7):1757–829.

Carbado, Devon, and Daria Roithmayr. 2014. "Critical Race Theory Meets Social Science." *Annual Review of Law and Social Science* 10:149–67.

Carter, Pamela, and Phoebe Roaf. 2004. "A Historic Overview of Brown v. Board of Education." *Los Angeles Business Journal* 51:410–13.

Cipriano-Walter, Mary. 2014. "Falling Off the Track: How Ability Tracking Leads to Intra-School Segregation." *Thurgood Marshall Law Review* 41(1):25–53.

Crenshaw, Kimberlé, Neil Gotanda, Gary Peller, and Kendall Thomas. 1996. *Critical Race Theory: The Writings That Formed the Movement*. New York: New Press.

Delgado, Richard, and Jean Stefancic. 2017. *Critical Race Theory*. New York: New York University Press.

Dreeben, Robert, and Rebecca Barr. 1988. "The Formation and Instruction of Ability Groups." *American Journal of Education* 97(1):34–64.

Ehrenreich, Barbara. 2009. "Is It Now a Crime to Be Poor?" *New York Times*. Opinion.

Fasching-Varner, Kenneth, Roland Mitchell, Lori Martin, and Karen Bennett-Haron. 2014. "Beyond School-to-Prison Pipeline and Toward an Educational and Penal Realism." *Equity & Excellence in Education* 47(4):410–29.

Gonzalez, Thalia. 2012. "Keeping Kids in Schools: Restorative Justice, Punitive Discipline, and the School to Prison Pipeline." *Journal of Law and Education* 41(2):281–335.

Hanson, Avarita. 2005. "Have Zero Tolerance Discipline Polices Turned into a Nightmare? The American Dream's Promise of Equal Education Opportunity Grounded in Brown v. Board of Education." *UC Davis Journal of Juvenile Law & Policy* 9:289–98.

Harris, Cheryl. 1993. "Whiteness as Property." *Harvard Law Review* 106(8):1707–91.

Ikemoto, Lisa. 1997. "Further the Inquiry: Race, Class, and Culture in the Forced Medical Treatment of Pregnant Women." Pp. 136–143 in *Critical Race Feminism: A Reader*, edited by A. Wing. New York: New York University Press.

Losen, Daniel. 2011. *Discipline Policies, Successful Schools, and Racial Justice*. National Education Policy Center.

Moody, James. 2001. "Race, School Integration, and Friendship Segregation in America." *American Journal of Sociology* 107(3):679–716.

Nussbaum, Lydia. 2018. "Realizing Restorative Justice: Legal Rules and Standards for School Discipline." *Hastings Law Journal* 69:583–644.

Oakes, Jeannie. 1985. *Keeping Track: How Schools Structure Inequality*. New Haven, CT: Yale University Press.

Rist, Ray. 1970. *The Invisible Children: School Integration in American Society*. Cambridge, MA: Harvard University Press.

Simson, David. 2014. "Exclusion, Punishment, Racism and our Schools: A Critical Race Theory Perspective on School Discipline." *UCLA Law Review* 61(506):507–62.

Skiba, Russell, Robert Homer, Choong-Geun Chung, Karega Rausch, Seth May, and Tary Tobin. 2011. "Race Is Not Neutral: A National Investigation of African American and Latino Disproportionality in School Discipline." *School Psychology Review* 40(1):85–107.

Solorzano, Daniel, and Tara Yosso. 2002. "Critical Race Methodology: Counter-Storytelling as an Analytical Framework for Education Research." *Qualitative Inquiry* 8(23):23–44.

Staff. 2013. *The Resurgence of Ability Grouping and Persistence of Tracking*. Brown Center Report on American Education.

Troyan, Brent. 2003. "The Silent Treatment: Perpetual in-School Suspension and the Education Rights of Students." *Texas Law Review* 81(6):1637–70.

Winfrey, Adia. 2018. "The Hate You Gave: The Prophetic Truth of Tupac's T.H.U.G.L.I.F.E." *National Monitor*.

Yosso, Tara. 2005. "Whose Culture Has Capital? A Critical Race Theory Discussion of Community Cultural Wealth." *Race Ethnicity and Education* 8(1):69–91.

Reading 4.2 Troubleshooting Racial Inequalities through a Collaborative Network in the Brazilian Educational System: The Case of "the Color of the Culture"

Otávio Rezende,[3] California State University

Rosiléia Milagres,[4] California State University

Keywords: Racial Inequalities, Black Movement, Collaborative Network, Education

Introduction

The black movement in Brazil has been inspired by the North American movement and was strengthened in the mid-1980s. By that time, a different profile of the black movement in the country emerged, denouncing the racism present in the social, political, economic, and educational structure (Gomes 2009). Nowadays, black people comprise 50.7 percent[5] of the Brazilian population, and they claim inclusion with equal rights and opportunities (Silvério, 2012).

The discussion on ethnic-racial issues, generated by a demand of the Brazilian society on promoting such debate, favored the creation of "the Color of the Culture" in 2004. This project refers to an inter-organizational network of private and public institutions, with the support of several nongovernmental organizations (NGOs) of the black and/or educational movements. It was created to implement the requirements of the Law 10.639/2003 in Brazilian primary and secondary schools. Such law has established national curriculum guidelines for the education of ethnic-racial issues and teaching of Afro-Brazilian and African history and culture in basic education. In sum, the project enhances inclusive initiatives and gives visibility to affirmative action promoted by the Brazilian society, contributing to the creation of inclusive teaching practices.[6]

"The Color of the Culture" developed a system of governance network to attend schools and social institutions across the country. The network involved the contractual integration of institutions and the procedural coordination of personal and organizational relationships. With this chapter, we intend to discuss the context in which such a network was formed and the management structure built to achieve results. We expect students do understand how public policy may be fundamental to work on people's understanding of their cultural heritage. The learning objectives involve the ability to describe how institutions can work together; to

---

[3] PhD in Business Administration–Affiliation: Centro Universitário Belo Horizonte–UNIBH–Brazil–e-mail: otrezende@gmail.com

[4] PhD in Economics–Affiliation: Fundação Dom Cabral–Brazil–e-mail: Rosileiam@fdc.org.br

[5] The 2010 Census reported that the black population exceeded the white population. There were 96.7 million (50.7 percent) who declared themselves black, compared with 91 million of whites (47.7 percent), 2 million of yellow (1.1 percent) and 817,900 of indigenous people (0.4 percent), from a total of 190,755,799 Brazilians (Ipea 2011).

[6] The network has produced some videos called *Heroes of the World*, which are short sketches showing the life and actions of outstanding Brazilian black people who have made a difference in society.

discuss how governance networks promote resource exchange; how to use social capital to put together people involved in social movements and promote affirmative actions; and to explain how ideas can be socially constructed and spread on a countrywide level.

To this end, besides this introduction, this work is divided into four sections: the context in which the network was formed, the convergence of the partners according to resources interdependence, the network structure, its interaction and results achieved. In the conclusion, we point out some research questions and recommended readings concerning the black movement in Brazil.

The System Context: Generating a Public-Private Collaborative Network[7]

The struggle of the Brazilian black people dates to the beginning of the country's republican history. Since then "organizations have been formed to increase the capacity of action in society, to stand up against racial discrimination, and to create mechanisms for recovery of the black race self-esteem" (Gonçalves, Gonçalves e Silva 2000, p. 139). Black protest organizations have emerged in different regions of the country, conquering the power of mobilization and visibility in the capitals and major cities. The coexistence between races in Brazil is marked by conflicts and tensions, and this trend was maintained almost throughout the twentieth century (Gonçalves, Gonçalves e Silva 2000). Despite past initiatives, organizations and the black movement have focused until the 1980s[8] on denouncing racism and discrimination and on proposing affirmative action policies (Gonçalves, Gonçalves e Silva, 2000; Menin and Shimizu 2006). By then, the struggle for racial equality emerges showing different characteristics. Later, a new profile of the black movement arises, denouncing both the racism present in the political, social, economic, and educational arena, and the myth of "racial democracy" present in the structure of the state and the school (Gomes 2009). Nowadays, their claims include an agenda: the study of African history and culture; the study of the black population struggle in Brazil; and the revision of textbooks containing racist content (Santos 2007, p. 171).

Along with these demands, there were public policies that favored the creation of the project "the Color of the Culture." The government of the former president Lula reaffirmed its commitment to ensure the right to education for millions of Brazilians who have not had access to education by defining literacy and inclusion as one of its four strategic educational policies.[9] All this has been effective due to a profound reorientation of policies implemented by the Ministry of Education (MEC) in 2004. One of them is the creation of SECADI,[10] a MEC's secretariat responsible for inclusive actions. This was an important step in the implementation of such a new strategic vision (Silvério, 2012).

Willing to strengthen the actions of Law 10.639/2003 and developing a national plan to define goals for its effective implementation, the government established a working group through means of ministerial decree

---

[7] A stable articulation between market and civil society, of mutually dependent actors, but functionally autonomous; whose interaction is guided by negotiated conflicts; which occurs in an institutionalized context of rules, norms, and shared knowledge and collective imagination; facilitates self-regulation of hierarchical policy decisions; and contributes to the production of "public value" in a broad sense of definition of problems, views, ideas, plans, and concrete regulations, and which are considered relevant to large sections of the population (SORENSEN, TORFING, 2009, p. 236).

[8] Compared to the United States, where affirmative action has taken place since the 1960s, there was a delay in this claim in Brazil, explained by the myth of "racial democracy" prevailing in the country throughout the twentieth century, which caused an ignorance of the existence of prejudice and race discrimination, beyond the defense of miscegenation as a race-strengthening standard (Menin and Shimizu 2006).

[9] Along with qualified basic education, expansion of vocational and technological education and reform of higher education.

[10] The Department of Continued Education, Literacy, Diversity and Inclusion implements educational policies in the areas of literacy and education of young people and adults, environmental education, human rights education, special education, the indigenous field school, maroon societies, and education for ethnic-racial relations. Its aim is to contribute to the inclusive development of education, valuing differences and diversity, promoting inclusive education, human rights, and social and environmental sustainability with a view to effective public policies (SECADI 2012).

No. 605, dated May 20, 2008, mandated from SEPPIR[11]/MEC. This measure assumes that, to democratize education, it is necessary to mobilize the whole society. In this way, MEC, through SECADI and its other offices,[12] recognized and appropriately prioritized the diversity of ethnic and racial experiences in educational systems (UNESCO, 2008). Because of the discussions promoted by this group, and seeking to ensure the wide participation of society, some "Regional Dialogues" occurred in six different states in Brazil from April to June 2008, putting together 720 participants. Among them, there were managers of the national school system, basic education teachers, academics, social movements, municipal councils, and state educational representatives; i.e., the main actors responsible for the implementation of Law 10.639/2003 (Silvério 2012).

"The Color of the Culture" was generated in this system context, with the main objective of developing audiovisual materials on the Afro-Brazilian history and culture. It was through that means that the project meant to enhance inclusion initiatives and give visibility to affirmative actions promoted by Brazilian society, contributing to the creation of inclusive teaching practices (Sant'Anna 2005). The core idea was that formal school education is an arena of struggle for the black movement. If, on one side, it can erase the contribution of African people in the construction of the Brazilian nation, on the other side it also represents the possibility "of changing the parameters of the effective educational system and educational policy in Brazil, since the history of people considered 'without history' starts to be told" (Silvério 2012).

The Convergence of Strategic Partners and Objectives

The participation of Africans and Afro-descendants in Brazilian society is often portrayed as a stereotype, folkloric or fictionalized, and out of focus (Sant'anna 2005, p.7). Discrimination occurs invisibly, supported by the "myth of racial democracy," which is based on the fallacy of undifferentiating difference. It covers key aspects of life for a significant portion of the population, allowing them to know in depth what they face and to value their effective participation in the history of building a nation.

Given this scenario, "the Color of the Culture" is aimed at the development of audiovisual material about the history and culture of Afro-Brazilians. The complexity of the project required dealing with a variety of factors involving the racial issue in Brazil, such as the involvement of different movements linked to democratic participation, religion, and the plural visions of academia and schools. The project worked "as a bridge, a meeting place, a place of dialogue between different groups and viewpoints; and Fundação Roberto Marinho (FRM) acted as a cornerstone for 'The Color of the Culture' since it stood alongside the diversity of views and discussions on the issue" (Brandão and Vassimon 2012).

FRM had a prominent position among the partners, since they conceived the project and presented it to Petrobras to obtain public funding for its implementation. For this purpose, FRM worked on partnerships with institutions which owned resources and capabilities to deal with the issue. The resource interdependence is noticeable in CHART 1, where the role (financial, technical, and human resources) of each institution is detailed:

CHART 1: Institutional Role Involved with the Project

Institution	Cooperation
Petrobras	Financial support.

[11] Secretariat of policies for promoting racial equality.
[12] Whose mission is to promote joint efforts with state and local governments, NGOs, social movements, trade unions, professional associations, research institutions, with the collaboration of international organizations to improve access, ensure continuity, and contribute to the improvement of practices and values that recognize and appropriately prioritize the diversity of ethnic and racial experiences in education systems (UNESCO 2008).

Roberto Marinho Foundation (FRM) and Futura Channel	Supply of personnel (FRM's team) for content development, executive production, programming, community mobilization, implementation, evaluation, planning, legal assistance, information technology (IT), institutional and communication relations, TV program production, and transmission of audiovisual works.
Education Ministry and SECADI	Institutional contacts with Educational Secretariats, reproduction and distribution of educational materials for public schools and institutions, material supply to Educational Secretariats.
SEPPIR (Secretary of Policies for the Promotion of Racial Equality)	Institutional contacts with Educational Secretariats, providing lists of distribution of training materials.
CIDAN (Brazilian Center for Information and Documentation of the Black Artist)	Mobilization and institutional contacts with their associates.
Ministry of Culture and Palmares Foundation	Institutional contacts with their local offices and other institutions.
Globo TV Channel	Production of a TV series named *Action* and dissemination of the project within their means.
Brasil TV Channel	Exhibition of the programs *Mojubá* and *Worldwide Heroes*.

Source: FRM (2009)

The project includes a series of cultural and educational activities focused on producing and broadcasting programs about the history of black people's contribution to Brazilian society (Silverio, 2000). Textbooks were distributed to public schools. All the products were developed as from the experience of FRM on creating attractive programs and educational materials (see CHART 2).[13] Their experience in communication and on mobilizing and training educators throughout the country has also contributed to a differentiated material. This production also received inputs from consultants and experts, with the participation of academics, educators, technicians, TV producers and directors, among others.

CHART 2: Products Developed for the Project

Product	Objective
Ação (Action)	News program showing positive experiences of organizations and social groups that work with young black people.
Nota 10 (Note 10)	Discloses experiences of basic education, educational resources, and research in the field of education aimed at the inclusion of African descendants.
Livros Animados (Cartoon Books)	Animation aimed to encourage reading and spread African and Afro-Brazilian legends and tales among children and educators.
***Heróis de Todo o Mundo* (Worldwide Heroes)**	Two-minute sketches that value the many roles of Africans and Afro-descendants as protagonists of Brazilian history.
Memória das Palavras	Educational game.

[13] See more on http://www.acordacultura.org.br/

(Word Memory Game)	
Onguê	Musical CD.
Mojubá	Videos showing the richness of Afro-descent heritage to restore local culture and the current Brazilian people's habits.
Coleção Saberes e Fazeres (Collection of Knowledge and Doings)	Notebooks with texts, articles, legislation, suggested activities, and methodology.
Mapas da África (Maps of Africa)	Maps of African diaspora and civilizing values of African Brazilians.

Source: Adapted from the Sponsorship Project (FRM, 2009) and Brandão (2011)

The creation of these materials involved discussions and knowledge exchanges between a diverse public and held in forums, meetings, documents, and training. Concerning the material, there were two big challenges: production and distribution. These two efforts could be taken as separate projects, giving important weight to the complexity of implementing such activities.

The Network Structure

The project aimed at providing methodological procedures to educators so they could optimize the use of materials and activities, adapting them to local conditions and forming a social network of multipliers. Its structure was based on three different levels: the "Managing Network" as national coordinators; the "Go-Between Network," responsible for methodological training; and the "Teacher's Network," which was responsible for implementing the methodology in the schools (see Figure 1).

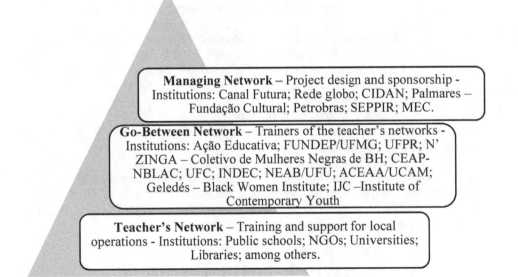

Figure 4.1: Governance Structure and Institutions Involved in Each of the Three Levels of Network

Source: Prepared by the authors.

The duties of each network sought to promote a dynamic relationship in the actions related to management, monitoring, and evaluation of activities (see Figure 4.2).

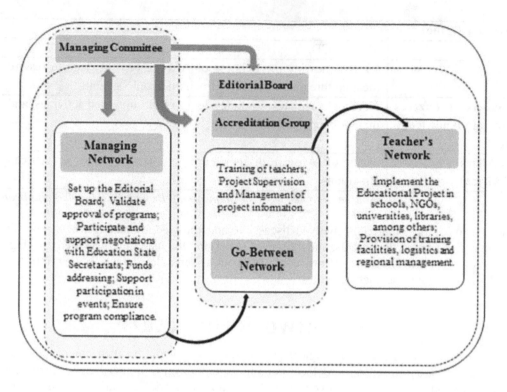

Figure 4.2: Governance Structure and Activities in Three Levels of Network

Source: Prepared by the authors.

In this structure, there were also three different working groups connecting the three-level networks:

1. The management committee, composed of representatives appointed by each of the partner institutions, members of the "Managing Network." It monitored and adjusted the scope and the project, endorsing products and processes and acting on partnerships. Their meetings were held bimonthly.

2. The "Editorial Board," composed of experts appointed by the "Management Committee," aimed to propose guidelines for the material production and ensure its adequacy in the training package (printed and audiovisual materials).

3. The "Accreditation Team," which was composed of the management team and representatives of the partners responsible for the formulation of bid documents and selection of institutions that took part in the "Go-Between Network." They were also responsible for defining the contractual and fiscal aspects of partnerships.

Network Interaction

There were different levels of governance within these networks. The Managing Committee, consisting of representatives of the institutions that sponsored the project (the "Managing Network"), designing the macro strategy of the network, with a separate and explicit regulation. In this level, Canal Futura acted as a leader that would define strategic issues when dealing with the project.

The "Go-Between Network" had a group of educational coordinators as members. They used to meet on a regular basis to plan and evaluate the work. According to the project's original design, this network would be related to the Editorial Board. However, it did not happen in practice. The original idea was that the Editorial

Board would represent the Go-Between Network to the Management Committee, so they could help with the conceptual thinking of the products and their subsequent implementation. Several factors led to the Editorial Board not playing the expected role, but it happened mostly because the project was already functioning when it was created. There was beforehand an existing editorial line of thinking, a well-constructed material in use, determining what should be done. Thus, the Editorial Board acted more as an adviser than as a governance actor. At the end of the day, it did not result as a negative impact on the quality of the project because the educational consultants overcame the task and the educational coordination group from Canal Futura ended up mediating the relations with the Go-Between Network.

For its part, the "Teacher's Network" was composed of representatives of several Educational State Secretariats, located in fourteen different states. These groups were responsible for implementing the project locally. Nevertheless, the reality found in schools was that members of the teacher's network, was quite distinct from the surrounding space in the Management and Go-Between networks. It is noticeable that the Teacher's Network did not realize the importance of the paradigm that the law intended to overcome. Moreover, this fact was perceived by the teachers more as a problem than as an issue to be addressed in the classroom in order to transform the actual reality.

The importance of FRM's role in the network is noteworthy. They had a formal central position in the management of these three-level networks. However, due to the fact of using the structure of Canal Futura to manage the network and their role as producers of the material, there was an ambiguity in the perception of the institutions of direct relationship with the management network. While FRM offered the structure, Canal Futura offered their intellectual capital, and both used their "symbolic capital" in external relations. This feature was used as a linkage mechanism of these organizations with other institutions (which belonged to the same group, Globo Organization). For example, while Canal Futura had an easy contact with universities and social movements, in turn, the Secretariat of Education would receive FRM very well due to its previous relationship with the production of a distance course broadcast by TV Globo.

Achieved Results

The network was structured and implemented in different regions of the country, conforming to three stages (see Figure 3).

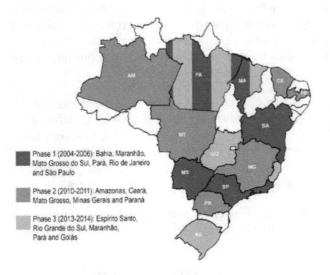

Phase 1 (2004-2006): Bahia, Maranhão, Mato Grosso do Sul, Pará, Rio de Janeiro and São Paulo

Phase 2 (2010-2011): Amazonas, Ceará, Mato Grosso, Minas Gerais and Paraná

Phase 3 (2013-2014): Espírito Santo, Rio Grande do Sul, Maranhão, Pará and Goiás

Figure 4.3: Geographic Distribution of Each Phase of Implementation of the Project

In the first stage, the objective was to provide methodological benefits to educators so they could optimize the potential of content, materials, and activities developed by the project, adapting them to local conditions and forming a social network of multipliers. Hence, the actions at this stage sought to: 1) contribute to the enforcement of Law No. 10.639/03; 2) enable NGOs to spread the methodology for using the products as an educational tool for reflection and development of local social capital; 3) strengthen this social capital through the formation of teachers of public schools and social educators from NGOs; 4) as well as to strengthen educational networks, with the participation of universities and NGOs working with the content on the training of the Afro-Brazilian culture and history.

At the time, 2,044 kits (teaching materials used in the implementation of the methodology) were distributed in the states of Bahia, Mato Grosso do Sul, Maranhão, Pará, São Paulo, and Rio de Janeiro, involving 31 Municipal Secretariats of Education and 3,000 educators trained. In total, the distribution of the materials involved 2,000 public and community schools, 115 NGOs, 20 universities, 36 specialists, and 199 partners and consultants, enabling a total average of 90,000 students to use the materials and experience the methodology in the classroom. More than 1,000 institutions had contact with the training and videos through Channel Futura in an audience at the time of 23 million viewers.

In the second phase, conducted between 2010 and 2011, the project aimed to provide the basis for sustainability and autonomy in the use of materials and methodologies for the strengthening of networks. To reach this goal, the project offered methodological subsidies to educators, so that they could improve the potential of contents, materials, and activities, adapting them to the local reality and forming a social network of multipliers. Actions were implemented in six other states: Ceará, Pernambuco, Amazonas, Minas Gerais, Paraná, and Mato Grosso. At the end of 2011, 26,517 educators were directly trained; 53,033 indirectly; 9,791 social educators (working with individuals in situations of socioeconomic vulnerability) directly; and 20,761 educators indirectly, making a total of 110,102 educators (teachers, coordinators, etc.).

The third phase started in 2013 and ended in 2014, covering the states of Espírito Santo, Rio Grande do Sul, Maranhão, Pará, and Goiás. Its purpose was to offer methodological subsidies through the provision of training educators and teachers established in different regions of the country, making the best use of the contents addressed in the products, materials, and activities. They were also expected to adapt such material to local realities, besides seeking the formation of a social network of multipliers.

First results found in evaluations done in the third phase relate to students' appropriation of the positive narratives about the black population, the quality of the material of the Color of the Culture, the dialogue with other projects with a perspective of an integrative education, as well as the implementation of the methodology in other disciplines. All these characteristics would provide continuous implementation of the methodology, the materials, and their contents (SEPPIR, 2015).

So far, the project "the Color of the Culture" has been present in 14 Brazilian states and 65 municipalities; trained more than 26,517 educators directly and 53,033 indirectly; 9,791 social educators directly and 20,761 educators indirectly. At the same time, 7,000 training materials have been distributed and reached more than 110,000 people (teachers, social educators, institutional managers, etc.) through training and use of its materials and methodology. Several pedagogical didactic resources, training, and monitoring of teachers were carried out and produced on a country level.

The project is an achievement of black social movements and allied organizations which stood up against racism and for democratization of education.

Conclusion

Our intention was to have a descriptive work, discussing the context in which the network was formed, and the management structure built to achieve results. We highlight the favorable scenarios for the struggle of social movements at the time of the project's implementation—in particular, the black power movement and the creation of an inter-organizational network to promote this discussion in the Brazilian basic school system. It all happened in a very positive social, political, and economic scenario; i.e., the Brazilian system context matured enough to create a private-public network that would work on that issue in the school system.

Since its implementation in 2004, the program began to take root in most of the schools by reviewing curriculum proposals, discussion of the pedagogical project, or creation of study groups related to the theme of racial inequality. When it comes to changing the social paradigm, students and teachers are more sensitive to the need of eliminating discriminatory practices. Most schoolteachers prioritize the discussion of issues, and it is easier to relate them to their content areas and disciplines (FUTURA, 2012).

Regarding the project management perspective, one concern was focused on two main streamlines: how to make the material most used by their public, the teachers; and how to create a network and a methodology for training educators. It is believed that the operation of a project of this size requires a well-defined timeline and strategic plan. Meanwhile, it is also believed that the conceptual design time, the "academic world" thinking, and the pedagogical advisers worked in a different time basis. More than that, these all differed for the time required to operate the project.

We understand that all these issues may bring research questions like: what should be the adequate theoretical background to better understand such phenomena? Can contractual and procedural governance help to better build such a model? Is the collaborative governance the adequate choice to fight racial inequalities in the Brazilian educational system?

Key words: Racial Inequalities; Black Movement; Collaborative Network; Education

Further Readings

Brazil census shows African Brazilians in the majority for the first time. Available at: https://www.theguardian.com/world/2011/nov/17/brazil-census-african-brazilians-majority. Accessed on January 2, 2018.

Brazil's New Black Power Movement. Available at: https://www.theroot.com/brazil-s-new-black-power-movement-1790856322. Accessed on January 2, 2018.

Race in Brazil. Available at: https://www.theglobeandmail.com/news/world/brazils-colour-bind/article25779474/. Accessed on January 2, 2018.

Unified Black Movement. Available at: http://www.blackpast.org/gah/movimento-negro-unificado-founded-1978. Accessed on January 2, 2018.

References

Brandão, A.P. 2011. *"Racial Diversity as a Positive Variable for the Construction of Strategies for Empowerment and Creation of Resources to Tackle Ethnic and Racial Prejudice in Brazilian Schools: The Experience of the Project 'The Color of Culture.'"* An International Workshop on Innovation, Diversity and Sustainable Development in Areas of Social Vulnerability, Boston. University of Massachusetts.

Brandão, A.P., and M. Vassimon. 2012. *Entrevista Concedida Por Videoconferência Pela Coordenadora De Conteúdo Do Canal Futura E Pela Gerente De Mobilização Comunitária.* Belo Horizonte/Rio De Janeiro.

FRM. 2009. *Projeto "A Cor Da Cultura" Apresentado Ao Programa Petrobrás Desenvolvimento Cidadania E Aprovado Para O Período De 2010/2011.* Rio De Janeiro: Fundação Roberto Marinho, 36 p.

FUTURA. 2012. Avaliação Do Progama "A Cor da Cultura"—2008. Available at: <http://www.Acordacultura.Org.Br/Sites/Default/Files/Documentos/Avaliacao032008.Pdf>. Acessed on August 20, 2018.

FUTURA. 2015. *Apresentação do projeto A Cor da Cultura,* por Lúcia Araújo, Diretora do Canal. Available at: <https://pt.slideshare.net/canalfutura/a-cor-da-cultura-apresentao-english-version>. Acessed on August 22, 2018.

Gomes, N.L. 2009. Evolução e Contexto Atual das Políticas Públicas no Brasil: Educação, Desigualdade e Reconhecimento In: M.E. De Paula and R. Heringer Eds.). *Caminhos Convergentes: Estado e Sociedade na Superação das Desigualdades Raciais no Brasil.* Rio De Janeiro: Fundação Heinrich Boll, Actionaid. Cap. 2, p.292. ISBN 978-85-62669-00-2.

Gonçalves, L.A.O., and P.B. Gonçalves e Silva. 2000. Movimento Negro e Educação. *Revista Brasileira de Educação.* Rio De Janeiro: 134–58.

IPEA. 2012. *Dinâmica Demográfica da População Negra Brasileira.* 2011. Available at: <http://Portal.Mte.Gov.Br/Data/Files/8a7c816a316b688101318aaf34bf324a/110512_Comunicadoipea91. Pdf >. Acessed on March 9, 2012.

Menin, M.S.D.S., and A.D.M. Shimizu. 2006. *Representações Sociais De Diferentes Políticas De Ação Afirmativa Para Negros, Afrodescendentes E Alunos De Escolas Públicas Numa Universidade Brasileira.* 29ª Reunião Anual da ANPED. Caxambu.

Santos, A.D.N. 2007. Adolescentes Negros e Não-Negros Na Escola: Identificando Estereótipos. In Iolanda De Oliveira, M.Â.D.S.A., Petronilha Beatriz Gonçalves e Silva, Rachel De Oliveira (Orgs.), Eds.. *Negro E Educação: Linguagens, Educação, Resistência, Políticas Públicas.* São Paulo: Ação Educativa; ANPED.

Sant'anna, W. 2005. *Marco Conceitual Do Projeto "A Cor Da Cultura".* P.68.

SECADI. 2012. *Secretaria De Educação Continuada, Alfabetização, Diversidade e Inclusão.* 2012. Available at: <http://Portal.Mec.Gov.Br/Index.Php?Option=Com_Content&View=Article&Id=290&Itemid=816 >. Acessed on April 9, 2012.

SEPPIR. 2015. *Projeto A Cor da Cultura é tema de reunião na SEPPIR.* Available at: < http://www.seppir.gov.br/central-de-conteudos/noticias/maio/projeto-a-cor-da-cultura-e-tema-de-reuniao-na-seppir>. Acessed on August 20, 2018.

Silvério, V.R. 2012. *Avaliação do Programa "A Cor Da Cultura".* Available at: <http://www.Acordacultura.Org.Br/ >. Acessed on April 15, 2012.

UNESCO. 2008. *Contribuições Para Implementação Da Lei 10.639/2003. Proposta De Plano Nacional De Implementação Das Diretrizes Curriculares Nacionais Da Educação Das Relações Étnico-Raciais E Para O Ensino De História E Cultura Afrobrasileira E Africana–Lei 10.639/2003.* Brasília: UNESCO/MEC: 58 p.

Reading 4.3 "I Know My Place": How Whiteness, White Culture, and White Educators Permeate and Shape Universities[14]

Demerris R. Brooks-Immel, EdD, and Susan B. Murray, PhD[15]

Keywords: Color-blind racism, aversive racism, white fragility, whiteness in education.

Goals of the Chapter

- To provide a sociological lens into the racialized worldview of white educators working in multiracial settings.
- To demonstrate how color-blind and aversive racism manifest in social interactions.
- To demonstrate how white educators embody and engage whiteness in working for racial justice.

Opening Quote

Interviewer: How do you think your white identity impacts your relationships with your students and colleagues of color?

White Administrator: I don't know. That is a good question. I don't know. One thing that is always there is that as a white person in America, you have privilege. It's just a fact. So the fact that I don't know if it has helped me get places, it probably has. You know. Because it is just the way we operate in America. So how do I think it affects my … you know, I don't really know. I'm hoping it doesn't have much of an effect. But it might. Um, I don't know. I treat all my colleagues and students as equals as best I can and um I hope that they see that. (Interview 2016)

Introduction

"I don't know." "I don't know." This was the rallying cry of most of the white educators we encountered when we asked about the impact of their white racial identities on their work in higher education. These educators, like most white people, had very little to say about their racial identities as white people. In fact, most white people have very little awareness that they even *have* white racial identities, or that whiteness and white racism are upheld by cultural values, institutional structures, and social interactions.

Most universities across the country operate as historically white spaces. Even institutions with diverse student populations are still being run by predominantly white-identified faculty, staff, and administrators (Feagin, Vera, and Imani 1996; Harris and Gonzalez 2012). And while much of the research on higher education

[14] Direct all correspondence to Susan B. Murray, Department of Sociology and Interdisciplinary Social Science, San Jose State University, One Washington Square, San Jose, CA 95092; susan.murray@sjsu.edu. This research was supported in part through a San Jose State University Research, Creativity, and Scholarship Grant.
[15] This is a collaborative research project and, as such, our names are listed alphabetically.

focuses on the experiences of students and faculty of color in predominantly white universities (Feagin, Vera, and Imani 1996; Hurtado, Carter, and Spuler 1996; Solorzano, Ceja, and Yosso 2000), very little has been written explicitly about the experiences of white-identified faculty, staff, and administrators as white people working in multiracial spaces.

Our qualitative research examines how white college faculty, staff, and administrators respond to multiracial environments and multicultural ideals. Specifically, we interviewed thirty white-identified faculty, staff, and administrators working in a "minority-majority" though predominantly white-run university asking: 1) how white people come to understand their own racial identities as white people; and 2) how they view their own "racial place" within a multiracial institutional context.

We invited whites to participate in confidential, one-on-one, in-depth interviews on whiteness and found most (but not all) unwilling and/or incapable of talking about their white racial identities. The majority of white administrators, faculty, and staff we interviewed, when asked direct questions about their white identities, exhibited what Robin DiAngelo (2016:247) calls white fragility, "… a state in which even a minimum amount of racial stress becomes intolerable, triggering a range of defensive moves." At the same time, a small minority of the white faculty we interviewed possessed a well-established practice of engaging in what we have come to term as *white countermoves*. These countermoves are characterized by a self-reflective and constant mapping of whiteness as a conscious practice. This chapter describes and analyzes the white defensive moves and countermoves made by white-identified faculty, staff, and administrators working in predominantly white-run multiracial "minority"-majority educational institutions.

Our goal in writing this chapter is to provide students with a racialized "map" of the university such that they are better able to mindfully traverse this institutional space (Wetherell and Potter 1992). Though advertised as race-neutral spaces celebrating "diversity and inclusive excellence," scholars have long argued that institutions of higher learning operate under "white supremacy values" (Feagin 2002; Okun 2001). Perfectionism, individualism, competition, paternalism, emotional neutrality, objectivity, and either/or thinking, are among those white cultural values promoted and rewarded in university settings (Okun 2001). White faculty, staff, and administrators, having internalized these values as neutral and normal, uphold these ways of thinking and doing as central to their work as educators. In this chapter, we argue that the institutional invisibility of white cultural values, coupled with white people's propensity toward white fragility, manifests among these white educators as aversive racism, a form of racism which "allow[s] well-meaning white people to maintain a positive (nonracist) self-image while still perpetuating racism" (DiAngelo, 2016:132).

Our initial interest in studying the racial literacy of white educators working in multiracial institutions of higher learning was to map how whiteness is undermined and/or sustained in this particular "geography of privilege" (Twine and Gardener 2013). Examining how white administrators, faculty, and staff come to understand and articulate their own racial locations and the place of whiteness in institutional structures leads to a deeper understanding of how universities as "structures in process" operate to perpetuate or dismantle existing racialized hierarchies. Our study, in other words, is sociological mindfulness (Schwalbe 2018) in practice, unveiling the direct and indirect patterns of racialization (Omi and Winant 1994) that structure university life.

Findings: Mapping Whiteness and the Language of White Educators

Our research unveiled three main patterned responses among the white-identified educators we interviewed: 1) color-blind racism: those who use the idea of color-blindness to avoid talking about race, including their own whiteness; 2) static awareness of white racial privilege: those who recognize how and when traditional power structures are reinforced and re-created in the university, but lack the confidence, skill, or will to challenge them effectively; and 3) embodied and engaged whiteness: those who consciously and consistently apply antiracist, antibias practices or pedagogy to interactions with students and colleagues.

Color-blind Racism and White Defensive Moves

When asked about the impact of their racial location as white people on their work as educators, most of the whites we interviewed responded with some form of color-blind racism. Color-blind racism refers to the practice by white people of pretending to not see race in an effort to appear "not racist" (Bonilla-Silva 2014). The logic behind this practice stands in direct contradiction to sociological mindfulness. Whites who profess to "not see race" are attempting to uphold a construction of reality that dictates: if I don't see race or name it, then it does not exist in my world and I cannot therefore ever be accused of being racist.

The Dunning-Kruger effect describes how people who lack proficiency in a skill overrate their actual competence because they are too unaware of the actual skill to understand what it means to have it. So is the case with many research participants who were asked to reflect on their own social location as white people in a majority-minority institution—because they have little to no experience reflecting on their whiteness, they lacked the tools to evaluate their own performance (Pennycook, Ross, Koehler, and Fugelsang 2017). The Dunning-Kruger effect, manifesting as color-blind racism, arose when educators were asked to discuss race in the context of childhood and family, social network, or work environments. In this instance, many research participants deflected from addressing whiteness by shifting the conversation to another "identity" which they were more comfortable discussing.

When asked if she thinks about her racial identity at work for example, a white female faculty member replied that it isn't an issue:

> "I mean, uh, you know if you're in the privileged group you don't see the other things. … I think more gender than race." In response to the same question, a white female administrator answered, "I think of myself as more of a scientist, which I feel is more of how I identify. But not the race part." And still another white female faculty member stated that she gets along well with her colleagues, not because she is white, but because she is attractive; "most men respond to that."

In each of these examples, when asked to reflect on their lived experience as white people, respondents quickly denied the salience of race on their interactions at work. In each case, the white educator deflects from race with a quick pivot to an alternate identity, *"more gender," "more scientist,"* or more about beauty.

The color-blind defensive move utilized by white educators was not limited to reflections on their own racial locations. Denying the relevancy of racialization extended to campus incidents, classroom interactions, and to the college students under their care. When asked, for example, how white people could have more effectively addressed a specific incident of racial bias that occurred in campus housing, many of the responses shifted the focus of the racial incident away from race. One white administrator opted to focus on bureaucratic process: *"I think what is running through my head is procedurally what could we have done better and I'm not sure how much that is tied into race."* Similarly, a female administrator asserted that an incident involving racist language and symbols was about bullying, not race:

> It was a terrible situation … But it's also very complicated. A very complicated situation. I don't think it's just about race. Uh huh. I think there was a lot of just plain old bullying going on that wasn't just about race. Uh huh. And I think it's unfortunate that it, it's become just about race, because I think there's a lot more to it.

In both cases, the urge toward a color-blind stance is so powerful that each university administrator attempts to transpose an explicitly blatant incident of white racism into something erasing racial meaning altogether, as a *"procedural"* problem or more simply as *"bullying."* In both examples, the transposition of white racism into something else is accompanied by an underlying accusation of blame: *"it's unfortunate that it, it's become just about race,"* paternalistically (Okun, 2001) shaming those who decry the significance of race over more *"complicated"* explanations.

In referencing their interactions with students, these white educators frequently engaged in what Bell and Hartmann (2007) refer to as "happy talk." Happy talk or " 'diversity discourse' …allows Americans to engage race on the surface but disavow and disguise its deeper structural roots and consequences" (Bell and Hartmann 2007:910). Generalizing race as "diversity" allows for "happy talk" (Bell and Hartmann, 2007) in which "white" and "people of color" are ignored as discrete categories, thereby conflating color-blindness with open-mindedness or lack of prejudice and providing an escape from the examination of white racial filters necessary to address structural and institutional inequality (DiAngelo 2016:7). A department chair, for example, happily offers evidence of her color-blind stance in reference to the students served in her department. When asked how her racial identity as a white person shapes her interactions with her students, she replied:

> I don't really look at it like that. I really don't look at my students and think, "you are a white student, you are an Asian student," I really don't look at them like that at all. And, so I don't really feel I know how to answer that question, I don't look at them like that.

Time and time again, the "happy talk" of color-blindness surfaced as the typical position for these white educators: *"I see students of color the same as everyone else. You know, I see the person. You might see someone is black, but once you get to know the person you don't see it anymore,"* similarly, *"… through my lens, it doesn't even, it doesn't even occur to me to think one way or another depending on whether someone is Asian or Black or a Mexican American or, whatever. I don't, I don't even think about that."* Even in cases where there are documented structured and historical inequalities between groups of students, white educators slide readily into happy talk. Dismissing the growing "achievement gap" between black, Latinx, and white students, one white faculty/administrator instead praises the "happy" feelings of the black and Latinx students she works so hard for:

> The achievement gap is growing, but just making sure our African American students and the Latino students feel really welcomed here. So we've worked really hard, … making everybody feel welcome … they're happy. You know we are not having problems, we could have gone down a slippery road. … It's hard. But I think it is by dialogue and by conversations and by breaking, like we did, break the bread. And being a part of that, things are better.

The "happy talk" of color-blindness provides a crutch that assuages the stress, burden, and discomfort many white people experience when discussing race and empowers participants to position themselves as racial innocents unaffected by race in their daily interactions (Bonilla-Silva 2014). Here the white educator emphasizes her *"hard work"* with students, and notes that despite a growing achievement gap, just by *"dialogue"* and *"breaking the bread,"* her African American students are *"happy,"* and things are *"better."* Although critical race theory regards racism as common, pervasive, and significant in how students of color experience higher education (Ledesma 2016), whiteness is neither discussed nor challenged (Wise 2015) in deference to happy talk.

The professed color-blindness of the white academics in our study is, of course, a fabrication. In their positioning as well-meaning whites in this particular setting and in this cultural moment, color-blindness equates with the "not-racist" side of the racist binary. Upholding color-blindness enables whites to hold fast to their position as individuals who are "just human" (DiAngelo 2016:194). It is, in other words, a self-preserving position that reinforces white supremacy cultural values concerning the invisibility of whiteness, the innocence of white people, and the denial of structured inequalities based on race.

Static Awareness of White Racial Privilege: Well-meaning Whites and Aversive Racism in Action

Static awareness was typified by those white educators who recognize how and when traditional power structures are reinforced and re-created in educational settings but lack the confidence, skill, or will to challenge them effectively. This group of white educators falls under DiAngelo's (2016) description of "well-meaning white people *[who]* maintain a positive (non-racist) self-image while still perpetuating racism" (p. 132). Like the white educators above who perpetuate color-blind racism, this group evidenced forms of "aversive racism" that defended their own racialized innocence while simultaneously calling out white racism in others. Even in cases where they recognize and name white supremacy and white privilege, they can fail to take effective countermeasures. The following confession, recounted by a white professor overwhelmed by her own inaction, illustrates one of these aversively racist moments:

> At one point during [a class] discussion a white male student said something really racist about black people. Now this student had been challenging me and making rude comments all semester, but I'd been ignoring him. This time, however, he crossed a line for me. When he made the comment, I was stunned. I didn't know what to do. I just gave him a look and told him his comment was inappropriate. As this was all happening a student walked out of class. This same student—a woman of color—came to me after class and implored me to do something. She said she had been feeling uncomfortable with this student's comments all semester to the point where sometimes she could not come to class because she was not up to facing him. I apologized to her and made sure she knew I hated what he said. I just didn't know what to do about him. Students like that can ruin a class for everyone.

In recounting this incident, this white professor inadvertently makes several aversively racist moves common to well-meaning whites (DiAngelo 2016). First, she assumes—as many whites do—that people of color have the same experiences that white people have (p. 229). In this case, though, her racist "line" was crossed during week ten of the semester; for her students of color, this line had been breached weeks earlier. The classroom is not a racially neutral space. Though individuals bring their racialized selves into the classroom (including whites), they are also met by an institutional space that reflects white supremacy culture. By failing to address the "disruptive" comments of the white male student from the start, her silence confirmed his right to be "disruptive"—regardless of her intentions. The white supremacy culture of the classroom allows white dominance to flourish. The second well-intentioned move underscored by this description is in the white professor's attempt to assert her not-racist position and "seek absolution" (DiAngelo 2016:224) from the woman of color who walked out of her class, *"I apologized to her and made sure she knew I hated what he said."* Rather than focusing on the student's experience, the professor's comments are centered on ensuring the student knows the professor *"hated what he said."* Here the perception of the white person as "not racist" becomes the goal of the interaction. This assertion, that the professor is not to blame for the white racism perpetuated in her class, reinforces the third "well-meaning" move she makes, "only acknowledging racism in other whites and not in ourselves" DiAngelo 2016:231). This white professor, socialized in white supremacy culture to the invisibility of whiteness, is immune to the everyday racial micro aggressions perpetuated by other whites. The "racial neutrality" of her classroom has not been "ruined" by the racism of one white student because classrooms are not racially neutral spaces. In this instance, from the perspective of the student of color, the class experience became untenable when micro aggressions were allowed to flourish without challenge. Like the white educators in our study, white students have few skills (and virtually no education) in naming and understanding whiteness. While blatantly racist statements made by white students must be interrupted and challenged, making them responsible for what happens afterward in the classroom is problematic. Instead, it is the responsibility of educators to understand how social inequalities manifest in the interactional dynamics of classrooms and to ready themselves with the skills to turn untenable moments into teachable ones.

This inability to take effective action was not limited to educators who claim little awareness of the impact of their racial identities. In explaining her constant awareness of her whiteness, one white faculty offered the following pedagogical example:

> Well, I'm always conscious of my race cause that's who I am … So I'm constantly saying, "I am white" … I'm constantly saying that because in my classroom, the white people are in the minority. The majority or the global majority is the majority of the class so for me to identify continuously to, to identify as white makes it safer for them because they, they see that I know my place.

This faculty member uses her admission of white privilege in the classroom to create a safe space for her students of color. *"To identify as white makes it safer for them because they, they see that I know my place."*

But acknowledging her privileged position in the dominant culture and *"knowing her place"* by itself does nothing to mitigate embodied power and privileges, nor does it create a "safe space." Without ground rules or other practical strategies for diminishing white privilege and white supremacy cultural values, the admission stands as a confirmation, not a repudiation, of the power hierarchy. As Smith (2013:277) notes, "the problem with safe space is the presumption that a safe space is even possible."

Calling out the racism of other whites, or naming and admitting white privilege, by themselves do little to dismantle the institutions holding that privilege in place. In the context of a white-run multiracial minority-majority university, white educators who call out the racism of others or name their privilege without simultaneously engaging in efforts to dismantle that privilege run the risk of reinforcing existing racial hierarchies.

Embodied and Engaged Whiteness: White Antiracist Practice in Action

Finally, a small minority of research participants were able to articulate a commitment to and recognition of the need for antiracist, antibias practices or pedagogy (beyond the simple acknowledgment of white privilege) and a conscious application of that awareness to interactions with students and colleagues. When asked for examples of being consciously aware of her racial identity at work, a white professor replied:

> I feel like the first years I was here, maybe it was me, and how I was starting these discussions, um, but students were less open to talking about it. And, now it seems, in part because of the general climate, something that students talk about more. And, I think I'm aware of trying to facilitate some of those discussions, as a white faculty member. And, I am aware that there are not enough faculty members of color on this campus, particularly, African American faculty members. And, um, yeah, so I think I'm pretty constantly aware of it, in the classroom.

Here the white faculty member engages with whiteness at both the interactional level, *"I'm aware of trying to facilitate some of those discussions, as a white faculty member"* and institutionally, *"And I am aware that there are not enough faculty members of color on this campus."* She is aware of the disproportionate lack of professors of color in the academy and the necessity of an embodied racial awareness for white faculty. Engaged action is exemplified by a simultaneous recognition of the responsibilities of white people as white people and an analysis of how the academy systematically disadvantages scholars of color (Bernal and Villapando 2002).

In another example, a faculty member recalls a time she was called upon by a student to assist with a housing program on the subject of race:

> In my, [GE] course we were talking about colorblind racism, and an African American student who was an RA in the dorms, came up to me, and said that she is in charge of dorm programming. And, would I come … and facilitate a discussion in the dorms, on colorblind racism. And, part of me was, like, why are you asking me? Like you're asking me, because you didn't have the words for this, and I'm the one who taught you those words, and directed you towards resources. But, I'm a white person. I shouldn't do this. I was like, I should direct you to …

An embodied understanding of whiteness, white identity, and white supremacy means knowing that regardless of individual circumstances, beliefs, or past histories, white people always move through a world structured by white supremacy and white privilege. In deference to her knowledge of this phenomenon, this faculty member's initial reaction is to concede both the opportunity and the expertise to a faculty member of color. She recognizes, however, that this invisible labor that is too often thrust upon and expected of faculty of color is not valued in the reappointment, tenure, and promotion process and is therefore a substantial burden that works against them.

And, so while on the one hand I was, like, I cannot speak to this, because, you know, I was well, wait a minute. Why shouldn't I do this? A, this student asked me. B, there's recent study that talked about how advising students of color, or supporting them, falls on faculty of color more. And so, of course … Maybe it's impactful for students to, to have a white faculty member talking about this stuff, and willing to go spend an evening in the dorms.

White educators who name and own their whiteness move through institutions of higher education fully cognizant of their white racialized selves. At first, her awareness inhibits, as she equates leading a discussion about race at the request of her black students with another example of institutionalized racism in which whites are the experts on all matters. She realizes, however, that this is an opportunity for the students involved to interact in a meaningful way with a race-conscious white person who can successfully model claiming one's white identity and articulate the role of whiteness and white racism in this multicultural community.

Realizing the importance of owning and embodying whiteness stands in direct contradiction to white cultural norms of invisibility and silence (Frankenberg 1993). Common to the interviewees who demonstrated such engaged awareness was evidence of and commitment to their own ongoing antiracist education. Ongoing antiracist education manifested as planned or executed proactive moves to acquire training and education on white racism. For some the training began in graduate school, for others it was "inspired" by colleagues calling them out, or simply as a result of them *developing as … a person."* In all cases where engaged white educators embraced the need for their own ongoing antiracist education, they also embraced it as necessary for their students. In referencing her work with graduate-level teaching assistants, one white professor acknowledges:

> … if they (teaching assistants) can't have a conversation with their students about race, then I have failed them deeply … but at least we can read bell hooks and we can talk about Ferguson and we can try to learn from that and I hope that is valuable for them. I hope that I'm modeling a kind of openness of spirit, but also a willingness to explore things that people don't really want to explore. It's so much easier not to, right?

Although educated and knowledgeable about race, the white faculty member does not present herself as an expert. Instead, she provides a space for herself and her teaching assistants to explore and discuss race in a manner fostering growth as individuals, instructors, and members of their multicultural community. Campus "diversity" efforts that do not incorporate ongoing antibias or antiracist education for all members of its community rely on "magical thinking" to address the challenges that come with the application of racial identities in the classroom and elsewhere (Chang, Chang, and Ledesma 2005; Tatum 1992). A white male faculty chair was forced to confront the issue when students expressed concern about racially insensitive comments made in some classes:

> The students complained last year that other students made very racially biased comments in class. Really nasty comments about how black people smell, about Latinos, really very shocking, and the faculty, at the time, didn't know how to respond to it. Some of the students felt that it created a pretty unsafe environment in the classroom … So, when the students brought that to our attention, that was pretty shocking to us, and we wanted to fix it which meant we needed to retrain our faculty, retrain ourselves, become more understanding about what the issue is.

Here the suggestion of "retraining" demonstrates engaged action as it includes all members of the department. No one person is blamed; the "incident" is not seen as an aberration in an otherwise racially harmonious environment; all are included in the need for further antiracist education and training. Instead of simply labeling and blaming the students responsible for racist comments and referring them to another campus office designated to deal with issues of race, this department acknowledges its responsibility in the education and socialization of its students *and its faculty.* Engaged critical multiculturalism necessitates, as part of the acclimation process for students, faculty, staff, and administration, an education that assures they are cognizant of and do their part to maintain a "safe, welcoming and inclusive place to live, work and study" (Fernandes, 2016).

Engaged action is demonstrated by white educators who can articulate awareness that, despite other statuses they may occupy, they move through multicultural spaces as white people. To arrive at this point, they must continually evaluate what it means to be a white person in a multicultural institution and are in constant search of opportunities to achieve equity and justice for themselves, their colleagues, and their students.

Conclusion

"Sociological mindfulness is a way to see where we are and what needs to be done. It is a path to heartfelt membership in conversations that ought to have no end" (Schwalbe 2018:281). This chapter examines the racialized worldview of white educators working in multiracial university settings. We offer this qualitative sociological analysis as a starting point for conversations about the impact and practice of color-blind, aversive racism by well-meaning white educators.

Instead of allowing white fragility and the "white defensive moves" it inspires to maintain institutional silences and individual ignorance, this chapter unpacks these socially constructed moments of institutional racism. The color-blind racism exhibited by these white educators upholds a construction of reality that reinforces the invisibility of whiteness, the racial "innocence" of white people, and the denial of structured inequalities based on race. Similarly, the static awareness exhibited by well-meaning whites who claim/name their white privilege, yet provide no counter-measures to undermine this scaffold of institutionalized racism, reinforces that privilege and the white supremacy culture of higher education. Unveiling institutional racism as structure-in-process provides a tool for both students and educators to engage in "heartfelt" and sociologically mindful conversations about racialized realities at their own institutions.

This analysis also examines "countermoves" made by whites who understand the embodied-nature of their whiteness and engage in their roles as educators in full cognition of the institutionalized racism upholding white privilege and supremacy. Engaged action is demonstrated by white educators who can articulate awareness that, despite other statuses they may occupy, they move through multicultural spaces as white people. White educators engaged in countermoves, in other words, act much like qualitative social scientists in that they appear to constantly racially code their interactions with themselves, others, and the social, political, historical, and cultural contexts surrounding them.

This analysis maps the complex contours of whiteness and white supremacy in an institution of higher education at a particular historical juncture. As critical multiculturalists, we understand these findings to be far removed from the intentions and self-definitions of some of these white educators. As such, we argue these findings are essential tools in enabling whites and others to recognize white moves and countermoves in situ, and thus disrupt the racial hegemony of whiteness. If the white social actors under study have the institutional power to determine how institutional resources are distributed, then understanding the racialized meanings they bring to their daily round of interactions is critical to an understanding of institutional structure, power, and process.

To students practicing sociological mindfulness as they study social inequalities, we offer the following message: remain mindfully skeptical of the institutions you traverse (Schwalbe 2018:275). Though you are surrounded by an environment of experts, you cannot assume they recognize, understand, or are able to articulate the white supremacy culture that surrounds them. Even the most supportive people have implicit biases shaping their thoughts, evaluations, language, and actions. If you want to understand how white supremacy cultural values may be operating in your institution, we urge you to read Tema Okun's (2001) analysis of characteristics of white supremacy values and identify those operating at your university. Explore your campus website for references to courses, events, films, or talks that explore white racism, white privilege, and white supremacy and participate in them. Analyze newspaper accounts of "racist" campus incidents, noting whether such accounts tie the perpetrators of such crimes to white cultural values or not. We believe that any movement toward racial justice must include open discussions and analyses of whiteness, white racism, white privilege, and white supremacy.

To the students of color reading this chapter: it's not you. Not your fault, not your imagination, and not (solely) your responsibility. To the white students reading this chapter: it could be you. You may be color-blind, aversely racist, or embodied in whiteness and engaged action. However, it's not your fault, not your imagination, and not (solely) your responsibility. Engaging in sociological mindfulness enables us to make conscious, informed choices about our acts and actions. Choose wisely.

Discussion Questions

1. Spend some time thinking about your first memory around the idea of race. Does your first memory center on people of your same racial location, or a different one? Discuss how this might differ between white people and people of color.

2. Think about your last conversation about whiteness or white people. Did this conversation happen in a same-race or mixed-racial space? Do conversations about race vary depending upon who is present? Why?

3. Think about all the formal education you have received. Can you recall any educational experiences centering on white racism, white supremacy culture, or white privilege? If yes, did the experience fit with the authors' depiction of an antiracist countermove? Why or why not? If no, what do the silences around these key concepts reflect about the institution of education?

Exploratory Research Questions

1. Compare and contrast how "race" is presented in Introduction to Sociology texts from the 1970s and 1980s compared with such texts today. How has sociology as a discipline shifted in its analysis of race and racism over the last fifty years?

2. Conduct a content analysis of news articles on campus racial incidents in 2015. Can you identify any patterns in how "cause" is determined in these articles? How often is dominant white culture tied to discussions and analyses of such incidents?

Suggestions for Further Readings

DiAngelo, Robin. 2016. *What Does It Mean to Be White?: Developing White Racial Literacy*. New York: Peter Lang Publishing, Inc.

Okun, Tema. 2001. "White Supremacy Culture." dRworks: www.dismantlingracism.org

Visit Project Implicit and take an implicit bias test: https://implicit.harvard.edu/implicit/takeatest.html

References

Bell, J., and D. Hartmann. 2007. "Diversity in Everyday Discourse: The Cultural Ambiguities and Consequences of 'Happy Talk.'" *American Sociological Review* 72 (6):895–914.

Bonilla-Silva, Eduardo. 2014. *Racism Without Racists: Color-blind Racism and the Persistence of Racial Inequality in the United States*. Lanham, MD: Rowman & Littlefield.

Chang, M.J., J. Chang, and M.C. Ledesma. 2005. "Beyond Magical Thinking: Doing the Real Work of Diversifying Our Institutions." *About Campus 10*(2), 9–16.

DiAngelo, Robin. 2016. *What Does It Mean to Be White?: Developing White Racial Literacy*. New York: Peter Lang Publishing, Inc.

Feagin, Joe R. (2002). *The Continuing Significance of Racism: U.S. Colleges and Universities*. Washington, DC: American Council on Education, Office of Minorities in Higher Education.

Feagin, J., H. Vera, and N. Imani. 1996. *The Agony of Education: Black Students at White Colleges and Universities*. New York: Routledge.

Fernandes, R. 2016. "How Bias Training Works in One Campus Police Department." *Chronicle of Higher Education*. Retrieved January 21, 2017, from https://rhs.msu.edu/sites/default/files/u44/Anti-bias%20story.pdf

Frankenberg, R. 1993. *White Women, Race Matters: The Social Construction of Whiteness*. Minneapolis: Minnesota University Press.

Harris, A.P., and C.G. Gonzalez. 2012. "Introduction." In G. Gutierrez y Muhs, Y.F. Niemann, C.G. Gonzalez, and A.P. Harris, eds. *Presumed Incompetent: The Intersection of Race and Class for Women in Academia* (pp. 1–14). Colorado: University Press of Colorado.

Hurtado, S., D. Carter, and A. Spuler. 1996. "Latino Student Transition to College: Assessing Difficulties and Factors in Successful College Adjustment." *Research in Higher Education* 37(2):135–57.

Okun, Tema. 2001. "White Supremacy Culture." dRworks: www.dismantlingracism.org

Omi, M., and H. Winant. 1994. *Racial Formation in the United States: From the 1960s to the 1980s*. 2nd ed. New York: Routledge & Kegan Paul.

Pennycook, G., R.M. Ross, D.J. Koehler, and J.A. Fugelsang. 2017. "Dunning-Kruger Effects in Reasoning: Theoretical Implications of the Failure to Recognize Incompetence." *Psychonomic Bulletin & Review*. doi: 10.3758/s13423-017

Schwalbe, Michael. 2018. *The Sociologically Examined Life: Pieces of the Conversation*. New York: Oxford University Press.

Smith, A. 2013. "Unsettling the Privilege of Self Reflexivity." In F.W. Twine and B. Gardener, Eds. *Geographies of Privilege* (pp. 263–80). New York: Routledge.

Solorzano, D., M. Ceja, and T. Yosso. 2000. "Critical Race Theory, Racial Microaggressions, and Campus Racial Climate: The Experiences of African American College Students." *Journal of Negro Education* 69(1–2):60–73.

Tatum, B.D. 1992. "Talking about Race, Learning about Racism: The Application of Racial Identity Development Theory in the Classroom." *Harvard Educational Review* 62(1), 1–24. Retrieved January 22, 2017, from http://www.siprep.org/uploaded/ProfessionalDevelopment/Minutes/Tatum_Talking_About_Race.PDF

Twine, F.W., and B. Gardener, eds. 2013. *Geographies of Privilege*. New York: Routledge.

Wetherell, M., and J. Potter. 1992. *Mapping the Language of Racism: Discourse and the Legitimation of Exploitation*. New York: Columbia University Press.

Wise, T. 2015. "Awareness, Sensitivity and Checking Our Privilege Are Not Enough: Reflections on Whiteness and American Higher Education." *JSCORE* 1(1):83–100.

Reading 4.4 Racial and Ethnic Macro and Micro Aggressions and White Privilege and Supremacy: The Experiences of College Students of Color on Predominantly White Campuses

Kenneth Sean Chaplin, John Carroll University

Keywords: Racial and ethnic macro and micro aggressions, White privilege and supremacy, Experiences of college students of color, Sociological imagination and mindfulness, Predominantly white campus

Learning Objectives

1. To identify racial and ethnic macro and micro aggressions, and sociological imagination and mindfulness.
2. To identify major areas of social life where racial and ethnic interactions and relations between white/European American students with students of color on predominantly white campuses occur.
3. To identify patterns of white privilege and supremacy, its overt and covert manifestations, and its ideological hold in and beyond white/European American students.

Introduction: Racial and Ethnic Sociological Imagination and Mindfulness

C. Wright Mills's (1959) *Sociological Imagination* is a classic text that still forges questions and queries about the influence of macro and micro social structures on people's everyday lives. In *Sociological Imagination*, Mills discusses the relationship between private troubles and public issues (i.e., social problems), and then explains how social structures unconsciously impact everyday people's mundane thoughts, patterns of action and interaction, and behavior. According to Mills (1959), many people misunderstand and misinterpret the problems in their lives and their patterns of behavior because it is devoid of deeper sociologically imaginative, connected, thinking. Mills also asserts, absent in people's minds is any significant consideration of the influence of race and ethnicity in structuring and organizing many people's lives and lifestyles (Hughes 1963).

Race and ethnicity in the United States is significantly related to fertility and mortality rates, cycles of poverty, rampant unemployment, and environmental pollution; many contemporary sociologists have explored the racial and ethnic gaps in US society as a way of increasing sociological awareness and mindfulness, and social justice and equality. Gitlin (2000) says,

Mills did not sufficiently apply his sociological imagination to the vexing, central problem of race. Mills himself hated racism, but although he lived through the early years of the civil rights movement, he wrote surprisingly little about the dynamics of race in American life … Today, race has become so salient in American social structure and discourse as, at times, to drown out other contending forces. (Gitlin 2000, p. 239)

Like Mills (1959), Berger (1963) proposed a *sociological perspective* that focuses on the influence of macro and micro social structures on people's everyday lives by "seeing generic social behavior and phenomena via the eyes of particular individual's life experiences," but to envision both of these as a product of historical and contemporary structural patterns of social interaction and behavior. Like Mills (1959), Berger's focus on social structures and forces is also absent of deeper sociological thinking, imagination, and mindfulness of the significance of race and ethnicity in US society. In this chapter, I examine a snippet of the sociological literature and research about race and ethnicity as I focus on racial and ethnic macro and micro aggressions in concert with the pervasive influence of white privilege and supremacy. Via racial and ethnic macro and micro aggressions—those real and/or perceived commonplace environmental and institutional slights and hostilities, and those verbal and nonverbal snubs and insults that communicate negative antagonistic messages to people of color—I examine structural and face-to-face social interaction and relations of white/European American college students with students of color on a predominantly white campus. I demonstrate how racial and ethnic macro and micro aggressions are embedded in an ideology of white privilege and supremacy (Solorzano 1998; Solorzano, Ceja, and Yosso 2000), which students of color often unconsciously engage in. The responses of students of color are captured, queried, and advanced using an approach that advocates for increased racial and ethnic sociological mindfulness. Special emphasis is given to the ways students of color respond to racial and ethnic micro aggressions on their predominantly white campus that is reflective of the pervasive influence of white privilege and supremacy. I conclude with some suggestions on how to increase all students' racial and ethnic sociological mindfulness.

From an Absent-minded Racial and Ethnic Sociological Imagination to Conscious Racial and Ethnic Sociological Mindfulness

The US presidential election of Barack Obama stimulated mass media and pop(ular) cultural conversation about a post-racial US society (Feagin 2013; Bonilla-Silva 2017). In a post-racial society, everyday obstacles and claims of racial and ethnic bias, prejudice, and discrimination would cease to exist; all peoples would be free from any impact of race and ethnicity on the social structuring and organization of their lives. Post-racialists have since insisted race and ethnicity are meaningless, and claims of racism and ethnic bias and discrimination are useless social forces. Some critics assert "race" is now used by anyone and everyone to attack another for thinking about race via being racist, ethnically biased, and discriminatory (Teasley and Ikard 2010).

Facilitating racial and ethnic sociological imagination must be embedded in racial and ethnic sociological mindfulness via the contemplation of a US society plagued by racism, ethnic bias, prejudice, and discrimination manifest in all major social structures, institutions, and organizations (Feagin 2014; Kucsera 2009). Such mindfulness must begin with acknowledging race and ethnicity as macro and micro social structures linked to racial and ethnic disadvantage, and privilege and supremacy. As part and parcel of US ideology, unpacking the influence of race and ethnicity on people's lives requires mindful recognition of historical and contemporary conditions and circumstances as manifest in social experiences and group relations of our constructions of racial and ethnic selves in relation to others. Such mindfulness must also contemplate "makings of difference" as political, intertwined with conscious and subliminal consequences and inequality reflected in ritual social interaction and relations. Incorporating mental and emotional development that involves deeper sociological thought and self-reflection about the impact of race and ethnicity as privilege and disadvantage and as hegemonic norms have to be considered and contemplated (Bonilla-Silva 2013 and 2017; Goldberg 2001; Feagin 2013 and 2014).

Advancement from imagination to mindfulness must include conscious and subconscious struggle against overt and covert racial and ethnic macro and micro aggressions that structure everyday face-to-face interactions and relations of white/European Americans with people of color (Cabrera 2014). By better understanding politics in the making of racial and ethnic difference, sociological mindfulness will aid the tearing down of racially and ethnically unjust hierarchical social order. Increased mindfulness must also acknowledge how racial and ethnic privilege promotes overt and covert constructions and refortifications of unjust, unmerited, racial and ethnic supremacy (Feagin 2014).

Advancing racial and ethnic sociological mindfulness advances thinking and reasoning about our everyday interactions and behavior and about the gaps and assumptions in the sociological literature and research filled with racial and ethnic bias, prejudice, and discrimination (Feagin 2013 and 2014; Zuberi and Bonilla-Silva 2008). Engaging intensively about race and ethnicity as purposeful political projects and processes can yield greater mindfulness that cultivates awareness, attentiveness, empathy, and respect for the experiences of people of color (Omi and Winant 1994). Such mindfulness heightens mental and emotional states via the consideration of people of color and reduces the stress and stressors of discussing experiences with racism, racial and ethnic bias, prejudice, discrimination, segregation, and xenophobia at the root of racial injustice and inequality. Having mindful conversations and discussions that consider multiple racial and ethnic positions, locations, and experiences can cultivate deeper sociological thinking and imagination.

Chief goals of racial and ethnic sociological mindfulness are to increase one's racial and ethnic: 1) self-awareness; 2) social awareness of others; 3) understanding of macro structures and institutions; and 3) micro patterns of everyday thought, interaction, and behavior. Encouraging racial and ethnic sociologically mindful thinking can reduce knee-jerk reactions and responses that are often perceived as hostile, aggressive, and threatening that are impediments to racial and ethnic justice and equality (Kucsera 2009; Womack and Sloan 2017).

Racial and Ethnic Macro and Micro Aggressions in Whites' Collegiate Space

Racial and ethnic macro aggressions comprise unmerited, unjust, state-sanctioned inequality that produces and perpetuates inferior systems of health care and education that manifest in inferior housing, employment, and occupational opportunities and outcomes (Wiberg 1983). Racial and ethnic micro aggressions (rooted in clinical psychology) refer to the demeaning social interactions and behavior that dominant populations have with minorities, often highlighted by unjust, inequitable treatment (Wong, Derthick, David, Saw, and Okazaki 2014).

Together these aggressions support social intolerance for racial and ethnic differences, which in turn promote racial and ethnic privilege and supremacy; in the United States, these aggressions reflect white-skinned people's racial and ethnic privilege and supremacy.

These aggressions do not always manifest as blatant, overt, deliberate acts of racial and ethnic bias, prejudice, and discrimination. Much often occurs in epithets and appellations intended to socially control and order minorities. Reliance on negative demeaning labels and stereotypes is routine, which is projected to minorities yielding significant influence on the social organizations of their lives (Pierce 1970). The casual degradation of minorities results in socioemotional and psychological harm and humiliation; much of this is attributable to the insulting, insensitive, inappropriate comments and jokes (attached to condescending statements and projections) of white-skinned peoples toward minorities largely documented in the ritual interaction people of color have reported with whites (Burdsey 2011; Cabrera 2014). Sue, Capodilupo, Torino, Bucceri, Holder, Nadal, and Esquilin (2007) propose such micro aggressions result in minorities' ritual suffering of daily verbal, behavioral, and environmental assaults and indignities of whites' struggle over place, space, and resources. Inherent in whites' struggle is ideological control of race and ethnicity, which routinely manifests in physical and symbolic forms of violence that promote racial and ethnic order and organizations of privilege and supremacy. US law, social work, and education manifest and reflect these aggressions embedded in white privilege and supremacy (Davis 1989; Ross-Sheriff 2012; Solórzano 1998; Solorzano, Ceja, and Yosso 2000; Yosso, Smith, Ceja, and Solórzano 2009). Thematic categories of minorities' experiences with these aggressions include, but are not limited to, the following:

1. Being considered an illegal alien and/or foreigner in the country of your birth.

2. Being ascribed lower intelligence and cultural and social class standing.

3. Being denied a racial reality linked to systematic racial discrimination, hostility, and aggression.

4. Being eroticized for your language and culture.

5. Being invalidated by complex overlapping intra-ethnic and intra-cultural differences.

6. Suffering the pathologization of culturally negative values connected to your language, dialect, communication style, and modes and means of expression.

7. Suffering negative hostile treatment related to second-class citizenship.

8. Suffering the avoidance and neglect of others due to the lack of acceptance and tolerance, which are characteristics of being made to feel social invisibility.

Below are specific examples students of color reported they experienced on my campus. After IRB approval was obtained, I compiled this list from the numerous focus groups and in-depth interviews I conducted with black/African, Latinx, Middle Eastern, and Asian American undergraduates.

Where are you from? No, where are you really from? That's so gay? Can you speak Indian? Just stay inside ... the sun will make you darker, you should stay inside. You don't act like a normal ... typical Asian. You're so pretty for an Asian girl. Can you teach me your language?

(Selena Chin, a twenty-year-old Asian female sophomore; Grinni Chatnee, a twenty-one-year-old Asian American female junior)

Can I touch your hair? It's so nice. OMG, it's so soft ... softer than it looks. It looks so real. You can't be black with hair like that! You're black and what else? You talk like a white girl. You sound so white. You're pretty for a dark-skinned girl. You're pretty for a black girl. No, really, are you mixed? You're too pretty to be just black.

(Marya Williams, an eighteen-year-old black/African American female freshman; Cheri Mabin, an eighteen-year-old black/African American female freshman; Shelly Grand, an eighteen-year-old black/African American female freshman; Kiera May, a nineteen-year-old black/African American female sophomore)

You're smart. You're so articulate ... well spoken. You dress like a white boy. What sport do you play? Do you play basketball? Are you Puerto Rican? {I'm black, but people always tell me I look Spanish.}

(Conner Bowman, a nineteen-year-old black/African American male sophomore; Marvin Mavis, a nineteen-year-old black/African American male freshman; Mark Tomlinson an eighteen-year-old black/African American male freshman)

You speak really good English. You're so spicy—I love it. You're so loud, but it's ok. I didn't know you were so smart. Do you know any coyotes? {I always hear a lot of border jokes.} Is that your real hair? I don't understand what you're saying—speak English, we're in America. You need to speak like an American. Mexicans antagonize the police, so that's why they end up having to shoot them.

(Jessica Lorena, a twenty-two-year-old Mexican female junior; Diane Mae, a nineteen-year-old Mexican female sophomore; Gaby Rosa, a nineteen-year-old Guatemalan female sophomore)

I hear so many jokes about being a terrorist, and questions like, "Am I here looking for oil?" A lot of people also make fun of our Prophet and they constantly ask me about the veil, and make burka jokes.

I also hear I don't look like a typical Arab. Someone told me the other day I'm probably used to the heat and hot weather because I'm a sandie from the desert.

(Mae Akadda, a nineteen-year-old Muslim female sophomore)

These aggressions often surface as tasteless demeaning attempts at humor via comments and jokes said (and often repeated) by friends and acquaintances. Although these appear as minor incidents and experiences of students of color on my campus, they too often are so numerous that they significantly influence the ability of students of color to adequately function and become a social weight equivalent to having to constantly lift and navigate "a ton of feathers" (Caplan and Ford 2014).

Reponses to Social Aggressions: Overt and Covert Manifestations of White Privilege and Supremacy in Students of Color

Predominantly white college/university campuses are social places and spaces that promote and perpetuate white privilege and supremacy, and racial and ethnic hostility and oppression (Feagin, Vera, and Imani 1996; Moore 2008; Fitzgerald 2015). White students on these campuses routinely advocate for a racially and ethnically conservative student body and campus culture opposed to racial and ethnic diversity and inclusion (Solorzano, Ceja, and Yosso 2000; Yosso, Smith, Ceja, and Solórzano 2009). With the exception of many black/African American varsity student-athletes, many of these school's sport programs are comprised of white, middle-class US Americans (Hawkins 2013). For many students of color, these collegiate places and spaces (and the social interaction that occurs within them) routinely remind students of color they are racial and ethnic outsiders, which is discouraging and a hindrance to their socio-educational achievement and advancement (Feagin, Vera, and Imani 1996; Moore 2008; Singer 2005).

Misunderstandings and misrepresentations of the impact of white privilege and supremacy is that it only manifests as hostile, aggressive, threatening face-to-face interaction and social relations (Sue et al. 2007 and 2008). The aforementioned responses of student of color on my campus do not always demonstrate that, which yields great insight into the ideology and logic of white privilege and supremacy (Bonilla-Silva 2017; Feagin 2013 and 2014). Explanations from students of color on my campus about their dealings with micro aggressions illustrate the pervasive ideological control of white privilege and supremacy.

I just say, you're not the only people on earth who actually have good hair! No, I actually do speak proper English... do you expect all of us to speak the same way—like talk ghetto and be ratchet? I went to an all-white high school and when some of my white friends find out, they are usually so surprised to hear... like, I went to a good school like they did.

(Marya Williams, an eighteen-year-old black/African American female freshman; Cheri Mabin, an eighteen-year-old black/African American female freshman; Shelly Grand an eighteen-year-old black/African American female freshman)

I hear I dress white ... look like a white boy all the time. It doesn't even piss me off to hear that anymore. I'm just trying to dress right. Look neat ... proper. Not all of us have our pants hanging low down around our ankles. I used to dress like that when I was a freshman in high school, but not anymore. I'm done with that.

(Immanuel Barry, a twenty-one-year-old black/African American male junior; Marvin Mavis a nineteen-year-old black/African American male freshman; Mark Tomlinson, an eighteen-year-old black/African American male freshman)

I don't wear a veil. I look normal, but I hear students making fun about it, and making burka jokes. They think I'm Italian or Eastern European most times. They have no idea I'm an Arab. It's really offensive, even if they are not saying it to my face.

(Mae Akadda, a nineteen-year-old Muslim female sophomore)

The students' responses reveal much about the ideological stronghold and logic of white privilege and supremacy, expressed via taken-for-granted whites' norms (Bonilla-Silva 2017; Feagin 2014; Moore 2008). These ideological norms manifest in the logic of what is "good," "proper," "neat," and "normal" within racial and ethnically restrictive discriminatory America, embedded in assumptions about whites' normalcy of privilege and supremacy. The responses of the students of color on my campus reflect conscious and unconscious ways they aligned themselves with whites' logic, privilege, and supremacy to pursue and obtain the societal benefits associated with white normalcy, devoid of their possession of white skin. These students' responses also demonstrate the desire to embrace socio-educational advantages via distancing themselves from the perceived negative cultural assumptions and labels associated with their racial and ethnic group.

The responses of my students are not without qualification. The racially and ethnically macro aggressive educational environment they are in emphasizes the ideological embrace of white thinking and reasoning, which distinguishes them as white-minded social aspirants. Their embrace of white privilege and supremacy on campus has provided many with social distance from seemingly culturally depressed, marginal, racial and ethnic groups that often face blatant, overt face-to-face racial and ethnic bias, prejudice, and discrimination. These students' embrace of whites' normalcy of privilege and supremacy as sociocultural standards of "good," "proper," "neat," and "normal" illustrates the stronghold of racial and ethnic ideological oppression and suppression of diverse and inclusive sociocultural expression and representation (Feagin 2013). Many African Americans in particular often feel under pressure to be positive sociocultural representatives of their racial and ethnic groups and consequently aligned themselves, their thinking, attitudes, speech, attire, and patterns of social interaction and behavior to mimic whites in order to ward off such aggressions (Sue, Capodilupo, and Holder 2008).

Acting and embracing whiteness as a normative racial and ethnic standard is a common racial, ethnic, and social class strategy of students of color who pursue socioeconomic advancement and upward social mobility (Tyson, Darity Jr., and Castellino 2005). Such pursuits and desires have damaging long-term racial and ethnic consequences. More sociologically mindful literature and research are needed to examine how students of color use their social class status and opportunities to validate their similarities to whites via the embrace of white privilege and supremacy. Such literature and research can reveal more about the intersection of race and ethnicity with sex and gender in the operation of class privileges and disadvantages of students of color in predominantly white collegiate institutions.

Discussion and Conclusion: Toward Racial and Ethnic Sociological Mindfulness

Acknowledging race and ethnicity (and its diverse manifestation of racism and ethnic prejudices and discrimination) is central to the development of racial and ethnic sociological mindfulness. Evasion, negligence, and repudiation invalidate institutional, interpersonal, and face-to-face experiences of people of color, which has impacted constructions of selves, identities, and realities. Choosing to deny the influence of race and ethnicity in people's lives is choosing to misunderstand and misrepresent racial and ethnic realities in a US social system erected by racism and ethnic prejudice and discrimination.

Circa sixty years ago, Mills (1959) and Berger (1963) stretched sociological thinking and understanding anew via promoting others to engage in deeper imagination and perspective. Their works, however, were devoid of substantive discussion of the structural and organizational impact of race and ethnicity. This absence, however, did not thwart sociologists' efforts to develop deeper racial and ethnic imagination and mindfulness.

Racial and ethnic sociological mindfulness contemplates how thought, feeling, and emotion operate in relation to one's actions and behavior with others. Deeper consideration of how structural relations and micro-level interaction is informed by race and ethnicity must also include the political "makings of difference" in terms of perpetuated racial privilege and supremacy, and disadvantage.

Contemporary racial and ethnic aggressions reveal much about US historical interactions and relations in and beyond predominantly white educational institutions. Responses from students of color to such aggressions demonstrate an ideology and logic of racial privilege and supremacy rooted in whites' whiteness that reveals much about the pervasive influence of white privilege and supremacy on US society.

Responses from students of color illustrate how whites' ideology and logic manifested as preferential forms of beauty, speech, language and dialect, attire, and leisurely activities that are consciously and unconsciously associated with racial and ethnic privilege and supremacy.

More sociological literature and research must consider the sociological movement from imagination to mindfulness, making central historical and contemporary understandings of race and ethnicity embedded in the macro and micro aggressions people of color experience. Attached to such mindfulness are approaches that must also consider the influence of racial and ethnic privilege and supremacy in US society maintained and perpetuated by whites. Mindful considerations of white privilege and supremacy are needed to process racial and ethnic ways of thinking and emoting as reflective experience of in and beyond predominantly white educational organizations and institutions.

Chapter Review Questions:

1. How did C. Wright Mills and Peter Berger develop, or not develop, a racial and ethnic sociological imagination? A sociological mindfulness perspective?

2. How is a racial and ethnic sociological imagination similar to, and different from, racial and ethnic sociological mindfulness?

3. How are racial and ethnic macro and micro aggressions similar and different?

4. In what kinds of social interactions and spheres do racial and ethnic macro and micro aggressions tend to occur?

5. What themes of racial and ethnic micro aggression stand out to you? Why? Which ones are difficult for you to understand and relate to?

6. How is white privilege and supremacy connected to the racial and ethnic macro and micro aggressions on and beyond collegiate environments?

7. How are the responses of students of color connected to a logic and ideology of white privilege and supremacy?

8. What are some suggestions for strengthening and developing goals and objectives for increased racial and ethnic sociological mindfulness?

Additional Readings

Brunsma, D.L., E.S. Brown, and P. Placier. 2013. "Teaching Race at Historically White Colleges and Universities: Identifying and Dismantling the Walls of Whiteness." *Critical Sociology* 39(5), 717–38.

Halley, J., A. Eshleman, and R.M. Vijaya. 2011. "Seeing White: An Introduction to White Privilege and Race." Lanham, MD: Rowman & Littlefield Publishers.

References

Berger, P. 1963. *Invitation to Sociology: A Humanistic Perspective*. New York: Anchor, Doubleday.

Bonilla-Silva, Eduardo. 2013. "'New Racism,' Color-blind Racism, and the Future of Whiteness in America." In *White Out* (pp. 268–81). Routledge.

Bonilla-Silva, Eduardo. 2017. *Racism without Racists: Color-Blind Racism and the Persistence of Racial Inequality in America*. Lanham, MD: Rowman & Littlefield.

Burdsey, D. (2011). "That Joke Isn't Funny Anymore: Racial Microaggressions, Color-Blind Ideology and the Mitigation of Racism in English Men's First-Class Cricket." *Sociology of Sport Journal* 28(3), 261–83.

Cabrera, N.L. 2014. "Exposing Whiteness in Higher Education: White Male College Students Minimizing Racism, Claiming Victimization, and Recreating White Supremacy." *Race Ethnicity and Education* 17(1), 30–55.

Caplan, P.J., and J. Ford. 2014. "The Voices of Diversity: What Students of Diverse Races/Ethnicities and Both Sexes Tell Us about Their College Experiences and Their Perceptions about Their Institutions' Progress Toward Diversity." *Aporia*, 6(4), 30–69.

Davis, P.C. 1989. "Law as Microaggression." *Yale Law Journal* 98(8), 1559–577.

Feagin, Joe R. 2013. *The White Racial Frame: Centuries of Racial Framing and Counter-Framing*. New York: Routledge.

Feagin, Joe R. 2014. *Racist America: Roots, Current Realities, and Future Reparations*. New York: Routledge.

Feagin, Joe R., H. Vera, and N. Imani. 1996. *The Agony of Education: Black Students at White Colleges and Universities*. Psychology Press.

Fitzgerald, Terence D. 2015. *Black Males and Racism: Improving the Schooling and Life Chances of African Americans*. New York: Routledge.

Gitlin, T. (2000) *The Sociological Imagination*: With a new Afterword by Todd Gitlin in Mills, C.W. (2000) The Sociological Imagination, Oxford University Press, London: Penguin, 40th anniversary edition, 239.

Goldberg, David Theo. 2001. *The Racial State*. Malden, MA: Wiley-Blackwell.

Hawkins, B. 2013. *The New Plantation: Black Athletes, College Sports, and Predominantly White NCAA Institutions*. Palgrave Macmillan.

Hughes, E.C. 1963. "Race Relations and the Sociological Imagination." *American Sociological Review* 879–90.

Kucsera, J.V. 2009. *Racial Mindfulness: Exploring the Influence of Mindfulness on Racial Biases*. Austin: University of Texas Press.

Mills, C.W. (1959/2000). *The Sociological Imagination*. Oxford University Press.

Moore, W.L. 2008. *Reproducing Racism: White Space, Elite Law Schools, and Racial Inequality*. Lanham, MD: Rowman & Littlefield.

Omi, M., and H. Winant. 1994. *Racial Formations in the United States*. New York: Routledge.

Pierce, C.M. 1970. "Offensive Mechanisms." In *The Black Seventies*, edited by Floyd B. Barbour, 265–82. Boston: Porter Sargent.

Ross-Sheriff, Fariyal. 2012. "Microaggression, Women, and Social Work." *Yale Law Journal* 98(8) 233–36.

Singer, J.N. 2005. "Understanding Racism through the Eyes of African American Male Student-Athletes." *Race, Ethnicity and Education* 8(4), 365–86.

Solórzano, Daniel G. 1998. "Critical Race Theory, Race and Gender Microaggressions, and the Experience of Chicana and Chicano Scholars." *International Journal of Qualitative Studies in Education* 11(1) 121–36.

Solórzano, Daniel, Miguel Ceja, and Tara Yosso. 2000. "Critical Race Theory, Racial Microaggressions, and Campus Racial Climate: The Experiences of African American College Students." *Journal of Negro Education*, 60–73.

Sue, D. W., Capodilupo, C.M., and A. Holder. 2008. "Racial Microaggressions in the Life Experience of Black Americans." *Professional Psychology: Research and Practice* 39(3), 329–36.

Sue, D.W., C.M. Capodilupo, G.C. Torino, J.M. Bucceri, A. Holder, K.L. Nadal, and M. Esquilin. 2007. "Racial Microaggressions in Everyday Life: Implications for Clinical Practice." *American Psychologist* 62(4), 271–86.

Teasley, M., and D. Ikard. 2010. "Barack Obama and the Politics of Race: The Myth of Postracism in America." *Journal of Black Studies* 40(3), 411–25.

Tyson, K., W. Darity Jr., and D. R. Castellino. 2005. "It's Not 'a Black Thing': Understanding the Burden of Acting White and Other Dilemmas of High Achievement." *American Sociological Review* 70(4), 582–605.

Wiberg, H. 1983. "Research on Aggression and the Study of Conflicts on Macro Level." *Aggressive Behavior* 9(2), 106.

Womack, V.Y., and L.R. Sloan. 2017. "The Association of Mindfulness and Racial Socialization Messages on Approach-Oriented Coping Strategies among African Americans." *Journal of Black Studies* 48(4), 408–26.

Wong, G., A.O. Derthick, E.J.R. David, A. Saw, and S. Okazaki. 2014. "The What, the Why, and the How: A Review of Racial Microaggressions Research in Psychology." *Race and Social Problems* 6(2), 181–200.

Yosso, Tara, William Smith, Miguel Ceja, and Daniel Solórzano. 2009. "Critical Race Theory, Racial Microaggressions, and Campus Racial Climate for Latina/o Undergraduates." *Harvard Educational Review* 79(4), 659–91.

Zuberi, Tukufu, and Eduardo Bonilla-Silva (Eds.). 2008. *White Logic, White Methods: Racism and Methodology*. Lanham, MD: Rowman & Littlefield Publishers.

Reading 4.5 Inequality in the Graduate School Admissions Process: The Chicanx/Latinx Experience

Elvia Ramirez

Keywords: race and class inequalities, underrepresentation, educational attainment, and educational experience

Introduction

Despite representing the largest racial/ethnic minority group in the country, the Chicanx/Latinx population remains tenuously represented in higher education. The Chicanx/Latinx high school dropout rate has dropped dramatically, and more Chicanx/Latinx students than ever before are enrolling in college (Krogstad 2016). Nonetheless, Chicanx/Latinx students are less likely than all other major racial/ethnic groups to obtain a four-year college degree. For example, in 2014, just 15 percent of Chicanx/Latinx individuals ages 25–29 had obtained a bachelor's degree or higher, compared to 22 percent of African Americans, 41 percent whites, and 63 percent Asian Americans (Krogstad 2016). Similarly, Chicanx/Latinx student enrollment in PhD programs has been increasing over time; quite notably, the number of Chicanx/Latinx doctorate recipients increased approximately 67 percent from 2006 to 2016 (National Science Foundation, National Center for Science and Engineering Statistics 2018). Still, Chicanx/Latinx students remain dramatically underrepresented in doctorate education. In 2016, for example, just 7 percent of all doctorate recipients were Chicanx/Latinx, while 71 percent were white (National Science Foundation, National Center for Science and Engineering Statistics 2018).

Because graduate (PhD) education plays an increasingly key role in elite formation (Posselt and Grodsky 2017) and is a critical mechanism for socializing aspirants to the professoriate (Ramirez 2017), it is critical that scholars analyze the graduate school admissions process, particularly as viewed and experienced by Chicanx/Latinx students. It is especially important that scholars examine how inequalities embedded in the graduate school admissions process exacerbate the underrepresentation of Chicanx/Latinx students in PhD programs. This chapter presents findings of a study examining Chicanx/Latinx students' views of the graduate school admissions process. The central research question guiding this study is: How does the graduate school admissions process, as viewed and experienced by Chicanx/Latinx students, reflect and perpetuate race and class inequality?

Literature Review

The process by which students prepare for, apply to, and are admitted into college, also known as "college choice" (McDonough, Antonio, and Trent 1997), is highly unequal. Research shows that low-income and historically underrepresented racial/ethnic minorities (i.e., African Americans, Chicanxs/Latinxs, and Native Americans) navigate the undergraduate college admissions process with fewer resources, guidance, and knowledge about college admissions than their middle-class peers (Hill 2008; McDonough 1997; Ramirez 2011; Walpole 2007). Studies also find that of all historically underrepresented racial/ethnic minority (URM) students, Chicanx/Latinx students are especially disadvantaged, as they are more likely than other students to attend high schools that provide limited college-related resources and information to students (Hill 2008). Inequalities in access to college-related resources and information negatively impact the educational attainment rates and opportunities of Chicanx/Latinx students and other URMs. For example, research shows that compared to their middle-class peers, low-income and URM students have lower college eligibility rates and lower four-year college attendance rates (Ramirez 2011).

Regardless of academic ability, women, URMs, and low-income students are less likely to attend prestigious undergraduate institutions compared to their white, male, and middle-class counterparts (McDonough 1997; Ramirez 2011). The type of undergraduate institution students attend is important and consequential, as research clearly shows there are greater educational and occupational returns to attending selective (versus nonselective) undergraduate institutions (Ramirez 2013). For example, graduates of private and prestigious undergraduate schools enjoy higher salaries than graduates of less selective universities (Kim 2004). Similarly, graduates of prestigious doctoral programs are more likely to secure academic employment, particularly at prestigious universities (Burris 2004).

Structural inequalities also shape students' access to graduate education. For example, students from middle-class, college-educated families have greater opportunities for obtaining a graduate education—particularly at prestigious doctoral institutions—than first-generation and working-class students (Mullen, Goyette, and Soares 2003; Ramirez 2014; Zhang 2005). Furthermore, studies consistently find a positive relationship between undergraduate college selectivity (prestige) and graduate school admission (Posselt 2018). That is, students who attend highly selective (prestigious) undergraduate institutions are more likely to be admitted to graduate school. Because URMs, women, and low-income students are less likely to attend selective institutions, these students are systematically disadvantaged in the graduate school admissions process.

Students, particularly URMs and working-class students generally, encounter various barriers as they navigate the graduate school application process. For example, Ramirez (2011) found that Chicanx/Latinx students navigate through various challenges while applying to graduate school, including: (a) lack of knowledge concerning graduate school admissions; (b) lack of guidance, support, and mentorship; (c) institutional abuse (i.e., abusive behavior by institutional agents and limiting students' opportunities for graduate school); and (d) the Graduate Record Examination (GRE) (a standardized exam required for graduate school admissions). Other studies also find that standardized college admissions exams such as the GRE pose barriers for URMs and working-class students (Walpole et al. 2005). Lower test scores on standardized exams constrain URM students' opportunities for college education, including graduate study (Ramirez 2011). Despite lacking predictive validity (Ibarra 2001), faculty often rely on GRE scores in their graduate school admissions and fellowship award decisions (Nettles and Millet 2006).

In addition to standard measures like grades and GRE scores, faculty at doctoral institutions often base their graduate school admissions decisions on: (1) the quality (measured as selectivity or prestige) of undergraduate institution; (2) the scholarly reputation of recommendation letter writers; and (3) faculty judgments of program alumni with similar characteristics (Posselt 2018). Posselt (2018) notes that "graduate programs' admission preference for students from elite colleges and universities contributes to inequality in graduate education and the labor market" (p. 518). The criteria used in graduate school admissions decisions, such as the focus on selectivity of undergraduate institution, thus perpetuate social inequality.

Overall, the extant scholarship on graduate education clearly reveals there is "persistent stratification" by race/ethnicity, class, and gender in graduate education application, admission, enrollment, and degree attainment processes (Posselt and Grodsky 2017:353). However, how Chicanx/Latinx students view and experience the graduate school admissions process has not been the subject of much scholarly investigation. To fill this gap in the literature, the present study examines, via the lenses of intersectionality theory, how Chicanx/Latinx students perceive and experience the graduate school admissions process.

Theoretical Framework

This study is grounded in intersectionality theory, a theoretical framework developed by women of color feminists (e.g., Baca Zinn and Thornton Dill 1996; Collins 2002; Crenshaw 1991) that examines multiple and interlocking structures of inequality. Emerging as a critique of unitary theories of gender, intersectionality theory problematizes race, class, and gender inequality. Though each of these systems of inequality is analytically distinct, they all intersect and influence one another.

Intersectionality theory eschews the "ranking of oppressions"; that is, it refuses to privilege one system of inequality over another, particularly because race-, class-, and gender-based systems of inequality are interconnected and collectively configure the structure of our society (Andersen and Collins 2001). Furthermore, intersectionality theory argues that intersecting forms of inequality produce both oppression and privilege. In other words, while systems of race, class, and gender create disadvantages for women, people of color, and the working class, they produce unacknowledged benefits for those at the top of these hierarchies (i.e., whites, members of the upper class, and men) (Baca Zinn and Thornton Dill 1996:327). Race, class, and gender thus simultaneously produce systems of oppression and privilege that affect *all* individuals.

Intersectionality theory is also guided by standpoint epistemology, a philosophy and methodology that calls attention to "social location in the production of knowledge" (Baca Zinn and Thornton Dill 1996:328). That is, intersectional analysis is grounded in the assumption that "marginalized locations are well suited for grasping social relations that remain obscure from more privileged vantage points" (Baca Zinn and Thornton Dill 1996:328). Indeed, as this study will demonstrate, the graduate school (PhD) admissions process appears very different from (and, I argue, more complex and comprehensive than) institutional/dominant accounts when viewed through the standpoint of historically underrepresented students. In sum, I employ intersectionality theory to examine the graduate school admissions process as perceived and experienced by Chicanx/Latinx doctoral students.

Research Methods

Data for this paper stem from a larger case study examining the graduate school experiences of Chicanx/Latinx students at "Western Region University" (a pseudonym), a doctorate-granting public research university located in the western region of the United States. The study is based on in-depth, semi-structured qualitative interviews conducted with Chicanx/Latinx individuals who had completed, or were in the process of completing, their doctoral (PhD) degrees at Western Region University (WRU) at the time of the study. Data for this study also stem from analysis of institutional data and official WRU documents.

A total of 24 interviewees—12 men and 12 women—were recruited for the study. Prospective interviewees were identified through an official list of enrolled Chicanx/Latinx doctoral students at WRU All enrolled Chicanx/Latinx doctoral students were sent a letter that both explained the nature of the study and requested their participation. Individuals who agreed to participate in the study were also asked to refer potential recruits for this study. All interviewees were asked to fill out a written questionnaire, which documented their background and family characteristics, as well as answer open-ended questions from an interview guide. The interview guide concentrated on a wide range of topics, including respondents' personal and familial backgrounds and their K–16 and graduate school experiences. Data for this chapter stem from questions concerning respondents' perceptions of the graduate school admissions process, specifically. Interviews lasted approximately two to four hours each and were conducted face-to-face and via telephone. Each interview was tape recorded and transcribed verbatim.

Respondents' disciplinary associations included the sciences, technology, math, and engineering (STEM) fields ($n = 3$), social sciences ($n = 16$), education ($n = 3$), and humanities ($n = 2$). Nineteen respondents were enrolled in the university at the time of the study and were at various stages of their graduate program, ranging from the first year to the dissertation stage. Five interviewees had already obtained their PhDs, having completed their programs from 1990 to 2005. The majority ($n = 22$) of respondents are of Mexican American descent; two interviewees are of South American origin. Additionally, most respondents are first-generation college students ($n = 19$) and from working-class backgrounds ($n = 15$). All study participants were assigned a pseudonym to protect their confidentiality.

Results

Unlike undergraduate admissions, graduate school admissions at Western Region University (WRU) are a highly decentralized process, insofar as admissions decisions are made at the departmental level. In the mid-1990s, WRU eliminated Affirmative Action because of state policies that required elimination of Affirmative Action programs in college admissions and public sector employment. Official WRU documents indicate that admission to WRU PhD programs generally depend on several measures, including undergraduate GPA, GRE scores, letters of recommendation, interviews, and/or an evaluation of "fit" between student interests and faculty expertise. WRU documents also indicate that most graduate applications are reviewed by multiple faculty to ensure a "balanced" and "fair" assessment and to improve the chances that the "very best" students are admitted to WRU graduate programs. Admissions decisions are thus reputedly based on a holistic/comprehensive review process that considers multiple factors and views standardized exams (e.g., GRE) as just one component of the evaluation process.

When asked to share their views of their department's graduate admissions policies, respondents provided a mix of responses. Some praised their departments for employing a holistic/comprehensive review admissions process, others criticized their departments for relying too heavily on GRE scores and/or selectivity of undergraduate institution, and still others critiqued the composition of admissions committees. These findings are further delineated below.

Holistic/Comprehensive Review

A few respondents offered positive appraisals of their department's graduate admissions process because they felt applications were evaluated holistically/comprehensively. For example, Alejandro described his department's admission policies as "fantastic" because applications, including his own, were evaluated holistically. He explained,

> [The department] looks at the whole academic profile and thank God they do. Because I was lacking in my GREs. But because I was strong in my research, my letters, my statement, and my GPA, that's what they looked at overall … They consider you based on your whole academic profile and not just scores.

Like Alejandro, Mariana was happy her department didn't rely only on GRE scores when evaluating applicants because her own GRE scores were not very high. "Because they were looking at everything, what I've done in the past, who I was, and all of that, I still got accepted," Mariana explained. Erica also praised her department's admissions process because decisions weren't based simply on applicants' GRE scores. "Our department is really good at not just looking at numbers," she shared. "They're really good at looking at past experiences, letters of recommendation, and future aspirations … I think our department is good in that regard."

Heavy Focus on the GRE

Though a few respondents felt admissions decisions were made according to a comprehensive review process, most felt that graduate admissions decisions in their respective programs hinged too heavily on GRE scores. Raymond, for example, stated, "I think sometimes they get starry-eyed over GRE scores … I think they emphasize too much the GREs." Similarly, Xochitl believes admissions committees in her department tend to emphasize GRE scores over other factors. Although Xochitl was generally unfamiliar with graduate admissions policies in her department, she learned from fellow graduate student peers who participate in her department's graduate admissions committee that faculty eliminate applicants from consideration based solely on applicants' GRE scores. She explained,

> I don't really know too much about the admission policies … Well, I've talked to, there's two graduate students that I know right now that are on the committee that help review the

applications. So, I've been asking because I'm curious. And one of them was telling me that a lot of the faculty just look at the GREs right away, and if you don't have them, then that's it, you're in the "not considered" pile. So, I thought that was pretty harsh … A lot of people don't even look at the [writing] statements. They kind of look for if you're a "good fit" with the faculty, that kind of thing. But the biggest factor is those GRE scores. Obviously, those aren't a good indicator. I think that's a barrier for a lot of people.

Thus, contrary to official WRU accounts, Xochitl's narrative suggests that applicants for graduate school are eliminated from consideration based simply on their GRE scores, at least in some departments.

Many respondents felt the use of GRE as a weeding-out mechanism is discriminatory, disproportionately impacting students of color and/or those from working-class backgrounds. Francisco, for example, felt that relying on GREs for admissions purposes perpetuated racial inequality, particularly because white students tend to score higher on standardized exams than URMs. Ada, on the other hand, felt that employing GRE scores as a filtering device perpetuated class inequality because not all students can afford to take costly GRE preparation courses. She said,

I don't like them [graduate admission policies]. I think they should get rid of the GRE. Because like the SAT, I don't think it's a fair judgment of a person's ability, especially if people don't have the means to prepare for the GRE. Of course, they're going to do worse than somebody who had the means to pay for a grad prep course. So, to me it's very classist. I think it reproduces a lot of inequality based on class.

Respondents thus felt employing the GRE as a "weeding-out" mechanism in the graduate school admissions process perpetuates the reproduction of race and class inequality.

Selectivity of Undergraduate Institution

Although existing research suggests selectivity of undergraduate institution is a key factor in graduate school admissions (Posselt 2018), only a minority of respondents identified this as a key factor in graduate school admissions decisions at WRU. Isadora felt that using both GRE scores and selectivity of undergraduate institution as criteria in graduate admissions decisions discriminates against working-class and racial/ethnic minority students, particularly because these students do not have access to the same educational opportunities as their more privileged peers. She stated,

I think they need to think about a better evaluation system than the GRE. I mean, it doesn't just affect us. It affects a lot of minorities or students from other backgrounds. It discriminates based on class too. And [also] where you went to school. You didn't always have the same opportunities, so you're not starting with a level playing field.

Composition of Admissions Committees

Study participants also underscored the effects that the composition of graduate admissions committees have in achieving graduate student diversity. Respondents felt that applicants to graduate school are not given a "fair" and "balanced" review, particularly when admissions committees are comprised of racially homogeneous (i.e., mostly white) and/or politically conservative faculty; respondents felt these faculty tend to emphasize GRE scores over other factors in the admissions process. For example, Emilio stated,

[In] our department, it's ugly. They give too much weight to the Chair, who's usually white, and the adviser … The Graduate Division [at WRU] has … supposedly sent a message to the Chair and adviser that they want the top GRE scores. So that just eliminates [a] whole bunch of people of color … I don't think that's good. I think they should have a wider variety of students and faculty involved in the committee—have some kind of review process that is more inclusive.

Berta also believes that only when "progressive" (liberal) faculty participate in graduate admissions committees do a diverse body of graduate students get recruited into her department. She remarked,

I think the graduate admissions is very mixed, because it's based on who's on the committee. And if you get really conservative folks on your committee, then you get really conservative graduate students. And if you have the progressive folks, then you tend to have much more ethnic diversity, and much more class diversity, gender diversity.

Respondents also perceived that graduate admissions committees often do not "look for" or value diversity. Fernando, for example, felt that faculty in his department failed to grasp both the intellectual and social value of a racially/ethnically diverse graduate student population. In short, respondents felt that lack of diversity in graduate school admissions committees perpetuated the exclusion of racial/ethnic minorities.

Elimination of Affirmative Action

While most respondents articulated trenchant critiques of their department's graduate admissions policies and practices, others expressed criticism of anti–Affirmative Action policies enacted at the state and institutional (WRU) levels. Clara, for example, felt that Affirmative Action policies were instrumental in opening up the pathway to graduate studies for students like herself. With the elimination of Affirmative Action at the state and institutional (WRU) levels, Clara felt that Chicanx/Latinx students would have less access to graduate education. She stated,

I think that it's unfair, barbaric! Because so many of the professors and people who work within the university are mediocre anyway ... I think it's a catastrophe because I know that for me, Affirmative Action was totally pivotal and that another student like myself, now under this [anti–Affirmative Action] climate, would be prevented from getting their PhDs.

Similarly, Vicki viewed the elimination of Affirmative Action as contributing to the underrepresentation of Chicanx/Latinx students in doctoral education generally and from the knowledge production process specifically. She explained,

[Anti–Affirmative Action policies] are policies of erasure. They're trying to erase the fact that they have discriminated, that they have prejudiced people [in power] ... I think they see us as threatening ... We manage knowledge, we create knowledge, and if you can keep a tight hand over who is allowed access to do that, to define what is acceptable knowledge to convey to future generations, that's very oppressive.

Interviewees thus felt that anti–Affirmative Action policies contributed to the underrepresentation of Chicanx/Latinx students in doctoral education.

Discussion and Conclusion

This study analyzed Chicanx/Latinx doctoral students' perceptions of the graduate school (PhD) admissions process. Findings reveal that some Chicanx/Latinx doctoral students believed their departments employ a comprehensive review process that entails analyzing applications holistically, rather than relying on a single factor (e.g., GRE scores) in admissions decisions. Respondents lauded comprehensive review policies because they felt these helped them secure admission to graduate school.

In contrast, most respondents felt their department's graduate admissions policies were not based on a comprehensive review process. Instead, most respondents felt the process was skewed in favor of applicants with high GRE scores and/or those who had attended prestigious undergraduate institutions. These respondents' perceptions are consistent with the extant social scientific literature, which clearly reveals the importance of GRE scores and selectivity of undergraduate institution in graduate school admissions and fellowship award decisions (Nettles and Millet 2006; Posselt 2018). Because URMs, including Chicanx/Latinx students, are less likely to attend selective undergraduate institutions and tend to score lower on standardized admission exams compared to their white and middle-class peers, graduate admissions policies that prioritize these admissions criteria perpetuate the underrepresentation of URMs in doctoral education. As Posselt (2018) insightfully observes about pedigree considerations in graduate admissions, "A narrow view of college quality when evaluating graduate school applicants is therefore one way that inequities are reproduced in U.S. graduate education" (p. 498).

Furthermore, respondents noted that composition of graduate school admissions committees was a critical factor shaping graduate admissions decisions. Respondents felt that white and/or politically conservative faculty are not genuinely invested in recruiting a racially and/or socioeconomically diverse graduate student population. Study participants thus underscored the importance of faculty diversity in recruiting a diverse graduate student population. Because racial/ethnic minorities, particularly Chicanxs/Latinxs, are drastically underrepresented among the nation's faculty (Ramirez 2017), the lack of diverse graduate admissions committees will undoubtedly continue to be a problem in the future.

Finally, some respondents viewed the elimination of Affirmative Action as a root cause of the underrepresentation of Chicanx/Latinx students in doctoral education. Respondents perceived anti–Affirmative Action policies as "policies of exclusion." These sentiments are consistent with the scholarly literature, which clearly documents the devastating effects that the elimination of Affirmative Action has had on URM enrollment and graduation rates from postsecondary educational institutions, particularly at selective institutions (Garces 2018). Recent and ongoing challenges to the use of race and/or gender in college admissions (i.e., Affirmative Action) portend negative consequences for URM students' access to and enrollment in higher education institutions (Garces 2018).

Overall, study participants viewed their department's graduate school admissions policies as perpetuating the reproduction of race and class privilege and inequality. Clearly, respondents' perceptions and experiences stand in stark contrast to institutional/dominant accounts, which typically characterize the graduate school admissions process as "fair," "neutral," and/or "objective." These findings are also consistent with intersectionality theory, as respondents' narratives clearly reveal the ways that graduate admissions policies are steeped in race and class inequality. Future studies should examine how gender inequality processes are also embedded in graduate admissions processes.

In conclusion, this study finds that notwithstanding its apparent neutrality, the graduate school admissions process is a highly subjective, unequal, and ostensibly discriminatory process. From a policy standpoint, the findings underscore the need for reform of graduate admissions policies and procedures, particularly at universities and departments that do not rigorously employ comprehensive review admissions procedures. Reforming the graduate admissions process to make it more equitable and inclusive would help open up the pathway to graduate studies for Chicanx/Latinx (and other historically underserved) students.

References

Andersen, Margaret L., and Patricia Hill Collins. 2001. "Introduction." Pp. 1–11 in *Race, Class, and Gender: An Anthology*, edited by M.L. Andersen and P.H. Collins. Stamford, CT: Wadsworth Publishers.

Baca Zinn, Maxine, and Bonnie Thornton Dill. 1996. "Theorizing Difference from Multiracial Feminism." *Feminist Studies* 2:321–31.

Burris, Val. 2004. "The Academic Caste System: Prestige Hierarchies in PhD Exchange Networks." *American Sociological Review* 69(2):239–64.

Collins, Patricia Hill. 2002. *Black Feminist Thought: Knowledge, Consciousness, and the Politics of Empowerment*. New York: Routledge.

Crenshaw, Kimberlé W. 1991. "Mapping the Margins: Intersectionality, Identity Politics, and Violence Against Women of Color. *Stanford Law Review* 43:1241–299.

Garces, Liliana. 2018. "Don't Lose Race-Conscious Policies." *Science* 361(6403):627. Retrieved August 30, 2018 (http://science.sciencemag.org/content/361/6403/627/tab-pdf).

Hill, Lori Diane. 2008. "School Strategies and the 'College-Linking' Process: Reconsidering the Effects of High Schools on College Enrollment." *Sociology of Education* 81(1):53–76.

Ibarra, Robert A. 2001. *Beyond Affirmative Action: Reframing the Context of Higher Education*. University of Wisconsin Press.

Kim, Dongbin. 2004. "The Effect of Financial Aid on Students' College Choice: Differences by Racial Groups." *Research in Higher Education* 45(1):43–70.

Krogstad, Jens Manuel. 2016. "5 Facts about Latinos and Education." Pew Research Center. Retrieved August 30, 2018 (http://www.pewresearch.org/fact-tank/2016/07/28/5-facts-about-latinos-and-education/).

McDonough, Patricia M. 1997. *Choosing Colleges: How Social class and Schools Structure Opportunity*. State University of New York Press.

McDonough, Patricia M., Anthony Lising Antonio, and James W. Trent. 1997. "Black Students, Black Colleges: An African American College Choice Model." *Journal for a Just and Caring Education* 3(1):9–36.

Mullen, Ann L., Kimberly A. Goyette, and Joseph A. Soares. 2003. "Who Goes to Graduate School? Social and Academic Correlates of Educational Continuation After College." *Sociology of Education* 76(2):143–69.

National Science Foundation, National Center for Science and Engineering Statistics. 2018. *Doctorate Recipients from U.S. Universities: 2016*. Special Report NSF 18-304. Alexandria, VA. Available at www.nsf.gov/statistics/2018/nsf18304/

Nettles, Michael T., and Catherine M. Millet. 2006. *Three Magic Letters: Getting to Ph.D*. Baltimore: Johns Hopkins University Press.

Posselt, Julie R. 2018. "Trust Networks: A New Perspective on Pedigree and the Ambiguities of Admissions." *Review of Higher Education* 41(4):497–521.

Posselt, Julie R., and Eric Grodsky. 2017. "Graduate Education and Social Stratification." *Annual Review of Sociology* 43:353–78.

Ramirez, Elvia. 2011. "'No One Taught Me the Steps': Latinos' Experiences Applying to Graduate School." *Journal of Latinos and Education* 10(3):204–22.

Ramirez, Elvia. 2013. "Examining Latinos/as' Graduate School Choice Process: An Intersectionality Perspective. *Journal of Hispanic Higher Education* 12(1):23–36.

Ramirez, Elvia. 2014. "'Qué Estoy Haciendo Aquí? (What Am I Doing Here?)': Chicanos/Latinos(as) Navigating Challenges and Inequalities During Their First Year of Graduate School." *Equity & Excellence in Education* 47(2):167–86.

Ramirez, Elvia. 2017. "Unequal Socialization: Interrogating the Chicano/Latino(a) Doctoral Education Experience." *Journal of Diversity in Higher Education* 10(1):25–38.

Walpole, Marybeth. *2007. Economically and Educationally Challenged Students in Higher Education: Access to Outcome*s. San Francisco: Jossey-Bass.

Walpole, Marybeth, Patricia McDonough, Constance J. Bauer, Carolyn Gibson, Kamau Kanyi, and Rita Toliver. 2005. "'This Test is Unfair': Urban African American and Latino High School Students' Perceptions of Standardized College Admissions Tests." *Urban Education* 40(3):321–49.

Zhang, Liang. 2005. "Advance to Graduate Education: The Effect of College Quality and Undergraduate Majors." *Review of Higher Education* 28(2):313–38.

Discussion Questions

1. What obstacles, if any, did you face in navigating the K–12 school system?

2. Double segregation refers to segregation based on race and economic status. As noted, this phenomenon seems to be worsening. What strategies or tactics can be employed to reduce this social phenomenon?

Resources

National Center for Education Statistics: https://nces.ed.gov/

UCLA Civil Rights Project: https://www.civilrightsproject.ucla.edu/

References

Cokley, Kevin O. 2002. "Ethnicity, Gender and Academic Self-Concept: A Preliminary Examination of Academic Disidentification and Implications for Psychologists." *Cultural Diversity and Ethnic Minority Psychology* (8):378–88.

Cornbleth, C., and Korth, W. 1980. "Context Factors and Individual Differences in Pupil Involvement in Learning Activity." *Journal of Educational Research* (73):318–23.

Du Bois, W.E.B. 1903. *The Souls of Black Folk*. Oxford University Press.

Institute of Education Sciences. 2017. "Public High School Graduation Rates." *National Center for Education. U.S. Department of Education.* Retrieved April 7, 2019, from https://nces.ed.gov/programs/coe/indicator_coi.asp

Institute of Education Sciences. 2018. "Public High School Graduation Rates." *National Center for Education. U.S. Department of Education.* Retrieved April 7, 2019, from https://nces.ed.gov/programs/coe/indicator_coi.asp

McFarland, Joel, Jiashan Cui, Amy Rathbun, and Juliet Holmes. 2018. "Trends in High School Dropout and Completion Rates in the United States: 2018." (NES 2019-117). U.S. Department of Education. National Center for Education Statistics. Washington, DC. Retrieved April 7, 2019, from https://nces.ed.gov/programs/dropout/ind_03.asp

Musu-Gillette, Lauren, Cristobal de Brey, Joel McFarland, William Hussar, William Sonnenberg, and Sidney Wilkinson-Flicker. 2017. "Status and Trends in the Education of Racial and Ethnic Groups 2017." (NCES 2017-051). U.S. Department of Education. National Center for Education Statistics. Washington, DC Retrieved April 7, 2019 from http://nces.ed.gove/pubsearch

Langhout, Regina D., and Cecily A. Mitchell. 2008. "Engaging Contexts: Drawing the Link between Student and Teacher Experiences of the Hidden Curriculum." *Journal of Community & Applied Social Psychology* (18):593–614.

Massey, Douglas S., and Mary J. Fischer. 2005. "Stereotype Threat and Academic Performance." *Du Bois Review* (2)1:45–67.

McFadden, A. 1992. "A Study of Race and Gender Bias in the Punishment of School Children." *Education and Treatment of Children* (15):140–46.

Mikel Brown, L. 1999. *Raising Their Voices: The Politics of Girls' Anger*. Cambridge, MA: Harvard University Press.

Morgan, H. 1991. "Race and Gender Issues: In-School Suspension." *Paper Presented at the Annual Meeting of the American Education Research Association.* (Chicago, 3–7 April, 1991).

Steele, Claude M. 1988. "The Psychology of Self-Affirmation: Sustaining the Integrity of the Self." *Advances in Experimental Social Psychology* (21):261–302.

Steele, Claude M. 1992. "Race and the Schooling of Black Americans*." Atlantic Monthly* (269):68–78.

Steele, Claude M. 1997. "A Threat in the Air: How Stereotypes Shape the Intellectual Identities and Performance of Women and African Americans." *American Psychologist* (52):613–29.

UCLA Civil Rights Project. 2016. "Brown at 62: Segregation by Race, Poverty, and State." Retrieved from https://www.civilrightsproject.ucla.edu/research/k-12-education/integration-and-diversity/brown-at-62-school-segregation-by-race-poverty-and-state/Brown-at-62-final-corrected-2.pdf

U.S. Department of Education. 2019. "IDEA Static Tables. Part B Child Counts and Educational Environments by ages 3–5, and ages 6–21, by race/ethnicity and state." Retrieved April 7, 2019, from https://www2.ed.gov/programs/osepidea/618-data/static-tables/index.html#partb-cc

Winton, Richard, and Hannah Fay. March 20, 2019. "Wealthy Parents in Admissions Scandal Under Intense Pressure to Make Deals." Retrieved April 12, 2019, from https://www.latimes.com/local/lanow/la-me-college-admissions-scandal-legal-analysis-20190320-story.html

Section V: Popular Culture and the Media

Student Narrative

I'm walking around Sac State with my headphones on, writing rap lyrics in my iPhone. As I scribe, I imagine my lyrics transcending the screen and penetrating the fabrics of society. These lyrics aim to inspire listeners to live a conscious lifestyle and to make a positive impact in their community. In 2019, I believe rap lyrics have the ability to influence and move people the way that an eloquent speech composed by Dr. Martin Luther King Jr. would have influenced people in 1964. Rap music that contains a positive message can generate enough social influence to redirect negative trends and destructive ideologies that drive popular culture today, particular within African American communities. A couple of destructive ideologies that have driven culture in African American communities are "get rich or die trying" and the "gangsta" lore. Both have been perpetuated within the black community, since Gangsta Rap's inception in the late 1980s. History has shown that lyrics within rap music often times become popular monikers within communities of color. This is why I'm convinced that artists can generate new ideologies that push positive narratives forward. Growing up in Oakland during a period known as the "Hyphy Movement" in the early 2000s, I was able to gain firsthand experience of how influential music can be in shaping culture. My experiences during that time inspired a new hunger in me to create positive change through music. Fortunately, we are living in a time in history where resources and platforms provide us with more access to people directly from their technological devices.

Today in the 21st century, we have the ability to influence popular culture more than any other time in history. Social media and the internet have given us the platform and access to reach people all over the world from our cellphones and computers. With this opportunity, we must put together a concerted effort to create positive images and narratives through music and media by educating as well as empowering our families and communities. We must rebrand ourselves through every form of media that is available to us. The time is now. As I scribe lyrics in the notes of my iPhone, I envision rap music changing the world. We all have an amazing opportunity to create change and redirect popular culture from unconsciousness to consciousness. It's important that you use your gift as a tool to reach, teach, motivate, and inspire others to be the best they can be! Stay conscious of your influence.

DeWayne Lamont Ewing Jr., also known as Consci8us, is an inspiring music artist, inspirational speaker, and educator from Oakland, CA. His mission is use music as a tool to change the world. He is an alumnus of Cosumnes River College and Sacramento State where he finished with Cum Laude honors within his major, Sociology. He plans to continue his education in the coming years after gaining more work experience.

Learning Objectives

1. Discuss the culture industry and how it influences popular culture.

2. Relate stereotypical imagery of marginalized groups to larger structural inequalities of race, class, and gender.

3. Give examples of how popular culture reinforces race and ethnic hierarchies through the use of derogatory imagery.

Editor's Introduction

Jacqueline Brooks, PhD

DeWayne creates community through music, relying on technology to broadcast his message to listeners. In a short time, he can create a song, upload it to a social media platform, and share it with the world. Access to social media platforms (e.g. Facebook, Snapchat, YouTube, Twitter, Instagram, Tik Tok, and LinkedIn), has turned consumers into producers of artistic expression, whether it's music, fashion designs, prank videos, or documentary film. Some have turned their social media ventures into high-paying jobs. In 2018, the top ten performers on YouTube collectively earned $180 million (Webb 2019). This predominantly male group includes Vloggers, video gamers, pranksters, and a seven-year-old who brings home about $22 million a year reviewing toys. According to the Pew Research Center, about 69 percent of Americans use some form of social media, with at least 50 percent of adults using the top three social media platforms—Facebook, Snapchat, and Instagram—on a daily basis (2018). Social media is no longer utilized mainly by young, white, middle-class consumers. Rather, its pervasiveness draws from the diverse riches of age, race, gender, and educational attainment.

Popular Culture and Social Inequalities

Culture operates as a **social structure**—an aggregation of persistent social relationships and interactions that endure over time. Given its ubiquitous nature, culture influences much of what we think and do, meaning it's essential to how we construct social reality. According to Foucault, popular culture represents a unique subgroup of ideas, practices, behaviors, and products born out of post-industrialization and urbanization. Technology remarkably changed how we think and behave, thereby greatly altering the culture. As the wealthy indulged in expensive, **high culture,** low-income and middle-income groups consumed **low culture**, mass-produced commodities that appeased their less-refined tastes. Critical theorists make note of the **culture industry**, controlled mostly by powerful, wealthy capitalists, it reflects a monolithic engine that saturates markets with commodities. The average consumer strolls the aisles—physical or virtual—under the guise of "free choice," when in fact, the culture industry has subliminally implanted the very idea of what to buy, when, and for how much in their minds. Those who own the means of production, create and control the consumer.

Yet, the culture industry is not only classed; it is gendered and raced as well. Gender and race hierarchies influence how the culture industry depicts women and people of color and ultimately how the consumer perceives these marginalized groups. In *Hunting Girls, Sexual Violence from The Hunger Games to Campus Rape* (2016), Oliver suggests that our behavior, in many ways, imitates fantasy. She states, "Unfortunately, increasingly life imitates pornography, particularly creepshot photographs of unsuspecting girls and women.

With uncanny regularity, college and university officials are discovering Facebook pages, and other social media, used by fraternities, or creepshooters off the street, to post photographs of women, sometimes, naked, or in compromising positions" (2016:17). In addition, she describes the culture's fascination with women who look "dead" or unconscious, implying that what happens to them is of no consequence. "Snuff porn and various varieties of pornography feature incapacitated girls and women, some looking dead. And, of course, there are fraternity photos of unconscious nude or semi-clad girls in embarrassing poses on closed Facebook sites across the country" (Oliver 2016:16). Think about the volume of advertisements you consume on a weekly basis. How many of these ads use sex to sell a product? By sex, we mean largely the objectification of women and girls. Now, how many television shows use similar themes? How about movies and books? Soon keeping count becomes overwhelming. Oliver explains that we have a history of selling and consuming images of objectified, weak, and submissive women, some of which stems from fairy tales (2016). Today, we have shifted to marketing portrayals of strong, independent, young women who can fight alongside men (e.g., Katniss/*Hunger Games*, Bella Swan/*Twilight*, Tris/*Divergent*, and Hit Girl/*Kick Ass 2*). Yet, these characters are often punished for their self-sufficiency by being demeaned, beaten, and/or sexually assaulted (2016). What we create and consume reflects how we view one another.

Oliver (2016) traces much of our present-day obsession with sexualizing young women and girls to fairy tales, which sold fantasies of princes, girls needing rescuing, and living happily ever after. In American popular culture, minstrel shows reflected an inevitable extension of systemic racial domination and exploitation. Between 1830 and 1910, white actors played African American characters by darkening their skin, whitening their lips, and speaking in broken English. Black characters were presented as docile and obedient to whites. Du Bois (1992) refers to social deference bestowed upon whites by African Americans as a **psychological wage**, rooted in slavery. Black codes prohibited enslaved Africans from challenging or questioning whites—even poor whites who did not own land or slaves. Thus, the forced deference of enslaved Africans reinforced whites' feelings of superiority and dominance, regardless of their class standing. Minstrel shows perpetuated whites' need for social deference, justifying their position in the social, political, and economic hierarchies. After emancipation, by controlling images of African Americans, minstrel shows allowed whites to satisfy their fantasies of keeping African Americans under white control.

Controlling images delivered through narratives and photos justify social oppression by "othering" social groups, particularly when these images highlight and exploit perceived differences via dichotomies (e.g., "citizen" versus "noncitizen," or "black" versus "white") (hooks 1984; Collins 1990). The oppression of black women specifically relies on abrogating, dichotomizing images that present them as mammies (subservient versus independent), matriarchs (mean versus kind), welfare mothers (poor versus rich), and jezebels (promiscuous versus pure) (Collins 1990). As Collins states, "Race, class, and gender oppression could not continue without powerful ideological justifications for their existence" (1990:66). When the George W. Bush administration sought to rally the United States to war after 9/11, Arab and/or Muslim communities were "othered," viewed as strange (versus familiar), foreign (versus citizen), and dangerous (versus safe). Muslim women in particular were presented as needing saving from harsh, authoritarian regimes, solidifying their "othering" as "liberated or oppressed." In an ideological war for the anger and rage of Americans against Muslim extremists, these images controlled what the Western world thought, saw, and believed to be "Muslim" or "Arab."

This use of derogatory imagery extends to demean other race and ethnic groups. For example, Asian American women are often portrayed as cold, evil characters ("Dragon Lady) or submissive, overly sexualized beings (geisha). Both stereotypes reinforce biased perceptions of Asian American women as "exotic." Asian American men are often portrayed as the **biracial buddy**, relying on stereotypes of ancient Asian cultures to help whites (e.g., in *The Karate Kid* and *The Matrix*) (Park 2010). The representation of Native Americans within American popular culture reflects a deep-seated, historical prejudice toward indigenous people. The depiction of Native Americans as shamans, sidekicks, and wise men, often guiding the experiences of whites, stems from racialized perceptions of Native Americans as "noble savages." Native American women are often reflected as innocent or promiscuous, offering dueling caricatures easily manipulated by smart white men. Latinas are often stereotyped as hot-blooded, oversexed characters, using their sexuality to win favors. In addition, Latina characters are employed as maids or other domestic workers. Even when Latina characters break out of these molds, the other always seems present. Sophia Vergara's character in *Modern Family* is wealthy but sexualized. Jennifer Lopez's sex appeal was downplayed in *Maid in Manhattan*; however, she worked as a domestic in a hotel.

A Historical Example: The Case of Little Black Sambo

Growing up, I was accustomed to bright neon signs advertising casual dining fare at restaurants throughout my town. However, one in particular bothered me. The sign read, "Sambo's Restaurants." The owners, **Sam** Battistone and F. Newell **Bo**hnett, claimed the name of their franchise was derived from combining their names (Bernstein 1984). Yet, they filled the walls of their restaurants with images of "Sambo," a child of South Indian descent, who played with tigers and enjoyed eating pancakes. It just happens that in Helen Bannerman's nineteenth-century book *Little Black Sambo*, the protagonist, a South Indian boy, outsmarts several tigers who stole his clothes. The tigers fight among themselves, resulting in a pool of "tiger butter," which Sambo and his family use to make pancakes.

Figure SV.1 Sambo's Franchise Restaurant. Opened in 1957, Sambo's diners presented a welcoming environment for families desiring a cheap, quick meal. At its peak, the franchise operated 1,114 restaurants in 47 states. A combination of operational failures and lawsuits from civil rights groups protesting the racialized connotations of the franchise's logo and brand led to its demise. The original Sambo's in Santa Barbara, California, is the last remaining diner. Photo retrieved from the Ferris State University Jim Crow Museum of Racist Memorabilia.

Since racism is embedded in America's social institutions, its presence in places such as restaurants is not shocking or abnormal. To think otherwise would be a denial of a racial hierarchy that commodifies racial stereotypes. Within the realm of American literature alone, images of African Americans have been repeatedly defiled, in ways that "conveniently bound and violently silenced black bodies" (Morrison, 1997). Publisher Grant Richards originally sold Bannerman's book to a European audience in 1899. The first American version appeared in 1900, published. Over a forty-year period, multiple American publishers would market various reprints and reinterpretations of the book. Soon the nation's bookstores and school libraries filled with *Little Black Sambo* or its derivatives. In the original book Sambo was drawn as a dark-skinned, black child with somewhat exaggerated features. Keep in mind his character lived in India. As the book increased in American popularity, the characters became darker and their features more exaggerated. In some books, "Mumbo" is characterized as a terrifying figure perpetuating the controlling image of the "Matriarch" stereotype.. Despite the racialized imagery, *Little Black Sambo* became a popular children's book, adored by many, even leading to a children's cartoon. In the late 1930s, charges of racism were levied against children's books that depicted "plantation stories" and denigrating images of people of color. Although Little Black Sambo was eventually banned in elementary schools and public libraries, a quick search of the Internet will reveal its continued treasured place in the minds of "color-blind" Americans. Beginning in the late 1980s, re-imaginings of the book, which offered realistic imagery, and sometimes new interpretations of the original story appeared (Lester and Pinkney 1996). These editions have been met with positive responses, yet the stain of racism, filtered through a popular children's book, remains.

Mindfulness

In October 2018, the host of *Megyn Kelly Today* asked of her all-white panel, "What is racist?" The segment addressed the use of blackface, specifically during Halloween by white Americans seeking to embody popular African American celebrities (Kludt 2018). Kelly describes the backlash reality TV star Luann de Lesseps received when she dressed as Diana Ross the previous Halloween. Although the panel expressed dismay with de Lesseps's choice, Kelly implies that blackface is common during Halloween. Basically, what's the big deal? Well, the American public clued Kelly in over the next few days; soon afterward, her NBC show ended, despite Kelly offering an apology. In early 2019, Virginia governor Ralph Northam came under fire after his 1980s medical school yearbook surfaced. One photo shows a person wearing blackface, standing next to someone dressed in a Ku Klux Klan costume. Initially, Northam admitted it was him wearing blackface and apologized. Within one day, he reversed his story. The problem of blackface in American popular culture transcends Kelly and Northam. It reveals America's sordid history with race, exposing an injurious racial hierarchy. Yet, that is part of the problem. We don't know our history, or it's been whitewashed, erasing the stain of white racial dominance. As noted above, whites donned blackface in minstrel shows to mock, humiliate, and demoralize African Americans, thereby controlling the image of "blackness." When members of the 1960s Black Power movement lifted their fists and proclaimed, "I'm Black, and I'm Proud!," this mantra was born out of resistance to the distorted images of blackness produced by whites. Although minstrel shows ended in 1935, their legacy has created historical scrutiny of how we present ourselves as black people, from the way we wear our hair to what we eat. When white people choose to "honor" us by putting shoe polish on their faces and whitening their lips, they attempt to reaffirm their power to control how we look, think, speak, and behave. It is not an honor. It is hatred. It is a problem we share with other race and ethnic groups, as they resist the derogatory images of themselves created by a white-dominated culture. Racist appropriations of caricatures such as the "hot Latina," "Indian chief," "Dragon Lady," and "Karate Kid" still abound in American culture. To be mindful of this imagery means to recognize that history is a process, and we each have a role in shaping what race relations mean today and in the future.

Section Readings

In "Not Just Child's Play: Race and Ethnicity in Children's Toys," Sweet bridges the representation of characters of color in advertisements to larger, structural race inequalities. Using content analysis, Sweet sampled catalogs published between 1905 and 1995, identifying how often characters of color were represented and how they were depicted in ads. Sweet addresses how advertisers employ racial stereotypes to sell children's toys.

In "Erasing Narratives of Racism at an American Amusement Park: The Absence of African American Lived Experience in the Depiction of Nineteenth-Century Convict Leasing," Morris and Arford describe the Flooded Mine Ride at a Branson, Missouri, amusement park. The ride takes people on a tour of a decaying mine occupied by "prison guards" and "inmates," forced to work in life-threatening situations. Morris and Arford question how the amusement park selected to distort the reality of "convict leasing" in American history. Their work challenges us to confront how whitewashing American history purifies it, rendering it a suitable commodity to be sold as entertainment.

In "Black Gazing in Digital Communities as a Form of Collective Activism," Moore discusses how new media platforms offer black Americans control over their media consumption and production, encouraging black activism. Her work moves beyond "Black Twitter," engaging innovative communication platforms, such as the *READ*, the *Friend Zone*, *Blavity News*, and the *Shade Room*, each putting a new spin on adding black voices to political, economic, and social discourse.

In "Investigating, Explaining, and Exposing the Racial Past in the Present: The Possibilities of Documentary Film," Williams and George detail their experiences in studying Confederate culture within a Southern community. They document the responses of community members and participants of Civil War reenactments. Their work addresses how people interpret American history, in many cases whitewashing the actual events of the Civil War, reinforcing racial hierarchies. Their work culminated in a documentary film titled *Southern Discomfort*.

In "The Denigrated Other: Popular Representations of Afro-Latinos," Noakes discusses the representation of Afro/Latinas within popular culture. Noakes addresses how the perception of "blackness," stereotyped as poor and unintelligent, shapes the depictions of Afro/Latinas within media, advertising, and television.

Reading 5.1 Not Just Child's Play: Race and Ethnicity in Children's Toys

Elizabeth V. Sweet, PhD, San Jose State University

Keywords: Racial imagery, Symbolic annihilation, Controlling images

Race and Ethnicity in Children's Toys and Material Culture

What do you remember about the toys you played with as a child? Did you see yourself reflected in the toy characters you interacted with? For most of us, thinking back on our childhood toys calls up good memories and a pleasant sense of nostalgia. Toys are certainly fun, but they can also be the subject of serious study. Sociologists like me are interested in toys as *cultural artifacts*. Cultural artifacts are human-created objects that can be studied to learn more about the culture of their makers and users. So while dolls and building sets are fun things that children use in their creative play, they are also cultural artifacts filled with ideas about race, gender, class, and many other aspects of the society in which they were created.

This chapter will help you to understand how sociologists use content analysis to study the ideas about race and ethnicity that are embedded into material objects like toys. It will also help you to recognize and become mindful of the messages about race and ethnicity that are woven into the objects that you encounter in your daily life. Lastly, it will help you to develop critical media literacy skills that will aid you in decoding and resisting these messages.

Why Study Toys?

My interest in studying children's toys began as I was parenting an infant while working toward my undergraduate degree in sociology. In my classes, I was studying about social inequalities related to gender, race, and class and learning how they structure society and the opportunities and constraints that each of us faces. I learned that ideas about race, class, and gender are woven into so many facets of our everyday lives, from the ads we see to the movies we watch. As a result, I began to be more mindful of how these cultural messages were woven into the fabric of my own everyday life. And I couldn't help but notice how the toys, clothing, and books that my young daughter interacted with on a daily basis were also infused with messages about gender and race.

As I moved on to graduate school and continued to learn more about social inequalities, my interest in the relationship between social inequalities and material objects like children's toys intensified. I was struck by how different contemporary toys seemed from the toys that I played with as a child, particularly when it came to gender. For example, toys today are nearly all sold in gender-coded aisles or online toy pages (Auster and Mansbach 2012), but I didn't remember this being the case when I was a kid. So I initially became interested in studying how the gender marketing of toys might have changed over time, but I was also interested in whether and how the ideas about race in toys had changed in similar ways. With my interest sparked, I began to come up with a plan for how to study this topic using the tools of sociological research.

Designing a Research Project

Laying the Groundwork

The first step in designing a research project is to formulate the questions you hope to answer with your study. This was relatively easy for me, as my questions were what brought me to my project. Ultimately, I was interested in whether and how the relationships between gender, race, and children's toys had changed over time. More specifically, I was interested in looking at two aspects of toys: first, I wanted to look at how the representations of gender and race in toys had changed over time, and second, I wanted to know whether there had been change over time in how toys were marketed in terms of gender and race. Ultimately, I was interested not just in *how* race and gender were portrayed in toys, but also in how these portrayals related to larger systems of racial and gender inequality.

The next step in a research project is to do a literature review to see what other research has already been done on your topic. As it turns out, there weren't many studies that looked at either race or gender and children's toys; the few that I did come across were focused broadly on the history of toys and not on the relationship between toys and social inequalities. So I began to look for studies that examined how other products for children—like books and clothing—might be related to gender and racial/ethnic inequalities. It was during this search that I found a sociological study on race in children's literature, which gave me a roadmap for designing my own project.

In this study, sociologists Pescosolido, Grauerholz, and Milkie (1997) analyzed the representation of black characters in over 2,400 children's picture books published between 1937 and 1993. The researchers were interested in how often black characters appeared in children's literature, and they were interested in the ways in which those characters were portrayed. They needed a way to take raw data—the books themselves—and systematically describe their content. To do this, they created a content analysis *coding scheme,* which laid out specific, concrete measures of the concepts of interest. One of the most important pieces of their coding scheme was a count of the number of black characters in each book.

Using this count, the researchers were then able to describe (1) the percentage of books in each year that portrayed at least one black character; and (2) the percentage of books in each year that represented only black characters. When they plotted these data in a graph, the results were striking. Although black characters were vastly underrepresented over the entire time period studied, there was still variation in representation, with black characters being most likely to appear in children's books in the earlier part of the twentieth century and again at the end of the century. Interestingly, black characters were virtually absent from children's picture books during the period between 1959 and 1964.

Next, to understand these changes in racial imagery and how they might relate to larger changes in race relations over time, the researchers used a news databank to measure the number of episodes of racial conflict (which included confrontations, protests, and legal actions) in each year of the study time period. When compared to the results from the content analysis of books, the results were striking. The number of racial conflicts spiked during the same period that black characters disappeared from children's literature. From this analysis, the researchers argued that there was a strong relationship between societal race relations and the portrayal of black characters in children's literature. When race relations were relatively stable, black characters were more likely to be represented in children's books, although the nature of that representation did vary over time. However, when race relations were contested during the civil rights movement, black characters were essentially erased from children's literature, reflecting, as the authors explain, "…indecision or unwillingness to portray racial contact in new (and at the time radical) ways" (Pescosolido, Grauerholz, and Milkie 1997, p. 460). Both the trivialization of and the erasure of black characters are a form of *symbolic annihilation* (Tuchman 2000), and these were the primary modes of racial representation in children's literature over most of the twentieth century (Pescosolido, Grauerholz, and Milkie 1997).

This study was a gold mine for me because it gave me good ideas about how to design my own content analysis project and, importantly, it established a strong link between children's material culture—in this case, picture books—and social inequality. With this in mind, I began the work of designing my own research project.

Designing a Research Project

I had decided on using content analysis methods for my project, but I needed to find a source of data to analyze. This data source had to show what toys were available and popular at a given time, and it needed to give a sense of whom each toy was designed for and how it was meant to be used. If you wanted to study children's toys today, where would you go to find them? Most likely, you would go online and study the toys being sold by a major retailer. I wanted to study toys that were sold historically, so I needed to find the twentieth-century equivalent of Amazon.com, and print catalogs proved to be the perfect resource for this.

The Sears, Roebuck and Co. Catalog, first published in 1893, was essentially the Amazon.com of the past. The catalog was published regularly for over a century, and it advertised a wide range of consumer products, including toys. It was impossible for me to study every Sears catalog published, so I had to select a *sample*—a smaller subset of objects selected to represent the whole. My sample included catalogs from the years 1905, 1925, 1945, 1975, and 1995 to represent toys in the key early, quarter, mid-, late-quarter, and end-of-century time points.

With my data source in hand, now I needed to come up with a coding scheme to analyze them. Along with a series of concepts related to gender, I was interested in the representation of different racial and ethnic groups over time in toys and toy ads. Race is a *social construct*—it is defined socially in ways that vary over time and across place. It is difficult to measure race or ethnicity in images or material objects without reinforcing the idea that race is something we can easily observe just by looking at someone (Chin 1999). However, the only information I had to go on was what was printed on the catalog pages, and so I had to rely on visual and textual cues in the ads to categorize the race/ethnicity of toy characters and ad models. This was easiest with toy characters, as ads would often clearly identify the race or ethnicity of nonwhite characters. Ad models of color only appeared in the 1975 and 1995 catalogs, and here I relied on cues in the ad image to make inferences about a model's race/ethnicity when possible. I coded data at the ad level, so if an ad showed more than one toy character or ad model, I documented the race/ethnicity of each. This allowed me to analyze the extent to which ads were racially inclusive. In a later stage of the project, a research assistant used the coding scheme to analyze the same ads so that I could ensure my coding scheme was *reliable*. Coding reliability means that different people using the same coding scheme will categorize the data in the same way.

Along with the numeric representation of racial/ethnic groups, I was also interested in *how* different groups were represented among toy characters. To what extent did those representations rely on racial and ethnic stereotypes? To document this, as I analyzed each ad, I made note of how the characters were described in the text and depicted in ad images. This allowed me to compare how different groups were represented over time. In addition, though I did not code data in these years, I studied toy advertisements in catalogs from 1915, 1935, 1955, 1965, and 1985 to supplement my qualitative analysis of racial and gender representations.

Using the coding scheme I developed, I analyzed all of the toy advertisements in my catalog sample. I recorded this information in a spreadsheet and, when the data collection was complete, I used a statistical software package to analyze my results. I describe these results in the next section.

Research Results

Representations of Race and Ethnicity in Toys

The results from my analysis show that the dominant image of race in children's historical toys is that of whiteness. In fact, there was remarkably little racial and ethnic diversity in terms of both toy characters and ad models over the twentieth century, although there was some variation over time in the extent to which different racial and ethnic groups were represented in the world of toys. In addition, with a few exceptions at the end of the century, toys were overwhelmingly marketed to a white audience. Until 1975, I saw no ad models of color in the toy pages of the Sears catalogs I studied. However, in the last quarter of the twentieth century, I did observe an increase in the representation of racial and ethnic minorities in toy advertisements and a decrease of racially stereotyped toy characters.

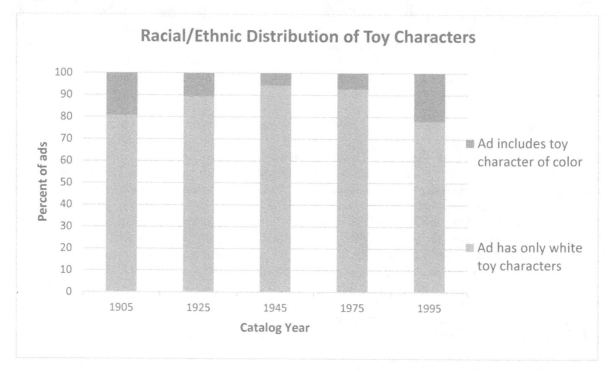

Figure 5.1: Racial Distribution of Toy Characters

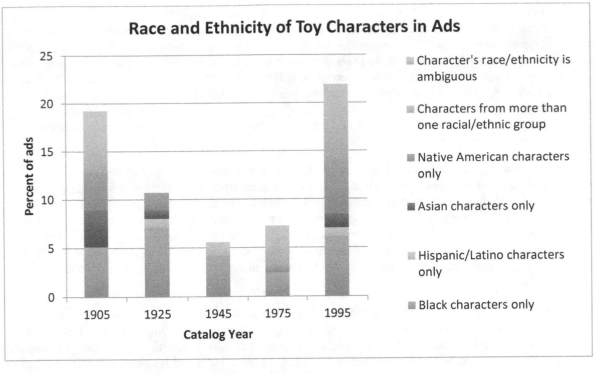

Figure 5.2: Race and Ethnicity of Toy Characters

As you can see in Figure 1, the overwhelming majority of toy ads[1] depicted only white toy characters across all time points studied. In all decades, characters of color were rare, but the lack of diversity is especially striking in the mid-century. Additionally, as you can see in Figure 2, while toy characters were most diverse at the beginning and end of the twentieth century, the representation of racial and ethnic minorities in these two time periods was very different. In the first half of the century, these representations were deeply infused with racial stereotypes. For example, in the 1905 Sears catalog, the "Negro Topsy Doll" was described as having "indestructible head and limbs" and wearing a "very loud and fancy striped topsy gown (p. 974). Mirroring the cultural narratives used to justify racial violence and oppression in adult society, this description plays upon racial stereotypes and encourages white children to play violently with the doll. Some ads were even more explicit in promoting racial violence, as was the case with the 1915 ad for the "Darkey Shooting Gallery," which encouraged children to make a game of using black characters for target practice. Such representations are examples of ***controlling images*** (Collins 2000) in that they work to sustain a system of racial domination.

African Americans weren't the only racial or ethnic group whose depiction relied upon racist stereotypes and promoted oppression. In the 1925 catalog, a page of masquerade costumes and masks advertised racial- and ethnic-inspired costumes based entirely on negative stereotypes about Mexicans, the Irish, and Gypsies, in addition to blacks (p. 532). And while the lack of racial and ethnic diversity among toy characters was even more pronounced in 1945, representations of black characters remained heavily stereotyped. For example, the board game "Little Black Sambo," based upon the popular children's book of the time, is built upon racial stereotypes.

In the 1975 Sears catalog, there was a small but notable shift in representation. For one, black and Asian children were included among the child models in toy advertisements, and there were two ads which depicted black and white children playing together. The inclusion of models of color in the Sears catalog seems to have happened rapidly, as in the 1965 catalog, all of the human models depicted in the catalog were white. Secondly, while the racial and ethnic diversity of toy characters in 1975 looked fairly similar to that in 1945, the nature of

---

[1] The graphs in Figures 1 and 2 show the racial and ethnic distribution of toy characters in ads for all toys that included a human character.

that representation had changed. For the first time, black dolls and action figures were presented as viable characters rather than as racist caricatures. Some ads identified doll versions by race in the ad caption, but aside from this, the descriptions, cost, and accessories for these versions were identical. For example, the ad for the "Bless You Baby Tender Love" doll (p. 451) shows both white and black versions of the doll in the image but offers just one text description of the dolls. There were still examples of racial stereotypes in the 1975 catalog, however. A Native American action figure in the "Big Jim" line, called "the Warpath," was shown with a bow and arrow and a menacing facial expression, playing upon stereotypes of Native American savagery. Nevertheless, the shift in the representation of black characters and the inclusion of ad models of color represents a substantive change from prior decades.

By the last decade of the twentieth century, the racial and ethnic diversity of toy characters increased substantially, though white characters remained vastly overrepresented. In the 1995 Sears catalog, 22 percent of the ads for toys with human characters included either a black, Hispanic/Latino, Asian, or Native American character. As in 1975, many dolls and action figures came in multiple versions labeled as either African American or white. In addition, there were two lines of dolls in the 1995 Sears catalog—the "African Queen" dolls and the "Kids of Color" dolls—which featured only black dolls and ad models. These two toy lines were the first (and only) instances that I observed which seemed to be explicitly designed for, and marketed to, children of color.

The representation of a more diverse set of ad models was also notable in the 1995 catalog. In this decade, the percentage of ads with only white models dropped to 84 percent (compared to 93 percent in 1975), and 11 percent of toy ads showed African American children either alone or with white children (compared to less than 2 percent of ads in 1975). There were also ads that featured Asian and Hispanic children, but they were more infrequent. Thus, while racial and ethnic minorities remained vastly underrepresented, there was nevertheless more racial and ethnic diversity in this decade than at any other time in the century.

Overall, the picture of race/ethnicity that emerges from twentieth-century toy advertisements is one of whiteness as racial default. When it comes to the representation of racial and ethnic minority groups, I observed an explicit reliance on racial stereotypes in the early century, a decrease in racial and ethnic diversity mid-century, and a broadening of racial and ethnic inclusivity in the last part of the century. My findings on the representation of race in children's toys were remarkably similar to what Pescosolido, Grauerholz, and Milkie (1997) described in their study of children's literature. As with their study, my results suggest that there was a fundamental shift in representation in the second half of the twentieth century that resulted from a direct and active challenge to the racial status quo. While early portrayals of nonwhite toy characters were ***controlling images*** riddled with blatantly racist stereotypes, during the middle of the century, characters of color virtually disappear from toy advertisements. Both of these patterns of representation are a form of ***symbolic annihilation*** (Tuchman 2000). The continued challenge to the racial status quo did eventually yield a more inclusive and positive representation of race and ethnicity in toys in the last decades of the century. Even then, white ad models and toy characters remained vastly overrepresented, and examples of racial and ethnic stereotypes and marginalization were still evident in toy ads.

From Representation to Lived Experience

When it comes to race in children's culture, things have improved over time, and yet the underrepresentation and stereotyped portrayals of racial and ethnic minorities remains a significant issue. The studies I have described suggest that the depiction of race in material objects like toys both reflects and reinforces societal racial inequality. But do the images of race in children's toys and culture actually affect kids? And if so, how?

In the 1940s, psychologists Kenneth and Mamie Clark conducted a series of influential experiments designed to study racial identification among children. In one of these studies, African American children between three and seven years of age were presented with both white and black dolls and then asked to select the doll that best fit a series of statements such as "give me the doll that is a nice doll" (Clark and Clark 1947). The children showed a clear, positive preference for the white doll, and the Clarks argued that this preference reflected the internalized oppression that comes from living in a society characterized by racial segregation and oppression.

The Clark and Clark (1947) study suggests that cultural messages have a direct effect on children's racial identity. In fact, we tend to think of children as little sponges who passively absorb messages they are given by adults and by society. Over the past several decades, however, sociologists who study childhood have begun to challenge this idea. In fact, children are—like all of us—active, creative, and imaginative beings who are capable of interpreting, and sometimes resisting, cultural messages (Corsaro 2005; Thorne 2009). Studies which examine how children actually experience and understand the cultural messages in products like children's books (Baker-Sperry 2007) and toys (Chin 1999; Bernstein 2011) show that children do actively interpret these objects, even though they generally don't do so in a way that fundamentally challenges their underlying cultural messages. Thus, the messages about race and ethnicity that children encounter in toys and products do play an important role in reinforcing and reproducing inequality, though the process isn't as simple as children passively taking these messages in. And the same is true of us as adults.

Becoming Mindful of Cultural Messages

In this chapter, you've learned how sociologists study the messages about race and ethnicity that are woven into the products we encounter in daily life. In addition, you've learned how race and ethnicity manifested in the toys and toy advertising of the past, and about the possible effects messages about race in children's culture may have. With all of this in mind, let's revisit the questions posed at the start of the chapter: When you think back to your own childhood, what do you remember about the toys you played with? Did you see yourself reflected in them? What messages did your toys convey about race and racial inequality? Do you think these messages had any impact on you?

In the days and weeks ahead, I encourage you to pay attention to how race is evident in the products and media that you interact with. Be mindful of who is represented and who is not, and notice the quality of that representation. Does the depiction rely upon, or convey, racial stereotypes? You can even use a modified version of the coding scheme I described from my study to conduct a systematic analysis of your own.

Along with being mindful of the messages you encounter in products and mass media, think about who is producing these products and media. A recent study found that black characters are much more likely to appear in films with black directors, but the same study shows that black directors are vastly underrepresented in the world of film (Smith, Choueiti, and Pieper 2013). Like the entertainment industry, women and persons of color are vastly underrepresented in the toy industry, particularly in leadership positions (Sweet 2013). How might the racial or ethnic position that content creators inhabit influence the images and messages they produce? What implications does this have for attempts to improve representations in the future?

Resources for Further Exploration

Everyday Sociology blog article by Karen Sternheimer: <u>Racism in Toyland</u>

Harvard Crimson article about research by Robin Bernstein: <u>Exploring Racism in Overlooked Objects</u>

Melissa Harris-Perry Show segment: *"Why Diversity Is Important in Dolls"* | MSNBC.

Parents Latina magazine article by Damarys Ocaña Perez: *"How Important Are Ethnic Dolls?"*

Scientific American blog article by Maia Weinstock: *"It's Time for More Racial Diversity in STEM Toys."*

Research Article by Dr. Sabrina Thomas

Thomas, Sabrina Lynette. 2005. "Black Dolls as Racial Uplift: A Preliminary Report." *Transforming Anthropology* 13(1):55–56.

References

Auster, C.J., and C.S. Mansbach. 2012. "The Gender Marketing of Toys: An Analysis of Color and Type of Toy on the Disney Store Website." *Sex Roles* 1–14.

Baker-Sperry, Lori. 2007. "The Production of Meaning through Peer Interaction: Children and Walt Disney's Cinderella." *Sex Roles* 56(11–12):717–27.

Bernstein, Robin. 2011. *Racial Innocence: Performing American Childhood from Slavery to Civil Rights.* New York: NYU Press.

Chin, Elizabeth. 1999. "Ethnically Correct Dolls: Toying with the Race Industry." *American Anthropologist* 101(2):305–21.

Clark, Kenneth B., and Mamie P. Clark. 1947. "Racial Identification and Preference in Negro Children." Pp. 169–78 in *Readings in Social Psychology*, edited by T.M. Newcomb and E.L. Hartley. New York: Henry Holt and Co.

Collins, Patricia Hill. 2000. *Black Feminist Thought: Knowledge, Consciousness, and the Politics of Empowerment.* New York: Routledge.

Corsaro, William A. 2005. *The Sociology of Childhood.* 2nd ed. Thousand Oaks, CA: Pine Forge Press.

Pescosolido, Bernice A., Elizabeth Grauerholz, and Melissa A. Milkie. 1997. "Culture and Conflict: The Portrayal of Blacks in U.S. Children's Picture Books Through the Mid- and Late-Twentieth Century." *American Sociological Review* 62(3):443–64.

Smith, Stacy L., Marc Choueiti, and Katherine Pieper. 2013. *Is the Key to Diversifying Cinematic Content Held in the Hand of the Black Director? Dr. Stacy L. Smith.* Retrieved June 10, 2017, from (https://pdfs.semanticscholar.org/067e/6a9196fe31c63e779a404e2b95a62b2251db.pdf).

Sweet, Elizabeth Valerie. 2013. "Boy Builders and Pink Princesses: Gender, Toys, and Inequality over the Twentieth Century." University of California, Davis. Retrieved (http://gradworks.umi.com/36/14/3614279.html).

Thorne, Barrie. 2009. "'Childhood': Changing and Dissonant Meanings." *International Journal of Learning and Media* 1(1):19–27.

Tuchman, Gaye. 2000. "The Symbolic Annihilation of Women by the Mass Media." Pp. 150–74 in *Culture and Politics.* New York: Palgrave Macmillan. Retrieved May 6, 2018, from (https://link.springer.com/chapter/10.1007/978-1-349-62397-6_9).

Reading 5.2 Erasing Narratives of Racism at an American Amusement Park: The Absence of African American Lived Experience in the Depiction of Nineteenth-Century Convict Leasing

Patricia Morris, Department of Sociology, California State University–Sacramento

Tammi Arford, Department of Crime and Justice, University of Massachusetts–Dartmouth

Keywords: Racial oppression, collective memory, historical representation, and convict leasing

Chapter Objectives

To highlight the ways in which racial oppression—a disquieting, but nevertheless fundamental, aspect of convict leasing—is so easily dismissed in this representation of the past.

To understand the ways in which "collective memory" is shaped, we must keep in mind that all constructed representations of the past, from those located in historically themed amusement parks to those in well-respected museums, are shaped by a variety of sociohistoric factors that we seek to draw into the open through this research.

To discuss the ways in which historical representations constructed within capitalist ventures are shaped by both the narrative the stakeholders wish to tell and the narrative that their customers wish to hear, or at a minimum, are willing to accept. The Flooded Mine serves as a tangible example of the intersection of these forces that allow the white nostalgia lens of Silver Dollar City and Branson, Missouri, to essentially remain unchallenged by decades of homogeneous, likeminded vacationers.

The nineteenth-century practice of convict leasing represents one of the most shameful chapters in American history—an era of essentially "neoslavery" where African Americans were arbitrarily arrested and pushed back into years of involuntary servitude after the Emancipation Proclamation, a practice that lasted until well into the twentieth century. Using laws enacted specifically to control and intimidate newly freed slaves, tens of thousands of African Americans were effectively sold as forced laborers. This chapter looks at the representation of convict leasing in an unexpected and seemingly inconsequential place, an amusement park. Located in Branson, Missouri, Silver Dollar City is a popular 1880s-themed amusement park which proudly claims to offer historical education and entertainment through "realistic" constructions of the past. In the Flooded Mine ride, park guests travel on "mine carts" through an animatronic depiction of a flooding mine from which the prisoners, forced to labor there, are trying to escape. Dozens of scenes depict this nineteenth-century practice of convict leasing with remarkably accurate detail from the use of replica uniforms and salvaged mining equipment, to the display of brutal methods of punishment used to control prisoners. In fact, when comparing the animatronic scenes at the amusement park to historical photographs of convict miners on display in the museum of the Missouri State Penitentiary, we found them remarkably similar—except for one key detail— nearly all the convict miners in the photographs are black and all the convict miners in the dozens of carefully constructed tableaux in the Flooded Mine are white.

We argue that the absence of African Americans not only renders the ride an inauthentic representation of convict leasing, but it obscures the incalculable human suffering produced by these systems of racialized control. In this paper, we seize upon the opportunity to reveal what the ride would have us forget and explore how the park distills a complex, troubling history of racial oppression into an easily digestible emotional experience that avoids social or political critique. In researching this topic, the authors employed a visual analysis framework to decode the meaning and messages of the Flooded Mine within the surrounding sociohistorical context. To this end we visited the park multiple times to conduct a nonintrusive form of participant observation, taking dozens of photographs, video, and notes on conversations and the behavior of guests and staff occurring around us. Additional data were retrieved from website content and other marketing material such as the official, promotional website for

Silver Dollar City and Facebook pages dedicated to the park and the Flooded Mine ride. Data analysis of the written and visual material involved inductive, open coding to identify key themes. In addition, to contextualize the events depicted in the ride, we toured the now defunct Missouri State Penitentiary and visited local historical societies researching the practice of convict leasing in the Ozark region.

Branson, Missouri, Silver Dollar City Theme Park, and the Flooded Mine Ride

Opened in 1960, Silver Dollar City theme park is situated in the heart of the Ozark Mountain region in a quaint vacation destination known to conservative Christians around the country simply as Branson. Described as "hillbilly Las Vegas," today's vacationers flock to the neon-lit streets of Branson, Missouri, to enjoy a mix of Christian, country, and Broadway music and dancing, along with other "wholesome" leisure opportunities for families (Aubrey 1996; Ketchell 2007). Like Arizona's Old Tucson or Virginia's Historic Williamsburg, history is a central theme of the tourism industry of Branson, Missouri, offering visitors the illusion of historical authenticity through carefully reconstructed simulations of a bygone era. Today Branson is a thriving tourist destination with more than 7 million visitors annually (Branson Tourism Center, 2018); 2 million more than visit the Grand Canyon (National Park Service, 2018).

Responding to growing national interest in the history of the Ozarks, Silver Dollar City theme park was developed in the early 1960s and became one of Branson's hallmark attractions. Silver Dollar City is designed to simulate a late-nineteenth-century mining town and, in the words of an advertisement for the park, allows guests to "discover new fun in America's past." Situated along tree-lined walkways with employees in period costume, the park features restored nineteenth-century buildings, including an 1843 country house complete with live farm animals, an 1880s-era schoolhouse, and an 1849 chapel "dismantled log by log, lovingly rebuilt" as well as a replica town square, firehouse, county jail, and saloon. In these spaces, guests can attend Christian church services on Sunday, test their knowledge of history with faux schoolteachers, or watch skits depicting historical figures such as Carrie Nation of the Women's Temperance Union fighting to end drinking in the town. From the thrill rides with names like Outlaw Run to the hundreds of resident craftspeople demonstrating and selling their work as glassblowing, metalsmithing, candle making, and print shop artisans, nearly every aspect of the 61-acre park is designed to evoke a sense of the "reality" of small-town life in the Ozark Mountain region.

Developed in 1968 (Payton 1997), the ride officially known as "The Great Shootout in the Flooded Mine" is one of the oldest rides in the park and depicts the nineteenth-century practice of convict leasing (Figure 1). Belying the brutality of forced prison labor, guests are greeted with the ride's irritatingly catchy theme song whose lyrics are clearly meant to warn riders of the dangers that await them in the flooded mine:

Welcome to the mine. Yeah. Welcome to our toil. Welcome to the trouble 'neath the earth and soil. You'll sweat a little water, you'll sweat a little blood, and you might get out if the mine don't flood.

Once aboard the ride, riders use laser guns (added in the 1980s) to hit infrared-sensitive targets, which activate the animatronic features such as dumping a bucket of water on the convicts or causing "explosions" by striking "dynamite" boxes labeled "TNT" (Figure 2).

Some prisoners are depicted as tricksters relying on the chaos of the flood to escape their incarceration, but others are shown as terrified, frantic, and panicking (Figures 3 and 4). Still others are exhibited as simpleminded, fun-loving convicts who seem blissfully unaware of their impending fate, smiling and happily working as the water levels continue to rise (Figures 5 and 6).

Regardless of their demeanor, by exclusively presenting the dozens of faux prisoners in every single carefully crafted tableau as white, the Flood Mine obscures the most important historical aspect of convict labor—these systems were fundamentally *Slavery by Another Name* (as revealed in Blackmon's 2008 book title on the subject) or perhaps even *Worse than Slavery* (as Oshinsky's 1996 title posits).

The Reality of Nineteenth-Century Convict Leasing

The Thirteenth Amendment officially abolished slavery and involuntary servitude in 1865 *except* for those convicted of a crime, opening the door for the creation of convict labor systems to perpetuate the control and exploitation of African Americans. **Convict leasing**, Blackmon (2008:68–9) argues, "solved two critical problems for southern whites … terrorized the larger black population into compliance" and "significantly funded the operations of government by converting black forced labor into funds for the counties and states." Southern states essentially constructed a set of vaguely defined vagrancy laws known as Black Codes, which varied from state to state, but all effectively restricted the lives and activities of African Americans, such that walking at night after curfew, loitering, unemployment, or changing employers without permission could result in lengthy imprisonment and involuntary labor (Blackmon 2008; Mancini 1996; Oshinsky 1996). Judicial records indicate these race-specific violations and other petty criminal charges accounted for the massive incarceration of black men in the late nineteenth century.

Laws regarding convict labor systems varied over time and from state to state; they typically involved government officials leasing inmates to large corporations, small businesses, or even individual families (Blackmon 2008; Mancini 1996; Oshinsky 1996). Under these systems, convicts were forced through beatings and physical torture to labor either inside prison walls or in factories, farms, brickyards, lumber camps, or mines. Thus, in the early decades of convict labor systems, emancipated people could be forced to live on the very plantations that had held them captive as slaves. In fact, some states literally converted slave plantations into prisons (for example, Parchman Farm became the Mississippi State Penitentiary and Angola Farm became what is today the Louisiana State Penitentiary). In nearly every aspect, Blackmon (2008:57) suggests from "the acquisition of workers, the lease arrangement, the responsibilities of the leaseholder to detain and care for them, the incentives for good behavior—convict leasing adopted practices almost identical" to slavery, often with deadly consequences.

Accounts of Ozark prisoners who worked the factories and mines consistently describe the harshness of prison labor practices, which demanded increasingly high productivity with brutal consequences for failing to meet unreasonable work quotas (Kremer 1992; Rasmussen 2012). A prisoner could be placed on a starvation diet, beaten or lashed, and kept in a "dungeon-like isolation cell" without furnishings (Schreiber, Moeller, and Stout 2004:84). Missouri prisoners who worked in mines were subjected to squalid living conditions, poor medical treatment, scant food, and frequent floggings, and hundreds died as victims of explosions, falls, fires, floods, neglect, and disease (Rasmussen 2012; Reynolds 1982). Thus, on one hand, the representation of convict laborers in the Flooded Mine is imbued with similar types of spectacular violence, albeit greatly toned down and a lot less bloody, but still consistent with historical accounts of the punishing conditions of convict leasing (see Figures 7, 8, and 9). On the other hand, by making all the convicts White, the Flood Mine erases the African

American lived experience and fails to acknowledge that the history of convict leasing is a history of racialized violence.

Erasing the History of Racial Conflict and Oppression

The inaccuracies of race in the depiction of convict labor in the Flooded Mine stands in stark contrast to the many times that Silver Dollar City is touted on their website and promotional material as an "educational experience" and as a place "dedicated to preserving 1880s Ozark culture." Not only did the creators of the Flooded Mine salvage materials from an inoperative local mine, but they also unmistakably researched information about what convict laborers would have worn and how they were treated in the Ozark mines. Yet, the racism that shaped convict leasing was selectively ignored. While evidence supports that this omission was likely an overt attempt to obfuscate racial violence, the possibility that the park was simply unaware of this reality is equally disturbing. In either case, in the decades since the ride's construction in 1968, the park never felt the need to address this aspect of the ride, even when the ride underwent massive renovations in the 1980s.

To better understand how racial oppression—a disquieting, but nevertheless fundamental, aspect of convict leasing—could be so easily dismissed, we must keep in mind that *all* constructed representations from those located in historically themed amusement parks to well-respected museums are shaped by a variety of sociohistoric factors. In the case of Silver Dollar City, for example, their historical representations are linked to the "Branson Brand," a carefully constructed citywide image that blends the nostalgia for a simpler time with conservative Christian values (Aubrey 1996; Ketchell 2007). In line with the city's self-proclaimed identity, the amusement park presents a genteel, *sanitized* vision of the Ozarks' past, selectively revealing some aspects of historical accounts, but intentionally hiding others:

> Unlike mining towns in rowdy 19th century America, there are no "blind tiger" saloons dispensing moonshine, no knife fights, no mule trains driven by profane miners with poor personal hygiene. Silver Dollar City avoids a rigid, literal interpretation of the past while keeping a frontier-friendly atmosphere. (Payton 1997:9)

Moreover, a common trope one encounters in both Branson and Silver Dollar City is that of being a place of "hillbilly history" that "focuses on a white, rural, yeoman farmer who is backward and antimodern," a trope which Brandon (2013:48) argues is deeply embedded in the **collective memory** of the Ozarks, such that it "obscures much diversity in the region and, more importantly, absolves the region from its history of racial conflicts." By focusing almost exclusively on white settlers and largely ignoring the Ozarks' indigenous people, the Osage Indians, as well as African Americans, the park presents a heroic, uncomplicated past that avoids discussion of racial tensions and conflicts. In both remembering and forgetting, the park amounts to a small-scale demonstration of the wider phenomenon inherent in the construction of national identities, what Hamilton (1994:23) calls "**socially organized amnesia**." Silver Dollar City constructs their identity through displaying a version of history that necessitates inclusion (of whiteness, rugged individualism, entrepreneurial capitalism, etc.) and exclusion (of racialized violence, heteropatriarchy, class struggle, etc.). Hence, it should come as no surprise that their portrayal of convict leasing is both present in its basic form, but absent of the moral complexities incongruent with a simplified, nostalgic past.

By telling some stories and silencing others, Silver Dollar City can create the unproblematic history they desire, but in doing so, they are selling a particular type of nostalgia to their audience: **white nostalgia**, "a mode of remembrance celebrating a specific time and place in history by erasing narratives of racism and by whitewashing memories" (Adamkiewicz 2016:17). Silver Dollar City provides a lens of white nostalgia through which to view the Ozarks' past by downplaying the social, political, and economic implications of race and racism. Not unique to Silver Dollar City, white nostalgia narratives are featured in many other places. For example, in a study of historic plantation museums, Adamkiewicz (2016:13) focuses on how plantation websites use white nostalgia to "deny the history of slavery or mention it only as a side effect" and to celebrate a sanitized, genteel narrative of the antebellum South. Scholars frequently note how slaves and the institution of slavery are often marginalized, while the slave owner family takes center stage in plantation tourism (Buzinde and Santos 2008; Eichstedt and Small 2002; Giovannetti 2009). For example, Moldin, Alderman, and Gentry (2011:4) describe most planation tours as painting "vivid, detailed accounts of the lives of members of planter families while reducing enslaved people … to stock characters who receive less attention than the furniture and china owned by the master."

Silver Dollar City, like any peddler of history as entertainment, reimagines facts to fit a narrative, but they are also a capital venture, constrained in part by the limits of what is palatable to paying audiences. By obscuring some of our more shameful history, the park frees the rider from the burden of facing truths they are either unaware of or would rather forget. Thus, to the extent that they are correct in their assumption that we don't want to confront these issues, any conjecture as to why Silver Dollar City developers, or any for-profit historical destination, chose to whitewash history, cannot ignore the possibility of our own culpability, our own cultural unwillingness to confront shameful and reprehensible parts of our past. Of course, people may be willing to confront troubling aspects of the past, but simply not while on an amusement park ride. Some of the park attendees and area residents suggested that experiences such as this are to be enjoyed in the "spirit of fun," and feeling pity for the ill-fated convicts and thinking about racial prejudice, even the racism of the past, "takes all the fun away." After all, it is just an *amusement* park ride. While appearing reasonable on the surface, this argument neglects the agency involved in the deliberate choice to construct the miners as *convicts*. In lieu of simply making them free miners, when confronted with the complex issues associated with showing the actual race of convict miners, the park has never questioned the premise that it was perfectly acceptable to simply change their race. Moreover, they assumed that there would be no backlash, and as it turns out, they were right. Either the audience is unaware of the race switch or they accept the alteration, continuously reaffirming the park's white nostalgia.

In addition to a refusal to acknowledge the racial prejudice of the past, we must also question if this whitewashed representation of convict leasing is a refusal to confront the racial prejudice of the present. In other words, to what extent is the assumption warranted that black bodies in the Flooded Mine might simply be unpalatable to (white) audiences? Based on "stereotypes that were first articulated in the nineteenth century but hold sway over the minds and imaginations of citizens of this nation in the present day" of black men as "brute— untamed, uncivilized, unthinking, and unfeeling," bell hooks (2004:xii) argues mainstream culture perpetuates and inculcates a fear of black men. This cultural fear of black male bodies, although an unfortunate reality, could, at least in part, explain the historically inaccurate portrayal of convict leasing that we see in the Flooded Mine.

Conclusion

The Flooded Mine stands as a testament to our willingness to whitewash history in the name of entertainment and, in doing so, we miss the opportunity to show a more humanizing and realistic historical depiction. For example, around the same time convicts are supposedly causing trouble for the warden during a mine flood in the imaginary town of Silver Dollar City, resistance occurred with some regularity in real mines that utilized convict labor throughout the Ozark region. Taking just one historical example, the park could have *accurately* depicted an incident in 1877 that involved over two hundred African American convicts toiling in the Montserrat Coal Company mine in Johnson County, Missouri (Kremer 1992; Reynolds 1982). Essentially, when two men, set to be whipped for lying and being "loud and unruly," refused to exit the barracks, a riot resulted (Schreiber, Moeller, and Stout 2004). Thus, the ride could have celebrated resistance to oppressive forces and been an object lesson on what happens when we lose compassion for a group of people and allow the pursuit of profit to outweigh human life. Yet, coming upon such a ride within the carefully constructed park, or anywhere in Branson for that matter, would be shocking and could never exist without dismantling their commodification of white nostalgia. However, as conscientious consumers, we are challenged to examine such representations with **sociological mindfulness**.

In the nearly fifty years following the unveiling of the Flooded Mine, the United States has experienced unprecedented growth in prisons, filled disproportionately with people of color, resulting in some of the highest incarceration rates in the world. The racial oppression that defined nineteenth-century convict leasing still shapes the criminal justice system today in every aspect, from police targeting to disparate sentencing and rates of conviction. Private businesses and the state continue to take advantage of disenfranchised prisoners and profit from their labor. In this racially skewed, murky new reality of mass incarceration, we cannot blindly consume narratives that make light of the harsh reality of prison life, past or present, when we ride the Flooded Mine, tour defunct prisons, or watch Hollywood comedies about prison life. To be sociologically mindful requires us to examine the social world that creates these narratives and uncover what those carefully designed cultural memories say about us as a society (see, for example, Cacho 2012; Ogletree and Sarat 2015; Wilson 2008). Rather than dismiss these representations of incarceration as trivial entertainment, Brown (2009:120) argues these spaces are worthy of investigation because they provide "evidence about how citizens attempt, or fail to attempt, to understand and process the meanings surrounding punishment" and, in this case specifically, the austere intersectionality between punishment, confinement, and race.

References

Aubrey, Karen. 1996. "Sinning Without Consequences and Other American Dreams: Southern Theme Parks, Restaurants, and Vacation Cities." *Studies in Popular Culture* 19(2):39–47.

Adamkiewicz, Ewa. 2016. "White Nostalgia: The Absence of Slaver and the Commodification of White Plantation Nostalgia." *Aspeers: Emerging Voices in American Studies* 9:13–31.

Blackmon, Douglas A. 2008. *Slavery by Another Name: The Re-enslavement of Black Americans from the Civil War to World War II*. New York: Doubleday.

Brandon, Jamie C. 2013. "Reversing the Narrative of Hillbilly History: A Case Study Using Archaeology at Van Winkle's Mill in the Arkansas Ozarks." *Historical Archaeology* 47(3):36–51.

Branson Tourism Center. 2018. Branson, Missouri, profile. Available at: http://www.bransontourismcenter.com/articles/bransonarticle87.

Brown, Michelle. 2009. *The Culture of Punishment: Prison, Society, and Spectacle*. New York: NYU Press.

Buzinde, Christine, and Carla Almeida Santos. 2008. "Representations of Slavery." *Annuals of Tourism Research* 35(2):469–88.

Cacho, Lisa Marie. 2012. *Social Death: Racialized Rightlessness and the Criminalization of the Unprotected*. New York: NYU Press.

Eichstedt, Jennifer L., and Stephen Small. 2002. *Representations of Slavery: Race and Ideology in Southern Plantation Museums*. Washington, DC: Smithsonian Institution Press.

Giovannetti, Jorge L. 2009. "Subverting the Master's Narrative: Public Histories of Slavery in Plantation America." *International Labor and Working-Class History* 76:105–26.

Hamilton, Paula. 1994. "The Knife Edge: Debates about Memory and History." Pp. 9–32 in *Memory and History in 20th Century Australia*, edited by K. Darian-Smith and P. Hamilton. Melbourne, Australia: Oxford University Press.

Herschend Family Entertainment. 2017. Silver Dollar City Official Website. Retrieved June 15, 2017 (www.silverdollarcity.com/theme-park/Attractions/Rides/The-Flooded-Mine).

hooks, bell. 2004. *We Real Cool: Black Men and Masculinity*. New York: Routledge.

Ketchell, Aaron. 2007. "I Would Much Rather See a Sermon than Hear One: Faith at Silver Dollar City." Pp. 56–84 in *Holy Hills of the Ozarks: Religion and Tourism in Branson, Missouri*. Baltimore.

Kremer, Gary R. 1992. Politics, Punishment, and Profit: Convict Labor in the Missouri State Penitentiary, 1875–1900. *Gateway Heritage* 13:28–41.

Mancini, Matthew. 1996. *One Dies, Get Another: Convict Leasing in the American South, 1866–1928.* Columbia: University of South Carolina Press.

Moldin, Arnold, Derek H. Alderman, and Glenn W. Gentry. 2011. "Tour Guides as Creators of Empathy: The Role of Affective Inequality in Marginalizing the Enslaved at Plantation House Museums." *Tourist Studies* 11(1):3–19.

National Park Service. 2018. Grand Canyon Park Statistics. Available at: https://www.nps.gov/grca/learn/management/statistics.htm.

Ogletree, Charles J., and Austin Sarat. 2015. *Punishment in Popular Culture.* New York: NYU Press.

Oshinsky, David M. 1996. *Worse than Slavery: Parchman Farm and the Ordeal of Jim Crow Justice.* New York: Free Press Paperbacks.

Payton, Crystal. 1997. *The Story of Silver Dollar City: A Pictorial History of Branson's Famous Ozark Mountain Theme Park.* Springfield, MO: A Lens & Pen Production.

Rasmussen, Jamie Pamela. 2012. *The Missouri State Penitentiary: 170 Years Inside the Walls.* Columbia: University of Missouri Press.

Reynolds, Bruce. 1982. "Convict Labor: The Montserrat Experience." *Missouri Historical Review* 77(1):47–63.

Schreiber, Mark S., Laura Burkhardt Moeller, and Laurie A. Stout. 2004. *Somewhere in Time: 170 Years of Missouri Corrections.* Marceline, MO: Walsworth Publishing.

Wilson, Jacqueline Z. 2008. *Prison: Cultural Memory and Dark Tourism.* New York: Peter Lang.

Reading 5.3 Black Gazing in Digital Communities as a Form of Collective Activism

Andrea L. Moore

Keywords: Black gaze, podcasts, digital communities, Black feminism, Womanism, collective activism, Black Lives Matter, intersectionality, the *READ*, the *Friend Zone*, *Blavity*, radical healing

Not only will I stare. I want my look to change reality.

—bell hooks

Introduction

Over the past few years, academia has increasingly developed research exploring the role social media sites (SMS) have on influencing individual political engagement (Conroy, Feezell, Guerrero 2012) and recently, activism shaping SMS racial discourse (Velasquez, LaRose 2014). Many of these studies exploring SMS activism or network activism in its earliest stages disproportionately underrepresented the role of intersectional marginalized communities—i.e., working-class, urban populations when examining sociocultural and economic political action (Jarvis, Montoya, Mulvoy 2005). Upon onset, these exact studies would suggest the importance of race, gender, or ethnic identities as being determining factors influencing how one politically engages with SMS. Yet, their samples identified mostly white participants with inconclusive data on "nonwhite" demographic variables with a focus on individual social media page content (Quinn-Thomas Project 2015).

A 2015 report on *Social Media's Influence on Public Discourse in the Pacific Northwest* by Quinn Thomas and the DHM Research Institute found that,

> While platform user rates among white and minority populations are roughly even, non-white social media users place a greater emphasis on these platforms as alternative forms of news and information. This seems to be underscored by national data showing higher levels of distrust of mainstream news among African American, Hispanic, and other minority groups in the U.S.— and a lack of media coverage about issues that affect them. (Quinn-Thomas Project 2015)

Such marginalization is a historical continuation of mainstream press ignoring black narratives and invalidating a myriad of their lived experiences and cultures. This is the reason for the distrust. Black press was created in the early nineteenth century as an alternative source of documentation and education by informing communities about political, social, and cultural issues relevant to black people. Black millennials engage with black-centered social media platforms not only to find out the latest in news and politics, but to be a part of popular culture (Quinn-Thomas Project 2015). Black-centered press creates a collective consciousness speaking back to **anti-blackness**. According to the Council for Democratizing Education, **anti-blackness** is a two-part formation that both voids blackness of value while systematically marginalizing black people and their issues (https://policy.m4bl.org/glossary/). This definition focuses on educational systems by which anti-blackness is incorporated and therefore learned. Global debates around anti-blackness include immigration and ways in which "Anti-Blackness even affects how Black people view themselves and each other" (*Huffington Post* 2017).

Despite the continuation of mainstream news exclusion of black-centered narratives, innovative ethnographic scholarship explores the influence social media has on impacting activism among black youth (Smith, Pew Research Center 2015).

This chapter aims to explore alternative intersectional frameworks in order to better understand what civic engagement and activism look like within marginalized black communities. Instead of employing individual efforts and which it refers to as the "scholarly gaze on Black life" (Dance 2002), it is imperative to search for collective spaces for activism that center the black gaze when dealing with black cultural politics and action. The **black gaze** is inclusive intersectional spectatorship by black people who contextually read themselves into what they are seeing. It is related to what bell hooks refers to as the **oppositional gaze** when analyzing film: "a political rebellion and resistance against the repression of black people's right to a gaze" (hooks 1992).

The black gaze operates as the dominant lens that validates participatory politics. "Participatory politics as practiced online provide for greater creativity and voice, as participants produce original content using video, images, and text … interactive, peer-based acts through which individuals and groups seek to exert both voice and influence on issues of public concern" (Cohen and Kahne 2011) by centering the contextualization of blackness as it is represented in popular culture. It is a seed of the Afrocentric and oppositional gaze, yet the black gaze originates from the center, not the margins. Centering in—order to subjugate blackness—requires interrupting space, thoughts, and disrupting hegemonic normalizing and lends itself to an intersectional narrative that speaks to black resistance and power in popular culture.

For example, social media networking site research has underestimated the correlations between **collective activism** and the creation of what are known as digital communities. Collective activism as a form of action refers to action taken together by a group of people whose goal is to enhance their status and achieve a common objective (Wright, Taylor, Moghaddam 1990). Here action is based on engagement. Black millennials experiencing trauma from systemic forms of oppression, have organically shared their responses to everyday lived experiences on social media and together formed black digital communities that show their collective power in numbers. A **digital community** is "a virtual community whose members interact with each other primarily via the Internet. For many, online communities may feel like home, consisting of a "family of invisible friends" (Rheingold 2001). Digital communities engage in conversations that create cultural content. Many of the same members go on to create black **digital artifacts** such as black podcasts (*the Read, the Friend Zone*) and black media tech sites (*Black Twitter and Blavity*). All provide communal spaces for black people to exercise their oppositional agency and "respond to sociocultural forces in ways that contribute … to what activist, Shawn Ginwright refers to as collective well-being" (Ginwright 2010). Ginwright understands the historical impact of collective action as a conduit for well-being and offers the process of **"radical healing"** as a form of activism. The digital artifacts listed above engage subscribers in radical healing as praxis by acknowledging the collective trauma black communities face. Their content designs "contribute to the individual well-being, community health and broader social justice where young people can act on behalf of others with hope, joy and a sense of possibility" (Ginwright 2010).

Intersectional Inclusion in the Mattering of Black Lives

"We have to acknowledge what it is. Right now, we know that injustice is pervasive in our communities, anti-black racism is a fact, and it's affecting all aspects of our lives, and we need an intervention here."

—Opal Tometi

As a response to the Black Lives Matter revolution, black feminist epistemology has taken the lead in facilitating the intersectional influences of radical, womanist, and socialist traditions evident in shaping the movement's political discourse. The academic works of Patricia Hill Collins's *Matrix of Domination* are understood as an intersectional "sociological paradigm that explains issues of oppression that deal with race, class, and gender, which, though recognized as different social classifications, are all interconnected" (Collins 2001:11,12). This in turn is shaping how millennials engage in racial discourse via social media (Cohen and Jackson 2016).

The recent intentional response of black gazing online as a form of collective activism was made prominent by two of the cofounders of the Black Lives Matter movement. Two of the founders are queer women who speak vehemently against the historical violence that has plagued their communities. They uplift the lives of those who share similar experiences while speaking against the erasure of activism. In a public love letter to people black gazing online, Alicia Garza wrote the phrase as an affirmation, and Patrisse Khan-Cullors (2018), coauthor of *When They Call You a Terrorist*, created the hashtag that soon set the tone for a new form of collective activism known as #hashtagactivism. In reference to the use of Twitter's hashtags for Internet activism, **hashtag activism** "is the act of fighting for or supporting a cause that people are advocating through social media like Facebook, Twitter, Google+ and other networking websites" (Techopedia.) While it was a direct response to the non-indictment of Officer Darren Wilson for the murder of Michael Brown, it was used as a social tool on Twitter to create political action relating to black visibility and liberation.

> While some have derided hashtag activism as ineffective, there is no denying the impact of social media in raising awareness of social issues this year … As 2014 closed, stories and unrest regarding police brutality in Ferguson and other parts of the country led to big outcry on social media. These events weren't the origin of the #BlackLivesMatter movement; however, throughout 2015, the deaths of Sandra Bland, Freddie Gray, and more recently Laquan McDonald helped give the movement more momentum. #BlackLivesMatter was Tweeted 9 million times this year, and the hashtag that started on social media, has become a social calling card for social justice and racial equality activists across the U.S. (Morrison, 2015)

#HASHTAG ACTIVISM #ONLINE #BLACKLOVE #COLLECTIVE

#SMS Vernacular

- #BlackLivesMatter
- #SayHerName
- #BlackGirlMagic
- #NeverForget
- #BlackBoyJoy
- #IntersectionalityMatters
- #LemonadeSyllabus
- #Beyhive
- #BlackExcellence

- #FB
- #BlackTwitter
- #Tumbler
- #JasmineBrand
- #BYF
- #NotMyPresident
- #Wayment

SM Digital Communities, Journalism, Podcasts & Radio

- #Blavity-Bulletin | BLAVITY tech company for forward thinking Black millennials pushing the boundaries of culture and the status quo.
- #TheShadeRoom-Where honest opinions on celebrity, community and political news live.
- #TheREAD-PodCast Throwing shade and spilling tea with a flippant and humorous attitude
- #TheFriendZone-PodCast Dustin Ross, HeyFranHey & Assante explore where pop culture and zen living meet
- #Stage30-PodCast- Navigating through life at 30 without a blueprint
- #TheBreakfastClub-iHeart Radio Show The World's Most dangerous radio show showcasing hip hop culture and politics.

Figure 5.3-1. Examples of trending #Hashtags and Social Media Digital Communities.

Image created by Andrea Moore 2017.

The BLM movement is an undeniable social, cultural, and political revolution. The work of Black Lives Matter supporters is based upon lifting up marginalized black people affected by systems of oppression. Moreover, the #sayhername mantra is based on a lack of mainstream acknowledgment of the number of women who are also murdered by police. Kimberlé Crenshaw authored a disturbing report on the need for representation as it relates to black women affected by police terror. "Although Black women are routinely killed, raped, and beaten by the police, their experiences are rarely foregrounded in popular understandings of police brutality" (Crenshaw 2016). The platform of the movement for black lives is focused on an intersectional approach to fight for liberation and bring awareness to a variety of injustices related to systemic oppression.

> We believe in elevating the experiences and leadership of the most marginalized Black people, including but not limited to those who are women, queer, trans, femmes, gender nonconforming, Muslim, formerly and currently incarcerated, cash poor and working class, disabled, undocumented, and immigrant. We are intentional about amplifying the experience of state and gendered violence that Black queer, trans, gender nonconforming, women and intersex people face. There can be no liberation for all Black people if we do not center and fight for those who have been marginalized. It is our hope that by working together to create and amplify a shared agenda, we can continue to move towards a world in which the full humanity and dignity of all people is recognized. (M4BL)

This collective activism informs as it requires the development of critical intersectional consciousness related to movement for Black Lives (Crenshaw, 1991:1241–299). Since being exposed to the fundamentals of an intersectional approach of overlapping social identities and related systems of oppression, domination, or discrimination, i.e., race, class, gender, age, citizenship, ableism, and their impact on interpersonal disciplinary, cultural, and structural forces, it is being offered as an analytic tool for community accountability in popular culture. #BlackLivesMatter

De-totalizing Stereotypes in Popular Culture

"There is an element of Black Twitter that generates slang to not be understood by the establishment. It's an authenticity check."

—"W.E.B.B.I.E. DuBois"

New scholarship has resoundingly noted a large black presence on social media emphasizing the burgeoning work within the digital community known as Black Twitter (Clark 2012; Newkirk 2015; Kidd 2017). De-totalizing stereotypes in popular culture from the black gaze in digital communities cannot be discussed without giving credit to Black Twitter. Black Twitter users are aware of the unapologetic freedom digital platforms give them to speak on topics of interest in ways that Stuart Hall discusses in the audience reception theory, de-totalizing hegemonic perspectives. The *oppositional position* becomes the coded reading that opposes the dominant meaning and typically occurs when the viewer is aware of her own social location and position in society. The viewer "de-totalizes the message in the preferred code in order to re-totalize the message within some alternative framework of references" (Hall 1980). Identity politics come into play, and a whole new set of meanings for deciphering codes become available as representations and their actual significance are debated. This interaction of decoding is a mutual conversation on which Hall elucidates: "Communication has always been linked with the intersectionality of power and knowledge, creating ideas in which matter and meaning are worth struggling over in order to regain control over image (Hall 1980).

The "twitterverse" is where the black-centered press resides and is then used to share in a communal conversation on the latest in black news and politics and pop culture. Inadvertently, it would not be until Black Twitter's undeniable presence was "realized" by outgroup members (mainstream journalists) who came across a topic that was "trending on Twitter," that advertisers began documenting the power presence of black meta-networks' digital subscriptions centralizing intersectional political discourse in popular culture (Meeder, Manjoo, Sicha 2010). Although digital subscription may be of importance for advertisers to financially capitalize on, it is the visibility of the oppositional narratives in mainstream spaces that serves a far greater purpose for black gazing online.

The power of black narratives within SMS via Black Twitter was originally popularized by W.E.B.B.I.E. DuBois, also known as @fivefifths, and later added to the academic canon by activist scholar

Meredith Clark. They were among the first to legitimize the unprecedented impact that young urban black cultural producers ahead of the techno-cultural game were having when "breaking the fourth wall" in cyber space allowing followers to join in the conversations on race and class. The "majority of race-related posts on Twitter were tied to current events. The nearly one billion race-related posts on Twitter during this period touched on a wide-ranging set of subjects, including social activism, pop culture and personal experiences" (Anderson, Hitlin 2016.) Black Twitter as a digital artifact is the original source for organically creating the blueprint for collective activism on a SMS. While many try to discredit the creators of this digital form of collective activism, the denial comes as no surprise and is thereby refuted by its members.

> To date, mainstream news media texts describe Black Twitter from the perspective of the deficiency model of technology adoption among African-American users. Early media framing of the phenomenon has been met with open rebuke and disdain among Black Twitter users, who counter that "Black Twitter" is resonant of key themes of community, social movements and private/public conversation. (Clark, 2014:186)

Clark's intersectional research on the racial discourse developed by Black Twitter found that it constitutes an influential meta-network of communicators with the ability to impact news media coverage on black American life. Clark defines Black Twitter as,

> a temporally linked group of connectors that share culture, language and interest in specific issues and talking about specific topics with a black frame of reference. And when I say "black," that isn't just limited to U.S. blacks, but blacks throughout the diaspora, and I think a lot of what we see reflects on blacks just in the U.S., but I do want to make that distinction clear, that it is not just of a matter of what we talk about here in the United States. (Clark, 2014:186)

Clark acknowledges the black gaze as the dominant one taking place on Black Twitter. This gaze allows Pan African communities to unite and share in their likeness and celebration of transnational cultures. The sociological imagination connected with centering blackness is what validates not only the presence of Black Twitter members but their collective power. Black Twitter is known as a collective because of the way in which the community galvanizes to bring attention to social protest, wrongdoing, or celebrating, such as #BlackExcellence, #BlackGirlMagic, #BlackBoyJoy. This can range from political issues like #ImWithKaep to #45 stating in 2017, "Frederick Douglass is an example of somebody who's done an amazing job and is getting recognized more and more," to being attacked by the #Beyhive, a black father teaching his children #DaddyDuties, to selling #Reallbbjudy hair products to Cardi B stunting in #FashionNova. Black Twitter will collectively "READ" any individuals or other social media sites—i.e., Instagram, Facebook—for acts of misconduct or appropriation of black culture. Hashtag activism is often rooted in feminists' movements; for example, #BlackGirlMagic is important because it is in itself a mantra associated with forms of digital activism via the use of a hashtag and other imagery. #BlackGirlMagic hashtag has been used over 9,000 times on Twitter. The hashtag was created in 2013 by CaShawn Thompson to celebrate the beauty, power and resilience and positive achievements of black women. "I say magic because it's something that people don't always understand. Sometimes our accomplishments might seem to come out of thin air, because a lot of times, the only people supporting us are other Black women" (*Los Angeles Times*).

This form of activism is in response to the commodification of the black body in pop culture and is yet another example of anti-blackness. Historically, physical features associated with African women have been commodified and put on display as objects and seen as grotesque, not beautiful or desirable. Yet, nonblack women are celebrated and admired for consuming similar physical features by way of purchasing them.

Commercial culture has tried to emulate by way of appropriating aspects of black cultural art forms; i.e., jazz, blues, R&B, soul, hip hop, etc. A reoccurring example of this is when something new about black culture is witnessed by voyeuristic *"nonblack"* people and its influences are transmitted into the culture of social media. The Internet may falsely broadcast an image of who the original cultural producers are; e.g., "Kardashians created box braids." #LIES. The fetishization and co-optation of black culture is part of a historical trajectory of what happens when black cultural forms of praxis become visible in public spaces. Millennials are not here for it; while black gazing, they in turn use their access to press to counter such narratives.

It is essential to examine the correlations between black gazing during the rise of the Black Lives Matter Internet discussions and the increase in black digital communities using their mediums to collectively express their reactions. As access to the Internet via smartphones increased, so did techno-cultural responses to the Black Lives Matter revolution. For many black digital natives, this was the first social movement they have participated in, and technology garners them to participate in new forms of activism. According to W.E.B.B.I.E. DuBois, Black Twitter is "… a very vital support network. It's an organizing platform, as the only way that Black Lives Matter exists. It gets play in entertainment a lot. What you're looking at is a hybrid entertainment network plus a fully functional and self-aware civil-rights network" (Vasilogambros, 2015).

Since BLM became a hashtag, an influx of black people began to search for the latest news and information from social media communities that do not conform to the typical dominant (hegemonic) reading vilifying the movement. They look to social media digital communities for missing details about recent accounts of police terror. These communities allow space to question and speculate upon "facts" presented by major news networks. Black digital communities create safe places online for people to begin to radically heal simply by sharing and discussing the latest intel related to black-centered narratives covering the movement.

Social media digital communities are in fact shaping perspectives on racial discourse as they weigh in on how one may interpret the movement for black lives. One must understand that the social and historical trauma of legalized systemic oppression is what black people are actively responding to when they engage on social media. Often, the collective information shared on Twitter informs people so they can come to their own understanding of events as they transpire. Black-centered narratives often foster knowledge that develop into trending topics and go viral. Case in point, the question, did Mike Brown have his hands up prior to being killed by Officer Darren Wilson in 2014 was debated on social media, which influenced mainstream media to incorporate it. These conversations help shift hegemonic narratives and create space for oppositional perspectives. #HANDSUPDONTSHOOT

Importance of Mental Wellness Awareness

"We haven't finished learning the tricks to developing as people, and we don't have a lot of spaces for that. Which I feel like is why wellness is so very important."

—Assanté

Although research on black podcasts is still cultivating, important works have begun to construct the importance of the listener and the community at large. In 2007, Dr. Rochella Ford wrote about black radio, in which she reminded PR practitioners of its influential power in media and community campaigns. Dr. Ford may have tried to warn these constituents of their future loss in its 15 million listeners to alternative digital communities such as podcasts if they did not offer more creative licensing or social and political news content into their programming. (Ford 2007). This message may have been received with resistance. In 2015, communications professor Sarah Florini noticed the major switch of black radio listeners tuning in to black podcasts. Dr. Florini wrote about the evolution of TWIB! This Week in Blackness Networks as being a contemporary form of the "Chitlin' Circuit" in digital communities. Florini states, "I have chosen to use the term ''Chitlin' Circuit'' because of its historical connotations. It positions these podcasters and their audiences in a long history of racial exclusion and resistance and highlights the legacy of Black entertainers creating for Black audiences outside of the white gaze" (Florini, 2015:209, 219). Florini's work helps support a foundational understanding of the social importance of black gazing in "enclave black spaces" like the barber/beauty shop and how podcasts simulate such experiences in a digital age. Both scholars highlight the ways in which black listeners cherish communal ways of being when discussing political or entertainment news.

Black Twitter has created a digital community in which such conversations take place 24 hours/7 days a week. Black Twitter has established itself as a major news conduit for most all Black digital communities and artifacts. They refer to Black Twitter as a source for engagement in weekly social, cultural, and political topics that listeners are already familiar with. Each week the Twitter community is incorporated into the formatting of *the Read, the Friend Zone, Blavity News,* and *the Shade Room. The Read directly* addresses Twitter comments about the latest in pop culture. Like *The Friend Zone,* which corresponds to the previous episode's wellness topic highlighting what they found in "the Twitter Streets," giving shout-outs to the person who tweeted and sharing their comments. Each week media tech publishes the *Blavity Bulletin* where they highlight "the Best of Black Twitter," showcasing a full news report of the topic and its larger connection to black history. *The Shade Room* compiles the funniest Twitter memes for the week and posts the laughs and upliftment. All utilize Afrocentric performance patterns of call-and-response to directly connect with their audience.

Black digital artifacts like podcasts provide communal spaces to discuss weekly news and entertainment. The black-owned Loud Speakers Network (LSN) serves as an umbrella agency for a variety of multicultural podcasts related to black press. LSN was the brainchild of the late and great Reginald Joseph Ossé, aka Combat Jack. He originally worked in hip hop promotion but saw a future in digital media. *The Read* and *the Friend Zone* are part of the flagship shows for the Loud Speakers Network and "bring in 1.2 million listens per month and has regular appearances on Apple's Top Podcast Charts" (Lebeau 2017). These podcasts have become so popular that subscribers want to connect offline.

Two reviews on iTunes speak to the radical way in which LSN podcasts provide an intersectional space for black communal sharing. "There's not enough Black-led traditional media platforms or Black focused content on existing platforms. So, I get my *fix* from podcasts which are useful for hearing a diversity of Black thought as well as perspectives that aren't ordinarily considered Black topics"—J. Another reviewer wrote, "I listen to Black podcasts to stay abreast of current events, Black politics and hear Black pundits that are often my age. The many stories reinforce that I am not alone in many of the *struggles and experiences* that I have"—J2. Both reviewers implied a need to connect with a shared Black community while acknowledging that podcasts provide a space for "individual well-being."

The Read, currently in its fifth year, was rated the number 1 podcast on iTunes under *Comedy* within four months of airing. While it is categorized as a comedy, it also provides serious conversations about mental health awareness as a form of self-care. Kid Fury, a known YouTuber/gamer from Miami, and Crissel from Oklahoma share a synergetic energy that allows the listeners to become a part of a conversation among friends sitting together in the living room. The hosts are known as the biggest Beyoncé stans on the planet, and while they may read one for filth each week, they will never allow anyone to speak negative on Beyoncé or her children. Jay Z, on the other hand, well that's another story. *The Read* follows a weekly formula that employs a black gaze on how people process controversial politics and hot topics in pop culture.

The Read unapologetically includes an intersectional advocation for marginally oppressed groups with centering a black queer narrative. Due to black women activists doing the work of employing intersectionality as an analytical tool, they have laid the foundation for new dialogues to be more inclusive of nonbinary cis perspectives in pop culture, and *the Read* is a perfect example of this inclusion. They both curse like somebody's grandmother while often engaging in conversations that explore systemic racism, transphobia, how homophobic the hip hop community is, depression, and why "break up with him" is often their go-to advice.

Each show begins with Kid Fury reading a monologue from a famous Hollywood film or television show in which Crissel is *supposed* to correctly guess its title. They introduce themselves as an important black person uplifting their names and the work they are known for. Next, they highlight an example of #BlackExcellence and share with the listeners why that person should be revered. This often informs the listeners about the amazing contributions black people are making in society. Both hosts are often asked questions in the listener letters section about life as queer black folx and how to deal with politically different relatives. The second part of the show focuses on hot topics of the week that venture from pop culture, politics, comedy, to trauma. The very end of the show is when they share their weekly "read." This is the heart of the show, and their opinions on political topics are what separate their podcasts from the others. The hosts center a raw and uncut delivery when sharing their weekly read. In lieu of the social climate under #45, podcasts may serve as a form of digital collective activism for communities seeking support in healing and self-care opportunities. The interesting point being that the socialization act of listening to these podcasts are somehow providing healing in the form of self-care. While technology is known for decreasing #IRL human social interaction, the nature of the topics that arise on the podcasts speak to the human need of processing lived experiences with other humans. It is not just reading comments behind a computer; it incorporates an audio cultural component that listener can identify with. Thus, the podcasts provide an identification comfort as a form of healing via the sharing in a digital age. #ProtectYourMagic

Conclusion

Mainstream news media and pop culture have historically centered Eurocentric narratives, thereby stereotyping, marginalizing, or completely ignoring all "other" perspectives. Therefore, the need for black people to seek and create separate press outlets to affirm their visibility and lived experiences is not new but unfortunately still necessary.

Black gazing employs a sociological mindfulness that offers a cultural studies analysis with an emphasis on self-reflection as a response to people seeking black-centered narratives to thoroughly discuss not only the ramifications of the ideology of the BLM movement but being black in America in its totality. Digital communities and the artifacts they produce make up modern forms of black press. These communities provide not only space but information where members can learn about and interact with each other on topics relevant to black people's everyday lived experiences.

While black podcasts research still has a lot of room for growth, it is essential that we continue to document the social impact these podcasts have on providing black spaces for celebration and anybody interested in an intersectional approach when analyzing life, pop culture, and the media.

Review Questions:

1. What is the black gaze?

2. How are digital communities applying a black gaze?

3. What is collective activism?

4. What is hashtag activism, and how does it appear in digital communities?

Critical Thinking:

1. How do black digital communities cultivate a form of socialization in lieu of social and political climate?

2. How do Black Twitter, podcasts, and digital news sites that discuss black culture intersect and impact history and popular culture socialization?

3. How have black digital communities that focus on popular culture and the media responded to the triggering traumas enveloped in the Black Lives Matter movement?

Recommended Reading

Collins, Patricia Hill. 2001. *Black Feminist Thought: Knowledge, Consciousness, and the Politics of Empowerment*. 2nd ed. New York: Routledge, 11–12.

Cohen, Cathy J., and Sarah J. Jackson. 2016. "Ask a Feminist: A Conversation with Cathy J. Cohen on Black Lives Matter, Feminism, and Contemporary Activism." *Signs: Journal of Women in Culture and Society* 41, no. 4:775–92. doi: 10.1086/685115

Crenshaw, Kimberlé. 2016. "Say Her Name: Resisting Police Brutality Against Black Women." https://musingsofawomanist.files.wordpress.com/2016/10/e945e-merged_document_228129.pdf

Garza, Alicia. 2014. "A Herstory of the #BlackLivesMatter Movement." thefeministwire.org (http://www.thefeministwire.com/2014/10/blacklivesmatter-2/);

Hall, Stuart. 1980. "Encoding and Decoding." In *Culture, Media, Language*, edited by S. Hall et al. London, UK: Hutchinson–CCCS.

hooks, bell. 1992. *Black Looks: Race and Representation*. Boston: South End Press.

Kellner, Douglas. 1995. "Cultural Studies: Multiculturalism and Media Culture." In Gail Dines and Jean M. Humez, *Gender, Race and Class in Media*. Thousand Oaks, CA.

Smith, Mychal Denzel. 2014. "How Trayvon Martin's Death Launched a New Generation of Black Activism." *Nation* (http://www.thenation.com/article/how-trayvon-martins-death-launched-new-generation-black-activism/)

References

References include digital press, i.e., social media, podcasts, and online news/journalism/sites.

Anderson, Monica, and Paul Hitlin. 2016. "Twitter Conversations About Race." http://www.pewinternet.org/2016/08/15/twitter-conversations-about-race/Jarvis, Sharon E., Lisa Montoya, and Emily Mulvoy. 2005.

Clark, Meredith. 2012.

Clark, Meredith D. 2014. "To tweet our own cause: A mixed-methods study of the online phenomenon 'Black Twitter.'" University of North Carolina at Chapel Hill, 2014.4

Cohen, C.J., and J. Kahne. 2011. "Participatory Politics as Practiced Online Provide for Greater Creativity and Voice, as Participants Produce Original Content Using Video, Images, and Text ... Interactive, Peer-Based Acts through Which Individuals and Groups Seek to Exert Both Voice and Influence on Issues of Public Concern." Participatory Politics, New Media and Youth Political Action. Oakland, CA: YPP Research Network.

Cohen, Cathy J., and Sarah J. Jackson. 2016. "Ask a Feminist: A Conversation with Cathy J. Cohen on Black Lives Matter, Feminism, and Contemporary Activism." Signs: Journal of Women in Culture and Society 41(4):775–92. doi: 10.1086/685115

Collins, Patricia Hill. 2001. Black Feminist Thought: Knowledge, Consciousness, and the Politics of Empowerment. 2nd ed. New York: Routledge.

Conroy, Meredith, Jessica T. Feezell, and Mario Guerrero. 2012.

Crenshaw, Kimberlé. 1991. "Mapping the Margins: Intersectionality, Identity Politics, and Violence against Women of Color." Stanford Law Review 43(6):1241–299.

Crenshaw, Kimberlé. 2016. Say Her Name: Resisting Police Brutality Against Black Women. https://musingsofawomanist.files.wordpress.com/2016/10/e945e-merged_document_228129.pdf

Dance, Janelle. 2002.

Ford, Rochella L. 2007. "The Power of Black Radio Public Relations."

Florini, Sarah. 2015. "The Podcast ''Chitlin' Circuit': Black Podcasters, Alternative Media, and Audio Enclaves." Journal of Radio & Audio Media 22(2):209–19. doi: 10.1080/19376529.2015.1083373 ISSN: 1937-6529 print/1937-6537 online

Ginwright, Shawn. 2010. "Peace Out to Revolution! Activism among African American Youth," Young Nordic Journal of Youth Research, Vol. (18):1.

Hall, Stuart. 1980. "Encoding and Decoding." In Culture, Media, Language, edited by S. Hall et al. London, UK: Hutchinson–CCCS, 515.

hooks, bell. 1992. Black Looks: Race and Representation. Boston: South End Press.

http://www.latimes.com/nation/nationnow/la-na-nn-everyones-saying-black-girls-are-magic-20150909-htmlstory.html

Khan-Cullors, Patrisse, and Asha Bandele. 2018. When They Call You a Terrorist: A Black Lives Matter Memoir. New York: St. Martin's Press.

Kidd, Dustin. 2017.

Lebeau, Jordan. 2017. "How Combat Jack and Loud Speakers Network Disrupted the Podcast Industry." https://www.forbes.com/sites/jordanlebeau/2017/06/02/how-combat-jack-and-loud-speakers-network-disrupted-the-podcast-industry/#6fe607895374

M4BL. https://policy.m4bl.org/glossary/

Meeder, Manjoo, and Sicha. 2010.

Morrison, Kimberlee. 2015. "2015's Top 5 Social Activism Campaigns: #BlackLivesMatter, #LoveWins & More." Adweek, December 28, 2015.

Newkirk, Vann R. 2015.

Quinn-Thomas Project. 2015. http://www.quinnthomas.com/wp-content/uploads/2015/10/QUINN-THOMAS_SocialMedia-Insights_Final.pdf

Rheingold, Howard. 2001. The Virtual Community: Homesteading on the Electronic Frontier. New York: Harper-Perennial.

Smith, Aaron. "African Americans and Technology Use." Pew Internet and American Life Project. Pew Research Center. Retrieved July 15, 2017, from http://www.pewinternet.org/2014/01/06/african-americans-and-technology-use/.

Smith, Sean Dajour. .2017 "Non-Black People of Color Perpetuate Anti-Blackness Too." Huffington Post, March 6. https://www.huffingtonpost.com/entry/non-black-people-of-color-are-not-exempt-from-being_us_58bdb5dbe4b0ec3d5a6ba143Techopedia. https://www.techopedia.com/definition/29047/hashtag-activism

Vasilogambros, Matt. 2015. "Black Twitter in Capital Letters Black Twitter Phenom 'W.E.B.B.I.E. DuBois' Discusses the Meaning of the Social Media Powerhouse." Interview Vann R. Newkirk @fivefifths Atlantic, October 7. https://www.theatlantic.com/politics/archive/2015/10/black-twitter-in-capital-letters/433047/

Velasquez, Alcides, and Robert LaRose. 2014.

Wright, Stephen C., Donald M. Taylor, and Fathali M. Moghaddam. 1990. "Responding to Membership in a Disadvantaged Group: From Acceptance to Collective Protest." Journal of Personality and Social Psychology 58(6): 994–1003. (June 1990). doi:10.1037/0022-3514.58.6.994

Reading 5.4 Investigating, Explaining, and Exposing the Racial Past in the Present: The Possibilities of Documentary Film

Dana M. Williams and Mark Patrick George

Keywords: Cultural hegemony, racist nostalgia, culture of resistance

There has been an effort on the part of white Southerners to keep the Civil War alive.

—Black Civil War reenactor

Introduction

We made a documentary film called *Southern Discomfort* about Civil War reenactments in the US South, in order to understand the complicated relationship between historic Southern culture and the still-racialized present. The South—as well as the rest of the United States—has never had a true reconciliation for past racial crimes like Native American genocide and African slavery, and we wanted to explore what that looked like in our backyard in southern Georgia. This chapter describes the personal and political motivations for this documentary, how we made it, and how others can replicate this approach where they live.

Both of us are white male sociologists. We grew up with more than our share of privileges. But, in particular, we are white people who benefited from a racially stratified society today as well as racial atrocities of the distant past. We have white frontier settlers and slave owners, respectively, in our family trees. While this alone doesn't make us "bad people," we know that how we choose to deal with such pasts and our current privileges is what gives merit to our self-identities as antiracists and applied social scientists. We believe that being white antiracists places a heavy burden upon us to work with our white brothers and sisters to grapple with the legacies of white supremacy in America.

Living in Georgia reminds you of the past every day. It's a place with lots of Confederate flags—on truck bumpers, buildings, T-shirts, and flag poles. There are also thousands of landmarks named for famous slave owners and racial segregationists. These names adorn everything from university buildings and elementary schools to counties and city streets. The ubiquity of such symbols is difficult to miss, but it's surprising how often people do not—or choose not to—think too much about it. For most people, this legacy is either too difficult to confront or painful to remember, or is simply "just the way it is" or even rather wonderful (depending on who you are).

So we wanted to make a documentary about something important in our local area, something that intersects with our past experiences with antiracist campaigns and struggles. Those experiences are diverse and illustrative: Mark has been involved for over two decades in antiracist organizing in the Deep South, while Dana has worked in the movement to eliminate racist representations of Native Americans in sports team nicknames and mascots. Given our personal histories, we thought it appropriate to try to address these commonplace representations where we lived and worked as sociologists (and, of course, as people of conscience).

We also knew that a lot of racial content in the United States is submerged. It is taken for granted and justified as "normal," thereby leaving that given reality alone and unchallenged. In relinquishing responsibility for addressing our past societal crimes, people give power to the historical forces that shaped the past, thus allowing them to continue to shape the future. We saw that the South is filled with symbols of slavery, the Confederacy, Jim Crow, and its white supremacist past. These symbols are not only like water is to a fish, but they are also indicative of devastating wounds that continue to bleed and never seem to heal. They also speak volumes about the South's racial order, where white Southerners pay little to no concern about what these symbols might mean to the millions of black people residing in the region.

Most importantly, this history constitutes **symbolic violence**, wherein Confederate culture attacks the socially disadvantaged, often with their complicity (see Bourdieu and Wacquant 1992). The streets named after slave owners and founders of the Ku Klux Klan like John Brown Gordon and Nathan Bedford Forrest (such as in the town where we lived) are driven upon by people who rarely stop to think about this honor and lionization. People who drive on Interstate 75 pass by Confederate monuments with distorted information and clear secessionist sympathies, and statues to Confederate soldiers can be found in most Southern counties, typically on public lands. Confederate flags that have historically been used by racist terrorist groups and segregationists opposed to integration and the civil rights movement during the 1950s and 1960s continue to fly around the South, including above government buildings. The Southern plantation, which prior to the Civil War housed and tortured hundreds of thousands of enslaved Africans, has also been converted into countless tourist sites, and the name "plantation" adopted by businesses and neighborhoods. These practices are deeply offensive to the millions of African Americans who live in the South and must drive down these roads, visit these government buildings, and pass by these monuments and Confederate flags each day. Of course, black people are also expected to not react to the symbol's subliminal message of both black subjugation and the Confederacy's boastful racism. This Confederacy—at least as a concept and a white-led power structure—was never truly defeated, despite the Civil Rights Act of 1964 and "color-blind" claims to the contrary.

Mark, a Southerner by birth, had been surrounded by these symbols his entire life and has become frustrated by the refusal of his fellow Southerners to address them. He asked Dana to attend a local Civil War reenactment with him in the winter of 2012. This was a subculture we were only tangentially aware of, and we wanted to figure out why Civil War reenactors did what they did and why it was so important to them. It seemed to us that reenactments and Southern culture generally tended to support certain mythologies about the Civil War, and in some instances glorify an openly racist past. To be honest, we were confused as to why the long-lost descendants of soldiers would choose to reenact the bloodiest conflict in the United States—a civil war that resulted in well over half a million deaths—something that no other society in the world does for their own civil wars. In sum, the practice of "reenacting" this conflict struck us as more than a little odd and disingenuous.

We thought that making a film was a way to document our exploration of this phenomenon, piece together an interesting story, and to share our interpretations with others. We are also both advocates of **visual sociological methods,** a data collection approach that uses "photographs, film, and video to study society and the visual artifacts of a society" (Harper 1988:54). Both of us have had some limited experiences making films before, so we knew that video footage can emotionally reach people in a way the written word often can't. And, most importantly in today's society, film can reach wider and more diverse audiences, too. A renaissance in documentary filmmaking has occurred since the beginning years of the twenty-first century, and film not only can reflect the ongoing struggles for social and racial justice, but also influence those struggles, too. Additionally, film can frame how diverse audiences understand important issues of conscience and help inspire action on those issues (Whiteman 2004). Innumerable documentaries, such as *An Inconvenient Truth, Sicko, The Weather Underground*, and *The Fourth World War*, have had a considerable impact upon both popular political consciousness as well as the agendas of social movements. We hoped that our efforts would have a comparable impact.

Making the Documentary

We traveled to northern Florida on multiple occasions for the purpose of interviewing reenactment participants, event attendees, local public officials (including a city mayor and a Park Service representative), and other residents. Since we were particularly keen to explore racial dynamics, we also went out of our way to pursue interviews with African Americans from the area, including local civil rights activists. We filmed these interviews, explaining to our interviewees that we were making a film on the subject of Civil War reenactments because we wanted to know why people participate in this hobby and what it meant for those participants. We later combined these interviews with many other sources of data, including photographs and other video footage, publications and websites created by reenactors, analysis of relevant historical texts, and unobtrusive observation at events focused on Civil War reenactment. This data collection lasted for about two years—when we thought we were missing important elements in our story, we pursued additional interviews or data sources.

What we found was fascinating. We were able to access the subculture of reenactment, as well as the motivations for and daily practices at these events. We also discovered cognitive disconnects between reenactors' personal biographies—often as the descendants of Confederate soldiers—and the actual social histories of the South. The biggest dissonance pertained to white reenactors' knowledge about the history of slavery, the role of slavery upon the Civil War, and the impact of racial ideology upon historical values. This knowledge was often either limited, or simply incorrect and rooted in a variety of popular mythologies. The greatest of these misconceptions was that slavery had (as many interviewees alleged) "nothing to do with the start of the Civil War" and that it was a minor force in the United States at the time. Consequently, their own admiration for Civil War ancestors was overwhelmingly positive and framed in the—generally misleading and simplistic—argument of "defending the South from Northern aggression." In order to contextualize these reenactors' voices, we also interviewed historians who specialize in Civil War history, who explained the various ways in which reenactors tend to misunderstand that history. Specifically, the expansion of slavery into western territories was the major cause of the Civil War; slavery itself was a thriving institution that involved approximately 4 million human beings; slavery in the South was expanding up until the start of the Civil War; and the South was not "unified" in its fight against the US government but rather divided along economic class lines.

While we were not greatly surprised, it was impressive to witness how rarely these white reenactors considered the present-day impact of their reenactments upon black residents in nearby communities. Our interviews with black residents of the local area illustrated how blacks often feel such events are not only white-led and performed for a nearly exclusively all-white audience, but also that black people's concerns and offense were openly flaunted. During our interviews with public officials and organizers of these events, the concerns of black residents were either unknown or dismissed by the anecdotal listing of a name or two of black elected officials who had participated in the past (despite the fact that the overwhelming majority do not, with many referring to the reenactment as the "red-neck festival"). One black woman refused to let her face be filmed out of fear of white backlash against her, while others spoke of the ways in which the white community marginalized dissenting voices.

After collecting all these interviews and other data, we spent a lot of time talking about what we learned. We discussed how the story we uncovered in northern Florida reflected patterns and practices in other areas of the United States, and how best to tell that story. Our goal was to create a film best suited toward long-term racial restitution and reconciliation. It seemed that repeating mistruths and ignoring a painful past did not serve the local community's interests, but rather helped one group of people feel better about themselves to the detriment of another group. We believe that filmmaking should encourage people to think differently about familiar and mundane circumstances, as well as enlighten audiences about phenomena that they knew nothing about. To that end, documentary films can be liberatory and useful in pursuit of racial mindfulness and justice.

As we began assembling the film by computer (using nonlinear video-editing software), the importance of the topic of persistent racism and ignorance in Southern history was brought into sharp focus. The very week we began production, a white supremacist and ardent admirer of the Confederacy named Dylann Roof murdered nine black worshippers in a Charleston, South Carolina, church. As we (and the rest of the world) learned of his racial views and motivations, we realized that our documentary's main focus—on how Civil War reenactments get much of the important racial history incorrect—was not only a small part of a much bigger problem, but we also realized that this was a very important and timely story to tell.

Mark did the vast majority of the film's production, with research assistance from and in regular consultation with Dana. As we debated different options for releasing *Southern Discomfort* for viewing, we decided we wanted as many people as possible to watch it. Thus, even though working with an official distributor or film company may have helped to widen its reach (and maybe even pay us a very small royalty for our labor), we still understood we were just antiracist sociologists who are only semiprofessional filmmakers. Official distribution was a world we didn't quite understand, so we simply released the film on the Internet. This made it immediately available to many people who simply wouldn't have the ability, opportunity, or resources to see it otherwise (see Tryon 2009).

Possible Applications

A powerful way to frame such an investigation and project is as "people's history." The historian Howard Zinn (1995) authored a comprehensive American history book called *A People's History of the United States: 1492–Present*, which was a structural analysis of US society from important and usually overlooked vantage points. People's history flips the typical "great man" narrative wherein rich, powerful white men, often businessmen, famous politicians, or military leaders are the main actors in history and driving force in society. History textbooks often uncritically glorify such individuals and treat them as uncomplicated, heroic figures who were solely responsible for the prosperous contemporary society (Loewen 1995). In fact, such powerful individuals possessed their power at the expense of the less powerful, just as the wealthy possess their riches at the expense of exploited poor workers. To reverse the perception of these "great men" requires an investigation of the major and important contributions of less powerful groups, such as African slaves, Native Americans, workers, women, immigrants, and others. Zinn's approach mirrors what others have called "history from below" (Thompson 1966) and power elite analysis (Domhoff 2006), all of which aim to explore the nature of power in a particular area or within a certain topical context. Describing the atrocities committed by the powerful and investigating the agency of average people—particularly the role of social movements as the engines driving social change—is a "people's history."

To begin a local, racial people's history study requires focus. The first step is to investigate a general phenomenon of interest that may have also occurred in your region. For us living on the West Coast, this might be a focus upon the long history of Chinese exclusion. Understanding a topic's abstract context will suggest how to pursue its local manifestations. For example, in Chico, California, exclusionary efforts occurred in the 1860s and 1870s to disempower and remove residents of Chinese ancestry—efforts that mirror other locales like Los Angeles, Portland, San Francisco, or Seattle (Pfaelzer 2008). Organizations like the Supreme Order of Caucasians attempted to boycott, marginalize and intimidate, and in some cases murder members of the region's considerable Chinese population (Shover 1998). Thus, Chico is a microcosm of the broader racial dynamics in the American West that turned the state into a white-dominated space, with few racial competitors.

We both participated in an organization—which Mark founded with students from his Race and Ethnic Relations course (see George and Williams 2018)—that used the public telling of local racial histories to pursue racial reconciliation. This organization is called the Mary Turner Project and takes its name from one of the black victims of a white lynch mob's murder spree in Brooks County Georgia, which resulted in the brutal death of ten people. Some of the Mary Turner Project's work has included the creation of educational materials and a website about the lynchings, a regular commemoration event that involves descendants of the lynching victims, and the installation of an official state historical marker at the site of Mary Turner's murder. Additionally, the Mary Turner Project has sponsored public forums on slavery, the use of the Confederate flag, and racial hostilities during the election of President Barack Obama. These all required doing relevant research on local racial history, organizing events that would be relevant and interesting to the local community in south Georgia, and finding a meaningful way to connect those histories to the present.

By bringing your sociological imagination into local racial history, one can practice sociological mindfulness (Schwalbe 2008). There are many things around us—although hidden from sight or lying dormant in old historical records—that have lasting social and structural impact today. By making an intervention where we live, regarding something important, it will touch others and affect their lives. The histories of white supremacy affect people all around the globe and have very acute consequences in the United States. Thus, there are innumerable local histories of race to explore and dig up. These histories often have personal connections to our families and hometowns. The more intimate and immediate that history's impact upon you, the more passionate and committed you'll be when investigating it and explaining its importance to others.

There are also many sources of data, including secondary data sources, lying in government documents and reports, covered in local and regional newspapers, stories repeated in oral histories and passed down through family lore, as well as materials collected by libraries, special archives, and historical societies. In addition, new sources of data can be acquired by interviewing people about their experiences, perceptions, and ideas. For example, by choosing to research a local atrocity—like a lynching—you may find crucial information from many of the above sources. By collecting many different kinds of data from various sources, you can construct a nuanced, interesting, and rich understanding of that atrocity.

In order to further contextualize those specific stories, interviews with sociologists, historians, or other scholars can be a powerful asset. Not only can such experts explain things in helpful ways, but they can also provide the necessary insight to understand some of the collected data that does not otherwise make sense. Many kinds of experts can be found in local areas that are often very willing to speak about areas in their expertise. Also, when trying to publicly reconcile a painful moment in the racial past, seeking assistance from potentially "apolitical" scholars is a catalyzing experience for you and them. To be mindful means going beyond simply understanding a problem, by acting upon an understanding of that knowledge. Being able to openly and "on-the-record" challenge inaccurate public versions of history makes one a mindful person who *exists within* a historical moment, rather than being someone who just *knows about* such history.

All this research and data collection can be powerfully assembled together. For instance, videotaped interviews are compelling and can be combined with old documents, photographs, maps, and archived video footage to dramatically augment a film's content. In fact, film is a wonderful multi-format medium in that sense: it can combine together many different sources of data, strung together strategically by a director to convey those ideas to a wider audience who otherwise would not make the effort to explore those various data sources separately.

Organizations

- Mary Turner Project
- Equal Justice Initiative
- Take 'Em Down NOLA

Reflection and Critical Thinking Questions

1. What documentary film has most provoked your sociological imagination and helped you to be sociologically mindful? Why?

2. How have historical racial symbols been used where you live, and what are the different ways that people interpret them?

3. What local historical event occurred that could benefit from sociological mindfulness? What could you do to help others be mindful about it?

Further Readings

Cutting, Hunter, and Makani Themba-Nixon. 2006. *Talking the Walk: A Communications Guide for Racial Justice*. Oakland, CA: AK Press.

Tolnay, Stewart E., and E.M. Beck. 1995. *A Festival of Violence: An Analysis of Southern Lynchings, 1882–1930*. Urbana: University of Illinois Press.

Williams, David. 2005. *A People's History of the Civil War: Struggles for the Meaning of Freedom*. New York: New Press.

Websites

Known Georgia Lynching Victims database: http://www.maryturner.org/database.htm

Was the Civil War About Slavery? (video): https://www.youtube.com/watch?v=pcy7qV-BGF4

Sundown Towns: https://sundown.tougaloo.edu/sundowntowns.php

Found SF: http://www.foundsf.org/index.php?title=Category:Racism

References

Bourdieu, Pierre, and Loïc J.D. Wacquant. 1992. *An Invitation to Reflexive Sociology*. Chicago: University of Chicago Press.

Domhoff, G. William. 2006. *Who Rules America? Power, Politics, and Social Change.* New York: McGraw-Hill.

George, Mark Patrick, and Dana M. Williams. 2018. "Teaching About Race and Social Action by 'Digging Up the Past': The Mary Turner Project." *Race, Ethnicity, & Education* 21(3):319–34.

Harper, Douglas. 1988. "Visual Sociology: Expanding the Sociological Vision." *American Sociologist* 19(1): 54–70.

Loewen, James W. 1995. *Lies My Teacher Told Me: Everything Your American History Textbook Got Wrong*. New York: Simon & Schuster.

Pfaelzer, Jean. 2008. *Driven Out: The Forgotten War Against Chinese Americans*. Berkeley: University of California Press.

Schwalbe, Michael. 2008. *The Sociologically Examined Life: Pieces of the Conversation*. New York: McGraw-Hill.

Shover, Michele J. 1998. *Chico's Lemm Ranch Murders and the Anti-Chinese Campaign of 1877*. Chico, CA: Association for Northern California Records and Research.

Thompson, E.P. 1966. "History from Below." *Times Literary Supplement*, April 7: 279–80.

Tryon, Chuck. 2009. *Reinventing Cinema: Movies in the Age of Media Convergence*. New Brunswick, NJ: Rutgers University Press.

Whiteman, David. 2004. "Out of the Theaters and Into the Streets: A Coalition Model of the Political Impact of Documentary Film and Video." *Political Communication*, 21:51–69.

Zinn, Howard. 1995. *A People's History of the United States: 1492–Present*. New York: HarperPerennial.

Reading 5.5 The Denigrated Other: Popular Representations of Afro-Latinos

Christian Noakes, Georgia State University

Popular commodities serve primarily as indicators of the socio-psychological characteristic of the multitude. By studying the organization, content, and linguistic symbols of the mass media, we learn about the typical forms of behavior, attitudes, commonly held beliefs, prejudices, and aspirations of large numbers of people.

—Leo Lowenthal (1968, xii)

Abstract

Popular culture tends to provide ideological support for socially and politically contingent inequalities. While mainstream collective perceptions of denigrated groups may be a product of systems of domination—e.g., ethno-racial, gendered, etc.—they can also help reproduce these structures by naturalizing disparities. Popular representations of people classified as Afro-Latino/a in Latin America reveal widespread ethno-racial beliefs. Given the wide reach of communication, they can also function as a reproductive instrument for these racialized assumptions and thus the social and symbolic domination which such assumptions support. Racial imagery created and propagated by cultural producers reinforces and informs the racial hierarchies from which such representations emerge. This reflexivity helps to sustain "the legitimate principle of vision and division" (Bourdieu 1989) of class and ethnicity in Latin America. The treatment of Afro-Latinos in popular culture and mass media plays an integral role in the subordination of the group in Latin American society.

Keywords: Afro-Latino/a, mass media, cultural production, social vision, racial imagery, popular commodity, mulato/a, mestizo

Chapter Goals

- Learn about popular conceptions of blackness and national and cultural identifies that are largely taken for granted in Latin America.
- Achieve a better understanding of the dialectical relationship between representation and power and the role of cultural production in social reproduction.
- Acquire a critical gaze to analyze implicit ideologies in popular culture.

While this paper focuses on Afro-Latinos, many of the same arguments and observations can be made of Latin America's other racialized subordinate group—indigenous populations. This shared experience is addressed in several sources that reference both black and indigenous populations. However, it has been observed that Afro-Latinos have generally been less successful than indigenous populations in gaining recognition and subsequent social, political, and economic gains (Hooker 2005). This paper looks at the popular assumptions of what it means to be black—i.e., essential character, behavior, and "place" in society—that pervade much of Latin American media and how such representations function to reinforce, reproduce, and actualize *social vision and division*.

The categorization of "Afro-Latino/a," while defined differently in many countries, has historically been the lowest and most reviled symbolic space in Latin America. This subordinate position has its roots in the slave economy of the "New World." Due largely to the fact that European contact wiped out large portions of indigenous populations and stirred rebellions—that, when successful, were due in part to native familiarity with the terrain—Africans became the predominant and "ideal" slaves. While the enslavement of Africans was initially economically—rather than ideologically—motivated (Fields 1990), the view of slaves as inherently different and dishonored (Patterson 2001) attached itself to a racialized vision as the Spanish and Portuguese slave systems developed. Just as in the United States, blacks in Latin America have been historically constricted in status and potential by the view of black foreignness and inferiority. This view has continued to justify and naturalize inequality. The consequence of this worldview has been the material and symbolic marginalization and impoverishment of Latinos perceived as belonging to an Afro-descended category. The popular stigmatization of Afro-Latinos influences the continuing trend of poverty and extreme inequality observable throughout much of the region. In creating products that ignore Afro-Latinos or depict them in a different, and often inferior, light than a perceived collective national or Latin American identity, the media is one of the most far-reaching and potent institutions of cultural production when it comes to reinforcing and reproducing a *sociodicy,* or justification myth, that serves to naturalize social relations and structures. Its depictions are often acts of symbolic violence (Bourdieu 1989) toward Afro-Latinos that have the consequence of naturalizing—and thus perpetuating—the socially constructed denigrated position in which they are confined. An ideological *stigma-theory* (Goffman 1963), which is defined through popular discourse and depicted in the media, serves to justify a perceived inferiority that has the consequence of limiting the life chances of those classified as black in Latin America.

A Popular Mythology

Transcendence Narrative

Today countries throughout the region often boast about how they do not have "race problems" like the United States. Such popular narratives include the belief that racial mixture has created a transcendent, or "cosmic," national race (as is the case in Mexico) or that while old racial divisions do exist, they are inconsequential due to a "racial democracy" that transcends racial antagonism, exploitation, or dehumanization (as is the case in Brazil). In official and popular discourse, Latin America sees itself as escaping the patterns of ethno-racial prejudice and discrimination that plague its northern neighbors (Hernandez 2013). However, such claims are based on the false assumption that all systems of ethno-racial domination adhere to the anomaly that is the American system. It is, however, true that Latin America does not have a history of massive race riots targeted at the black population as is the case with the United States. This may be in part due to the fact that Latin American ethno-racial structures that determine who is or is not black are far less rigid than in the United States, where a "one-drop rule" defines a black person as someone with any known African ancestry (Davis 1991, 5). While no longer enforced by law, the one-drop rule in the United States eliminated intermediate or gradational categories. Rather than a descent-based criterion, Latin American countries tend to determine an individual's ethnicity by relying more heavily on phenotype and various sociocultural markers (language, education, class, etc.). Latin American countries also have gradational systems with several intermediate categories rather than a rigid black/white dichotomy. This is due partly to the fact that miscegenation in popular and official discourse is seen as improving the non-European population instead of degrading a supposed white purity like in the United States and elsewhere. These characteristics have meant that individual mobility in the racial hierarchy is at least a possibility for the individual. However, none of these structural differences justify claims that blacks are treated as equals in Latin American society. It only means that some people/families can strategize a way out from the denigrated position of "black." In his comparative study of the United States and Brazil, Carl Degler (1971) calls this the "mulatto escape hatch (225)." The ability to "escape" an ethnic classification suggests in itself a popular view in which such designation is inferior and therefore should be transcended whenever possible. The fact that understandings of "race" are different from—and far less rigid than—US racial discourse does not mean that perception and categorization along racial lines is not highly consequential.

Blackness Portrayed

In many countries the myth of transcending racial antagonism is paired with a tendency to erase African contributions to national identities. This can be seen clearly when one looks at Latin American media. A 2011 study on *telenovelas* found that white people were overrepresented while people of African descent were underrepresented when compared to actual populations (Rivadeneyra 2011, 216). This trend holds true in countries where a relatively low percentage of the population is assigned an African-descended classification as well as in countries where they make up a significant percentage of the population. The practice of black erasure also persists in most other popular media formats in Latin America. Misrepresentation via the prevalence of white faces and the lack of people of color can be seen in television, film, magazines, and advertisements, thereby playing an essential role in the continued valorization of "whiteness" and the denigration of "blackness."

One of the most pervasive forms of ethno-racial domination acted out by Latin American media against Afro-Latinos is the clear demarcation and thus alienation of the latter from the rest of society. A common example of this strategy is the portrayal of inherent class differences between black people and perceived collective national and regional identities. Given the prevalent representations of blacks as "childish" or irresponsible—such as Mexico's Memin Pinguin (see Figure 1)—it comes as no surprise to find that blacks are also more likely to appear in the media as being poor or lower-class. In her research, Rocio Rivadeneyra (2011) found that Afro-Latinos are also often overrepresented as wealthy characters in *telenovelas*. In contrast, most of the non-African characters are portrayed as middle class (218). While Rivadeneyra had not anticipated this finding, it is consistent with the portrayal of Afro-Latinos as inherently poor. Such depictions of blacks in the extremes of society clearly delineate a middle-class "us" (white/*mestizo*) from a lower- and upper-class "them." It is common for nations and cultures to construct their collective identities around their middle-class populations. In other words, nations prefer to present and even perceive themselves as dignified (not poor) as well as modest (not rich). This suggests that the depiction of Afro-Latinos as disproportionately both rich and poor shows audiences the "alien within," which in turn perpetuates the tendency toward black erasure throughout Latin America in both the media and other fields. Such depictions suggest blacks are not as "Latino" as other groups. As the following testimony from L.G. Murillo-Urrutia, the former governor of Choco, Colombia, illustrates, blacks are also often seen as foreign regardless of shared cultural characteristics.

> In my own Latino neighborhood my wife was seen as Latina and I was assumed to be either from the African continent or African American, particularly when I had not yet spoken. Even when I spoke in plain Spanish people still assumed that I learned Spanish as a second language somewhere in Latin America. Interestingly, my kids with lighter complexions who speak fluent Spanish and English are always assumed to be Latinos. (32)

This statement attests to the firm boundary imposed on Afro-Latinos in an otherwise fluid and gradational system of ethno-racial classification. Depicting a black identity that is explicitly different and foreign to a collective, middle-class *mestizo* identity is essential in the symbolic and social exclusion of Afro-Latinos.

The representations of those perceived as "black" goes further than to suggest partial citizenship. Rivadeneyra's (2011) study of *telenovelas* also found that black characters are also nearly four times as likely to be wearing clothes that depict them in a hypersexualized manner (216). Black women in particular are often objectified in this way by Latin American media in part because of the intersectionality of being both black and female—two categories traditionally made subordinate throughout Latin America. According to Rivadeneyra, "being seen as sexual objects is one way in which individuals of African or Indigenous descent are subjugated and given positions of little power in society (218)." Portraying Afro-Latina/os in this fashion is an act of symbolic violence that reinforces the association of blackness with lowliness. This subjugation, like that of the various forms of differential representation, is filtered through television, advertising, and other forms of media into the public psyche, which then preserves the racialized hierarchy throughout Latin America.

The objectification of black women is often more complex than the suggestion of a link between African heritage and eroticism. Were this the case, the desire for a black sexuality would contradict and thus undermine the racialized monopoly of honor. Therefore, the representation of Afro-Latinas as highly desirable sexual objects often requires making them appear whiter. Beauty supplies, such as whitening creams and hair straighteners meant to make Afro-Latinas more "European," are often used on black women when appearing on television or in advertisements. It is this "whitening" that creates the image of Afro-Latinas as highly desirable and hypersexualized objects for the dominant culture.

> [T]he *mulata* is attractive because the hypersexual imagery around black women is tempered by the idea that the *mulata*—understood in the context of ideologies of mixture in these countries—is seen to be taming herself, morally improving herself, bringing herself closer to the heart of the dominant society. (Wade 2013, 188)

The selling of Afro-Latinas as sexual objects of desire often involves "subduing" African traits so as to make a more enticing "product." It is not the full "Europeanization" of Afro-Latinas that makes them most desirable as this is not possible; unlike the boundaries between other popular or official categories, the category of "white" is based on a supposed purity of descent and therefore nonporous by comparison. What makes the representation of Afro-Latinas as hypersexualized objects so powerful is that "whitening" suggests both an aesthetic "improvement" and an obedience. The former makes them desirable, while the latter makes objectification socially acceptable. The "whitening" of Afro-Latinas serves to justify sexual desire and objectification while maintaining ethno-racial boundaries that associate African traits with ugliness and a general lowliness. As Frantz Fanon (1952) pointed out long ago, the Manichean dichotomy of whiteness and blackness is internalized in the psyche of many Afro-descendants, who then participate in promoting the glorification of whiteness—an act of self-defamation that entails psychological and physical damage (see Figure 2).

Lived Realities

Class and Citizenship

Let us now consider the positions Afro-Latinos occupy in social space in order to better understand the potential consequences of such "popular commodities" and the dialectical relationship between the material and symbolic subjugation. Both their lack of representation and their misrepresentation as inherently poor or "alien" naturalize the disproportionately high rates of poverty among Afro-Latinos. This is in part due to the popular view of the "Latino identity" as being non-African, which suggests that people designated "black" are not entitled to the same rights as other citizens. The depiction of Afro-Latinos as "outsiders" or the "other" naturalizes racial disparities in collective social, political, and economic rights. In the case of depicting blacks as lower-class, it suggests that poverty is an inherent condition of such classification. As Tanya Kateri Hernandez (2013) states, "[r]acial stereotyping … facilitates the exclusion of Afro-descendants because racialized views have become so embedded in the social fiber of Latin American societies that the subordinated positions of Afro-descendants in the labor force is naturalized and viewed as logical (81)." It is thus taken for granted that they are naturally inclined to be disproportionately poorer than other groups. The extreme racial disparities throughout Latin America suggest that poverty is the social norm for Afro-Latinos. For instance, in 2005, 80 percent of Afro-Colombians lived below the poverty line and 98 percent of the nation's black communities lacked basic utilities, while only 6 percent of white communities suffered from similar deprivation (Hernandez 2013, 75). Such disparities can be observed throughout the region. The UN Development Program's 2010 Regional Human Development Report for Latin America and the Caribbean found the proportion of Afro-Latinos and indigenous people living on less than a dollar a day was roughly twice that observed for European descendants in most Latin American countries (36). While income distribution in Latin America is responsible for some of the worst class inequalities in the world, the distribution of wealth and resources along ethnic lines is even more drastic (Dulitzky 2001, 41). The overrepresentation of Afro-Latinos as poor naturalizes the disproportionate poverty that results from a tradition of discrimination. The same can be said with regard to the overrepresentation of wealthy Afro-Latinos (Rivadeneyra 2011). Racialized class distinctions delineate "black" and "Latino" identities. Such depictions carry with them the power to naturalize inequality and discrimination and therefore reproduce the racialized social hierarchy.

Commodification of Flesh

Just as class-based representations of Afro-Latino/as "alien" create conditions in which it is acceptable that they are denied equal rights as citizens, the popular depiction of blacks as purely sexual beings or objects has influenced social relations toward the realization of such distorted visions. In Brazil, discourses of black hypersexuality are internalized by locals and tourists alike to make places such as Salvador "sites of desire" for sex tourism (Williams 2009). The representation of Afro-Latinas as objects for sexual domination shapes popular categorical assumptions and therefore creates highly racialized social and economic interaction. As one Afro-Brazilian woman testifies:

> My own color draws attention in Pelourinho. I go to Pelourinho with no makeup, with jeans, tennis shoes, and clothes that cover my body. … Just by being a black woman, you become a tourist attraction. [The tourist] approaches you, thinking you're a sex worker—even the domestic tourist who comes on a business trip. (Williams 2013, 45)

This shows a strong association between being categorized as black and being hypersexualized to the point where an individual's intended signals of modesty (choice of dress) go unnoticed or are disregarded. In Brazil, Colombia, Costa Rica, Cuba, and Venezuela, this has driven many Afro-descendant women to become sex workers, as it is one of the few sectors in which they are not customarily excluded and can earn higher wages than in other informal sectors (Hernandez 2013, 81). This demand has its origins in the perception of both nationals and tourists—which is itself nourished by popular depictions—in which black women are reduced to sexual objects. In seeing these women as hypersexualized objects, the behavior directed toward them actualizes this objectification. Therefore, the hypersexualization of Afro-Latinas (as appears to be the case with other prejudices directed at Afro-Latinos) becomes a self-fulfilling prophecy in that the representation/prejudice of black women as highly sexualized objects often means they are treated as such. This can take the form of racially motivated sexual harassment or highly racialized sex industries.

Conclusion

In closing, images of black inferiority, foreignness, and hypersexuality are vital instruments in the reification of a public identity of Afro-Latinos via delineation and denigration. As a reflexive manifestation of what Lowenthal (1968) refers to as a "popular commodity," symbolic violence in the form of racialized assumptions in Latin American media serve to, as Bourdieu (1977) says, create *the world of tradition experienced as a "'natural world'"* (164). The stereotypical representations of Afro-Latinos help confine blacks to denigrated positions in social space because social agents then assume that such representations reveal the essential identity of blacks as inevitably or inherently subordinate. As a result, Afro-Latinos are overrepresented in the informal economies—especially sex work and other low-paying jobs—of most Latin American countries with available data (Gradin 2011), thus perpetuating the patterns of poverty and sexual objectification that are normalized by the dominant social vision. Collective actions toward Afro-Latino/as are informed by popular myths which affect the availability of resources and life chances so as to mirror consumed racial imagery. The inherently foreign and the hypersexualized are perceptive agreements that serve to objectify and restrict the rights of Afro-Latino/as. In a sense, this is to begin to make the unreal real via the misrecognition of symptoms of inequality as justification for inequality. Therefore, both the lack of representation and the misrepresentation of blacks in Latin American mass media is one of the more subtle and taken-for-granted forms of ethno-racial domination exercised against the region's black population. The media, in wielding such power, is a fundamental institution in realizing and maintaining the dominant racial vision of Latin American society.

Discussion Questions

1. How do widespread assumptions around race and/or gender inform the construction of place? What are some examples of racialized and/or gendered space? Are these places exclusive to a subordinate group, or do dominant groups have regular access? Do these places serve the needs/interests of subordinate or

dominant groups? What is the role of pop culture (television, film, advertising, etc.) in defining and reinforcing racialized spatial barriers?

2. Is the "mulatto escape hatch" a means of undermining or solidifying racial subordination?

3. What messages do the Memin Pinguin covers presented above convey about blackness and cultural assumptions of racial tolerance?

4. In addition to the above example of Sammy Sosa, what other examples of internalized denigration of blackness/black people are there in popular culture?

5. Who has the power to produce racialized images and meaning? What are some ways these images are consumed on a mass scale?

Research Questions

1. There are several examples of popular culture used as a means to reinforce hierarchies (racial, etc.). Can popular culture be used instead to undermine, expose, or dismantle these hierarchies, or does the power structure around the production of meaning presuppose its function in maintaining relations of power?

2. What sort of racial imagery is in US popular culture? How do these images relate to the material and symbolic positions of different groups? Do messages of blackness vary between US and Latin American culture?

3. What sorts of Muslim images are most prevalent in US popular culture? How do these images relate to the position of Muslims in our society and US presence in the Middle East? How do racial images fit into popular understandings of Islam?

4. The above focused on the cultural production of dehumanizing or degrading racial imagery. What are some images of blackness that are either positive (culture of affirmation) or defiant (culture of resistance)? Are these representations prevalent in pop culture?

Additional Links

Stuart Hall's Representation and the Media Lecture (Kanopy)

https://www.kanopy.com/product/stuart-hall-representation-media

Al Jazeera clip on Stuart Hall, representation, and contestation

https://www.youtube.com/watch?v=FWP_N_FoW-I

Edward Said on Orientalism

https://www.youtube.com/watch?v=fVC8EYd_Z_g

Al Jazeera clip on Edward Said and Orientalism

https://www.youtube.com/watch?v=4QYrAqrpshw

Class Dismissed Documentary

https://www.youtube.com/watch?v=by9SEhBPrJY&t=2s

Suggestions for Further Reading

Dorfman, Ariel, and Mattelart, Armand. 1971 (1991). *How to Read Donald Duck: Imperialist Ideology in the Disney Comic*. Chile.

Fanon, Frantz. 1952. *Black Skin, White Masks*. New York: Grove Press.

Hall, Stuart. 1986. "Gramsci's Relevance for the Study of Race and Ethnicity." *Journal of Communication Inquiry* 10(5).

Hall, Stuart. 1997. "Representation and the Media." Lecture Transcript. Retrieved from https://www.mediaed.org/transcripts/Stuart-Hall-Representation-and-the-Media- Transcript.pdf.

Monk, Ellis P. Jr. 2016. "The Consequences of 'Race and Color' in Brazil." *Social Problems* 63:413–30.

Patterson's "Taking Culture Seriously: A Framework and African American Illustration." Pp. 202-218 in *Culture Matters: How Values Shape Human Progress*. Lawrence Harrison and Samuel Huntington, 2000, New York: Basic Books.

Roth-Gordon, Jennifer. 2017. *Race and the Brazilian Body: Blackness, Whiteness, and Everyday Language in Rio de Janeiro*. University of California Press.

Said, Edward. 1979. *Orientalism*. New York: Vintage Books.

Wacquant, Loïc. 1997. "For an Analytic of Racial Domination." *Political Power and Social Theory* 11:221–34.

References

Bourdieu, Pierre. 1989. "Social Space and Symbolic Power." *Sociological Theory*, Vol. 7, No. 1 (Spring), 14–25.

Bourdieu, Pierre. 1977. *Outline of a Theory of Practice*. Cambridge, UK: Cambridge University Press.

Davis, F. James. 1991. *Who Is Black? One Nation's Definition*. University Park: Pennsylvania State University Press.

Degler, Carl N. 1971. *Neither Black nor White: Slavery and Race Relations in Brazil and the United States*. New York: Macmillan.

Dulitzky, A.E. 2001. "A Region in Denial: Racial Discrimination and Racism in Latin America." *Beyond Law* (8):85–107.

Fanon, Frantz. 1952. *Black Skin, White Masks*. New York: Grove Press.

Field, Barbara. 1990. "Slavery, Race and Ideology in the United States of America." *New Left Review*, 181.

Goffman, Erving. 1963. *Stigma: Notes on the Management of Spoiled Identity*. New York: Simon & Schuster.

Gradin, Carlos. 2011. "Occupational Segregation of Afro-Latinos." Society for the Study of Economic Inequality. *Universidade de Vigo*.

Hernandez, Tanya Kateri. 2013. *Racial Subordination in Latin America: The Role of the State, Customary Law, and the New Civil Rights Response*. New York: Cambridge University Press.

Hooker, Juliet. 2005. "Indigenous Inclusion/Black Exclusion: Race, Ethnicity, and Multicultural Citizenship in Latin America." *Journal of Latin American Studies* 37(2):284–310.

Lowenthal, Leo. 1968. *Literature, Popular Culture, and Society*. 1962. Palo Alto, CA: Pacific Books.

Patterson, Orlando. 2001. "Slavery as Social Institution." Elsevier Science Ltd.

Rivadeneyra, Rocio. 2011. "Gender and Race Portrayals in Spanish-Language Television." Springer Science & Business Media.

UN Development Program. Regional Human Development Report for Latin America and the Caribbean 2010.

Wade, Peter. 2013. "Articulations of Eroticism and Race: Domestic Service in Latin America." *Feminist Theory* 14(2):187–202.

Williams, Erica Lorraine. 2009. "Anxious Pleasures." PhD diss., Stanford University.

Williams, Erica Lorraine. 2013. *Sex Tourism in Bahia: Ambiguous Entanglements*. Champaign: University of Illinois Press.

Discussion Questions

1. In what ways has your race and/or ethnicity been portrayed within popular culture? Provide concrete examples.
2. What examples of antiracism exist within popular culture? Provide concrete examples.

Resources

Flooded Mine Ride: https://www.youtube.com/watch?v=FZD5fVSm40g

Southern Discomfort. Documentary Film: https://www.youtube.com/watch?v=8u9GMrYOydw

References

Bannerman, Helen. 1921. *Little Black Sambo*. Bedford, MA: Applewood Books.

Bannerman, Helen, and John R. Neill. 1908. *The Story of Little Black Sambo*. Chicago: Reilly & Lee Co.

Bernstein, Charles. 1984. "Sambo's: Only a Fraction of the Action: The Inside Story of a Restaurant Empire's Rise and Fall." Burbank, CA: National Literary Guild.

Collins, Patricia Hill. 1990. *Black Feminist Thought: Knowledge, Consciousness, and the Politics of Empowerment*. New York, NY: Routledge.

Du Bois, W.E.B. 1992. *Black Reconstruction in America: 1860–1880*. New York: First Free Press.

hooks, bell. 1984. *Feminist Theory from Margin to Center*. New York: Routledge.

Kludt, Tom. October 2, 2018. "Megyn Kelly Apologizes for Defending Blackface Halloween Costumes." CNN Business. Retrieved. April 12, 2019, from (https://www.cnn.com/2018/10/23/media/megyn-kelly-blackface/index.html).

Lester, Julius, and Jerry Pinkney. 1996. *Sam and the Tigers*. New York: Dial Books for Young Readers.

Oliver, Kelly. 2016. *Hunting Girls: Sexual Violence from The Hunger Games to Campus Rape*. New York: Columbia University Press.

Pew Research Center, Internet and Technology. 2018. "Social Media Fact Sheet." Retrieved April 15, 2019, from (https://www.pewinternet.org/fact-sheet/social-media/).

Webb, Kevin. 2019. "The 10 Highest-Paid YouTubers Include the Paul Brothers and a 7-year-old Toy Reviewer." Retrieved April 15, 2019, from (https://www.businessinsider.com/highest-paid-youtube-stars-2018-12#1-ryan-toysreview-22-million-10).

Section VI: Family and Partnerships

Student Narrative

It was about 20 years ago at the age of five that I learned my place in society. It was like any other day in my Kindergarten class where we would sit around a circle and say our prayers out loud except on this particular day I learned what it meant to be a black girl. What was supposed to be a positive learning environment soon turned into a racially charged environment, but of course at the time I didn't know that. As we went around the prayer circle one of the white boys in class said "I pray for everyone in the world but black people." I instantly felt like he was talking directly to me. I was confused and wondered why he would say that. I remember looking to my teacher for clarification but she didn't say or do anything. As a child that had never been confronted with racism I couldn't understand why he didn't want God to help black people. I kept thinking what is wrong with black people? I'm black, What is wrong with me? When I went home that day and told my parents about what happened they were very upset and stared asking me a bunch of questions about the incident. Of course, I didn't know what they were so upset about, I just wanted to know why he didn't want to pray for black people. They explained to me that there would always be people who would have a problem with the color of my skin. They told me that there were going to be some people in life that were going to judge me before they even knew me because of the color of my skin. They wanted me to understand that racism wasn't fair, but it was just the way things were. I learned quickly that the color of my skin was going to be something that I would have to deal with for the rest of my life. They didn't want me to feel bad about being black; they just wanted me understand that unfortunately this was the life I had to look forward to. A life with which they and so many other black people had to become familiar.

Alisha Jones was a master's student in the Department of Sociology at California State University–Sacramento at the time of writing this narrative. She is from Fairfield, California. She is now a sociology PhD student at University of California–Merced.

Learning Objectives

After you read this section on families and partnerships, you should be able to:

1. Understand the concept of racial socialization.

2. Recognize the challenges and resilience of the immigrant community in raising children.

3. Understand the historical background of, as well as current trends in, interracial marriages.

Editor's Introduction

Aya Kimura Ida, PhD

Sociologists argue that the family is an important agent of socialization. **Socialization** refers to "the process by which individuals adapt to and internalize the norms, values, customs, and behaviors of a shared social group" (Perez-Felkner 2013:119). Socialization takes place through interactions with **agents of socialization,** or the individuals, groups, or entities that facilitate the socialization process. Families, peers, teachers, school, and media are often seen as major forces influencing our socialization experiences and what we learn. Individuals learn about norms, values, customs, and behaviors of the social group explicitly through verbal interactions with the socialization agents or implicitly by observing how they react toward a person, task, issue, and/or situation in daily lives. It is important to note that we never stop learning; that is, socialization is a lifelong process. Interacting with the agents of socialization, we develop the images and social locations of our own and other ethnic and racial groups. These images, in turn, serve as the reference in shaping our identities and behaviors. The images of other racial and ethnic groups developed through socialization may be biased and sometimes held at the unconscious level, but have real consequences in our thoughts and behaviors (see Lisa Harrison's chapter in Section II, *"Identity, Wellness, and Society"*). For that reason, whether you are conscious or not, the type of person you prefer to date or marry may partly be shaped by your socialization process, while other structural forces also shape your relationship patterns. In this section and the following chapters, you will learn about diverse families and relationships. First, you will learn about racial socialization, childrearing practices in immigrant and/or transnational families, and then about factors influencing interracial marriages.

Racial Climate in the Society and Racial Socialization

Minority youth learn about their race, ethnicity, and social position from an early age and throughout adolescence (Perez-Felkner 2013), and most minority families are shown to engage in **racial socialization** (Hughes and Johnson 2001). The vignette written by a graduate student, Alisha Jones, shows three agents of socialization at play, triggering her to learn about her social location as a black person at age five: her peer, teacher, and parents. Her peer intentionally excluded "black people" in his prayer, which showed her a glimpse of how people who had the same skin color as hers are treated in the society. Then, when she looked to her teacher, she did not say or do anything. This lack of intervention also fueled into her confusion about her first recognizable encounter with the discrimination and likely communicated to her the notion that discrimination is something that is accepted or too touchy to be addressed. Her parents reacted strongly to the incident and immediately engaged her in *preparation for racial bias*—an aspect of racial socialization that often takes place in minority racial groups (Hughes and Johnson 2001:983). In preparation for bias, minority parents prepare their children for potential encounters with racial discrimination and stereotyping. In racial socialization, minority parents also often warn children about interacting with other groups (i.e., *promotion of mistrust*) and emphasize their own group culture, history, and heritage (i.e., *cultural socialization*). Racial socialization is associated with a host of positive outcomes for minority youth, such as higher self-esteem, academic performance, and sense of efficacy and lower depressive symptoms, while overemphasis on racial discrimination may contribute to withdrawal from activities that are linked to success in dominant society.

While we know more about racial socialization and its consequences for minority youth, how about in white families? How do white parents socialize their children about race and ethnicity? In the following section, Megan Underhill shows how middle-class white parents communicated with their children when Michael Brown's death and the Ferguson protests made the headline news. Based on her interview data, she found that most parents did not engage their children in conversations about racial tension and protests in efforts to maintain a protected, worry-free childhood. This suggests a stark difference in racial socialization in racial minority and white families.

Transnational and Immigrant Families and Parenting

While anti-immigration sentiment still exists and is prevalent in some parts of the United States, immigrant families are an expanding segment of the US population. The US Census showed, in 2013, 13 percent of the total population was first-generation immigrants (i.e., the foreign-born or people who were born in a country other than the United States), and 12 percent was second-generation (i.e., the native-born with at least one foreign-born parent) (Trevelyan et al. 2016). By 2060, it is projected that about one in five US residents will be foreign born. Some immigrants move to this country as a family, while other families make a voluntary or involuntary decision to physically separate between two or more countries while maintaining close ties and relationships with one another. Those families that are physically separated between nations but maintain close ties are called **transnational families** (Schmalzbauer 2004; Shih 2016). Transnational families are not a new phenomenon, but have gained more scholastic attention since the 1990s. These families are similar to immigrant families in that they must adopt to a new culture, language, secure housing and employment, and learn how the educational and social systems work in the host country. Nonetheless, transnational families have the additional challenge of coping with family separation. Many research on transnational families focus on the separation of a nuclear family; for example, a parent(s) leaving children in their home country for employment opportunity and a child sent to a relative in another country for educational opportunity. Far fewer studies recognize extended families being separated from a nuclear family as transnational families. In the following section, my colleagues and I present a case of Japanese immigrant or transnational families navigating through childrearing in the United States, leaving their extended families in Japan. Some are married to American citizens and had children in the United States, while others moved here with their Japanese spouse and children on their expatriate assignment for work. What they all have in common is a strong tie maintained with their extended families in Japan; in that sense, they are transnational. The Japanese parents in this study report problems that many immigrants face when adapting to the new society, such as language barrier, unfamiliarity with culture and social systems, and discrimination, and recognize ethnic community based on a Saturday Japanese School as a significant resource to cope with such difficulties. While studies show the benefits of biculturalism (LaFromboise, Coleman, and Gerton 1993) and many parents do desire to raise their children to become bicultural, such a task was not easy even for the relatively affluent parents with higher educational attainment level. This demonstrates the complexity of childrearing when one is a minority and/or newcomer in the soceity.

A Half Century After *Loving v. Virginia*

Until only about fifty years ago, it was illegal to marry a person of different race in many states in the United States. **Anti-miscegenation laws** had been enforced to prevent whites from marrying a member of another racial and ethnic group until 1967, when the US Supreme Court in the *Loving v. Virginia* case legalized interracial marriages. At that time, only 3 percent of the newlyweds were in such marriages (Livingston and Brown 2017). In 2015, however, the proportion of interracial newlyweds jumped to 17 percent. The statistical report by the Pew Research Center found that Asians and Latinx newlyweds were most likely to marry someone of a different race in the United States, but gender mattered. For example, black men were more likely to marry interracially than black women, and Asian women were more likely to marry someone of a different race than Asian men. Education also mattered; college graduates were more likely to marry interracially than people with lower educational attainment level. With the increase in the actual number of interracial marriages, the public opinion regarding interracial marriages has been also changing. In 2017, 39 percent of the surveyed individuals reported that interracial marriage is good for society. Political identification seems to matter in the attitudes in that Democrats are more likely to agree that interracial marriage is a good thing for society than Republicans. It is important to study the acceptance level of interracial intimacy and family and the actual proportion of interracial marriages as research recognizes them as indicators of progress made in race relations in a society (Yancey and Lewis 2009).

Although interracial marriage is on the rise and has become more accepted over the past fifty years, research shows that interracial relationships are less likely to result in marriage than same-race relationships, suggesting that people are more likely to engage in interracial dating and cohabiting than interracial marriage (Joyner and Kao 2005). Also, whites, blacks, and Latinx were more likely to be in a relationship with someone of another race when they are younger, and interracial sexual relationships declined with age. Drawing from the idea of **anticipatory socialization,** where individuals adapt the values and norms of the group which they aspire to join, Joyner and Kao (2005) explain the decline of interracial relationships with age may be due to "anticipatory mate selection." In **anticipatory mate selection**, "individuals are thought to select partners they expect to be more acceptable marriage partners, and consequently favor same-race partners over different-race partners" increasingly with age as they become more conscious about marriage potential (566). Marriage requires more commitment; it involves a public acknowledgment of the partnership and an assumption of sharing family, friends, financial, and other types of resources, and possibly children. When people think of the ideal family in the United States, most individuals still imagine a family with parents of the same race (Yancey and Lewis 2009). In addition, there is a long history of interracial families facing ignorance, harassment, and discrimination often by whites in this country. Thus, one's preference for interracial marriages may be more susceptible to social pressures. In the following section, Xing Zhang and Sharon Sassler summarize literature on the various individual, interpersonal, and structural factors shaping one's likelihood to be in an interracial relationship.

Mindfulness

"I'm not Japanese. I'm American!," said my three-and-a-half-year-old daughter one day when I asked why she did not want me to speak to her in Japanese at her daycare. Caught off guard, and probably feeling a little sad and rejected, I did not know what to think and what to say. However, this incident gave me an opportunity to reflect more mindfully about what I say, how I frame, and how I act as a mother—an influential socialization agent for my daughter. This incident also reminded me that, as young as she was, she was also being socialized by her peers and teachers. After all, she was the only Japanese kid in her daycare where she spent most of her day on weekdays since she was six months old. Literature on socialization recognizes individuals as not just passive receivers of information, but rather an active participant in shaping their own socialization process and culture in which they participate (Corsaro 2011). Though I was not able to react effectively when the incident happened, I made sure to take an advantage of every other opportunity to have conversations with my daughter about ethnic culture and race. We talked every time when her friends or she commented how "weird" it was to speak another language, bring seaweed-wrapped rice balls for lunch, and have unfamiliar toys and objects at our home and every time she said she wanted "yellow" (blond) hair. Being a novice parent in the United States (a "foreign" country to me), I was not sure if it was appropriate to speak with her teacher about my concerns, but I did. Now, at age five, she seems more confident as a bicultural kid at school. Thanks to her teachers who embraced various ethnic and racial heritages students bring to their class, my daughter and her friends somehow came to redefine her and other children's cultural backgrounds as something that they add to the class. Her friends urge her to teach them how to count in Japanese, and she is learning how to say things in Spanish and proudly shows off newly learned Spanish words to me. These observations in my family make me realize that children and adults are active participants in our own socialization process and the cultures of the community into which we are socialized.

It is important to realize that we are not only the recipient of socialization, but also a socialization agent to someone else—our partner, family members, peers, neighbors, school, and wider community. Like my experience shared above, you may be a socialization agent to younger ones—your child, niece, or nephew. You are also a socialization agent for your parents and grandparents, perhaps influencing their views on race and ethnicity. What you post on social media also shapes other people's views and sense of reality. Thus, it is very important to take a moment and be mindful about the potential consequences of your voices, actions, and representations. In a positive light, this means that you do have the opportunity to influence the people around you and the greater society in a positive way. This positive change you may create in society is only possible when you become mindful about your own observations and experiences and realize that you are a socialization agent to someone else.

Parenting during Ferguson: making sense of white parents' silence

Megan R. Underhill

Department of Sociology and Anthropology, University of North Carolina Asheville, Asheville, USA

KEYWORDS Parenting; racial socialization; whiteness; silence; racial protest; Ferguson

Introduction

On 9 August 2014, an unarmed black teenager named Michael Brown was fatally shot by Darren Wilson, a white police officer in Ferguson, Missouri. Brown's death, and the multi-week protest that followed, riveted the attention of the United States and also the world.[1] Activists' protests called attention to the continued problem of racial inequality in the United States but they accomplished something more: Brown's death and protesters calls for racial justice revealed once again a deep divide between the racial perspectives of black and white Americans.

This divide was evidenced in series of surveys conducted by the Pew Research Center in 2014. Results from a survey published 18 August 2014 revealed that 80 per cent of black respondents believed Brown's death "raised important questions about race" as compared to only 37 per cent of whites. This sharp attitudinal divide was evidenced yet again in a Pew study conducted after Officer Wilson's 2014 acquittal and published on their website 8 December 2014, wherein 80 per cent of black and 23 per cent of white respondents indicated "the grand jury's decision not to charge Darren Wilson in the death of Michael Brown was the wrong decision". That the majority of white survey respondents doubt the racial significance of Brown's death is not entirely surprising. As Lewis (2004) has argued, one consequence of being a member of the dominant racial group is that members give less thought to how their dominant status shapes their life outcomes.

While there is research that examines the racial attitudes and beliefs of white adults (Croll 2007), we know little about how these racialized worldviews are learned by white children. Racial socialization research offers some insight into this process; it illuminates how and what people learn about race and racism. Most of the parenting-related, racial socialization research indicates that white parents refrain from speaking with their children about race and racism because they subscribe to a colourblind ideology and believe talking about race is impolite, or worse – racist (Hagerman 2016; Vittrup 2016).

Thus, the purpose of this paper is to add to research on white racial socialization by studying what white parents report communicating to their children about racial tension, violence and protest – subjects we know something about among black (see Thomas and Blackmon 2015; Threlfall 2016) but not white families. Findings from this study are important because they illustrate what white parents believe are the best racial practices to pursue during a period of heightened public attention to issues of racial violence and protest.

To examine these issues, I use data from interviews with forty white, middle-class parents in Cincinnati, Ohio – a city that possesses a history of racial tension and protest.[2] In brief, study results indicate that few parents reported speaking with their children about racial tension or racial protests, even when such discussions were highly visible in the news and on social media. Parents reported various reasons for their silence, the most notable being a desire to create a protected, worry-free childhood. Many parents were also unable to see how such subjects related to their family's white life. Not all parents, however, were silent. Twelve parents recalled speaking with their children about racial tension, Brown's death, and the Ferguson protests but most of their discussions were communicated from a neutral or a defensive colour-blind frame. Only two parents highlighted issues of power and privilege.

Findings

Silence as a protective parenting practice

Most of the parents in this study (*n* = 28) said they had not conversed with their children about racial tension or protests in Cincinnati, Ohio (2001) or Ferguson, Missouri (2014). When I asked parents why they remained silent, half said it was because they believed their children were too young to discuss such matters. The other half placed responsibility at their children's feet, noting that their children "never asked". Further questioning revealed that parents' silence was also associated with a third factor – they did not know what to say due to the pervasiveness of their white worldview.

Parents like Hannah said they refrained from speaking with their children about racial tension in the United States, including protests in Cincinnati and Ferguson, because the subject matter was too mature and they preferred to keep their children "in a little bubble, if possible". Most parents who cited this concern had children between the ages of three to eight (*n* = 9) but a few parents with older children expressed similar reservations (*n* = 3). Charlotte, for example, a mother of three who worked part-time as a book-keeper, said she shied away from such discussions because she did not want her children – ages nine, eleven and thirteen – "worrying about things they don't have to worry about". Other parents' concerns ran deeper. For example, Lauren a stay-at-home mother of two, explained she had no intention of talking to either of her sons, age four and seven, about Ferguson because she did not want to "scare them":

> My sons get very scared of things. I'm still trying to shelter them both. I don't want them to have bad dreams. I want to keep them kids as long as I can. The only thing they should worry about is going outside and playing.

Most participants (*n* = 37) said they had spoken with their children about race before. Parents' discussions relied on the theme that "we're all the same but different", and were also informed by the "happy" diversity rhetoric described by Bell and Hartmann (2007). For example, parents like Justin, an entrepreneur in his early thirties, reported telling his children, age five and three, that racial differences are "what makes the world beautiful and interesting. We should celebrate them". Consequently, among this subset of parents, happy discussions of race were common; unhappy racial conversations were not. This happy race-talk sustained the worry-free childhood participants believed was the cornerstone of a successful upbringing (Shanahan 2007).

Discussions of racial tension on the other hand, ran counter to parents' positive racial messaging and were minimized or positively reframed. In a few instances, this positive reframing of negative racial topics extended all the way to discussions of slavery. For example, when Patricia, a human resource manager in her early forties, was confronted with a question from her eight-year-old daughter about "how people could have been so mean as to own slaves", Patricia immediately altered the emotional tenor of the conversation. She adopted a "feminist point of view" and shifted the conversation away from race and towards gender, urging her daughter to think about "black women and how strong they were … " in the hope her daughter would "think about how you can be a strong woman too". Not only did Patricia avoid the subject of racial violence in response to a question about slavery, but she sidestepped the issue of race altogether, recasting slavery as a black feminist victory.

Other parents made conscious decisions to isolate their children from unhappy racial news. For example, Julia, a mother of four who worked part-time at her children's school, acknowledged she did not speak with her children about racial protests in Ferguson because she did not like to "foster the negative". In fact, she and seven other parents pursued a "no-news" policy in their household and car. Julia explains:

> We don't watch a lot of news because there is really nothing good on it. So no, we haven't [spoken about Ferguson]. Um, instead of pointing out that there is this black-white thing, we just tell our children that we all love each other.

Not only does Julia not teach her children about Ferguson, but she sends her children the message that that there is no tension between whites and people of colour. She chooses to ignore the "black–white thing" in favour of a positive racial message that emphasizes how people of all races "love each other".

In an effort to cultivate a childhood that was "virtuous in its naiveté", parents like Julia adopted a protectionist parenting strategy (Shanahan 2007, 413). They isolated their children from information or people that undermined the innocence of their children's youth. These were parents who were deeply uncomfortable thinking or talking about racial tension or protest. They dealt with this discomfort by shutting out the upsetting news.

Parents' silence may have also stemmed from a desire to be seen as a "good white" parent. For white parents in this study and others, being a "good white" means being non-racist and colour-blind (Lavelle 2015). Because parents understood racism as a psychological rather than a structural phenomenon, they believed they could prevent racism by thinking positive thoughts about people of colour and avoiding "negative" race-talk.

One of the consequences of this protective parenting practice was that parents hindered their children from learning about current events. This became important in light of the second reason parents cited when explaining why they refrained from these discussions; parents claimed their children "never asked". In line with research that positions whites as reactive discussants of racial subjects, this subset of parents said they would have spoken to their children about racial tension or protests if their children asked but "they never did" (Vittrup 2016). Given the predominance of this no-news policy among participants, it is possible their children never heard about Michael Brown or the Ferguson protests. However, children's ignorance was by no means accidental. Parents' no-news policy created a structure of silence around their children wherein challenging conversations were excluded from participants' homes.

Parents felt a sense of pride about the positive, colourblind bubble they created around their children. None considered the racialized consequences of their silence. By not speaking with their children about racial tension or the past or recent racial protests, parents implicitly signalled that such topics were either conversationally inappropriate or immaterial to their and their children's lives. Parents' silence reinforced white normativity by making it seem as if whites were not implicated in racial matters.

White normativity: "racial tension has never been a big part of my life"

None of this subset of silent parents reported feeling a sense of urgency to speak with their children about racial tension or the underlying factors that contributed to racial protests in Cincinnati or Ferguson. All described feeling uncertain about what they would or should say to their children. Ten parents said they planned to speak with their children about racial tension and protests "one day, when my kids are older" but when pushed for details about the hypothetical conversation, parents admitted they "really don't know".

Few parents appeared knowledgeable about racial tension or racial inequality in the United States – past or present. When trying to make sense of it, most cited slavery as the source of present day racial discord. A few participants also mentioned Jim Crow segregation. Only three offered a contemporary example of racial inequality and each cited police brutality towards African Americans. They were the only participants in this subsample who provided a post-Civil Rights example of racial inequality *and* who connected the racial protests in Cincinnati and Ferguson to police violence against communities of colour. Despite this, none felt prepared to speak with their children about the subject. Two parents attributed this to their privileged status as a white American. Penelope, a mother of three white sons explains:

> I think growing up being white, I think there's a lot of anger there that I couldn't even begin to understand. When I think about the conversations black parents have to have with their sons, you know – "this is how you need to behave with the police." I know I will never have to do that. So I don't know how I would address Ferguson.

Penelope recognized it was critical for black parents to have a police-talk with their children, but that she, a white parent "would never have to do that". She was one of the only parents in this subsample who alluded to – but never directly discussed – the idea of white privilege. She understood her white skin allowed her to create a protected bubble around her children, something black parents could not necessarily guarantee.

So prominent was this worldview among some participants that they were unable to see how or why the subject of racial tension or protests related to their life. For example, eight parents claimed their silence was not purposeful; they simply had not considered either topic. As countless participants told me, "it isn't really part of my life". Though the 2001 Cincinnati protest was distant from participants' day-to-day lives, the Ferguson protest was not. Twenty-nine parents were interviewed days, weeks, and months after Brown's death.

Most of these participants had difficulty interpreting world events outside of a white normative frame. For a handful of participants, the only events that burned brightly in their memory were those that involved white people. There are many problems associated with teaching children about past or present racial events through a lens of white normativity. When parents avoid, downplay, or positively reframe uncomfortable or unhappy matters of racial inequality, they contribute to an intergenerational "collective forgetting", which helps sustain racial inequality into the next generation (Feagin 2013, 17). As Feagin argues: "when such a momentous and bloody past is suppressed, downplayed, or mythologized … ordinary Americans, especially whites … have difficulty seeing or assessing accurately the present day realities of unjust enrichment and impoverishment along racial lines" (2013, 19).

Breaking the silence: white parents' discussions of racial tension and protest

A third of the parents in my sample reported speaking with their children about racial tension and the Ferguson protests. Most adopted a *neutral* or a *defensive colourblind* frame, wherein they deemphasized racism, avoided discussions of power, and adhered to an individual rather than a structural understanding of race and racial inequality. Additionally, two parents evidenced a race-conscious frame. They spoke with their children about Michael Brown and connected his death to systemic racial inequality. None of the parents in this subsample spoke with their children about the 2001 Cincinnati protest.

Ten of the twelve parents in this subsample adopted a *colourblind* frame when speaking with their children about racial tension and the Ferguson protests. By colourblind I mean that parents discussed racial events using a non-racial frame or they attributed race-related outcomes to non-racial phenomena (Bonilla-Silva 2014).

Most of the colourblind parents discussed in this subsection were those who reported providing their children with neutral, power-evasive explanations. These parents were reluctant to speak with their children about challenging racial subjects but they did not want to raise them in an anesthetized bubble either. Hence, they read, watched, and listened to the news in the presence of their children. Still, few thought discussions of racial tension or protest developmentally appropriate for children six years of age or younger. In fact, only one parent, a high school guidance counsellor in her early thirties, recalled speaking with her child, age five, about Ferguson. She too drew upon race and power-evasive language:

> I did tell her there was a man but I didn't identify color. So I don't know if that's good bad or indifferent. I just said there was a man who was killed by a police officer and some people think it was an okay thing and some people think it was a really bad thing. And that's what the protests are about.

Caitlyn, the mother quoted above, adopted an air of neutrality when communicating with her daughter about Brown's death, noting that "some people think it was an okay thing and some people think it was a really bad thing". In so doing, Caitlyn depoliticized the Ferguson protests. She positioned them as connected to the shooting death of an abstract individual and failed to discuss how Brown's death and the Ferguson protests were directly informed by racial concerns. True to a colourblind frame, her explanation ignored race.

Parents with children seven and older were less reticent to speak with their children about racial tension, but their conversations, like Caitlyn's, tended to be child-initiated, brief, and power-evasive. For example, Stephen, a self-avowed progressive father of one, admitted he might not have spoken with his daughter, age seven, about the Ferguson protests had it not been "all over the news":

> It's in everything you hear. We have NPR on in our house and our car and it was just like all the time in your face. And so we were processing it as adults and she had question about it. We just had a little conversation about how not all people get along. And unfortunately sometimes they are a different color. We were trying to be honest but also trying to help her understand at her level.

In contrast to Caitlyn, Stephen makes no mention of the shooting death of Michael Brown but does briefly allude to race when he states that the protests were related to "different color people" not "getting along". Though Stephen's explanation of the Ferguson protests is somewhat less colourblind than Caitlyn's, it maintains a neutral, power-evasive frame. As evidenced in Stephen's comment, colourblind parents do not see themselves as being better positioned than people of colour. From their perspective, whites and people of colour are "equal". Consequently, the Ferguson protests are interpreted as an unfortunate dispute between equal status groups.

This type of neutral, colourblind framing was also evident in the way Ilene, a day-care provider and mother of three, spoke with her son, age eleven, about Ferguson:

> Everybody just has such a strong opinion on whether the police officer was guilty or innocent and whether he should have been punished and whether he, [sighs] killed, I can't remember the kids name now, um whether he was shot because of race or because he was charging the officer. And because everyone feels strongly and none of us were there, I just thought it would be better for him not to talk about it because it's very sensitive for a lot of people. I don't want him to say something that's going to like ... cause trouble or make people feel upset.

Like Caitlyn, Ilene attributes the Ferguson protests to the death of a "kid" whose name she "can't remember". Ilene is reluctant to side with either Brown or Wilson supporters because she is unsure whether Brown's death was triggered by the officer's racial bias or his need for self-defence. Consequently, she expressly forbids her son from speaking with his classmates about Brown's death. Caitlyn is able to maintain a position of silent neutrality because she understands Brown's death as an isolated incident. She does not connect his death to larger patterns of police brutality against people of colour or to ongoing racial inequality. Ilene's message to her son is clear. Do not talk about race; it might offend someone. In this way, Ilene communicates to her son that conversations about race are best avoided.

A smaller subset of colourblind parents ($n = 3$) rejected the neutral framing described above. They too possessed a colourblind worldview but approached the subjects of racial tension and the Ferguson protests from a more defensive perspective. They did not believe white Americans were responsible for racial tension in the United States. If racial tension continued, they reasoned, it was because of the black community's inability to "let go of their anger". Helen, a stay-at-home mother of two, described how she addressed the subject of racial tension with her son, age eleven:

> We talked a little bit about how people of a different color were treated differently in the past and that a lot of people have a lot of bitterness over that and they can't let go of it. It may not have anything to do with how they are being treated today, they just can't let go of that anger.

Jaime, a part-time administrative assistant and mother of three, engaged in similar reasoning with her ten-year-old son:

> I told him the tension in this country goes back hundreds of years. You know, back to the Civil War. But that's hard because he doesn't know the history and I can only look at today. I mean, I don't own a slave. I've never owned a slave.

In the above quotes, we see that Helen and Jaime believe racism and racial inequality are a thing of the past. Neither denies people of colour were "treated differently" "hundreds of years ago" but they reject the idea that racism continues to shape their day-to-day experiences and life outcomes. These parents minimize the reality of racism when speaking with their children, a trend that is consistent with previous research on white families (see Hagerman 2016). They do this through their adoption of what Bonilla-Silva, Lewis, and Embrick (2004) identify as the "past is the past" and the "I didn't own a slave" storylines. Both storylines justify the current racial status quo by depicting contemporary society as progressive and race-neutral (Bonilla-Silva, Lewis, and Embrick 2004).

This disavowal of contemporary racism also informed how this subset of parents evaluated Michael Brown's death and the Ferguson protests. All three dismissed the idea that racial bias had anything to do with why Officer Wilson shot and killed Michael Brown. According to Charlotte, a mother of three, Officer Wilson fired at Brown because Brown was unable to "manage his emotions and act like an adult". Brown was thus believed to have provoked and incited Officer Wilson.

Jaime conveyed a somewhat similar message to her son. She believed Brown was shot because he disobeyed Wilson's instructions:

> I have a hard time being able to explain to my child, the right and wrong of the situation because in my book, it doesn't matter who you are. You don't run from the police. I'm trying to teach my kids that the police are there to help you. They're here to protect you. They don't just come and arrest you. But if you do something wrong, they will come. It doesn't matter if you're white or black, Asian, you know, Indian. I said, "these men robbed a store. They scared people and then when police were coming after them, they ran. And the one guy was shot, he didn't have gun. He wasn't armed so he couldn't have hurt the police officer. But the police officer did shoot and kill him." And my son's comment was, "he shouldn't have run from the police." I'm like, "yeah. He shouldn't have run."

Elements of a white normative frame are evident in Jaime's discussion of the police. She does not think the police are biased as promulgated by Ferguson protesters. Instead, she counsels her child that "the police are here to help you". It never occurs to Jaime how her race and class inform this positive assessment. Indeed, research indicates that people of colour have different experiences with police than whites (Alexander 2010). They are more likely to be stopped and arrested by police (Alexander 2010; Rojek, Rosenfeld, and Decker 2012) and according to the 8 April 2016 *Washington Post* story, unarmed black men were also seven times more likely to be fatally shot by a police officer than an unarmed white in 2015. Though this discrepancy may elude white parents like Jaime, it does not escape the notice of black parents. They understand they will have to have "the talk" with their children – especially their sons – regarding appropriate ways to interact with the police (Threlfall 2016). One of the privileges of whiteness is that white parents do not feel compelled to have similar conversations with their children. Like Jaime, most envision the police as protectors rather than threats to their children's safety.

Discussion and conclusion

Writing over 100 years ago, DuBois ([1903] 2009) described a "conspiracy of silence" concerning the subject of race in the United States. The silence DuBois described was so deafening and absolute that even the "astonished visitor is inclined to ask if after all there *is* any problem here" (DuBois [1903] 2009, 50). Results from this study provide insight into why this "conspiracy of silence" is reproduced among middle-class, white families even at a time when discussions of race are featured prominently in protests and news coverage.

Michael Brown's death and the Ferguson protests brought discussions of racial inequality to the fore of the public's attention – or at least that is how it appeared based on a perusal of news coverage and social media postings. But the findings here reveal that these public discussions of race and racial inequality did not necessarily filter down into the white, middle-class home. In fact, the majority of parents said nothing to their children about racial tension or racial protests in Cincinnati or Ferguson. When I pushed parents for a reason why, they noted their children were "too young" or "never asked".

I argue parents' silence was driven by a belief that their white children's early and middle childhood should be a protected, worry-free period of life.

Consequently, parents isolated their children from subjects they deemed upsetting. When racial discussions did occur, they were first distilled through a "happy" diversity rhetoric wherein challenging aspects of a subject were omitted or positively reframed leaving behind a narrower and more celebratory message (Bell and Hartmann 2007). While well intentioned, parents' silence purposefully ignored the reality of race relations in the United States. For the majority of participants, the result was a childhood structured by racial silence.

Parents' silence also stemmed from another factor. They did not know what to say to their children about racial tension in the United States, or how it informed the Ferguson protests. Few possessed an awareness of contemporary racial inequality, which meant that many of the protesters concerns were lost on parents. Several parents also explained they did not think about racial tension or protests because they did not directly "impact my life".

In some ways, participants' self-reported conversations about racial tension and the Ferguson protest, teach us about what white, middle-class parents believe it means to be a "good parent" to a white child when events like Michael Brown's death and the Ferguson protests are featured prominently in the media. We know, for example, that in today's colourblind world, being a "good" white means being non-racist – a position many whites associate with racial silence and colourblindness (Lavelle 2015). However, as Zerubavel (2006) argues, silence is also a form of denial. People adopt a position of silence when a subject inspires discomfort or pain. For whites in the United States, race and racial inequality are upsetting subjects that challenge white claims of moral goodness. Thus, by remaining silent, white parents are able to distance themselves and their children from a negative collective identity as a white American and to assert a positive identity as an individual (Lavelle 2015).

White parents' desire to protect their children from unsettling information or news is interesting, especially when compared to research documenting black parents' protective racial socialization practices. The fact that protection guides both white and black parents' racial socialization, but motivates them to make drastically different decisions – silence vs. bias preparation – speaks to the position of whites and blacks in the racial hierarchy. As members of the dominant racial group, whites do not have to think about race when reflecting on their children's physical or psychological well-being. If anything, white parents' cultivation of racial silence allows whites to maintain their position of dominance with a guilt-free conscience. The opposite applies to parents of colour. They are incentivized to speak with their children about racial discrimination, violence, and police brutality so as to protect their child from the threat of physical or psychological harm.

A third of parents did speak with their children about racial tension and the Ferguson protests. Most adopted a neutral or a defensive colourblind frame. Parents who opted for a neutral frame avoided speaking with their children about racial inequality. None connected Brown's death to issues of police violence or to a larger pattern of racial inequality. Parents who espoused a defensive, colourblind frame also provided their children with ahistorical, power-evasive explanations. But they also did something more. In subtle and not-so subtle ways they communicated to their children that Brown's death was Brown's fault, thereby individualizing his death and invalidating protesters message that Brown's death was emblematic of an enduring racial problem in the United States. By downplaying the racial significance of Brown's death, parents deftly protected their family's privileged structural location and made inaction a defensible recourse.

Though the overwhelming majority of parents did not report speaking with their children about racial tension or the significance of the Ferguson protests, two parents did. These parents acknowledged the presence of racism in the United States and engaged their children in a discussion of white power and privilege. Though their numbers were few, their actions provide modest evidence of heterogeneity in white parents' racial socialization efforts. In line with Hagerman's (2014, 2016) findings, they suggest that some white parents – perhaps only a minority – actively work to raise children who are attendant to the structural basis of racial inequality.

Although I believe this study contributes important findings to the question of how white parents believe they ought to talk about controversial racial topics with their children, this study features two important limitations, and therefore opportunities for future research. First, this study cannot comment on the ways in which children themselves understand the messages their parents give them about racial tension and protest. We know, for example, that children interrogate and reinterpret racial messages they are exposed to by parents, peers, and schools (Hagerman 2014; Winkler 2012). Consequently, future research should also examine how white children make sense of these parent–child discussions.

Second, all of my respondents were, broadly speaking, middle class. Hence, an important question for future researchers to consider is whether parents' class status contributes to their racial silence. It is possible that poor whites are less capable of cultivating a childhood structured according to racial silence due to resource constraints. Additional research is needed to assess whether white racial silence is a protective practice all whites engage in, or whether it is specific to whites with class privileges.

Notes

1. I use the term "racial protests" to describe the actions of activists in Ferguson (2014) and Cincinnati (2001). I do not use the word "riot" to describe these events because of the word's racially charged, negative connotation.

2. I define "racial tension" as a sense of discord or distrust between members of different racial groups.
3. Like other researchers, I also established rapport with participants by informing them that I too was a parent, and as a parent, could empathize with the challenges they faced (Mose 2016). Being a parent created a point of commonality between myself and participants, which may have helped attenuate participant discomfort speaking about race.

Acknowledgements

The author thanks Jennifer Malat, Sarah Mayorga-Gallo, David Brunsma and two anonymous reviewers for their constructive feedback on earlier drafts of this article.

Disclosure statement

No potential conflict of interest was reported by the author.

Funding

This research was supported by the Charles Phelps Taft Research Center (Charles Phelps Taft Dissertation Award, Charles Phelps Taft Graduate Enrichment Award) and the Kunz Center for Social Research (Kunz Center Graduate Student Research Award) at the University of Cincinnati.

References

Alexander, Michelle. 2010. *The New Jim Crow: Mass Incarceration in the Age of Colorblindness*. New York: The New Press.

Allen, Quaylan. 2016. "'Tell Your Own Story': Manhood, Masculinity and Racial Socialization among Black Fathers and Their Sons." *Ethnic and Racial Studies* 39 (10): 1831–1848.

Bell, Joyce M., and Douglas Hartmann. 2007. "Diversity in Everyday Discourse: The Cultural Ambiguities and Consequences of 'Happy Talk'." *American Sociological Review* 72 (6): 895–914.

Bonilla-Silva, Eduardo. 2014. *Racism Without Racists: Color-Blind Racism and the Persistence of Racial Inequality in the United States*. Lanham, MD: Rowman and Littlefield.

Bonilla-Silva, Eduardo, Amanda Lewis, and David G. Embrick. 2004. "'I Did Not Get That Job Because of a Black Man … '": The Story Lines and Testimonies of Color-Blind Racism." *Sociological Forum* 19 (4): 555–581.

Burton, Linda M., Eduardo Bonilla-Silva, Victor Ray, Rose Buckelew, and Elizabeth Hordge Freeman. 2010. "Critical Race Theories, Colorism, and the Decade's Research on Families of Color." *Journal of Marriage and Family* 72 (3): 440–459.

Croll, Paul R. 2007. "Modeling Determinants of White Racial Identity: Results from a New National Survey." *Social Forces* 86 (2): 613–642.

Doane, Ashley W. 2003. "Rethinking Whiteness Studies." In *White Out: The Continuing Significance of Racism*, edited by Ashley W. Doane and Eduardo Bonilla-Silva, 3–18. New York: Routledge.

DuBois, W. E. B. [1903] 2009. *The Souls of Black Folk*. New York: Simon and Schuster.

Feagin, Joe. 2013. *The White Racial Frame: Centuries of Racial Framing and Counter-framing*. New York: Routledge.

Frankenberg, Ruth. 1993. *White Women, Race Matters: The Social Construction of Whiteness*. Minneapolis: University of Minnesota.

Hagerman, Margaret Ann. 2014. "White Families and Race: Colour-Blind and Colour-Conscious Approaches to White Racial Socialization." *Ethnic and Racial Studies* 37 (14): 2598–2614.

Hagerman, Margaret Ann. 2016. "Reproducing and Reworking Colorblind Racial Ideology." *Sociology of Race and Ethnicity* 2 (1): 58–71.

Hughes, Diane. 2003. "Correlates of African American and Latino Parents' Messages to Children about Ethnicity and Race: A Comparative Study of Racial Socialization." *American Journal of Community Psychology* 31 (1–2): 15–33.

Hughes, Diana, Emilie Smith, Howard Stevenson, James Rodriguez, Deborah J. Johnson, and Paul Spicer. 2006. "Parents' Ethnic-Racial Socialization Practices: A Review of Research and Directions for Future Study." *Developmental Psychology* 42 (5): 747–770.

Lavelle, Kristen M. 2015. *Whitewashing the South: White Memories of Segregation and Civil Rights*. Lanham, MD: Rowman and Littlefield.

Lewis, Amanda. 2003. *Race in the Schoolyard: Negotiating the Color Line in Classrooms and Communities*. New Brunswick, NJ: Rutgers University Press.

Lewis, Amanda. 2004. "'What Group?' Studying Whites and Whiteness in the Era of 'Color-Blindness'." *Sociological Theory* 22 (4): 623–646.

Logan, John R., and Brian J. Stults. 2011. "The Persistence of Segregation in the Metropolis: New Findings from the 2010 Census." Census Brief prepared for Project US2010.

Mayorga-Gallo, Sarah. 2014. *Behind the White Picket Fence: Power and Privilege in a Multi-ethnic Neighborhood*. Chapel Hill: University of North Carolina Press.

Mose, Tamara R. 2016. *The Playdate: Parents, Children, and the New Expectations of Play*. New York: New York University Press.

Rojek, Jeff, Richard Rosenfeld, and Scott Decker. 2012. "Policing Race: The Racial Stratification of Searches in Police Traffic Stops." *Criminology; An Interdisciplinary Journal* 50 (4): 993–1024.

Shanahan, Suzanne. 2007. "Lost and Found: The Sociological Ambivalence Toward Childhood." *Annual Review of Sociology* 33 (1): 7–28.

Thomas, Anita Jones, and Sha'Kema M. Blackmon. 2015. "The Influence of the Trayvon Martin Shooting on Racial Socialization Practices of African American Parents." *Journal of Black Psychology* 41 (1): 75–89.

Threlfall, Jennifer M. 2016. "Parenting in the Shadow of Ferguson." *Youth and Society*. Advance online publication. doi:10.1177/0044118X16670280.

Vittrup, Brigitte. 2016. "Color Blind or Color Conscious? White American Mothers' Approaches to Racial Socialization." *Journal of Family Issues*. Advance online publication. doi:10.1177/0192513X16676858.

Winkler, Erin N. 2012. *Learning Race Learning Place: Shaping Racial Identities and Ideas in African American Childhoods*. New Brunswick, NJ: Rutgers University Press.

Zerubavel, Eviatar. 2006. *The Elephant in the Room: Silence and Denial in Everyday Life*. Oxford: Oxford University Press.

Reading 6.2 Raising a Child in a "Foreign" Country: The Case of Japanese Parents in the United States

Aya Kimura Ida, California State University–Sacramento

Naoko Oyabu-Mathis, University of Mount Union

Thais Forneret, California State University–Sacramento

Daphne Kennelly, California State University–Sacramento

Abstract

How do immigrant parents navigate parenthood in the United States? Using qualitative data, we examine challenges faced by Japanese immigrant parents and reveal how they cope with these challenges. The participants reported that they struggled with language barriers, discrimination, unfamiliarity with the social systems, and the complexity of bicultural/bilingual childrearing. The Japanese Saturday School provided socially, psychologically, and culturally important resources to cope with the difficulties.

Keywords: Parenting, immigrant parents, immigrant community, Japanese, *ibasho*, fictive kin

I feel like I cannot do what other adults can do. There was a time when my child was hit in the face by a ball during a little league game and began bleeding very badly. But I had never been to an emergency room and didn't even know where to take him and I was in a panic about what to do. Over the phone, my husband told me to wait until he got there. Other (American) parents at the game couldn't believe that I would wait for my husband while my son was in such a terrible condition. So they looked up which hospital I could take him to under our insurance and took us to the emergency room; they did the paperwork for me, and stayed with us. I was very thankful. But this incident made me feel so ashamed that I cannot do what an adult or parent (typically) does for their child.

Akane, a forty-year-old Japanese mother, shared this story to illustrate the difficulty she faced as an immigrant parent. In this chapter, we introduce the challenges of this mother and a number of other Japanese parents who recently moved to the United States. We use the term *immigrants* to refer to Japanese parents in this study, encompassing various situations they are in, but recognize their experiences might be very different from those of *issei* who had migrated to this country a long time ago and/or immigrants from other countries.

More than 421,600 foreign-born Japanese currently live in the United States, and about 79,900 of them are children under eighteen (Ministry of Foreign Affairs of Japan, 2017). Although smaller in size than other immigrant groups, the number of Japanese immigrants has also been steadily growing, and they are one of the fastest-growing Asian segments of the US population. While adult immigrants arrive in the United States with dreams for and optimism about their children's future, immigrant parents also face a dual challenge: managing their own sociocultural adjustment *and* becoming an effective parent in a "foreign" environment by learning new definitions of parental roles in the receiving society and culture (Ali 2008). While adjusting to a new culture and society, having an *ibasho* may be critical for Japanese immigrants. *Ibasho* is a Japanese concept referring to "a sense of comfort and psychological security that a person feels in specific locations they regularly visit"

(Herleman et al. 2008:282). Research has shown that a sense of *ibasho* is important in providing social support and decreasing stress, and a lack of *ibasho* means a lack of psychosocial security . This chapter first describes Japanese parents' views on raising a child in the United States, then explains the challenges faced in their daily lives, and concludes by describing the role of Japanese School in providing important resources, including *ibasho*, for navigating parenthood in this country.

Methods

The data used in this chapter come from foreign-born Japanese parents residing in California (n=54) and Ohio (n=64), whose child(ren) attended a supplementary Japanese Saturday School (hereafter Japanese School). Anonymous online qualitative surveys were conducted, asking to describe their own adjustment processes and childrearing experiences in the United States. Although both Japanese and English language options were given, only one participant responded in English. The data collection took place in the early summer of 2011 in California and two years later in Ohio (see Table 1 for more information about the sample). About 40–50 percent were permanent residents (i.e., green-card holders), and the rest were long-term visitors who moved to the United States temporarily for work or schooling.

Table 1. Sample Characteristics (n=119)

	California (n=54)	Ohio (n=64)
Female (%)	81%	72%
Age (average)	41 years	41 years
Married (%)	96%	98%
Japanese Spouse (%)	50%	61%
Years in the US (average)	10	10
Employed Men (%)	100%	94%
Employed Women (%)	36%	36%
College Educated+ (%)	66%	77%
Number of Children (average)	2	2
Permanent Resident (%)	48%	39%
N	55	64

Participants were recruited at the Japanese schools in California and Ohio. Both schools had about 100 elementary, middle, and high school students attending every Saturday, and the students went to the local American school (hereafter, local school) from Monday to Friday. The Japanese government subsidizes these Japanese schools, provides the standardized curricula, tests, and textbooks used in Japan, but it is primarily the volunteering parents who run and sustain the school instrumentally and financially. It was originally established for the families who lived in the areas (in the United States and other countries) with a high concentration of Japanese families on temporary work assignment in order to adhere to the same curricular standards held for the public schools in Japan and to prepare the children for returning to, and having easy adaptation in, the Japanese education system. While there have been an increasing number of permanent resident families, the expectation and purpose of these schools remain the same. The Japanese school taught students not only Japanese language and culture, but also other subjects taught in public schools in Japan, including math, social studies, and sciences. Speaking English is highly discouraged among peers and teachers and at home. Today, these schools are known to be academically rigorous and tough for some children who cannot keep up with the weekly assignments and are not proficient in Japanese language and culture.

Findings

Biculturalism and bilingualism are highly romanticized in Japan, and there is an assumption that children become bicultural and bilingual naturally. However, as shown, immigrant parents often face a complex reality in raising a child in a multicultural environment.

Almost all respondents conceptualized and admired American mainstream culture as valuing diversity and the uniqueness of individuals. In contrast, Japanese culture was viewed somewhat negatively as having too much emphasis on homogeneity and uniformity. They believed that living in America without the strict constraints and emphasis on collectivism of Japanese society would foster their children's individuality. The parents also reported that childrearing in the United States liberated them from the strict standards held for them as parents regarding discipline, ideals, and norms surrounding parenting in Japan and gave them freedom to pick and choose the parenting practices and ideals that worked for them without feeling shame and guilt for not conforming to the norms.

However, this American emphasis on individualism also posed challenges for Japanese parents. One mother explained:

> Japanese culture emphasizes harmony and not standing out from others, while American culture emphasizes the opposite, that assertiveness is important, and individualism is accepted. So, there are different norms emphasized in American schools and Japanese schools. Teaching my children about this contradiction is very difficult.

As shown in this mother's quote, some parents reported that they wished, but struggled, to teach their children norms like discipline and harmony, which were valued in Japan but not so valued in mainstream US society. One of the challenges immigrant parents face is simultaneously teaching their children their own culture while exposing and encouraging them to also adopt the host culture when there is a contradiction between cultures. Further, many felt that in the United States, individual parents are held more accountable in childrearing, whereas in Japan, the community, school, and parents share equal responsibility for childrearing. Thus, although they were relieved not being judged by the strict parenting standards of Japanese culture, they also felt the weight of responsibility as individual parents.

Acculturative Stress

Many parents in the study reported experiencing **acculturative stress,** or stress endured while adjusting to a new dominant culture, such as language barrier, unfamiliarity with the education and medical systems, and discrimination. Several respondents blamed acculturative stress for their physical illness (e.g., frequent colds, stomach ulcers) as well as psychological struggles (e.g., feeling sad and lonely, or experiencing social anxiety or suicidal thoughts). One respondent implied that they once developed a suicidal thought while adjusting to their life in America.

The Language Barrier

In addition to cultural conflicts, the parents' own language barrier was most frequently mentioned as the source of problems and was commonly reported as a source of depression. Parents with a language barrier found assisting their children with homework, reading notices from school, and communicating with teachers and other parents to be extremely stressful (see also Ali 2008; Turney and Kao 2009). Some described spending hours with a dictionary in hand, helping their children with their homework. A mother described the difficulty in the following way:

> Because my husband was not good at English either, it was very stressful whenever we had to check our children's homework, go to the hospital, or do any kind of paperwork, and whenever some trouble came up. I once told my husband that I would go back to Japan with my children

because it became too hard to read the handouts my kids brought home from school and help the children with their homework in English.

The language barrier resulted in parents being unable to provide their children not only sufficient instrumental support (e.g., homework help), but also social networking support. Some mentioned feeling guilty about not being able to volunteer at the school, and others who did volunteer found it emotionally taxing because of the language and cultural barriers. Respondents found it difficult to socialize with and befriend American parents and feared that this might hurt their children's ability to make friends. One mother stated:

[It's hard when] I cannot keep up with the conversation even if I try to join the circle of American parents. I'm not sure how to help my children when they have a problem. I didn't attend school here, so I'm anxious and uncertain about how I should best guide my children.

Respondents also described the language-related difficulties faced by their children. One father described such struggles as follows.

I originally thought my children would find it natural and easy to acquire English, but that wasn't the case for my children. It took my children a long time to get used to English, and when we had just arrived here, we spent hours together on their homework.

These quotes demonstrate how the language barrier challenged the parents' self-efficacy and the assumptions about ease of bicultural and bilingual parenting. Given that most of the parents had higher educational attainment, the inability to help their own children in school due to the language barrier might have been perceived as especially hard on the parents. Things that would have been easy for them in Japan, such as helping with their kids' homework, were seen as a source of significant stress for parents with language barriers.

Unfamiliarity with Education and Medical Systems

Parents also reported that their limited knowledge of the K–12 education system in the United States prevented them from getting more involved at their children's local school. One mother described her situation as follows.

I didn't understand the school culture, events, and rules here in the U.S. and felt inadequate as a support for my child. When my child started junior high, I couldn't help him even though he was struggling academically. It took us half a year to feel adjusted.

Another frequently mentioned problem was being unfamiliar with the US medical system. In addition to the difficulties caused by unfamiliarity with procedures such as using medical insurance and having to make appointments rather than dropping in, language barriers also caused parents to be uncertain about the care their children received and to feel not confident enough to seek medical care independently. The language barrier and being unfamiliar with the US medical system made them feel "incapable as an adult" because they were unable to perform tasks that would have been considered trivial in Japan. The mother in the opening quote, for example, was thankful for the help she received from American parents to get the emergency medical care her son needed, but she also felt inadequate and ashamed for not being able to meet the needs of her son without help, which compromised her confidence as a parent. A father in the study expressed similar sentiments:

Although I am getting used to living in the U.S., I would find it difficult to live here permanently. My kids are well adjusted here, but I feel like we, the parents, are not taking care of them well enough in various situations. I feel that we may end up not satisfying the societal expectations as parents in our kids' daily lives and education.

Because both US and Japanese societies conceptualize a parent as someone who guides and protects their children, when immigrant parents must rely on their children for help or are unable to guide or stand up for them due to the language barrier and cultural unfamiliarity, their self-efficacy as parents may be threatened, especially among the parents with higher education.

Discrimination

Although we did not ask specifically about discrimination, discrimination came up as one of their most difficult experiences in the United States. Often, the parents attributed the discriminatory experience to xenophobia and racism (see also Yeh et al. 2003). Parents reported these discriminatory incidents happening in stores, local schools, or playgrounds and framed these not as isolated incidents, but more as ongoing problems they face as immigrants. Interestingly, there was a regional difference with regard to discrimination: one in five Ohio respondents mentioned it as a problem, whereas only one in twenty California residents did so. California is known for its diversity and higher concentration of Japanese immigrants and Japanese Americans, which may have shielded these parents against discrimination. Also, it was only mothers who mentioned discrimination in their responses, and none of the fathers did, which may have been in part the results of underreporting among Japanese men about their experiences, as well as the intersectionality of gender and minority status exposing Japanese women to more discrimination. One mother described how discrimination experiences interfered with her involvement at the local school.

> I feel that no matter how hard I tried, I would never be treated equally to a native [US-born] person. When I was volunteering at my child's [local] kindergarten, I was in charge of collecting tuition. One day, I requested a parent to pay a tuition that was overdue. The parent got so mad at me and made me leave. Later, another volunteer with blonde hair went to the same person to collect the tuition. This time, the person willingly communicated her payment plans. I don't want to think it was because of my race, but I kind of have to wonder if it was because I am not native.

Another mother explained that her child faced discrimination at the local school and she could not intervene effectively due to her language barrier. Interestingly, but not surprisingly, many of the mothers described their child facing discrimination as their own struggle. For example, one mother recounted the following.

> When my child went to his friend's house, his friend's father just yelled at my child at the door, "Get out!" My son told me about this incident days later, and it broke my heart when I found out. Later, I heard he was racist. I thought no child should be treated that way.

Many mothers described their inability to intervene and protect their children due to the language barrier as the most heartbreaking and frustrating experience in the United States and made them feel less capable as parents.

Japanese School as *Ibasho*, an "Oasis"

Parents' descriptions of the Japanese School were overwhelmingly positive. Parents reported wanting their children to be bicultural and bilingual, and this was the main motivation for sending their children to a local school during the week and to Japanese School on Saturdays. Not surprisingly, all parents agreed that the Japanese School was a reliable educational resource that made bicultural parenting possible. Parents on temporary work assignment in the United States often characterized the school as a critical resource helping their children keep up with the academic curriculum in Japan. These parents emphasized the importance of ensuring a smooth transition back into the Japanese school system and their children being prepared for the competitive entrance exams they would face upon their return to Japan. For permanent resident parents, the Japanese School was primarily a place where their children could maintain ties to the Japanese language, culture, and identity and befriend other children of Japanese descent. Although parents' expectations of the school differed slightly depending on their status in the United States, all agreed that Japanese School lessened the burdens that accompany bicultural parenting.

Japanese School seemed to play a significant role in providing *ibasho, which* made bicultural parenting less stressful. When asked about what helped them persevere during difficult times, many respondents discussed the importance of knowing other Japanese immigrant parents in the same situation, with whom they could talk about their concerns and from whom they could seek advice (see Noh and Kaspar 2003). The parents felt as though their uncertainties, difficulties, and ambivalence were not easily understood by others, including their family and friends back home who admired biculturalism and bilingualism while not realizing the difficulties.

For these parents, the Japanese School was more than just an educational institution for children, but an important social networking site for themselves. Some characterized the school as the center of the community and a place to meet others whose values, experiences, and concerns reflected their own. Parents relied on this social network for emotional, informational, and social support. Mothers often described finding *mama tomo*—friendship networks of mothers who shared concerns, emotional support, and information. They shared information from where to buy fresh fish and Japanese groceries to how to navigate mainstream school and medical systems. The networks helped these Japanese immigrants form a ***fictive kinship***, in which non-related individuals act as members of an extended family based on close friendship ties rather than blood or marriage (Ebaugh and Curry 2000). These networks helped them effectively enact their role as parents in the United States.

Two mothers described the school as an "oasis" where they could reaffirm their authentic selves and could be "Japanese" without hesitation. Several other parents explained that the school was a place where they could be who they really were, implying difficulty of being authentic to themselves outside the school. A mother said, "I can speak Japanese all I want there, so I used to look forward to Saturday [when the school takes place], especially when I first arrived here." Being around "similar others" and having a sense of *ibasho* gave them the comfort to knowing that they were not alone in feeling overwhelmed with acculturative stress and the difficulty of bicultural parenting (see also Kunikata et al. 2011). Thus, the Japanese School also provided a sense of *ibasho* through a sense of community and inclusion.

It is, however, important to recognize that a few parents, especially permanent residents, also mentioned that the school was occasionally a source of stress because of its overemphasis on uniformity and homogeneity, which they saw as negative characteristics of Japanese culture. Some parents, who described themselves as different from "typical Japanese [people] who always hang out with similar people," felt the school was sometimes stressful because it required them to deal with other parents who expected to adhere to the close-knit social networks. These claims may illustrate the concept of negative social capital in the immigrant community or the idea that gaining benefits from that community demands conformity and requires individuals to sacrifice individual freedom (Portes 1998).

Conclusion

Japanese as an ethnic group have been socially constructed as a model minority in the United States and are often seen as a relatively well-adjusted immigrant group. While it is true that many Japanese immigrants are highly educated, skilled workers with a higher socioeconomic status than many other immigrant groups and the average American (Duleep and Dowhan 2008), socioeconomic privileges did not always shield the immigrant parents against the difficulties of childrearing in a foreign environment. These challenges included language barriers, unfamiliarity with the medical and school systems, and experiences of discrimination.

When facing such challenges, Japanese School helped share the burden of bicultural/bilingual childrearing and created a space to form social networks with others in similar situations, which provided a mechanism for coping with acculturative stress. It was in these school-based social networks that the parents were socialized to learn about American children's peer culture and customs and found ways to navigate the unfamiliar medical and education systems in the United States. These social networks also provided a sense of not being alone in the challenge of raising children in an unfamiliar culture and society. At the same time, some parents recognized the price they paid for this resource, such as the significant amount of parental investment and commitment.

Although the current study focused on Japanese immigrants, some of the findings may be relevant for immigrant parents of other national origins. By understanding the complex experiences of immigrant parents, the mainstream schools, the health care system, and immigrant service organizations can better aid immigrant families and provide *ibasho*, or a sense of belonging.

Acknowledgments

Faculty Summer Research Fellowship, Probationary Faculty Development Grant, CTL Faculty Learning Community Professional Development Fund, and Provost's Research Incentive Fund at California State University–Sacramento funded this research. We would like to thank our student assistants Rina Fukushima, Christina Macias, and Nicole Guzman for their work.

Reflection Questions

- If your parents or you were immigrant parents, what are the differences and similarities in their or your experiences of raising a child in America?
- What can you or your communities do to help immigrant parents overcome the difficulties?

Exploratory Research Questions

- Find immigrant parents in your community and ask about their experiences of raising a child in a "foreign" environment. Are their experiences different from or similar to those described in this chapter? How? What would be the source of difference or similarity?

Further Resources

Berry, J.W., Uichol Kim, Thomas Minde, and Doris Mok. 1987. "Comparative Studies of Acculturative Stress." *International Migration Review* 21(3):491–511.

Migration Policy Institute's Interactive Website on "Children in U.S. Immigrant Families (By Age Group and State, 1990 versus 2016). Available at https://www.migrationpolicy.org/programs/data-hub/charts/children-immigrant-families

References

Ali, Mehrunnisa Ahmad. 2008. "Loss of Parenting Self-Efficacy among Immigrant Parents." *Contemporary Issues in Early Childhood* 9(2):148–60.

Duleep, Harriet Orcutt, and Daniel J. Dowhan. 2008. "Research on Immigrant Earnings." *Social Security Bulletin* 68(1):32–50.

Ebaugh, Helen Rose, and Mary Curry. 2000. "Fictive Kin as Social Capital in New Immigrant Communities." *Sociological Perspectives* 43(2):189–209.

Herleman, Hailey A., Thomas W. Britt, and Patricia Y. Hashima. 2008. "Ibasho and the Adjustment, Satisfaction, and Well-being of Expatriate Spouses." *International Journal of Intercultural Relations* 32(3):282–99.

Kunikata, Hiroko, Yuko Shiraishi, Kazuo Nakajima, Tetsuya Tanioka, and Masahito Tomotake. 2011. "The Relationship between Psychological Comfort Space and Self-Esteem in People with Mental Disorders." *Journal of Medical Investigation* 58(2011):56–62.

Ministry of Foreign Affairs of Japan. 2017. *Annual Report of Statistics on Japanese Nationals Overseas*. Tokyo, Japan: Ministry of Foreign Affairs.

Noh, Samuel, and Violet Kaspar. 2003. "Perceived Discrimination and Depression: Moderating Effects of Coping, Acculturation, and Ethnic Support." *American Journal of Public Health* 93(2):232–38.

Portes, Alejandro. 1998. "Social Capital: Its Origins and Applications in Modern Sociology." *Annual Review of Sociology* 24:1–24.

Turney, Kristin, and Grace Kao. 2009. "Barriers to School Involvement: Are Immigrant Parents Disadvantaged?" *Journal of Educational Research* 102(4): 257–71.

Yeh, Christine, Agnes K. Arora, Mayuko Inose, Yuki Okubo, Robin H. Li, and Pamela Greene. 2003. "The Cultural Adjustment and Mental Health of Japanese Immigrant Youth." *Adolescence* 38(151):481–500.

Reading 6.3 Parents, Peers, and Pressure: The Dynamics of Interracial Relationships

Xing Zhang and Sharon Sassler, Cornell University

Keywords: Anti-miscegenation laws, contact hypothesis, homogamy, individual preferences, racial socialization, structural opportunities, third parties, social exchange theory

You're officially entering the interracial big leagues, and you're doing it without a warm-up. Everyone knows you're supposed to ease into interracial dating. You know, make your way up the color scale.

—CeCe, Issa Rae's friend from the *Awkward Black Girl* YouTube Series

Learning Goals from This Chapter

This chapter focuses on the unique challenges that those in interracial relationships may face from their parents and peers. In particular, we review the various pressures young couples may face at different relationship stages. How do parents and peers shape the likelihood of entering into and progressing a relationship that crosses racial or ethnic lines? What pressures are brought to bear on those who embark on interracial relationships? How do these pressures influence the behaviors of individuals embarking on relationships with those from other racial or ethnic backgrounds? We provide background information on the history of race relations with regard to marriage in the United States, and how race, ethnicity, gender, and immigration status factor into interracial relationships and union formation.

Introduction

Racial and ethnic diversity in the United States is growing, and by mid-century the country is projected to become a majority-minority society. Much of this is driven by an increase not only in the proportion of racial and ethnic minorities within the United States, but to a growing acceptance of interracial dating and union formation. The growth in interracial relationships is often portrayed by scholars who study race relations, immigrant adaptation, and stratification, as well as by the popular media, as a sign that social distance between racial and ethnic groups has declined (Gordon 1964). In fact, some portray the increase in interracial relationships as indicating that the United States is really on its way to be an actual melting pot. But the path to intimate unions that cross racial and ethnic boundaries is not necessarily strewn with roses. This chapter focuses on the dynamics shaping the chances that interracial relationships and unions will form and progress. In particular, we discuss how parents and peers, as well as legal barriers and social norms, have influenced the progression (or dissolution) of interracial relationships. We conclude by reflecting on the composition of those in such unions.

In the United States, **anti-miscegenation laws** historically prevented particular racial and ethnic groups from marrying each other. Such laws, which were primarily found in Southern states, prevented whites from marrying other racial and ethnic groups. They were not overturned until 1967, when the US Supreme Court case *Loving v. Virginia* found such laws to be unconstitutional.[i] Since then, the overall prevalence of interracial relationships and unions has increased. As of 2017, approximately 17 percent of all first marriages were interracial in the United States. Asians and Hispanics are more likely to intermarry than blacks and whites

(Livingston and Brown 2017). Figure 1 shows an overview of differences in the prevalence of intermarriage by race, ethnicity, and gender in 2017.

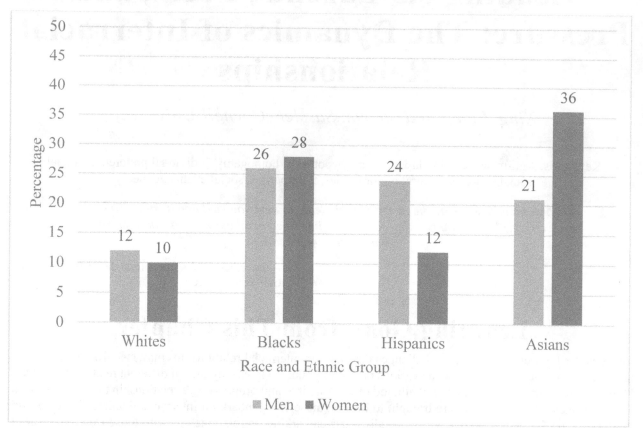

Figure 6.3-1. Percentage of Interracial Marriages in the Previous 12 Months by Race, Ethnicity, and Gender, as of 2015.

Source: Livingston and Brown, 2017.

Data is from the 2014–2015 American Community Survey, and data was analyzed by the Pew Research Center.

How Are Interracial Relationships and Unions Formed?

Interracial dating, cohabitation, and marriage are affected by the following factors: **individual preferences**, **structural opportunities**, and **third parties** (Kalmijn 1998). **Individual preferences** are an individual's choice over his or her romantic partner. For example, an individual may express preferences to date within their own racial, ethnic, or religious group. Such preferences, however, are implicitly shaped by portrayals of different groups as well as status hierarchies, or, in the words of Herbert Blumer (1958), one's own group position. **Structural opportunities** are the places where people meet, such as in neighborhoods, in educational settings (such as in high school, at a community college, or in a university setting), places of worship or employment, or while engaging in leisure activities. These places are structured in the sense that they provide opportunities to meet romantic partners, given the racial and ethnic composition of the setting. **Third parties** may not be directly related to the relationship but can prevent the relationship from occurring. For example, government authorities established laws that prohibited intermarriage. Nowadays, parents and peers are more likely to intervene in the formation of new romantic relationships, by emphasizing group belongingness, challenging those who may look beyond skin color or ethnic origin, or exerting pressure (social, economic) to impede relationships.

The Role of Parents on Interracial Relationships and Union Formation

Parents, an example of a third party, have considerable influence over their children's romantic relationship choices. For example, they can provide advice and opinions on prospective dating partners, have oversight on their children's curfew, and may monitor the activities and types of behaviors their children participate in. Parental influence over relationships can vary by race, ethnicity, gender, and immigration status. The research suggests that parents exert more control over the relationships of their daughters, and that parental control is often greater among minority groups than for whites (Dubbs, Buunk, and Li 2012). Among immigrant generations, parental conflict tends to be highest among first- and second-generation immigrant children, where differences in values, norms, and behaviors may arise (Chao and Aque 2009; Foner and Dreby 2011). Children of immigrants may be open to dating and marrying other races but are also aware that their parents may not necessarily approve of their selection of romantic partners (Kasinitz, Mollenkopf, and Waters 2009). The likelihood of interracially dating and marrying increases as immigrant generational status in the United States increases (King and Harris 2007; Qian and Lichter 2007); that is, the second generation is more likely to partner across racial or ethnic lines than is the first generation.

Research on Parental Approval of Interracial Relationships

Parents may discourage interracial dating in the ways they socialize their children, through **racial socialization**. Racial socialization is the process through which parents teach their children, either directly or indirectly, about race, including their attitudes toward other racial and ethnic groups (Lesane-Brown 2006). In fact, adolescents involved in interracial relationships are more likely to hide the relationship from their parents than are those in monoracial relationships (Lee and Bean 2010; Wang, Kao, and Joyner 2006). In addition, less familial and parental support is offered to those in interracial unions compared to those in same-race unions (Hohmann-Marriott and Amato 2008). Qualitative studies of parents' opinions on interracial relationships show that parents who disapprove of their children's mate choices have threatened to sever family ties and are also likely to cut off financial resources (Lee and Bean, 2010; Rosenblatt, Karis, and Powell 1995). Demonstrating the persistence of group positioning (Blumer 1958), parents are more likely to disapprove of a black partner than a nonblack partner (Kasinitz, Mollenkopf, and Waters 2009; Lee and Bean 2010). Greater contact and support from the partner's family has been associated with longer relationship duration and transitioning into more formal commitments (Sassler and Miller 2015; Surra 1990). Research shows that adolescents involved in interracial relationships are less likely to reveal their relationships to their families, meet their partners' parents, and appear together in public (Wang, Kao, and Joyner 2006) than adolescents involved in intraracial (racially homogamous) couples. Perhaps not surprisingly, those involved in interracial relationships are also more likely to terminate their romances than their counterparts in racially homogamous couples.

Research finds considerable heterogeneity in how parents support (or discourage) the formation of interracial partnerships. Conservative families are found to be more resistant to ethnic intermarriage, compared to less religious and more expressive families (Huijnk, Verkuyten, and Coenders 2010). In the United States, black family members have been found to be the most supportive and accepting of biracial marriages, while white family members were the least supportive (Lewis and Yancey 1995). At the same time, a sense of familial obligation, or pressure to comply with the family's wishes, may be higher among minority groups (Uksul, Lalonde, and Cheng 2007), especially those who are first- or second-generation immigrants. Children of immigrants were often aware of their parents' preferences for their romantic partner and felt pressure to date within the same racial and ethnic group (Kasinitz, Mollenkopf, and Waters 2009). Of course, parental attempts to control their children's partner choice may not succeed, as children may not comply with their parents' views or wishes.

Challenges of Being in an Interracial Relationship from Peers

Interracial couples may face pressures from their peers to remain in racially and ethnically **homogamous** relationships, or relationships that remain within the same race and ethnic group. Friends do have influence in romantic relationships; in fact, studies have shown that friends' opinions are more important than are parents' opinions in determine romantic partner choice (Wright and Sinclair 2012). How do peers contribute to the process of interracial relationships and union formation? Sociologists describe the importance of the **contact hypothesis**, which states that greater interpersonal contact between racial and ethnic groups contributes to decreased prejudice and discrimination. Those who grew up in more diverse communities are more likely to have interracial friendships and are more likely to be in interracial relationships later in life (Huschek, De Valk, and Liefbroer 2010; Vanhoutte and Hooghe 2012). Those who received randomly assigned roommates from a different racial and ethnic group were more likely to have favorable attitudes toward them (Shook and Fazio 2008).

But what about the unique challenges that those in interracial relationships may face on a day-to-day basis? Those in interracial relationships may face pressure from peers to date and marry within the same racial and ethnic group. Due to scrutiny from peers and the public, interracial couples are less likely to show public displays of affection relative to homogamous couples (Vaquera and Kao 2005). Examples of these negative experiences include being stared at by strangers, hearing slurs muttered, or experiencing differential treatment at restaurants or stores (Datzman and Brooks Gardner 2000). Couples in interracial relationships may cope with these experiences by ignoring their surroundings, avoiding public settings, choosing to stay at home, or changing their locations and friendships to only go to places where they feel supported (Datzman and Brooks Gardner 2000). These negative experiences in public can lead to shame, sadness, resentment, and anger for those in interracial relationships (Datzman and Brooks Gardner 2000).

Making Sense of Peer Influence on Interracial Relationships: Social Exchange Theory

Why might interracial couples face scrutiny from peers? Interracial relationships have long been viewed as evidence of status-caste exchange, which we will refer to as **social exchange**. Specifically, minority groups are seen as trading something—their attractiveness or socioeconomic status—for the dominant group's racial caste status. The persistence of a racial hierarchy and its consolidation with economic status, reinforces patterns of racial homogamy. Nonetheless, interracial romances occur. As mentioned by CeCe in Awkward Black Girl in the opening quote, sometimes racial minorities who date whites are portrayed as trying to elevate their position in society, or having internalized their racial self-hatred (Chito Childs 2005). More recently, scholars have suggested that while status-caste exchange may be applicable to some marriages involving whites and minorities, it is not the dominant tendency (Kalmijn 2010; Rosenfeld 2005). As evidence of this, marriages between whites and minorities are more likely than not to include partners with similar levels of education (Qian 1997; Rosenfeld 2005).

Pressure to Tie the Knot or Break Up?

The prevalence of interracial relationships varies by relationship type. Interracial relationships are most often found among couples who are dating; the prevalence of interracial couples among those who are cohabiting is much lower, and it declines even more among those who are married. In the United States in 1995, for example, racial homogamy was highest among married couples and lowest among couples who were dating (Blackwell and Lichter 2004). Scholars account for this dramatic change across relationship types by suggesting that a process of **winnowing** is occurring; as relationships get increasingly more committed, they become more selective and prone to social pressures (Blackwell and Lichter 2004; Qian and Lichter 2001), and more heterogamous unions are less likely to persist. In fact, interracial relationships are more likely to end, while racially homogamous unions often continue on to marriage (Blackwell and Lichter 2004). Other studies have found that interracial friendships are more likely to transition to sex than friendships that are monoracial (McClintock 2010) and do so faster (Sassler and Joyner 2011). Interracial relationships are less likely, however, to transition to cohabitation and marriage, and less likely to last longer than three months (D'Souza 2010; Qian and Lichter 2001).

Minority groups are more likely to partner with others from a different racial background, which may be due to their smaller within-group partner market. Although they have grown in recent years, blacks, Asians, and Latinos are still numerical minorities in the United States. In fact, very high rates of interracial relationship formation are found for Asian women. Nonetheless, variations—by gender and group—in the prevalence of interracial partnering provide further evidence of **status exchange**. Black and Hispanic men are more likely to cohabit with white women then white men are to cohabit with black and Hispanic women (Qian and Lichter 2007). Nonetheless, when white men cohabit with minority women, they enter into shared living at a significantly faster pace than when minority men partner with white women or minority women (Sassler and Joyner 2011). Asian women are more likely to cohabit with a partner of a different race than Asian men (Qian and Lichter 2007).

Conclusion

The role of this chapter was to examine how parents, peers, and pressure to transition to different relationship stages factored into interracial relationships. The prevalence of interracial relationships and unions has been increasing over time since **anti-miscegenation laws** were declared unconstitutional in 1967. Interracial relationships and unions occur due to varying reasons, such as **individual preferences** and **structural opportunities.** However, **third parties,** such as parents and laws, have considerable influence over whether or not these interracial relationships occur in the first place, or endure, and may encourage racially and ethnically **homogamous** relationships. Sociologists have also described other reasons for interracial relationships, such as the **contact hypothesis**, and **social exchange**. Research on the role of parents, peers, and pressure to transition to different relationship stages within the realm of interracial relationships indicates that there remain difficulties on the path toward a society that is racially and ethnically tolerant. Even as the United States becomes more racially and ethnically diverse, the rise of interracial relationships and unions is not inevitable. That will depend on the receptiveness of the dominant group to minorities, social attitudes toward those from other groups, and the laws and regulations shaping who arrives in our country, as well as the opportunities available to those who reside here. The current trend, however, is one of tolerance and growing acceptance of interracial relationships.

Reflection and Critical Thinking

Vignette

Andrew, a Latino twenty-one-year old, has been dating Sally, a black American twenty-year old, for a year. His parents are in town to visit for graduation, and he is interested in introducing her to his parents. Once they meet, his parents disapprove of Sally and strongly encourage him to find a romantic partner of the same ethnic background.

- Discuss what you would do if you were Andrew. Would you listen to your parents?
- How would you feel if you were Sally?

Discussion Questions

Would your parents allow you to be in an interracial relationship? What about an interracial marriage? Does the race or ethnicity of the partner matter, or would they be open to all racial and ethnic groups? If your opinions from your parents differed, would you choose to listen to your parents or decide against them? Why or why not?

Vignette

Dexter, an Asian American male, expresses frustration to his long-time friend Melanie, an Asian American female dating a white guy. He asks her, "Why are all the Asian women dating white guys? What's left for us? I just get so angry whenever I see an Asian girl and a white guy on the street."

- What do you think of Dexter's reaction to Melanie's relationship?
- What assumptions does he make about interracial pairings?
- What would you say to Dexter if you were Melanie?

Discussion Questions

What would your friends think of you if you got into an interracial relationship? Would the opinion differ based on the race and ethnicity of the partner? Would their opinions matter to you?

Exercise

Come up with a list of traits you would look for in a potential romantic partner. Would these traits be the same for someone you dated, moved in with, or married?

Discussion Questions

Did you find evidence of the winnowing hypothesis as you completed the exercise? If so, why do you think this was the case?

Exploratory Research Questions

1. What are the factors that contribute to acceptance and tolerance of interracial relationships among parents? Do they vary by gender and the race or ethnicity of the partner?

2. Aside from parents and peers, what roles do siblings or extended family members play in approval or disapproval of interracial relationships?

3. Do interracial relationships where both partners are a racial and ethnic minority face greater challenges than those partnered to a white? Why?

List of Organizations

1. Mavin Foundation: http://www.mavinfoundation.org/index.html

Further Readings and Websites

1. Yellow Fever—Asian American men's perspective on interracial relationships
   http://www.youtube.com/watch?v=vC_ycDO66bw

2. *Awkward Black Girl*—Interracial dating comedy short
   http://www.youtube.com/watch?v=ELMgw3FToXY

3. *All American Girl*—The role of parents in interracial relationships
   https://www.youtube.com/watch?v=I4Q8HhKT3MY

4. *Dear White People*—The role of peers in interracial relationships
   https://www.netflix.com/title/80095698

References

Blumer, Herbert. 1958. "Race Prejudice as a Sense of Group Position." *The Pacific Sociological Review* 1(1): 3-7.

Blackwell, Debra, and Daniel T. Lichter. 2004. "Homogamy Among Dating, Cohabiting and Married Couples." *Sociological Quarterly* 45(4):719–37.

Chao, Ruth K., and Christine Aque. 2009. Interpretations of Parental Control by Asian Immigrant and European American Youth. *Journal of Family Psychology* 23(3):342–54. doi:10.1037/a0015828

Chito Childs, Erica. 2005. "Looking Behind the Stereotypes of the "Angry Black Woman:" An Exploration of Black Women's Responses to Interracial Relationships." *Gender & Society* 19(4):544–61.

Datzman, Jeanine, and Carol Brooks Gardner. 2000. "In My Mind, We Are All Humans': Notes on the Public Management of Black-White Interracial Romantic Relationships." *Marriage and Family Review* 30(1–2):5–24.

Dubbs, Shelli L., Abraham P. Buunk, and Jessica Li. 2012. "Parental Monitoring, Sensitivity toward Parents, and a Child's Mate Preferences." *Personal Relationships* 19(4):712–22. doi:10.1111/j.1475-6811.2011.01388.x

D'Souza, Rhiannon A. 2010. "A Multilevel Analysis of Interracial Relationship Characteristics among Young Adults." *Race and Social Problems* 2(2):92–100.

Foner, Nancy, and Joanna Dreby. 2011. "Relations between the Generations in Immigrant Families." *Annual Review of Sociology* 37:545–64. doi: 10.1146/annurev-soc-081309-150030

Gordon, Milton. 1964. *Assimilation in American Life.* New York: Oxford University Press.

Hohmann-Marriott, Bryndl E., and Paul Amato. 2008. "Relationship Quality in Interethnic Marriages and Cohabitations." *Social Forces* 87(2):825–55.

Huijnk, Willem, Maykel Verkuyten, and Marcel Coenders. 2010. "Intermarriage Attitude among Ethnic Minority and Majority Groups in the Netherlands: The Role of Family Relations and Immigrant Characteristics." *Journal of Comparative Family Studies* 41(3):389–414.

Huschek, Doreen, Helga A.G. de Valk, and Aart C. Liefbroer. 2011. "Does Social Embeddedness Influence Union Formation Choices among the Turkish and Moroccan Second Generation in the Netherlands?" *Journal of Comparative Family Studies* 42(6):78–808.

Kalmijn, Matthijs. 1998. "Intermarriage and Homogamy: Causes, Patterns, Trends." *Annual Review of Sociology* 2:395–421.

Kalmijn, Matthijs. 2010. "Educational Inequality, Homogamy and Status Exchange in Black-White Intermarriage: A Comment on Rosenfeld." *American Journal of Sociology* 115(4):1252–263.

Kasinitz, Philip, Mary C. Waters, John H. Mollenkopf, and Jennifer Holdaway. 2010. *Inheriting the City: the Children of Immigrants Come of Age.* New York: Russell Sage Foundation.

Lee, Jennifer, and Frank D. Bean. 2010. *The Diversity Paradox: Immigration and the Color Line in Twenty-First Century America.* New York: Russell Sage.

Lesane-Brown, Chase L. 2006. "A Review of Race Socialization within Black Families." *Developmental Review* 26(4):400–26.

Livingston, Gretchen, and Anna Brown. 2017. "Intermarriage in the U.S. 50 Years after *Loving v. Virginia*." Pew Research Center Report. http://www.pewsocialtrends.org/2017/05/18/intermarriage-in-the-u-s-50-years-after-loving-v-virginia/

Qian, Zhenchao, and Daniel T. Lichter. 2001. "Measuring Marital Assimilation: Intermarriage among Natives and Immigrants." *Social Science Research* 30 289–312.

Qian, Zhenchao, and Daniel T. Lichter. 2007. "Social Boundaries and Marital Assimilation: Interpreting Trends in Racial and Ethnic Intermarriage." *American Sociological Review* 72(1): 68–94.

Rosenblatt, Paul C., Terri A. Karis, and Richard D. Powell. 1995. *Multiracial Couples: Black & White Voices.* New York: Sage.

Rosenfeld, Michael J. 2005. "A Critique of Exchange Theory in Mate Selection." *American Journal of Sociology* 110(5):1284–325.

Sassler, Sharon, and Kara Joyner. 2011. "Social Exchange and the Progression of Sexual Relationships in Emerging Adulthood." *Social Forces* 90(1):223–45.

Sassler, Sharon, and Amanda J. Miller. 2015. "The Ecology of Relationships: The Effect of Meeting Patterns on Cohabiting Couples' Relationship Progression." *Journal of Social and Personal Relationships* 32(2):141–60.

Surra, Catherine A. 1990. "Research and Theory on Mate Selection and Premarital Relationships in the 1980s." *Journal of Marriage and the Family* 52(4):844–65. doi:10.2307/353306

Uksul, Ayse K., Richard N. Lalonde, and Lynda Cheng. 2007. "Views on Interracial Dating among Chinese and European Canadians: The Roles of Culture, Gender, and Mainstream Cultural Identity." *Journal of Social and Personal Relationships* 24(6):891–911. doi: 10.1177/06265407507084189

Vanhoutte, Bram, and Marc Hooghe. 2012. "Do Diverse Geographical Contexts Lead to Diverse Friendship Networks? A Multilevel Analysis of Belgian Survey Data." *International Journal of Intercultural Relations* 36(3):343–52. doi:10.1016/j.ijintrel.2011.09.003

Vaquera, Elizabeth, and Grace Kao. (2005). "Private and Public Displays of Affection among Interracial and Intra-Racial Adolescent Couples." *Social Science Quarterly* 86(2):484–508.

Wang, Hongyu, Grace Kao, and Kara Joyner. 2006. "Stability of Interracial and Intraracial Romantic Relationships among Adolescents." *Social Science Research* 35(2):435–53.

Wright, Brittany L., and H. Colleen Sinclair. 2012. "Pulling the Strings: Effects of Friend and Parent Opinions on Dating Choices." *Personal Relationships* 19(4):743–58. doi:10.1111/j.1475-6811.2011.01390.x

Discussion Questions

1. Did your family members talk to you about your ethnicity and/or race? If so, which of the following did your family do: "preparation for bias," "promotion of mistrust," or "cultural socialization?"

2. When was the first time you recognized your race? Share the story of your earliest memory of realizing your race.

3. List and compare the challenges faced by interracial couples fifty years ago and now. How has the nature of the challenges changed?

4. Examining the personal story that the author shared under Mindfulness, discuss how the experience might have been different if the parent had a language barrier and were less familiar with the US school system and culture. What else might have changed the experience for the child and/or parent if the parent were a different race, ethnicity, nationality, gender, and educational level?

Resources

A Family Guide to Talking About Race—the RACE Project (American Anthropological Association)

Available at: http://understandingrace.org/pdf/family_guide.pdf

TED Talk "Color Blind or Color Brave" by Mellody Hobson

Available at: https://www.ted.com/talks/mellody_hobson_color_blind_or_color_brave

References

Corsaro, William A. 2011. *The Sociology of Childhood. 3rd ed.* Thousand Oaks, CA: Pine Forge Press.

Hughes, Diane, and Deborah Johnson. 2001. "Correlates in Children's Experiences of Parents' Racial Socialization Behaviors." *Journal of Marriage & Family* 63(4):981–95.

Joyner, Kara, and Grace Kao. 2005. "Interracial Relationships and the Transition to Adulthood." *American Sociological Review* 70(4):563–81.

LaFromboise, Teresa, Hardin L.K. Coleman, and Jennifer Gerton. 1993. "Psychological Impact of Biculturalism: Evidence and Theory." *Psychological Bulletin* 114(3):395–412.

Livingston, Gretchen, and Anna Brown. 2017. "Intermarriage in the U.S. 50 Years After Loving v. Virginia: One-in-Six Newlyweds Are Married to Someone of a Different Race or Ethnicity." Washington, DC: Pew Research Center. Retrieved April 9, 2019 (https://www.pewsocialtrends.org/2017/05/18/intermarriage-in-the-u-s-50-years-after-loving-v-virginia/)

Perez-Felkner, Lara. 2013. "Socialization in Childhood and Adolescence." Pp. 119–50 in *Handbook of Social Psychology*, edited by J. DeLamater and A. Ward. New York: Springer.

Schmalzbauer, Leah. 2004. "Searching for Wages and Mothering from Afar: The Case of Honduras Transnational Families." *Journal of Marriage and Family* 66:1317–331.

Shih, Kristy Y. 2016. "Transnational Families." Pp.1–7 in *The Wiley Blackwell Encyclopedia of Family Studies*, edited by Constance L. Shehan. John Wiley & Sons, Inc.

Trevelyan, Edward, Christine Gambino, Thomas Gryn, Luke Larsen, Yesenia Acosta, Elizabeth Grieco, Darryl Harris, and Nathan Walters. 2016. *Characteristics of the U.S. Population by Generational Status: 2013: Current Population Survey Reports*. Washington, DC: U.S. Bureau of the Census.

Yancey, George A., and Richard Lewis. 2009. *Interracial Families: Current Concepts and Controversies*. New York: Routledge.

---

[i] Of course, sexual contact between whites and nonwhites had long occurred, but anti-miscegenation laws prohibited couples from legalizing such unions via marriage in the states that upheld such laws. Other laws, such as the War Brides Act, enabled alien spouses and children of members of the US armed forces to enter the United States after World War II. Enacted in 1945, this act enabled Japanese and Korean wives of American soldiers to immigrate, while the Alien Fiancées and Fiancés Act of 1946 (also known as GI Fiancée Act) eliminated barriers for Filipino and Indian war brides. In essence, these laws allowed wives of (mostly male) American military to immigrate to the United States. Such unions were largely between white or black military men and Asian wives.

Section VII: Racialized Immigration Policies

Student Narrative

In high school I was a high achieving student. I took Honors and Advance Placement classes and enrolled at the local community college, but during my sophomore year of high school I realized that I would not be able to attend college because I lacked a social security number. I felt anxious, depressed, and hopeless, but I also knew that graduating from high school and attending college were the only ways to justify the journeys across the desert of my loved ones, the burns on my mother's arms caused by the griddle at her job, and the years that had passed since I last saw my grandparents waving goodbye. Through my dedication and the support of my family, friends, and mentors, I earned an AA degree in 2013. That same year I became a DACA recipient, I received the Jack Kent Cooke Foundation Undergraduate Transfer Scholarship, and I transferred to the University of Pennsylvania. In 2016, I graduated with a B.A. in sociology. Life after graduation has been challenging. As most recent college graduates, I have struggled with the post-grad blues and an overall lack of sense of direction. Being a first-generation, low-income, undocumented college graduate has intensified those feelings, but I am continuing to be patient and to persevere.

Aida Rodriguez earned a bachelor's degree in sociology with a concentration in global and international studies from the University of Pennsylvania. Her undergraduate coursework and research focused on immigration and migration, specifically that of Central American unaccompanied children. She is currently gaining work experience before attending graduate school.

Learning Objectives

After you read the introduction and the chapters in this section, you should be able to:

1. Identify how immigration laws and policies in the United States have operated in the context of a racialized state.

2. Connect how immigration patterns have impacted demographic changes in the United States.

3. Articulate how illegality is part of the racial project in the United States.

Editor's Introduction

Heidy Sarabia

Like Aida, I also came to the country as a child, I excelled in school, and found myself fighting to continue my education—which shaped my sense of identity, belonging, and membership in the United States. Being an immigrant, a newcomer, in the United States is not easy, and as Aida Rodriguez shared, being undocumented makes the immigrant experience that much more difficult and painful. Historically, citizenship in the United States has been intimately connected to whiteness. In this introduction to the section of immigration, we want to first highlight how citizenship has been tied to whiteness and then highlight how Mexicans—the largest immigrant and racial group in the United States—became "illegal." I will end by discussing how immigration and race have been kept as separate fields of study in sociology, and summarizing the chapters in this section.

Historical Overview

White Citizenship

Most of us are immigrants in the United States, except for the Native Americans of the American continent, who lived in the continent before the arrival of Europeans. Hence, **colonialism** is at the core of the formation of the United States as a country, and **historical immigration policies** have enacted a racial project from the beginning. From the first **Naturalization** Law of 1790, naturalization was restricted to "any alien, being a free white person" (US NAT ACT 1790:103). Immediately after the American Revolution, **slave codes** were enacted to establish slavery, a set of laws that defined the status of slaves and denied citizenship rights to blacks. While nonwhites, as individuals, could sometimes pass or were able to attain citizenship rights, as a group, African Americans, Indian Americans, Asian Americans, and Latinos have been systematically denied access to the legal status of citizenship and the rights that are accorded to such status, such as the right to vote, own property, or testify in court.

In *Dred Scott v. Stanford* (1857), the US Supreme Court ruled that African Americans, enslaved or free, could not be US citizens. As a group, African Americans were not granted automatic citizenship until the Fourteenth Amendment to the Constitution was ratified in 1868 and were finally guaranteed the right to vote with the Fifteenth Amendment in 1870. The Naturalization Act of 1870 also extended the right to naturalized African immigrants.

While Indian Americans were able to gain some rights based on specific treaties or intermarriage, as a group, they had not gained citizenship rights until 1924 with the Indian Citizenship Act, which declared that "all non-citizen Indians born within the territorial limits of the United States be, and they are hereby, declared to be citizens of the United States" (US Indian Citizenship Act 1924). Aside from having formal citizenship rights, from the 1940s to the mid-1960s, the US government implemented **Indian termination** policies that attempted to assimilate Native Americans into Western-mainstream American society by dismantling **tribal sovereignty** through the process of giving criminal or limited-criminal jurisdiction to states over tribes and reservations.

The Chinese Exclusionary Act of 1882, renewed in 1892 and 1902, not only restricted immigration but also naturalization of Asian immigrants and Asian Americans. By the 1910s, states were already passing laws using language that prohibited "aliens ineligible for citizenship" in the Naturalization Act of 1870 from owning or leasing land, which directly affected Asians and Asian Americans. The Chinese Exclusionary Act and the Gentlemen's Agreement of 1907 restricted migration, especially female migration, as well as the mobility of Asian men—as a result, the practice of **picture brides** emerged, in which mostly Japanese, Okinawan, and Korean men selected brides from their native countries using matchmakers and photographs. Asian Americans as a group only gained access to rights through immigration and naturalization laws in 1954 with the McCarran-Walter Act, which abolished all racial barriers to naturalization.

Mexicans: In-between Citizens and Prototypical "Illegal Aliens"

The **indigeneity** of Mexicans, who are for the most part indigenous to the American continent, has been completely ignored. Considered foreign, for Latinxs in general and Mexicans in particular, US citizenship has historically been a complicated form of belonging due to a series of legislative mandates passed in the nineteenth and twentieth centuries. With the passage of the Treaty of Guadalupe Hidalgo in 1846, Mexicans attained *de jure* citizenship rights automatically—a legal status, delineated by the state—although they were treated as *de facto* second-class citizens throughout the nineteenth and twentieth centuries (Fox and Guglielmo 2012). The Immigration Act of 1924 changed the legal positionality of Mexican migrants. While this act did not limit the number of visas available for those citizens of the Western Hemisphere, it did not specify how many would be available either (Ngai 2005).

Immediately after the passage of the Immigration Act of 1924, the State Department acted to implement the law and "moved in 1929 to restrict Mexican immigration through administrative means" (Ngai 2005:54). By limiting visas to Mexicans—and the means to legally enter into the United States—"Mexicans would become racialized aliens in the United States in large part by their illegal presence in the region that was once Mexico" (Ngai 2005:55). By the 1930s, legal status became central to the racialization process of Mexicans, as mass repatriation campaigns, also known as **Mexican Repatriation Programs**, effectively expulsed close to 1 million migrants back to Mexico—effectively equating illegality with Mexican migration. In the 1950s, the United States and Mexico reached bilateral accords to bring temporary workers to the United States in order to have cheap and disposable labor workers who could be returned to Mexico once their work was not needed or once they created problems for the system. This program, known as the **Bracero Program**, lasted from 1942 to 1964. Then, the Immigration Act of 1965 further created "more severe restrictions on the conditions of 'legal migration from Mexico'"(DeGenova 2004:130–1).

Throughout the 1970s, migration from Mexico continued, but largely unauthorized. By the 1980s, the undocumented population in the United States had reached the millions. Thus, the Immigration Reform and Control Act of 1986 (IRCA) was significant immigration legislation that sought to incorporate the undocumented population in the United States at the time, which was mostly composed of Mexican immigrants. Yet, IRCA also engendered the militarization of the border through important budget allocations, paradoxically legalizing a segment of the unauthorized Mexican population already living in the United States while encouraging the settlement of the unauthorized population here through the border buildup. IRCA also gave rise to the mixed-status families by providing **permanent legal residency** to some, while keeping in place the structural limit on who can adjust their legal status. In the context of these truncated legal rights—as immigrant illegality was never eliminated by IRCA—research on migrant illegality emerged as a field of study.

Racial and Ethnic Understandings of Migration

Two theories have dominated our understanding of racial relations in the United States. On one hand, race theories have been used to make sense of the experience of African Americans brought to this country as slaves. On the other hand, ethnic theories have been used to make sense of the experiences of European immigrants who arrived during several waves—but with a particular focus on the second migration wave that brought to US shores migrants from southern and eastern Europe, considered to be unassimilable to the US society due to the cultural and religious differences with the Anglo-Saxon, Protestant mainstream US culture (Omi and Winant 1994).

There have been four waves of mass migration to the United States. In the first wave, during the colonial and postcolonial era in the seventeenth century, migrants from Europe arrived and slaves from Africa brought against their will repopulated the United States in the context of indigenous genocide and depopulation. The second major wave of migration took place in the eighteenth century, when German, Irish, and Italian immigrants dominated the migration waves. The third wave of migration occurred at the end of the nineteenth century, and it was dominated by Asian migration flows from China and Japan. The last wave of migration, after 1965, has been dominated by Asian and Latinx immigrants.

The main theory of immigration, based on the experiences of southern and eastern Europeans, posited **assimilation** as the process by which immigrants became incorporated into the mainstream. Robert E. Park theorized that race relations would follow a cycle from contact (marked differences), to competition, accommodation, to assimilation (indistinguishable from the mainstream); under this theory, ethnic and racial identities become less salient over time. Milton Gordon later added detail to this theory by proposing different stages to the assimilation process: cultural, structural, and marital assimilation, and added that the process of assimilation could take three or more generations. Under this tradition of assimilation, Richard Alba and Victor Nee argued for a "new assimilation theory" that included the economic and racial context of reception as a key factor that shaped assimilation. Then, Herbert Gans argued that there were different paths into the mainstream. Alejandro Portes and Min Zhou combined these theories into the **segmented assimilation** framework. These theories, however, are not able to explain or did not take into consideration the experiences of black Americans and Mexicans in the United States—who, after multiple generations in the United States continue to be considered outsiders. Critiques of assimilation theory argue that this theory focuses on the experiences of European immigrants to the United States, and race is completely ignored.

Immigration and Race

Scholars have begun to explicitly incorporate race theories into their study of immigration. Scholars have also explored the connections between racial identities, anti-immigrant sentiment, and politics, especially in times of heightened **nationalism**. For example, in a study conducted by Major, Blodorn, and Major Blascovich (2018), they found that the changing racial demographics of America contribute to Trump's success as a presidential candidate among white Americans whose race/ethnicity is central to their identity (Major, Blodorn, and Major Blascovich 2018) and how racial anxiety becomes "white-lash" in the political arena. Other scholars have begun to explore the connections between the racialized law enforcement practices of criminalizing people of color and the mass incarceration of immigrant Latinxs in the United States (Armenta 2016). Now scholars pay close attention to "**crimimmigration**"—the merge of immigration and criminal law. In connecting current trends with historical patterns, Manuel Barajas argued for an analysis that he calls interactive colonialism (XC), which "grounds the migration and incorporation experiences [of Mexicans] in a historical context shaped by colonialism (various and overlapping forms), dialectical relations (intersecting systems of racial, class, and gender oppression), and social interactions (transnational networks)" (Barajas 2012:271–2). In other words, colonialism, intersectionality, and borders matter in the migrating experiences of Mexicans—an indigenous population in the American continent that is viewed and framed as "alien" in the United States.

The election of Trump in 2016 has brought to the forefront the racialized anxieties that US Americans feel as a result of drastic demographic changes that forecast a new nonwhite majority in the United States by

2045 (Frey 2018). The current policies of the Trump administration, asking for a concrete wall, calling the National Guard to the border, even threatening with closing the border—although temporarily—highlight the racialized anxieties brown migrants from the American continent have awoken in the United States. Today, unauthorized migration is at an all-time low (Burnett 2017) and Mexico deports more Central Americans than the United States (Melendez 2018), and yet fears of a brown invasion from the south continue to be popular in the United States (Fabian 2018).

Mindfulness

The story of Aida Rodriguez, the immigrant who provided the introduction vignette, highlights that we are the product of past immigration and racial laws and policies that determined how we got here (for most of us), and the rights afforded to us as a group once we are here—some of us are given the opportunity to thrive, while others must struggle to get basic opportunities such as going to school. But she also highlights the agency, resiliency, and power we have to also shape our society through activism and thus create political changes for a better society tomorrow. Ultimately, we can use our sociological understanding of how race shapes immigration laws and policies to inform our own understanding of current immigration proposals, and also inform and shape how others view and understand racial inequality and immigration. For example, in 1994, 63 percent of US Americans thought immigrants were a burden for the nation, and 31 percent thought immigrants were a strength for the nation. Twenty years later, views flipped: 51 percent of US Americans think immigrants are a strength to the nation, and 41 percent think immigrants are a burden to the nation (Lopez, Passel, and Rohal 2015). This is in part due to the work young immigrant activists, known as the DREAMers, did to change perspectives on what it meant to live as undocumented in the United States.

Section Readings

The chapters in this section present a complicated picture of how immigration is racialized in the United States—at the border, within the interior, and institutionally by US government agencies and the media. In the first chapter, Sarabia and Perales show how the government racializes unauthorized migration at the border through the mass prosecution of unauthorized entry and reentry into the United States—which targets and affects Mexican migrants disproportionately. In the second chapter, Valadez shows how federal judges also play a role in the racialization of migration in the interior of the United States through systematic biased and unconscious racism. Finally, in the last piece, Elias highlights how the media frames policies in ways that draw moral boundaries around "deserving" and "undeserving" migrants—thus perpetuating the racialized views the general people have about unauthorized migration. Elias also highlights, in consideration of such framings, how migrants contest and resist these framings actively.

Reading 7.1 Operation Streamline: Producing Legal Violence, Racialized *Illegality*, and Perpetual Exclusion

Heidy Sarabia, California State University–Sacramento

Maria Perales, Princeton University

Keywords: Operation Streamline, Racialized Illegality, Perpetual Illegality, Crimmigration, US-Mexico Border

Sara had attempted to cross the US-Mexico border without documents through deserts, water canals, ports of entry, jumping through fences, and running through mountains. She had failed seventeen times when I met her, and even though she was determined to continue trying, she had concluded that she would not attempt crossing through Arizona and would only try in California. When she was caught in Arizona, she had to see a judge and was put in prison for fifteen days, while in California she was only jailed for a few hours each time she was caught. Nevertheless, prosecuted for "illegal" entry" (a misdemeanor) in Arizona, she could be considered a "criminal" now and face prosecution for "illegal reentry" (a felony) if she were caught again. Sara was crossing unauthorized to try to reach her husband and children, as well as an ill mother living in the United States—her only crime was trying to reunite with her family. Yet, she is the type of immigrant who is the main target of today's fierce focus on stopping unauthorized migration.

When Trump delivered his immigration plan in the summer of 2015, the US-Mexico border wall was a key delivery point: "There must be a wall across the southern border. … Mexico must pay for the wall" (Corasaniti 2016). A year later, Trump continued to emphasize the border wall as a key component of his plan to curb unauthorized immigration: "We will build a great wall along the southern border. And Mexico will pay for the wall. One hundred percent. They don't know it yet but they're going to pay for it" (Corasaniti 2016). Yet, Trump's comments obscure a reality in immigration and enforcement tactics: border apprehensions are at an all-time low (Gonzalez-Barrrera 2016), and border enforcement tactics have dramatically changed in the last ten years.

In this chapter, we discuss three issues related to immigration enforcement along the US-Mexico border. First, we discuss the most important shift in immigration enforcement along the border, from physical (walls) to legal (prosecutions) barriers. Second, in light of this new shift in enforcement tactics, we argue that this new type of enforcement results in racialized criminalization of unauthorized immigrants. Finally, we show how the long-term consequences of this new immigration enforcement technique focused on legal enforcement results in perpetual exclusion from the social fabric of the United States.

Methods

This chapter draws from primary data collected along the US-Mexico border in California and Arizona by the authors. Sarabia conducted participant observation from June 2009 to August 2010 at a migrant help center located along the US-Mexico border in the city of Mexicali, Baja California, Mexico, right across from Calexico, California, where she talked to migrants deported from California and Arizona—some prosecuted under Operation Streamline. Perales spent a week in Arizona, in Nogales, Phoenix, and Tucson. There, she met with several immigrants' rights organizations that work either directly or indirectly with migrants who had been prosecuted under Operation Streamline. She also sat in on an Operation Streamline procedure and spoke with long-time *End Streamline Coalition* volunteers. Their coalition includes several key local and regional human and migrants' organizations, seeking to end the mass criminalization and deportation of migrants at the border. Not only does the *Coalition* advocate for the termination of Operation Streamline but also it demands a more humane, legal, and cultural treatment of migrants in the United States. In addition to the primary data collected by both authors, we also rely on secondary data on detentions, prosecutions, and deportations reported by the Department of Homeland Security (DHS) and the Transactional Records Access Clearinghouse (TRAC) to supplement our ethnographic data.

Literature: Border Enforcement, from Walls to Courts

Since its inception, US immigration enforcement, though less serious in nature, displayed a racialized component. From the creation of the US Border Patrol to the early 1990s, enforcement of immigration laws at the border was based on apprehending unauthorized immigrants after they crossed and physically moving (most of) them to Mexico—these "deportations" were administrative matters (much like a traffic ticket).

In 1992, however, Operation Blockade changed how the border was patrolled. Operation Blockade, implemented by a new chief of Border Patrol in the El Paso, Texas, sector, changed two things. First, it moved most Border Patrol agents to the border itself in order to prevent migrants from crossing (rather than catching them once inside). In addition, it also used military tactics, equipment, and personnel to support the operation (Andreas 1998:596). Operation Blockade, later renamed Operation Hold-the-line, also marked two important changes in border policy. First, it marked the dramatic and sustained increased in the INS budget (see Table 1). In fact, the Border Patrol budget doubled from 1990 to 1996 and would double again from 1996 to 2001. In 1990, the Border Patrol budget was less than $300 million; by 2016, the budget was $3.6 billion. Second, it began the tactic of concentrating resources and personnel on a relatively small segment of the border to prevent crossings from these segments that have traditionally been used by unauthorized migrants (Cornelius 2001). Operation Blockade was deemed to be a success by Border Patrol given that it decreased the number of border crossings and apprehensions on the segments of the border heavily patrolled (Bean et al. 1994).

Operation Blockade became the model for other operations, using the same tactics—Operation Gatekeeper (1994) in California, Operation Safeguard (1994) in Arizona, and Operation Rio Grande (1997) (Dunn and Palafox 2005). Yet, critics argued that rather than curb unauthorized immigration into the United States, these operations merely rerouted immigrants to other, more dangerous, sectors of the border (see Table 2). As a result, deaths at the border began to climb as immigrants crossing clandestinely began to look to more remote alternatives to enter the United States. It has been estimated that more than 6,000 migrants have perished on their way to the this country (USBP 2016). The number could be much higher because this data only accounts for migrant bodies found, and not for "missing" persons.

In 2003, INS was reorganized under the umbrella of the DHS (USCIS 2011), and in 2005, a new operation was implemented along the border that would have lasting effects.

Targets of Policing: The Racialized Consequences of the "Neutral" Application of the Law

When the US Border Patrol was created in 1924, the main were Chinese immigrants, but soon after, they were replaced by poor Mexican unauthorized border crossers (Hernandez 2010). Historically, most unauthorized immigrants in the United States are from Mexico—due to the lack of permits that would allow Mexican nationals to enter here legally (Hernandez 2010). Border Patrol has classified migrants apprehended as "Mexicans" and

"Other Than Mexican (OTM)." From 2004 to 2005, the apprehension of OTM migrants in Texas soared.[2] In 2004, 9,896 OTM were apprehended in the Del Rio border sector; a year later, 15,642 OTM were apprehended (Lydgate 2010:491). While Mexican unauthorized migrants were simply moved/deported back to Mexico, these OTM migrants could not be simply deported, and Border Patrol did not have the space to detain these immigrants. They were given a "Notice to Appear" in immigration courts—but few returned to appear in court.

Border Patrol decided to criminally prosecute all the OTM migrants in order to send them to the criminal justice system where there was more space to detain them. But the US Attorney's office (USAO) determined that detaining and prosecuting people based on their national origin would be considered an equal protection violation. Consequently, Border Patrol decided to continue with the plan, adopt a "zero tolerance" stance, and prosecute all migrants crossing unauthorized (Lydgate 2010:492). This new plan became the basis for Operation Streamline.

Operation Streamline, now implemented in eight of the nine border sectors in the Southwest (Boyce and Launius 2013), has changed unauthorized border entry and reentry from an administrative matter to a criminal offense—effectively criminalizing immigration law (Coleman 2007). This operation marks the shift in tactic, from "prevention through deterrence" to "high consequences" (Argueta 2016). Today, migrants crossing unauthorized face detention, incarceration, and prosecution of unauthorized entry or reentry as criminal offenses (Martinez and Slack 2013). From 2007 to 2008, prosecutions of unauthorized entry and reentry doubled (see Table 3). In addition, by prosecuting all immigrants crossing unauthorized, the group most affected is Mexican nationals.

Scholars have argued that Operation Streamline does not work. For example, Amuedo-Dorantes and Pozo (2014) found that intent to return to the United States unauthorized does not differ whether or not migrants were detained in a sector where Operation Streamline operates. But research has focused mostly on the legal consequences of Operation Streamline: eroding procedures in the criminal law system (Chacon 2009), undermining due process (Boyce and Launius 2013), and reducing migrants' ability to gain legal status in the United States (Martinez and Slack 2013). Yet, we still know little about the social process and social consequences of Operation Streamline and its consequences as it criminalizes unauthorized presence in the United States.

The names of these operations, intended to stop the flow of unauthorized migrants—Operation Blockage, Hold the Line, Gatekeeper, and Safeguard—point to the increased militarization of the US-Mexico border (Dunn 1996) and increased reliance on framing the issue of unauthorized immigration as an issue of "us versus them" and thus "othering" undocumented immigrants (Caldwell 2016). Mexican unitized migrants increasingly became caught between larger economic, political, and social forces that pushed them to migrate unauthorized into the United States and the national immigration policies that are extremely restrictive for Mexican immigrants. In addition, at the local level, as Border Patrol tried to "game the system" by forcing OTM immigrants into the criminal justice system, Mexican immigrants became the primary targets of these new enforcement tactics.

In the rest of the chapter, we want to highlight three aspects of Operation Streamline that have had a serious and long-term impact for unauthorized migrants crossing the border, for those framing unauthorized migration as an issue of criminality, and for the settlement prospects of those who reenter unauthorized into the United States.

How Unauthorized Migration Became Criminalized

While border enforcement changed in the 1990s with increased military presence along the border, Operation Streamline changed border enforcement in ways that increased legal violence, not just physical violence. In this

---

[2] See Lyndgate 2010 for an excellent review of why numbers of OTM soared and the institutional challenges this created.

section, we show how and why Operation Streamline (focused on prosecutions) differs from the physical (i.e., militarization and walls) tactics used to discourage unauthorized border crossing.

Recall that Sara, the story we open the chapter with, had attempted to cross the border through both California and Arizona. Given that in Arizona, through Operation Streamline she faced the judge and had to spend time in prison, she had decided to cross only through California. Even though the last time she had attempted to cross, through the All-American Canal, she almost drowned. The legal threads had routed her to take more physically dangerous border-crossing paths. In another case, Rita, a young woman from Tabasco, had been given legal residency papers so she could cross through the "line," that is, an official point of entry. Yet, she was caught and imprisoned for two months in Arizona. She subsequently decided to cross through California and broke her right leg trying to cross the border fence. Again, the legal threats had routed Rita to cross through more dangerous terrain.

The migrants we met in our research expressed fear about the explicit legal threats they encountered while crossing through Arizona. Jail time was the most explicit form of legal violence that migrants disliked and tried to avoid. In addition, migrants were also told that they were banned from returning to the United States and that subsequent arrests could result not only in jail time but also in heavy fines. For example, Ramiro was given a letter of deportation that threatened him with up to twenty years in prison and a $250,000 fine if he was caught unauthorized in the United States again. Ramiro was not sure if this was true or not but felt "fearful" and did not know what to do next. He desperately wanted to reunite with his wife and five children in the United States, but the legal threat weighed on him heavily.

By criminalizing immigrants for unauthorized entry and reentry, through Operation Streamline, it made migrants take even more risks when crossing unauthorized. While border apprehensions are at an all-time low, deaths in the deadliest border sector (Tucson) are up five times from a decade ago (Blust 2016). In the March 2016 procedure, one of the authors observed and was told by long-time volunteers how apprehended migrants were legally advised by their counsel to take the smaller plea deal: unauthorized entry. Few of those in court that day sought to appeal any of the accusations as doing so meant longer trials and consequently longer periods in detention. Nonetheless, after serving the sentence for unauthorized entry, according to the volunteers, these migrants were likely to embark on the trip once again, but this time, with the knowledge that capture by immigration officials meant facing the more serious offense: unauthorized reentry. The offense also meant longer periods in detention.

How Criminalization Produced Racialized Illegality

The current criminalization of unauthorized entry and reentry, carried out *en masse* by the implementation of Operation Streamline, is fed by and also feeds on racist and xenophobic attitudes toward unauthorized migrants.

This is exemplified by Donald Trump. As he announced his run for the nomination for president in the Republican Party, he stated,

> When Mexico sends its people, they're not sending their best. … They're sending people that have lots of problems, and they're bringing those problems with us. They're bringing drugs. They're bringing crime. They're rapists. And some, I assume, are good people. (Trump cited in Kopan 2016)

Trump depicted all Mexican immigrants as drug dealers, criminals, and rapists, making an explicit racial categorization of all Mexicans as criminals. But then, to make it more palpable, he turned his focus on "criminal aliens," stating,

> Zero tolerance for criminal aliens. Zero. Zero. Zero. They don't come in here. They don't come in here. According to federal data, there are at least 2 million, 2 million, think of it, criminal aliens now inside of our country, 2 million people criminal aliens. We will begin moving them

out day one. As soon as I take office. Day one. In joint operation with local, state, and federal law enforcement. (Trump cited in Bump 2016)

Trump exaggerated figures about the number of immigrants who have been prosecuted for a crime, ignored the fact that most "crimes" are immigration or drug-related offenses (Gramlich and Bialik 2017), and overlooked the role the US government plays in actively producing these "criminalized" migrants. For example, once in office, Trump actively expanded who is considered a "criminal alien" through his executive power. This broader definition now includes immigrants who use fraudulent documents to seek work and anyone who, "in the judgment of an immigration officer," poses a risk to public safety or national security (Medina 2017).

While all the rhetoric focuses on legality and criminality—that is, a focus on those who commit illegal and criminal acts—the reality is that most immigrants targeted as "criminal aliens" have committed immigration or drug-related offenses. Yet, the rhetoric posits these immigrants as a danger to society. In addition, due to the demographics of the undocumented population, most immigrants targeted for, apprehended, and prosecuted for immigration and drug-related activities are Latino and black immigrants. In fact, half of all federal prosecutions are immigration related (Gramlich and Bialik 2017). Thus, a language of legality and criminality hides the racialized anxieties driving a discourse about immigrants as dangerous criminals.

Along the border, for example, Operation Streamline produces criminality through mass prosecutions. The human rights organization Coalición de Derechos Humanos and law scholar Doris Provine point to the racism the Streamline process upholds, derived from a process that disproportionately targets Central American and Mexican migrants. Derechos Humanos contends that more than half of the detainees continue to be of Latinx descent and of a darker complexion. During her observations at the Operation Streamline procedure, one of the authors found this to be almost universally the case, as the majority of all apprehended migrants possessed darker skin tones. Furthermore, Provine highlights that although more than 40 percent of unauthorized migrants are visa over-stayers, Operation Streamline allows the government to geographically target areas of high Latinx migrant influx (Provine 2013:33).

The mass criminalization of Latinx migrants is perpetuated under the premise of border security, among others reasons. For example, former governor of Arizona and secretary of the Department of Homeland Security, as well as current president of the University of California system, Janet Napolitano, supports and promotes Operation Streamline and similar methods on the basis that it ensures safer, more secure and prospering borderland communities. In a speech given before the Senate committee, Napolitano contended that these policies played a pivotal role in creating safer communities with constant, "almost flat" crime and drug-related violence levels (Napolitano 2011). Inevitably, Operation Streamline produces racialized outcomes because prosecution along the US-Mexico border means that most migrants who are caught and prosecuted along the border are Mexican/Central American immigrants. Thus, when Trump or Napolitano talks about criminals and the need for border community, they are associating a threat with a very particular subset of migrants: Mexican immigrants. When Trump is targeting Mexican immigrants and Latinx immigrants for deportation, he is highlighting the generalized fear of the browning of the United States.

How Criminalization Resulted in Perpetual Exclusion

The legal tactics of border enforcement, focusing on prosecuting immigrants for entering and reentering unauthorized, have long-lasting consequences for the migrants crossing unauthorized. Sara, for example, the immigrant who began the chapter, will not be able to adjust her status even if she has the opportunity. And even in the event of an immigration reform that could allow unauthorized immigrants to gain legal status in the United States, these past prosecutions for immigration and drug-related offenses will probably make many immigrants ineligible for legalization, as they are already being left out of immigration reform efforts (Caldwell 2016).

The consequences of criminalizing immigration and drug-related offenses are that those criminalized immigrants end up in a revolving door of exclusion. When immigrants deported as "criminal aliens" return to the United States, and they are caught again, they are automatically imprisoned (without a right to see a judge), and then automatically deported (again, without a right to see a judge). For example, ICE reported in its news bulletin, "Mexican national sentenced to 41 months for illegal re-entry" (ICE, April 8, 2010) and "Mexican man receives 5-year sentence for re-entry after deportation" (ICE, May 20, 2009). These Mexican immigrants served prison time in the United States for the "crime" of unauthorized reentry into this country. Thus, deported immigrants as "criminal aliens" who return to the United States live in *perpetual illegality* (Sarabia 2011) because they are ineligible to adjust their status.

For example, such was the experience of Sebastian, who moved to here at the age of fourteen and had married a US citizen in the 1990s. As a legal resident, he felt no need to become a naturalized citizen. But in 2002, he was arrested and charged for selling drugs. In addition to the prison term he served, he lost his legal permanent residency and was deported to Mexico. He had left his life, family, and home behind in the United States, so he returned immediately. Being deported as a "criminal alien," however, meant that he would no longer be eligible to adjust his legal status in the United States, and four years later he was arrested again for possession of a firearm. Again, he served time for the charge and then was deported once again, but returned here immediately. Two short years later, he was driving to pick up one of his daughters and was stopped for a traffic violation—he was driving in a bus-only lane on the freeway—and was deported again to Mexico. Sebastian, now living in *perpetual illegality*, can't escape the revolving door of arrests and deportations. As a Latino man, he is more likely to be targeted for minor crimes (Gardner and Kohli 2009), and as a deportable immigrant, he is ineligible to go in front of a judge to change his legal status (Martinez and Slack 2013). Given that unauthorized entry is a felony, the fact of living in the United States—even without doing anything else—is itself his crime.

Conclusion

Operation Streamline is a program that dehumanizes undocumented immigrants, specifically those of Central American and Mexican origin, through the process of criminalizing their unauthorized entry and reentry into the United States. Operation Streamline overlooks the push-and-pull factors that drive migration, and instead, through an individualistic lens, attempts to deter unauthorized migration through criminalization. Though it claims to successfully stop immigration and extols its efficiency, the process, in conjunction with other enforcement policies, has pushed immigrants to more dangerous areas along the desert. On average, a person dies in the desert every day. Until we begin to address the structural factors that impact communities as a whole—and drive migration—we will not have a humane system of managing migration. In fact, the only humane way to deal with migration might be to accept that human mobility is a human right—one that does not deserve to be criminalized.

Reflection/Critical Thinking Questions

1. In what ways do you think the US government is intentional in the production of perpetual exclusion?

2. Who benefits from this perpetual exclusion?

3. What factors might drive/shape perpetual exclusion locally, nationally, and globally?

Exploratory Research Questions

1. What are the long-term effects of this perpetual exclusion for immigrants?

2. What are the long-term effects of this perpetual exclusion for US society?

Further Readings and/or Web Links

- Explore more data on immigration enforcement using the Yearbook of Immigration Statistics: https://www.dhs.gov/immigration-statistics/yearbook
- Explore more data on the handling of immigration cases by the US Department of Justice: https://www.justice.gov/eoir/statistical-year-book
- Explore more data on immigration published by the Transactional Records Access Clearinghouse (TRAC): http://trac.syr.edu/immigration/
- Visit a website focused on crimmigration: http://crimmigration.com/
- Visit the Pew Research Center site focused on immigration trends: http://www.pewresearch.org/topics/immigration/
- Visit the Gallup Poll to see how the US public thinks about and views immigration: http://news.gallup.com/topic/immigration.aspx

Tables

Table 1. Border Patrol Budget (1990–2016)

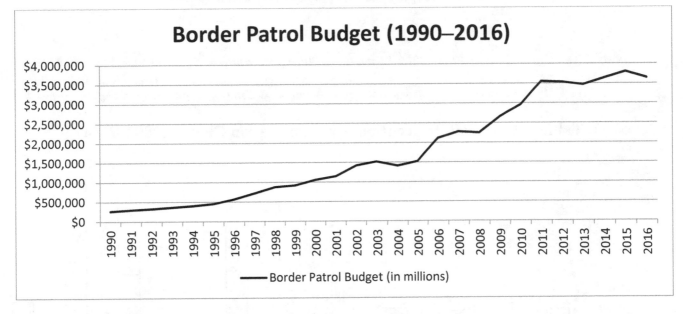

Source: USBP. 2016. "Southwest Border Deaths By Fiscal Year." Retrieved 7/5/17. (https://www.cbp.gov/sites/default/files/assets/documents/2016-Oct/BP Southwest Border Sector Deaths FY1998 - FY2016.pdf).

Table 2. Border Patrol Apprehensions by State (1990–2016)

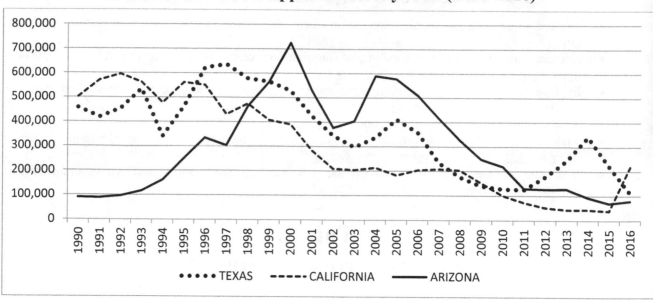

Source: USBP. 2016. "Total Illegal Alien Apprehensions By Fiscal Year." Retrieved 7/5/17.
(https://www.cbp.gov/sites/default/files/assets/documents/2016-
Oct/BP%20Southwest%20Border%20Sector%20Apps%20FY1960%20-%20FY2016.pdf).

Table 3. Criminal Prosecutions by Immigration Charge (2004–2014)

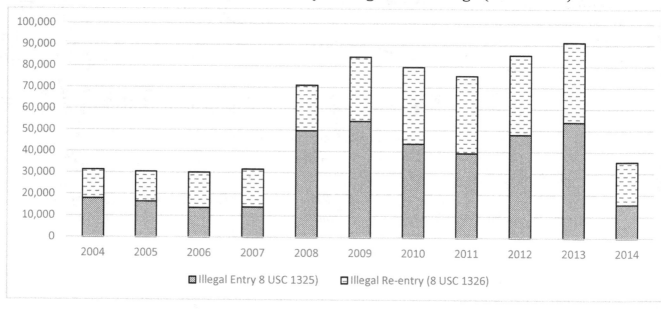

Source: TRAC. 2014. "Charges in Criminal Enforcement of Immigration Laws." Retrieved 7/5/17.
(http://trac.syr.edu/immigration/reports/354/).

References

Amuedo-Dorantes, Catalina, and Susan Pozo. 2014. *On the Intended and Unintended Consequences of Enhanced Border and Interior Immigration Enforcement: Evidence from Deportees.*

Andreas, Peter. 1998. "The Escalation of U.S. Immigration Control in the Post-NAFTA Era." *Political Science Quarterly* 113(4):591–615.

Argueta, Carla N. 2016. *Border Security Metrics Between Ports of Entry.* Retrieved (https://fas.org/sgp/crs/homesec/R42138.pdf).

Bean, Frank D., et al. 1994. *Illegal Mexican Migration & the United States/Mexico Border: The Effects of Operation Hold the Line on El Paso/Juárez.* University of Texas at Austin: Population Research Center.

Blust, Kendal. 2016. "Deaths per 10,000 Border Crossers Are up 5 Times from a Decade Ago." *Arizona Daily Star,* May 21, 1–7. Retrieved (http://tucson.com/news/local/border/deaths-per-border-crossers-are-up-times-from-a-decade/article_c1279aaf-4ad8-51c9-82d8-3143b836f52e.html).

Boyce, Geoffrey, and Sarah Launius. 2013. *Warehousing the Poor: How Federal Prosecution Initiatives like "Operation Streamline" Hurt Immigrants, Drive Mass Incarceration and Damage U.S. Communities.* Retrieved (https://dspace.hampshire.edu/bitstream/10009/935/1/popdev_differentakes_082.pdf).

Bump, Philip. 2016. "Here's What Donald Trump Said in His Big Immigration Speech, Annotated." *Washington Post,* August 31, 3–7. Retrieved (https://www.washingtonpost.com/news/the-fix/wp/2016/08/31/heres-what-donald-trump-said-in-his-big-immigration-speech-annotated/?utm_term=.e22b8e1da7c9).

Caldwell, Beth. 2016. "The Demonization of 'Criminal Aliens.'" Retrieved June 14, 2018 (http://crimmigration.com/2016/10/25/the-demonization-of-criminal-aliens/).

Chacon, Jennifer M. 2009. "Managing Migration Through Crime." *Columbia Law Review* 109:135–48.

Coleman, Mathew. 2007. "Immigration Geopolitics Beyond the Mexico-US Border." *Antipode* 39(1):54–76. Retrieved (https://www.researchgate.net/profile/Mathew_Coleman2/publication/229688673_Immigration_Geopolitics_Beyond_the_Mexico-US_Border/links/5748618308ae008e3c912ddd.pdf).

Corasaniti, Nick. 2016. "A Look at Trump's Immigration Plan, Then and Now." *New York Times,* August 31. Retrieved (https://nyti.ms/2jSho8v).

Cornelius, Wayne A. 2001. "Death at the Border: Efficacy and Unintended Consequences of US Immigration Control Policy." *Population and Development Review* 27(4):661–85.

Dunn, Timothy J. 1996. *The Militarization of the U.S.-Mexico Border, 1978–1992: Low-Intensity Conflict Doctrine Comes Home.* CMAS Books, University of Texas at Austin.

Dunn, Timothy J., and José Palafox. 2005. "Militarization of the Border." *The Oxford Encyclopedia of Latinos and Latinas in the United States Border.* Retrieved (http://www.uua.org/sites/live-new.uua.org/files/documents/washingtonoffice/immigration/studyguides/handout4.1.pdf).

Gardner, Trevor, and Aarti Kohli. 2009. *The C.A.P. Effect: Racial Profiling in the ICE Criminal Alien Program.* Chief Justice Earl Warren Institute on Race, Ethnicity & Diversity. University of California, Berkeley Law School.

Gonzalez-Barrrera, Ana. 2016. "Apprehensions of Mexican Migrants at U.S. Borders Reach Near-Historic Low." *Pew Research Center* 2006:2014–17. Retrieved (http://www.pewresearch.org/fact-tank/2016/04/14/mexico-us-border-apprehensions/).

Gramlich, John, and Kristen Bialik. 2017. *Immigration Offenses Make up a Growing Share of Federal Arrests.* Retrieved (http://www.pewresearch.org/fact-tank/2017/04/10/immigration-offenses-make-up-a-growing-share-of-federal-arrests/).

Hernandez, Kelly Lytle. 2010. *Migra! A History of the U.S. Border Patrol.* University of California Press.

Kopan, Tal. 2016. "What Donald Trump Has Said about Mexico and Vice Versa." *CNN,* August 21, 1–6. Retrieved (http://www.cnn.com/2016/08/31/politics/donald-trump-mexico-statements/index.html).

Lydgate, Joanna Jacobbi. 2010. "Assembly-Line Justice: A Review of Operation Streamline." *California Law Review* 98(2):481–544.

Martinez, Daniel, and Jeremy Slack. 2013. "What Part of 'Illegal' Don't You Understand? The Social Consequences of Criminalizing Unauthorized Mexican Migrants in the United States." *Social & Legal Studies* 22(4):535–51. Retrieved (http://sls.sagepub.com/cgi/doi/10.1177/0964663913484638).

Martinez, Daniel E., and Jeremy Slack. 2013. *Bordering on Criminal: Part II: Possessions Taken and Not Returned.*

Medina, Jennifer. 2017. "Trump's Immigration Order Expands the Definition of 'Criminal.'" *New York Times,* January 26, 26–28. Retrieved (https://nyti.ms/2k9rO7n).

Napolitano, Janet. 2011. *Secretary Janet Napolitano, before the Senate Committee on Homeland Security and Governmental Affairs: "Securing the Border: Progress at the Federal Level."* Washington, DC. Retrieved (http://www.dhs.gov/ynews/testimony/testimony_1304459606805.shtm).

Provine, Doris Marie. 2013. "Institutional Racism in Enforcing Immigration Law." *Norteamérica* 8:31–53. Retrieved (http://linkinghub.elsevier.com/retrieve/pii/S1870355013717828).

Sarabia, Heidy. 2011. "Organizing 'Below and to the Left': Differences in the Citizenship and Transnational Practices of Two Zapatista Groups." *Sociological Forum* 26(2):356–80.

USBP. 2016. *Southwest Border Deaths By Fiscal Year.* Retrieved (https://www.cbp.gov/sites/default/files/assets/documents/2016-Oct/BP Southwest Border Sector Deaths FY1998 - FY2016.pdf).

USCIS. 2011. "Our History." *DHS.* Retrieved June 14, 2018 (https://www.uscis.gov/about-us/our-history).

Reading 7.2 Crimmigration: Understanding the Effects of Immigrant Status on the US Court System

Mercedes Valadez, California State University–Sacramento

Keywords: nativism, legal permanent resident, focal concerns perspective, federal sentencing guidelines, fast-track departure, general deterrence, specific deterrence, unwarranted disparity

Introduction

Negative immigrant stereotypes emphasize the beliefs that immigrants are criminally prone and a threat to social order. This leads to the conclusion that implementing and enforcing punitive measures will curb that crime, which in turn supports identifying, locating, imprisoning, and deporting immigrants. Even though immigrants have lower crime rates compared to native-born Americans, the myth of the criminal immigrant persists. One of the recent cases that drew attention to the myth of the criminal immigrant was *People of the State of California v. Jose Ines Garcia Zarate aka Juan Francisco Lopez Sanchez.*

In the News: Case Study

On July 1, 2015, Kate Steinle, her father, and a friend were walking along Pier 14 in San Francisco when Steinle was fatally struck in the back by a single bullet. Approximately one hour later, Garcia Zarate was arrested for suspicion of murder. The following day, police recovered the weapon from the San Francisco Bay off Pier 14. Roughly two months later, Garcia Zarate was charged with the second-degree murder of Kate Steinle. His trial began on October 23, 2017. Garcia Zarate's defense argued that the shooting was an accident. Garcia Zarate claimed that he found the gun wrapped in a T-shirt under a bench and that it had gone off by accident. An expert witness testified that the bullet ricocheted off the ground and traveled approximately 78 feet before it struck Steinle. During closing arguments, the jury was instructed to consider first-degree murder, second-degree murder, and manslaughter charges. On November 30, 2017, Garcia Zarate was acquitted of all charges besides firearm possession (James 2017).

This case was one of the most polarizing in recent history because of Garcia Zarate's immigrant status. Garcia Zarate had previously been deported five times and scheduled for his sixth deportation in 2015. However, he had no prior violent criminal record. He was briefly held in custody for felony unlawful reentry but was released by the federal authorities to San Francisco, where he had a twenty-year-old drug warrant for marijuana possession. The possession charge was dropped, and Garcia Zarate was released by the sheriff's department despite a federal detainer request. As a sanctuary city, San Francisco local law enforcement agencies do not need to honor federal retainer requests. After the Steinle shooting, federal and state authorities blamed each other for Garcia Zarate's release. The state argued that if Garcia Zarate had been deported, then Steinle would not have been shot. To that end, federal authorities argued that if the retainer had been observed, this tragedy would have been avoided. This case ignited a firestorm of controversy surrounding punishing and deporting immigrants, especially those with a prior criminal history.

Politicians, including President Trump, used the Garcia Zarate trial to vilify immigrants, promote nativism, argue for a border wall, and make the case to eliminate sanctuary cities. While Garcia Zarate was found not guilty by a jury of his peers, he was guilty in the court of public opinion. Not only was he guilty of the murder of Steinle, but he also deserved to be punished for being undocumented. Following the trial, President Trump tweeted, "A disgraceful verdict in the Kate Steinle case! No wonder the people of our Country are so angry with Illegal Immigration," and "This is exactly why we need the wall. It's time to put the safety of our citizens before illegal immigrants!" Former attorney general Jeff Sessions followed Trump's sentiments by stating:

> When jurisdictions choose to return criminal aliens to the streets rather than turning them over to federal immigration authorities, they put the public's safety at risk. San Francisco's decision to protect criminal aliens led to the preventable and heartbreaking death of Kate Steinle.

These statements echo and reinforce distrust of immigrants and foster an environment focused on identifying, locating, and deporting immigrants using the courts. Because of fear, myths, and misconceptions, immigrants may be more at risk of harsher treatment in the US court system. The push toward punitive legislation has served to increase the number of immigrant-related cases in federal courts, which has created a burden on these courts. Judges, like the rest of the public, are not immune to prejudice and bias. Even though judges are supposed to be fair and impartial, they may be also be influenced by negative immigrant stereotypes during their decision-making process. When comparing similarly situated offenders, native-born Americans, we can see this bias more clearly. In this chapter, I will discuss judicial bias and the factors that judges often consider at the time of sentencing and how these may be detrimental to immigrant defendants. In addition, I will discuss the influence of immigrant status on federal sentencing outcomes.

Judicial Bias

Section 2.3(a) of the Judicial Code of Conduct notes that judges are to perform the duties of the judicial office without prejudice or bias. They are supposed to be fair and impartial during their decision-making process rather than apply the law arbitrarily. However, there are times when judges deviate from the expected norms and express their bias against immigrants. In *U.S. v. Onwuemene* (1991), for example, the trial judge used the defendant's immigrant status as a factor in the sentencing process. The trial judge stated:

> You are not a citizen of this country. This country was good enough to allow you to come in here and to confer upon you … a number of the benefits of this society, form of government, and its opportunities, and you repay that kindness by committing a crime like this. We have got enough criminals in the United States without importing any.

Following the trial, the appellate court ordered that the defendant be resentenced because the defendant's due process rights had been violated. They also found that the trial judge had given undue weight to the defendant's immigrant status during the sentencing process. Similarly, trial judges have used a defendant's country of origin to assign negative stereotypes to a defendant and later used these assumptions to justify disparate treatment. The case of *U.S. v. Borrero-Isaza* (1989) highlights this issue. Borrero was arrested by Drug Enforcement Administration (DEA) agents for possessing approximately 1 kilogram of cocaine. During Borrero's sentencing, the judge made several disparaging remarks about Borrero's nationality. He stated,

> I just finished a case with two Colombian aliens. *Not only aliens. Illegal aliens* … People, such as Mr. Borrero are emboldened to undertake this type of crime because they don't think they are going to pay for it that much, if they are caught, number one … If they are caught, some of these lax sentences they are meted out, if you will, cause people of Mr. Borrero's ilk to feel that they can do this. It has gone so far … that an illegal alien who doesn't speak the language from Colombia—come here, and with impunity … sell kilogram quantities of cocaine … And somehow the people who are selling narcotics, *particularly from source countries* have to know that we in the United States mean business, and we are going to put a stop to this.

Borrero was sentenced to twelve years in prison and five years of probation, but appealed his sentence citing that his due process rights had been violated. He argued that his white codefendant received a substantially shorter sentence for the same drug trafficking conviction. The appellate court ordered that the defendant be resentenced because a harsher sentence cannot be imposed based on the defendant's nationality.

Judicial use of a defendant's nationality and/or immigrant status is not meant to be used for discriminatory purposes. However, judges have used bias and negative immigrant stereotypes to sentence offenders to the maximum penalty allowed by the Federal Sentencing Guidelines.[3] While some immigrant-related cases are sent back to trial court (see *U.S. v. Onwuemene*), not all cases are resentenced. In fact, judges are able to use a defendant's immigrant status or nationality during their decision-making process if used as a means of general deterrence[4] (*U.S. v. Gomez* 1986). In the case of *U.S. v. Gomez* (1986), the appellate court agreed with the ruling of the lower court and allowed the defendant's nationality to be considered during sentencing. Gomez, who was a Colombian national, faced charges of conspiracy to distribute narcotics, among other charges. During his trial, both the prosecutor and trial judge referred to the defendant's nationality and immigrant status. The prosecutor mentioned the "disturbing trend" of the recent drug cases involving immigrants from Latin America. During the sentencing phase, the trial judge noted that he intended to make an example out of Gomez with the purpose of deterring others from migrating to the United States with the purpose of committing drug-related offenses. As such, Gomez was sentenced to fifteen years in prison. He appealed his case, but the appellate court let the lower court decision stand because the trial judge focused on the goal of general deterrence rather than specifically focusing on the defendant's ethnic background. The appellate court supported using the reasoning of general deterrence to dissuade other immigrants from entering the United States with the intent of committing drug-related crimes. While bias and prejudice can factor into judicial decision-making, judges tend to rely on key case characteristics and individual specific characteristics during the decision-making process.

How Do Judges Decide?

Judges rely on key case characteristics, such as prior criminal history, to sentence an offender. However, they often lack the information and/or time to effectively assess a defendant's likelihood of reoffending (Steffensmeier, Ulmer, and Kramer 1998). As such, they rely on "focal concerns" during their decision-making process. According to the focal concerns perspective, judges rely on the following three key concerns during the sentencing phase: (1) the blameworthiness of the offender; (2) protection of the community; and (3) organizational constraints and practical consequences (Steffensmeier et al. 1998). As such, judicial decision-making is often influenced by both negative and positive stereotypes. In the case of most immigrants, this proves to be detrimental because immigrant stereotypes that often drive judicial decision-making tend to be negative.

Blameworthiness

Immigrants, especially those who are undocumented, are often linked to negative stereotypes, resulting in severe punishment (Valadez and Wang 2017). Offender blameworthiness refers to the offender's culpability or dangerousness. Immigrants, particularly those who are undocumented, are considered to be a threat to public safety, national security, and to be more criminally prone. Traditionally, judges use prior criminal history and offense seriousness as indicators of blameworthiness (Steffensmeier et al. 1998). However, individual level characteristics such as citizenship status, nationality, education, race/ethnicity, and age influence sentencing outcomes (Logue 2009; Steffensmeier et al. 1998; Valadez and Wang 2017). Immigrants are often viewed as more violent, threatening, more likely to reoffend, and more likely to participate in criminal lifestyles (Alba, Rumbaut, and Marotz 2005; Massey 2009; Newton 2008; Steffensmeier and Demuth 2006). Due to the proximity

---

[3] The United States federal courts system uses the Federal Sentencing Guidelines, which are set of rules aimed at creating uniform sentencing practices for individuals and corporations convicted of felonies and (Class A) misdemeanor offenses (United States Sentencing Commission 2016a).

[4] General deterrence refers to punishing one person with the intent that it will influence others not to perpetrate the same or similar offense. Specific deterrence refers to punishing an individual so that that specific person does not reoffend.

and perceived threat of the US-Mexico border, Mexican nationals face additional scrutiny and perceptions of dangerousness compared to other Latino immigrant subgroups (Logue 2009). Perceptions based on myths and stereotypes can lead to harsher treatment of immigrants in the courts.

Immigrants, including those who are undocumented, are less likely to commit crime compared to their US-born counterparts (Sampson 2008). However, the spread of misinformation about the dangerousness of immigrants affects public perception of immigrants (Wang 2012). For example, the 2000 General Social Survey found that 73 percent of US respondents thought that immigrants were either somewhat or very likely to commit crime (Ipsos Public Affairs 2010). The fear of immigrants is on the rise. The number of Americans who considered immigration a "bad thing" rose from 31 percent in 2001 to 36 percent in 2009 (Morales 2009).

High-ranking politicians reinforce harmful and false statements about immigrants. For example, the Trump administration reinforces perceptions of immigrant threats. In his June 16, 2015, announcement for candidacy for president, Donald Trump made a series of statements disparaging and negatively stereotyping immigrants, particularly Mexican nationals. Referring to Mexico, he stated "They are not our friend, believe me. They are bringing crime. They are rapists. And some, I assume, are good people" (cited in Reilly 2016). Federal judges have lifetime appointments made by the president and confirmed by the US Senate. Trump inherited approximately 100 vacancies for federal judges and has focused his efforts on nominating conservative white males. There is widespread concern that the federal judges nominated by Trump will neither be impartial nor unbiased, which may have a detrimental effect for immigrant defendants. For example, in September 2017 Trump nominated Gregory Katsas to the DC Court of Appeals. Prior to his nomination, Katsas served as counsel to the president and advised him on DACA and the travel ban. While judges are supposed to be impartial and unbiased, that is not always the case. Similar to other members of the public, they may be influenced by the social times and moral panic surrounding immigrants. The makeup of newly appointed federal judges may shift the sentencing landscape to reflect a more punitive position against immigrants, especially Latinos.

Protection of the Community

Judges consider protection of the community, which is based on the premise that dangerous offenders should be removed from their community. Incapacitation is used to remove an offender from society. In the criminal justice system, incapacitation is primarily accomplished through imprisonment (Steffensmeier et al. 1998). In addition to incarceration, immigrant defendants face an additional form of incapacitation through the use of deportation. Unlike US-born offenders, immigrants can be deported upon serving their sentence. Deportation is not exclusively used against undocumented immigrants. Legal permanent residents are also at risk of being deported. Deportation is the ultimate form of incapacitation because it permanently removes individuals from the community. Judges use what is commonly referred to as a "perceptual shorthand" to identify those whom they consider pose the greatest threat or risk to a community (Albonetti 1991; Steffensmeier et al. 1998). To better assess a defendant's risk or threat level, defendant-specific characteristics, such as community ties, employment, and educational level are considered (Steffensmeier et al. 1998). Immigrants, especially those who are undocumented, are more likely to be economically disadvantaged, to reside in socially disorganized neighborhoods, and to have unstable employment (Newburger and Gryn 2009). Unstable employment is commonly used to describe employment in the secondary labor market. Undocumented immigrants are often employed in seasonal work, including farming and construction, which requires that employees move frequently, thus creating the perception of instability. Migrant and seasonal farm workers may be viewed as being less stable and having fewer social ties to their community, which can influence their sentencing outcomes. In addition to the uncertainty and unpredictability of employment, immigrant defendants are also more vulnerable to additional scrutiny because of their non-US citizen status. For example, they are usually considered a flight risk, which increases the odds of pretrial detention, which impacts sentencing outcomes (Wolfe, Pyrooz, and Sphon 2001; Valadez 2013). Because judges fear that immigrant defendants might flee the United States rather than go to trial, they might be more willing to hold them in pretrial detention. Research suggests that being held for pretrial detention leads to a greater likelihood of being incarcerated (Valadez and Wang 2017). In addition, immigrants are generally considered less economically stable, to have few social ties, and limited or no opportunities for informal social control. These factors serve to influence judicial decision-making during the sentencing process and often result in unfavorable sentencing outcomes for immigrant defendants.

Organizational Constraints and Consequences

Lastly, organizational constraints and consequences are additional concerns that judges consider during the sentencing process. Practical constraints involve concerns about the social costs of incarceration and the resources spent going to trial. Organizational concerns involve relationships between the courtroom actors (e.g., prosecutor, judge, defense), safeguarding the courtroom workflow, being cognizant of correctional resources, and prison overcrowding (Dixon 1995; Ulmer and Kramer 1996). Judges also consider the practical consequences, including an offender's ability to serve time in prison, special needs, health concerns, and disruption to the family unit. The social cost of incarcerating immigrant offenders may not be viewed as devastating to their community (Steffensmeier et al. 1998). US district courts with large caseloads of immigrant defendants may be influenced by organizational constraints connected with the overload of immigrant cases and the problems this creates in workflow. For example, district courts that have greater caseloads of immigrant defendants may encourage them to participate in a fast-track[5] departure to save the resources and time associated with going to trial. Immigrant defendants who choose to forgo a fast-track departure may be punished more harshly for using the court's time and resources by choosing to proceed with a trial. Finally, judges consider local and community politics (Mishler and Sheehan 1993). They consider the impact that an offender's likelihood of reoffending might have on the court's standing. Together, the use of these "focal concerns" can put immigrants at a greater disadvantage compared to US citizens. The rise of immigrant-related prosecutions at the federal level has had an impact in the workflow and resources of the US federal court system. The section that follows provides an overview of how immigrants fare in the US court system.

Immigrants and the Federal Courts

Immigrants are said to be at a greater disadvantage compared to nonimmigrant groups in the US courts. This is due in part to the role of the state in its construction of the crime-immigration debate. Creating the myth that immigrants are more criminally prone and more deserving of punishment fuels public distrust of immigrants and encourages bias and unfair treatment of immigrants. In the courts, immigrants receive double punishment (Sayad 2004). First, they are punished for the offense committed/convicted. Second, they are punished for their immigrant status, which is considered a form of delinquency. Not only are immigrants more at risk of severe punishment in the courts, but "any trial involving a delinquent immigrant puts the very process of immigration on trial, first as a form of delinquency and second as a source of delinquency" (Sayad 2004:282). Since immigrants are considered to be more threatening, it can lead to enforcement of punitive policies that focus on punishing immigrants. As a result, this will increase the number of immigrant-related cases in US court districts. Some district courts, especially those near the southern border, have had to make adjustments to their workflow due to immigrant case overload.

As the United States continues to wage war against immigrants, federal enforcement of punitive immigration policies is actively being enforced. The threat of terrorism, coupled with the War on Drugs, increased attention and enforcement around the southern border, which has resulted in an increased number of prosecutions against immigrants in federal courts (Cottam and Marenin 2005; Logue 2009). The number of immigrant-related cases has been on the rise over the last decade (United States Sentencing Commission 2009). The number of immigrant defendants rivals the number of US native-born defendants (see Figure 1). In 2016, US citizens made up the majority of federal offenders convicted in the federal court system (58.30 percent), with

---

[5] A fast-track departure (5K3.1) can be initiated by a government motion or by a judge (Office of the Attorney General 2003). Fast-track programs are especially relevant in cases with immigrant defendants (Hartley and Tillyer 2011). This program is designed so that defendants who agree to participate in these programs waive their preliminary rights, plead guilty to all charges, and are sentenced immediately (United States Sentencing Commission 2003). By waiving their preliminary rights, defendants eliminate the costs associated with going to trial. Fast-track departures often lead to reduced sentence length, which is viewed as a reward for freeing up resources to prosecute others.

noncitizens not far behind (41.70 percent), whereas in 1996, non-US citizens made up only 27.3 percent of federal offenders compared to US citizens (72.7 percent). In addition to increased enforcement efforts, severity of punishment has also increased. The average amount of prison time served by immigrant offenders increased from four months in 1986 to twenty-one months in 2000 (Scalia and Litras 2002). During fiscal year 2015, immigration-related offenses (e.g., unlawful entry, remaining unlawfully in the United States, and human smuggling) were most commonly committed by noncitizens (92.1 percent), followed by drug offenses (United States Sentencing Commission 2016b). Immigrant offenders are primarily Hispanic (95.4 percent), have less than a high school education (80.7 percent), and are primarily men (93.1 percent) (United States Sentencing Commission 2016b).

With the increase in immigrants processed in the federal court system, it is critical to understand how they fare in the criminal justice system. The sentencing literature continues to find unwarranted disparities[6] based on offender-specific characteristics, such as age, race, ethnicity, education, and gender. For example, younger offenders, males, those with less formal education, and racial/ethnic minorities are more likely to be sentenced to prison and serve longer prison terms (Albonetti 1991; Spohn 2000; Steffensmeier and Demuth 2000; Valadez and Wang 2017) compared to their counterparts. Two recent court cases reflect this bias. Judge Aaron Persky sentenced Stanford University swimmer Brock Turner to probation and six months in jail for felony sexual assault compared to Raul Ramirez, an immigrant from El Salvador, who received three years in prison for a similar offense (Silverstein 2016). The obvious contrast between these offenders is reflected in their race/ethnicity, nationality, education level, and socioeconomic status. Unlike Ramirez, Turner was likely considered a salvageable offender, whereas Ramirez fit the stereotype of a dangerous violent criminal. Two offender characteristics that have often been overlooked in the sentencing literature are citizenship status and legal status. This is a considerable oversight, since noncitizens make up almost half of the offenders processed in the federal court system.

With respect to certainty of punishment (e.g., the likelihood of imprisonment), noncitizens (e.g., legal permanent residents and undocumented immigrants) are more likely to be incarcerated compared to US-citizen offenders. However, the results on severity of punishment are mixed (Demuth, 2003; Light 2014; Valadez and Wang 2017)—meaning that immigrants are more likely to be incarcerated, but once incarcerated, they are not necessarily sentenced to longer prison terms compared to US citizens. However, there are notable differences in the treatment among immigrant groups. For example, young Hispanic male noncitizens and undocumented immigrants are among the groups that have the greatest odds of being sentenced to prison (Valadez and Wang 2017). In addition, Mexican nationals are more likely to be incarcerated and serve longer prison terms compared to other Latino subgroups (Valadez 2013). This finding is not surprising considering the negative stereotypes attached to young Hispanic male immigrants, especially Mexican nationals. However, the length of imprisonment varies and is not always more severe compared to US citizens.

There are a growing number of studies that examine the influence of immigrant status on the likelihood of imprisonment and length of incarceration. Their findings are mixed. For example, Demuth (2002) found that noncitizens and undocumented immigrants were more likely to be incarcerated compared to US citizens. However, he did not find significant differences in the length of imprisonment between the two groups. Wolfe and colleagues (2011) again found that noncitizens had higher odds of imprisonment compared to US citizens. However, they found that undocumented immigrants received shorter prison sentences compared to US citizens. Perhaps rather than using additional resources for long-term imprisonment, immigrants may be given shorter prison sentences so that they can be deported sooner. Other studies have delved deeper into the issue of citizenship and made distinctions by defendant nationality (Logue 2009; Valadez 2013). Research suggests that Mexican nationals are treated more harshly compared to non-Mexican offenders and more likely to be incarcerated. The influence of citizenship status on federal sentencing outcomes varies. One reason that might contribute to these inconsistent findings may be related to the years of data analyzed. Some periods reflect years of greater or lesser judicial discretion. Several other factors can also explain the conflicting findings, including districts (e.g., U.S.-Mexico border districts) and offense type (e.g., immigration) examined.

---

[6] Unwarranted disparity refers to the residual variation due to variables outside of legally relevant factors.

The rise of immigrant offenders in the criminal justice system is alarming. There is a focus on identifying, locating, prosecuting, incarcerating, and deporting immigrants. Once they enter the criminal justice system, they face several disadvantages, including financial, language barriers, and negative stereotypes.

Conclusion

The sentencing literature suggests that negative immigrant stereotypes may influence the judicial decision-making process. If that's the case, then sentencing isn't being conducted in a fair and impartial manner. Instead, it can be arbitrary and capricious. Criminalizing immigrants has resulted in mass deportations, family separation, and misuse of funds and wasteful spending. This is done in the name of combating a false immigrant threat. In 2015, there were an estimated 43.2 million immigrants living in the United States. This makes up approximately 13.4 percent of the US population (Lopez and Radford 2017). The majority are Mexican nationals (26.8 percent), non-US citizens (52 percent), female (51.4 percent), and have less than a high school education (51.6 percent). Nationality, citizenship, educational attainment, and sex put an immigrant at higher risk of being treated more punitively in the courts. The effort to vilify one group of people in the courts is creating a system based on discriminating against those deemed to be unworthy of living in the United States.

Discussion Questions

1. Look for a similar case/offense in which one defendant is an immigrant and the other is a US citizen. Did their courtroom outcomes differ? If so, why do you believe they differed? If not, why not?

2. Do you think it's fair to consider immigrants to be a greater flight risk compared to US citizens? If so, should this affect their case outcome? Why or why not?

Exploratory Research Questions

1. Does judicial political party can influence courtroom outcomes for immigrant offenders? Find evidence to support your position.

2. Do you think that judges are more punitive in their sentencing practices when there is a Republican presidential administration in power?

Websites

https://www.ussc.gov/

https://www.ice.gov/

https://www.ussc.gov/guidelines

Suggested Readings

Huntington, Samuel P. 2004. "The Hispanic Challenge." *Foreign Policy* 141:30–45.

Kanstroom, Daniel. 2007. *Deportation Nation: Outsiders in American History*. Cambridge, MA:

Harvard University Press.

References

Alba, Richard, Ruben G. Rumbaut, and Karen Marotz. 2005. "A Distorted Nation: Perceptions of Racial/Ethnic Group Sizes and Attitudes Toward Immigrants and Other Minorities." *Social Forces* 84:901–19.

Albonetti, Celesta A. 1991. "An Integration of Theories to Explain Judicial Discretion." *Social Problems* 38:247–66.

Cottam, Martha L., and Otwin Marenin. 2005. "The Management of Border Security in NAFTA: Imagery, Nationalism, and the War on Drugs." *International Criminal Justice Review* 15:15–37.

Demuth, Stephen. 2003. "Racial and Ethnic Differences in Pretrial Release Decisions and Outcomes: A Comparison of Hispanic, Black, and White Felony Arrestees." *Criminology* 41:873–908.

Demuth, Stephen. 2002. "The Effect of Citizenship Status on Sentencing Outcomes in Drug Cases." *Federal Sentencing Reporter* 14:271–75.

Dixon, Jo. 1995. "The Organizational Context of Criminal Sentencing." *American Journal of Sociology* 100:1157–98.

Hartley, Richard D., and Rob Tillyer. 2011. "Defending the Homeland: Judicial Sentencing Practices for Federal Immigration Offenses." *Justice Quarterly* 29:76–104.

Ipsos Public Affairs. 2010. Ipsos/McClatchy Poll conducted May 6–9, 2010. Washington, DC.

James, Mike. 2017. "Undocumented Immigrant Not Guilty of Murder in Polarizing San Francisco Case." Retrieved December 9, 2017, from (https://www.usatoday.com/story/news/2017/11/30/undocumented-immigrant-not-guilty-murder-polarizing-san-francisco-case/911849001/).

Logue, Melissa A. 2009. "The Price of Being Mexican": Sentencing Disparities between Noncitizen Mexican and non-Mexican Latinos in the Federal Courts." *Hispanic Journal of Behavioral Sciences* 31:423–45.

Lopez, Gustavo, and Jynnah Radford. 2017. "Facts on U.S. Immigration, 2015: Statistical Portrait of the Foreign-Born Population in the United States." Retrieved September 25, 2017, from (http://www.pewhispanic.org/2017/05/03/facts-on-u-s-immigrants-current-data/)

Massey, Douglas S. 2009. "Racial Formation in Theory and Practice: The Case of Mexicans in the United States." *Race and Social Problems* 1:12–26.

Mishler, William, and Reginald S. Sheehan. 1993. "The Supreme Court as a Countermajoritarian Institution? The Impact of Public Opinion on Supreme Court Decisions." *American Political Science Review* 87(1):87–101.

Morales, Lymarie. 2009. "Americans Return to Tougher Immigration Stance: More Want Immigration Decreased than Kept the Same or Increased." Gallup Organization online report, retrieved August 29, 2011 (http://www.gallup.com/poll/122057/AmericansReturn-Tougher-Immigration-Stance.aspx).

Newburger, Eric, and Thomas Gryn. 2009. "The Foreign-Born Labor Force in the United States: 2007." Retrieved August 7, 2009 (http://www.census.gov/prod/2009pubs/acs-10.pdf).

Newton, Lina. 2008. *Illegal, Alien, or Immigrant: The Politics of Immigration Reform*. New York: New York Press.

Sampson, Robert. 2008. "Rethinking Immigration and Crime." *Contexts* 7:28–33.

Sayad, Abdelmalek. 2004. *The Suffering of the Immigrant*. Cambridge, UK: Polity.

Silverstein, Jason. 2016. "Judge Who Gave Brock Turner 6-Month Sexual Assault Sentence Delivers Harsher Punishment to Immigrant in Similar Case." Retrieved September 1, 2017 (http://www.nydailynews.com/news/national/brock-turner-judge-harsher-sentence-immigrant-article-1.2689471).

Scalia, Jason, and Marika F.X. Litras. 2002. *Immigration Offenders in the Federal Criminal Justice System, 2000*. Bureau of Justice Statistics Special Report. Washington DC: U.S. Department of Justice. http:/www.ojp.usdoj.gov/bjs/abstract/iofcjs00.htm.

Spohn, Cassia. 2000. "Thirty Years of Sentencing Reform: The Quest for a Racially Neutral Sentencing Process." Washington, DC: National Institute of Justice: Criminal Justice.

Steffensmeier, Darrell, and Stephen Demuth. 2000. "Ethnicity and Sentencing Outcomes in U.S. Federal Courts: Who Is Punished More Harshly?" *American Sociological Review* 65:705–29.

Steffensmeier, Darrell, Jeffrey Ulmer, and John Kramer. 1998. "The Interaction of Race, Gender, and Age in Criminal Sentencing: The Punishment Cost of Being Young, Black, and Male." *Criminology* 36:763–97.

Ulmer, Jeffrey, and John Kramer. 1996. "The Use and Transformation of Formal Decision-Making Criteria: Sentencing Guidelines, Organizational Contexts, and Case Processing Strategies." *Social Problems* 45:248–67.

U.S. v. Borrero-Isaza, 887 F.2d 1349, 1352 (9th Cir. 1989).

U.S. v. Gomez, 797 F.2d 417 (7th Cir. 1986).

U.S. v. Onwuemene, 933 F.2d 650, 651 (8th Cir. 1991).

United States Sentencing Commission (USSC). (2016a). Guidelines Manual. Washington, DC: USSC.

United States Sentencing Commission (USSC). (2016b). "Overview of Federal Criminal Cases Fiscal Year 2015." Washington, DC: USSC.

United States Sentencing Commission (USSC). (2009). "Overview of Federal Criminal Cases Fiscal Year 2008." Washington, DC: USSC.

United States Sentencing Commission (USSC). (2003). "Downward Departures from the Federal Sentencing Guidelines." Washington, DC: USSC

Valadez, Mercedes. 2013. *"We Have Got Enough Criminals in the United States Without Importing Any": An Examination of the Influence of Citizenship Status Legal Status and National Origin Among Latino Subgroups in Federal Sentencing Outcomes."* Retrieved from (https://search.proquest.com/openview/ec0bc0d38ebed675c18308f51c41dd70/1?pq-origsite=gscholar&cbl=18750&diss=y)

Valadez, Mercedes, and Xia Wang. 2017. "Citizenship, Legal Status, and Federal Sentencing Outcomes: Examining the Moderating Effects of Age, Gender and Race/ethnicity." *Sociological Quarterly.*

Wang, Xia. 2012. "Undocumented Immigrants as Perceived Criminal Threat: A Test of the Minority Threat Perspective." *Criminology* 50:743–76.

Wolfe, Scott E., David Pyrooz, and Cassia Spohn. 2011. "Unraveling the Effect of Offender Citizenship Status on Federal Sentencing Outcomes." *Social Science Research* 40:349–62.

Reading 7.3 DREAMers, DACA, and Neoliberalism: Undocumented Resistance to Neoliberal Cooptation of the Dreamer Narrative

Edwin Elias

Chapter Goals

The goal of this chapter is to highlight the reasons why undocumented youth are cautious of media and politicians using the DREAMer narrative for their own political, economic, and ideological agenda that supports neoliberalism. Undocumented youth are now hesitant to identify as a DREAMer due to some of its exclusions of the rest of the undocumented population.

Keywords: Coded Language, Identity Politics, Superficial Representation, Neoliberalism

Introduction

It is estimated that 22 percent of the 11 million undocumented immigrants are under the age of twenty-five (Baker and Rytina 2013). Many of these youth only recognize the United States as their home as a result of migrating at an early age and have been largely socialized with American cultural norms and educated in American educational institutions. Today, they have become a focal point in American politics that has generated contentious debates surrounding whether they should obtain a pathway toward citizenship. A majority of Democrats and Republicans have become advocates for their worthiness to remain in the United States due to their economic and cultural benefits. Yet, this attention and advocacy for "DREAMers" and DACA recipients are often aligned with social, political, and economic interests that correspond with neoliberal logics.

History of Undocumented Youth

In *Plyler v. Doe (1982),*[7] the US Supreme Court viewed the denial of a free public education for undocumented kids as a violation of the Fourteenth amendment (Olivas and Bowman 2011).[8] This seminal case allowed undocumented youth access to a K–12 education. Unfortunately, access to a postsecondary education was not addressed.[9]

Upon completing high school, attending a four-year university is an extremely difficult task for undocumented youth to pursue (Abrego 2006; Gonzales 2008a, 2015). They would have to self-finance education due to their ineligibility to access any form of federal financial aid and, in some states, pay tuition as

---

[7] *Plyer v. Doe*, 457 U.S. 202 (1982).

[8] Two central points guided the Court's decision: First, the Court viewed that children should not be held accountable for their parents' decision to migrate to the United States, over which they had no control. Secondly, denying them an education would create a "subclass of illiterates within our boundaries, surely adding to the problems and costs of unemployment, welfare, and crime ... [and] deny them the ability to live within the structure of our civic institutions, and foreclose any realistic possibility that they will contribute in even the smallest way to the progress of our Nation."

[9] It is estimated that every year, 65,000 undocumented students graduate from high school, and a growing number attend institutions of higher education (Perez 2014).

a foreign student (Olivas 1996; Rincon 2008). For many, even the small number who completed their bachelor's degrees, the most viable option was entering the informal labor market (Gonzales 2008a, 2011, 2015).

By 2001, the Senate introduced the DREAM (Development Relief and Education for Alien Minors) Act that would create a pathway toward citizenship for undocumented youth.[10] The bill failed to get sufficient votes to pass the House.[11] Despite the failure to enact the bill, the DREAM Act invigorated undocumented youth to be at the forefront of the immigrant rights movement. They have continuously mobilized to share their stories of success and struggle to highlight the current anachronistic immigration policy and the pressing need for immigration reform (De la Torre and German 2014). Also, undocumented youth began to identify as DREAMers, as individuals who would have benefited from the DREAM Act.

DACA and Education

On June 12, 2012, DACA,[12] although not a pathway toward citizenship, came into effect, which would provide undocumented youth a two-year renewable work permit and defer their deportation.[13] DACA allowed undocumented youth to "come out of the shadows" and economically, socially, and institutionally integrate into American society (Gonzales and Bautista-Chavez 2014; Gonzales and Terriquez 2014). Formally entering the labor market has increased their wages by 69 percent, from $10.29 per hour to $17.46 per hour (Wong et al. 2017).[14] Their financial integration has created new jobs and opened a new market of consumers to the global economy.[15]

Coupled with DACA, several states passed their own bills to aid undocumented students in accessing higher education and to decrease the fear of the immigrant population residing therein. Twelve states and the District of Columbia now issue driver's licenses to undocumented immigrants. In 2011, California became the first state to allow undocumented college students access to state financial aid that decreased their financial burden and increased their enrollment in California public universities.[16] Today, there are eighteen states that allow undocumented students to pay in state tuition, and six allow undocumented students aid to financial aid. Medical and law schools are admitting undocumented students. Undocumented immigrants are allowed to practice law in California, Florida, and New York,[17] and in California they are allowed to apply and be admitted to its professional boards.[18] At the same time, their experiences and chances of upward mobility are based on the intersection of state and federal immigration laws (Gonzales and Ruiz 2014).

---

[10] Among the various requirements, the bill required undocumented youth to have completed high school, be admitted to an institution of higher education, or have a GED.

[11] Since 2001, a version of the DREAM Act has been reintroduced in 2009, 2010, 2011, and 2012, but failed to pass each time.

[12] Similar to the DREAM Act, DACA has similar qualifications: those who were under the age of 31; came to the United States before reaching their sixteenth birthday; had continuously resided in the United States since June 15, 2007; were physically present in the United States; had no lawful status; were currently in school; had graduated or obtained a certificate of completion from high school; had obtained a general education development (GED) certificate; or were an honorably discharged veteran of the Coast Guard or Armed Forces of the United States; and had not been convicted of a felony, significant misdemeanor, or three or more other misdemeanors, and do not otherwise pose a threat to national security or public safety. For more information, see https://www.uscis.gov/archive/consideration-deferred-action-childhood-arrivals-daca

[13] It has been estimated that nearly 2 million people were eligible for this program (Zong and Batalova 2017). Since the enactment of this executive order, approximately 800,000 have received DACA, and nearly 700,000 are enrolled today as of 2017 (U.S. Citizenship and Immigration Services).

[14] Opening a bank account, getting a credit card, and having a driver's license are some of the first new experiences of DACA recipients (Gonzales et al. 2016). Some have purchased new cars, bought homes, and opened new businesses. State tax revenues increased primarily through car registration and title fees (Wong et al. 2017).

[15] It is projected that DACA beneficiaries would contribute $433.4 billion within the next decade (Wong et al. 2017).

[16] Known as the California Dream Act, CA AB 130 & CA AB131 allows undocumented students to obtain state financial aid and be eligible for private scholarships.

[17] CA AB 1024 (2013); FL HB 775 (2014); and 2015 NY Slip Op 04657 [131 AD3d 4].

[18] CA AB 1159 (2013) requires all 40 licensing boards under the California Department of Consumer Affairs to consider applicants regardless of immigration status.

Undocumented Youth and Identity

As the majority of undocumented youth have primarily partaken of American rites of passage toward adulthood—getting a driver's license, applying for FAFSFA, and applying for part time jobs—it informs them of the limitations of their legal status; their relationship with the state as they learn how to be "illegal" (Gonzales 2008, 2011, 2015; Gonzales and Chavez 2013). The realization of the life that awaits them once they reach adulthood has caused depression and other mental health problems (Gonzales 2008, 2011, 2015; Gonzales and Chavez 2013; Gonzales et al. 2013; Pila 2015).

Living in a dichotomous world (undocumented/documented), the politicization of their existence, constantly living in fear, and the never-ending threat of deportation has deeply shaped their understanding of membership in American society (Gonzales 2008, 2011, 2015; Elias 2016). Similar to the impact of CA-AB 540 (Abrego 2006), the enactment of DACA, a temporary legal status, improved emotional and economic well-being, but it did not change how youth chose to identify. From their viewpoint, their lives continue to face similar problems: their family members and friends are facing heightened threats of deportation; they are limited or denied full access to rights of citizens or permanent residents; their right to be in the United States is debated every day; and they fear DACA's repeal. The election of Donald Trump has reinforced their framework of understanding their relationship with the state and continuing to live under constant uncertainty.

Thus, most DACA recipients continue to choose to identify as undocumented because their situation remains precarious and their identity is also connected with their family and friends (Elias 2016). Undocumented youth will continue to identify as undocumented until they become American citizens. Still, living as an undocumented immigrant during their formative years continues to play such a monumental role in subsequent experiences that some continue to identify with the struggles of the undocumented even post-citizenship (Elias 2016).

Resistance Toward Neoliberalism and the DREAMer Narrative

Neoliberalism is the dominant social, economic, and political ideology centered on "the elevation of the market—understood as a non-political, non-cultural, machine-like entity—over all other modes of organization" (Lee Mudge 2008:705).[19] It places responsibility of well-being on the individual—the individual should not be an economic burden on the state, and instead be self-sufficient. Ideal citizens are "individualistic and self-reliant producers and consumers within the capitalist free market" (Berger 2009:215) and are evaluated based on the social, economic, or cultural assets they provide (Ong 1996).

Neoliberal logics have dichotomized immigrants as deserving or undeserving (Lamont and Duvoux 2014; Huber 2016a, 2016b; Nicholls et al. 2016), and emphasis of evaluating the worth of an individual to be admitted to the national community (Berezin 2009; Fassin 2005, 2012; Joppke 2007; Lamont and Duvoux 2014; Nicholls et al. 2013; Nicholls 2016). In this context, DREAMers are now viewed as cultural and economic assets for the neoliberal state (Nicholls 2016). The DREAMer narrative has now been coopted by the neoliberal media and state to support their specific agendas—namely, to increase the immigration-detention apparatus and to justify their continued assault on social welfare by showcasing their self-sufficiency and success without any state help. There tends to be an association of DREAMers with college-educated undocumented youth. Yet, only 54 percent of undocumented youth have at least a high school degree, and only 5 to 10 percent enroll in an institution of higher education—far fewer complete their degree.[20] Using neoliberal logic, DREAMers tend to be positively portrayed by the media in contrast to Central American youth, who are portrayed as a burden on

---

[19] Currently, most politicians, media, and policy experts adhere to this political, social, and economic outlook. Some of the tenets of the ideological framework of neoliberalism are the deregulation of capital; that the free market will solve most problems; limited state intervention; limited taxation; and the necessity of decreased social welfare spending. This framework has spread to previously protected institutions such as health care and education (Harvey 2007).

[20] "National Institutions Coming Out Day Toolkit: Institutional Policies and Programs with and for Undocumented Students," United We Dream, 2015.

the state (Huber 2016). This focus on undocumented students, or DREAMers, upholds the neoliberal vision of self-sufficient, entrepreneurial people who are not a burden on the state. Their success and upward mobility with DACA have gained the sympathy of neoliberals who previously stood in opposition to their stay. This shift, from being demonized to becoming a group that must be protected, in particular by individuals who worked to prevent the passage of an immigration bill, was noticed immediately by undocumented youth and activists (Elias 2016).

For example, former House speaker Paul Ryan came out to defend DACA, stating, "[t]hese are kids who know no other country, who were brought here by their parents and who know no other home … I think the president as well has mentioned that he wants to have a humane solution to this problem" (Bernal 2017). Undocumented youth's uneasiness of having these allies stems from concern about their objectives when they previously were not advocates of undocumented youth and continue to strongly oppose legalization programs for other segments of the undocumented population.

After the passage of DACA, many undocumented students and activists have made an effort to refrain from using the term DREAMer, as it could be problematic and create a hierarchy of immigrants, contrary to the goal of a humane immigration reform. In addition, by the time DACA came into effect, some of the original DREAMers' age made them ineligible for this program. Thus, the meaning and political message of identifying as a DREAMer had changed for those who found themselves locked out of the benefits from DACA. In many ways, DACA recipients were not able to celebrate their newly gained rights with some of their ineligible peers who were also DREAMers or with their family members who were not DACA eligible.

For example, Victoria, twenty-five, now in a prestigious dental school, and an individual who is not politically active, noticed an inherent problem with DACA:

> I don't like that people with DACA are the only ones that are getting benefits … DREAMER, it has a connotation to it. I feel like saying DREAMER is a bit condescending. … If I say that I am undocumented I am not differentiated from my parents.

She observed being unintentionally separated from her parents by using the term DREAMer, based on their lack of DACA eligibility in comparison to her. In another example, Leo, twenty-seven, a long-time community college student, also highlighted the limitations of the term.

> Well dreamer has a connotation of the perfect student. [I] think there [are] other people who say they finish high school but they didn't go to college … I think they should also … qualify for that [DACA].

Leo's viewpoint sheds light on the small population that fit the DREAMer archetype. In response, undocumented college student organizations in California have begun to change the name of their organization for political and practical purposes. They found that DREAMer is not inclusive of undocumented students on their campus who are older or do not view themselves as DREAMers.

Hardt and Negri (2001) posit that social movements critical of imperialism are eventually coopted by mainstream culture. Coopting takes away control of the narrative from the subject, and it also pacifies the movement. Robinson and Barrera (2011) argue that neoliberal logics coopt counterhegemonic movements by incorporating some of its leaders into positions of power and conceding to some of their demands but not to the detriment of the status quo. Undocumented youth, students, and activists were thus correctly concerned with neoliberal advocacy utilizing the term for the interest of the political and media mainstream.

President Donald Trump has offered to create a pathway toward citizenship at the cost of erecting a new Berlin Wall on the Southwest border, increasing the number of ICE agents, and deporting millions of undocumented immigrants. Thus, undocumented youth and immigrant rights organizers' concerns came to the forefront during bill negotiations to protect DREAMers as a result of President Trump terminating DACA. They have voiced their concern to former House minority leader and current speaker of the House Nancy Pelosi by stating that they will not be "used as a bargaining chip." DACA recipient Lizette Diaz (2017) correctly stated:

[t]hey want to force us—in a desperate attempt to save Dreamers—to throw the very people who taught us how to dream under the bus: our parents. The people who came before us and who fought before us. Saving Dreamers should not mean that more detention centers are built or funding for the wall.

The resistance to this Faustian[21] bargain presented by policies based on neoliberal logics highlights the tense political climate and the attempts by those in power to coopt the immigrant youth movement to advance a neoliberal agenda.

Conclusion

President Trump's decision to end DACA provoked a massive rally by millions of Americans voicing their aversion to wrongfully penalize DREAMers. Global corporations,[22] politicians, Republicans and other conservative figures, and mainstream media voiced their support for DACA. In this context, undocumented youth noticed the shift in how the term DREAMer is understood in the United States. After the enactment of DACA, many became aware that advocates of neoliberalism were using a narrative of individualism and continue to create a hierarchy of immigrant worthiness. This is evidenced by the Koch brothers' network's advocacy for DACA, arguing that the United States "has benefited tremendously from a history of welcoming people from all cultures and backgrounds. This is a hallmark of free and open societies." Through their *Libre* initiative, an entity that focuses on Latinx issues, they have asked "lawmakers to act as expeditiously as possible on a bipartisan fix that allows Dreamers to remain here, achieve their potential, [and] help build a stronger nation" (Markay 2017).

Yet, as I have shown, undocumented youth have resisted the cooptation of the DREAMer narrative. They have observed politicians' and the media's use of their stories to promote neoliberal immigration policies that support productive members of society as an economic benefit—while simultaneously supporting harsh immigration policies that increase deportations and continue to leave family and communities "in the shadows." These youth have understood how the meaning of the term DREAMer, initially a term of empowerment and one that highlighted the need for just immigration reform, is now being used by those in power to portray an image that is against the root of their identity—humane immigration reform for 11 million undocumented immigrants. Their resistance toward neoliberalism is currently occurring through their refusal to accept a pathway toward citizenship at the cost of their family, friends, and the growth of the immigration industrial complex.

Reflection/Critical Questions

1. How would you lead your everyday life knowing the rest of society is divided over whether you should remain in the United States?

2. If you were undocumented, would you reveal your status to your friends and teachers?

3. How can the current immigration problem be fixed?

Exploratory Research Questions

1. Which racial and ethnic groups will be affected by increased border enforcement and deportations?

2. Will the erection of a large border in the Southwest deter undocumented migration?

---

[21] A Faustian bargain is a deal that focuses on the present without considering any of the long-term consequences it may have.
[22] Such as Apple, Microsoft, and Google.

Further Readings and Materials

ACLU: https://www.aclu.org/issues/immigrants-rights

American Immigration Council: https://www.americanimmigrationcouncil.org/

CARECEN: http://www.carecen-la.org/

Center for American Progress: https://www.americanprogress.org/issues/immigration/view/

Define American: https://defineamerican.com/

United We Dream (Toolkit and Resources): https://unitedwedream.org/tools/toolkits/

University of California Undocumented Students Resources: http://undoc.universityofcalifornia.edu/

Film

Documented (2013): http://documentedthefilm.com/

Podcasts

This American Life: Our Town (Parts 1 & 2): https://www.thisamericanlife.org/632/our-town-part-one

References

Abrego, Leisy J. 2006. "I Can't Go to College Because I Don't Have Papers: Incorporation Patterns of Latino Undocumented Youth." *Latino Studies* 4(3):212–31.

Baker, Bryan, and Nancy Rytina. 2013. "Estimates of the Unauthorized Immigrant Population Residing in the United States: January 2012." Office of Immigration Statistics.

Berezin, Mabel. 2009 "Illiberal Politics in Neoliberal Times." *Culture, Security and Populism in the New Europe*. Cambridge, UK: Cambridge University Press.

Berger, Susan. 2009 "(Un)Worthy: Latina Battered Immigrants Under VAWA and the Construction of Neoliberal Subjects." *Citizenship Studies* 13(3):201–17.

Bernal, Rafael. 2017. "Ryan Says Trump Shouldn't End DACA." *The Hill*, September 1. Retrieved October 15, 2017 (http://thehill.com/latino/348863-ryan-says-trump-shouldntend-daca).

Diaz, Lizette. 2017. "As a Dreamer, I Will Not Be a Bargaining Chip for Trump's Attack on Immigrants." *Common Dreams*, September 6. Retrieved October 29, 2017 (https://www.commondreams.org/views/2017/09/06/dreamer-i-will-not-be-bargaining chip-trumps-attack-immigrants).

Elias, Edwin. 2016. *New Dreams: The Impact of DACA on Undocumented Youth in Southern California*. ProQuest.

Fassin, Didier. 2005. "Compassion and Repression: The Moral Economy of Immigration Policies in France." *Cultural Anthropology* 20(3):362–87.

Fassin, Didier. 2012. "Humanitarian Reason: A Moral History of the Present." Trans. *Rachel Gomme. Berkeley: University of California Press*, 254.

Gonzales, Roberto G. 2008a. *Born in the Shadows: The Uncertain Futures of the Children of Unauthorized Mexican Migrants*: ProQuest.

Gonzales, Roberto G. 2011. "Learning to Be Illegal: Undocumented Youth and Shifting Legal Contexts in the Transition to Adulthood." *American Sociological Review* 76(4):602–19.

Gonzales, Roberto G. 2015. *Lives in Limbo: Undocumented and Coming of Age in America*. University of California Press.

Gonzales, Roberto G., and Angie M. Bautista-Chavez. 2014. "Two years and Counting: Assessing the Growing Power of DACA." In *American Immigration Council Special Report*.

Gonzales, Roberto G., and Leo R. Chavez. 2012. "'Awakening to a Nightmare': Abjectivity and Illegality in the Lives of Undocumented 1.5 Generation Latino Immigrants in the United States." *Current Anthropology* 53(3):255–81.

Gonzales, Roberto G., Benjamin Roth, Kristina Brant, Jaein Lee, and Carolina Valdivia. 2016. "DACA at Year Three: Challenges and Opportunities in Accessing Higher Education and Employment." *American Immigration Council*.

Gonzales, Roberto G., and Ariel G. Ruiz. 2014. "Dreaming beyond the Fields: Undocumented Youth, Rural Realities and a Constellation of Disadvantage." *Latino Studies* 12(2):194–216.

Gonzales, Roberto G., C. Suárez-Orozco, and M.C. Dedios-Sanguineti. 2013. "No Place to Belong: Contextualizing Concepts of Mental Health Among Undocumented Immigrant Youth in the United States." *American Behavioral Scientist* 57(8):1174–99.

Gonzales, Roberto G., and V. Terriquez. 2014. "Becoming DACAmented: Assessing the Short-Term Benefits of Deferred Action for Childhood Arrivals (DACA)." *American Behavioral Scientist* 58(14):1852–72.

Hardt, Michael, and Antonio Negri. 2001. *Empire*. Harvard University Press.

Harvey, David. 2007. *A Brief History of Neoliberalism*. Oxford, UK: Oxford University Press.

Huber, Lindsay Perez. 2016a,b. "Constructing 'Deservingness:' DREAMers and Central American Children in the National Immigration Debate." *Association of Mexican American Education* 9(3):22–34.

Lamont, Michèle, and Nicolas Duvoux. 2014. "How Neo-Liberalism Has Transformed France's Symbolic Boundaries?" *French Politics, Culture & Society* 32(2):57–75.

Markay, Lachlan. 2017. "Koch Brothers Will Push Congress to Protect DREAMers." *Daily Beast*, September 9. Retrieved January 5, 2018 (https://www.thedailybeast.com/kochbrothers-will-push-congress-to-protect-dreamers)

Massey, Douglas S., and Karen A. Pren. 2012. "Unintended Consequences of US Immigration Policy: Explaining the Post-1965 Surge from Latin America." *Population and Development Review* 38(1):1–29.

Nicholls, Walter. 2013. *The DREAMers: How the Undocumented Youth Movement Transformed the Immigrant Rights Debate*. Palo Alto, CA: Stanford University Press.

Nicholls, Walter J., Marcel Maussen, and Laura Caldas de Mesquita. 2016. "The Politics of Deservingness: Comparing Youth-Centered Immigrant Mobilizations in the Netherlands and the United States." *American Behavioral Scientist* 60(13):1590–612.

Olivas, Michael A., and Kristi L. Bowman. 2011. "Plyler's Legacy: Immigration and Higher Education in the 21st Century." *Michigan State University Law* 216:261–273.

Ong, Aihwa, Virginia R. Dominguez, Jonathan Friedman, Nina Glick Schiller, Verena Stolcke, and Hu Ying. 1996. "Cultural Citizenship as Subject-Making: Immigrants Negotiate Racial and Cultural Boundaries in the United States." *Current Anthropology* 37(5):737–62.

Perez, Zenen Jaimes. 2014. "Removing Barriers to Higher Education for Undocumented Students." *Center for American Progress.*

Robinson, William I. 2014. *Global Capitalism and the Crisis of Humanity.* Cambridge, UK: Cambridge University Press.

Robinson, William I., and M. Barrera. 2011. "Global Capitalism and Twenty-First Century Fascism: A US Case Study." *Race & Class* 53(3):4–29.

Wong, Tom K., Greisa Martinez Rosas, Adam Luna, Henry Manning, Adrian Reyna, Patrick O'Shea, Tom Jawetz, and Philip E. Wolgin 2017. "DACA Recipients' Economic and Educational Gains Continue to Grow." Center for American Progress. August 28. Retrieved December 15, 2017 (https://www.americanprogress.org/issues/immigration/news/2017/08/28/437956/daca recipients-economic-educational-gains-continue-grow/)

Zong, Jie, and Batalova, Jeanne. 2017. "Frequently Requested Statistics on Immigrants and Immigration in the United States." *Migration Policy Institute.* March 8, 2017. Retrieved December 15, 2017 (https://www.migrationpolicy.org/article/frequently-requested-statistics-immigrants-and-immigration-united-states#Unauthorized)

Student Narrative

I end this section with another student narrative, how Laura felt the day Trump was elected, to highlight the pain and panic many immigrant families and communities have felt since the election of Trump and the consequences of his policies.

> Seeing my mother crying the night of November 8, 2016, was when I realized what was coming, I dreaded this day for months, the thought of a Trump presidency was daunting. Since he began his campaign the anti-immigrant and anti-Mexican rhetoric was very clear, and it scared me. I remember crying after midnight as the acceptance speech came and the following day feeling like my world was collapsing before my eyes. Despite the clear threat of DACA ending what scared me the most was that my parents could be deported, that many families like mine were going to be broken, and that my parents' sacrifices had been for nothing. My family has been my source of inspiration in these hard times. My parents are a reminder of the strength that I have within me, they have made it work in a foreign country despite the odds being against them. In a few days I will become the first in my family to receive a graduate degree. Walking across that stage will be a homage to my parents and their resiliency because they are the original Dreamers.

Laura Zaragoza is an undocumented graduate student in the Sociology Department. She was born in Mexico City and came to the United States along with her mother and siblings when she was ten years old. They came to reunite with their father.

Discussion Questions

1. What is the immigration story of your family? Or if you are Native, what is the story your family has shared about the immigration/colonization into this country and how that shaped your family's history?

2. What are your views about immigration today, and how has your background, what you hear in the news, and your family and friends shaped those views?

3. What do you think you can do to shape the type of immigration policies that are developed and how these are implemented in the United States?

Resources

Explore the *New York Times* interactive map about immigration to the United States:

http://www.nytimes.com/interactive/2009/03/10/us/20090310-immigration-explorer.html

Explore the Gallop Poll's data on view on immigration: http://news.gallup.com/poll/1660/immigration.aspx

Explore the Pew Research Center interactive data about undocumented immigrants in the United States: http://www.pewhispanic.org/interactives/unauthorized-trends/

Visit Jose Antonio Vargas's site Define American: https://defineamerican.com/

Visit an alternative view of belonging by the organization 67 Dreams: https://www.afsc.org/program/67-sue%C3%B1os

Also visit the largest immigrant coalition in the United States. United We Dream: https://unitedwedream.org/

References

Armenta, Amada. 2016. "Racializing Crimmigration: Structural Racism, Colorblindness, and the Institutional Production of Immigrant Criminality." *Sociology of Race and Ethnicity*. Retrieved (http://sre.sagepub.com/lookup/doi/10.1177/2332649216648714).

Barajas, Manuel. 2012. "Societies Without Borders A Comparative Analysis of Mexican—and Europe and European—Origin Immigration to the United States: Proposing an Interactive Colonization Theory." *Societies Without Borders* 7(3):264–94. Retrieved (http://scholarlycommons.law.case.edu/swb).

Burnett, John. 2017. *Arrests for Illegal Border Crossings Hit 46-Year Low*. Retrieved (https://www.npr.org/2017/12/05/568546381/arrests-for-illegal-border-crossings-hit-46-year-low).

DeGenova, Nicholas. 2004. "The Legal Production of Mexican/Migrant 'Illegality.'" *Latino Studies* 2:160–85.

Fabian, Jordan. 2018. "Trump: Migrant Caravan 'Is an Invasion.'" *The Hill,* October 29. Retrieved (https://thehill.com/homenews/administration/413624-trump-calls-migrant-caravan-an-invasion).

Fox, Cybelle, and Thomas A. Guglielmo. 2012. "Defining America's Racial Boundaries: Blacks, Mexicans, and European Immigrants, 1890–1945." *American Journal of Sociology* 118(2):327–79.

Frey, William. 2018. *The US Will Become "Minority White" in 2045, Census Projects.* Retrieved (https://www.brookings.edu/blog/the-avenue/2018/03/14/the-us-will-become-minority-white-in-2045-census-projects/).

Lopez, Mark Hugo, Jeffrey Passel, and Molly Rohal. 2015. *Modern Immigration Wave Brings 59 Million to U.S., Driving Population Growth and Change Through 2065.* Retrieved (https://www.pewhispanic.org/2015/09/28/modern-immigration-wave-brings-59-million-to-u-s-driving-population-growth-and-change-through-2065/).

Major, Brenda, Alison Blodorn, and Gregory Major Blascovich. 2018. "The Threat of Increasing Diversity: Why Many White Americans Support Trump in the 2016 Presidential Election." *Group Processes and Intergroup Relations* 21(6):931–40.

Melendez, Jose. 2018. "Mexico Deports More Central Americans than the U.S." *El Universal*, October 23. Retrieved (https://www.eluniversal.com.mx/english/mexico-deportation).

Ngai, Mae M. 2005. *Impossible Subjects: Illegal Aliens and the Making of Modern America.* Princeton, NJ: Princeton University Press.

Omi, Michael, and Howard Winant. 1994. *Racial Formation in the United States: From the 1960s to the 1990s.* 2nd ed. New York: Routledge.

Section VIII: Coloniality in the Twenty-first Century

Student Narrative

As an undocumented Latina woman, who arrived to the US at the age of two I experience race on a daily basis. I have come to understand the experience as one surpassing immigration status. Living in the US as an undocumented individual and then having my immigration status shifted to Dacamented did not change the way I am treated in the United States, it only changed the way I experience racism. As an undocumented person the racism I experienced was overt, dehumanizing, and unfair and as a Dacamented person I receive this same treatment but in a covert form. The color of my skin, my country of origin, and my immigration status constantly places me in a position where I have to explain my identity to society on a daily basis and in every interaction, I encounter. In college a simple question regarding financial aid would turn into a full disclosure of my identity only to be asked by the financial aid representative why I did not just go apply for citizenship. In an employment setting I have been asked about how I obtained my work permit, and when I visit a department store in a "predominantly white neighborhood" I am overtly subject to racial gaze that is disapproving and is there to cast me in a non-belonging category.

Jannet Esparza is a graduate student in the Department of Sociology at California State University–Sacramento.

Learning Objectives

After you read the introduction and the chapters in this section, you should be able to:

1. Identify the global emergence of a racial order as expressing both different iterations but the same underpinnings processes.

2. Connect how global economic, political, and social interconnectedness has shaped views and understandings of race in a local and global context.

3. Articulate how racial categorization is both a global and local process.

Editor's Introduction

Heidy Sarabia

As Jannet reveals, moving across borders without state sanction can shape your experiences of race, and changing legal status often masks how race and legal status are often intersectional. My own experiences across the US-Mexico border highlight how racial meanings and categories change, but are also stable, across international boundaries.

In 2009, as I was crossing the US-Mexico border, a border patrol agent was walking around my car, moved the sniffing dog too close to my opened car window, and scared me. I felt disrespected, became furious, and demanded to know the officer's name. He passed by me, smiled, and kept walking with the dog. So I turned to the officer inspecting my US passport; he said he did not have to give me the other officer's name. I started complaining, "Who did they think they were? I wanted his name!" But then, the officer looked at me and said, "Just because you are a US citizen you think you have rights! I don't have to let you in the US" I was in shock. I was in the border, the borderlands where as a US citizen I did not have any rights. I am sure white citizens are not told they have no rights as they try to enter the United States, but as a Chicana the officer could say out loud what many must think and know silently: "they have the bureaucratic power to determine who gets in and who does not into the United States." It was then that it dawned on me how tenuous my rights were as were the rights of the thousands of unauthorized migrants who risked their lives to cross into the United States.

As a dark-skinned Chicana, my racial markers rendered my citizenship questionable in the eyes of US border patrol officers. In Mexico, I pass as a *mestiza* woman—part of the majority—but my dark skin often means people assume I am working class and not a professor at a US university. At the border, in-between nations, I am both treated as a suspect by US immigration authorities and treated as a working-class Mexican on the Mexican side—this in-between, borderland positionality (Anzaldua 1987) has deeply shaped experiences— just like Jannet, there are daily reminders of our status as outsiders—yet, these experiences have also shaped my critical perspective about the construction of political, ideological, and physical borders and boundaries.

Historical Overview

Race, as a global phenomenon, emerged with the conquest and colonization of the American, Asian, and African continents by Europe. Upon the arrival of European colonizers in the American continent in 1492, questions of whether the indigenous inhabitants of the Americas were in fact human, and thus deserving of rights, were entertained by Spanish colonizers (Mignolo 2000). After diseases, war, and genocide killed most of the indigenous population in the American continent, about 12.5 million African slaves were imported to the continent (Henry Louis Gates 2017), and the idea of race solidified as a concept to justify unequal rights.

In the United States, the **one-drop rule** defined racial categories, as those with one drop of African blood (descendants) were considered black and thus ineligible for rights as US citizens. In Latin America, the logic of **castas** (meaning lineage/bleed/race) and the ideology of **whitening** prevailed, whereby hereditary transmission of white blood or any mixture with European descendants was considered a whitening and improving of one's racial status (Graham 2010).

In 1789 the US Constitution was adopted, which declared that "all men are created equal" but also forbade the federal government from preventing states from importing slaves for twenty years. Yet, in 1792, Denmark outlawed the slave trade, and by 1801, Haitians led a successful slave rebellion that abolished all slavery in Haiti—making it the first antislavery nation in the world. After 1824, in a wave, Guatemala, Argentina, Peru, Chile, Bolivia, Paraguay, and Mexico outlawed slavery. It would take a civil war for the United States to abolish slavery in 1865 through the Thirteenth Amendment to the US Constitution (ISM 2019).

While the one-drop rule was used in the United States to maintain spatial segregation between whites and nonwhites, more mixture and interaction were allowed in the rest of Latin America. In the early nineteenth century, eugenics, a pseudoscientific effort to prove that certain races were biologically superior, took hold in the United States. As a response, Jose Vasconcelos, a Mexican intellectual, developed the idea of **raza cosmica**, the idea that **mestizaje**—the mixture of races—creates something much better. While mestizaje was adopted by the Mexican state as a way to develop a nationalist agenda, it has often been critiqued as an explicit erasure and pressure for indigenous people to assimilate and lose their language and customs. Likewise, in Brazil, Gilberto Freyre developed the ideology of **racial democracy** to highlight their tolerant and conflict-free society—but this perspective has also been criticized as an ideology that masks gross racial inequality in Brazil. As Telles and Sue argue, arguments of "racial democracy" and race mixture in Latin America have often masked and maintained racial inequality (Telles and Sue 2010).

Coloniality: The Legacy of Colonialism

In many ways, race as a social construction has been localized—with specific meanings in different locales. Hence, nation-states differ on how they collect data on racial categories. For example, when collecting racial data in the United States—five racial groups are listed in the US census (white, black, American Indian and Alaska Native, Asian, Native Hawaiian or Other Pacific Islander). In Mexico, historically, a language question has sought to capture indigenous ancestry, and now a new question about African background has been added (Rao 2015). In Brazil, the census question is: Is your color or race white, black, yellow, brown, or indigenous?[23] Nevertheless, the global racial hierarchy that has positioned those racialized as white on top of this hierarchy has been solidified.

In light of the continuities, divergences and convergences globally, and the legacy of colonialism, scholars have theorized **coloniality** as the simultaneous economic capitalist expansion and racial division of labor that the colonial European project implemented globally (Quijano 2000). Hence, coloniality connects the simultaneous racial and economic legacy of colonialism that continues to produce intense racial inequality and wealth accumulation—which continues to benefit those who have benefited from the exploitation of formerly colonized people and territories.

Mindfulness

Global conceptions of race are ultimately informed by both local histories but also by global flows of ideas about race, rooted in colonialism and imperialism, that have established whiteness at the top of the totem pole. Yet, we are all responsible for the way in which racial hierarchies are perpetuated or challenged both locally and globally. Historical examples of transnational and global action against racial projects—such as the divestment activism in the United States that challenged apartheid in South Africa—highlight the power of mobilizing both local and global notions of race to create change locally and globally. We must be mindful of both the ways race is (re)inscribed in the local and global contexts as we mobilize to challenge old racial hierarchies; and how living

---

[23] https://unstats.un.org/unsd/demographic/sources/census/quest/BRA2010enl.pdf

in a context where we must understand "race without racists" (Bonilla-Silva 2006) also is a process that occurs simultaneously at the local and global levels. We must navigate being mindful but also fearless about challenging racial hierarchies that perpetuate inequality.

Section Readings

The chapters in this section present historical, theoretical, and empirical rich material on the legacies of colonialism. In first chapter, focused on the global south, Vargas presents the concrete case of genocide in Guatemala and how racialized responses—both in how genocide has been framed and how it has been addressed—show the extent of the colonial legacy of power and race, and how this legacy has determined how humanity has been evaluated. The second chapter, focused on the global north, also presents a very concrete example of a current colonial concept—nation-state borders. Young shows how race and racism operate in the production and policing of these nation-state borders. Using the specific example of Canada's visa requirements for Mexican citizens, Young highlights how coloniality "normalizes" these racialized policies that also produce undocumented migration as "illegal and fraudulent." Reminding us that nation-states produce illegality (DeGenova 2004) on a global scale—as highlighted by Jannet's story of living undocumented in the United States.

In the third chapter, Rosado turns our attention to how race in South America, in Colombia specifically, has historically and contemporarily shaped access to land and resources. Both Vargas and Rosado highlight the resistance shown in the part of the state to acknowledge racialized systems of exploitation, while overwhelming evidence suggests race matters. In the last piece, Forneret and Nihn present a historical piece that makes the connections that scholars of coloniality have argued about, the simultaneity between economic and racial systems—that is, capitalism exists in part because a global-racial system exists. Forneret and Nihn end their chapter by describing current coloniality—that is, the way the colonial system has changed and evolved, but has not ended.

Reading 8.1 Race and Ethnicity in Guatemala

Maria Vargas

Keywords: Guatemala, Civil War, Genocide, Indigenous People.

Sí, Hubo Genocidio (Yes, There Was Genocide)

Guatemala made international headlines in 2013 when former president Efraín Ríos Montt was accused of the most grievous human rights violations in recent Latin American history. Ríos Montt was found guilty of acting as the intellectual that ordered his Guatemalan military to commit "72 specific incidents where 1,771 people were killed, 1,485 acts of sexual violence were committed, and 29,000 Guatemalans were internally displaced" (Willard 2012). Ríos Montt was found guilty of enacting a genocidal campaign during his rule between 1981 and 1982 against Ixil Mayans. The 1,771 people killed were all Mayan and lived in the towns of San Juan Cotzal, San Gaspar Chajúl, and Santa María Nebaj, known as the Ixil Triangle in the Western Highlands, home to mostly Mayans in Guatemala.

Article II of the 1948 United Nations Genocide Convention defines genocide as:

Any of the following acts committed with intent to destroy, in whole or in part, a national, ethnical, racial or religious group, as such: (a) Killing members of the group; (b) Causing serious bodily or mental harm to members of the group; (c) Deliberately inflicting on the group conditions of life calculated to bring about its physical destruction in whole or in part; (d) Imposing measures intended to prevent births within the group; (e) Forcibly transferring children of the group to another group.

Therefore, under the understanding of the Genocide Convention and documentary evidence used to prove that despite Ríos Montt not personally committing these crimes, he ordered and was aware of the murders, rape, and torture that were occurring when he was in control of the Guatemalan army. However, shortly after charges were read and Ríos Montt was sentenced to eighty years in prison and escorted in handcuffs by Guatemalan security, the Guatemalan Constitutional Court annulled the historic verdict. Ríos Montt's defense team claimed that he was subjected to illegal proceedings because the trial continued without the presence of his lawyers, who had walked out of the courtroom because they were upset at how the tribunal was handling the case. According to the Constitutional Court, "the trial should have been halted at this point while the challenges filed by Mr. García (Ríos Montt's lawyer) were being resolved" (Willard 2012). There have been countless attempts from human rights and local activist organizations to hold a retrial, but Ríos Montt's legal team counters with legal petitions that cause severe delays in the legal process.

The Guatemalan genocide case further splintered what Guatemalan anthropologist Diane Nelson calls a "finger in the wound," a metaphor symbolizing the continuous genocidal violence against indigenous people that is perpetrated by a militarized nonindigenous elite. In other words, Nelson perceives the Guatemalan nation as a body in which ethnic difference is a historical traumatic wound, and the finger represents the resistance of Mayan communities against a murderous state (Nelson 1999). Ríos Montt represents the racist, militarized, Guatemalan oligarchy that has historically targeted the indigenous people for extermination and justified such violence by claiming it is in the interest of creating a less indigenous and more modern nation. Therefore, Ríos Montt was supported not only by his defense team and family but also by the military and oligarchy who claimed that no genocide had occurred. Instead, they understood the violence committed under his command in the context of war and that his army was fighting armed guerrillas and their docile indigenous followers. However, countless forensic evidence has shown that the indigenous civilians, most of them women and children, were not part of any revolutionary group or guerrillas, and most were massacred while they were unarmed (Snow and Peccerelli, 2008). Thus the "genocide debate," whether there was genocide or not, became a convenient way for the pro-military sector in Guatemala to hide the glaring role that race played in the genocide. In this chapter, I will address how racial and ethnic difference in Guatemala enabled genocidal violence against the Ixil Mayans during the Internal Armed Conflict. I will provide historical background of Spanish colonialism to clearly demonstrate the racial and ethnic hierarchies of *ladino versus indio* that the Spanish oppressor introduced to a territory such as Guatemala where its inhabitants were all indigenous people. I will also discuss the role of Ríos Montt during the IAC to show how under his command he drew from the American National Security Doctrine to specifically target Ixil Mayans and not *ladino* rebels. In addition, I will focus on the Commission of Historical Clarification and their interpretation of genocide that further indicted the Guatemalan military, who profusely denied their participation in genocide crimes.

Historical Background

The Spanish colonial project began in 1524 when Spanish conquistadores led by Pedro de Alvarado invaded Guatemala and attacked the Mayan indigenous peoples of the Americas (Martinez-Pelaez 2009). Guatemalan scholar Egla Martinez-Salazar refers to this invasion as the "first genocide" that marked the brutal legacy of conquest in Central America. Martinez-Salazar states, "It was cruelly implemented through the destruction of bodies, cultures, epistemologies, and spirits. It set the pace for the institutionalized terror that persists to the present day and has been one of the hallmarks of Guatemala's history, even if transformed in ideology and in practice" (Martienz-Salazar 2012:31).

In colonial Guatemala, the term *Criollo* was used for Spanish descendants, the first-generation settlers; it is a racial classification that proves that the individual is not from a mixed union but rather pure Spanish. *Criollismo* was the belief that the Criollo was at the top of the racial hierarchy because he was of Spanish ancestry and had superior European qualities compared to mestizos and Indians. Consequently, Guatemalan indigenous communities were targeted by the military, but it was not to maintain a purity of race since this was not possible in a nation whose ideal national subject is a mixed offspring or *mestizo* meaning the union of Spanish and indigenous persons. Historically, it has been the nonindigenous elite that controls the state and the military in Guatemala. Guatemalan scholar Egla Martinez-Salazar calls this system of domination the "*Creole-Ladino-Bourgeois-Militarized state*" responsible for the slaughter of rural indigenous people to not only exploit their land but to transform Guatemala into a "whiter" ladino race, where the criollo ideal of racial purity was closer in reach. *The Creole-Ladino-Bourgeois-Militarized* state desired to exterminate the indigenous race and establish not a pure race but a mixed race where Spanish ancestry is most prevalent and indigenous ancestry disappears. Subsequently, the survival of the colonial project in Guatemala depended on the birth of the cosmic race, the mestizo, to inhabit the New World and accomplish the *blancamiento* (whitening) through the erasure of indigenous people and their culture.

According to Historian Greg Grandin, the term *ladino* emerged in the sixteenth and seventeenth centuries in Guatemala and initially referred to the elite, Spanish-speaking and acculturated Mayan indigenous people. *Ladino* was also a derogatory term that referred to the poor and homeless population, but in the nineteenth century, the term shifted and was used to "refer to all who could not be considered Indian." (84). Ultimately, what the introduction of the term accomplished was the reduction of colonial racial categories of Criollos, mestizos, Indians to the binary of indigenous/ladino, thus highlighting the intersection of race and cultural assimilation. Therefore, the term *ladino* is not only understood in physical features as race is understood in the United States, but in Guatemala, race is also understood in "cultural rather than biological terms, with all those not engaged in an identifiable indigenous lifestyle referred to as *ladinos*" (84). In other words, in Guatemala, the color of your skin is not the sole determining feature of your race; culture is also important because race is understood in terms of economic development. A dark-skinned man who does not belong to an indigenous community and does not speak an indigenous language or practice indigenous traditions is, in the eyes of the Guatemalan state, a *ladino*. It is the existence of indigenous culture, not physical characteristics, that historically has posed an obstacle for the *Ladino-Bourgeois-Militarized state* because through their eyes culture represents a primitive savageness and docile people who need to be exterminated for the good of the *ladino* nation.

The Internal Armed Conflict

The book *Guatemala: Causas y Orígenes Del Enfrentamiento Armado Interno* (Guatemala: Causes and Origins of the Internal Armed Conflict) by truth commission report, "the Commission of Historical Clarification" (CEH) situates the armed conflict within a Guatemalan society dominated by an agricultural economy and specific notions of race and ethnicity (CEH 2000). The CEH traces the emergence of the armed conflict to the CIA-sponsored coup of President Jacob Arbenz, which took place in 1954, following increasing political violence between Arbenz and the Guatemalan oligarchy. Arbenz believed that the Agriculture Reform Act would economically transform Guatemalan society because it would more evenly distribute the land and thereby reduce poverty levels in the indigenous communities. Indigenous communities had been struggling for their land rights for centuries, and their fight had intensified in 1944 with the emergence of modernity in Guatemala. Arbenz's support of the Agriculture Reform Act angered the United States, which owned the United Fruit Company in Guatemala. Consequently, the US and Guatemalan landowners devised a strategy linked to Cold war anti-Communist sentiments to create a political practice that portrayed the Arbenz government and its followers as Communists (CEH xix). With the overthrow of the Arbenz government, Guatemala retained its practices of extracting economic wealth from the land of indigenous peoples and maintained an amicable relationship with the United States that would extend to military aid for the civil war.

Guatemala's Civil War, or Internal Armed Conflict (IAC) as referred to in Guatemala, ensued shortly after the 1954 CIA-sponsored coup and lasted thirty-six years, making it the longest civil war in Latin America. From 1960–1996, more than 200,000 people were killed. The IAC left countless human rights violations in its aftermath, most committed by the military and the state, such as enforced disappearance, torture, sexual violence, and genocide. According to the CEH, 80 percent of the victims were indigenous, and the military committed 93 percent of the atrocities (CEH 1999). How could such atrocities and terror occur in the twenty-first century, and why did an indigenous population receive the brunt of the violence that accumulated into genocide?

1982 Ixil Triangle Genocide

The counterinsurgency campaign designed and deployed by Ríos Montt in 1982 is known as the peak of ruthless violence during the Internal Armed Conflict. Ríos Montt's counterinsurgency campaign created a geopolitical division that targeted the vast Western Highlands of Huehuetenango and El Quiche, the majority of which is composed of rural terrain and home to the long-marginalized and forgotten indigenous population. The military was concerned with the growth of guerrilla groups in the Western Highlands, specifically the Guerrilla Army of the Poor (EGP), who they believed had garnered thousands of indigenous sympathizers who had aided the EGP to escape the General Romeo Lucas García counterinsurgency (Alvarez Bobadilla 2011).

According to forensic anthropologists Clyde Snow and Freddy Peccerelli, who have led the efforts of exhuming mass graves in Guatemala City and the Western Highlands, the Civil War consisted of two "overlapping campaigns best characterized as *rural* and *urban*."[24] The urban campaign targeted union leaders and student activists who were captured by death squads and illegally detained. Many of these victims experienced excruciating torture aimed at extracting information from them to use against the revolutionary movement. The peak of the urban campaign occurred under the General Romeo Lucas García regime in 1978–1982; according to Snow et al., the rate of violent deaths that were pronounced at the scene rose to 25.2 percent above normal in the period of 1978–1983.[25]

---

[24] Snow, Clyde Collins. "Hidden in Plain Sight: X.X. Burials and the Desaparecidos in the Department of Guatemala, 1977–1986," 105.

[25] Snow, Clyde Collins. "Hidden in Plain Sight: X.X. Burials and the Desaparecidos in the Department of Guatemala, 1977–1986," 105

The new counterinsurgency campaigns, which would become rural and led by Ríos Montt, believed that the historical neglect by the Guatemalan government of rural and indigenous populated areas made these areas vulnerable to manipulation by guerrilla groups. Historian Betsy Konefal writes, "When General Efraín Ríos Montt took over the government, authorities claimed that repression was lessening, and it was marginally true in Guatemala City. But the army was killing far greater numbers in the countryside. The army, in fact, militarized the countryside to an extent previously unseen."[26] With the rural regions as the main target of the new counterinsurgency plan, this placed the indigenous people of the countryside in a dire imperilment.

In contrast to the terror carried out by Lucas García, Ríos Montt ignored Guatemala City where Lucas García had focused on kidnapping, torturing, and executing mostly *ladino* male (not their entire family) politicians, labor union leaders, and students who opposed the state. Instead, rural spaces where Mayan families, including children, women and the elderly, lived peacefully became the targets and epicenter of the war. This change in geography from the urban center of Guatemala City mostly populated by *ladinos* to the Western Highlands, mainly home to Ixil Mayans, exposed a malicious ulterior motive contradicting the army's denial that race played a central role during the IAC. It was this shift from urban to rural that marked a turn toward genocide because it placed the indigenous population in the fire of intensified militarized violence perpetuated by the army.

Acts of Genocide

As part of the 1996 Peace Accords, the United Nations organized the CEH to launch an investigation into the human rights violations committed during the armed conflict and publish their findings in a truth commission report. The CEH was published in 1999 and contained collected testimonies from the survivors of the conflict, especially in the rural regions. Subsequently, the CEH became an instrumental tool that aided in the validation of a Guatemalan genocide supported by international human rights. Crucial to the CEH's claims was that "acts of genocide" against Mayans had occurred in 1981–1985. The commission defined genocidal acts as "means that are utilized to achieve a political, economic, or military end."[27] End or goal refers to the extermination of a particular group such as the Ixil Mayans. "The CEH describe how the army came to define entire Maya communities as "internal enemies"; thus, the annihilation of the Mayan populations was intentional, even though the military's overarching motivation was to defeat the insurgency."[28] The CEH further exposed the genocidal crimes that had occurred in the IAC and challenged popular military and media discourse after the war, insisting that the deaths, tortures, and disappearance were simply the consequences of a war, and that since ladinos had also been affected, therefore, race has nothing to do with the violence. To the contrary, the CEH showed how the application of the American National Security Doctrine created a strategy that justified "annihilation of the internal enemy" because it positioned Ixil Mayans as subversives.

The American National Security Doctrine

The American National Security Doctrine exposes the depth of complicity of the United States and the transnational connection between Guatemala's genocidal campaign and the US capitalist agenda. In the context of the Cold War, US president Dwight D. Eisenhower and Secretary of State John Foster Dulles justified the 1954 overthrow of democratically elected president Jacobo Arbenz with anti-communism rhetoric that hid the capitalist policies and institutions that Arbenz did not support. After the 1954 coup d'état, a thirty-six-year war ensued, carried out by US-backed dictators who not only defended the corporate interests of the United States, but also secured capitalist "free market" policies that functioned in the favor of the elite in Guatemala. As a

---

[26] Konefal, Betsy. 2010. *For Every Indio Who Falls: A History of Maya Activism in Guatemala (1960–1990)*. Albuquerque: University of New Mexico Press, 152.

[27] CEH, Memoria, Vol. 10, 813.

[28] CEH 386.

result, the Guatemalan oligarchy and the US government formed a powerful alliance to defeat anti-capitalist or Communist revolutions in Latin America from the 1960s onward.

Consequently, the army undertook an anti-Communist crusade in Guatemala, developed from a US national doctrine that stabilized new ideological and political strategies, which were transformed into military curriculum and taught in the US School of the Americas. These programs aimed to prevent internal revolutionary warfare and thus constructed an internal enemy where the military was no longer neutral, but politicized. Latin Americanist and political economist Robinson Rojas states, "The new concept of 'internal war' involved the military in a process of surveillance and intelligence-gathering. From here, internal war was a political process in which a section of the population not only had to be defeated but destroyed."[29]

The political strategy of the National Security Doctrine adopted by Ríos Montt, a former student at the School of the Americas, would manifest itself into one of the deadliest counterinsurgency campaigns in Latin America, known as scorched-earth policy, in which the goal of the Guatemalan state as learned from US national security doctrine was to redesign an entire indigenous culture. Guatemala offered fertile soil for the US Empire's genocidal tendencies against indigenous populations. For example, Guatemala's geopolitical landscape, made up of an ultraconservative elite ruling class to which Ríos Montt belonged enabled the National Security Doctrine to function as another tool of systemic racism that transformed those who challenged capitalist policies and institutions into the undesirable internal enemy. Ríos Montt states, "Naturally, if a subversive operation exists in which the Indians are involved with the guerrilla, the Indians are also going to die. However, the army's philosophy is not to kill Indians, but to win them back, to help them" (389).

Operation Sofia

Operation Sofia, a military log composed of hand-written reports made by the commanding general of individual paratrooper battalions, provided specific details of Ríos Montt's counterinsurgency operation that took place in the Ixil Triangle during the months of July and August of 1982. Kate Doyle, senior analyst of US policy in Latin America at the National Security Archive,[30] was in charge of authenticating the document and preparing it for use in international human rights courts. In 2009, Doyle's testimony was crucial to establishing authenticity of the OD and exposing a chain of command that implicated Ríos Montt. Doyle states, "After months of analysis … we have determined that these records were created by military officials during the regime of Efraín Ríos Montt to plan and implement a 'scorched earth' policy."[31] Doyle's analysis unveiled the chain of command that implicated Ríos Montt as the person responsible for giving the orders. Doyle's analysis of OS also highlighted how written reports identified all citizens living in the village, including women, children, and the elderly, as "subversives" and would use the word "eliminated" to imply they were killed by the soldiers.

Furthermore, Guatemalan historian Marta Casaus Arzu examines the relationship between racism and genocide and the roles that the Guatemalan army, oligarchy, and US military intelligence played in designing genocidal military campaigns. Arzu argues that OS was a product of racism and functioned as a technology of power because the military and the oligarchy took advantage of Guatemala's history of exclusion and exploitation toward the indigenous population. In other words, the Guatemalan army took advantage of the *Creole-Ladino-Bourgeois-Militarized* that imagined ladinos as the only legitimate homogeneous nationhood representing Spanish ancestry. Arzu states: "Out of the total number of human rights violations that affected life and physical integrity, 70% were committed against Mayans and only 10% against ladinos."[32]

---

[29] Rojas, Robinson. "Notes on the Doctrine of National Security." http://www.rrojasdatabank.info/natsec1.htm.
[30] The NSA is a nonprofit research institute located in New York City, founded in 1985 by American journalists committed to declassifying US documents by using the US Freedom of Information Act and acting as a public-interest law firm working toward expanding access to government information.
[31] NSA.
[32] NSA.

Final Conclusions

The objective of this chapter is to understand the role that race and ethnicity played in the 1984 genocide against Ixil Mayans under the Ríos Montt regime. How was it that while Ríos Montt was convicted of genocide in 2013, a vast portion of the country denied genocide had occurred at all? Rather than focusing on whether or not there was genocide was the focus of the conversation after the genocide trial, it is important to center race and contextualize the historical roots of an elitist and racist Guatemalan society that reduced all racial and ethnic diversity to simply ladino and indigenous. Indigenous people, or *los indios*, as referred to in Guatemala, have historically been seen through the eyes of the nonindigenous oppressor as inferior, backward, and subhuman. Therefore, as occurred in the IAC, this historical racism was not only present but also a driving force of Ríos Montt's opportunistic deployment of the national security doctrine that targeted the Ixil Maya as the internal ancestral enemy.

References

Commission for Historical Clarification (CEH). 2000. *Guatemala: Causes and Origins of the Internal Armed Conflict*. Guatemala: F & G Editors.

Commission for Historical Clarification (CEH), xix.

Commission for Historical Clarification (CEH). 1999. "Guatemala: Memory of Silence." Guatemala City.

2011. Guatemala City: The Archives of Peace, 35.

Martinez Pelaez, Severo. 2009. *La Patria Del Criollo*. Durham, NC: Duke University Press.

Martinez-Salazar. 2012. *Global Coloniality of Power in Guatemala: Racism, Genocide, Citizenship*. Lexington Books.

Álvarez Bobadilla, Marco Tulio, editor. 2011. *Presidential General Staff in Guatemala: An Approximation*. Guatemala City: The Archives of Peace, 35.

Willard, Emily. 212. "Genocide Trial against Ríos Montt: Declassified Documents Provide Key Evidence." http://nsarchive.wordpress.com/2012/02/02/genocide-trial-against-Ríos-montt-declassified-documents-provide-key-evidence/.

Reading 8.2 The Differential Impacts of Nation-state Borders and Bordering Practices

Julie E.E. Young

Keywords: Borders; categorization; interdiction; externalization; internalization.

> *I was indistinguishable from the border; I* was *the border.*

> —Shahram Khosravi 2010, p. 98 (emphasis in original)

Introduction

In June 2016, during the visit of Mexican president Enrique Peña-Nieto to Ottawa in advance of the Three Amigos Summit, Canada's prime minister Justin Trudeau announced plans to lift the visa requirement on Mexican nationals wishing to come to Canada. The visa requirement had been in place since 2009 and a diplomatic irritant from the moment it was implemented, not to mention its impact on Mexican nationals seeking protection in Canada or attempting to visit their loved ones. The announcement was framed through the lens of strengthening the bilateral relationship and underscored that the decision to lift the visa was primarily an economic calculation. At the same time, statements from Canadian officials clearly articulated the role of the visa in refugee deterrence, and concerns that lifting the visa may prove to be "unsuccessful" due to an anticipated increase in asylum claims or "other irregular migration" (Government of Canada 2016). Making an asylum claim is not unauthorized or irregular migration, although it has increasingly been constructed as such by officials in Canada and other countries in the Global North (Macklin 2005). Statements from the Canadian government that accompanied the announcement focused on "irregular" migration and an equation of Mexican asylum claims with this kind of migration: "Canadian officials continue to work with their Mexican counterparts to support a sustainable visa lift. This includes collaborating on combating irregular migration – to maximize the benefits of the visa lift for both countries" (Government of Canada 2016).

Thinking about the ways in which Canadian border-control policies aim to deter refugee claims by people of Mexican descent opens a window into considering the racialized and classed dimensions of these policies. Moreover, the case demonstrates that borders are implemented and worked out by a range of actors across multiple spaces and relationships—from customs lines at airports, to visa offices in capital cities, to schools, workplaces, hospitals, and public transit where people go about their daily lives. The goals of this chapter include: deepening understandings of the consequences of nation-state borders; examining the ways in which race and class distinctions are embedded in how borders are implemented and enforced; considering the differential impacts of border-control policies; and rethinking borders as social and political processes.

Border Control as Social and Political Practice

Borders are often understood only as lines on a map that mark the edges of a nation-state's territory. While these international boundary lines are the most visible expression of borders, in fact the border exists in a number of forms, places, and relationships. William Walters (2004) has described the border as a "membrane" to highlight the selectivity of borders and the ways in which bordering practices act as a sorting mechanism (see also Lyon 2002). He has also used the metaphor of the "firewall" in the sense that officials use data collected about individuals attempting to cross borders to assign them to a category that determines the conditions of entry or refusal. Over the past decade, border regimes have increasingly made use of pre-clearance programs and biometric information (e.g., fingerprints, iris scans, DNA testing) to verify identity and assess potential risks associated with people attempting to cross the border. Data is collected in advance of an individual's arrival at the border to better profile "risky" versus "un-risky" or "desirable" versus "undesirable" border crossers (Amoore 2006; Lyon 2002; Pratt 2005).

It is in this sense that Emily Gilbert (2007) has described the border as producing "calculable subjects operating in calculable spaces" (p. 86). The nation-state governs by making its population knowable and therefore manageable. Border regimes assign people to categories that mask the complexity of reasons for moving, imposing order onto human mobility, which is inherently disorderly. Parvati Raghuram (2004) identifies three "modes of control" that the state exercises over its migrant population (p. 196):

1. Entry – by determining who gets in and who does not, and under what conditions;

2. Integration – by shaping access to services and programs, rights, and responsibilities;

3. Citizenship – by establishing formal membership in society and thus deciding who can become a citizen and how.

How a person is categorized as they cross state borders matters. It has impacts on their experiences, outcomes, and sense of identity and belonging. Jennifer Hyndman (2004) refers to the "politics of mobility" to emphasize the uneven access to mobility and rights that exists globally. People can be treated differently at the same border, and borders have differential impacts on the basis of race, gender, class, nationality, geographical location, and immigration status, among other factors. Race and class, in particular, intersect to shape how global borders are enforced and whether they are opened to a given border crosser.

Several researchers argue that racism is institutionalized in the practice of nation-state borders (see Anderson, Sharma, and Wright 2009; Boyce 2018; Doty 2011; Sharma 2006). Racial profiling is embedded in migration controls—in both external and internal border control practices. The border and its differentiating functions appear not only at physical boundaries between states but also in encounters at health clinics, schools, workplaces, and courtrooms, and in less formal spaces like newspaper pages and bus stops (Anderson et al. 2009; Bailey, Wright, Mountz, and Miyares 2002; Polanco 2016; Ong 2003; Vukov 2003). This is also referred to as the "internalization" of border control practices whereby local police forces cooperate with national immigration enforcement officials (Coleman 2007; Gilbert 2007; Gilbert 2010; Ridgley 2008; Varsanyi 2008). In the United States, the geography and deployment of internal immigration checkpoints and "random stops" within the country show that Latinx communities are overwhelmingly targeted, revealing the systemic racism underlying these practices (Boyce 2018; Chacon and Davis 2006). As such, it is important to consider the micro-scale at which the border intersects with individual bodies, whereby people are fixed into particular identities that ignore actual embodied experiences and dimensions of identity (Gilbert 2007).

Meanwhile, countries are increasingly putting their borders on the move to prevent unwanted forms of migration. They appear and are enforced in locations far from the territories of nation-states where one would expect to encounter them. Jennifer Hyndman and Alison Mountz (2007) argue that states use geography to curb access to rights of asylum and legal representation. These spatial tactics—often referred to as interdiction or deterrence practices—include the location of visa offices and imposition of visas on particular countries, the designation of so-called "safe third countries" and "safe countries of origin," and the offshoring of refugee processing zones. These policies and practices make it almost impossible to arrive on the territory of wealthier and more powerful states in the Global North for the purposes of migration or to make a refugee claim. They are also part of a broader trend toward the criminalization and securitization of migration.

The contemporary preoccupation with "illegal aliens" and "bogus refugees" is connected to a longer history of marking out "deserving" and "undeserving" population groups for differential treatment by state institutions as well as more recent concerns with fraud and abuse (Pickering and Weber 2006; Pratt 2005). The depiction of migrants and refugees as criminals and security concerns justifies and perpetuates national policies that restrict access to nation-state territory. Audrey Macklin (2005) refers to this as the "discursive disappearance of the refugee": interdiction practices discredit the legitimacy of individuals who arrive at or within state borders to make a claim for refugee status without the requisite preselection and documentation by visa officers abroad and render "illegal" those people who manage to evade these policies. The equation of refugee claimants with illegality then reinforces the need for these laws and practices (Macklin 2005; Pickering and Weber 2006; Pratt 2005). In the North American context, illegality has been further linked with Mexican-ness, and this racialized criminalization influences how both internal and external borders are policed, with particular impacts on individuals and communities of Mexican descent living within and/or attempting to cross US and Canadian borders (Gilbert 2010). At the same time, the overarching national security framing of border-control policies masks the underlying racism and discrimination that are expressed through the selectivity of border enforcement that targets people of color, and especially those who appear to be Muslim, for heightened surveillance and suspicion (Pratt 2005; Sharma 2006).

Illustrative Case Study: Mapping the Mexican Visa Requirement in Canada

Returning to the case introduced above, Canada's 2009 visa implementation was part of the construction of refugee claimants from Mexico as a policy problem. In 2005, Mexico became the top source country for refugee claims lodged in Canada and maintained this position through 2009, with a peak of 9,400 in 2008. Along with the rising number of claims over the 2000s and a low acceptance rate for these claims by Canada's refugee tribunal (11 percent in 2008), 632 people with Mexican or Haitian passports had arrived in the Detroit-Windsor border city over a five-month period (from August 30, 2007, to February 8, 2008) to make refugee claims. This was more than double the number of claims lodged at this border crossing over the same period the previous year. These arrivals elicited a response from the Canadian government, which started to talk a lot about Mexican refugee claimants and compile data into graphs comparing claims by Mexicans to claims by people from "all other countries."

Rather than interpreting the rising numbers of refugee claims as symptomatic of protection concerns in Mexico,[33] they were instead used as evidence that Mexicans were abusing Canada's refugee determination system. Indeed, even with the lifting of the visa requirement in December 2016, Canadian officials indicated that it could be re-implemented if the numbers rose too high. Sources say a threshold of 3,500 Mexican claims annually would trigger re-imposition of the visa, although this is not spelled out in the policy (Harris 2016).

Canada's Mexican visa requirement presents several points of entry for analysis, given its trajectory and the long history of visa policies in the country. In a sense, it was further evidence of an ongoing reliance by officials on a visa policy to deter unwanted arrivals in the country. This approach was first analyzed by Gerald Dirks (1995), who said that Canadian officials had settled on the visa policy as a tool for managing undesirable refugee claims, and is illustrative of Macklin's (2005) framing of the "discursive disappearance of the refugee." In the case of the visa policy, it is one in a chain of discursive links that produce refugee claimants as illegal if they manage to arrive on the territory of a state that allows them to make a claim for asylum. Indeed, the need for the Mexican visa was framed in relation to "illegal migration" debates in the United States. These bordering practices contribute to framing asylum seekers as criminals and security threats.

In the Mexican case, there was a direct line drawn between refugee claimants arriving in Canada and "illegal aliens" in the United States that bolstered the argument for visa imposition. Liette Gilbert (2010) describes this as the "discursive migration of illegal immigration rhetoric" from the United States into Canada. Her analysis of local and national newspaper coverage of the 2007 episode found a focus on Mexicans arriving at the Detroit-Windsor border, although 67 percent were actually of Haitian origin. She found that Mexicans were depicted five times more frequently than were Haitians: the word "Mexican" appeared 270 times, while the word "Haitian" occurred 58 times in the 56 articles analyzed. In explaining this focus on Mexican over

---

[33] Violence in Mexico increased dramatically in 2006.

Haitian refugee claimants, Gilbert reminds us that there was a moratorium on deportations to Haiti, which meant that Canadian officials were more likely to see Haitians as legitimately in need of political protection. Moreover, racialized as black, Haitian claimants matched the essentialized assumption about what a "real" refugee looks like. Conversely, media coverage deployed the term "illegal" to describe Mexican asylum seekers, which functioned to de-legitimate their refugee claims. Media representations of the people arriving revealed that US discourses of Mexican illegality had crossed the border into Canadian debates (Gilbert 2010). In interviews carried out with Mexicans living in Toronto after the visa imposition, Paloma Villegas (2013) documented that these migrants felt they had been illegalized through the policy and public discussions that ensued in relation to the visa requirement. Mexican identity and tenure in Canada were increasingly seen as suspect.

Related to this illegalization of Mexican claimants and other people of Mexican descent living in Canada, Mexican refugee claims continue to be deployed by Canadian officials as a barometer to evaluate the integrity of the Canadian refugee system. "Too many" claims by Mexican nationals became viewed as an indicator of problems with and justification for changes to the system. Consequently, there is an ongoing refusal to consider protection issues in Mexico and instead a focus on the security of Canada's borders over any contemplation of or response to insecurities within Mexico. Indeed, following the visa implementation, Mexico was also added to Canada's list of designated "safe" countries in 2013. This means that refugee claims filed by a person from Mexico are subjected to an expedited decision-making process and, prejudged as fraudulent, they are excluded from the right of appeal. After the visa policy was lifted on December 1, 2016, policy makers and the media resumed tracking Mexican claims amid fears of a "rush" on the border of undocumented Mexicans living in the United States (Harris 2016).

The visa policy is part of what Young (2018) refers to as "the Mexico-Canada border"—or the ways in which Canada polices Mexico's borders through multiple sites and tactics. It is important to analyze these discrete policies as components of a larger, coherent structure because Canada's increasing involvement in policing Mexico's borders has shifted the material and discursive terrain of mobility and displacement both within and across North American boundaries. An important aspect of the Mexican visa case is its role in constructing Mexico as the lynchpin of regional migration management, similar to the ways in which Turkey and Libya have been used in relation to the European Union's attempts to manage migration practices and routes (Andersson 2016). As such, it is crucial to insist that Canada's interventions in enforcing Mexico's borders are not just about deterring migration from Mexico, since policing Mexico's borders also results in preventing the movement of Central American migrants. By far the largest groups of people seeking to transit Mexico are nationals from Honduras, Guatemala, El Salvador, and Nicaragua (Alba and Castillo 2012; Isacson, Meyers, and Morales 2014). The ways in which the Canadian border materializes within Mexico influence migration into and through Mexico itself.

Canada's visa policy is part of a broader strategic approach to managing migration regionally, as it is one tactic in a suite of measures targeting migration from, throughout, and into Mexico. Although the policy explicitly focused on preventing Mexican nationals from having access to the right to asylum in Canada, its impacts cast a wider net that also ensnared Central Americans displaced by poverty and violence into Mexico. As such, Canada's border control efforts have wider regional impacts with consequences for Central American and other origin migrants attempting to transit through Mexico and arrive in the United States and Canada. At their core, policies like Canada's visa requirement represent judgments about the bodies of Mexican and Central American people on the move, even as the dire situations in that region are increasingly understood as a crisis (Beuze 2017).

Conclusion

This chapter examined the uneven and differential impacts of nation-state borders. It also presented the border as a practice—i.e., bordering as an active and ongoing process that **categorizes** and sorts people as they attempt to cross it as well as before they arrive (**interdiction** or **deterrence** measures) and after they have crossed (**internalization** of border control practices). Similar to the ways in which social boundaries are policed, nation-state borders are enacted and performed by a range of actors across a host of spaces and relationships—from the workplace to the bus stop to newspaper pages. The discussion of Canada's decision to implement a visa requirement on Mexico illustrated the construction of Mexican refugee claimants as a policy problem that needed to be resolved as well as the broader consequences of Canada's border-control practices that target migration from Mexico. Moreover, it demonstrated how border-control policies and practices are racialized, in the sense that refugee claimants of Mexican descent were targeted differently than those from Haiti when they attempted to enter Canada via the same border crossing. Based on their racialized identities and their presumed "illegal" status in the United States, Mexican border crossers were criminalized, their claims for refugee protection were dismissed as fraudulent, and their attempts to enter Canada were depicted as abusing the country's immigration system. As such, borders act as expressions of power that enforce divisions and exclusions based on race, socioeconomic status, and other forms of distinction.

Reflection/Critical Thinking Questions

1. Where have you encountered the border in your daily life? Think about the times and places where you are required to show a piece of personal identification in order to access a program, service, or location.

2. What are some of the benefits or disadvantages that you experience due to your citizenship or immigration status?

3. In the quote that opens the chapter, Khosravi (2010) states that he was "indistinguishable from the border; [he] *was* the border" (p. 98). Drawing from the discussions in this chapter and your own experiences with crossing borders, reflect on and analyze this description of his experience of having crossed the border "illegally" into Europe.

Exploratory Research Questions

In thinking about nation-state borders as social and political processes, a number of questions arise regarding their broader impacts:

1. What are some examples of the uneven or differential impacts of borders?

2. In what ways can we argue that systemic racism operates via border control policies?

3. What are some of the local and regional consequences of Canada's migrant interdiction and deterrence practices?

4. How do migrant justice and indigenous activists challenge or resist the racialized, classed, and colonial logics of nation-state borders?

Further Readings

Books

Andersson, R. 2014. *Illegality Inc.: Clandestine Migration and the Business of Bordering Europe*. Oakland: University of California Press.

Anzaldúa, G. 1987. *Borderlands/La Frontera: The New Mestiza*. San Francisco: Aunt Lute Books.

Nevins, J. 2002. *Operation Gatekeeper: The Rise of the "Illegal Alien" and the Making of the US-Mexico Boundary*. New York: Routledge.

Ngai, M.M. 2014. *Impossible Subjects: Illegal Aliens and the Making of Modern America*. 2nd ed. Princeton, NJ: Princeton University Press.

Simpson, A. 2014. *Mohawk Interruptus: Political Life Across the Borders of Settler States*. Durham, NC and London, UK: Duke University Press.

Website

Border Criminologies: Themed Week on *Race and Border Control*

https://www.law.ox.ac.uk/research-subject-groups/centre-criminology/centreborder-criminologies/blog/2015/04/race-and-border

References

Alba, F., and M.A. Castillo. 2012. *New Approaches to Migration Management in Mexico and Central America*. Washington DC: Migration Policy Institute.

Amoore, L. 2006. "Biometric Borders: Governing Mobilities in the War on Terror." *Political Geography* 25(3):336–51.

Anderson, B., N. Sharma, and C. Wright. 2009. "Editorial: Why No Borders?" *Refuge*, Special Issue on No Borders as Practical Politics. 26(2):5–18.

Andersson, R. (2016). "Europe's Failed 'Fight' against Irregular Migration: Ethnographic Notes on a Counterproductive Industry." *Journal of Ethnic and Migration Studies* 42(7):1055–75.

Bailey, A.J., R.A. Wright, A. Mountz, and I.M. Miyares. 2002. "(Re)producing Salvadoran Transnational Geographies." *Annals of the Association of American Geographers* 92(1):125–44.

Beuze, Jean-Nicolas. 2017. "As a Refugee Crisis Unfolds, Central America Needs Canada's Help." *Maclean's*, 23 December.

Boyce, G.A. 2018. "Appearing 'Out of Place': Automobility and the Everyday Policing of Threat and Suspicion on the US/Canada Frontier. *Political Geography* 64. https://doi.org/10.1016/j.polgeo.2018.02.001

Chacon, J.A., and M. Davis. 2006. *No One Is Illegal: Fighting Racism and State Violence on the US-Mexico Border*. Chicago: Haymarket Books.

Citizenship and Immigration Canada. 2009. *Backgrounder: The Visa Requirement for Mexico*. Accessed at: http://www.cic.gc.ca/english/department/media/backgrounders/2009/2009-07-13.asp

Coleman, M. 2007. "Immigration Geopolitics Beyond the Mexico-US border." *Antipode* 38(1):54–76.

Dirks, Gerald E. 1995. *Controversy and Complexity: Canadian Immigration Policy During the 1980s*. Montreal & Kingston: McGill-Queen's University Press.

Doty, R.L. 2011. "Bare Life: Border-Crossing Deaths and Spaces of Moral Alibi." *Environment and Planning D: Society and Space* 29(4):599–612.

Gilbert, Emily. 2007. "Leaky Borders and Solid Citizens: Governing Security, Prosperity and Quality of Life in a North American Partnership." *Antipode* 39(1):77–98.

Gilbert, Liette. 2010. "North American Anti-Immigration Rhetorics: Continental Circulation and Global Resonance of Discursive Integration." In I. Hussain, editor, *The impacts of NAFTA on North America: Challenges Outside the Box* (pp. 63–91). New York: Palgrave Macmillan.

Government of Canada. 2016. *News: Canada to Lift Visa Requirements for Mexico*. Prime Minister of Canada, 28 June. Accessed at: https://pm.gc.ca/eng/news/2016/06/28/canada-lift-visa-requirements-mexico

Harris, K. 2016. "Canadian Officials Preparing for Potential Flood of Mexican Migrants After Trump Wins Presidency." *CBC News*, 10 November. Accessed at: http://www.cbc.ca/news/politics/canada-mexico-visa-requirement-trump-1.3845957

Hyndman, Jennifer. 2004. The (Geo)politics of Gendered Mobility. In L.A. Staeheli, E. Kofman, and L. Peake, editors, *Mapping Women, Making Politics: Feminist Perspectives on Political Geography* (pp.169–84). New York: Routledge.

Hyndman, Jennifer, and Alison Mountz. 2007. "Refuge or Refusal: The Geography of Exclusion." In D. Gregory and A. Pred, editors, *Violent Geographies* (pp. 77–92). New York: Routledge.

Isacson, A., M. Meyer, and G. Morales. 2014. *Mexico's Other Border: Security, Migration and the Humanitarian Crisis at the Line with Central America*. Washington, DC: Washington Office on Latin America.

Khosravi, Shahram. 2010. *"Illegal Traveler": An Auto-Ethnography of Borders*. New York: Palgrave MacMillan.

Lyon, D., ed. 2002. *Surveillance as Social Sorting: Privacy, Risk and Digital Discrimination*. London: Routledge.

Macklin, Audrey. 2005. "Disappearing Refugees: Reflections on the Canada-US Safe Third Country Agreement." *Columbia Human Rights Law Review* 36:365–426.

Ong, A. 2003. *Buddha Is Hiding: Refugees, Citizenship, the New America*. Berkeley: University of California Press.

Pickering, S., and L. Weber, eds. 2006. *Borders, Mobility and Technologies of Control*. Dordrecht, Netherlands: Springer.

Polanco, G. 2016. "Consent Behind the Counter: Aspiring Citizens and Labour Control Under Precarious (Im)migration Schemes." *Third World Quarterly* 37(8): 1332–350.

Pratt, A. 2005. *Securing Borders: Detention and Deportation in Canada*. Vancouver: University of British Columbia Press.

Raghuram, Parvati. 2004. "Crossing Borders: Gender and Migration." In L.A. Staeheli, E. Kofman, and L. Peake, eds., *Mapping Women, Making Politics: Feminist Perspectives on Political Geography* (pp. 185–197). New York: Routledge.

Ridgley, J. 2008. "Cities of Refuge: Immigration Enforcement, Police, and the Insurgent Genealogies of Citizenship in US sanctuary cities." *Urban Geography* 29(1): 53–77.

Sharma, N. 2006. White Nationalism, Illegality and Imperialism: Border Controls as Ideology. In K. Hunt, ed., *Gendering the War on Terror: War Stories and Camouflaged Politics* (pp. 121–43). Aldershot, UK: Ashgate.

Varsanyi, M.W. 2008. "Immigration Policing through the Backdoor: City Ordinances, the 'Right to the City,' and the Exclusion of Undocumented Day Laborers. *Urban Geography* 29(1):29–52.

Villegas, Paloma. 2013. "Assembling a Visa Requirement Against the Mexican 'Wave': Migrant Illegalization, Policy and Affective 'Crises' in Canada." *Ethnic and Racial Studies* 36(12): 2200–219.

Vukov, T. 2003. "Imagining Communities through Immigration Policies: Governmental Regulation, Media Spectacles and the Affective Politics of National Borders." *International Journal of Cultural Studies* 6(3):335–53.

Walters, W. 2004. "Secure Borders, Safe Haven, Domopolitics." *Citizenship Studies* 8(3):237–60.

Young, J.E.E. 2018. "The Mexico-Canada Border: Extraterritorial Border Control and the Production of 'Economic Refugees.'" *International Journal of Migration and Border Studies* 4(1–2):35–50.

Reading 8.3 Race, Space, and Displacement: An Overview of Ethno-racial Dynamics in Colombia

Shantee Rosado, University of Pennsylvania

Keywords: Colombia, Blackness, Indigeneity, Multicultural Constitution, Displacement, Civil War, Census.

Introduction

To understand the importance of race and ethnicity in Colombia, researchers often point to the role of stark regional differences that generally align with racial and ethnic groups in the country.[34] According to Wade (1995), race and region operate in tandem within Colombia, where the Pacific and Atlantic coasts are still regarded as "black" regions, the Amazon region is regarded as "indigenous," and the Andean highlands are referred to as "white and *mestizo*" areas. Although migration has been, and is, commonplace in Colombia, scholars still find that since colonization, "the population of Colombia has not historically moved toward anything like complete racial integration" (Green 2000, p. 118).

Three main ethno-racial groups encompass most of the Colombian population. Whites and *mestizos* are often jointly regarded as the majority group in Colombia, making up 85.9 percent of the population (DANE 2005b). The second largest group is Afro-Colombians, or blacks and *mulatos* (those with mixed black and Spaniard ancestry), who comprise 10.6 percent of the population (DANE 2005b). Lastly, the small yet significant population of *indígenas*, or indigenous Colombians, make up 3.4 percent of the nation (DANE 2005b). These numbers should be considered cautiously, though, given they change depending on who collected the data and how they phrased questions regarding racial and ethnic identity (Paschel 2013).

In the following chapter, I briefly outline the history of ethno-racial categorization in Colombia, tracing its origins from the colonial era until the present day, as the country endures the lasting effects of an ongoing—though waning—civil war. Following this is a discussion of the impact of the civil war on black and indigenous Colombians. Here, I highlight the importance of the fifty-three-years-long conflict between the Colombian Armed Forces and armed guerrillas and paramilitaries to understand existing racial and ethnic disparities. This is followed by a discussion of the Colombian national census and its recent reintroduction of questions on race and ethnicity. I conclude by outlining several social, economic, and health disparities that persist for indigenous and Afro-Colombians, relative to the white/*mestizo* majority in Colombia.

Spanish Colonization and Slavery

Spaniards started to colonize the region encompassing Colombia, known then as *Nueva Granada*, in 1510. Using the port town of Cartagena, Spanish and other European enslavers unloaded millions of kidnapped Africans onto Colombia's shores from the sixteenth to the mid-nineteenth centuries. Spaniards hoped to use these enslaved Africans as a replacement for indigenous laborers in the region, whose population had been significantly reduced

---

[34] The distinction between race and ethnicity remains widely debated among scholars. Researchers have found that "racial" categories, as understood in the United States, are often ascribed "ethnic" elements in Latin America, such as language and cultural practices (Wade 2010). Conversely, members of ethnic groups in Colombia, such as Indigenous people, are often racialized (e.g., by making reference to physical characteristics common to group members) (Wade 2010). Hence, I use the terms "race and ethnicity" and "ethno-racial" to acknowledge the permeable boundaries between these concepts in Colombia.

since colonization (Lane 2000). Additionally, the Spanish crown was indecisive about forcing indigenous peoples into labor, given their scarce numbers (Lane 2000). Cartagena was one of the most widely used slave ports in the Americas (Newson and Minchin 2004), from where enslaved Africans were shipped down the country's Pacific coast to work at the grueling task of gold mining in the tropical jungles of the region (Lane 2000). Enslaved Africans were also transported along the Caribbean coast of the country and further into the Andes region into present-day Ecuador and Peru.

During colonization, Spaniards developed the *castas* (castes) system of classification, which used skin color and other features to designate social status for Latin Americans based on the purported "blood" of their direct ancestors (Wade 2010). These castes were meant to document who had "pure" Spanish "blood" in the colonies and deserved special privileges and rights, versus those who had African or indigenous "blood" and should be afforded little or no rights (Carrera 2003). In eighteenth-century Mexico, a series of over 200 *casta* paintings were commissioned by Spanish elites, each depicting up to sixteen pairings that illustrated, for example, what the offspring of a Spaniard and an African should be called—*mulato*—or what the child of an indigenous person and a Spaniard should be called—*mestizo*, among other labels (Katzew 2005). These paintings reflected the idea of "race" as synonymous with "ancestry" and were some of the earliest depictions of the process of *mestizaje* in the Spanish colonies. Race mixing, or *mestizaje*, was never illegal in Colombia or Latin America as it was in the United States, though it was widely discouraged (Wade 2010).

Independence and the Nation-building Period

During the early 1800s, a wave of independence movements swept Latin America, as *criollos*, or Latin America–born people of Spanish descent, sought autonomy from their Spanish rulers. In Colombia, the call for independence came in 1810, when Spaniards in the capital of Bogotá gathered to renounce their rule by the Spanish monarchy (Lasso 2003). In 1853, Colombia established its first constitution, which also abolished slavery in the country.

During this period, Colombian governmental officials strove to construct a sovereign nation. This process involved diminishing perceived differences between citizens and emphasizing their common Colombian-ness. The high number of African descendants and indigenous people within the new nation complicated these attempts, though (Lasso 2003). How would Colombian elites reconcile an image of the country as unified and singular given the diversity within its borders? The answer in Colombia, as in many other Latin American countries, was to present themselves as a "mixed" nation and to emphasize the importance of *mestizaje*, or race mixing, for the progress of the nation (Lasso 2003; Wade 2010).

This embrace of *mestizaje* might sound progressive for the time, especially given the proliferation of racial violence just north in the United States. In fact, the wide appeal of *mestizaje* in Colombia and other Latin American nations led outsiders to label the region a "racial democracy," where divisions based on race or ethnicity did not exist (Lasso 2003; Paschel 2010; Wade 1995, 2010). The largest racial group became *mestizos*, Colombians of mixed indigenous and European ancestry. In the past few decades, scholars and social activists have debunked the notion of racial democracy in the region by noting the persistence of a racial hierarchy favoring whiteness and trenchant inequalities faced by black and indigenous people (Green, 2000; Hooker, 2005; Lasso, 2003; Radcliffe, 2007). Scholars have also argued that *mestizaje* was meant as a process of *blanqueamiento*, or whitening, in which blacks would be excluded altogether from the national imaginary and the indigenous population would eventually be absorbed into the white population (De Ferro, 1995; Wade, 1995).

From the colonial period through independence, race in Colombia was understood in largely geographic terms (Appelbaum 1999). In this ethno-racial and spatial configuration, black Colombians were viewed as largely residing in rural areas along the Pacific and Caribbean coasts (Wade 1995). Indigenous Colombians were also seen as rural dwelling, living in the *Amazonas* region in the south of the country, and along the Pacific and Caribbean coasts (Wade 2010). The center of the country, which was also the center of power within Colombia, was perceived as predominantly white and *mestizo* (Appelbaum 1999). To this day, when asked about race in

Colombia, many discuss this notion of racialized regions, despite considerable migration within the country over time.

Adopting a Multicultural Constitution and Granting Ethnic Land Rights

In the 1960s, indigenous Colombians began organizing for autonomy over their communal lands under the premise they had specific needs and ways of living that differed from the rest of the Colombian population (Asher 2009). International indigenous movements fighting for their right to land around this same period inspired this movement for indigenous Colombians (Paschel 2016). After decades of activism and negotiations with the Colombian state, the first indigenous reservations, or *resguardos*, were formally established by the Colombian government in the early 1980s.

In 1991, Colombian officials drafted a new constitution that recognized, after centuries of *mestizaje* as a national ideology, that its population was multicultural and pluri-ethnic. The move came about through lengthy proceedings and took as a model the fourteen other countries in the region working to adopt a multicultural constitution (Hooker 2005). This "multicultural turn" in the region took different forms depending on the country, though the general premise was that countries like Colombia needed to acknowledge the presence and importance of its indigenous populations, who were gaining land rights and had the backing of international NGOs (Ng'weno 2007).

Black organizers in Colombia saw this new constitution as a political opening to advocate for their own rights over territory in the Pacific region (Paschel 2010). With significant international backing, black social movements fought for the implementation of laws that would grant land rights to black Colombians (Paschel 2016). Black organizers stated they, too, had specific needs and ways of living that differed from that of *mestizos* and whites, and used similar language to that of past indigenous rights activists to advocate for themselves (Asher 2009). Under these conditions, the Colombian government passed Law 70, or the Law of Black Communities, in 1993.

Law 70 granted black Colombians living along the Pacific Coast the right to communal land ownership within the nation, conditioned on their identification as "culturally different" from the white and *mestizo* majority (Paschel 2010). Further, Law 70 stated that black Colombians living in these communally owned regions had the right to *consulta previa*, or prior consultation, a requirement that anyone seeking to develop the land within these regions had to consult with black community leaders prior to implementing their projects (Asher 2009). The passage of the multicultural constitution and designation of ethnic communal lands were lauded as major wins for black and indigenous Colombians. Nevertheless, members of these groups remained cautious about the limitations of laws and constitutions, which often led to different results once implemented (Paschel 2016). The lands secured as indigenous *resguardos* today encompass over 25 percent of all land in the country, while black communal lands make up 3 percent of all land in the country (Chaves and Zambrano 2006).

Violence and Displacement as Extensions of Racism

Since 1954, the Colombian national army has been at war with left-wing Marxist guerrilla groups seeking land ownership and political power. While these guerrillas began their struggle as one for the rural poor, when faced with the need for continued funding, they began engaging in the illicit drug trade. Thus, the growing, processing, and transportation of cocaine became a major funding source for guerrilla groups (Saab and Taylor 2009). Throughout the 1980s, the Pacific region of the country, home to a large concentration of indigenous and black communal land, became attractive to guerrillas seeking land and potential recruits (Oslender 2007). Right-wing paramilitary groups also became active during this period, further adding to unrest in the region (Saab and Taylor 2009). These right-wing groups were composed of wealthy landowning elites and their recruited underlings.

The civil war has been especially harmful to Afro-Colombians and indigenous Colombians. First, militants have targeted black and indigenous communal landowners in their attempts to seize land (Oslender 2007). After the passing of Law 70, rural black communities used local methods of establishing land ownership, which often did not align with the documentation methods of the Colombian government. These informal land agreements were attractive to armed groups, who could seize the land and later claim it was not previously owned (Asher 2009). Second, given the rural presence of many black and most indigenous Colombians and the mostly rural presence of the civil war, the conflict has disproportionately affected these minority groups relative to their urban-dwelling white and *mestizo* counterparts (Oslender 2007). Third, the lack of state presence (e.g., police, military, and other government officials) in these regions makes addressing violence there complicated, if not impossible. This makes these regions especially attractive to armed groups and others engaged in the drug trade (Sánchez-Garzoli and Cordoba 2017).

Many wonder whether the disproportionate impact of the civil war on black and indigenous Colombians is intentional. In other words, is it because they are black and indigenous that members of these groups are targeted? Or is it simply a by-product of them living in rural areas, which tend to be more attractive to those seeking land? The answers to these questions are complicated. It is difficult to prove that armed groups have intentionally targeted black and indigenous people. Nevertheless, several factors have made these regions especially vulnerable to civil war conflict. For example, the southern and Pacific coast regions of the country have been under-resourced for centuries, which explains their persistent lack of state presence and state funding (Asher 2009; Oslender 2007). Thus, one might argue that civil war conflict has affected these regions not explicitly because of race, but rather due to the Colombian government's ongoing neglect of black and indigenous Colombians.

By 2005, and after decades of civil war conflict, Colombia had seen some of the highest numbers of internal displacement in the world. Internal displacement occurs when an individual migrates within a country's borders due to violence or the threat of violence (Cohen and Deng 2012). Current estimates state that roughly 5 million people, or 10 percent of the entire Colombian population, have experienced internal displacement (NRC/IDMC 2015). Black and indigenous activists as well as human rights organizations have argued that minority groups are overrepresented among the internally displaced (CODHES 2006; Sánchez-Garzoli and Cordoba 2017), though the exact number of black and indigenous Colombians impacted by the war is hard to ascertain.

Those who are displaced often move to nearby or major cities, where they hope to escape civil war violence (CODHES 2006; Vélez-Torres and Agergaard 2014). Today, cities including Quibdó, the capital of Chocó, and Bogotá, the capital of the country, have received large numbers of displaced black and indigenous Colombians. The transition to life in these cities is often harsh for these individuals, as they face hardships due to racial discrimination in the labor market, police brutality, economic hardships from having left their land, and health problems, among other adversities (Ibáñez and Vélez 2008).

In 2011, given the crisis of displacement after decades of armed conflict, the Colombian government implemented the Law for Victims and Land Restitution, or Law 1448. This law stated that individuals who had been violently displaced had a right to resources to improve their economic, social, and health outcomes. The law allows displaced people to register with a state agency to reclaim land they lost due to displacement and receive reparations for their losses. The work on this front is both arduous and slow moving. Those who have been displaced face a quandary—missing their homes, while negotiating a return to areas still facing armed conflict (Summers 2012). Scholars and local activists have also reported evidence of collusion between the government and armed paramilitary groups, stating that paramilitary groups are paid by government officials to "clear the land" of residents for agribusiness and large infrastructure projects (Asher and Ojeda 2009; Escobar 2003; Oslender 2007). These claims have caused further mistrust of the government among displaced peoples in the ongoing land restitution process.

Classifying Race and Ethnicity in the Colombian National Census

The 2005 Colombian General Census was a fortuitous occasion for sociologists looking to understand ethno-racial disparities in the country. In 2005, Colombian government officials made several changes to how they collect information on Colombians' race and ethnicity. In the previous national census (in 1993), individuals were classified as part of an ethno-racial group only if they resided on indigenous or Afro-Colombian communal land (DANE 2005b). For the 2005 census, the Colombian state uncoupled race and ethnicity from residence on ethnic communal land (DANE 2005a). The 2005 Colombian Census question for race and ethnicity now asked,

> Given your culture, tribe, or physical features, are you, or do you consider yourself as:
>
> 1. Indigenous? (if yes, please list the name of your tribe)
>
> 2. Roma?
>
> 3. Raizal from the archipelago of San Andres and Providencia?
>
> 4. Palenquero from San Basilio?
>
> 5. Black, mulato, Afro-Colombian, or Afro-descendant?

According to Paschel (2013), it took Afro-Colombian organizers several campaigns to make progress in their efforts to properly enumerate the Afro-Colombian population. Given the centuries-long adherence to the ideology of *mestizaje*, black organizers were faced with a difficult task—increasing black consciousness among those with African ancestry (Paschel 2016). One notable campaign titled "*Las Caras Bonitas de Mi Gente*," or "The Beautiful Faces of My People," included a series of commercials showing a variety of people with different skin colors and features, all of whom identified as *afrodescendientes* (Paschel 2013). The commercials and posters sought to encourage those with African ancestry to self-identify as such on the 2005 census. The numbers gathered in the 2005 census did, in fact, reflect an undercount of black Colombians in the previous census. While in 1993 the percent of the population identified as black was only 1.5 percent, the 2005 census showed that 10.6 percent of the Colombian population self-identified as Afro-descendant or black (DANE 2005b).

Improvements in census enumeration are critical for understanding ethno-racial disparities in places like Colombia. For example, Colombia has only collected nationwide information on Afro-descendants during the colonial era and for the past two national censuses in 1993 and 2005 (DANE 2005b). This lack of data makes it difficult for sociologists seeking to make claims about long-standing ethno-racial inequalities on a national level.

Conclusion

In this chapter, I provided a brief overview of major factors impacting the lives and outcomes of black and indigenous Colombians. Research on racial and ethnic disparities in Colombia has been hampered by the government's lack of data on the Colombian population by race and ethnicity. This changed significantly with the reintroduction of ethno-racial questions on the 1993 and 2005 Colombian General Censuses.

Using recent data, researchers have shed light on ethno-racial disparities still plaguing Colombia, though studies on disparities in education, income, and health are limited (Bernal and Cárdenas 2005; Romero P. 2010). For example, research by Peña and Wills (2010) found that both indigenous and black Colombians experience a wage gap relative to whites and *mestizos*, and shows that this gap can only be explained in the Afro-Colombian case by accounting for place of residence, age, and education. Another study found that Afro-Colombian men received 6.4 percent less in annual incomes than their white and *mestizo* counterparts (Rojas-Hayes 2008). In the case of indigenous Colombians, Romero P. (2010) used national survey data and found that indigenous Colombians, on average, earned 29.5 percent less income than other Colombians. Research on health also shows worrisome results for indigenous and black Colombians. For example, a report using the Living Standards Survey (LSS) showed that black and indigenous Colombians had worse health outcomes than their white and *mestizo* counterparts—these included chronic illness, hospitalization in the past year, and episodes of illness in the previous month (Bernal and Cárdenas 2005). The same report showed that while 31 percent of whites and *mestizos* report being uninsured, 48 percent of their black and indigenous counterparts lack health insurance.

Most recently, and after many failed attempts, the Colombian government succeeded in signing a peace accord with the largest guerrilla group in Colombia, the *Fuerzas Armadas Revolucionarias de Colombia*, or FARC, in late 2016 (Brodzinsky 2017). News outlets have deemed this historic peace agreement as the end of the civil war in Colombia. Black and indigenous activists have been cautiously celebrating, though. First, members of these groups struggled to ensure the peace agreement addressed the violent displacement of, and resettlement options for, indigenous and black Colombians (Sánchez-Garzoli and Cordoba 2017). Second, the agreement was signed amid continuing violence in areas with large concentrations of black and indigenous people, such as Chocó (Charles 2018). Future research on Colombia should examine the multilayered disparities facing black and indigenous victims of the civil war. Scholars should also address the lack of research on ethno-racial disparities in socioeconomic status and health within Colombia and in Latin America as a whole.

Critical Reflection Questions

1. In what ways did the 1991 Colombian constitution impact black and indigenous people?

2. How has the Colombian civil war impacted the lives of indigenous and black Colombians?

3. Why do national census data matter for researchers studying race and ethnicity in Colombia?

Exploratory Research Questions

1. What are the state agencies involved in the land restitution process?

2. To what extent are government officials involved in the displacement of black and indigenous Colombians?

3. What organizations have been fighting for displaced indigenous and black Colombians? How do they approach this issue?

Further Reading and Resources

To understand the role of black Colombian organizations in gaining land rights, read Karen Asher's *Black and Green: Afro-Colombians, Development, and Nature in the Pacific*.

To better understand black Colombian organizations' role in gaining broader civil rights, read Tianna S. Paschel's *Becoming Black Political Subjects: Movements and Ethno-Racial Rights in Colombia and Brazil*.

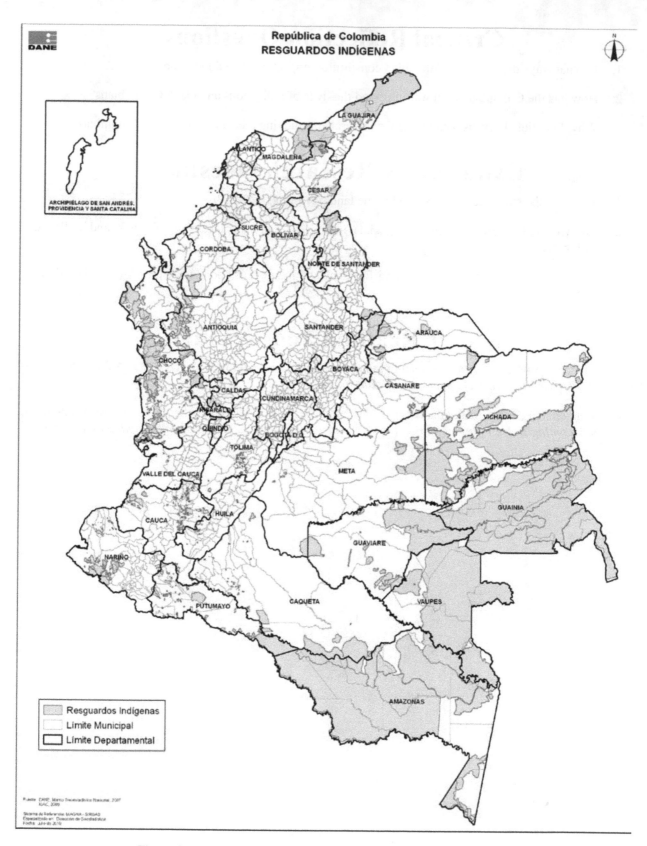

Figure 8.1-1 Indigenous *Resguardos* (Reservations) in Colombia, 2010.

Source: DANE

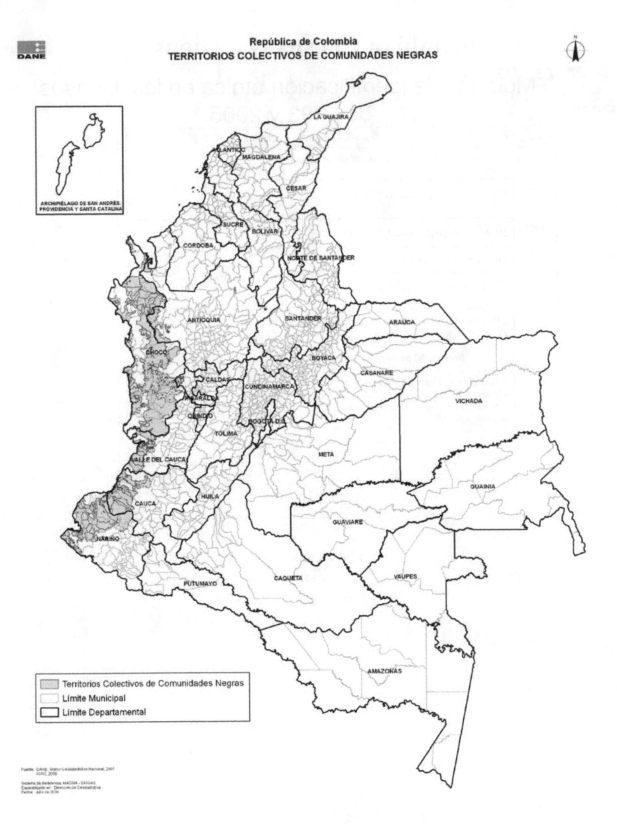

República de Colombia
TERRITORIOS COLECTIVOS DE COMUNIDADES NEGRAS

Figure 8.1-2 Black communal land in Colombia, 2010.

Source: DANE

Colombian Census Questions

Para tomar decisiones
DANE

Módulos de identificación étnica en los Censos de 1993 y 2005.

Año	Módulos de identificación étnica	
1993	¿Pertenece a alguna etnia, grupo indígena o comunidad negra ? SÍ__ ¿A cuál? _____ NO	Para todas las personas
	¿Habla su lengua indígena? SI NO	Sólo para las personas censadas con F 2 en áreas predominatemente indígenas
	¿Habla otra lengua indígena? SÍ__ ¿Cuántas? _____ NO	
2005	¿ De acuerdo con su CULTURA, PUEBLO O RASGOS FÍSICOS ... se reconoce como: 1. Indígena? Nombre del pueblo: _____ 2. Rom? 3. Raizal del archipiélago de San Andrés y Providencia? 4. Palenquero de San Basilio 5. Negro(a), mulato(a), Afrocolombiano(a) o afrodescendiente? 6. Ninguno de los anteriores?	Para todas las personas
	¿Habla la lengua de su pueblo ? 1 SI 2 NO	Para indígenas, rom, raizales del archipiélago de San Andrés y Providencia y palenqueros de San Basilio

55
AÑOS

Figure 8.1-3a

33. ¿De acuerdo con su **CULTURA, PUEBLO** o **RASGOS FÍSICOS**, ... es o se reconoce como:

1 ○ Indígena?

1.1 ¿A cuál **PUEBLO INDÍGENA** pertenece?

(Escriba el nombre del pueblo)

2 ○ Rom?
3 ○ Raizal del Archipiélago de San Andrés y Providencia?
4 ○ Palanquero de San Basilio?
5 ○ Negro(a), mulato(a), afrocolombiano(a) o afrodescendiente? ⎫ Pase
6 ○ Ninguna de las anteriores? ⎭ a 35

34. ¿Habla... la **LENGUA** de su pueblo?

1 ○ Sí
2 ○ No

55
AÑOS

Figure 8.1-3b

References

Appelbaum, Nancy. 1999. "Whitening the Region: Caucano Mediation and 'Antioqueño Colonization' in Nineteenth-Century Colombia." *Hispanic American Historical Review* 79(4):631–67.

Asher, Karen. 2009. *Black and Green: Afro-Colombians, Development, and Nature in the Pacific*. Durham, NC: Duke University Press.

Asher, Kiran, and Diana Ojeda. 2009. "Producing Nature and Making the State: Ordenamiento Territorial in the Pacific Lowlands of Colombia." *Geoforum* 40(3):292–302.

Bernal, Raquel, and Mauricio Cárdenas. 2005. "Race and Ethnic Inequality in Health and Health Care in Colombia." *Fedesarrollo* 29.

Brodzinsky, Sibylla. 2017. "'Welcome to Peace': Colombia's Farc Rebels Seal Historic Disarmament." *Guardian*, June 27.

Carrera, Magali M. 2003. *Imagining Identity in New Spain: Race, Lineage, and the Colonial Body in Portraiture and Casta Painting*s. University of Texas Press.

Charles, Mathew. 2018. "Farc Deal Opens Path for Colombia's Other Rebels: 'The Future Has to Be about War.'" *Guardian*, January 7.

Chaves, Margarita, and Marta Zambrano. 2006. "From Blanqueamiento to Reindigenización: Paradoxes of Mestizaje and Multiculturalism in Contemporary Colombia." *European Review of Latin American and Caribbean Studies* 80:5.

CODHES, ed. 2006. *Desafíos Para Construir Nación: El País Ante El Desplazamiento, El Conflicto Armado Y La Crisis Humanitaria, 1995–2005*. 1st ed. Bogotá: Consultoría para los Derechos Humanos y el Desplazamiento (CODHES).

Cohen, Roberta, and Francis M. Deng. 2012. *Masses in Flight: The Global Crisis of Internal Displacement*. Brookings Institution Press.

DANE. 2005a. *Censo General*. Colombia: Departamento Administrativo Nacional de Estadística.

DANE. 2005b. *La Visibilización Estadística de Los Grupos Étnicos Colombianos*. Colombia: Departamento Administrativo Nacional de Estadística.

Escobar, Arturo. 2003. "Displacement, Development, and Modernity in the Colombian Pacific." *International Social Science Journal* 55(175):157–67.

Hooker, Juliet. 2005. "Indigenous Inclusion/Black Exclusion: Race, Ethnicity and Multicultural Citizenship in Latin America." *Journal of Latin American Studies* 37(2):285–310.

Ibáñez, Ana María, and Carlos Eduardo Vélez. 2008. "Civil Conflict and Forced Migration: The Micro Determinants and Welfare Losses of Displacement in Colombia." *World Development* 36(4):659–76.

Katzew, Ilona. 2005. *Casta Painting: Images of Race in Eighteenth-Century Mexico*. Yale University Press.

Lane, Kris. 2000. "The Transition from Encomienda to Slavery in Seventeenth-century Barbacoas (Colombia)." *Slavery & Abolition* 21(1):73–95.

Lasso, Marixa. 2003. "A Republican Myth of Racial Harmony: Race and Patriotism in Colombia, 1810–12." *Historical Reflections/Reflexions Historiques* 29(1):43–63.

Newson, Linda A., and Susie Minchin. 2004. "Slave Mortality and African Origins: A View from Cartagena, Colombia, in the Early Seventeenth Century." *Slavery & Abolition* 25(3):18–43.

Ng'weno, Bettina. 2007. "Can Ethnicity Replace Race? Afro-Colombians, Indigeneity and the Colombian Multicultural State." *Journal of Latin American and Caribbean Anthropology* 12(2):414–40.

NRC/IDMC, Norwegian Refugee Council/Internal Displacement Monitoring Centre. 2015. "Global Overview 2015: People Internally Displaced by Conflict and Violence—Protracted Displacement in Colombia." *Refworld*. Retrieved September 14, 2017 (http://www.refworld.org/docid/554c6cd51d.html).

Oslender, Ulrich. 2007. "Violence in Development: The Logic of Forced Displacement on Colombia's Pacific Coast." *Development in Practice* 17(6):752–64.

Paschel, Tianna S. 2010. "The Right to Difference: Explaining Colombia's Shift from Color Blindness to the Law of Black Communities." *American Journal of Sociology* 116(3):729–69.

Paschel, Tianna. 2013. "'The Beautiful Faces of My Black People': Race, Ethnicity and the Politics of Colombia's 2005 Census." *Ethnic and Racial Studies* 36(10):1544–563.

Paschel, Tianna S. 2016. B*ecoming Black Political Subjects: Movements and Ethno-Racial Rights in Colombia and Brazil*. Princeton, NJ: Princeton University Press.

Peña, Ximena, and Daniel Wills. 2010. "Ethnic Earnings Gap in Colombia." *Banco de La República's Seminario Semanal de Economía, Bogotá, June 16.*

Rojas-Hayes, Carolina M. 2008. "Race Determinants of Wage Gaps in Colombia." *Economía Del Caribe* (2):31–65.

Romero P., Julio. 2010. *Educación, Calidad de Vida Y Otras Desventajas Económicas de Los Indígenas de Colombia*. Banco de la República.

Saab, Bilal Y., and Alexandra W. Taylor. 2009. "Criminality and Armed Groups: A Comparative Study of FARC and Paramilitary Groups in Colombia." *Studies in Conflict & Terrorism* 32(6):455–75.

Sánchez-Garzoli, Gimena, and Marino Cordoba. 2017. "Despite Obstacles, Colombia's Ethnic Minorities Integrate Themselves into Peace Accord." *LASA Forum* 48(1):17–20.

Summers, Nicole. 2012. "Colombia's Victims' Law: Transitional Justice in a Time of Violent Conflict?" *Harvard Human Rights Journal* 25(1):219–35.

Vélez-Torres, Irene, and Jytte Agergaard. 2014. "Political Remittances, Connectivity, and the Trans-Local Politics of Place: An Alternative Approach to the Dominant Narratives on 'Displacement' in Colombia." *Geoforum* 53:116–25.

Wade, Peter. 1995. *Blackness and Race Mixture: The Dynamics of Racial Identity in Colombia*. JHU Press.

Wade, Peter. 2010. *Race and Ethnicity in Latin America: Second Edition*. New York: Pluto Press.

Reading 8.4 Racial Hierarchy and Colonialism: How the World Understands Race Today as a Result of the Colonial Conquests

Thais Forneret, California State University–Sacramento

Thien-Huong T. Nihn, PhD, Cosumnes River College

Keywords: Colonialism/Neocolonialism, Capitalism, Global Color Hierarchy, Caste, Whitening/Mestizaje, Globalization

> *From the first ships that landed in Virginia in 1607, to the ships that survived the Great Hurricane of 1635, to the first slave ships, some British settlers of colonial America carried across the sea Puritan, biblical, scientific, and Aristotelian rationalizations of slavery and human hierarchy. From Western Europe and the new settlements and Latin America, some Puritans carried across their judgement, of the many African peoples as one inferior people. They carried across racist ideas—racist ideas that preceded American slavery, because the need to justify African slavery preceded colonial America.*
>
> —Ibram X. Kendy (2016)

Introduction

Current conventional wisdom assumes a social order in which race-based discrimination is unacceptable. Events such as the Holocaust in Europe during World War II (Siebers and Dennissen 2015) and the passage of the Civil Rights Act in the United States (Bonilla-Silva 2006) signaled to the world that the era when overt racism was acceptable was coming to an end and that a new, more equitable racial code was in place. That was the beginning of the current idea of a "post-racial" society. Yet, a vast number of people around the world continue to live under the ever-present shroud of racial discrimination. To understand the socioeconomic world today, we must understand the historical shifts and the continuities in the global political-economic arena that have led to the current inequalities. This paper argues that colonialism shaped how race is perceived worldwide, and how economic systems today reproduce and maintain relationships of domination. To this end, this chapter demonstrates how: 1) colonialism shaped racial hierarchy; 2) today's global economy resulted from colonialism; 3) racial exploitation is vital to the subsistence of capitalism; and 4) colonialism did not end but evolved into neoimperialism.

The Legacy of Capitalism and Colonialism

We live in the age of late capitalism and post-colonialism, in contrast to modern capitalism and imperialism. Modern capitalism and imperialism saw their height during the nineteenth century and were characterized by the search for economic trade routes and natural resources (i.e., the establishment of colonies), to be exploited in service of industrialization in the West. Late capitalism and post-colonialism, on the other hand, form today's global capitalism and are a result of the colonial era. The current social order has its roots in the exploitation of peoples of color and is now maintained through economic interventions that benefit former colonizer nations to the detriment of former colonized territories.

Take the history of the Xaripus, a pueblo that lives in Michoacán (Mexico) and Stockton (United States). For centuries, this pueblo inhabited a vast and wealthy territory until European colonizers became interested in mapping pueblos and pillaged their wealth. Indigenous peoples were stigmatized and were displaced to the bottom rung of society. Racism at the institutional level was manifested in laws that targeted indigenous peoples, while European immigrants were unaffected by those laws (Barajas 2017; Sánchez 2015). The ideology of *mestizaje* was advanced by politics and privatized lands. According to Barajas (2012), **mestizaje** "refers to racial and/or ethnic mixing," a process of racial and cultural amalgamation that favored Spanish lineage and light skin (p. 289).

Another way of describing *mestizaje* is through the concept of castes. A **caste** system is a form of social stratification that hierarchically divides the population into distinct social groups. For example, when Spaniards sailed to Latin America, they brought black and white people to the New World; the introduction of European colonizers and blacks led to the miscegenation of racial groups and ultimately, to a racial hierarchy in which whites were at the top, mestizos were the middle/buffer layer, and blacks were at the bottom of the racial order (Sánchez 2015). As a result, *mestizaje* was used as a strategy of *blanquiamiento* (**whitening**) of the population— what was a desirable trait (light skin) became a state-enforced mechanism of social control. A direct consequence of mestizaje/blanquiamiento was that fewer individuals self-identified as *mestizo negro* because "[b]eing categorized as black would deprive them from accessing to some spaces and benefits" (Sánchez 2015:49). For example, in the late 1800s and early 1900s, only 3–4 percent of the Mexican-born population owned land (Barajas 2017). By the time World War II ended in the mid-1900s, many of the colonies under Western imperial rule revolted and became independent nation-states politically; hence, a situation of post-colonialism arose. Transnational corporations (TNCs) usurped Mexican resources, while Mexican-born individuals became *braceros* at the service of foreigners (Barajas 2012; Harvey 2005). Sadly, the Mexican revolutions of the 1970s did not undo the damages of mestizaje and institutional racism. The stigma associated with indigenous identities persists in the former colony to this day.

A holistic way of contextualizing the history of exploitation of peoples of color is through the lens of Interactional Colonialism, a theory proposed by sociologist Manuel Barajas (2012). This model postulates that colonialism intersects with the dialectical relations of gender, race, class, and with social interactions to further contemporary neocolonial politics of empire. According to this framework, colonial exploitation was facilitated by sexist, capitalistic, and white-supremacist patterns.

Race and Hierarchy

The history of the Xaripus shows how colonization and imperialism shaped racial structures around the world, and how former colonized nations struggle to subsist in the global market today. The concept of *race* is global. It emerged during the colonial expansion and the "scientific" knowledge disseminated by European settlers. Race informs a person's social interactions, as it legitimizes racial identities and often perpetuates prejudice (especially for nonwhite persons). Thus, we use the term *race* not to describe biological characteristics, but a social product created and reinforced through daily interactions. Societal understanding of race does not occur in a vacuum. It is a long, sociohistorical process exemplified by the *color line*: a barrier of laws and customs that establishes a dominant class based on skin pigmentation (Karenga 2011). The **global color hierarchy** is a universal phenomenon; it is a common understanding that dark-skinned peoples are at the bottom of the social strata, while their light-skinned counterparts are at the top of the hierarchy. Where does this universal understanding of racial hierarchy originate?

Historically, racial demarcation has been used to exclude mostly nonwhites from socioeconomic gains through legally sanctioned and implemented discriminatory practices. In the United States, immigrants of color have been barred from entering the country (such as exclusionary acts), and did not have the legal rights enjoyed by white males (disenfranchisement, segregation) (Feagin 1997; Haney-López 1994; Katznelson 2005; Kendi 2016). The history of tenuous race relations in the United States is as old as the foundation of the country itself.

Racist ideas about the inferiority of people of color provided a justification for Europeans to enslave sub-Saharan Africans (Kendi 2016). The Greeks subscribed to Aristotle's racial hierarchy, in which the Greeks were superior to other peoples. Similarly, the Romans used Aristotle's "climate theory"—an argument that extreme temperatures engender morally degenerate, intellectually incapable, physically unattractive, and overall inferior humans—as a justification for slavery (Kendi 2016:17). Enlightenment intellectuals in the 1700s argued that the perceived moral flaws of the natives were a sort of White Man's Burden—a paternalistic and ethnocentric discourse put forward by imperialist forces to *redeem* colonized peoples by replacing their culture and social structure with that of the colonizer (Escobar 1999; Kendi 2016; Said 1979). The assertion of the inferiority of the colonized was a necessary component of imperialism: colonies of exploitation provided natural resources while native peoples were simultaneously a commodity to be traded and a source of labor. Racist ideas present today are inherited from the past and continue to shape social norms (Olsson 2009). As racism was used in the past to excuse colonial exploitation, contemporary "[r]acially discriminatory policies have usually sprung from economic, political, and cultural self-interests" (Kendi 2016:9) and benefit the elites.

The current social order decries racism and fosters a color-blind ideology in which meritocracy is solely responsible for individuals' socioeconomic status. Take the American Dream, for example. It posits that anyone can "make it" in the United States as long as they work hard enough. Accordingly, the story goes, the elite and dominant class earned their high status through their own merit, not privilege. Therefore, race is no longer an accepted variable to explain people's predicament.

Racism Enabled Colonialism

In order to achieve its goal (accumulation of wealth), the elite often plays divide-and-conquer and pits one marginalized group against the other. In the United States, the separation between low-class whites and blacks was concocted in the aftermath of Bacon's Rebellion in 1676, when Nathaniel Bacon gathered an army of 500 men demanding freedom for poor whites and blacks (Bush 2011; Kendi 2016). The rebellion dwindled with Bacon's death, but the white ruling class, fearing that poor whites would join free blacks in union-like organizations, granted poor whites rights such as ownership of property, liberty, and voting while denying those rights to people of color (Feagin 1997). White rebels were pardoned, offered goods such as money and weapons (Bush 2011), and given power to control blacks as they wished, while blacks were flogged (Kendi 2016). Hence, poor whites permanently moved to a higher status in society, above slaves, while permanently keeping blacks at the very bottom of the social ladder. Being white became a form of social and psychological wage for poor whites (Roediger 2007) who accepted their newly crafted social position as superior to that of slaves and blacks and equal to the white ruling power. By pitting one group against the other, the elite stigmatized blacks, solidified its dominance, and maintained the status quo. Similarly, in Mexico, blacks remained at the bottom of the social pyramid, poor whites (or mestizos in Mexico) occupied a position above blacks, and the white elite stayed at the top and exploited the classes and resources beneath it.

Politics of Empire

Europe's and the United States' colonialism disseminated structural racism and social inequality worldwide (Kendi 2016; Said 1979). Despite former colonies gaining their political independence, colonialism has not ended, but has evolved from a situation of settler colonialism to "economic colonialism." What imperial powers used to accomplish through formal territorial rule through the early twentieth century is now accomplished covertly through control of the global economy. As the United States became an economic superpower in the decades following World War II and the World Bank was created during the European reconstruction (Goldman 2005), financial institutions became the main weapon for developed nations in the Global North to continuously exploit developing countries in the Global South.

With military coercion and the facilitation of international financial institutions, such as the World Bank, the International Monetary Fund (IMF), and the World Trade Organization (WTO), the international influence of the former imperial powers continues. The difference today is that their agendas are accomplished not only on the basis of nationalist identities, but also by employing the help of transnational geopolitical and economic institutions. This unequal relationship is known as **neoimperialism**: the re-subordination of former developing countries through economic, geopolitical, and military force (Harvey 2005). The neoimperial powers are mostly former imperial countries: United States, United Kingdom, France, Germany, Italy, Canada, Japan, and Russia, while the "economic colonies" are mostly formerly colonially occupied countries located in the Southern Hemisphere, such as in Africa, South America, and some parts of Asia. As the former colonizers relied on ideas of racial inferiority of the occupied territories, we see the Global North (high-income countries, or HICs) continue to exploit the Global South (low-income economies) under the guise of globalization. Colonialism imposed a new social order in the colonies based on race, class, and gender inequalities. This new structure firmly delineated venues for upward mobility by superimposing male, capitalistic, and European dominance on indigenous populations. In this intersectional context, globalization is a form of resubmission of low-income countries (LICs), whose populations comprise majorly of people of color (United Nations 2018) and a continuation of colonization.

Capitalism Today

The neoliberal policies furthered by the IMF clearly stipulated austerity measures that the borrowing countries should abide by, but the lending organization did not enforce social protections that would ensure that the LICs would maintain a safety net for its population living in poverty. On the contrary, the pillars of fiscal consolidation (deregulation, privatization, and cutback of social services) worsened preexisting levels of poverty. In other words, structural adjustment policies served as a forfeiture of public assets to benefit TNCs (Harvey 2005). Opening developing countries to foreign investment occurs through the establishment of export processing zones, free trade zones, or special economic zones, where local taxes and protective laws are relaxed. These special zones allow TNCs to operate like separate countries within foreign countries, without accountability to local laws. This is United States imperialism in a nutshell: HICs will almost invariably have the upper hand and will dictate the rules. Opponents of the World Bank argue that its structural adjustment policies are "catalysts for the collapse of economies throughout Latin America, Africa, and Asia" (Goldman 2005:47), mostly former colonies. Capitalists from financial institutions such as the IMF argued that lending money to low-wage workers was a social good since the loans subsidized homes, cars, and living expenses. However, the result of such loans has largely been accumulation by dispossession. This type of debt trap is a fundamental component of neoimperialism, and it exists in all societal levels, from individuals to sovereign states. The IMF has a special power over borrowing countries. LICs are usually unable to get loans elsewhere and are coerced into implementing structural adjustment policies that limit services to poor peoples of color and women.

Who benefits within this new international division of labor? Borrowing governments benefit from the foreign exchange gained through the remittances immigrant laborers send home (Chang 1997). HICs benefit from taxpayer savings from not having to pay for public benefits and social services for temporary laborers (p. 140). The "host" countries also benefit from the products of immigrant labor or the labor themselves, such as service (sex work, domestic services, and health services) (p. 135), manufacturing (garments and electronics) (Tran 2013:9), and agriculture. Finally, TNCs benefit from the profits gained from their cheap and highly exploitable labor (Chang 1997:137). Immigrant and Global South women not only serve as an ideal source of economic labor, but they also serve as tools of international relations. For example, the labor of South Korean women working in American military camp-towns, in a sense, "greases the wheels" of foreign relations between the US and South Korean governments (Kim-Gibson 2000).

Who loses within this international division of labor? Primarily immigrant and Global South women bear the burden of globalization: "In both their home and 'host' countries, and for both their own and their employers' families, these women pay most dearly for 'adjustment'" (Chang [1977] 1997:133). The super-exploitation of Global South and immigrant women, whose products and labor are exported for the world market, is known as the *racialized feminization of labor and migration*. Due to **globalization**, a socioeconomic process of international integration, developing economies and immigrant women end up at the bottom of the global economic ladder.

As proposed earlier by interactive colonialism (Barajas 2012), capitalism acts as a system of domination along with patriarchy and white supremacy. In a global economy, dialectic relations occur within countries and between them. Frequently, light-skinned individuals amass wealth, while their dark-skinned counterparts have lower to negative net worth. Note that the median household income of whites in the United States in 2015 was $62,950 versus $36,898 for blacks and $45,148 for Hispanics (Proctor, Samega, and Kollar 2016).

Where Do We Go from Here?

The profit-making business is racialized because it has its roots in colonialism, a system based on a specific racial hierarchy. Colonization was a global event and so is the stratified understanding of race and skin color. It is of utmost importance to understand race relations today in light of colonial exploitation. Peoples of color have been subjugated and exploited for centuries. As previously stated, TNCs act in self-interest and manipulate governments to finance the interest of the private sector. Trade agreements today are a form of politics of empire because they turn LICs into new colonies of exploitation and force upon them a social order that is rooted in inequality. When LICs borrows from the IMF or enter trade agreements with the Global North, they "become absorbed into capitalist relations […] and lose their local autonomy and become part of a global division of labor, serving the corporate interests and consumer needs" of HICs (Barajas 2012:268). As such, it is unwise to expect that capitalists will fund social change.

As capitalism is based on class struggle and on the pursuit of profit (i.e., exploitation), leaving the source of corporate power unchanged will not solve social inequalities. It can, however, be attenuated. Policies that create poverty and inequality (e.g., structural adjustments and cuts in safety nets) need to be replaced with policies that lead to fair trade among nations (e.g., granting LICs access to G-7 markets while strengthening regional trade associations; disempowering the IMF, WTO, and the World Bank) and that reduce social inequality in the Global South (e.g., restorative measures that will return the plundered wealth of former colonies—i.e., restitution). Such policies would allow governments in low-income economies to invest in their domestic markets, expand the production of goods and services that benefit the population (education, health care, living wages), and lift impoverished households out of extreme poverty.

Restorative justice is fundamental to the economic independence of former colonies. Colonial expansion left the world fractured: HICs of the past remain rich today; women occupy a subjugated position in relation to men; light skin grants benefits that are denied or far-reaching for dark-skinned individuals. Former colonies that gained political independence are currently economically dependent on the former masters. Racially, HICs are majorly white, while LICs are mostly nonwhite. The common necessity that ties poor nations together is economic liberation from neoimperial powers. *Divide and conquer* is an old tactic that can be overcome by unity and solidarity. This idea is not new: the Landless Workers Movement in Brazil and the Zapatistas in Mexico have shown that it is possible to overcome class struggles and racial divides and fight for freedom and the general welfare of the population. Social inequality and racist policies are not innate characteristics of social life, but a result of long-lasting exploitative capitalist forces.

Discussion Questions

1. What were the key components of colonialism, as identified in the text?

2. Describe Barajas's Interactional Colonialism. Why do you think this theory is called *interactional*?

3. What is the dominant narrative about the origins of race, and how does it relate to colonization?

4. How is globalization a women's issue?

5. How do financial institutions, such as the IMF and the World Bank, benefit from colonialism?

6. Why should we care about colonialism?

7. Define the concept of race.

8. How did colonialism shape understandings about race?

Further Readings

Barajas, Manuel. 2009. *The Xaripu Community: Labor, Migration, Community and Family Across Borders*. Notre Dame, IN: University of Notre Dame Press.

Bhattacharyya, Gargi, John Gabriel, and Stephen Small. 2002. *Race and Power: Global Racism in the Twenty-First Century.* New York: Routledge.

Chang, Howard F. 2008. "The Economics of International Labor Migration and the Case for Global Distributive Justice in Liberal Political Theory." *Cornell International Law Journal* 41(1):1–25.

Coulthard, Glen S. 2007. "Subjects of Empire: Indigenous Peoples and the 'Politics of Recognition' in Canada." *Contemporary Political Theory* 2007(6):437–60.

Winant, Howard. 2006. "Race and Racism: Towards a Global Future.*" Ethnic and Racial Studies* 29(5):986–1003.

References

Barajas, Manuel. 2012. "A Comparative Analysis of Mexican- and European-Origin Immigration to the United States: Proposing an Interactive Colonization Theory." *Societies Without Borders* 7:(3):264–94.

Barajas, Manuel. 2017. "The Xaripu Community Across Borders: A Case Study of Colonial Dislocation, Continuities and Resistance." In *Indigenous Peoples Day Conference at Sacramento State University*. Sacramento, CA.

Bonilla-Silva, Eduardo. 2006. *Racism Without Racists: Color-Blind Racism and the Persistence of Racial Inequality in America*. Lanham, MD: Rowman & Littlefield.

Bush, Melanie E.L. 2011. *Everyday Forms of Whiteness: Understanding Race in a "Post-Racial" World*. Lanham, MD: Rowman & Littlefield.

Chang, Grace. [1977] 1997. "The Global Trade in Filipina Workers." Pp. 132–52 in *Dragon Ladies: Asian American Feminists Breathe Fire*, edited by S. Shah. Boston: South End Press.

Escobar, Arturo. 1999. "The Invention of Development." *Current History,* Nov. 1999(98):382–86.

Feagin, Joe R. 1997. "Old Poison in New Bottles: The Deep Roots of Modern Nativism." Pp. 13–43 in *Immigrants Out!: The New Nativism and the Anti-Immigrant Impulse in the United States*, edited by Juan F. Peres. New York: New York University Press.

Goldman, Michael. 2005. "The Rise of the Bank." In *Imperial Nature: The World Bank and Struggles for Social Justice in the Age of Globalization* (pp. 46–99). New Haven, CT: Yale University Press.

Haney-López, Ian F. 1994. "The Social Construction of Race: Some Observations on Illusion, Fabrication, and Choice." *Harvard Civil Rights-Civil Liberties Law Review,* 29(2):1–62..

Harvey, David. 2005. *A Brief History of Neoliberalism*. Oxford, UK: Oxford University Press.

Karenga, Maulana. 2011. "Du Bois and the Question of the Color Line: Race and Class in the Age of Globalization." *Socialism and Democracy,* 17(1):141–60.

Katznelson, Ira. 2005. *When Affirmative Action Was White: An Untold History of Racial Inequality in Twentieth-Century America*. New York: W.W. Norton.

Kendi, Ibram X. 2017. *Stamped from the Beginning: The Definitive History of Racist Ideas in America*. London, UK: Bodley Head.

Kim-Gibson, Dai Sil. 2000. *Silence Broken: Korean Comfort Women*. Parkersburg, IA: Mid-Prairie Books.

Olsson, Ola. 2009. "On the Democratic Legacy of Colonialism." *Journal of Comparative Economics* 37(2009):534–51.

Proctor, Bernadette D., Jessica L. Samega, and Melissa A. Kollar. 2016. "Income and Poverty in the United States: 2015." *U.S. Bureau of the Census*. Retrieved November 20, 2017 (https://www.census.gov/library/publications/2016/demo/p60-256.html).

Roediger, David R. 2007. *The Wages of Whiteness: Race and the Making of the American Working Class*. New York: Verso.

Said, Edward W. 1979. *Orientalism*. New York: Vintage Books.

Sánchez, Paloma Fernández. 2015. "Racial Ideology of Mestizaje and Its Whitening Discourse in Memín Pinguín." *Revista de Lenguas Modernas* 23(2015):45–49.

Siebers, Hans, and Marjolein H.J. Dennissen. 2015. "Is It Cultural Racism? Discursive Exclusion and Oppression of Migrants in the Netherlands." *Current Sociology* 63(3):470–89.

Tran, Ngoc Angie. 2013. *Ties That Bind: Cultural Identity, Class, and Law in Vietnam's Labor Resistance*. Ithaca, NY: Cornell University Press.

United Nations. 2018. "LDCs at a Glance | Economic Analysis & Policy Division." *Department of Economic and Social Affairs*. Retrieved July 22, 2018 (https://www.un.org/development/desa/dpad/least-developed-country-category/ldcs-at-a-glance.html).

Discussion Questions

1. Have you traveled outside of the United States? Are you viewed differently, in terms of race/ethnicity, inside and outside of the United States? How come?

2. Do you interact with people who come from a different context? Do they see your race/ethnicity differently? How come?

3. In what ways do you think living in the United States shapes the way to see, understand, and approach issues of race/ethnicity in unique ways?

Resources

How census data on race is collected in many countries: http://www.understandingrace.org/lived/global_census.html

Data on global racial inequality: https://inequality.org/facts/racial-inequality/

Research data on global attitudes and trends: https://www.pewglobal.org/

Poll data from around the world: https://www.gallup.com/analytics/232838/world-poll.aspx

References

Anzaldua, Gloria. 1987. *Borderlands/La Frontera: The New Mestiza.* 3rd ed. San Francisco: Aunt Lute Books.

Bonilla-Silva, Eduardo. 2006. *Racism without Racists: Color-Blind Racism and the Persistence of Racial Inequality in the United States.* Rowman & Littlefield Publishers.

DeGenova, Nicholas. 2004. "The Legal Production of Mexican/Migrant 'Illegality.'" *Latino Studies* 2:160–85.

Graham, Richard. 2010. *The Idea of Race in Latin America, 1870-1940.* edited by R. Graham. University of Texas Press.

Henry Louis Gates, Jr. 2017. *How Many Slaves Landed in the U.S.?* Pantheon.

ISM. 2019. "Abolition of Slavery in the Americas." *International Slavery Museum.* Retrieved August 4, 2019 (http://www.liverpoolmuseums.org.uk/ism/slavery/americas/abolition_americas.aspx).

Mignolo, W. D. 2000. "The Many Faces of Cosmo-Polis: Border Thinking and Critical Cosmopolitanism." *Public Culture* 12(3):721–48.

Quijano, Anibal. 2000. "Coloniality of Power and Eurocentrism in Latin America." *International Sociology* 15(2):215–32.

Rao, Sameer. 2015. "Mexico Finally Recognizes Afro Mexicans in National Census." *ColorLines2*, December.

Telles, Edward E. and Christina A. Sue. 2010. "Race Mixture: Boundary Crossing in Comparative Perspective." *Ssrn* 35(2009):129–46.

Section IX: Mobilizing for Social Change

Student Narrative

One day, during an internship at a resource center for the homeless in my senior year in college, I received a call from a homeless man called Thomas. He said that he had only $14 and needed an ID card to apply for benefits, so he requested a waiver to pay a reduced fee of $8.00 for the document. After that, only $6.00 would be left for food, accommodation, and transportation. He also said that he was hungry and asked if we had a bag of food to give him. Thomas was diabetic and toothless, which limited his food options. As a resource center, we could provide him with the waiver, but we had no food to donate or shelters to refer him to as all the beds were unavailable. Thomas taught me that even small actions that I would consider insignificant can mean a lot to someone in need. Thomas was grateful when he arrived at the resource center. The reason for his gratitude was beyond the material benefits that we provided: he was thankful for the fact that I listened to him on the phone and let him talk freely. I used to see myself as this poor-dark-skinned-female-Latina immigrant at the intersection of multiple subordinate categories. But I was not powerless at all. Empathy and critical thinking are important traits to have, but they need to be accompanied by actions, even small ones, if we want to shape the world we live in.

Thais Forneret graduated with a master's degree in the Department of Sociology at Sacramento State University. Her research focused on conducting content analysis on white nationalism following the Unite the Right rally in August of 2017.

Learning Objectives

After you read the introduction and the chapters in this section, you should be able to:

1. Identify how racial projects are not static and how people have always mobilized to challenge racial inequality.

2. Connect how social movements in the United States have been influenced by racial projects.

3. Differentiate between mobilizing around racialized identities and mobilizing around racism.

Editor's Introduction

Heidy Sarabia

The United States is a place with many vast, visible, and painful inequities, but as Thais Forneret reminds us, small acts of kindness can often go a long way; and when these acts of kindness are organized by groups and mobilize many people, the changes can be much more significant and lasting. I was introduced to the world of social movements in 1994, when I first heard about an indigenous group in Mexico—the Zapatistas—who were demanding land, food, health care, education, and the freedom to practice their language, customs, and religion. What inspired me most was their demand for a "world where many worlds fit." I was very inspired by the Zapatistas in the 1990s and then became inspired by the immigrant activists of the 2000s—demanding to be treated as equals in the United States.

In this introduction to the section of social change, I want to first highlight how, from the foundation of the United States of America as a nation-state, racial structures were firmly established. Yet, from the beginning people have also mobilized to challenge these racial inequities, and how today people continue to mobilize to challenge racial injustice but also to maintain the racial project of inequality.

Historical Overview

The Founding of a Racial Dictatorship

From the foundation of the United States of America as a nation-state, a **racial dictatorship** was firmly established, defined by Omi and Winant as a system where "most non-whites were firmly eliminated from the sphere of politics" (Omi and Winant 1994:65). During this period, individuals resisted and fought back against the racial dictatorship; the most famous examples include Harriet Tubman, who helped many slaves to escape, or Nat Turner, who led a rebellion of slaves to gain freedom. While these might seem as exceptions, resistance against slavery was actually not uncommon (Aptheker 1983).

The period of racial dictatorship in the United States lasted from 1607 to 1865, and was disrupted by the Civil War, followed by a brief period of Reconstruction that ended shortly in 1877 (Omi and Winant 1994:66). Immediately after the end of slavery, Southern states began to pass laws that would restrict the promises of the Fourteenth Amendment to the US Constitution—that promised to grant full citizenship rights and equality to those born in the United States. These **Jim Crow** laws established legal segregation in public spaces—including schools, transportation, restrooms restaurants, pools, even drinking fountains—for whites and blacks (Packard 2002). Jim Crow law mandated *de jure*, or legal, separation between blacks and whites, mostly in Southern states, while in the North, *de facto*, or by custom, segregation between blacks and whites was also observed. Jim Crow laws also affected Mexicans in the Southwest who were not legally segregated (as Mexicans were officially categorized as white), but Mexicans were also barred from public spaces by de facto or by custom (Fox and Guglielmo 2012).

Given that segregation was legal, the battles to change society were fought in the legal arena. For African Americans, they focused on challenging laws as unconstitutional. For Latinos and Asians, they often argued that they should be treated equally because they were officially (or should be considered) white (Haney-Lopez 1996). In 1954, when the US Supreme Court ruled in **Brown v. Board of Education** that "separate but equal" was unconstitutional, the legality of segregation finally ended. But things did not change much. The law had changed, but it would take people to mobilize to actively demand the enactment and guarantee of such changes, like the nine African American students in Little Rock Arkansas, who desegregated the school system by enrolling in Little Rock Central High School (Fitzgerald 2006).

Mobilizing to Create Change

The **civil rights movement** in the United States of the 1950s and 1960s, led mostly by African Americans, included the mobilization of thousands of people in different arenas, seeking equal access to opportunities. People mobilized around desegregation struggles in the educational system (Fitzgerald 2006), public transportation (Kohl and Brown 2007), public spaces such as lunch counters (Chafe and Chafe 1981), public pools (Wiltse 2007), the use of drinking fountains (Wiltse 2007); equality in public and private spaces has been a battle. Other groups—women, Native Americans, Chicanxs, Asian Americans, LGBTQ+, farmworkers, among others—were inspired from the mobilization among the African American community and also began mobilizing to demand changes.

In 1957, President Eisenhower signed the Civil Rights Act of 1957 into law, the first major civil rights legislation since Reconstruction that allowed federal prosecution of anyone who tried to prevent someone from voting. By 1964, President Lyndon B. Johnson signed the Civil Rights Act of 1964, which guaranteed equal employment for all, limited the use of voter literacy tests, and allowed federal authorities to ensure public facilities were integrated. Simultaneously, the Freedom Summer, or the Mississippi Summer Project, took place—a mass voter registration campaigned organized by the Congress on Racial Equality (CORE) and the Student Nonviolent Coordinating Committee (SNCC) to increase voter registration among African American voters in the South (McAdam 1988).

Mobilization to create change, however, has also created a backlash. In the 1960s, the US government began surveilling civil rights activists (Wiltse 2007), leaders were assassinated; whites also moved en masse to suburban areas or moved their children to private and charter schools rather than integrate with African American students (Wiltse 2007). Today, school segregation is more severe than when the US Supreme Court ruled on **Brown v. Board of Education** (Wiltse 2007).

Mobilizing for Change in a Post-Racial Society

Things have certainly changed. Today, few people agree that public spaces should be segregated. Yet, as sociologist Eduardo Bonilla-Silva highlights, once we dig deeper into people's views of racial relations, many still hold on to old ideas about the racial order (Bonilla-Silva 2006) . Thus, while the election of Barack Obama marked a momentous occasion that represents all the changes undergone by US society, the election of Obama also obscured the institutional racism that is difficult to eradicate (Bonilla-Silva and Ray 2009). Simultaneously, the election of Donald Trump also points to the backlash and the racial anxieties aroused by the demographic changes that are browning the United States (Bonilla-Silva and Ray 2009). The election of Trump signals a movement to mobilize around racism.

While the explicitly racist comments of Trump are jarring—such as his comments about how "When Mexico sends its people, they're not sending their best … They're bringing drugs. They're bringing crime. They're rapists. And some, I assume, are good people" (Trump cited in Burns 2015), less visible and more institutionalized forms of racial inequality continue to define life in the United States. The multiple ways in which institutionalized racism keeps creeping up in society range from the medical disparities experienced by people of color (Sewell 2016), to the vast gap in wealth accumulation (Oliver and Shapiro 2013), to the targeting of people by the criminal justice system—what Michelle Alexander calls the new caste system in the United States. (Alexander 2012). Nevertheless, these racial disparities also bring about the desire to create change and work more toward equality. For example, today's use of social media and cell phones has brought to the forefront the current struggles for racial equality—as black and brown bodies become the targets of police brutality. In the face of these challenges, the cry and mobilization for Black Lives Matter has taken momentum. Today's activism reflects the historical fact that people are never passive in the context of oppression. For example, Laura Zaragoza's vignette of how she and her family reacted to Trump's election reminds us of the resiliency of those who are targeted for exclusion in the United States.

> Seeing my mother crying the night of November 8, 2016 was when I realized what was coming, I dreaded this day for months, the thought of a Trump presidency was daunting. Since he began his campaign the anti-immigrant and anti-Mexican rhetoric was very clear, and it scared me. I remember crying after midnight as the acceptance speech came and the following day feeling like my world was collapsing before my eyes. Despite the clear threat of DACA ending what scared me the most was that my parents could be deported, that many families like mine were going to be broken … that my parents' sacrifices were for nothing … but I promised myself that I would not give up on my dreams, that my education was going to be part of my resistance … Walking across that stage, the first in my family to receive a graduate degree, will be a homage to my parents and their resiliency because they are the original Dreamers.

> Laura Zaragoza is an undocumented graduate student in the Sociology Department. She was born in Mexico City and came to the United States along with her mother and siblings when she was ten years old. They came to reunite with her father.

Mindfulness

The story of Thais Forneret and Laura Zaragoza, the students who provided the vignettes in this section, highlight that we have a choice on how we treat each other, how we care for each other, how we react to each other, how we move forward in difficult times, and how we act in the context of racial oppression. Activists have shown us that it takes a lot of work to create change, that it is difficult to eradicate racial inequality, and that the fight for radical change is far from being over. Thus, we must be mindful of how we interact with each other, how we avoid perpetuating systems of inequality, and how we must work every day to treat each other humanely. Respect cannot be legislated, so treating each other with respect can be a very powerful first step in establishing firmly that we are all created equal. Beyond the first step, of treating each other with respect, social, cultural, political, and economic changes must be legislated in order to produce the desired result—a society where one's race does not determine the opportunities and outcomes for people.

Section Readings

The chapters in this section present a broad range of mobilizations—from marches to online activism, from spoken word to militancy—and many chapters also offer a comparative viewpoint that allows us to consider the intersectional ways in which alliances form. In the first chapter, Perez documents how undocumented Latino youth activists put their bodies on the line as they become agents of social change through their participation in rallies, marches, public protests, and sit-ins as they demand changes in immigration laws. In the second chapter, Escudero highlights how Asian and Latinx undocumented immigrant experiences are both similar but also racialized differently, which shapes how activists are strategic and purposeful in their efforts to reframe immigration issues as multiracial and not merely affecting Latinx communities. In line with the focus on intersectionality, in the third chapter, Anne Luna addresses how location, gender, and race shape how Native women's environmental justice work is reoriented from urban areas to address specific crises such as Standing Rock in a rural locale. Luna also demonstrates how reacting to an imminent crisis, the construction of the Dakota Access Pipeline (DAPL), also presents opportunities to generate and sustain community life among Native activists and their allies. Perez and Luna bring to the forefront how racialized bodies put themselves on the line to create social change.

In the fourth chapter, Walkington presents another example of how racialized bodies and voices press for social change in the context of oppression. This chapter focuses on how spoken-word poetry is utilized to address the experiences and obstacles experienced by racialized bodies, highlights how performance is used both as a way to challenge mainstream narratives of inequality, but also to provide counter-narratives around issues, such as the war on drugs, military policing, and mass incarceration, among others. The last chapter presents a historical view of two groups that have often been framed in opposition in the mainstream news media: African Americans and Asian Americans. Hence, Hope presents a parallel historical trajectory of these two groups in California that informs how they have also become allies on multiple occasions, as the racialization of both groups operate in tandem to maintain racial inequality.

Reading 9.1 "Targeted but Not Shut Down": Latino Undocumented Immigrant Activists Fighting for Social Change

Joanna Perez, California State University–Dominguez Hills

Keywords: Latinos, Undocumented Immigrants, Political Activism, Policies

Introduction

Although anti-immigrant legislation and messages have deeply impacted the lives of Latino undocumented immigrants living in the United States, Latino undocumented immigrant young adult activists are putting their bodies on the line and participating in marches, rallies, public protests, sit-ins, and other forms of activism in order to fight for their rights. In this chapter, I discuss the struggles of Latino undocumented immigrant young adults as well as the ways in which they cope with their lack of legal status, demonstrate resilience, and engage in activism in order to have access to better life opportunities. This chapter draws on fieldwork and in-depth interviews with Latino undocumented immigrant young adult activists in the United States, particularly Illinois and California. First, I examine intersectional oppressions that Latino undocumented immigrant young adults face throughout their lives, particularly with regard to the intersection of race and immigration status. Second, I provide a brief policy review that highlights the multiple ways in which Latino undocumented immigrant young adults are excluded and included in society, particularly regarding their access to education. Lastly, I discuss the various ways that Latino undocumented immigrant young adults have become agents of social change through activism.

During the Coming Out of the Shadows event, undocumented immigrants and allies chant "UNDOCUMENTED" followed by a resounding "UNAFRAID" as they march in the busy streets of Chicago, Illinois. As the march concludes, everyone gathers around an open public space while undocumented immigrant youth and young adults walk up to the stage. One by one, undocumented immigrant youth and young adults tell their story of self, followed by a statement, "My name is ____, I am undocumented and unafraid." While each story of self is uniquely powerful, all narratives demonstrated the importance of fighting for social change. In fact, during an interview with Rosa, I asked her about the Coming Out of the Shadows event, and she stated, "Though we are targeted, we will not shut down! It is time to come out of the shadows, fight for our rights, and let everyone know why it is important to join our efforts so that together, we can fight for social change." In the eyes of Rosa and several Latino undocumented immigrant activists, lack of legal status does not define a person; it is what drives one to fight for a better tomorrow.

Certainly anti-immigrant legislation and messages have deeply impacted the lives of Latino undocumented immigrants living in the United States. While Latino undocumented immigrants are often physically present and embraced in the US workforce, because they lack legal status, they are not given the same rights or treated the same as their US citizen or permanent resident counterparts. In other words, Latino undocumented immigrants are invisible as they work in factories, in the back of restaurant kitchens, picking produce in secluded farms, cleaning houses, and doing other "low-skill" work, but instantly become visible when they are used as a scapegoat to explain social problems in this country. For example, Latino undocumented immigrants are depicted as "criminals" and as people who take away jobs, resources, and opportunities from US citizens. In the process, these images and labels are used to legitimize the passage of immigration law and policies meant to instill fear, shame, and ultimately push undocumented immigrants to leave the United States. Yet, rather than remaining in the shadows to prevent the risk of deportation, Latino undocumented immigrant young adult activists like Rosa are putting their bodies on the line and participating in marches, rallies, public protests, sit-ins, and other forms of activism in order to fight for their rights and change their life circumstances.

In this chapter, I discuss the struggles of Latino undocumented immigrant young adults as well as the ways in which they cope with their lack of legal status, demonstrate resilience, and engage in activism in order to have access to better life opportunities. This chapter draws on fieldwork and in-depth interviews with Latino undocumented immigrant young adult activists in the United States, particularly in Illinois and California, from 2010–2016. First, I examine intersectional oppressions that Latino undocumented immigrant young adults face throughout their lives, particularly with regard to the intersection of race and immigration status. Second, I provide a brief policy review that highlights the multiple ways in which Latino undocumented immigrant young adults are excluded and included in society, especially regarding their access to education. Lastly, I discuss the various ways that Latino undocumented immigrant young adults have become agents of social change through activism.

Intersectional Oppressions

While race is often conceptualized as a social construction, race has also been used as a sociohistorical concept that marks differences among groups of people (Omi and Winant, 2007). This includes individuals being racialized based on phenotype and or genotype. However, that notion has been contested by scholars such as Burton, Bonilla-Silva, et al. (2010), who posit that racializing people in this form legitimizes racial hierarchy, resulting in the marginalization and oppression of people of color. Furthermore, ethnicity refers to membership based on ancestral origins and/or cultural traits. The prevalence of slavery and colonization led to the dominant American ideology of racial and ethnic hierarchy, where "white" and European ancestral origins are placed at the top versus "people of color" and non-European ancestral origins are placed at the bottom (Cobas, Dunay, and Feagin 2016). This racial and ethnic hierarchy has thus been used to classify racial/ethnic minorities as inferior.

While the placement of Latinos within American racial hierarchy has changed throughout history, Latinos are portrayed as a threat (Chavez, 2013). For instance, Latinos are depicted as dark skinned, foreigners, working class, unable and unwilling to assimilate, and individuals undeserving of basic human rights (Cobas, Dunay, and Feagin 2016). This process of racialization for Latinos establishes "whiteness" and reinforces the racial hierarchy as it is equal to acceptance and belonging as well as associated with certain privileges afforded to whites only (Tafoya 2007). In essence, the intersectionality of race, immigration status, class, language, gender, and other identity markers not only defines the social position of Latina/o undocumented immigrant young adults, but also the multilayers of oppression that they face due to their social position.

Policy Review

Despite dealing with intersectional oppressions, Latinos have gained visibility as a political group. For instance, Latinos began to fight for their right to an equal education. The key US Supreme Court ruling of *Brown v. Board of Education* desegregated schools, which was significant for the educational trajectory of Latinos and other nonwhite racial groups in the United States (Salomone, 1986). Yet, Latinos continued to be denied equal rights. Hence, during the 1960s and 1970s, Latinos became new political subjects who challenged existing power and social relationships in order to gain equal status in mainstream America. Given that Latino youth fought for access to higher education, it resulted in institutional action, change in admission policies, and curricula (MacDonald, Botti, and Clark 2007). To be sure, given the demands for civil rights by all students of color, policy changes like the Higher Education Act of 1965 was passed to address these historical inequalities.

As Latinos in the United States began to gain visibility in mainstream society, so did undocumented Latino students. In 1982, the *Plyler v. Doe* US Supreme Court ruling granted undocumented students the right to a K–

12 public education based on the premise that no child should be denied access to an education, irrespective of their immigration status, especially given that most enter the United States not knowing about their status (Perry, 2006). Although this permitted undocumented students to become high school graduates, it did not address their access to higher education. In fact, because of the passage of state and federal immigration policies, many undocumented students were not able to reach their full potential. In 1996, Congress passed the Illegal Immigration Reform and Immigration Responsibility Act (IIRIRA), which denied any higher education benefits and often prevented states from passing any legislation that aids undocumented students who wish to pursue higher education (Olivas, 2004). To make matters worse, undocumented immigrant students from low socioeconomic backgrounds who wanted to pursue a postsecondary education were adversely affected by the anti-Affirmative Action movement across the nation, including Proposition 209 in California (Chapa, 2008). In addition, undocumented immigrant students who had limited English proficiency were deeply impacted by anti-bilingual education programs. In 1998, California Proposition 227 eliminated bilingual education with the purpose of establishing English-only language classrooms (Gutierrez, Bosquedano-Lopez, and Asato 2000). Lastly, after September 11, 2001, any prospects of passing comprehensive immigration reform vanished and led undocumented immigrants to become categorized as a threat by the Department of Homeland Security.

Certainly, anti-immigrant sentiment and legislation forced undocumented immigrant students to overcome several obstacles in order to move along the educational pipeline. Yet, hope was found with the passage of various in-state tuition policies across the United States. According to the National Immigration Law Center, as of 2017, "at least twenty states and the District of Columbia have 'tuition equity' laws or policies that permit certain students who have attended and graduated from secondary schools in their state to pay the same tuition as their 'in-state' classmates at their state's public institutions of higher education, regardless of their immigration status" (NILC, 2018). Although in-state tuition policies make college more affordable for Latino undocumented students, financial issues persist because access to financial assistance (i.e., financial aid, loans, work-study, etc.) is limited or denied. At the national level, even if Latino undocumented students are able to secure the funds to pursue a higher education, their lack of legal status still presents certain risks, especially with regard to deportation. Hence, undocumented immigrants and allies have been fighting for access to a pathway to legalization.

Since 2001, the Development, Relief, and Education for Alien Minors (DREAM) Act has been proposed in the United Sates Congress, which would ultimately provide a way for undocumented youth to attain legalization and pursue a higher education or join the military (Olivas 2012). Although the DREAM Act has secured bipartisan support, it has not yet passed in Congress. In fact, though several elected officials have publicly expressed their support to provide a pathway to citizenship to "DREAMers," no permanent solution has been approved. After mass nationwide mobilization among undocumented immigrant young adults gained public recognition, elected officials were pressured to take action. This eventually led President Obama to issue an executive order known as Deferred Action for Childhood Arrivals (DACA), which was implemented on August 15, 2012. Under DACA, eligible undocumented immigrants have access to a work permit and temporary relief from deportation. Though becoming DACAmented was not a permanent solution, nor did it resolve all issues faced by Latino undocumented immigrant youth and young adults, it did alleviate some of their main concerns, especially as they transitioned into adulthood (Gonzales 2016). For once, those with DACA status began to gain a sense of belonging in the United States. However, on September 5, 2017, the Trump administration decided to rescind DACA, leaving thousands of DACAmented people in legal limbo and without an opportunity to make their dreams a reality. Given the countries of origin for DACA recipients (see Figure 9.1), Latino DACAmented immigrants are the largest population being impacted by the current state of DACA (Lopez and Krogstad 2017). As of August 2018, DACA continues to be under constant change based on debates in Congress, decisions in the courts, and the political agenda under the Trump administration.

Given today's political climate, undocumented immigrants and allies are campaigning to pass a Clean Dream Act. The Clean Dream Act would provide eligible undocumented immigrants with a pathway to citizenship without experiencing further criminalization by not providing funding for increased border security, interior enforcement, and detention centers. In other words, the passage of the Clean Dream Act should not come at the expense of expanding institutional racism. Though the Clean Dream Act has gained massive support, it has not passed. Nonetheless, Latino undocumented immigrant youth and young adult activists continue to remain hopeful and are resilient agents of social change.

Social Change Through Activism

Indeed, though substantial changes have been made since 2001, it is clear that the US government is not yet willing to provide undocumented immigrants with a pathway to citizenship. Yet, Latino undocumented immigrant young adult activists are putting their bodies on the line and fighting for social justice. Across the country, undocumented immigrant young adult activists have created nationwide organizations like United We Dream. At the state and local levels, organizations, including "Dream teams" and "Undocumented alliances," have been created to provide undocumented immigrants with a safe space, resources, and overall support. Often, these organizations "are affiliated with high schools and higher education institutions, non-profit organizations, or are independent" (Seif 2011:70). During an interview, Jacob shared,

> You know, before I found out about my local dream team, I felt alone, like I was the only one who was thinking, feeling, and going through certain things because of my status. But once I joined the organization, I have not only gained support, but I have also become empowered.

In the case of Jacob and several other interviewees, being able to have access to an organization and network of other immigrants who share similar experiences is crucial in not only feeling validated, but also becoming aware that they have power despite their lack of legal status.

In addition to organizations, Latino undocumented immigrant young adult activists have become involved with various forms of activism in order to make their voices heard. This has included their participation in pro-immigrant rallies and marches, lobbying, creating and getting petitions signed, and even testifying in congressional hearings. It is through these forms of mobilization that Latino undocumented immigrant young adult activists have managed to gain political visibility and support. As Ernesto recalls,

> Growing up, I was always told to never share about my undocumented status. It was almost like I had to do it because I did not want to feel any shame or put myself in a vulnerable position. But, when I first told my story during a congressional hearing, I felt liberated. For once, I felt like my status did not define me.

Like Ernesto, other interviewees revealed that participating in political activism is not only a way to deconstruct the intersectional oppressions that they have been dealing with all their lives, but also a way to demonstrate the complexities of their identity and ability to change dominant ideology of what it means to be an undocumented immigrant in the United States. Furthermore, by sharing their narratives, Latino undocumented immigrant young adult activists are able to showcase a sense of empowerment and agency where their legal status does not define their voice or worthiness in society.

Though political activism became the initial form of pushing back against anti-immigrant rhetoric and legislation, due to the lack of action from Congress to provide a permanent solution, Latino undocumented immigrant young adult activists escalated their forms of activism. For example, Latino undocumented immigrant young adult activists began to participate in acts of civil disobedience. While civil disobedience among US citizens has been used as a tactic in several social movements, it is a significant tactic used among undocumented immigrant activists, given that it could not only lead to their arrest but threat of deportation, a permanent form of removal. For example, after seeing the ways that undocumented immigrants are constantly criminalized and oppressed in her community, Cristina decided to participate in a sit-in hoping to change established forms of social inequality. As she remembers seeing the police officer approach her and asking her to move, Cristina shares,

> I remember my heart starting to beat faster, my palms sweating uncontrollably, but all I could think about was how day after day, my community began to get smaller because more and more people were being deported. I could not let this happen anymore. I needed them to know that

what they were doing was not right, they were separating families just because they lacked nine digits.

By participating in a public sit-in, Cristina put herself at risk of being detained and eventually deported. Yet, she knew that just like her, several other marginalized communities had to engage in activism in order to create change.

Certainly, whether it is joining an organization and/or either engaging in political activism or acts of civil disobedience, Latino undocumented immigrant young adult activists have clearly demonstrated that though they lack legal status, they are not powerless. Instead, rather than keeping their immigration status a secret, they are proudly self-identifying as undocumented and unafraid. While no form of comprehensive immigration reform has passed, these efforts of valor have not gone unnoticed. In fact, even in today's political climate, Latino undocumented immigrant young adult activists are transforming the immigrant rights movement and keeping those in power accountable. For this reason, not only are Latino undocumented immigrant young adult activists resilient and powerful, they are also agents of social change.

Conclusion

Gaining visibility in spite of anti-immigrant sentiment, messages, and legislation is not an easy task. Yet, Latino undocumented immigrant young adult activists have beat the odds and have made it a point to push boundaries in an effort to call out injustices and work to create social change. Their efforts have not only complicated established racial hierarchies and other institutional forms of oppression, but also challenged what it means to be an undocumented immigrant in the United States today. In the process, Latino undocumented immigrant young adult activists have demonstrated what it means to embody resilience.

Though you yourself might not be Latino, think about the ways in which race and ethnicity have impacted your life. Likewise, though you might not be undocumented, think about the ways in which marginalized communities continue to struggle in their everyday lives simply because they do not fit the status quo. Remember that in order to fully understand why we are who we are and where we are in life today, we must understand how history, law, and the larger society have shaped our life trajectory and our access to life opportunities. Lastly, think about the ways in which you can create social change. Perhaps you do not want to become an activist, but one way that you can become an agent of social change is by taking what you learn back to your communities. In other words, share your knowledge and find ways to apply what you learn for the betterment of your respective communities.

If you want to become more invested in learning about the lives of Latino undocumented immigrant young adult activists or marginalized communities that are using activism to create social change more generally, start doing your own research! Some potential research questions are: How does legal status shape racialized experiences of racial/ethnic minorities? How does legal status impact activism? More broadly, other research questions include: How do social inequalities shape the lives of racial and ethnic minorities? How can social media be used as a way to promote awareness of racial/ethnic inequality? How can students fight for social justice on and off campus?

Further Readings

Books

Gonzalez, Roberto G. 2016. *Lives in Limbo: Undocumented and Coming of Age in America.*

Muñoz, Susana M. 2015. *Identity, Activism, and the Pursuit of Higher Education: The Journey of Undocumented and Unafraid Community.*

Nicholls, Walter. 2013. *The DREAMers: How the Undocumented Youth Movement Transformed the Immigrant Rights Debate.*

Pabon Lopez, Maria, and Gerardo R. Lopez. 2009. *Persistent Inequality: Contemporary Realities in the Education of Undocumented Latina/o Students.*

Perez, William. 2009. *We Are Americans: Undocumented Students Pursuing the American Dream.*

Perez, William. 2012. *Americans by Heart: Undocumented Latino Students and the Promise of Higher Education.*

Rincon, Alejandra. 2010. *Undocumented Immigrants and Higher Education: Si Se Puede!*

UCLA Labor Center. 2012. *Undocumented and Unafraid: Tam Tran, Cynthia Felix, and Immigrant Youth*

Websites & Social Media

United We Dream (https://unitedwedream.org)

#Not1More (http://www.notonemoredeportation.com)

UndocuMedia (https://www.undocumedia.org)

Dreamers Adrift (http://dreamersadrift.com)

Films

Advance Parole (http://www.advanceparole.org)

Documented (http://documentedthefilm.com)

Don't Tell Anyone, No Le Digas a Nadie (http://www.nodigasfilm.com/about/)

Forbidden (http://www.forbiddendoc.com/educational-distribution/)

Papers (https://www.grahamstreetproductions.com/papers-stories-of-undocumented-youth/)

Top countries of origin for DACA recipients

Current DACA enrollees

	Total	%
Mexico	548,000	79.4
El Salvador	25,900	3.7
Guatemala	17,700	2.6
Honduras	16,100	2.3
Peru	7,420	1.1
South Korea	7,310	1.1
Brazil	5,780	0.8
Ecuador	5,460	0.8
Colombia	5,020	0.7
Argentina	3,970	0.6
Philippines	3,880	0.6
India	2,640	0.4
Jamaica	2,640	0.4
Venezuela	2,480	0.4
Dominican Republic	2,430	0.4

Note: Only refers to individuals who are active DACA recipients, as of Sept. 4, 2017. Figures rounded by USCIS. Only top 15 countries shown.
Source: U.S. Citizenship and Immigration Services.

PEW RESEARCH CENTER

Figure 9.1-1

Figure Link: http://www.pewresearch.org/fact-tank/2017/09/25/key-facts-about-unauthorized-immigrants-enrolled-in-daca/

References

Burton, L.M., E. Bonilla-Silva, V. Ray, R. Buckelew, and E. Hordge Freeman. 2010. "Critical Race Theories, Colorism, and the Decade's Research on Families of Color." *Journal of Marriage and Family* 72(3) 440–59.

Chapa, J. 2008. "A Demographic and Sociological Perspective on Plyler's Children, 1980–2005." *Northwestern Journal of Law and Social Policy* 3(2):186–200.

Chavez, L. 2013. *The Latino Threat: Constructing Immigrants, Citizens, and the Nation.* 2nd ed. Stanford, CA: Stanford University Press.

Cobas, J.A., J. Duany, and J.R. Feagin. 2016. "Introduction: Racializing Latinos: Historical Background and Current Forms." In *How the United States Racializes Latinos: White Hegemony and Its Consequences* (pp. 1–15). New York: Routledge.

Gonzales, R.G. 2016. *Lives in Limbo: Undocumented and Coming of Age in America.* Oakland, CA: University of California Press.

Gutierrez, K.D., P. Basquedano-Lopez, and J. Asato. 2000. "English for the Children: The New Literacy of the Old World Order, Language Policy and Educational Reform." [Electronic version]. *Bilingual Research Journal 24*:1–24.

Lopez, G., and J.M. Krogstad. 2017. "Key Facts about Unauthorized Immigrants Enrolled in DACA." Pew Research Center. (http://www.pewresearch.org/fact-tank/2017/09/25/key-facts-about-unauthorized-immigrants-enrolled-in-daca/).

MacDonald, V.M., J.M. Botti, and L.H. Clark. 2007. "From Visibility to Autonomy: Latinos and Higher Education in the U.S. 1965–2005." *Harvard Educational Review* 77(4):474–504.

NILC. 2018. "Basic Facts about In-State Tuition for Undocumented Immigrant Students." Retrieved from: https://www.nilc.org/issues/education/basic-facts-instate/

Olivas, M.A. 2004. "IIRIRA, the DREAM Act, and Undocumented College Student Residency." *Journal of College and University Law 30*(2):435–64.

Olivas, M.A. 2012. *No Undocumented Child Left Behind: Plyler v. Doe and the Education of Undocumented Schoolchildren*. New York: New York University Press.

Omi, M., and H. Winant. 2007. "Racial Formations." In P.S. Rothenberg (ed.), *Race, Class, and Gender in the United States: An Integrated Study*. 7th ed. (pp. 13–22). New York: Worth Publishers.

Perry, A.M. 2006. "Toward a Theoretical Framework for Membership: The Case of Undocumented Immigrants and Financial Aid for Postsecondary Education." *Review of Higher Education* 30:21–40.

Salomone, R.C. 1986. *Equal Education Under Law: Legal Rights and Federal Policy in the Post-Brown Era*. New York: St. Martin's Press.

Seif, H. 2011. "'Unapologetic and Unafraid': Immigrant Youth Come Out from the Shadows. *New Directions for Child Adolescent Development* 134:59–75).

Tafoya, S. 2007. "Shades of Belonging: Latinos and Racial Identity." In P.S. Rothenberg, ed. *Race, Class, and Gender in the United States: An Integrated Study*. 7th ed. (pp. 218–21). New York: Worth Publishers.

Reading 9.2 Immigrants and Their Activism: A Differential Racialization Approach

Kevin Escudero, Brown University

Abstract

While the issue of undocumented immigration is often depicted in the mainstream political imagination as affecting members of the Latinx community, this is not necessarily this case nor has it been true historically. Through the use of a differential racialization approach, this chapter examines the seemingly disparate yet interrelated racial positioning of Asian and Latinx undocumented immigrants within the US racial order. In doing so, this chapter centers the online activism of Asian and Latinx undocumented immigrant activists to illustrate how community members have been both strategic and purposeful in their efforts to reframe the issue of immigration reform as a multiracial issue: one that affects Asian, Latinx, and other immigrant communities.

Keywords: Comparative Racialization; Racial Formation Theory; Individual and Collective Action; Immigrant Youth; Media Activism

Introduction

Immigrant communities in the United States today consist of a heterogeneous group of individuals hailing from many different regions across the globe. Immigrant youth, members of the 1.5-generation, born abroad and having arrived in the United States before adolescence, have been at the forefront of social movement activism (Gonzalez 2008; Lopez and Marcelo 2008; Nicholls 2013).[35] Given immigrant youth's leadership in the contemporary immigrant rights movement and their high levels of civic engagement, one might ask: What factors explain immigrant youth's high levels of civic engagement and political activism? Relatedly, what role do the youth's ethno-racial identities play in this process?

In other writing (Escudero forthcoming), I answer these questions by drawing on extensive ethnographic fieldwork conducted with undocumented Asian and Latinx[36] immigrant activists in San Francisco, Chicago, and New York City, three of the immigrant rights movement's primary epicenters. In this chapter, I draw on a close reading of a Dreamers Adrift *Undocumented and Awkward* video series episode to highlight the centrality of race, in particular differential racialization processes, as related to the depiction of undocumented Asian and Latinx immigrants in the United States today. This chapter begins with an overview of the immigrant community in the United States and its racial/ethnic makeup, prior to transitioning to a discussion of the theoretical frameworks of race, racial formation, and differential racialization. The next section consists of a close reading

---

[35] For a further discussion of Latina/o youth immigrant and nonimmigrants' civic engagement, see https://www.wilsoncenter.org/sites/default/files/Seif percent20- percent20Challenging percent20Boundaries percent20and percent20Creating percent20Safe percent20Spaces.pdf.

[36] I purposefully use the term "Latinx," given that up until recently, the term *Latino* was used as a term of self-identification for individuals residing in and/or born in the United States whose families have Latin American origins. The term Latino was preferential to Hispanic as it was a means of self-identification rather than a category created by the federal government to classify individuals. The term therefore has a broader and more capacious reach as compared to the term *Hispanic*. (For a greater discussion of these two terms, see https://www.npr.org/sections/parallels/2015/08/27/434584260/hispanic-or-latino-a-guide-for-the-u-s-presidential-campaign). Latinx rather than Latino is gender inclusive acknowledging the multiple, overlapping gender identities among community members. For further discussion on the debate regarding the term Latinx, see https://www.nbcnews.com/news/latino/be-latinx-or-not-be-latinx-some-hispanics-question-n817911.

of the *Undocumented and Awkward* series episode, then concludes with a discussion of how these frameworks are also relevant for analyzing examples of immigrant racialization in other social movement and activist contexts.

An Overview of the Immigrant Population in the United States Today

According to estimates from the Pew Hispanic Center, a national nonpartisan think tank, there were an estimated 43.2 million immigrants residing in the United States, which constituted 13.4 percent of the overall US population as of 2015 (Lopez and Radford 2017). *Immigrants*, in this context, refers to members of the foreign-born population: US citizens and noncitizens. Among members of the foreign-born population, 48 percent are US citizens and slightly more than half, or 52 percent, are noncitizens (Pew 2015).

Of the 43.2 million immigrants in the country, significant proportions hail from Asia and Latin America. In fact, almost one third—26.9 percent—were born in South and East Asia, followed closely by another third—26.8 percent—who were born in Mexico (Ibid). Latinx immigrants comprise 34.4 percent of the total US population (Ibid). In this chapter, I intentionally distinguish between Hispanic and Latinx on the basis that Hispanic primarily refers to individuals hailing from a particular region, while Latinx identity is a term of self-identification among members of the diaspora (Lopez et.al. 2017).

While measures of migrants' countries of origins are important, research has also shown that upon arrival in the United States, immigrants draw upon racial categories and processes of racialization in their previous countries of residence and in the United States when asserting a racial/ethnic identity.[37] With regard to racial self-identification, the majority of immigrants in the United States—or 73.1 percent—self-identify as white. This can potentially be attributed to the fact that race is a socially constructed category, as will be discussed in further detail in the following section[38] and that there exists immense variation in racial/ethnic identification among members of the Latino community (Rodriguez 2000).[39]

Sociological Theories of Race, Racial Formation, and Differential Racialization

Social science scholars of race have importantly argued that race is a social construct, which sociologists Michael Omi and Howard Winant have drawn upon in their development of what they term a Racial Formation Theory Framework. According to Omi and Winant, the process of racial formation "… [can be defined as] … the sociohistorical process by which racial identities are created, lived out, and destroyed" (Omi and Winant 2014: 109). Thus, the very act by which racial categories are created, operationalized, and then replaced by another master category, is all part of an interconnected, constitutive process.

---

[37] For a greater discussion of this topic, see Wendy Roth's book *Race Migrations* or Tiffany Joseph's book, *Race on the Move.* Also see the work of sociologist Edward Telles at the University of California–Santa Barbara.

[38] Though often used interchangeably, it is important to note the differences and similarities between the concepts of "race" and "ethnicity" to assist in providing context as to how they will be used in this chapter. As defined by sociologists Michael Omi and Howard Winant, "ethnicity" is rooted in two concepts: "*biologistic understandings of race*, and *Puritanism*, the founding religious/political orientation of the White Anglo-Saxon Protest (and actually Calvinist) settlers of North America" (Omi and Winant 2014, p. 23). On the other hand, "race" is "… a concept that signifies and symbolizes social conflicts and interests by referring to different types of human bodies. Although the concept … invokes seemingly biologically based human characteristics (so-called phenotypes), selection of these particular human features for purposes of racial signification is always and necessarily a social[ly] and historical[ly] shaped process" (Omi and Winant 2014, p. 110). A key difference is that while ethnicity is rooted in pseudoscientific notions of biological differences between groups with the central reference point being a White European identity, race takes into account social and historical processes that have led to the understanding of how a particular group of people are constituted and understood in relation to other racialized groups.

[39] Also see https://www.migrationpolicy.org/article/pigments-our-imagination-racialization-hispanic-latino-category.

While often recognized as a central framework for analyzing race in the world today (HoSang et.al. 2012: 9), Racial Formation Theory has also been pushed to look beyond the United States and to pay further attention to categories of analysis, such as class and other axes of marginalization (Ibid: 9-10). For critical scholarship addressing these issues and discussing the relevance of Racial Formation Theory in an increasingly complex world, a central work to examine is the edited volume *Racial Formation in the Twenty-First Century (HoSang et.al. 2012)*.

Ethnic studies and geography scholar Laura Pulido has in her research utilized a racial formation approach and emphasized the importance of race as an ideology as part of the racialization process that communities undergo (Pulido 2006). According to Pulido, ideologies relate to the means by which individuals both consciously and unconsciously make sense of the world around them, leading to the production of hegemonic ideologies: "Hegemonic ideologies, or what Gramsci calls 'common sense,' are ideologies that become so widespread and accepted that they not only become naturalized but determine boundaries of acceptable thought ..." (Pulido 2006: 24-25). Race, as a hegemonic ideology, is a pervasive category in the lives of racialized peoples in the United States today, and as Omi and Winant argue, can be understood as a "master category" (Ibid).

Building on these two theoretical conceptualizations—race as a social construct and as an ideology—this chapter utilizes what Pulido calls a *differential racialization approach* to examine the ways in which individuals and groups are racialized in relation to one another. According to Pulido, differential racialization can be understood as "... the fact that different groups are racialized in distinct kinds of ways" with racialization explained as shaped by "the particulars of history, geography and the needs of capital [or labor needs]" (Pulido 2006:25). Though racialization is a continually shifting and socio-historically contingent process, as the differential racialization paradigm demonstrates, this process does not necessarily play out in the same way for all groups. Acknowledging these differential histories and the relative nature of racialization processes, the following section offers an analysis of the differential racialization of Asian and Latinx undocumented immigrant activists in the present-day period. In doing so, I seek to emphasize the processes by which community members have worked to overcome such structural and ideological divisions to present a united front.

Though these theoretical frameworks offer important, multifaceted approaches to analyzing race, one might ask, what is the relationship between processes of racialization and the migration experience? While immigrants are racialized (both in their sending countries and after their arrival in the United States), are they also subject to experiences of anti-immigrant sentiment and nativism differently from their nonimmigrant counterparts? Race and education scholars Lindsay Perez Huber, Corina Benavides Lopez, Maria Malagón, Veronica Velez, and Daniel Solórzano have developed the concept of "racist nativism," building on the work of historian George Sánchez, defined as "... the assigning of values to real or imagined differences, in order to justify the superiority of the native, who is to be perceived white, over that of the non-native, who is perceived to be People and Immigrants of Color, and thereby defend the rights of whites, or the natives, to dominance" (Perez et.al. 2008). For immigrant rights activists, it is critical that an analysis of their racial/ethnic identities includes a discussion of the intersection between racialization and immigrant identities formation processes such as is evident in the racist nativist theoretical formation.

An Example from the Immigrant Rights Movement: Dreamers Adrift's *Undocumented and Awkward* Series

A San Francisco Bay Area collective, Dreamers Adrift is self-described as "... a media platform led by undocumented [artists] with the goal of taking back the undocumented narrative ..." (DreamersAdrift 2019). This work is achieved, "... through [the use of] videos, art, music, spoken word and poetry" (Ibid). Important for its centering of undocumented immigrants' lived experiences, this platform not only prioritizes community-driven self-representation, but works to engage community members through the use of innovative new media techniques. As other scholars have noted, new and social media technologies have played an elected role in the immigrant rights movement as it has facilitated the formation of connections among members of a highly marginalized community at a moment when publicly sharing one's undocumented status was gradually becoming a risk that activists were willing to take (Zimmerman 2016). As will be discussed in this section, one of the site's two original series, *Undocumented and Awkward* confronts daily awkward encounters that undocumented immigrants face and facilitates consciousness raising regarding these interactions among allies.

The episode that I will focus on here, Episode 7 in the series, is particularly noteworthy as it confronts the issue of Asian undocumented immigrants' invisibility within the larger narrative of undocumented immigration nationally. This episode opens at a bus stop in what appears to be a local suburban neighborhood during the late afternoon as the sun is beginning to set. Two individuals are already standing at the stop, fidgeting with their hands as they eagerly await the bus's arrival. They are seen playfully joking with one another in English about how one of the two individuals "looks good" for their upcoming day, donning some sunglasses even though the sun is about to set.

Shortly thereafter, an Asian presenting individual appears on the screen and takes his place, waiting alongside the other two individuals. All three carrying backpacks or a messenger bag, one can infer that these are three students waiting to head to campus or perhaps to work. A few moments after the Asian character's arrival, the other two characters who were previously conversing in English, switch to Spanish. "Dude, since when do 'chinitos' [Asians] here ride the bus?" one asks. "Since they're stingy," the other replies. "I find it so annoying that the folks who have proper documentation and a license could drive to school, while we're forced to take the bus because we don't have documents. And here they are taking up space," the first character continues. Egging him on, the second character states, "I bet he's got a car at home, but he just doesn't want to pay for gas." After a few more brief exchanges, the two characters then become curious about the time, with one of the two Latinx presenting characters asking the Asian presenting individual, in English, for the time. "Yes, it's 2 o'clock in the afternoon." As the two Latinx presenting characters debate whether the Asian character understood them, he quickly replies, in Spanish, "Yes, I understood you. And you know what? I'm also undocumented and I don't have a license. That's why I'm here waiting for the bus." After a few more exchanges, the Latinx presenting characters learn that not only is the Asian presenting individual undocumented, but that he is from Peru, not from an Asian nation. The episode then ends with the original two characters starting into the camera with looks of disbelief on their face in light of the information they just learned.

This episode is extremely powerful in not only shattering mainstream media's stereotypes of undocumented immigrants as solely consisting of Latinx immigrants, but also confronting assumptions among undocumented community members regarding who is undocumented. These artificial divisions in how undocumented Asian and Latinx immigrants in the United States are represented can be understood through a lens of what Pulido articulates in her work as differential racialization. Asian immigrants are a unique immigrant group, given their status as the first undocumented immigrants in the United States, entering the country through illicit channels during the Chinese Exclusion Era (1882–1943) (Lee 2003; Ngai 2014; Romero 2011). Moreover, as historian Kelly Lytle Hernandez demonstrates in her research, the border patrol was initially established to detain and police Chinese undocumented immigrants, but over time, gradually was used to surveil Latinx migrants (Hernandez 2010). Latinx immigrants, though at the forefront of the immigrant rights debates today, have only become subjected to quota restrictions since 1965 with the passage of the Hart-Cellar Act (Ngai 2004). The powerful effects of racialization, however, have worked to depict undocumented immigrants as a Latin American issue, what anthropologist Leo Chavez has termed the "Latino Threat Narrative" (Chavez 2013), with Latin American migrants being depicted as dangerous criminals and a drain on the US economy (Santa Ana, Otto and González de Bustamante 2012). Today, Asian immigrants are typically depicted as deserving of inclusion, assimilable, and high achieving (in part due to the model minority myth) (Chow 2017). On the other hand, Latinx immigrants are usually deemed unworthy of inclusion and a threat to US society as well as the racial order.

Seeking to overcome these artificial and top-down approaches to analyzing Asian and Latinx undocumented immigrant experiences, activists with whom I collaborated have actively worked to advance a two-part approach to rectifying this issue. First, activists have foregrounded a discussion of Asian and Latinx immigrant community histories through the use of popular education strategies. By understanding and knowing one's own community history and that of other similarly situated communities, community members draw upon their own knowledge when working to combat these immensely pervasive stereotypes. Instances of such efforts include the use of new and social media such as the videos in Dreamers Adrift's *Undocumented and Awkward* series. Second, through the cultivation of a greater understanding of what undocumented immigrant experiences encompass—Asian and Latinx migrant experiences, but also queer immigrant narratives—activists have work to showcase a broader narrative regarding the "undocumented immigrant experience" in the United States today. As part of these efforts, some organizers have also worked to link the targeting of Muslim migrant communities in the post-9/11 period with the treatment of Latinx and other undocumented immigrants. Collectively, these two strategies have facilitated undocumented immigrant activists' success in lessening the effects of the differential racialization of Asian and Latinx undocumented community members to refocus efforts around justice for all undocumented immigrants.

Conclusion

As this chapter has demonstrated, theories of race, racialization, and differential racialization are central theoretical frameworks with important implications for undocumented Asian and Latinx immigrants' daily lives. Two groups, which are situated "between" blacks and whites in the US racial order, Asian and Latinx communities are also two groups that have been racialized in relation to one another and as part of an interstitial group within the black/white divide present in US race relations (Park and Park 1999). Immigrants' identity, however, also plays a key role in the racialization processes that Asian and Latinx immigrant communities undergo. With a focus on Asian and Latinx undocumented immigrant political activism, this chapter has shown how even though differential racialization can lead to the emergence of artificial divisions among members of similarly situated groups, these communities have in fact devised innovative strategies to overcome these barriers to collective organizing. As immigrant communities continue to find themselves under attack and with limited opportunity to exercise full or partial citizenship, such efforts will become increasingly important in the fight for migrant and refugee justice.

Reflection Questions

1. In what ways is a multiracial/ethnic approach important in understanding the immigrant rights movement and other social movements (e.g. civil rights, environmental justice, LGBTQ rights, etc.), both historically and in the contemporary period?

2. In employing a differential racialization approach to examine the case of the immigrant rights movement, how would you propose balancing the use of community-based narratives, academic research, and media discourse?

3. In your opinion, what has been social and digital media's impact on transforming the ways in which knowledge is shared in the immigrant rights and other social movement contexts?

Websites for Further Research on Asian and Latinx Undocumented Immigrant Youth Activism

- Asian Students Promoting Immigrant Rights through Education (ASPIRE) in the San Francisco Bay Area: http://sfbay.aspireforjustice.org/
- Dreamers Adrift: http://dreamersadrift.com/
- My Undocumented Life Blog: https://mydocumentedlife.org/
- Revolutionizing Asian American Immigrant Stories on the East Coast (RAISE): http://aaldef.org/raise.html
- UPLIFT in Los Angeles: http://www.upliftlosangeles.org/

Reading 9.3 Journey to Standing Rock: Environmental Justice on the Frontlines

Anne Luna

Yah hey people stand up and fight, Yah hey it's all right, Yah way hey water is life.

—Iroquois gratitude song sung at Standing Rock

Keywords: Native Americans, Political Activism, Standing Rock, Dakota Access Pipeline (DAPL)

The grassroots movement in response to the Dakota Access Pipeline (DAPL) constructed by Energy Transfer Partners offers a unique opportunity for understanding research in Native American communities. In turn, research on Native environmental justice organizing can offer unique insights into cultural transformation and continuance, gender and identity politics, social action, and resistance. The goals of this chapter are to address urban Native American environmental justice organizing in relation to Standing Rock and the central role Native women play in generating and sustaining community life. The chapter opens with pathways to decolonize research on the subject. Next, it addresses historical materialism and how it can be applied to Native experience. Finally, it presents an analysis of principles of Native women's environmental justice work in urban areas as well as at Standing Rock.

Researchers of oppressed people tend to view social groups or identities as fixed units of analysis, which is especially problematic when researching groups who experience multiple layers of identity. Although speaking of Native Americans as a monolithic group may be convenient, it is deeply problematic. As Seidman (1993:134) argues, "identity is a site of on-going social regulation and contestation rather than a quasi-natural substance or an accomplished social fact." While Native American women may identify with some constructions fixed upon them, they also experience and embody many other intersecting constructions involving identity and the self. As a queer, pale-faced, mixed-race, urban, Native American woman, this is something I am especially aware of in research, teaching, and social movement spaces.

In the United States, urbanization has affected everyone. In particular, the experience of Native American peoples has been one of forced migration and, eventually, induced urban migration. Native Americans, like other ethnic groups, have had to find ways to fit into urban centers while still trying to maintain their cultures. Urban Indian communities are now centered around Native organizations that have helped to organize activities and contributed to a growing pan-Indian identity. Pan-Indian social movements have created unique spaces for Native women's environmental justice work in urban areas while simultaneously connecting them with tribal homelands across the Americas.

Researching Native Americans

Social research into Native American communities has evolved since the beginning of colonization. This is a concern, given that most of such research is initiated by agencies or non-Native individuals (John 1990). Native Americans have been exploited by researchers whose motivation was to conduct research for the sake of advancing their profession (Swisher 1993). Conducting research without respect for or benefit to subjects or their communities can be seen as a form of exploitation. The desire to remedy the imbalances that occur during the research process has pushed some researchers toward defining and producing ethical research practices.

Historically, groups of researchers and institutions have been able to access federal, state, or other resources to study Native populations for research that was mainly conducted from an *etic* perspective. The goal of an etic approach is to reveal patterns of behavior as defined and perceived by the researchers' priorities (as an outsider looking in). Vine Deloria Jr. (1991) referred to these types of researchers as academic hustlers. In addition, studies have been conducted in Native communities that incorrectly framed the research problem and failed to increase understanding of the types of problems and their possible solutions. "Whether racially prejudiced or guilt-ridden, patronizing, paternalistic, or romantic, Indian history mainly has been perceived from a white perspective, based on the idea that 'the conquerors write the history'" (Mihesuah 1998:86). Whether through ignorance or intention, the research process and results of these studies have reinforced the existing power imbalance and had a negative impact on Native communities and cultures (LaFromboise and Plake 1983).

Another issue to consider is that there is no single Native American culture. Researchers must avoid stereotyping and "lump[ing] peoples from vastly different cultures under the umbrella term *Indian*" (Davis and Reid 1999:756). Tribal nations and cultures are numerous and varied. There are 567 federally recognized tribes and at least 30 state-recognized tribes; meanwhile, hundreds of other groups remain unrecognized (Anner 1990). According to 2010 Census estimates, only 30.7 percent of self-identified American Indians and Alaska Natives alone live on reservations and in other tribal areas, while over two-thirds live outside of tribal areas (Norris, Vines, and Hoeffel 2012).

Given the history of Native experiences with researchers, ethics and community input are of paramount importance. Recent studies of Native communities have demonstrated the value of participatory research to engage the *emic* (insider's) perspective in social research. Increasingly, research is being conducted in collaboration with urban and reservation Indian communities. These studies emphasize a research process that addresses issues of importance to the affected Native communities (Swisher 1993). The best research and practice models engage Native communities and organizations as active partners in the research. They are no longer seen as research subjects or passive recipients by non-Native researchers (Teufel-Shone, Siyuja, Watahomigie and Irwin 2006).

One cannot overemphasize that frameworks using universal membership do not guarantee the successful analysis of members of Native communities. It is likely that a Native woman researcher will have an understanding of what Native women may face. However, the researcher must remain aware of, make transparent, and constantly seek out and question the appropriateness of spaces in which they meet research participants.

Ladson-Billings (2000:260) utilizes a framework of multiple consciousnesses that avoids oversimplifying people or groups with labels. Rejecting essentialized views of research subjects forces researchers to work within fluid intersecting concepts of identity. Although a Native woman researcher may have a "perspective advantage" when researching populations of Native women, they still may not appreciate the diverse experiences that Native women face (Ladson-Billings 2000:272). Including Native communities in this process will help to enrich the research experiences of both researchers and participants.

The Importance of Place

Lobo (1998) notes that urban Indian identity and sense of community often circulate around cultural activities associated with a Native organization. The urban community lends a sense of belonging along with a social obligation to contribute to the well-being of its members. There is a shared understanding of participation and informal consensus. Aspects defining Native identity in the urban community include: ancestry, appearance, cultural elements, and community participation. Women who work with urban Indian organizations are thus able to find a sense of place and belonging that ties them to their community.

In regard to tribal homelands, a major source of identity is rooted in the land, as articulated by songs and stories connecting personal reality to time and space, while in urban Indian communities, the only land base is that associated with community organization buildings and the like. Although the majority of Native people now live in urban areas, this does not necessarily separate them from their homelands. Even third- and fourth-generation urban people maintain a feeling of connection to their land of origin. Given this connection, staggering numbers of Native peoples were bound to join the pipeline protests at Standing Rock.

The American Indian Movement (AIM) and other Red Power (American Indian rights) groups arose out of urban settings where young people acted to strengthen their intertribal connections within urban areas and into reservations settings (Straus and Valentino 2003). Although the 1972 Trail of Broken Treaties, a cross-country protest, initially magnified strains between urban and reservation Indians, it eventually strengthened connections between these groups. Red Power protests shifted from short-term urban actions to longer events, often on or near reservations, thus turning the primarily urban movement into one that was rooted in reservation communities. The results of intertribal political action in this era was increased federal funding, expanded programs, and enhanced self-determination for tribes. According to Donald Fixico (2000:124), "'Group' emphasis or 'community' represented the way of life for Indian people, and this outlook has extended noticeably into urban Indian communities. …" In the most basic sense, Indian people enjoyed and benefited from being with each other, especially in the context of settler colonialism. This helped pave the way for the Native women's environmental justice organizing in relation to Standing Rock.

Historical Development of Capitalist Society

In terms of understanding the relationship of rural and urban Native environmental justice organizing, analyzing the role of the state is of paramount importance. Historical materialism is a methodological approach to the study of society, economics, and history first articulated by Karl Marx. The theoretical perspective looks at the causes of change and development in society in terms of the means by which humans collectively produce the necessities of life. The noneconomic features of a society, like social classes, ideologies, and political structures, are an outgrowth of its economic activity.

In 1884, Friedrich Engels argued that although modern humans have existed as a species for over one hundred thousand years, humans only began living in family units in the last several thousand years. Previous societies were egalitarian and only later did they eventually divide into classes. Pre-class human social organization was based on large clans and collective production, distribution and childrearing. Although a division of labor often existed between women and men in pre-class societies, there was no evidence to suggest that women were systematically oppressed (Engels 1975 [1884]:66).

Historical materialism emerged from a fundamental reality of human existence: in order for people to survive and continue from generation to generation, it is necessary for them to produce and reproduce the material requirements of life. According to Marx 1961 ([1844]), in order to carry out production and exchange, people have to enter into productive relations. People collectively work on nature but do not do the same work. There is a division of labor in which people not only do different jobs, but some people live off of the work of others by owning the means of production. This is accomplished in different ways, depending on the form of society. Production is carried out through definite relations between people. In turn, these relations of production are determined by the level and character of the productive forces that are present at any given time in history. For Marx, forces of production refer to the means of production, such as the tools, instruments, technology, land, raw materials, and human knowledge and abilities (Marx 1961 [1844]).

Through the lens of historical materialism, we can see that society has moved through a number of types or modes of production; that is, the character of the relations of production is determined by the character of the productive forces. The main modes of production Marx identified include primitive communism or tribal society, ancient society, feudalism, and capitalism (Marx 1961 [1844]). In each of these modes of production, people interact with nature and produce their living in different ways; surplus from that production is allotted in different ways. Land was held in common in communal tribal societies, and although a division of labor existed, everyone's contribution was valued. Ancient society was based on a ruling class of slaveowners and slaves; feudalism was based on landowners and serfs; and capitalism is based on the capitalist class and the working class. The capitalist class privately owns the means of production, distribution, and exchange like factories, mines, shops, and banks, while the working class lives by exchanging their labor with the capital class for wages (Marx 1961 [1844]).

The relationship between owners and workers is the economic and social basis of our modern American society. In a class-based society, class relations determine the character of the dominant mode of production (Marx 1961 [1844]). This sets up the political superstructure, including the state and other ideological and political establishments, that serves the interests of the ruling class. The state, therefore, is a tool of class rule and domination (Marx 1961 [1844]). Democracy in a capitalist society is constrained by the restrictions set by capitalist exploitation. As a consequence, it will always be a democracy for the rich property owners and not for the working people. A few people will always be at the top; the rest will be exploited and oppressed. This domination can be seen in the colonization of the Americas, the oppression of tribal cultures and identities as well as gender roles, and the continued exploitation of Native lands for capitalist profit against the wishes of the affected Native communities.

This perspective also offers some interesting explanations for the movement of Native populations between urban and reservation areas in the United States. The realities of poverty and unemployment that Native Americans face in urban and rural areas are a direct result of poorly conceptualized programs and a failing capitalist system. Common experiences among relocated Indians eventually led to the formation of a socially conscious, pan-Indian identity in urban areas. As a result, when the lives and environmental health of Lakota peoples were in crisis at Standing Rock, Natives from all over the country were drawn to the frontlines.

Settler Law in Relation to Standing Rock

This section will outline the history of federal Indian law and policy and illustrate how the exercise of government power has oppressed Native people. Federal Indian law and policy has evolved through many shifts over the course of settler colonialism. During some periods, the dominant view was that tribes are enduring independent bodies for whom the geographic base should be protected. During other periods, the disruption of tribes was the goal, with the hope that their members would be assimilated. These two opposing views have worked together to form a complicated patchwork of policies. Whatever the policy, the law is an aspect of the superstructure of our capitalist society. These laws have worked predominantly to oppress Native peoples in the United States.

After the War of Independence, the nation found itself in a situation in which they wished to prevent wars between state citizens and Natives. Congress set the pattern of federal Indian law through a series of Trade and Intercourse Acts passed between 1790 and 1834 (Getches et al. 2005:89). The policy was intended to subject all interactions to federal control and minimize contacts between Indians and non-Indians. The acts established the boundaries of Indian country and were intended to protect them against incursion.

Regardless of the acts, conflicts continued to grow as non-Indian pressure for land intensified. The solution to remove tribes toward the west was pushed in the early nineteenth century by Presidents Monroe, Adams, and most vigorously by Jackson, who called for removal in his 1829 state of the union address. Simultaneously, the US Supreme Court independently built legal doctrines that gave the power to treat with tribes to the federal government. The tribes had inherent aboriginal title to their lands, and only the federal government could extinguish that title (Getches et al. 2005:68). As population pressures from the east continued, the federal government restricted tribes to specific reservations. Most of this was done through treaties, wherein tribes would cede most of their land in order to reserve outright title to a smaller portion. Reservations were intended to help keep the peace by creating space between Indians and non-Indians (Getches et al. 2005:140–41). Regardless of this intention, most reservations were dramatically reduced through a variety of congressional acts placing Natives at odds with the development efforts of non-Native interests.

In the case of the Standing Rock reservation, the Sioux Nation ceded their vast territory in the Plains for lands set aside by the 1851 Treaty of Fort Laramie (Getches et al. 2005). The Standing Rock reservation also retained water rights from the 1851 treaty and subsequent treaties. These water rights give the tribe jurisdiction over the Missouri River south of the Heart River, which would eventually include the DAPL route. A later treaty in 1868 established a permanent reservation for the Sioux with a northern boundary at the current border between the states of North and South Dakota, which is south of the DAPL route, but left their water rights intact. Under Article 16 of the 1868 treaty, lands north of the permanent reservation were deemed "unceded Indian territory." According to the Indian Claims Commission (ICC), in a 1978 decision, the northern boundary of the unceded Article 16 lands was the Heart River—the same boundary recognized by the original Treaty of Fort Laramie. Later on, the US Supreme Court upheld the ICC's decision, stating that a "more ripe and rank case of dishonorable dealing will never, in all probability, be found in our history" (448 U.S. 371 (1980)).

After a limited review of the DAPL route, the US Army Corps of Engineers found no significant impact. In spring 2016, however, the Advisory Council on Historic Preservation, the Environmental Protection Agency, and the Department of the Interior requested that the Army Corps of Engineers conduct a formal environmental impact assessment. The Standing Rock Sioux Tribe filed suit against the Corps of Engineers in July 2016, but the motion was denied by the court. In December 2016, in the last moments of the Obama administration, the Corps of Engineers denied an easement for construction of the pipeline under the Missouri River. Although an environmental impact assessment was finally to be conducted by the Corps of Engineers, many water protectors continued to occupy the site (Stand With Standing Rock 2016). President Trump signed an executive order on January 24, 2017, expediting the environmental review to complete the pipeline (Mufson 2017). Trump then authorized the Corps of Engineers to proceed on February 7, 2017, ending the environmental impact assessment and the required public comment period (Harder and Matthews 2017). The number of water protectors at the encampment gradually decreased due to harsh winter conditions, police violence, and Trump's approval of the pipeline. On February 23, 2017, law enforcement officers from numerous states and the National Guard evicted the remaining water protectors from the site (Wong 2017). The DAPL was completed in April, and the first oil was delivered on May 14, 2017 (Renshaw 2017).

The Standing Rock Tribe has vehemently opposed the route of DAPL since 2014, stating that the pipeline would negatively impact the tribal water supply, threaten ancient burial grounds, and violate its water rights. The tribe's position is supported by treaties codified by their tribal constitutions. Both the DAPL crossing site and the anti-pipeline encampment, while technically outside reservation limits, are nevertheless on these unceded treaty lands. Given this history, the situation was ripe for transcontinental environmental justice organizing.

Native Women in Action

Given that community work is family focused, many women become involved in it as a way to improve life for their children. Most Native women are motivated to participate in environmental justice work because of the interconnectedness of all things, by the value of inclusivity, and their drive to improve the world for all living beings. They are stimulated "by a desire to achieve fundamental changes in existing social, political, and economic systems in order to make these more egalitarian and equitable for children, for women, and for racial/ethnic minority groups" (Prindeville 2002:78–87). Leadership is a cooperative undertaking for Native people. Mentoring, advising, and supporting future leaders "through the use of a traditional American Indian worldview that involves collectivism, collaboration, compassion, and courage" develops effective Native leadership (Portman and Garrett 2005:287). Native women organizers share the experience of being on the frontline of the immediate educational, employment, health, and social needs of their people in urban and rural areas. Hence, they are in a unique position to lead their communities for collective and collaborative action for a just society.

In many ways, Native American emphasis on cultural continuity runs counter to contemporary American ideals. Native communities value members who maintain traditions, "even after centuries of concerted and brutal effort on the part of the American government, the churches, and the corporate system to break the connection between individuals and their tribal world" (Gunn Allen 1992:210). If Americans followed indigenous traditions, women's contributions would be honored, and the necessities of life would be distributed based on need. Native people must remember the traditions of this continent; otherwise, we will remain trapped by an exploitative patriarchal capitalist system. "Indeed, the basic ideas of socialism, the egalitarian distribution of goods and power, the peaceful ordering of society, and the right of every member of society to participate in the work and benefits of that society, are ideas that pervade American Indian thought and action" (Gunn Allen 1992:220).

Indigenous women leaders and organizers share the experience of being on the front-line of the immediate educational, employment, health and social needs of Native people. Indigenous women are in a unique position to lead their communities for collective and collaborative action for a just society. In April 2016, LaDonna Brave Bull Allard, an elder, established a spiritual resistance camp on her land on the Standing Rock Sioux reservation. Over the summer, the camp exploded with thousands of water protectors from across the country.

Water is my blood, air is my breath, fire is my spirit, earth is my body.

—Prayer song sung on the frontlines at Standing Rock

Media coverage raised public awareness attracting thousands of non-Native folks to Standing Rock. In some ways, the camp was in danger of being colonized by the disproportionate number of non-Native folks with no experience moving in Native spaces. In response to this, women organizers stepped up to create a camp orientation meeting. In this meeting they imparted important information to guide one's time at the camp. The facilitators explained how environmental justice organizing at Standing Rock was to be informed by and supportive of the Seven Lakota Values. These values include prayer, respect, compassion, honesty, generosity, humility, and wisdom.

Prayer: It was a resistance ceremonial prayer camp. Participants were asked to do their work in ceremonial prayer, regardless of whether it was how they usually operated. Water protectors were reminded to listen more than they spoke and to observe what was happening around them.

Respect: Respect at the camp was demonstrated by listening, and coming from a place of agreement. Regardless of the organizing expertise water protectors brought with them, they were reminded that they should respect the leadership of local elders. Indigenous organizing is different from many other social movement spaces, and visitors were reminded that they should let go of control. Conflict is not an indigenous value, but respect is, so water protectors were asked to be respectful toward law enforcement.

Compassion: Water protectors were reminded to have compassion for themselves. They were reminded that it was okay to make mistakes because you learn from mistakes. They were also reminded to be compassionate toward everyone regardless of where they're coming from. Organizers reminded water protectors that accountability and compassion are the basis of love. Participants were responsible for taking care of one another. They were asked to be self-sufficient, but to understand interdependence. Everyone was expected to help each other out.

Honesty: Water protectors were asked to be honest about their intentions and any stereotypes they might carry. They should understand that they might not have complete information. They should be honest with themselves about their reactions and perceptions of things. They should have their eyes open. They were reminded that they would have particular interactions with people of different backgrounds, which they couldn't control. Support and solidarity are impossible if one does not examine their attitudes. Water protectors were also reminded to be honest about what they were capable of doing. Many people involved in the movement have experienced trauma, and they were encouraged to take time to sit and do internal work.

Generosity: Water protectors were told to be generous with each other. Resources must be shared, especially if one was only there for a short time. The focus was to give more than you received. All donations were directed to be taken to the donation center. Extra firewood or food were to be shared to make sure people had access to them when they needed them. It was very cold, so if people had space in their tent they were encouraged to be generous and offer their space. Visiting water protectors were also reminded that they had privilege because they could come and go whenever they wanted. People of color were reminded that they also had privilege. If they brought their traumas to camp, it was problematic; it didn't entitle them to access body work or healing, especially if they had access to those things at home. They were reminded that the Indian Health Service is underfunded, so that the limited amount of money that goes to IHS means that Native access to health care is also limited. For folks who are Native or who were at camp a long time, it was okay to access necessary supports, but they should also be prepared for people to say no.

Humility: The organizers acknowledged that many visitors were experts in their own right but were reminded to check their egos. They can't defeat the black snake overnight, and the indigenous centered fight probably already considered their solution. Water protectors were reminded that if they had a brilliant idea, they should sit with it before they start telling people. Savior mentality is not welcome in Native spaces. Then, as for ideas, water protectors were encouraged to think about who would follow through, to think about intention versus impact. Many were taking away things from the movement but also leaving things behind.

Wisdom: Water protectors were reminded that way over 500 years of wisdom were present where the seven council fire met. Tons of wisdom in that space may look different from what visitors were familiar with. They were told to trust and let that wisdom guide what you did. Some people may not explain things, but they were encouraged to trust and know that wisdom was moving them forward to defeat the black snake.

These guiding principles helped to center an increasingly non-Native movement around Native values in a way that was specific to the culture with which they were visiting. This is an example of the way Native women, rooted in their traditions, lead people and create and support egalitarian social relations. This anticolonial approach highlighted fundamental differences between Native societies and the capitalism imposed on them by settler colonists.

Reflections on Urban Women's Contributions to #NoDAPL

Native women have been central to building and sustaining Native communities. This is due to their direct participation in social movements, as well as through the roles they play in the organization of family, the maintenance of culture, and securing the material necessities of life. Native women have provided the foundation for the organizations and networks that are the backbones of their communities.

Women have been instrumental in maintaining the connection with traditional values that helps to bind the Native community together. Women leaders in urban and rural Native organizations have helped the Native community maintain a sense of belonging and have created a forum in which to address issues facing American Indians. Native women have played key roles in the development of pan-Indian identity and a sense of urban social consciousness. As such, Native women are in a particularly powerful place to lift up the screen of capitalist ideology and expose the history of domination that still works to oppress the majority of American society. They have the power to set an example to other peoples and organizations by creating and reinforcing ideology that is inclusive of broader worldviews and life ways. Native American women leaders, who historically held respected positions in their communities, can help modern American people understand alternative modes of being and thinking. They can help drive the development of class-consciousness in America. This development is the first major step down a long road to create true equality and freedom in America.

References

Anner, J. 1990. "To the U.S. Census Bureau, Native Americans Are Practically Invisible." *Minority Trendsetter* 4(1):15–21. Oakland, CA: Center for Third World Organizing.

Davis, S.M., and R. Reid. 1999. "Practicing Participatory Research in American Indian Communities." *American Journal of Clinical Nutrition* 69:755S–759S.

Deloria, Vine. 1991. "Research, Redskins, and Reality" [Commentary]. *American Indian Quarterly*, Fall, 457–67.

Engels, Friedrich. 1975. [1884]. *The Origin of the Family, Private Property and the State*. New York: International Publishers.

Getches, D.H., C.F. Wilkinson, and R.A. Williams Jr. 2005. *Cases and Materials on Federal Indian Law*. 5th ed. American Casebook Series. St Paul, MN: Thompson West.

Gunn-Allen, P. 1992. *The Sacred Hoop: Recovering the Feminine in American Indian Traditions*. Boston: Beacon Press.

Harder, Amy, and Christopher M. Matthews. 2017. "Trump Administration Gives Final Approval for Dakota Access Pipeline." *Wall Street Journal*. Retrieved November 2, 2018. https://www.wsj.com/articles/trump-administration-gives-final-approval-for-dakota-access-pipeline-1486500445 (February 7, 2017).

John, R. 1990. "The Uninvited Researcher in Indian Country: Problems of Process and Product Conducting Research among Native Americans." *Mid-American Review of Sociology* 14:113–33.

Ladson-Billings, G. 2000. "Racialized Discourses and Ethnic Epistemologies." In N.K. Denzin and Y.S. Lincoln (Eds.), *The Handbook of Qualitative Research* (257–77). Thousand Oaks, CA: Sage.

LaFromboise, T.D., and B.S. Plake. 1983. "Toward Meeting the Research Needs of American Indians." *Harvard Educational Review* 53:45–51.

Lobo, Susan. 1998. "Is Urban a Person or a Place? Characteristics of Urban Indian Country." Los Angeles: *American Indian Culture and Research Journal* 22(4):89–102.

Marx, Karl. 1961. [1844]. *Economic and Philosophic Manuscripts of 1844*. Moscow, Russia: Foreign Languages Publishing House.

Mihesuah, D.A. (Ed.). 1998. *Natives and Academics Researching and Writing About American Indians*. Lincoln: University of Nebraska Press.

Mufson, Steven. 2017. "Trump Gives Green Light to Dakota Access Keystone XL Oil Pipelines." *Washington Post*. Retrieved November 2, 2018. https://www.washingtonpost.com/news/energy-environment/wp/2017/01/24/trump-gives-green-light-to-dakota-access-keystone-xl-oil-pipelines/?noredirect=on&utm_term=.1823f387fbc9 (January 24, 2017).

Norris, T., P.L. Vines, and E.M. Hoeffel. 2012. "The American Indian and Alaska Native Population: 2010." *2010 Census Briefs* (Census Publication No. C2010BR-10). Washington, DC: U.S. Bureau of the Census.

Portman, T.A.A., and M.T. Garrett. 2005. "Beloved Women: Nurturing the Sacred Fire of Leadership from an American Indian Perspective." *Journal of Counseling and Development* 83:284–291.

Prindeville, Diane-Michele. 2002. "A Comparative Study of Native American and Hispanic Women in Grassroots and Electoral Politics." *Frontiers* 23(1):67–89.

Renshaw, Jarrett. 2017. "East Coast Refiner Shuns Bakken Delivery as Dakota Access Pipeline Starts." *Reuters*, April 4, 2017. Retrieved November 2, 2018.

Seidman, S. 1993. "Identity and Politics in a 'Postmodern' Gay Culture: Some Historical and Conceptual Notes." In M. Warner (Ed.), *Fear of a Queer Planet: Queer Politics and Social Theory* (105–142). Minneapolis: University of Minnesota Press.

Stand With Standing Rock. 2016. "Standing Rock Sioux Tribe's Statement on U.S. Army Corps of Engineers Decision to Not Grant Easement." Retrieved November 2, 2018. https://standwithstandingrock.net/standing-rock-sioux-tribes-statement-u-s-army-corps-engineers-decision-not-grant-easement/

Straus, Anne Terry, and Debra Valentino. 2003. "Gender and Community Organization Leadership in the Chicago Indian Community." *American Indian Quarterly* 27(3&4):523–32.

Swisher, K. 1993. "From Passive to Active: Research in Indian Community." *Tribal College* 4:4–5.

Teufel-Shone, N.I., T. Siyuja, H.J. Watahomigie, and S. Irwin. 2006. "Community-Based Participatory Research: Conducting a Formative Assessment of Factors That Influence Youth Wellness in the Hualapai Community." *American Journal of Public Health* 96(9):1623–628.

United States v. Sioux Nation of Indians, 448 U.S. 371 (1980)

Wong, Julia Carrie. 2017. "Police Remove Last Standing Rock Protesters in Military-Style Takeover." *Guardian*. Retrieved November 2, 2018. https://www.theguardian.com/us-news/2017/feb/23/dakota-access-pipeline-camp-cleared-standing-rock (February 23, 2017).

Reading 9.4 Fight the Power: Community Resistance to Structural Oppression

Lori Walkington

Necks stretch forward, trying to reach that long boulevard at the furthest edge of the reserve—

always named after Malcolm, or Dr. King.

Last chance to drop their kill, I wonder if our girls will be locked in sights

before their feet touch the Promised Land ... and I am afraid.

"I Am Afraid"

—Walkington, 2016

Abstract

Spoken-word poetry, and the knowledge we can gain from the poets who perform it speaking of subjective experiences and obstacles, are integral toward social change for structurally oppressed communities. Also known as performance poetry, these powerful testimonials mirror oral traditions such as speaking circles from the African diaspora, indigenous oral traditions in the Americas, and the spoken-word poetic communities of color and marginalized peoples. Within the spoken-word poetry communities of San Diego, California, community members who have been oppressed by the war on drugs, military policing, mass incarceration, state, interpersonal violence, sexism, racism, poverty, marginalization, and other systemic inequalities, learn from and support one another in moving their communities toward social change.

Keywords: Community Healing, Community Trauma, Oppressed Communities, Social Change, Spoken-Word Poetry, Transformative Social Justice

Chapter Goals

After reading this chapter, you should be able to:

- Identify and explain structural oppression
- Identify and explain transformative social justice models
- Analyze the relationship between public performances and understanding structural oppression
- Analyze the interlinking systems of structural oppression as they are impacted by race and class and gender and documentation status
- Identify some avenues toward social change within communities suffering the effects of structural oppression

Introduction

Structural oppression can be understood as the intersecting power systems and institutions that result in a socially constructed and complex set of social inequalities. In the form of spoken-word poetry, community members participate in open-mic events performances which may assist communities and members impacted by structural oppression by interrogating these systems (Williams 2012). Therapeutic models teach the packaging of pain in poetic prose and have the potential toward healing as social change in two ways. First, making pain into an object distanced from the self has potential healing power for poets. Second, audience members can heal by associating their own pain with that of the poets', in this case, that which was suffered due to structural oppressions. This can be particularly powerful in the case of shame. Additionally, poetry has the power to evoke empathy in audiences (Williams 2012). For communities impacted by structural oppression, this empathy could lead to recognition of humanity, of social and community value. While the ongoing process of receiving and giving empathy may begin on an individual level, addressing structural oppression through these communities may begin healing as social change at the community level. The ways in which community members identify the locus of community pain, and how this pain is associated with structural oppressions, can lead to social change through practical community-level resistance via transformative justice models.

Transformative Social Justice

Key to transformative social justice is the focus on transforming structural forms of injustice, such as racism, sexism, and classism, and connecting past experiences to the present health of individuals, families, and communities in envisioning a better future. In this way, transformative justice includes a component directed beyond the immediate needs of all community members and toward the structural oppressions impacting them (Capeheart and Milovanovic 2007). This perspective recognizes harm at the political, social, and economic levels while addressing imbalances of power. Transformative social justice seeks to empower individuals and communities through needs-based justice that remains restorative while also seeking to "affect social-structural, structural, institutional arrangements, while simultaneously helping those whose lives have been affected by interpersonal conflict" (Capeheart and Milovanovic Kindle Locations 1023–1024).

My approach is also rooted in black feminist frameworks that seek everyday experiences and actions to ask the right questions in investigations of intersecting systems of oppression. This perspective utilizes a humanistic vision of community struggles requiring agents of social change to view these as part of the "wider struggle for human dignity, empowerment, and social justice" (Collins 2000:41). Spoken-word performances are rich with themes related to structural oppression, including experiences with racism, sexism, mass incarceration, deportation, state, gang, and interpersonal violence. Community members linked with open-mic events are cannons for social change in their communities.

Oral Traditions: Storytelling and Spoken-Word Poetry

Spoken-word, or performance poetry, was born through "Nommo," or the concept of "the generative power of the word" unique within African traditions of orality. This tradition includes indirection, lyrical quality, rhythm, repetition, soundin' out, historical perspective, mythication, and protests white domination (Walker and Kuykendall 2005:2–3). This concept encompasses performance as an integral component of the telling of stories. Much like the working-class black intellectual blues women of the 1920s, spoken-word community members in contemporary settings might be combining their ideals with activism in relating their understanding of their everyday experiences. Spoken-word poetry, like blues music, has the potential to build social solidarity toward social change by relating and commenting on social realities (Collins 2000). This may be particularly powerful for black women, who have historically been denied male protection, and who bear the brunt of what Collins calls the "love and trouble tradition" (2000:151) between black women and black men. Spoken-word poetry has been a growing part of culture for people of color. These performances have been lauded as a means by which community members open their own minds and those of others to the realities of their communities (Walker and Kuykendall 2005).

We can learn about healing as part of social change for structurally oppressed communities through oral traditions, storytelling, and spoken-word poetry. Central to this change is agency, political engagement, and identity. Social change through spoken-word poetry has been engaged in several American cities and communities. In San Diego, California, members of spoken-word communities link with other community organizations and activists toward social change against poverty, racism, mass incarceration, and other forms of state violence (Walkington 2018).

Research suggests spoken-word poetic performance as public testimonies serves as instruction for not only academics, but also civic, political, and community members toward healing communities of color (Chepp 2014; Williams 2015). It is within such cultural expression that we learn lessons illuminating avenues toward transformative social justice and healing for other oppressed communities. While the spoken-word communities in San Diego address the realities of communities and their members in this region, community members here engage performance as social protest (Flynn and Marrast 2008) and collaborative listening (Ellis and Rawicki 2013). At a time when the president of the United States makes statements supporting-violent white supremacist groups and spews racist vitriol about Mexican immigrants, members of structurally oppressed communities must find radical approaches toward social change and away from oppression.

Testimonios

Testimonios are intended to educate community members about systemic racism, white privilege, and complex power relations that foster a more relational consciousness among Chicanas that attends to their unique histories with and impacts of structural oppression. The intent is that the education provided through Testimonios about the social, racial, and economic barriers will inspire other individual responses to systems of oppression in these communities that engage in the struggle against these systems.

Testimonios serve as more than just stories to educate others to foster continued dedication to the struggles Latinx communities face. This perspective is particularly useful in lessons that guide transformative social justice practices to address trauma in communities of color, as it encourages the use of painful memories, lived experiences, and traumatic events by which individuals learn to navigate various forms of oppression, emerging as active political agents in service of helping others. This both heals the individual, but also humanizes the experiences of the oppressed, making it particularly useful in seeking pathways toward positive social change. Beyond the psychological and emotional impacts of oppression, these perspectives provide a framework to examine the mechanisms of institutional, social, and economic oppression individuals and communities of color face, which can inform avenues toward transformative social justice toward social change.

Resisting Racism: Defensive Othering and Claiming Histories

While community members certainly express trauma and pain related to structural oppression, these public testimonies are also used as social instruments to motivate resistance. True to their roots in the African diaspora and Testimonios, community members also express and make calls for resistance to the forms of structural oppression impacting their communities. Resistance to the structural oppression of racism and related stereotypes, poverty, and systems of residential segregation, gendered and state violence in the forms of police brutality, mass incarceration, immigration, and border patrol was present in poems across all four open-mics reviewed for this project.

Black Xpression open-mic began mid-2016 with a group of student performers from the community at a local restaurant before moving to its current location in La Bodega Art Gallery (*Daily Aztec* 2017). Links to local colleges are evident each Friday night as young and creative people of color come from around the county to share themselves, experiences, joy, and pain with one another. One of the cofounders described the open-mic in four words "Black. Empowerment. Unity. Community" (*Daily Aztec* 2017), but also pointed out that this community is for anyone who has felt silent or "othered."

Othering, or the process by which a dominant group defines an inferior group through invented categories, usually results in and reproduces inequality and can take three forms: oppressive othering, implicit othering, and defensive othering. Oppressive othering takes place when one group defines another as morally and intellectually inferior, as with racial classification schemes (Schwalbe et al. 2000:422–23). Defensive othering occurs within subordinate groups via deflection of stigmas placed upon them by the dominant group (Schwalbe et al. 2000:425). Members of the Black Xpression community engage in defensive othering each Friday night as they engage in a collective positivity that goes against the stigma of black urban youth in the United States.

The poetry at Palabras open-mic also contained expressions of resistance to racism and its mechanisms. In the Testimonios tradition, poets at Palabras performed pieces that link historical events and policies of racist oppression and violence to the segregation and containment of Native, Chicanx, and Mexican peoples. Toward this end, the cofounders of Palabras resist structural oppression by rehabilitating an abandoned warehouse in the historical Barrio Logan community. In providing this space for local community members, the Palabras Art Gallery also engages in transformative justice through art, education, community involvement, and racial integration. Honoring the history of this vibrant community through art is the most prevalent way the Palabras open-mic community engages in defensive othering as resistance to the pervasive racist construction of Latinx people in contemporary United States society.

The 2nd Tuesday/Revolutionary community members at Café Cabaret are the most diverse group included in this research, so much that I was struck at the diversity of this space. Not just the community members, but of the diverse understanding of intersecting systems of oppression community members reflect through their words. Middle-aged and slightly older-appearing white community members package painful memories of racist family members as primary agents of socialization and shedding those lessons. One such poet spoke of the shame she felt in not knowing of the atrocities of race as a child, or why she could no longer play with her childhood friend. In calling out the ways in which racism is taught to them as white children, community members at Café Cabaret are in direct resistance to that socialization. Further, in calling themselves out, relating how coming to the realization in the ways in which they were impacted by these lessons and calling for other whites to do the same, resists racism by offering a way out of racist thinking. The diversity of this community leads to poetry that indicates poets are keenly aware of the ways in which systems of oppression work against racial and ethnic groups not their own.

White, middle-aged, and slightly older, often veterans of wars and social justice movements of the 1960s era, the Revolutionary Poets' Brigade and 2nd Tuesday/Jihmye community members express strong resistance to racism in their poetry. Like Palabras, trauma and pain related to racism emerged in poems at Café Cabaret open-mics and was historically situated but with a slightly different point of focus. The emcee here speaks often about growing up in a home where racism was pervasive, and the reframing of a nonracist consciousness an ongoing process. While some of the white community members at the open mics resisted racist socialization in their homes, one of the featured community members at Café Cabaret, a middle-aged black woman, resists racism by calling out the ways in which borders shift and move not only to prevent entrance, but also movement, advancement, and resistance. One piece from this poet stood out as she spoke about borders crossing bodies, not the other way around. In this way, audience members are called in to the realization with her. Where they are used to be somewhere else. Belonged to a different people. The impact of a black woman speaking these histories was not lost on me. It speaks to the necessity for understanding systems of oppression and how they work, for all oppressed peoples.

Poems at Café Cabaret are not only situated in past historical context, but also include resistance to racist stereotypes perpetuated and supported by the Trump administration against migrant Mexican laborers. In one such piece, the president was directly called out for his statements about Mexico sending drug dealers and rapists to America. This piece, performed by a Latino, was an indictment in direct resistance to racist public sentiments about migrant Mexican workers and families. Resisting the common stereotype of Mexican migrant workers as lazy, immoral, and without work ethic, several community members read pieces wherein defensive othering can be seen.

Resisting Poverty

Resisting one structural mechanism of poverty, Black Xpression collaborates with a local entrepreneurial organization aimed at establishing and growing black wealth in one of the historically black neighborhoods in Southeast San Diego. Community members from Black Xpression also collaborate to feed homeless youth in the area with freshly baked goods. Providing fresh-baked food is a measure of humanity that is often held from homeless and indigent community members. Having my own experience with the dehumanization of county-managed food banks, I was struck at the humanity of this gesture. This mode of resistance also links with another structural factor impacting poverty in black communities—unequal access to adequate public education and the school-to-prison pipeline. Rather than engaging in the brain and cultural drain of black communities, the young black college students give back to the community by making connections between college students and social justice organizations and local community members.

In March 2018, the Black Xpression community joined forces with "Soulcial Workers" for the "Benefit 4 Brotherhood" clothing drive focused on obtaining professional menswear appropriate for ages twelve to twenty-six. Soulcial Workers is a local San Diego area nonprofit community arts organization with a mission "to restore hope, inspire healing, and nurture creativity for all youth in vulnerable populations" through "Attitudes, Awareness, and Relationships Training." Through this collaboration, the Black Xpression community is working within a transformative justice approach toward social change against the fallout of structural oppression in their community.

According to their website, the Soulcial Workers organization "works specifically with transition evidence based and rooted in a unique collaboration between creative process and restorative practices" that use performance "to engage youth in creating reflections that enhance self-awareness and incite critical thinking, … gain problem solving and leadership skills, develop artistry and gain a better sense of identity" in a safe environment, "where youth can create meaningful connections with their peers, empowering one another through the exploration and sharing of lived experiences" that culminates in "team presentations that tell the story of how these issues impact their community and role they would like to play in affecting change" through the process of "directly from its youth about how they see themselves reflected in the world around them" (http://www.thesoulcialworkers.com/). Through this collaboration, the Black Xpression community is engaging in positive social change through transformative social justice actions.

Members of the Café Cabaret open-mics joined together with the group 100 Thousand Community Members for Change, a community of poets, writers, artists, musicians and activists joined together in a movement of transformative justice. The goal of the organization is to create global transformation and social change by creating and organizing events based on local needs. Poets from Café Cabaret took their poetry across the border to Tijuana for a food drive at a local café run by a young couple from Seattle, Washington. This community space provides free food to the community four days a week, offers classes in art, dance, and other educational sources. Here, community members were engaging in binational transformative justice efforts in bridging the 2nd Tuesday Jihmye and Revolutionary community members with community members and activists across the border in Tijuana. In an area that is rife with state, drug, and gang violence on both sides of the border, this work is transformative.

Resisting State Violence: Higher Education, Mass Incarceration, and the School-to-Prison Pipeline

The Café Cabaret poets also engage transformative social justice via collaborations with local colleges. At one Café Cabaret open-mic, a poet announced that her campus community was hosting an event produced and organized by students that featured poetry from formerly incarcerated students. Events such as these are transformative in that they provide a different vantage point through with the larger community can understand and empathize with these members of their community. When held on college campuses, these events have the power to transform the minds and ideas of young people who will go out in the world, make and enforce laws and policies, and attend to those most vulnerable in our communities.

Working directly against structural oppression, community members from the Café Cabaret community have worked together to write grants and organize volunteer efforts across the area. One of them funds a poetry-writing workshop in local juvenile halls. Working in the juvenile and criminal justice systems is important to this community. In keeping with the goal of transformative justice that seeks to highlight local issues of structural oppression for those on the outside, publishing these works in the San Diego Poetry Annual may help to humanize these kids to members of the larger San Diego community. Further, in attending and completing writing workshops, kids who have been adjudicated delinquent have an avenue for packaging their pain and receiving empathy not only from the workshop facilitators, but also their peers, and perhaps even law enforcement and social workers.

Like the poet community at Black Xpression, the Café Cabaret community also works with youth before they are swept up in the juvenile criminal justice system though their kids' version of the San Diego Poetry Annual. By conducting workshops with local youth, community members engage in transformative justice as social change through poetic intervention. Community members understand that children are also impacted by structural oppression, and taking a proactive, community-level intervention-based approach to healing through poetry has the possible added impact of reaching members of the larger community who may relate to or empathize with them.

Resisting the Borders of Body and Nation

Members of the Café Cabaret and Jihmye 2nd Tuesday open-mics joined together with the group 100 Thousand Community Members for Change, a community of community members, writers, artists, musicians and activists joined together in a movement of transformative justice (http://100tpc.org/about-2/). The goal of the organization is to create global transformation and change by creating and organizing events based on local needs. Several of the community members from the Café Cabaret site took up this challenge and took their poetry across the border to Tijuana for a food drive at a local café run by a young couple from Seattle. On one observation night, organizers were collecting cans of food as a form of donation prior to their trip. From what I can gather, this is an ongoing process, and have seen social media planning future can drives and poetry readings from the Revolutionary Poets Brigade (subset of Café Cabaret poets) and 100 Thousand Community Members for Change.

Through collaborations that are binational, the Revolutionary Poets Brigade engages in resistance to white supremacy in that many of the community members involved are white, male, and at least middle-aged. Engaging with community members in Tijuana, this group actively resists racist constructions of Mexican people by engaging with them on a personal level and sharing in their pain through the art of poetic expression. Perhaps some of these community members engage in this work as change agents with some form of insider status as whites. The meanings community members make of the process of packaging their own pain and receiving others through a process of mutual empathy is a question for future research. However, it is clear the community members observed for this research are acutely aware of and able to express how structural oppression in the form of immigration and border policies has impacted their communities.

Community members at Palabras also resist the borders of nations through their poetry. During one reading, community members took audience members through the history of borders invading their land, communities, and families. Community members here resist the idea that borders are a space or place; instead, bodies are the border. In resisting the body as a border, community members remind their audiences that borders cross bodies, not the other way around. There is a dreamlike sense to these pieces, as community members imagine themselves into birds, flying and crossing and free from borders, resisting their placement and meaning.

Performing poetry in a mix of Spanish and English, community members at Palabras resist the southern border by speaking in the language indigenous to the land. It is a useful reminder of the transitory and superfluous nature of borders being drawn over, between, and among people. Community members at Palabras remind us of the bloody histories attached to this land. Of prisons and guns and economic exploitation. Of horses and schools and liquor brought to their people as a means of disruption and division. They remind us that the placing of borders across bodies deemed as "others" is not new or aberrant, but a part of the fabric and history of this nation.

Conclusion

Community members at both open-mic sites expressed resistance to structural oppression in their poetry. As knowledge agents, community members clearly identify racism, state violence, and poverty as structural disruptions to their communities. Related to transformative social justice, these community members don't just speak about it, they be about it! It is clear the Black Xpression and Café Cabaret open-mic communities engage in community-level efforts fighting poverty and homelessness through canned-food drives and distribution of fresh-baked goods. Black Xpression community members' collaboration with black entrepreneurial organizations with the goal toward growing black home and small business ownership in the local historically black community of Southeast San Diego works toward social change against systemic poverty. Café Cabaret poets work toward social change in collaboration with local and binational social justice organizations.

Community members across both sites engage in resistance against racial stereotypes. For the Black Xpression community members, this takes the form of black joy as defensive othering. Every Friday night, over one hundred (mostly young) people crowd into the Palabras Art Gallery to engage in black positivity. In an era when black death pervades newscasts on what seems like a daily basis, black positivity and joy are necessary for healing from the damage caused to members of communities blighted by the war on drugs, police brutality, and the poverty that has remained in many of these communities. Resisting mass incarceration and the school-to-prison pipeline, community members from the Café Cabaret and Palabras engage in poetry-writing workshops for vulnerable populations such as juveniles both in and not yet in the juvenile justice system.

Maintaining identity and speaking truth to each other about their pain, community members at these open-mics call for resistance to several forms of structural oppression. They resist the silencing of their histories by speaking of resistance movements through time and space. They resist racist constructions of Mexican migrants by telling stories of mothers looking for work so they may feed their children. They resist state violence by calling out specific forms of it, lest we forget it is ever present. They resist shame by speaking about sexual and interpersonal violence, depression, anxiety, and addiction. They resist white supremacy by coming together across racial and ethnic identities, sharing their pain and their histories. Finally, they resist by engaging in social change through healing via the expression of their pain, empathizing with each other, and addressing the structural causes of that pain within their communities.

Critical Thinking Questions

1. The forms of structural oppression impacting any one community vary by the culture, demographics, and history of such communities. Therefore, what poets speak to will vary depending on the communities and space in time and place the poetry is performed. If you were to write a poem about structural oppression in your community, which forms would you be sure to include?

2. This chapter focused specifically on spoken-word poetry as a catalyst for identifying and attending to social change in structurally oppressed communities. What other forms of performance might be useful toward transformative justice models seeking positive social change in structurally oppressed communities?

Further Reading/Web Links

https://sandiegopoetryannual.com/

http://www.kpbs.org/events/ongoing/black-xpression-open-mic/

https://www.poetryinsandiego.com/

http://www.thesoulcialworkers.com/

http://100tpc.org/

References

Capeheart, Loretta, and Dragan Milovanovic. 2007. *Social Justice: Theories, Issues, and Movements.* New Brunswick, NJ: Rutgers University Press.

Chepp, Valerie. 2014. "Speaking Truth to Power: Spoken Word Poetry as Political Engagement among Young Adults in the Millennial Age." University of Maryland.

Collins, Patricia Hill. 2000. *Black Feminist Thought: Knowledge, Consciousness, and the Politics of Empowerment.* New York: Routledge.

Collins, Patricia Hill. 2015. "Intersectionality's Definitional Dilemmas." *Annual Review of Sociology* 41(1):1–20.

Ellis, Carolyn, and Jerry Rawicki. 2013. "Collaborative Witnessing of Survival during the Holocaust an Exemplar of Relational Autoethnography." *Qualitative Inquiry* 19(5):366–80.

Flynn, Karen, and Evelyn Marrast. 2008. "Main Content Area Spoken Word from the North: Contesting Nation, Politics, and Identity." *Wadabagei: A Journal of the Caribbean and Its Diaspora* 11(2):3–24. Retrieved March 3, 2016 (http://search.proquest.com.ezproxy.csusm.edu/docview/200337322?accountid=10363&rfr_id=info:xri/sid:primo).

Neiderland, Paula. 2017. "Black Xpression open mic empowers and unites community." *Daily Aztec.* (http://thedailyaztec.com/85737/artsandculture/black-xpression-open-mic-event-seeks-to-empower-and-unite-community/.) Retrieved March 22, 2018.

Pearlman, Jeanne. 2010. "CHRONICLES OF RESISTANCE: A BORDERLANDS TESTIMONIO." PhD dissertation, University of Pittsburgh, ProQuest Dissertations Publishing.

Schwalbe, Michael et al. 2000. "Generic Processes in the Reproduction of Inequality: An Interactionist Analysis." *Social Forces* 79(2):419–52.

Somers-Willett, S. 2005. "Slam Poetry and the Cultural Politics of Performing Identity." *Journal of the Midwest Modern Language Association* 38(1):51–73.

Walker, F., and V. Kuykendall. 2005. "Manifestations of Nommo in 'Def Poetry.'" *Journal of Black Studies* 36(2):229–47.

Williams, Todd O. 2012. *A Therapeutic Approach to Teaching Poetry: Individual Development, Psychology, and Social Reparation.* New York: Palgrave Macmillan.

N.A. 2018. 100 Thousand Poets for Change. Retrieved January 25, 2018.

N.A. https://www.facebook.com/pg/enclavecaracol/about/?ref=page_internal

N.A. "Poetry in San Diego." Poets.org. Retrieved November 30, 2017 (http://www.poetryinsandiego.com/).

N.A. 2018. "Read a Poem at an Open Mic." Retrieved April 15, 2018. (https://www.poets.org/poetsorg/text/read-poem-open-mic)

Reading 9.5 Solidarity Thwarted: The Racialization of African Americans and Asian Americans in California

Jeanelle K. Hope

Keywords: racialization, orientalism, model minority, solidarity, racial hierarchy, assimilation, racial intelligence, activism, social movements, diaspora, systemic change, radicalism, coalition building.

Chapter Goals/Learning Objectives

1. Understand the history of racial stratification/hierarchies in a US context and its implications on marginalized communities, in particular blacks and Asian Americans.

2. Understand black and Asian relations, or Afro-Asian relations, as historically changing and imbricated with race, class, nationality, and other relations of difference.

3. Understand the potential of radical solidarity and coalitional politics.

Introduction

SOMArts, one of the leading art galleries in San Francisco, curated a contemporary art exhibit in the summer of 2017 dedicated to providing space for black women—"The Black Woman is God: Divine Revolution." The exhibit featured a piece of a smiling black girl holding a bottle of orange juice. The canvas was adorned with gold medallions featuring images of Catholic saints and their Yoruba names. The center image of the young girl lay surrounded by the words "Say Her Name," a rallying cry and popular social media hashtag created by the Movement for Black Lives (M4BL) to call attention to state-sanctioned violence faced by women of color.

The painting was of Latasha Harlins, a fifteen-year-old black girl who has often been at the center of discussions on the 1992 Los Angeles riots. On March 16, 1991, Harlins went into a liquor store owned by Soon Ja Du, a Korean American, and her husband, Billy Heung Ki Du, in South Central Los Angeles. Harlins intended on purchasing a bottle of orange juice, later placing the bottle in her backpack. Before she could pay for the item, Soon Ja Du determined that Harlins was stealing, and she began grabbing the young girl. Harlins attempted to defend herself but was shot in the head by Du during the scuffle. Harlins died with the money she planned on using to pay for the juice in her hand. The murder of Latasha Harlins catapulted an intense discussion on black and Asian relations, as the mainstream media characterized the event as the "black-Korean conflict," and rappers, such as Tupac Shakur and Ice Cube, would later write songs honoring Harlins and vilifying Korean storeowners (Ice Cube 1991; Shakur 1993).

Harlins was killed just thirteen days after the infamous beating of Rodney King by the Los Angeles Police Department (LAPD).[40] These two events—compounded by years of swelling racial tensions, an inequitable distribution of wealth throughout Los Angeles that created gross living conditions for those in South Central Los Angeles, and a police force that was being investigated for its racist actions toward black and Latinx

---

[40] On March 31, 1991, Rodney King, an African American man and taxi driver, was pulled over by officers of the Los Angeles Police Department (LAPD). Videotape footage showed four officers repeatedly beating King until much of his face was disfigured. All four officers were charged but later acquitted. The acquittal helped spark the 1992 Los Angeles uprising.

citizens—served as a catalyst for the 1992 LA uprising. The uprising—labeled as riots by the media—was a significant moment in US urban history as it highlighted the layered racial tensions within the country in the post–civil rights era. But these racial tensions were not just a black and white problem, but also a black and yellow issue, a brown and white issue, a black and brown issue, and so on.

This chapter (1) examines how African Americans and Asian Americans are racialized within the United States, in particular throughout California. It (2) delves into how these groups have systematically been racialized against each other in an effort to suppress their attempts at racial cohesion or solidarity; and (3) this work argues for the necessity of Afro-Asian solidarity as a means to seek systemic social change by highlighting past and current moments of solidarity and recognizing their connection to broader social movements.[41]

Creating a Third-World Liberation Front

Both African Americans and Asians began migrating to the Golden State during the nineteenth century. African Americans were being brought by their enslavers to mine gold or were fleeing the conditions of the antebellum South. Chinese immigrants began entering the state in search of employment—primarily working on the construction of the transcontinental railroad—following the first Opium War of 1839–1842, which devastated China. While California presented great opportunities for both groups, they were met with great anti-immigrant sentiment and staunch anti-blackness. This discrimination manifested in the form of anti-immigration legislation, racially restrictive housing covenants, racially motivated taxation, and other forms of de jure and de facto segregation. Because of this marginalization, the growing Asian and black populations were often relegated to similar communities away from white neighborhoods. Marginalized communities throughout Los Angeles, Oakland, San Francisco, and Sacramento served as sites of this interracial comingling (Shizue 2016).[42]

These conditions persisted well into the twentieth century, and by the 1960s, California urban cities such as Oakland and San Francisco were rocked by deindustrialization, leaving many of those who relied on the once plentiful factory work jobless. City governments divested from their urban cores, leaving whole neighborhoods economically disadvantaged. Instead, city officials put public dollars behind "white flight," funding sprawling suburban communities (Santangelo 2001; Self 2003). Persistent inequitable living conditions, coupled with a heightened national awareness of police brutality, transformed the social movements of that era as a new generation of young activists grew disillusioned with nonviolent tactics and respectability politics, opting for a more militant stance to seeking justice. By 1966, the Black Power, Asian American, and other movements, including the Disability Rights, Anti-War, Feminist, and Chicano movements were materializing. Collectively, these movements called for civil rights for marginalized people both domestically and globally. The Black Power and Asian American movement activists were making similar demands at the time: fair housing, the end of systemic racism and discrimination, greater access to education, jobs, and the creation of Ethnic Studies departments at colleges and universities, to name a few.

Additionally, much of this organizing fervor emanated out of high school and college campuses around the San Francisco Bay Area, such as the University of California–Berkeley, Merritt College, San Francisco State College (now San Francisco State University), and McClymonds High School. This student activism spread into surrounding communities due to close proximity, overlapping issues, and the push for solidarity (Murch 2010). In 1968, solidarity was actualized at San Francisco State College when student leaders formed the Third World

---

[41] Drawing on Fred Ho and Bill Mullen's work, I define Afro-Asian as the range of historical, political, and cultural connections between Asian/Asian Americans and African/African Americans. I focus on black and Asian relations as opposed to black and Latinx, or black and Native American relations to highlight the shared struggle, migration patterns into California, and how these two groups, unlike the others, have been racialized against each other. Moreover, I focus on black and Asian relations in an effort to grow scholarship within the budding field.

[42] By the late nineteenth century, Chinese were no longer the only Asian immigrants looking for opportunity in California. Japanese, Koreans, Filipinos, and other East and South Asians also began immigrating to California. During World War II, African Americans migrated from the Jim Crow South to California, in particular Los Angeles, Oakland, and San Francisco in search of wartime jobs.

Liberation Front (TWLF), a coalition of student activists from black, Latinx/Chicanx, Native American, and Asian American student political groups.

The TWLF drew their ideas from Third World leaders and philosophers such as Malcolm X, Mao Zedong, Ho Chi Minh, and Kwame Nkrumah, developing a global consciousness that was steeped in revolutionary internationalism and socialism. Moreover, the TWLF took its lead from the Bandung Conference—the 1955 convening of African and Asian countries in an effort to combat Western imperialism and capitalism. This conference is often heralded as one of the first moments of Afro-Asian solidarity on the global stage, and was seen as a source of inspiration for many Asian American and Black Power groups during the late 1960s.[43]

Beyond the TWLF, Afro-Asian solidarity was actualized around the Bay Area. During the Black Panther Party's (BPP) infancy, leaders Bobby Seale and Huey P. Newton were greatly influenced by Maoism, with Mao Zedong's *Red Book Quotations from Brother Mao Tse Tung* being recommended reading for new members. Mao, the founding leader of the People's Republic of China, was a supporter of black liberation, calling for Third World solidarity within the United States. His work helped transform the Black Power movement, as it provided a framework that was more inclusive and dynamic, highlighting the need for a Marxist model that stressed the global class struggle (Kelley 2008:99). Furthermore, Newton and Seale received support early on from one of their childhood friends, Richard Aoki. Aoki was Japanese American and grew up near Newton in West Oakland. Having recently returned from serving in the military, Aoki had access to guns and other weapons, which he donated to the Party, becoming the first Asian American member of the organization.

The BPP would go on to work with groups like the Asian American Political Alliance (AAPA) and Red Guards, two radical Asian American organizations in the Bay Area that also emerged during the Black Power era. The BPP and aforementioned Asian American groups collaborated on political education classes, rallies, and survival programs, like free breakfast for children and the elderly and the Free Huey campaign (Ibid).

Within these movements and organizations African Americans and Asian Americans raised similar concerns with regards to their material conditions in the United States as well as in contesting Western imperialism and capitalism. However, there were key distinctions in what motivated them. For African Americans, it was the ubiquity of anti-blackness and legacy of enslavement that left generations of African Americans at a deficit. For Asian Americans, it was the need to rebuild their communities following internment, strict immigration laws, and language barriers, to name a few. While both groups drew criticism for their militancy and radicalism during the period, the media simultaneously deemed Asian Americans the "model minority," even though many were living in poor conditions, lacked access to higher education, and were underemployed. This shift would not only impact the US racial hierarchy, but also re-charter the future of black-Asian relations.

The Model Minority: Juxtaposing Blacks and Asian Americans

First used in a January 1966 *New York Times* article entitled, "Success Story Japanese-American Style," by sociologist William Petersen, "model minority" was used to describe Asian Americans, mostly Japanese and Chinese Americans, who were able to attain middle-class status in the United States (Petersen). Their success was highlighted as proof that Asian Americans were no longer impacted by racial and economic discrimination and largely accepted by whites because they were able to assimilate into the dominant culture because they

---

[43] Many scholars trace the infancy of Afro-Asian solidarity back to the Bandung Conference in 1955. While this event is central to understanding the non-aligned movement and Pan African collaboration, it does not necessarily mark the beginning of Afro-Asian solidarity or encounters. Moreover, much of the scholarship on this event has been romanticized. Tamara Nooper argues that the event was more symbolic (Fraser 1945; Jones 2005).

valued entrepreneurship, education, and authority (Ibid). The work also sought to theorize why non-Asian minorities had yet to achieve the level of success as their peers.

In creating the "model minority-problem minority dichotomy," Petersen juxtaposes and pits Asian Americans and African Americans against each other, challenging the very grounds of Afro-Asian solidarity by focusing on their differences rather than their commonalities, setting the stage for a tumultuous future for black-Asian relations. Moreover, this portrayal of Asian Americans was a shift from their prior depiction in mainstream media. Since their arrival to the United States, Asians had overwhelmingly been portrayed negatively in the media—early political and editorial cartoons often depicted Asians as barbaric, dangerous, and villainous, instilling a fear of people from "the East." White-led media stoked anxieties about the "Yellow Peril," the belief that those of the East sought to overthrow the Western world. With no looming threat from the East, yellow peril can only be surmised as a myth born out of xenophobia and racism.

Edward Said's framework of orientalism best captures American anti-Asian xenophobia. Said contends that the Orient, or the East (the Middle East, Asia, and Africa), was integral to the development of the Occident, or the West (Europe and European-colonized Americas). Slavery, colonialism, and imperialism provided the material means for the development of Western capitalism primarily via the control of the Orient's natural resources and people (Said 1978: 9). Orientalism is an extension of yellow peril in that it describes how Western artists, writers, and even early political leaders viewed the East as monolithic and static, without recognizing their own role in the underdevelopment of many countries in the Orient. Orientalism argues that the West not only views the Orient as less civilized and developed, but also uses that very belief as a justification to further exploit the Orient.

Orientalism and notions of yellow peril are still pervasive in contemporary mainstream media. While depictions of Asians are not as brazen as the Fu Manchu character of the 1930s, mainstream news outlets, for example, often characterize China as this monolithic illusive force constantly challenging the United States for global supremacy. There is certainly some validity to those claims, as China has become a key fixture within global markets; however, the portrayal of China often harkens back to a history of fear and xenophobia. This history of anti-Asian rhetoric is why Petersen's portrayal of Japanese Americans was so stark, even though it was no more than a refashioning of orientalist ideas to stereotype Asians because of their perceived assimilation and likeness to whiteness.

Ultimately, Petersen's analysis lacked a serious discussion of global anti-blackness and the legacy of enslavement and colonialism, which would have exposed Petersen's simplistic arguments. Moreover, he places the burden of success on African Americans and Asian Americans without accounting for how policies and systems steeped in white supremacy continuously work to oppress both groups. The model minority myth validated Asian American identity (arguably a particular type), stratifying them closer to whiteness and what it meant to be "American." This stratification inherently created tension and animosity, as Asian Americans were now seen as "greater than" and in some cases afforded certain social and economic privileges that other communities of color were not. Moreover, this stratification becomes internalized, as witnessed with the Latasha Harlins case. Soon Ja Du operated out of a place of anti-blackness when she shot Harlins, and the lax sentencing she received, similar to that of the white officers who brutalized Rodney King, only highlighted for African Americans that Asian Americans were privy to certain aspects of whiteness. Because of these beliefs, anti-Asian sentiment within the African American community became prevalent.

Eroding Model Minority and Rebuilding Afro-Asian Solidarity

For decades, activists and scholars have been refuting Petersen's "model minority" myth, as it often reflected the experiences of a few—mostly affluent East Asians—while the narratives of South, Southeast, and other Asian and Pacific Islander groups were largely erased (Wu 2015; Hsu 2017; Lee 2015; Ancheta 2010). The "model minority" myth was also devoid of any gender or class analysis. For example, Vietnamese, Hmong, and Cambodians refugees immigrated to the United States largely for political reasons and have remained relatively disadvantaged. But moving into the 1980s and 1990s, the idea of Asian Americans as the "model minority" shifted from a problematic argument to a widely believed stereotype that oversimplified, distorted, and rendered the experiences of Asian Americans monolithic (Lee 2015).

Claire Jean Kim, an Asian American studies scholar, offers a counter to the "model minority" myth with her theory of racial triangulation. She posits that Asian Americans, being neither black nor white, have been valorized in comparison to blacks, but both Asians and Blacks remain culturally and racially subordinate to whites (Kim 1999). Refuting Petersen's claims, Jean-Kim asserts that Asian Americans occupy an angle between blacks and whites. This triangle illustrates how Asian Americans are situated between the two racial groups and navigate between blackness and whiteness. Racial triangulation also details just how connected African Americans and Asian Americans are due to a shared struggle against white supremacy and imperialism. Conversely, Kim's work is not without its own limitations. Racial triangulation, similar to "model minority," does not account for the nuances around race or gender and class.

Still, Kim's work pushes us to move beyond racial scapegoating, toward understanding racial power that largely upholds white supremacy and the racial status quo. Kim's work also leaves room for the creation of coalitional politics and solidarities that seek to obliterate existing racial hierarchies. Beyond the era of Afro-Asian solidarity that emerged following Bandung and during the Black Power and Asian American movements, there have been contemporary periods of improved black-Asian relations and even solidarity building.

Today, Asian American millennials are speaking out against the model minority myth and how it is used to pit Asian Americans against other people of color, especially within higher education.[44] When an anti-Affirmative Action lawsuit was brought against Harvard University by a conservative organization using a young Asian American as the plaintiff, Harvard students rebuffed attempts to be used as "tools" to further suppress minority enrollment. Christina Qiu, a Harvard University student, responded to the case by stating that "model minority status was granted as a counter to black activism" (Qiu 2017). She highlights that the "model minority" is grossly flawed and has been weaponized to divide communities of color and reinforce white supremacy. Qiu warns that these efforts by anti-Affirmative Action organizations only facilitate the resegregation of institutions using Asian bodies as disposable tools. To her point, white college students across the nation have also expressed with great dissatisfaction the swelling Asian and Pacific Islander populations on college campuses.[45] Qiu's article in *the Harvard Crimson* is a call for solidarity, one that was echoed in the 2016 "A Letter for Black Lives."

In a post-Ferguson era, following the case of Peter Liang and Akai Gurley, a collective of Asian American millennials, led by ethnographer Christina Xu in 2016, came together to discuss how Asian Americans are imbricated within issues raised by the M4BL. "A Letter for Black Lives" was written to begin conversations about police brutality, anti-blackness, and racial justice with members in their communities; calling for Asian American elders to have empathy and support for their children and youth who support the Movement for Black Lives (BLM 2016a). Since its publication, the letter has been shared online through social media millions of times and has been translated into over thirty languages, also spawning a YouTube video and a comic edition (BLM 2016b). The letter has also been edited for different communities, providing more nuanced discussions. For example, the South Asian American version details how Indians and other darker-skinned Asian Americans have also become victims of anti-black racism.

---

[44] In 1996, with the passage of Proposition 209, California voters decided to do away with affirmative action in the state, including in higher education. Since then, eight other states have followed California's lead. African Americans and Latinx Americans were disproportionately impacted by this decision, with their enrollment plummeting at California's public universities, while Asian Americans witnessed exponential growth. See Erica Perez, "California Proposition 209: Minority Enrollments Down in UC Schools Despite Diversity Efforts," HuffPost, last modified April 25, 2012, accessed February 3, 2018, https://www.huffingtonpost.com/2012/02/24/proposition-209_n_1300122.html.

[45] The University of California–Los Angeles made news in 2012 for its nickname, "University of Caucasians Lost among Asians," highlighting the sheer anti-Asian sentiment brewing at the university.

Conclusion

The "Letter for Black Lives" is certainly a step in the right direction to begin having discussions around US racialization, and more importantly on building Afro-Asian solidarity within the current M4BL. In an era fraught with blatant xenophobia and racism being espoused from the federal government, strengthened black-Asian relations are critical to dismantling the systems of oppression that have stratified these groups based on their proximity to whiteness, instead of their shared humanity.

Strengthening black-Asian relations is essential to toppling a racial hierarchy that situates African Americans at the bottom, Asian Americans near the top, and other populations of color, such as Native Americans and Chicanx/Latinx Americans, scattered between the two. Solidarities between black, Chicanx/Latinx, and Native Americans have garnered greater longevity and focus because of the consistent framing of these populations as "problem minorities." This chapter highlighted some of the key moments of Afro-Asian solidarity throughout history, and while much is still being carried out by activists and organizers in the name of building solidarity among blacks and Asian Americans, the impact of the model minority myth is still present as communities remain disconnected. The rebuilding of black-Asian relations and Afro-Asian solidarity will help collapse the racial hierarchical structure by shrinking their "distance" from each other, which can only be accomplished by returning to an engagement rooted in a shared struggle and liberation. Furthermore, this hierarchical collapse will also help facilitate the dissolution of systems oppression, such as capitalism, white supremacy, anti-blackness, and anti-Asian sentiment, which have been internalized and thwarted the possibilities of another Bandung or Third World Liberation Front.

Reflection/Critical Thinking Questions

1. How has US racialization shaped your lived experience?

2. What role do systems and other people have in shaping our identities?

3. What are the consequences and legacies of exclusion for the dominant and marginalized groups?

4. What does solidarity mean to you?

Exploratory Research Questions

1. How has/does Afro-Asian solidarity manifest(ed)?

2. What is solidarity, and what does solidarity look like for communities that are invested in dismantling systems of oppression?

Further Readings and Resources

Articles and Books

Anderson, Crystal. 2013. *Beyond the Chinese Connection: Contemporary Afro-Asian Cultural Production*. Jackson: University of Mississippi Press.

Asian Community Center Archive Group, comp. 2009. *Stand Up: An Archive Collection of the Bay Area Asian American Movement 1968–1974*. Berkeley, CA: Asian Community Center Archive Group.

Frazier, Robeson Taj. 2014. *The East Is Black: Cold War China in the Black Radical Imagination*. Durham, NC: Duke University Press.

Lowe, Lisa. 1996. *Immigrant Acts: On Asian American Cultural Politics.* Durham, NC: Duke University Press.

Maeda, Daryl. 2012. *Chains of Babylon: Rethinking the Asian American Movement.* New York: Routledge.

Mullen, Bill. 2004. *Afro-Orientalism.* Minneapolis: University of Minnesota Press.

Mullen, Bill. 2006. *Afro-Asian Encounters: Culture, History, Politics.* New York: NYU Press.

Nakagawa, Scot. 2015. "When Blacks and Asians Clash." Race Files. Last modified May 5, 2015. Accessed February 12, 2017. https://www.racefiles.com/2015/05/05/when-blacks-and-asians-clash/.

Onishi, Yuichiro. 2014. *Transpacific Antiracism: Afro-Asian Solidarity in 20th Century Black America, Japan, and Okinawa.* New York: NYU Press.

Prashad, Vijy. 2002. *Everybody Was Kung Fu Fighting: Afro-Asian Connections and the Myth of Cultural Purity.* Boston: Beacon Press, 2002.

Films/Videos

Mountains That Take Wing: Angela Davis and Yuri Kochiyama—A Conversation on Life, Struggles & Liberation (film).

Mike Cheng & Ben Wang. *Aoki.* https://www.youtube.com/watch?v=HqF2fLGjf9U (film).

Podcasts

Code Switch Episodes: "Japanese Americans Exiled in Utah," May 19, 2017. "Encore: Asian American Letter on Behalf of Black Lives," November 26, 2016.

References

Ancheta, Angelo N. 2010. "Neither Black Nor White." Race, Class, and Gender in the United States: An Integrated Study 120-29.

BLM. 2016a. "Letters for Black Lives," last modified July 12, 2016, accessed January 31, 2018, https://lettersforblacklives.com/.

--. 2016b. "Letters for Black Lives Inaugural ENG Letter," video file, 5:39, YouTube, posted by Letters for Black Lives, July 11, 2016, accessed May 24, 2018, https://www.youtube.com/watch?v=vrR-8_odGh4.

Ice Cube. 1991. Death Certificate. Priority Records, compact disc.

Fraser, Cary. 1945. "An American dilemma: race and realpolitik in the American response to the Bandung Conference, 1955." Window on Freedom: Race, Civil Rights, and Foreign Affairs 1988: 115-140.

Hsu, Madeline Y. 2017. The good immigrants: How the yellow peril became the model minority. Princeton University Press.

Jones, Matthew. 2005. "A "Segregated" Asia?: Race, the Bandung Conference, and Pan-Asianist Fears in American Thought and Policy, 1954–1955." Diplomatic History 29.5: 841-868.

Kelley, Robin D.G. and Betsy Esch. 2008. "Black Like Mao: Red China and Black Revolution," in Afro Asia: Revolutionary Political & Cultural Connections Between African Americans & Asian Americans, ed. Fred Ho and Bill Mullen. Durham, NC: Duke University Press.

Kim. Claire Jeam. 1999."The Racial Triangulation of Asian Americans." Politics & Society 27(1): p. 107.

Lee, Stacy J. 2015. Unraveling the" model minority" stereotype: Listening to Asian American youth. Teachers College Press.

Murch, Donna Jean. 2010. *Living for the City: Migration, Education, and the Rise of the Black Panther Party. Chapel Hill: University of North Carolina Press.*

Petersen, William. "Success Story, Japanese-American Style." *New York Times Magazine*, 21–45.

Qiu, Christina. 2014. "Asian Americans Are Not Tools," Harvard Crimson, last modified August 7, 2017, accessed February 3, 2018, http://www.thecrimson.com/article/2017/8/4/qiu-asian-americans/.

Said, Edward. 1978. Orientalism. London, UK: Routledge.

Santangelo, Gretchen L. 2001. "Deindustrialization, Urban Poverty and African American Community Mobilization in Oakland, 1945 through 1992" in Seeking El Dorado: African Americans in California, ed. Lawrence DeGraff, Kevin Mulroy, and Quintard Taylor. Seattle, WA: University of Washington Press.

Self, Robert. 2003. American Babylon: Race and the Struggle for Postwar Oakland. Princeton, NJ: Princeton University Press.

Shakur, Tupac. 1993. Strictly 4 My N.I.G.G.A.Z. Interscope Records.

Shizue Seigel. 2016. *Standing Strong! Fillmore & Japantown: Voices from Write Now! Fillmore and Write Now! Japantown.* San Francisco: Pease Press.

Wu, Ellen D. 2015. The color of success: Asian Americans and the origins of the model minority. Vol. 100. Princeton University Press.

Discussion Questions

1. Have you ever participated in a march, rally, boycott, or demonstration? What motivated you to participate? What did your family, friends, peers think about your actions?

2. Given today's ubiquitous presence of technology, how do you think this helps or hinders the way we think about and go about advocating and pressing for social change?

3. In what ways do you think you can be more involved today or in the future to press for social change? What are the issues that are important to you today that might motivate you to become involved in advocating or pressing for changes?

Resources

Black Lives Matter: https://blacklivesmatter.com/about/

Radical Monarchs: http://radicalmonarchs.org/

Say Her Name: http://aapf.org/sayhernamereport

United We Dream Network: https://unitedwedream.org/

67 Sueños: https://www.afsc.org/program/67-sue%C3%B1os

References

Alexander, Michelle. 2012. *The New Jim Crow: Mass Incarceration in the Age of Colorblindness*. New York: New Press.

Aptheker, Herbert. 1983. *American Negro Slave Revolts*. Intl Pub (1700).

Bonilla-Silva, Eduardo. 2006. *Racism without Racists: Color-Blind Racism and the Persistence of Racial Inequality in the United States*. Lanham, MD: Rowman & Littlefield Publishers.

Bonilla-Silva, Eduardo, and Victor Ray. 2009. "When Whites Love a Black Leader: Race Matters in Obamerica." *Journal of African American Studies* 13(2):176–83.

Burns, Alexander. 2015. "Choice Words from Donald Trump, Presidential Candidate." *New York Times (Web Edition)*, June 16, 16–18. Retrieved (https://nyti.ms/1Grykcn).

Chafe, William H., and William Henry Chafe. 1981. *Civilities and Civil Rights: Greensboro, North Carolina, and the Black Struggle for Freedom*. Oxford University Press.

Fitzgerald, Stephanie. 2006. *The Little Rock Nine: Struggle for Integration*. Compass Point Books.

Fox, Cybelle, and Thomas A. Guglielmo. 2012. "Defining America's Racial Boundaries: Blacks, Mexicans, and European Immigrants, 1890–1945." *American Journal of Sociology* 118(2):327–79.

Haney-Lopez, Ian F. 1996. *White By Law: The Legal Construction of Race*. New York: New York University Press.

Kohl, Herbert R., and Cynthia Stokes Brown. 2007. *She Would Not Be Moved: How We Tell the Story of Rosa Parks and the Montgomery Bus Boycott*. New York: New Press.

McAdam, Doug. 1988. *Freedom Summer*. New York: Oxford University Press.

Oliver, Melvin, and Thomas Shapiro. 2013. *Black Wealth/White Wealth: A New Perspective on Racial Inequality*. New York: Routledge.

Omi, Michael, and Howard Winant. 1994. *Racial Formation in the United States: From the 1960s to the 1990s*. 2nd ed. New York: Routledge.

Packard, Jerrold M. 2002. *American Nightmare: The History of Jim Crow*. New York: St. Martin's Press.

Sewell, Abigail A. 2016. "The Racism-Race Reification Process: A Mesolevel Political Economic Framework for Understanding Racial Health Disparities." *Sociology of Race and Ethnicity* 2(4):402–32.

Wiltse, Jeff. 2007. *Contested Waters: A Social History of Swimming Pools in America*. University of North Carolina Press.

Credits

Patricia Hill Collins, "Intersectionality's Definitional Dilemmas," Annual Review of Sociology, vol. 41, pp. 3-5, 11-20. Copyright © 2015 by Annual Reviews. Reprinted with permission.

Michael Omi and Howard Winant, "Conclusion: Racial Formation Rules: Continuity, Instability, and Change," Racial Formation in the Twenty-First Century, ed. Daniel Martinez HoSang, Oneka LaBennett, and Laura Pulido, pp. 302-330. Copyright © 2012 by University of California Press. Reprinted with permission.

David R. Williams and Michelle Sternthal, "Understanding Racial-ethnic Disparities in Health: Sociological Contributions," Journal of Health and Social Behavior, vol. 51, no. 1, pp. 18-27. Copyright © 2010 by SAGE Publications. Reprinted with permission.

Fig. 4.3: Adapted from https://pt.slideshare.net/canalfutura/a-cor-da-cultura-apresentao-english-version

Fig. SV.1: Source: https://commons.wikimedia.org/wiki/File:Sambos.jpg.

Megan Underhill, "Parenting During Ferguson: Making Sense of White Parents' Silence," Ethnic and Racial Studies, vol. 41, no. 11, pp. 1934-1935, 1939-1946, 1947-1951. Copyright © 2017 by Taylor & Francis Group. Reprinted with permission.

Fig. 8.1-3a: Source: DANE.

Fig. 8.1-3b: Source: DANE.